2

ECONOMICS AND POLITICS WITHIN SOCIALIST SYSTEMS

A Comparative and Developmental Approach

Klaus von Beyme

Translated by
Barbara Evans and *Eva Kahn-Sinreich*

PRAEGER

PRAEGER SPECIAL STUDIES • PRAEGER SCIENTIFIC

Library of Congress Cataloging in Publication Data
Beyme, Klaus von.
    Economics and politics within Socialist
systems.
    Translation of: Ökonomie und Politik im
Sozialismus.
    Bibliography: p.
    Includes index.
    1. Communist countries—Economic policy.
2. Industrial management—Communist countries.
I. Title.
HC704.B4713   338.947   81-10750
ISBN 0-03-046671-7   AACR2

Originally published in 1975 as *Ökonomie und
    Politik im Sozialismus*

Published in 1982 by Praeger Publishers
CBS Educational and Professional Publishing
A Division of CBS, Inc.
521 Fifth Avenue, New York, N.Y. 10175 U.S.A.
©1975 (German edition) and 1982 (English edition)
by R. Piper & Co., Verlag

23456789 145 987654321
Printed in the United States of America

dedicated to
Dietrich Geyer

CONTENTS

LIST OF TABLES

INTRODUCTION

Comparative research on socialist systems is both easier and more difficult than it was at the time when the first socialist countries were developing. It is easier because most of the socialist countries have developed their own original features and are no longer as dependent on imitation of the Soviet model as they used to be in their early days, and because most of them are publishing more and more data that can serve in comparison, whereas in the early days an official atmosphere of secrecy and a distrust in quantitative analysis made comparative studies impossible. The integration of statistical systems within Comecon has unified accounting systems and made quantitative data more open to comparison.

On the other hand, however, comparison would seem to be more difficult than in the 1950s because the socialist countries are becoming increasingly divergent in their ideology, and growing neo-Marxist criticism of the so-called real socialism of existing systems is tending to make the concept of what can actually be called "socialism" more and more uncertain.

A social scientist who tries to compare socialist and capitalist societies, either as a whole or solely in specific aspects, is always in danger of falling between two stools. If comparison not only constitutes a "method" but also a "state of mind," as a well-known writer on international politics put it,[1] then, in the eyes of the established mainstream on both sides of the iron curtain, this objectivist comparative politics approach would seem to have a stance of subversion in it when applied to socialist countries. It seems to question established loyalties to the systems. There is, of course, little hope that the scholars of socialist countries will accept the results of an intersystem comparison. They usually work on comparisons solely for apologetic purposes in order to prove that workers under capitalist conditions have a much worse life than workers in socialist countries—a hypothesis that has at times survived even among Eurocommunists in the West.[2] The greatest degree of success that an attempt at comparative analysis can hope to achieve among the scholars of socialist countries is to be recognized as trying to understand the socialist countries.[3]

The defenders of state socialism are, however, not the only ones to misinterpret most attempts at comparison. Western critics also brand certain studies as "Trojan Horses" intended to undermine the democratic system, as has been demonstrated by a right-wing politician in a parliamentary debate: "These [the comparative scholars] are not communist scholars teaching at the Humboldt University in East Berlin or at the Karl-Marx University in Leipzig, but West German professors, one in Munich, the other at Heidelberg. Both of them advocate a democratic socialism for the future, applying formulations which I have quoted. How do you dare to ask us why we think the choice is between freedom and socialism."[4] These familiar suspicions about comparative research into socialism make it necessary to take three preliminary steps before proceeding to an analysis of socialist policies, namely:

1. a discussion of problems regarding the theory of socialist society;
2. the typology of socialist systems and their constituent elements;
3. operationalization of these elements through the use of indicators.

1. The theory of socialist society

The comparative approach of today is equally far removed from the conservative view that socialism is the incarnation of all the evils of our time and can only be compared to other "totalitarian systems," such as fascist regimes, as it is from the apologetic view of the socialist countries, where most scholars—apart from some notable exceptions in Poland[5]—can never admit that "bourgeois scholars" are able to acquire insight into the developmental laws of socialist societies. Nevertheless, the prospects for reaching agreement on some methodological rules for comparison within the socialist camp, as well as for comparison between capitalist and socialist countries, are not so bleak:

1.   Socialist planners aim to carry out comparisons in a large number of sectors, even if they reject or do not care for the comparison of global societies. This is reflected in a joke the author heard in Moscow: An American expert on railways wanted to compare Soviet and American performances. He was given impressive data on the number of trains running in the Soviet Union. When he asked if he could check the figures for himself with a visit to the capital's busiest railway station and then began to query the figures after having waited half an hour for a single train to depart, he was stopped by his Soviet host with the counterargument "and you are treating your negroes badly." The counterargument may not be without foundation, but it can only be used in an overall comparison of the two systems. In a sectoral comparison of transportation the argument is nonsense because of the fallacy of "misplaced concreteness" on a different level of comparison. Planners in socialist countries make use of comparative figures and are becoming increasingly interested in correcting gaps and lags in their own system through quantitative studies of other countries' performances. They do, however, continue to use data in fields favorable for socialist countries, such as social security, education, and employment, but refuse comparisons of equivalent data in the name of the "superior quality of socialism" in other fields where comparisons tend to be less flattering for the performance of socialist systems, such as housing, environmental protection, or the production of consumer goods and services for the population.

2.   Even neo-Marxist critics of socialist countries have come increasingly to abandon their approach, which one could define as a *hailing of the ontological qualities of the socialist system,* and have started asking the question as to whether there is not an inherent danger of the rise of a "Gulag Archipelago" in every forced trans-formation toward socialism.[6]

3.   The chances of achieving partial agreement on typologies and methodology have become all the greater since socialist scholars have taken over a large number of Western paradigms—such as systems theory, cybernetics, survey research—that had been branded

as bourgeois deviance when they were first brought into application. On the other hand, the ideological basis of Western scholars has also been smoothed down with the progression from the totalitarian model, via convergence theories, to modern functional comparisons of systems.

Totalitarian models only admitted comparison of socialist countries with fascist regimes, and in the earlier versions of Friedrich and Brzezinskii there was no room for an internal development of socialism toward liberalization, pluralism, and democracy.[7] *Convergence theories*, working on the assumption that postindustrial societies were growing more and more alike, envisaged peaceful change in socialist countries, but the tacit underlying assumption was that socialist countries would borrow more from the West than the West would borrow from them. Only a few economists, such as Jan Tinbergen,[8] kept a fair balance between the elements of interest for the other system as well.

Only recent, functional *system comparisons*, however, have been ready to accept the fact that the two systems are basically different and have given an unbiased analysis of the functions, forms of behavior, and attitudes that certain institutions hold for the development of respective systems. Leftist critics of "bourgeois democracy," together with Parsonian systems theoreticians, have long put forward the hypothesis that one-party rule in socialist countries can be considered as a functional equivalent of Western multiparty systems. The only difference would seem to be that Marcusians meant this statement as an accusation whereas the Parsonians claimed to give a value-free analysis since the ideologies of systems were regarded as being interchangeable.[9] However, modern systems analysis is no longer interested in classifying ontological material that shows some similarities; instead, it prefers to pinpoint functional equivalences, despite blatant *prima facie* dissimilarities.

What the author terms "comparative functional analysis" does not need the acceptance of the whole metatheoretical basis of functionalism. Area studies in general and comparative communist students in particular remain skeptical about the benefits of fashionable new approaches, be this systems theory or the behavioral revolution.[10] Even economists are generally more wary of losing themselves in the abstract games of econometrics than are their counterparts in the field of research on capitalist systems.

The functional approach has two advantages:

1.   it shares with Marxism the assumption that the variable attributes

of the system are highly related to each other and that inter-relationships maintain certain variables in the system;[11]

2. after overcoming the static bias of the older Parsonian form of systems theory, it was combined with a historical interest in modernization and development; modernization theory was far from having lost all its bias of a U.S.- or Europe-centered view, but it was at least more receptive to the differences in roads to development than were the older theories of totalitarianism, the "bureaucratic model" (Alfred Meyer), movement regimes (Robert Tucker), "administered society" (Allen Kassof), "ideocratic apparatocracy" (Robert Conquest), and "authoritarian society" (Christian Peter Ludz).

The older institutional political science was mainly interested in the mechanisms of social control. These approaches had difficulty in accepting that the *"prokuratura"*—one of the main institutions of repression—claimed to have the functions of an ombudsman and that the Soviet "general'nyi prokuror" asked permission to participate in round tables on ombudsmen.[12] Modern functional comparisons can duly acknowledge certain protective functions of the prokuratura without embellishing the repressive functions, which also still remain in the institution.

The most important feature of modern functional comparison is that it no longer adopts a generally hostile approach toward the ideological self-definition of socialist systems. Ideology is not considered material for Sunday speeches alone, and systematic comparison searches for operationalization, so as to measure the impact of ideological proposition. The unbiased comparatist, however, will adopt an agnostic stance toward rabulistic periodization schemes and may have some reservations as to whether there is a "necessary development toward socialism." There is, however, no doubt that communist ideology shapes the system, and in many countries this has become a self-fulfilling prophecy. Thus we have to accept the criteria for the mature socialism stage,[13] which, it is claimed, is the stage most Comecon countries have now reached; only Poland is more prudent here and does not claim to have constructed socialism. These are criteria such as:

1. full development of a socialist way of production;
2. sociopolitical unity of society with increasing rapprochement of the social classes;
3. full use of the scientific–technical revolution;

4. developed socialist democracy;
5. a deep-rooted socialist conscience in the masses;
6. cooperation of states and parties in the socialist world system.

We can even accept the criteria for the "construction of communism." One of the most important indicators, which is frequently mentioned, is that more than 50% of income is paid via social consumption and services supplied free of charge by the state. It is highly unlikely that Marx envisaged realization of the *"principle of needs"*—as opposed to the "principle of achievement," which prevails in capitalist societies and in the first stage of communism, the socialist subperiod—in terms of social services organized by the State. But it is not the exegetic interest in what Marx really meant that concerns comparative scholars; their real interest lies in seeing whether, by using these indicators as a yardstick, progress made toward communism can be taken from the realm of ideological declaration into the sphere of scientifically controllable statements (see Chapter 5).

2. The typology of socialist societies and their constituent elements

Socialist systems aim to have the capacity to create a consistent set of *ex ante* planned policies without the rationality of the party's plan being disturbed through the struggles of parties, interest groups, or elites. This coherent system of plans cannot, however, be directly deduced from Marx' and Engels' work. Neither of them compiled a well-defined theory for socialist society. In opposing utopian socialism, they came close to a Jewish *Bilderverbot*. Engels stated that, "to speculate about the mode of distribution of food and housing in the society of the future leads straight into utopia" (MEW, Vol. 18, p. 285). A few writings, such as Marx's "Critique of the Gotha Programme' (1875) or Engels' "On the housing question" (1872), deal with the socialist society of the future. Most of their concepts have been developed as a "critique of bourgeois economy" and cannot simply be applied to socialist societies. Comparisons of a socialist ideal with the social reality in the Moscow-oriented countries, which one so frequently finds in neo-Marxist writings, are therefore highly problematical and unfair.

In the meantime, socialist development can be analyzed using empirical methods; it can no longer simply be inferred from the Soviet development. Soviet works on socialism stress the "one essence" under "different forms."[14] In more descriptive treatises, however, the Soviet-centered bias of the selection and definition of socialist countries emerges quite clearly.[15] Even Third-World countries that call themselves "socialist" but do not directly belong to the Soviet sphere of influence are labeled by the Soviet Union as "countries of socialist orientation" on the basis of a number of criteria, the most important of these being "friendship with the Soviet Union."[16] Only Polish comparative scholars have no difficulty in separating socialist countries into "Comecon" and "others." Among the latter, Albania, China, North Korea, and Yugoslavia are recognized as being "socialist."[17]

Neither in the East nor in the West is every country that claims to be socialist defined as such in scholarly treatises. Three criteria are most frequently used in the literature of both camps: Marxist-Leninist ideology, state ownership of the means of production, and Soviet orientation—the latter hardly being applicable to China since 1960.[18] Some authors take as their criterion not the mere fact that a party of Marxist orientation is in power (as in Angola, Ethiopia, Cambodia, Laos, Afghanistan) but that the whole state has been permanently converted to the socialist way of life.[19]

Whereas Moscow-oriented Communists normally accept descriptive typologies of socialism (if these are "ideologically correct"), Western neo-Marxists at times reject any definition of socialism on the basis that it is artificial; in their opinion only the "overcoming of the logic of capitalist development" can be a test for a noncapitalist social structure, and one cannot simply apply a group of descriptive indicators.[20] Without the operationalization of global features such as "logic of capitalism" we will hardly ever know what socialism actually is. On the other hand, most typologies tend to be unsatisfactory since they start from very partial phenomena such as the extent of social control, planning systems, or the recruitment of elites. It is only recently that classifications of socialist systems which take in a wide range of indicators of socioeconomic and political change have been added to the prevailing typologies of economic systems.[21] The danger here, however, is that if classifications are begun from the sets of data available, then it will not necessarily be the most relevant clusters of problems that are selected.

Figure 1

Societal sphere	Prevailing principle	Social formation	
		Capitalism	Socialism
sphere of production	exchange or planning	private ownership of the means of production prevails	public ownership of the means of production prevails
		steering *ex post* by market mechanisms	steering of the economy *ex ante* through central planning
		motivation of the individual by material incentives	motivation of the individual by appeals to socialist conscience, with use of material incentives as a reluctantly acepted substitute for ideological motivation
sphere of distribution	bargaining or central steering of distribution	inequality of income and opportunity ideologically accepted	sets out to create greater equality of income and opportunity than in capitalist systems
		highly organized collective interest groups with potential for conflict	small autonomy of collective interest and no potential for conflict
		distribution according to the	distribution by work achievement, which,

In order to improve the consensus of scholars on definitions of socialism, we can consider the three most important spheres of society as used by Marx and which come close to typologies applied in policy analysis of Western democracies, namely, the sphere of production, the sphere of distribution, and the sphere of legitimation or the political sphere. For purposes of differentiating between capitalism and socialism, we can then pinpoint three elements

Societal sphere	Prevailing principle	Social formation	
		Capitalism	*Socialism*
		"principle of achievement," with accepted inequalities limited by welfare state devices	according to the ideology, is more oriented toward the quality of work (lesser privileges for academic professions?) and increasing distribution on the *principle of needs* (social services and provision of infrastructure free of charge)
sphere of legitimation or political sphere	integration by gratification, organization, repression, and ideology (in socialist societies the rank order is reversed)	ideology is hidden behind the "technical necessities" pluralism of ideologies on the basis of a consensus on the market economy	primacy of Marxist–Leninist ideology; dissent seen mostly as deviant behavior
		pluralism of parties and interest groups	hegemony of the Communist party as the alleged expression of the dominance of the working classes
		primacy of the economy	primacy of politics

within these spheres, on which even most of the different Marxist groups could probably agree (see Figure 1). Most of the nine criteria listed under socialism are fulfilled in the various countries that are called socialist, even if in some cases one or another of the criteria is not emphasised as strongly by the political and ideological decision-makers. Some of the criteria are less essential than others. It would be quite possible to imagine a form of democratic socialism without a one-party hegemony, organized instead on the pluralist basis of the Soviets, without any manipulation from above. But socialism without the socialization (and not simply nationalization!) of the means of production is inconceivable.

Only in the case of Yugoslavia have serious doubts been formulated both in the East and the West as to the socialist character of the country. Marx sometimes defined socialism simply as the "abolition of private property" (MEW, Vol. 4, p. 475, 493), and Yugoslav communists have rightly argued that it was not the mere outward juridical form of public ownership that was considered essential by Marx. Yugoslavia is not classified among the market economies even in most Western comparisons (an exception here being Frederic Pryor in his seminal study), because about half her productive capital was privately owned during the period under examination, and a number of other Socialist countries rejected at that time the notion that the country was socialist.[22] Even China gave up its dogmatic discrimination against the Yugoslav road to socialism. Moreover, by taking more sophisticated indicators than simply the number of plants that are no longer privately owned, such as the proportion of industrial production contributed by the public sector (Table 1, p. 29) or the number of workers employed in non-private industry, Yugoslavia could even have claimed in the 1960s to be predominantly socialist in character. In addition, the Yugoslav communists rightly argue that by the token of the "withering away of the state," measured in terms of workers' participation in economic decisions, Yugoslavia comes closer to Marx's ideas than does any other state and is, in fact, more socialist than those "etatist" socialist countries that denigrate the Yugoslav model.

Orthodox Marxists will also criticize the amount of attention paid to the sphere of distribution in this classification. Marxist catalogues of criteria for socialism tend to overemphasize the sphere of production, even though Engels (MEW, Vol. 20, p. 138) has warned us against rating the sphere of distribution solely as a "passive result of production." Normally the emphasis on distribution is branded as being "revisionist." Once again, Engels can be quoted here, when he warned in his *Anti-Dühring* against endorsing a socialist way of distribution while conserving a capitalist mode of production. On the other hand, in the case of China, underemphasis of the needs of consumption under socialist conditions at the time when the "gang of four" came into prominence has been branded old-fashioned "equalization" (*uravnilovka*), which tries to enforce communist distribution patterns before a socialist mode of production has been achieved.[23]

This schedule can certainly not be used as a doctrinaire checklist which justifies the exclusion of certain countries which fall short on one or two criteria. It might, however, serve to explain why certain countries have been included in this study and others (such as Tanzania or Algeria) not. Nevertheless, we can hardly hope that all the dissent among Marxists as to the extent to which a country can deviate from this catalogue and still be called "socialist" will be resolved. The main differences relate to:

1. *the extent of remainders of private property* in agriculture and trade—this is a problem in Poland and Yugoslavia;
2. *the extent of centralization* necessary for a socialist planned economy—again Yugoslavia would seem to be a deviant case here, at least since 1965;
3. *the hegemony of the working class* and its party, which is doubted by Trotskyists and Maoists as far as most countries are concerned: they can only see "an elitist substitute for the rule of the workers" in the Comecon countries;
4. the extent to which *dictatorship of the proletariat* may be substituted by the "state of the whole people"—a device that has been emphasized since Khrushchev in the Moscow-oriented countries;
5. the survival of an important role for money in a more-or-less independent *"sphere of circulation"*—the fourth category in Marx's classification, which marked a feature of capitalism and was to wither away in socialist society;
6. the extent of social *inequality* admissible in socialism;
7. the amount of *independence that can be granted to the social organizations by the party*, which claimed to rule over all of them with the Leninist concept of the "transmission belt"— at least in Poland and Yugoslavia greater autonomy for trade unions is under discussion even in leading circles of the party;
8. the extent to which gratifications—*material incentives*—or negative sanctions—*repression*—are justifiable in order to construct socialism.[24]

Some of these ideological divergences result from differences in the periodization of history. The greater the emphasis placed on the utopian idea of transition to communism, the greater the emphasis on different policies to further this goal, in particular the construction of communes with complete integration of production (China), self-administration (Yugoslavia), and renunciation of material incentives for purposes of motivating the people (Cuba in its initial phase).

3.   The problem of operationalizing typologies
     through the search for indicators

Only once the theoretical concepts of socialism have been
clarified and some typological work carried out on the divergences
can the data for quantitative comparison be discussed. Without
theoretical clarification, the measurement of individual indicators
would be meaningless.

When comparing different systems, in particular, we need
indicators in order to make evaluations. It makes no sense to compare
the Supreme Soviet with the U.S. Congress, even if both institutions
do seem to be parliaments. But *policy output* can be compared in
a variety of ways, the extremely different nature of the institutions
that produce this output notwithstanding. A particular drawback
encountered in the case of socialist countries is that there is still
less *survey data* available to back up the *aggregate data*. Thus satisfaction with output is still more difficult to measure than in capitalist
countries. Sometimes the mere application of the word "indicator"
has been criticized—the Russian word "*pokazately*" or the East
German expression "*Kennziffer*" mean, it is claimed, something very
different. The Rumanians, however, make it unlikely that *pokazatel*
has a completely different meaning from the word "indicator" since,
true to the tradition of Latin languages, they use precisely the same
word as Western scholars, namely, "*indicatori.*"[25] Furthermore,
a familiar argument put forward by socialist countries to the effect
that the search for indicators in comparative studies marks an
attempt to ignore the "systematic differences" between systems does
not seem very logical in light of the assertion in Soviet textbooks
that comparisons with indicators can serve to reveal both differences
and uniformities in systems. This is an essence of knowledge on
comparisons that dates from the *Logic* of John Stuart Mill, with his
differentiation between the "method of agreement" and the "method
of difference."[26] Criticism of the quantitative bias of gross units of
production when used in research will hurt Western science less than
the socialist countries. The "ideology of tons" has only recently
been substituted by the search for "qualitative indicators," officially
emphasized at the twenty-fifth party convention, and in the meantime
the most important periodical *Sotsiologisheskie issledovaniya* is being
allowed to discuss the problem even under its Western term of
"social indicators" (*sotsial'nye pokazately*).[27] Whatever may still be
the shortcomings of the social indicators movement in the West,
there is no doubt that it represents an important countermovement

against gross output figures in macroeconomic analysis and in the attempt to measure the "quality of life."

The search for indicators would only become meaningless if we were naive enough to believe that by comparing systems on the basis of some 100 indicators we would obtain a quantitatively reliable figure on the efficiency of a system as a whole. Even economists have given up measuring comparative effectiveness, because there are quite a few differences that are due less to the system than to certain features in political and social culture. As a Polish economist once put it: "Our economic reform model is far superior to the East Germans', but East German performance is far superior to ours."[28] This he explained as resulting from a superior work ethic on the part of East German workers. Indicators do, however, help to get sectoral comparisons away from a mere exchange of ideological statements of superiority.

Soviet scholars cooperate in many international statistical enterprises. There is still some criticism of the categories used in international statistics, and typologies are offered that better meet the conditions of socialist countries. The search for indicators as such, however, is no longer condemned as being "bourgeois."[29]

Comparisons of socialist countries on the basis of indicators are facilitated by the unified accounting system adopted by the Comecon countries, which was, in many ways, a copy of the Soviet model, but with certain exceptions, such as the German Democratic Republic, which relied on the old German fiscal tradition. In addition, data in socialist countries are sometimes less divergent than in Western democracies since juridical definitions of notion do not hold the same role there,[30] and, in the Comecon countries at least, there is a high degree of homogeneity in the ideological basis underlying the definition of phenomena in the various countries. On the other hand, comparison with countries outside Comecon is still more difficult than comparison among OECD countries. Even Che Guevara admitted that the organization of planning and the collection of data at the outset of Cuban planning was guerrillero-like.[31] Since Cuba's integration into Comecon, the situation has become much better, although the late-developers, Mongolia and Cuba, are sometimes dropped from the statistics in some years so as not to highlight certain lags too drastically.[32] It was 1952 before China created a central statistical system and 1955 before her statistics could be considered to be reliable.[33] Since the 1960s there have been few figures available, and even standard Soviet textbooks on the Chinese economy stop at 1960 in most tables.[34]

Deliberate falsification of data is usually no longer imputed to socialist countries by Western scholars. It is recognized that data are no longer produced for propaganda purposes and that the planners themselves are making increasing use of them.[35] Even in China the time is past when statistics seemed to be tantamount to subversion because of their "bourgeois objectivism."[36]

But even the Soviet Union (where hardly any reliable data is available between the late 1930s and 1956) has serious gaps in its data handbook. There are no data on nonferrous metals or on strategic goods such as ships, aircraft, and most electronic products. There are virtually no data on important social phenomena, such as alcoholism and other forms of deviant behavior. Financial statistics and the national budget are incomplete.[37]

The most important source of error, however, is the reporting system used by the state-owned industries. Keen interest in the indicators for future plans and hopes for an easy plan permitting surplus production and hence additional bonuses for the workers may distort the reliability of data, especially as far as economic data are concerned, despite the honesty of central statistical officers. Statistics in socialist countries (and this is unfortunately true of social statistics in Western countries as well) can be compared to a bikini: "interesting parts are revealed, but the essentials remain covered."[38]

Any attempt to use these available sources will reveal only an incomplete picture. The author is prepared for criticism quoting the truism that the search for indicators is incomplete because there are too few indicators in some relevant spheres such as "participation"[39] —"*Ein Schelm, der mehr gibt als er hat*" (A villain who gives more than he has to offer—German proverb). A process-oriented view of the development of socialist countries must proceed with care when generalizing certain indicators for all the socialist countries. Familiar indicators for modernization are always in danger of reflecting Western biases. A typical example here is "urbanization," which figured so prominently as an indicator in early developmental research —it is of little value as an indicator once we are aware of the fact that socialist systems have tried to prevent their big cities from growing bigger; China has even experimented with a reversal of the urbanization process during sending-down movements (see Chapter 2, Section 1).

Sometimes figures for Western systems are given for purposes of comparison. It should be borne in mind, however, that data groups fall roughly into three different categories when it comes to the comparability of indicators taken from capitalist and socialist countries:

1. Some data, such as working days lost through accidents, drop-out rates in the school system, or interview data on how people spend their time during a day, are comparable without great difficulty. Some differences in counting methods may, however, distort the results even in this group. The two German states, for example, have developed different time spans for reporting accidents at work.
2. Most data are comparable after suitable adaptation by the statisticians; here we can cite comparisons of GNP and the national income of socialist countries (see Chapter 4, Section 1).
3. A large amount of data is easy to come by but is not comparable at all. It makes no sense to compare the degree of unionization in the Soviet Union (97%) with that in the United States (about 24%) without discussing the qualitative differences in trade unions in the socialist countries, where they administer the social welfare system and therefore hold more gratifications and sanctions to motivate workers to join them.

Only for the first two types of data are cross-systemic figures occasionally offered. This does not mean, however, that these data are comparable without qualitative comments on differences within the respective systems.

Research on aggregate data needs to be backed up by *subjective indicators* and *survey data,* because *policy output* is not automatically converted into an *input of legitimacy* on the part of the people. "Satisfaction" does not necessarily correlate with government performance. Behavioralist students in microsocial science have been more optimistic in this respect than have the macroresearch-oriented pioneers of the social indicator movement, who have some doubts as to the availability in the foreseeable future of reliable subjective indicators.[40] Nevertheless, we have an increasing need for subjective indicators, since in capitalist and socialist countries alike certain crises of legitimacy are caused less by a *performance crisis* than by a *satisfaction crisis* with the performing state, which cannot always be explained by the population's rising expectations.

For a long time Marxist planners were even more reluctant to admit the importance of subjective indicators than they were in the case of objective aggregate data. Marx himself was apparently anti-behavioralist in that he refused "to judge a period of transformation on the basis of conscience," and he also held that an individual could not be assessed through his self-image (MEW, Vol. 13, p. 9). This contempt for subjective opinions did not, however, prevent Marx from using surveys himself when he needed evidence to show that the workers did not share the assessments of bourgeois governments. An example of this is represented by his "questionnaire for workers" (1880) (MEW, Vol. 19, pp. 230ff, 570). He even used the survey data to question objective social data on the alleged improvements in the living conditions of the working class. If one analyzes this questionnaire, however, it becomes evident that the opinions of the workers were less important to Marx than were the informational questions about their objective social condition. Nevertheless, this example is sometimes quoted by nonorthodox socialist thinkers, such as Garaudy, to show that Marx himself would not approve of the elitist approach adopted by ruling parties, who for a long time were not concerned about the opinion of the people, except under the guise of secret service reports.

Survey data are still harder to come by than objective social indicators, though this has been available to Western scholars through surveys carried out among emigrés. In the early days these were U.S. surveys; recently they have been mainly conducted in Israel.[41] Foreign scholars have only rarely been allowed to carry out surveys in socialist countries, such as in the early days in Cuba and more recently in Yugoslavia.[42] Occasionally survey data from socialist countries have been brought to the West by the person who had collected them and then published.[43]

Survey studies in socialist countries were initially conducted in the production sphere in order to increase working discipline and control deviant behavior. Whereas capitalist societies mostly develop deviant behavior in the distribution sphere, socialist societies tend to develop as much deviant behavior in production because of the rigid rules of the planned economy. One of the favorite forms of deviant behavior is the illegal exchange of goods for fulfillment of the plan (see Chapter 6, Section 2).

The poorest data basis we have is certainly that in the political sphere. Political questions are generally excluded from those surveys that are published. Even research into nonpolitical areas, such as inquiries into professional prestige, leaves out political posts (unlike certain surveys conducted during the Dubček era in Czechoslovakia) (see Chapter 2, Section 2).

This study tries to provide evidence for the development of socialist countries by means of quantitative data, although it also tries to avoid any data-fetishism and to describe the different evolutions of socialist systems with a historical approach so as not to simplify the results on the rather formalistic basis of available data. The author also tries to avoid the dangers of a kind of *"outputism,"* whereby only facts that are open to politometric analysis are deemed worthy of study. The use of *"symbolic politics"* is still found more frequently in socialist countries than in capitalist societies, since the whole of the state's activity is less oriented toward conflict resolution and aimed instead at transforming the attitudes and perceptions of its citizens. Thus outputs are influenced to a large extent by the necessities of symbolic politics, within the framework of an ideological theory as to the course of history.

4.   Normative goals and the typology of policies in socialist systems

Marxist ideologists are more goal-oriented than most Western scholars, who implicitly stick to the notion of piecemeal engineering. The two basic values of socialist ideology are *security* and *freedom.* These values have two preconditions that need to be fulfilled by socialist policy, namely *equality* and *justice.* Further process-oriented notions play a dominant role in Marxist ideology: The negative aspect of that which is to be overcome is *alienation;* the positive aspect of that which is to be realized is *emancipation.* Some Freudo-Marxists—mostly deriving their ideas from the Frankfurt school— have tried to combine these notions with modern theories of basic needs, ranging from Maslow to Etzioni. Most Marxists, however, would not accept psychological classifications of needs, considering them too ahistorical. Marx taught that needs develop historically. Their development is limited not by basic anthropological predispositions but rather by the limits of production in a given historical period (MEW, Vol. 25, p. 269). Thus so-called *goal culture* (the utopian image of a final society) has too little bearing on *transfer culture,*[44] which develops the norms for everyday decisions in socialist states. This gap is only partly filled by the middle-range projections of the party program. In many cases the priorities have been uncovered with the aid of content analysis.[45]

These priorities, however, do not always reflect the concrete typology of policies emphasized by party leaders in a given period. As in capitalist societies, policies are frequently defined by the competences of ministries. The administrative framework of governments in socialist countries is so fragmented into a large number of highly specialized policy areas that these are not very useful for a fair classification of policies. Hence the author has chosen to take the three spheres of society given in Marxist theory—the sphere of production, the sphere of consumption, and the political sphere—and to combine these with the four main *middle-range goals* of socialist politics, *redistribution, efficiency, protection*, and *participation*. This leads on to the policy classification shown in Figure 2, which underlies the structure of this study. This classification is open to criticism, but it seems to be fairer than a number of other typologies that have been developed. Some do not have a common logical basis and contain *goals* (such as redistributive functions of the states) together with mere *instruments* for realizing goals, such as "regulative" or "repressive" functions of states.[46]

The author's system of classification does not mean that all socialist countries try to combine the same mixture of goals and instruments so as to achieve these goals in an identical manner. Even an individual system will shift its emphasis from one goal to another depending on its stage of development. Once the revolution is over, the *redistribution functions* are at the center of state activity. This generally leads to a loss of *efficiency*, especially with the nationalization of the means of production. Thus, in the second phase, attention is focused on maximizing measures to increase efficiency, and through this overemphasis *protective and participatory measures* are neglected. Participation, in particular, which has played an important role in the revolutionary phases, is now increasingly replaced by manipulated pseudoparticipation from above. These historical differences are not always reflected in time-series of indicators. Again, verbal historical analysis will have to differentiate between the different socialist systems.

The four main instruments of legitimation (ideology and socialization, organization, repression, gratification) are important when it comes to realizing the basic goals. But again, these instruments are dependent on the period of revolutionary politics: in the first phase, particularly in countries that have experienced long civil wars, such as Russia and China, *ideology* and *repression* are the most important instruments. Later, *organization* and *gratifications* play a predominant role when the initial impetus toward revolutionary change is beginning to weaken.

Comparative research has to shed light on the different developmental roads and stages of socialist countries. But no "ideal road to socialism" can be expected to emerge as the result of such an analysis.

Figure 2

Societal sphere	Basic goals	Policies
production	REDISTRIBUTION	redistribution of the means of production (nationalization, collectivization)
distribution		incomes policy, price policy, tax policy, social policies, consumer goods policy, education
legitimation		cadre selection
production	EFFICIENCY	economic policies of growth and stability
distribution		social welfare, infrastructural policies
legitimation		mass mobilization, social control
production	PROTECTION	labor protection
distribution		health policy, social policy, housing construction, protection of the environment
legitimation		legal policy
production	PARTICIPATION	codetermination at work
distribution		codetermination in central planning
legitimation		organizational policy

Certain generalizations will, however, be possible as to typical mistakes committed by revolutionary elites in a large number of socialist countries, which have taken their toll in terms of economic efficiency and human well-being, and which must be considered as excessive when weighed against the benefits achieved by the socialist transformation of society.

I

REDISTRIBUTION

1

Redistribution
in the production sphere

Even within the economies of capitalist countries there is a spreading view that promotion of a high level of social outcome only represents half the task of state politics. The other half consists in redistributing social outcome among the members of society (J. Berliner).[47] In many cases, however, this view is only put into practice in the distribution sphere. In the production sphere measures tend to be sporadic and coupled with measures in the distribution sphere (such as profit-sharing schemes). Only socialist countries have made redistribution a prime target of politics for any length of time. As a rule, redistribution measures are concentrated in the construction phase of socialism when reorganization of production and ownership patterns enjoys high priority on the list of state measures. In capitalist systems, on the other hand, incremental ad hoc policies, with no ultimate target, take precedence over an equitable distribution structure in society and are merely accompanied by vague comparative targets such as "more social justice." Hence, in the event of a conflict of targets and a shortage of resources, redistribution measures in the distribution sphere are put back in favor of radical redistribution in the production sphere. Redistribution takes on different proportions in the three sectors of trade, industry and commerce, and agriculture.

1.   Socialization of the means of production in industry

At the end of 1917 Lenin saw the dilemma of a revolution confined to one country and acknowledged that a "definitive victory of socialism in one country is, of course, impossible (LPSS, Vol. 35, p. 277). Yet it was not solely because of the isolated position of the Soviet power that he believed immediate construction of a comprehensively planned socialist economy to be impossible. Abolition of private ownership would, he felt, be possible with the help of the masses, but he had no magic recipe for further planning for industry once it had been expropriated—"It is easy to issue a decree on abolition of private ownership, but this must and can only be put into effect by the workers themselves. Should mistakes occur then these are the mistakes of a new class building up a new life. No concrete plan exists for organizing economic life, nor could it ever exist" (LPSS, Vol. 35, p. 147).

A combination of action both from below and from above was to serve to achieve the first step in propelling worker control beyond the dual leadership phase and to tackle expropriation of the bourgeoisie. An initial step toward this was outlined in mid-December in the draft decree on socialization of the national economy. This, however, went far beyond the measures that actually proved feasible. It was proposed that the banks be nationalized, mandatory syndicates be set up, a state monopoly be established for foreign trade, capitalist speculation be combatted, unemployment be eliminated, and the food situation be improved. So that checks could be made on the bourgeoisie, all citizens with assets of more than 1000 rubles and a monthly income of 500 rubles were to keep a consumption and work book in which they were to enter work done (LPSS, Vol. 35, p. 156).

These far-reaching requirements came up against resistance in the party, however, and only nationalization of the banks and cancelation of the national debt were able to be implemented immediately. Even in nationalizing the banks Lenin met with misgivings, to which he alluded when addressing the All Russia Central Executive Committee on December 14 (27), 1917, as he took to task the "criticizing learned experts" who only declared themselves in agreement "in principle" with the Council's decisions and with proletariat dictatorship. "Why," he asked the scrupulous members of the party in helpless passion, "if you know everything so well and are so experienced, do you not help us? Why do we see nothing but sabotage on your side as we plough our difficult way?" (LPSS, Vol. 35, p. 172). In the face of this resistance even the theory of comprehensive socialization of industry as a whole had to be abandoned in favor of the theory of a state capitalist transitional economy. The concept of workers' self-administration also had to make way for the authoritarian labor charter concept set up under the German war economy, which led to the left-wing opposition, under Bukharin, reproaching Lenin with betrayal of his earlier ideals.

Only the banking system and the fleet were nationalized in 1917/18; for the rest, capitalist ownership patterns were left largely untouched. The Soviet state restricted itself to isolated measures against enterprises suspected of resistance to and sabotage against the new system. Alongside this, however, expropriations occurred in the country which were not controlled on a centralized basis but were instead carried out by the local cadres or through spontaneous action on the part of the workers. Since the latter generally led to production stoppages, the Council of the People's Commissars felt itself compelled on February 1, 1918, to ban expropriations without the approval of the newly established Supreme Council of the National Economy. Trotski proceeded to criticize strongly the "flood of comradeship," and more than a few party leaders recommended that the running of enterprises be left to the bourgeois experts and not to the elected councils.[48] In his speech on nationalization of the banks, which also contained even further-reaching ideas, Lenin had already judged cooperation of the bourgeois specialists to be of importance: "We will call upon the experts in this field to help us but only when the keys are in our hands. Then we will be able to employ former millionaires as experts" (LPSS, Vol. 35, p. 172). Lenin now saw state capitalism as the "saving grace" that could secure the transition to socialism, "since state capitalism is something centralized, thought-out, controlled, and socialized and that is precisely what we are lacking" (LPSS, Vol. 36, p. 255). Although Lenin had virtually no other choice than the one he took during the years of war communism, his option was to have far-reaching consequences. Since redistribution in the production sphere was only successful in a very sporadic manner in the initial stages, the increase in efficiency in the NEP period was interposed, as it were, in the redistribution process, and the end of the 1920s saw a cumulation of several targets, such as redistribution (particularly in the agricultural sector), increased efficiency through introduction of the plan system, and forced industrialization. These targets were to some extent incompatible. It was only at the price of extreme intensification in the dictatorship that they could be tackled in parallel at all. The socialist systems that came about after the Second World War encountered less difficulty in their redistribution policy since they were protected externally by the Soviet protecting power and internally had only to combat a bourgeoisie greatly weakened through war.

Stages in redistribution policy

As a rule, nationalization of industry was tackled with greater speed than collectivization of agriculture, with the exception of Bulgaria. Given the fact that several socialist countries were under-developed, sweeping expropriation of the widely scattered small-holdings was not possible. Despite the reproaches of left-wing Western communists, Lenin went on to develop the concept of "state capitalism" (LPSS, Vol. 36, p. 293). Today Soviet economics still regards state capitalism as an unavoidable transitional phase for many countries, one that can be divided into three phases:

1. a phase of indirect control of the mainly private sector through tax, price, and credit policies;
2. a phase of mixed state/private enterprises;
3. a nationalization phase.

The country that followed this pattern most closely in its politics was China. Soviet economists believe,[49] however, that the policy of special treatment for the "national bourgeoisie" (that is, the section of the bourgeoisie that was neither "imperialist" nor "counter-revolutionary"), consisting in compensation and in the maintenance of many former industrialists at the head of their enterprises, meant that only superficial nationalization (*ogosudarstvlenie* rather than *natsionalizatsiya*) came about, even during the third stage of state capitalism. Nationalist and great-power chauvinistic interests had in fact prevailed behind the state façade—Chinese foreign trade and cooperation with the Chinese abroad are cited in attempts to prove this. The Maoist reproach that a "state bourgeoisie" had substituted itself for the proletariat vanguard in the Soviet Union has recently led to retaliation with the theory of a "national state bourgeoisie" in China. Both these designations are of little analytical value, however. The process of regularizing the private sector and creating a nationalized industry was effected in stages (as was the collectivization of agriculture) that differed from one socialist country to another. If we look for a systematic pattern, then four stages do emerge:[50]

1. In systems that made the transition to socialism after the Second World War, the first groups to be expropriated were those suspected of being *war criminals, fascists,* or *collaborators* with the fascist occupying power. In East Germany this took place up to 1948, mainly upon the orders of the Soviet occupying power. The basis for this was Command No. 124 issued by the Soviet occupying power in Germany (SOPG), the so-called Sequester Command, dated October 30, 1945, in which three lists were drawn up. List A covered enterprises that were to be put to a referendum; List B covered less important enterprises whose owners had a clean political record—these enterprises were to be handed back; and List C covered the 200 most important enterprises that were transformed into some 251 Soviet limited liability companies. Ownership of these passed to the Soviet Union. In 1950 this group accounted for 22% of GDR production. The Soviet limited liability companies (with the exception of Wismut AG) were not handed back to the German Democratic Republic in the form of state-owned enterprises until 1953. This instance of nationalization serving for purposes of monitoring reparations was, however, unique and atypical. In the German Democratic Republic, nationalization was driven on at a slower pace than in the other countries, partly on account of political considerations associated with the fact that Germany was not as yet definitely divided. In Poland the socialist sector already accounted for 96.7% of gross output as early as 1950. In Czechoslovakia the figure had reached 96% by 1950, yet in the German Democratic Republic the Soviet limited liability companies and socialist and cooperative undertakings only made up 77.6% of gross output in 1950 (see Table 1).[51] The Soviet limited liability companies, however, provided the Soviet Union with a pawn for controlling the whole economy. This was an instrument of control that did not exist in the other countries, and hence socialist steering capacity was greater than the proportion of nationalized property implied.

The last wave of nationalization in the German Democratic Republic was initiated relatively later on (between February and May 1972). This covered seminationalized enterprises, private enterprises, and some of the craft cooperatives (PGHs). The campaign was the subject of careful preparation. It even proved possible to preprogram a certain degree of self-initiative on the part of the bourgeois parties (in particular the Liberal Democratic party, the LDPD).[52]

2. In systems that made the transition to socialism in confrontation with imperialist powers, nationalization of *foreign capital* played an initial role. In China foreign firms were first subjected

mainly to indirect pressure with, for example, a ban on dismissal of workers making these firms unprofitable for foreign capitalists.[53] In Cuba nationalization through the law of July 6, 1960, constituted retaliation for the cancellation on the part of the United States of the sugar quota, and in Chile even the nonsocialist opposition parties agreed to nationalization of the American firms. Contrary to the complete stop put on capital investment from capitalist powers in the Eastern bloc countries, Chile at this time was encouraging joint ventures between foreign firms and the Chilean state.[54] In some cases there were protracted negotiations in the people's democracies as regards compensation for capitalist proprietors.

3.   In all systems nationalization policy was initially focused on the *basic materials industries*—even the bourgeois parties had demanded that these be nationalized after the Second World War. In many Eastern bloc countries—as in Hungary—this firstly involved the mines and large enterprises in the metalworking industry.[55] In countries with a different structure and virtually no mineral resources, the most important processing industry was to be found in other branches of the economy—in Cuba, for instance, in the sugar mills, with the first expropriations of plantations following with the law of October 13, 1960.

4.   At a subsequent stage, the *number of workers* criterion was laid down in a large number of systems. This, however, did not provide a sufficiently sound basis for expectation since—as was the case when the hectare limit was set during the expropriation of large estate holdings—the permissible ceilings fluctuated rather frequently; in Hungary, for example, Law No. XXV in 1948 set the limit at 100 workers, yet in 1949 only 10 workers were allowed to be employed privately[56]; in Yugoslavia in the 1970s the number of workers permitted was said to have been increased from 10 to 50.[57] Even in countries where these nationalization campaigns appeared to have the support of wide majorities, there was always criticism, and rightly so, that they did not create uniform criteria and did not permit reliable expectations, hence causing unnecessary cutbacks in production due to investment strikes. After Allende had taken over power in Chile, it was announced that some 200 enterprises would have to reckon on being nationalized, with additional criteria being tacked on subsequently—monopolies and ologopolies or certain branches of the economy. These were primarily the subject of contention when nationalization seemed to have repercussions on political pluralism, such as when it was announced that ex-president Alessandri's paper factory was to be nationalized, and the opposition

feared that this would lead to discrimination in the allocation of the paper ration for opposition pamphlets.[58]

Although the parties proceeded gradually in the individual countries, obliged to give varying degrees of consideration to the "nationalist bourgeoisie," they had nonetheless achieved clear dominance of the socialist sector after a few years, measured in terms of gross production, although not always in terms of retail trade turnover as well in all countries. According to Soviet figures (see Table 1) the redistribution process in the people's democracies of Eastern Europe progressed comparatively more rapidly than had been the case in the Soviet Union and was later to be the case in China.

The underlying causal factors determining the relative extent of public ownership in socialist countries lie, no doubt, outside the sphere of economics. But if we compare the branches showing the highest proportions of nationalized enterprises, socialist countries follow patterns that are similar to those of capitalist countries. Branches with tendencies toward a monopoly, heavy industry, and nationally prestigious branches of economics and especially

Table 1

Proportion accounted for by the "socialist sector"
(in percentages)

Country	Year	Socialist sector		Private sector	
		Gross industrial production	Retail trade turnover	Gross industrial production	Retail trade turnover
Bulgaria	1950	97.5	94.3	2.5	5.7
China	1952	52.8	42.0	39.0	57.8
Czechoslovakia	1950	96.0	91.7	4.0	8.3
GDR	1950	77.6	47.2	22.4	52.8
Poland	1950	96.7	83.0	3.3	17.0
Rumania	1950	92.4	88.5	7.6	11.5
Soviet Union	1924	76.0	47.3	24.0	52.7

Source: V. I. Vanin, *Gosudarstvennyi kapitalizm v KNR* (Moscow: Nauka, 1974), p. 16. Slightly deviant figures in: K. I. Mikul'skii, *Klassovaya struktura obshchestva v stranakh sotsializma* (Moscow: Nauka, 1976), p. 47.

Table 2

Nationalization ratios for major economic sectors
(in percentages)

Country	Year	Total	Manu-facturing, mining	Commerce	Construc-tion	Transpor-tation, communi-cation
Bulgaria	1956	37	85	96	96	100
GDR	1964	71	84	55	67	96
Poland	1960	48	83	53	90	96
Soviet Union	1959	59	93	92	100	100
Yugoslavia	1953	30	72	79	100	100
for comparison:						
Austria	1966	31	25	18	4	78
France	1954	17	8	5	1	69
Israel	1959	24	2	1	6	32
Japan	1960	10	0	0	14	42
Sweden	1960	20	4	5	12	53
United Kingdom	1962	25	9	n.d.	8	70
United States	1960	15	1	1	12	18
FRG	1950	9	1	0	0	74

Source: F. L. Pryor, *Property and Industrial Organization in Communist and Capitalist Nations* (Bloomington: Indiana U.P., 1973), pp. 46f.

the necessity of socialist regimes to control transportation and communication show the highest impetus toward rapid nationalization after seizure of power by communist parties (see Table 2).

Instruments of redistribution policy

The extensive range of expropriation criteria was backed up by an extensive range of instruments that were applied in the subsequent stages of nationalization policy. These instruments were employed to very varying degrees. They included:

1. material incentives (such as state holdings, tax and personal benefits for those concerned);
2. ideological mobilization of the masses and democratic decision mechanisms;
3. indirect repression, through a tightening-up of legal measures for dealing with economic offences and provocation of labor conflicts.

1. *Material incentives* were employed most extensively in countries that had to give the most consideration to a strong "nationalist bourgeoisie," that is, mainly in China and the German Democratic Republic.

In 1955, China launched a campaign among industrialists, encouraging them to surrender their property to the state in return for five years' relatively high compensation. In many cases former capitalists were appointed directors of state enterprises and were able to continue receiving dividends even after the set deadline of 1962. Despite criticism during the cultural revolution of the privileges accorded to the nationalist bourgeoisie, there is virtually no indication that these have been fully abolished. In 1956 roughly one-third private/seminationalized enterprises existed alongside the state sector.[59]

"Persuasion" was also rated above repression in policies relating to the nationalist bourgeoisie, although the methods of persuasion used always contained an element of psychological coercion and did not bring about a true change of attitude in every case. Only "bureaucratic capitalists" and the closest supporters of the Kuomintang were excluded from this tolerance policy. Even renegade Kuomintang officials and those belonging to the Manchu dynasty were given the opportunity to convert. However, since they could not, as a rule, become party members, they were granted a channel to represent their interests in the Democratic party. This party remained undisturbed up to the cultural revolution, and it is estimated that in the sixties more than 110 nationalist capitalists were members of the National People's Congress.[60] The law on inheritance was not revoked de jure, but the system succeeded in convincing people through social pressure to renounce their inheritance.

The German Democratic Republic also made extensive use of material incentives during the third phase of its nationalization policy, creating seminationalized enterprises in the form of a *Kommanditgesellschaft* (limited partnership), in which the state was represented via a bank or via a state-owned enterprise. The owners were granted tax concessions. Managing directors' salaries were subject to a maximum tax rate of only 20%, whereas income tax for capitalists could run as high as 90%.[61]

2.   A second instrument used to advance the pace of the socialization of the means of production consisted in *ideological mobilization of the masses* and *democratic decision mechanisms*. The first form emerged predominantly in opinion-molding processes aimed at winning the full backing of the people and was used in China in 1952/53 with the "Five-Antis" campaign, when industrialists were intimidated with the fight against the five evils: tax evasion, fraud, bribery, production espionage, and theft of state property. A variant on this is the "Cuban strategy" in Latin America, which since Allende's takeover of power has been renamed the "Vuskovic strategy" (after the Chilean Minister of Foreign Affairs). Not infrequently labor disputes were triggered off externally, and the state, claiming it had to maintain public supplies, took recourse to Decree No. 520, left over from the short-lived Socialist Republic of the thirties and now being cited once more. According to this decree, enterprises could be expropriated under certain circumstances where this served the public interest.[62] In this way, 30% of national production was brought under state control, as against the previous figure of 10%.[63]

In a bid to stop this nationalization via administrative channels, the Chilean opposition attempted to bind nationalization to a law of Congress. This it did by introducing a law modifying the Constitution, which was passed on February 19, 1972, against the votes of the Unidad Popular. Allende placed his veto on this law, thereby provoking constitutional conflict. It proved impossible to resolve the legal bottleneck, and this contributed toward accelerating the 1973 counterrevolution.

Whereas representative, democratic attempts to legalize the channel nationalization policy have little prospect of success and are rejected by all states committed to dictatorship of the proletariat (and are certainly not capable of producing rapid nationalization), plebiscitary, democratic means have also been employed in other systems that had to contend with a strong bourgeoisie. In the German Democratic Republic, a referendum was to be held for List A enterprises. This marks a clear continuation of the left-wing initiatives taken in the plebiscitary expropriation of the princes of the Weimar Republic. An actual vote was, however, only held in the then *Land* (Province) of Saxony; this was on June 30, 1946, when 82% of votes cast were in support of the law. Citing the Saxony result, the authorities issued a decree for expropriation of the other "Länder," on the legal basis of SOPG Command No. 110, dated October 22, 1945.

All the same, a referendum held under guaranteed democratic conditions would nonetheless have been one way of advancing redistribution policy with true majority approval.

3.   A third set of instruments covers various types of *repression*, ranging from a tightening-up of the law on penalties for economic offences (GDR 1948) to the invervention of state agents, as happened not infrequently in Chile. It is, however, striking that the very systems that today regard themselves as resolutely prepared for revolution, such as Cuba and China, were not the countries that made a predominant use of repression. Instead, they employed material incentives, which, once redistribution was completed in the production sphere, were categorically rejected in the distribution sphere.

Concentration and monopolization

The redistribution process in the production sphere was accompanied by a simultaneous concentration of enterprises, brought about by the party with a view to increased efficiency. However, marked differences also exist here between the various socialist systems. In some socialist countries there seems to be no indication that this concentration, which followed on from nationalization, was by any means orientated toward the degree of monopolization achieved with capital during the presocialist period. While Czechoslovakia headed the concentration league in the sixties, the German Democratic Republic, for example, had no concentration movement of comparable proportions, despite its high level of productive resources and despite considerable concentration in a large number of sectors in presocialist times (see Table 3).

The size of production establishment in socialist countries is determined by various factors, such as the extent of the domestic market of a nation. The greater the barriers to trade, the smaller establishment size would be[64] (which can explain the relatively small size of GDR establishments only in the first phase of the East German experiment). The vicissitudes of centralization and decentralization of the planning systems (see Chapter 6, Section 2) also affected the degree of monopolization. A uniform trend is similarly lacking in countries such as Rumania and Bulgaria, where indus-

Table 3

Breakdown of industrial enterprises according to number of workers (1965) (in percentages)

Country	up to 500	501– 1,000	1,001– 5,000	5,001– 10,000	over 10,000
Bulgaria	31.8	20.9	39.2	4.3	3.8
Czechoslovakia	7.2	8.1	55.4	16.7	12.6
GDR	42.7	16.8	29.8	8.2	2.5
Hungary	9.7	7.9	47.9	20.0	14.5
Poland (1964)	21.2	16.5	47.2	11.9	3.2
Rumania	13.6	20.6	51.9	8.8	5.5

Source: M.Os'mova. "Kontsentratsia promyshlennosti v stranakh SEV," *Voprosy ekonomiki* No. 8 (1971): 99.

trialization took place at a later stage. In Bulgaria the number of small firms has remained relatively high, whereas in Rumania this has been the case for medium-sized firms. In all socialist countries, however, a number of sectors—particularly newly established lines of business —are highly concentrated, with a degree of monopolization which in itself holds new dangers. Even though the monopolization of a number of sectors permits efficient production, it nonetheless has an increasingly detrimental effect on the distribution sphere, since once firms have a greater say in price formation the abuse of monopoly positions cannot be entirely excluded, despite the better price-monitoring channels open to socialist states (see Chapter 2, Section 3).

2.   Cooperativization and nationalization
in trade and industry

In countries such as Poland and Czechoslovakia, which had known a strong cooperative movement before the transition to socialism, there was a large potential of anticapitalist feeling to tap, yet great difficulty was experienced in integrating the cooperatives into the socialist sector, with many half-hearted attempts being made to find a solution. This stemmed from the fact that many leaders of the cooperative movement favored the idea of a "third course" midway between capitalism and socialism, and their initial position of supporting the socialist government's redistribution policy gave way to a position constituting a hindrance in the transformation process.[65]

In trade and industry, concessions similar to those in the agricultural sector were granted to private enterprise. Whereas in the large socialist states—the Soviet Union and China—private enterprise no longer accounts for a significant market share, it has always accounted for a high share in the smaller countries. The highest percentage is to be found in Yugoslavia, where in 1959 only 11.6% of enterprises were organized along nationalized or cooperative lines. As late as 1964, 43.6% of those working in this branch were still employed by private enterprises.[66]

In Yugoslavia the proportion of output originating from the private sector is on the increase, chiefly in the craft, building, gastronomy, and transport sectors; consequently, the relative proportion of agriculture is falling (see Table 4).

In the German Democratic Republic—which in other areas was striving to be the "star pupil" of redistribution policy—despite establishment of the state retail stores (HO) in 1948, it proved impossible to step up either nationalization or cooperativization in this sector to the same rate as in other countries on account of the particular bottleneck in supplies experienced after the war.

Table 4

Breakdown of the private sector in Yugoslavia according to branches
(in percentages)

Branch	1962	1971
private sector as a whole	100.0	100.0
agriculture	87.6	75.3
crafts	7.1	10.5
building	4.2	9.1
restaurant businesses	0.2	2.2
transport	0.9	2.8

Source: *Materijalni i drustveni razvoj SFR Jugoslavije 1947–1972* (Belgrade; Savezni zavod za statistiku, 1973), p. 45.

According to GDR statistical yearbooks, the private craft sector still accounted for 53.6% of output in 1968, compared with 46.6% for the cooperative sector, and the private retail stores still made up 11.6% of turnover, compared with 9.2% for seminationalized stores, 34% for cooperative stores, and 45.2% for the state-owned sector[67] (see Table 5).

The biggest campaign against the private sector, in particular in trade and the service industries, was waged in Cuba. On March 26, 1968, 55,636 enterprises were nationalized and either allocated to state undertakings or placed under the management of the Revolution Defence Committees (CDR)—mass organizations divided up according to residential areas.

Shattering the "new petit-bourgeoisie" was a costly business, since rationing had to be tightened for all important commodities. Castro briefly founded this measure with the words "We haven't held a revolution here to establish the right to trade! That revolution took place in 1789—the era of the bourgeois revolution—nearly everyone has read about it. That was the revolution of the merchants, the bourgeoisie. When will people finally understand that this is a socialists' revolution, a communists' revolution."[68] There has probably been no other transitional society that has implemented its redistribution process so systematically right through to the end, taking an

Table 5

Ownership structure in trade
(in percentages)

Country	Year	State-owned	Cooperative	Private
Bulgaria	1977	66.7	33.3	0
Czechoslovakia	1977	74.3	25.7	0
GDR	1977	87.5		6
Hungary	1977	62.9	36.4	0.7
Poland	1977	28.2	70.5	1.2
Rumania	1977	71.2	28.8	0
Soviet Union	1976	69.3	28.2 (kolhoz trade)	2.5

Source: Selected statistics. From: *Jahrbuch der Wirtschaft Osteuropas/Yearbook of East-European Economics,* Vol. 8 (Munich: Olzog, 1979), pp. 458ff.

unusually high toll in terms of economic growth rates, and one that has been prepared to achieve equality in the production sphere at the cost of leveling down the population to frugality in the distribution sphere.

3. Collectivization of agriculture

Since all the autonomous and autochthonous socialist revolutions that have taken place to date have been staged in developing countries, redistributive policy in agriculture has always had a decisive impact on the major part of the population. The agricultural work force accounted for the majority of the working population in all systems, with the exception of Cuba and some highly industrialized states such as the German Democratic Republic and the Czechoslovakian Socialist Republic (see Table 6).

Time and pace of redistribution

In all socialist countries apart from Yugoslavia, Marxist theory assumes that the process of redistribution must lead on to indivisible collective property. The idea that state-owned enterprises must belong collectively to the workers involved is rightfully rejected for reasons of differences in development, and this is considered as anarchist–syndicalist degeneration of Marx and Engels' thought. Marx and Engels themselves had already feared that group owner- ship would only bring about a partial change in attitudes toward property and society and not the fundamental change required.[69]

The only exception to this rule was the Marxist classics' attitude to agricultural property. In his paper on the "Peasants' Question" of 1894, Engels expressed the view (MEW, Vol. 22, p. 502) that the party should not set out to conceal from the small peasants the inevitable decline of their class, because large-scale capitalist produc- tion would sweep over their powerless, outdated smallholdings, "like a railway train over a wheelbarrow." He did not, however, consider it to be the party's task to accelerate the extinction of the small peasantry. He therefore warned against "forceful expropriation" of the smallholders—either with or without compensation—once the

Table 6

Percentage of workers employed in agriculture

Country	%	Year	Rank out of 98 cases	Percentage 1960	1970	1979
Albania	72	1950	17	57.0	54.0	
Mongolia	71	1955	18	60.8	47.3	40.4
Rumania	70	1956	21	65.6	49.3	31.1
People's Republic of China	69	1950	28			64.0 (1975)
Yugoslavia	67	1953	30	63.7	49.8	
Bulgaria	64	1956	35	55.5	35.8	24.9
Poland	57	1950	46	44.1	34.6	26.9
Soviet Union	48	1959	60	38.8	25.4	20.6
Cuba	42	1953	65		27.2 (1975)	23.9 (1978)
Hungary	38	1960	70	38.9	26.4	21.8
Czechoslovakia	38	1950	71	25.9	18.6	14.3
GDR	19	1956	85	17.2	13.0	10.5

Source: B. M. Russett (ed.), *World Handbook of Political and Social Indicators* (New Haven and London, 1964), pp. 177ff. Figures for 1979: *Statisticheskii ezhegodnik stranchlenov SEV 1980* (Moscow: Statistika, 1980), pp. 403ff. On China: W. Kraus, *Wirtschaftliche Entwicklung und sozialer Wandel in der VR China* (Heidelberg: Springer, 1979), p. 535.

A comparison of different sources in: K. E. Waedekin, *Sozialistische Agrarpolitik in Osteuropa,* Vol. 2 (Berlin [West]: Duncker & Humblot, 1978), pp. 100f.

state power had been conquered, "even though we have to expropriate the big landowners." The collectivization of agriculture in socialist systems was based on Engels' instructions: "Our first task when it comes to the small peasant is to turn his private enterprise into a cooperative enterprise—not by force but by giving an example and by offering social assistance to this end" (ibid., p. 499). He held the view that one should spare the peasants the "real fall into the proletariat" and should try to win them over before capitalist production had developed through to its final consequences everywhere.

The special treatment reserved for agricultural property and, in some ways, for craftsmen's property too, once a socialist power had established itself in a state, was based on the fact that precapitalist structures predominated in the countryside. This was not so in the case of the large estates, and Engels recommended straightforward expropriation here. However, he did advocate complete frankness. The party should never give the impression of wanting to perpetuate plot ownership, as did the petit-bourgeois "rabble-rousing anti-semitism." This stipulation of absolute frankness, however, greatly handicapped the party in its job. No one had adequately forecast the very marked lack of interest that the peasants would show in further transformation once the first wave of redistribution had been completed, showing distrust toward the party whenever there was mention of the need to further reorganize production conditions in the countryside.

Thus the first socialist state, that is, Soviet Russia, was able to take a relatively long time over the transformation process in the countryside. Lenin polemized against the cooperative concept of the older utopian socialism, which believed in a peaceful transformation of society through cooperatives without revolution. However, once the political revolution was completed in Russia, his advice to people during the NEP period was to "first adapt to the level of the commonest peasant" and not to ask "anything higher" from him.

He felt it was up to the party to first make the population civilized enough "to appreciate all the advantages to be gained from general participation in cooperatives and to organize this participation by themselves." As far as Lenin was concerned, this transitional period could readily have taken even longer than his successor, Stalin, subsequently allowed for it. He spoke of a period of one or two decades for this "cultural revolution"—this was precisely the context in which Lenin used the term (LPSS, Vol. 45, p. 377). In the first phase of the land reform only big landowners were expropriated, as Engels had advocated. The first measures were taken on November 7, 1917, in the famous "Decree on the Land," but the crop failure of 1921, which yielded only half the prewar harvest, meant it was necessary to suspend redistribution and to tolerate a transitional phase of private capitalism during the NEP period.

In 1917 the Bolsheviks did not have a program for redistribution in the countryside and, unlike the redistribution process in China, they were lacking cadres with agricultural experience. Not infrequently they adopted the social revolutionaries' program—particularly since the Soviet government had very little control over events in the countryside in most parts of the former Tsardom. Compared to the Chinese redistribution process in the country, this was a largely uncontrolled and anomic process.[70]

Unlike the first phase of redistribution, the second phase, between 1929 and 1933, was conducted much more firmly and was implemented without taking local peculiarities into account, despite warnings from the opposition, which advocated a pragmatic approach; among these was Bukharin, for example: "We have no rich peasants in the Western sense, our kulaks cannot be compared with the rich peasants in Germany or France or with the American farmers. Everybody owning two horses and a few agricultural machines has been labeled a kulak. It will take years before this peasant economy is converted into a modern agricultural system. The party's monopoly will not be jeopardized if a few of these kulaks get rich; we hold the top commands and are able to maintain control. Compulsory collectivization would alter the regime's very character and would entail disastrous consequences. The most appropriate peasants' policy for Russia would be to raise agriculture to a higher level through a network of state-supported cooperatives."[71] There are many interpretations of Stalin's motivation for this doctrinaire approach: the wish for total control, even in the country; a means to combat undersupply in the rapidly growing cities; or a tool for fighting Trotskyist opposition by adopting their agricultural program so as to win over the left wing of the party. Under the terms of the party's project, 20% of land was to be collectivized by the end of the first plan. However, when this target was announced, it led to an unprecedented acceleration of the redistribution process through overzealousness on the part of local cadres. As early as 1932, 75% of land was collectivized, and by 1934 the figure had already reached 90% (see Table 7).

Some of the socialist systems created after the Second World War acted more swiftly in implementing collectivization:

1.   The fastest start was made in Bulgaria: by 1945, 3% of all arable land was already in the hands of collectives.[72]

2.   A more cautious and gradual approach was adopted by some of the relatively highly developed systems of Eastern Central Europe, such as Czechoslovakia and Hungary. Poland was the only Eastern bloc country where major party leaders—such as Gomulka—advised against collectivization and where hardly any pressure was exerted on the peasants even during the Stalinist period of the regime. When collectivization was at its peak, only 9.5% of land was in the hands of cooperatives, while the remaining collectives were generally not formed through the amalgamation of what had previously been independent peasants, but instead by penniless new settlers and farm laborers.[73] One of the reasons for this reluctant attitude held by the Polish leaders was the problem of potential unemployment. They feared that pooling plots into cooperatives would lead to redundancy of labor.[74] In the East European countries

Table 7

Forms of ownership in Soviet agriculture
(in 1,000,000 hectares)

	1928	1940	1965	1970	1979
kolkhoz	1.37	117.72	114.42	99.1	95.7
average size					
(in 1000 ha)	0.1	1.4	6.1	6.1	6.7
sovkhoz	1.37	13.26	94.83	91.7	112.4
average size					
(in 1000 ha)	2.0	3.7	8.3	6.9	5.8
private land					
private land					
of kolhozniks	1.15	4.50	4.20		
of public ser-					
vants	—	0.82	2.53		
private peasants	108.74	14.11	—		

Source: A. G. Gruchy, *Comparative Economic Systems* (Boston: Houghton Mifflin, 1966), p. 737. *SSSR v tsifrakh 1979* (Moscow: Statistika, 1980), pp. 135ff.

that expropriated substantial German minorities up to 1945, collective farms developed mainly in the territories previously inhabited by Germans, particularly in Yugoslavia (Voivodina), Czechoslovakia (the Sudeten regions), and Poland. In comparative terms, the Polish voivodeships of Poznan and Bydgoszcz had the highest percentage of cooperative and state-owned farms, ranking second to the former German Eastern Territories (see Tables 8 and 9).

Even in the newly gained Western territories, however, collectivization was not pushed through with any great impetus. Occasionally the settlers were even ordered to establish individual households and to divide up the land within a certain time limit. Quite often, the individual settlers would abandon the land again, and this would eventually be turned over to state farms—not to collective farms.[75]

3.   The scheme was slowest getting underway in the German Democratic Republic (1952-60) but was then carried out most thoroughly there. The district of Suhl was the last district to report complete collectivization, on April 14, 1960.

To begin with, the holdings expropriated during the first wave of redistribution were not turned over to collective operation. The

Table 8

Forms of ownership in the Polish voivodships
(in percentages)

Voivodship	Private farms	Cooperatives	State farms
Szczeczin	49.3	2.6	46.7
Koszalin	54.4	0.4	44.0
Olsztyn	65.8	0.5	32.8

Source: *Rocznik statystyczny* (Warsaw: G.U.S., 1970), p. 221; Z. A. Kruszewski, *The Oder-Neisse Boundary and Poland's Modernization* (New York: Praeger, 1972), p. 125.

GDR literature justifies this by arguing "that one must by no means press ahead of the evolution of the masses." Moreover, since consideration had to be given to a potential all-German development, it was felt preferable not to push ahead too far in the Eastern part of the country.

4.   A further variant was developed in Cuba, where land reform was carried out without the intermediate stage of extensive land distribution to private peasants. Given the cultivation of sugar cane and the plantation system, large-scale units naturally appeared to be more profitable in a developing country such as this. Before the revolution, the majority of the working population had been wage earners, whereas the independent peasantry were by tradition less important than in the other Latin American countries. The model of state farms became predominant here.[76] In recent Comecon statistics no collective farms are mentioned any more (cf. Table 12, last figure).

As a rule, collectivization was tackled once industry had been nationalized, although in Bulgaria collectivization and nationalization were implemented in the reverse order. In most cases the redistribution process was implemented in three phases:

1.   the first phase was devoted to *expropriation of the big land-owners* and of collaborators with the preceding regime or with foreign countries;
2.   in the second phase the actual *collectivization* was begun (exception: Cuba);
3.   in the third phase, a *higher type* of integrated cooperative farming system was established;

Table 9

Percentage of socialist sector in agriculture
(in percentages of arable land)

Country	Year	Socialist sector	Of which collective	Of which state
Albania	1959	95.1	73.5	
Bulgaria	1959	96.2	92.1	4.1
	1978	99.9		
China	1956		96.0	4.0
Cuba	1963			65.0
	1970			70.0
Czechoslovakia	1960	88.0		
	1972	91.6		
GDR	1960	92.5		
	1968		85.0	7.0
	1978	94.8		
Hungary	1960	77.8		
	1978	98.3		
Mongolia	1960	100.0		
	1978	100.0		
North Korea	1957		93.7	
Poland	1969		1.2	14.5
	1978	24.2		
Rumania	1959	72.7	44.1	28.6
	1978	90.6		
Soviet Union	1960	100.0		
	1978	100.0		
Yugoslavia	1967		14.2	

Sources: Figures for 1960 and 1978: *Statisticheski ezhegodnik stran-chlenov SEV 1976* (Moscow: Statistika 1973), p. 42; China: Li Choh Ming, *Economic Development of Communist China* (Berkeley/Los Angeles: University of California Press, 1959), p. 16; North Korea: R. A. Scalapino & Ch. S. Lee, Communism in Korea, Vol. 2 (Berkeley/Los Angeles: University of California Press, 1972), p. 1061; I. T. Sanders (ed.), *Collectivization of Agriculture in Eastern Europe* (Lexington: University of Kentucky Press, 1958), p. 70; Cuba: J. I. Dominguez, *Cuba. Order and Revolution* (Cambridge/Mass.: Belknap, 1978), p. 202.

4.   in the future, coexistence of collective and *state farms* is due to be phased out.

For a breakdown of this three-phase process in the various countries, see Figure 3.

The greatest differences naturally occurred in the first phase of the redistribution process, because the property situation, the distribution of latifundia and minifundia, and also the production systems in the agricultural sector—plantation farming or small-scale cultivation, extensive or intensive agriculture—differed greatly among the countries that were aiming to introduce socialist production conditions. Consequently, the upper limit for property ownership varied from one country to another, and the criteria determining how many hectares a peasant had to own before being considered a "kulak" varied according to the economic conditions and the vehemence of the class struggle in the countryside (in South Eastern Europe the hectare limit was 15 hectares and in Yugoslavia between 25 and 30 hectares[77]). The German Democratic Republic started out in 1945 with a 100-hectare limit, and Cuba even had a 400-hectare limit in 1959 (30 caballerias in the Agrarian Reform Law). In 1961 there were still as many as 11,000 kulaks in Cuba—the limit for private property had by then been reduced to 67 hectares. In Chile, the land reform was based on a 70-hectare limit. Czechoslovakia applied a criterion of "more than 50 employees or fifty hectares of land" in 1948.[78] In Rumania, the 50-hectare limit became compulsory on March 2, 1949, and the land mostly remained in the hands of the state.[79] In some Eastern European countries less land was distributed during the first wave of redistribution than in the agrarian reform that took place after the First World War.[80]

In China, which had its own specific property situation, the acreages that Eastern European countries permitted in private ownership during the initial stages would in themselves have been considered a kind of "kulakdom." Big landowners and large-scale farmers, who accounted for 10% of the rural population, owned some 70% of the land, with the remaining 90% of the rural population owning only 30% of all arable land[81] (see Table 10).

China proceeded relatively warily during the first phase, and about 40% of land was redistributed. The percentage of leasehold land dropped from 30 to 5%. The transition to collectivization was conducted much more cautiously than in other socialist countries inasmuch as "mutual aid teams" took on a propagandist function immediately after land distribution and started promoting collective forms of farming, supplying both a model and assistance. In 1950 collective farms accounted for only 10.7% of rural households, although by 1954 the figure had already risen to 58.3%.[82]

In regions liberated earlier than 1949, the improvement brought about in the poor peasants' condition was quite remarkable—even before the Chinese revolution had been completed. Regional surveys have shown that through various reforms, about one-third of rural families had been raised from the level of impoverished small peasantry to the status of new middle peasants by means of redistribution policy.

Whereas the national bourgeoisie was treated with the utmost care, the stratum of parasitic landowners was handled much less considerately—and this with the approval of the overwhelming majority of the population[83]—although they were at least left with a minimum subsistence level (unlike in the Soviet kulak persecutions). The methods of transformation, despite a considerable amount of repression, were mainly based on education, exemplary actions, and mutual assistance, and these had a considerable publicity effect among the poor rural populations in other parts of the country as well.[84]

It is true that the first wave of redistribution policy brought about a greater degree of equality in China, but it was certainly not able to abolish social stratification in the countryside. In fact, it had never been intended to reach this goal in the first wave of redistribution. The only goal here was "the abolition of the landlords as a class, not as individuals." Mao warned his cadres in 1948: "Therefore a landlord should be given as much land and property as a peasant and have the opportunity to learn how to do productive work." Only the worst "counterrevolutionaries" were excluded from this idea.[85] Some of the middle peasants were even allowed to keep more land than was distributed to the poor peasants. Ho Chi Minh went a step further in 1956 with concessions to "kulaks"—"We must show absolute confidence in the poor peasants, form a close alliance with the middle peasants, and a trustworthy alliance with the rich ones." This applied in particular to those who had backed the struggle for liberation.[86] During the first phase, both Mao and Ho Chi Minh applied Stalin's polemic against "absolute leveling-out" to property conditions in the country—an application for which Stalin had not meant it.

This reduced objective has its political repercussions: according to Chinese data, as late as 1954 there were still about 29% poor peasants and agricultural workers. Many small peasants were hardly

Figure 3

Country	First phase	Second phase	Third phase
Soviet Union	1917–21	1929–33	sovkhozization announced as of 1952
China	1950–53: land reform; about 40% of the land redistributed; in 1954, mutual-aid teams comprise 58.3% of households	1953: general line of transition to socialism; 1955: forcing of a higher type of cooperative	1958: formation of communes
Bulgaria	1944–48: about one-half collectivized	1948–49: new impetus owing to First Five-Year Plan	1953–55: stagnation, 1955: 62.5% collectivized
Cuba	1959: Agrarian Reform Law	1963: second agrarian reform (67-hectare limit)	as of 1968: campaign against the private sector

GDR	1945: land reform, 100-hectare limit	1952: first Agricultural Producers' Cooperatives (APC)	1954–60: promotion of second type of APC; by 1960: materialized to about 2/3
Hungary	1949–53: coexistence of different types	1953–55: retrograde movement during the New Course	from 1955: return to the first phase
North Korea	before the Korean War, only experimental cooperatives	1953–54: mutual-aid teams	1956/57: conversion to the higher type; 1957: 93.7%
Poland	1949–51	1956: retrograde movement	
Rumania	1949–51	1951–52: first type becoming more frequent again as a concession	1952: forcing of the higher type
Yugoslavia	1945: agrarian reform, 25 to 35	as of 1948: stagnation following the break with Cominform	1953: law on national land policy: above 10 hectares integration in the land pool

Table 10

Land distribution in China
(in mou*)

Size of farms	1929/33	Change	After reform
poor peasants	8.89	+ 3.57	12.46
middle peasants	22.18	− 3.17	19.01
rich peasants	47.22	− 22.13	25.09
former landlords		+ 12.16	12.16
all households	16.19	− 0.19	15.28

* 1 mou = 0.0667 hectare, 0.1647 acre

Source: P. Schran, *The Development of Chinese Agriculture, 1950–1959* (Urbana, Ill.: University of Illinois Press, 1969), p. 24.

able to subsist. Moreover, there was evidence of a trend toward a renewed concentration of land, despite constant propagandist efforts from the top to foster artificially the threat of a "return to capitalism in the countryside."[87]

Tendencies toward decollectivization

In some countries the agrarian redistribution process underwent a retrograde trend. This was particularly so in Poland, where the cooperatives were allowed to dissolve again from 1956 onwards, after Gomulka's takeover; the same was true of Czechoslovakia and Hungary (1953/54) and also of Yugoslavia from 1950 onwards. In Yugoslavia even the acquisition of private agricultural equipment was progressively liberalized between 1960 and 1967.[88] In Poland, as much as 81% of the land was farmed by private farmers in 1973. Under Gierek there were constant rumors that there would be a further, cautious attempt toward the collectivization of agriculture. Other countries in the Eastern block, such as Bulgaria, experienced stagnation but no retrograde development.

In the course of these trends toward decollectivization the party leaders did not, to their regret, succeed in preventing a partial backslide into primitive and futureless small-scale farming. This meant that the consolidation of arable land and the reorganization of agricultural enterprises had to be carried out at a later date, involving considerable expense, especially in Poland and Yugoslavia.

Even in China there were setbacks, which the party took with relative flexibility but generally countered with new, tougher measures after a short breathing space. Thus, sudden communization was interpreted as a slightly delayed answer to the difficulties experienced in collectivization. In China, in particular, the success of what had initially been a popular redistribution policy was jeopardized by the zigzag course adopted by the leadership: between 1953 and 1955 three attempts were made at accelerating the collectivization process, each of these then giving way to a slack period for purposes of resorbing political opposition.[89]

From 1959 onwards, a retrograde trend also began to emerge in the communization movement. The leadership showed extensive irritation at the radicalization and growing independence of the commune movement in the countryside.[90] The 26,000 or so communes created up to December 1958[91] were divided into production units (200 to 300 households), and these were then subdivided into production teams. In 1961/62 these teams were reduced to some 20 to 30 households. A production brigade was frequently regarded as the equivalent of one of the former production cooperatives, but a comparison of figures shows that quite often several cooperatives were united in one brigade.

The three-level system was not abolished de jure, but the production team had, in fact, become the decisive unit.[92] In some of the communes created after 1960 there were no longer any brigades at all. It is the commune that owns the land, but the lower-ranking units largely have their own independent sources of income and hold responsibility for management. This is despite efforts by commune management to impose centralized control, since tractors and machines are generally still owned or centrally administered by the commune, or at least via the repair stations—providing services that have to be paid for by the production teams—and this still provides a certain measure of central control. Special brigades and industrial enterprises (whose numbers dropped again in the communes after 1961) can procure special incomes in some communes.[93]

Certain retrograde trends were also apparent in other Far Eastern countries as well, particularly in Mongolia, where collectivization of the herds met with resistance.[94] The only countries that escaped noteworthy retrograde tendencies were the German Democratic

Republic—except for the dissolution of a few hundred APCs after the crisis of 1953—and the Soviet Union. In the Soviet Union, however, the process stagnated for some decades, and often a stop had to be put to the development of over-large enterprises.[95]

Types of collective farming

The various steps in the redistribution process in the country-side were characterized by different types of enterprises and different forms of integration. During its starting period, the Soviet Union experimented with several types of collective farming at one and the same time:

1.   the *toz*—T.O.Z. = *tovarishchestvo po obshchestvennoy obrabotke zemli*, featuring common tillage, privately owned draft animals, and collectivization of machinery and of half the land;
2.   the *artel'*—both the land and means of production collectivized;
3.   the *commune*—without private land or marketing facilities.

In the 1929/30 campaign the artel' became the predominant form, and from 1935 onwards it was the only admissible form of kolkhoz. With the artel', the Soviet leadership tried to achieve a compromise between the loosely organized form of the toz and the fully integrated commune (see Table 11).

Table 11

Forms of collective farming at the beginning of Soviet collectivization
(in percentages)

Date	Toz	Artel'	Commune
June 1, 1929	60.1	29.4	10.5
October 1, 1929	68.2	22.7	9.1
May, 1930	14.0	76.9	9.0

Source: Th. P. Bernstein, "Leadership and Mass Mobilization in the Soviet and Chinese Collectivization Campaigns of 1929/30 and 1955/56. A Comparison," *China Quarterly* No. 31 [1–47] (1967): 5.

The commune type, which had also developed to a small extent in the Soviet Union, was cut down by state policy to the artel' type of collective farming, because the egalitarian tendencies of the commune obviously proved to be incompatible with other targets, namely efficiency and development of productive resources. To date, it is primarily the Chinese model of commune that has been polemized against as an "adventurous" form of economy, which offends against the objective economic laws governing the construction of socialism.[96]

The Eastern bloc states mostly created variations of the three Soviet types of collective agriculture. In Hungary and Czechoslovakia as many as four different models coexisted for a time, whereas in Rumania and China there were at times only two variations.[97] In the German Democratic Republic the two lower types—cooperatives for common cultivation of land—resembled the lower Soviet form of the toz. Type III, that is, the APC, was organized along the lines of a Soviet kolkhoz. Even in this type of collective farming, however, a certain percentage of earnings (up to a maximum of 20%) was distributed in proportion to the amount of land, with a minimum of 80% distributed on the basis of labor units. However, those APCs that regarded themselves as the pacemakers of this evolution soon began to abandon their land percentages.[98] Promotion of the third type of collective agriculture went hand in hand with a concentration of enterprises. In the sixties the average size of enterprise increased from 280 to 550 hectares, such that the number of units operating shrank by nearly a half. In 1960, at the end of the collectivization process, just under two thirds of these enterprises were of type III and, by 1969, the figure had reached 85%.

Although the land still remains the property of the members in the third type of collective farm, it is the cooperative that holds the right of use. In the most common type of collective farming in the Eastern bloc (with the exception of Poland and Yugoslavia), the collective farmer is remunerated according to the work he does. The farmers continue to own their houses and a small plot of land. Differences have developed with respect to the legal status of property. In Hungary (from 1967 onwards) and in Rumania, the cooperatives are the landowners, whereas in Bulgaria and Czechoslovakia it is the farmers who hold the nominal land ownership. They have no right to sell their land, however.[99] Even nowadays in some countries it is not easy to establish the actual practice by studying the statutes of collective enterprises. In countries where the resistance against collectivization was greatest, as in Poland or Czechoslovakia, members have often got round practical application of the statutes.

State farms

Transformation of cooperative property into state property was periodically propagated in a large number of socialist countries and then the move presented as evidence that alignment of working conditions for the urban and agricultural working populations was well underway. The 1961 CPSU party program mentions that kolkhoz villages will gradually develop into larger, urban-type settlements, but the party refrained from committing itself to a policy of converting kolkhozy into sovkhozy. In fact, however, there were waves of sovkhozization in the Soviet Union, particularly in 1954 at the beginning of the New Lands Program, then in 1958 after liquidation of the Machine Tractor Stations (MTS), and again on repeated occasions during Khrushchev's term of office—one of Khrushchev's most cherished ideas was the transformation of the countryside into agrotowns. Four arguments were put forward to substantiate the need for further conversion of collective farms to state farms:

1.   *State farms have higher productivity*

Figures are quoted again and again in the literature in favor of this argument. However, in most countries the drop of productivity for cooperatives as compared to state farms (and even to private smallholdings) is not as blatant as in some figures for Poland. In the 1960s many state farmers in Eastern Europe had no profit because of a higher capital investment and lower prices for their products as compared to cooperative farms. As far as the Soviet Union is concerned, doubts have even been voiced on repeated occasions about the higher productivity of state farms and these substantiated by figures. By a straightforward weighing-up of the input of production factors against incremental yield, as compared to the kolkhoz, it will be seen that the result is not quite so clear-cut. Soviet literature abounds with complaints about unfulfilled targets in the sovkhozy,[100] and increasing demands are being made for the introduction of modern industrial accounting systems in the sector of state agriculture. Insofar as the sovkhozy or goskhozy do actually prove to be more productive, consideration must be given to the much greater capital investment required to produce this result.

2.   *Improvement of social security for the rural population*

It was only in the sixties that the *kolkhoz* workers were granted similar social benefits to those of industrial workers (see Chapter 8, Section 2), and the attainment of the same status as sovkhoz workers had always been one of the motives for promoting state farms. But owing to the expenses involved, the Soviet leadership did not dare to make use of this particular argument for fear of creating excessive expectations from the state.

Khrushchev often publicly warned against wanting to load all the worries of cooperatives onto the shoulders of the state in the times to come.[101]

3. *Simplification of administration in the country*

This argument was put forward mainly by the local cadres.

4. *Efforts toward phasing out the commodity–money relationship between town and country*

This argument came up time and again in the ideological discussion, under the pressure of the leftist polemic. In the Soviet Union, in Rumania and Czechoslovakia, the share of state farms is unusually high. The German Democratic Republic in this respect seems still to have the least socialist agriculture (cf. Table 9). There is no uniform trend toward the average size. If the state farms are much bigger then the kolkhozy in the Soviet Union, this is also due to a higher proportion of land that is extensively used.

Despite these arguments in favour of sovkhozization, the movement has repeatedly been broken off, due mainly to the following two reasons:

1. *Shortage of money*

Full alignment of the kolkhozniks to the individual and social consumption level of the sovkhoz workers was still beyond the financial means of the Soviet Union.

2. *Labor policy considerations*

At a higher level, the Soviet Union experienced a problem similar to that experienced during collectivization in Poland, where even the first redistribution process could not be pushed forward for fear of liberating considerable quantities of labor. In the Soviet Union, dissolution of the kolkhozy often led to "frictional unemployment" (see Chapter 4, Section 1) since the new state farms were under no obligation to take on all the former kolkhozniks. The sovkhozy were more inclined to hire seasonal workers than to engage too many permanent workers on their farms.

In the light of this experience, the Soviet Union's agrarian structure policy tended more toward aligning the working conditions of the sovkhozy and kolkhozy, such as by guaranteeing minimum wages to the kolkhoz workers and by allowing sovkhoz workers to run private subsidiary farms, which were really only supposed to be tolerated on a temporary basis so as to increase the kolkhozniks' earnings. As far as opportunities for participation and management methods were concerned, the differences between kolkhozy and sovkhozy had always been much less significant here than in the protective sphere of social security or in the redistributive sphere of income distribution.

In all other countries—with the exception of Cuba—the development of state enterprises in agriculture underwent an even more pronounced stagnation than in the Soviet Union. During the first phase of redistribution in the German Democratic Republic, four-fifths of the estates that had already belonged to the state beforehand were divided up, in a manner incomprehensible to some socialists. But even China followed the Soviet idea of the superiority of state farms prior to the Great Leap Forward. These were developed especially in the frontier areas, for purposes of settling returning Chinese expatriates. Among the four provinces that had the largest number of state farms in 1957 (the beginning of the commune movement) were the three regions of Sinkiang, Inner Mongolia, and Heilungkiang. As in the Soviet Union, these state farms were better equipped with machinery and offered better wages and social conditions for their workers. Nevertheless, they only accounted for 4% of China's arable land in 1964.[102] With the expansion of communes during the Great Leap Forward, the boundaries between the two types of collective farms became more fluid. Occasionally, transformation of a state farm into a commune would be tolerated. As the communes grew in size and their functions multiplied, due to their merging with the local authorities, it became increasingly difficult to draw a systematic distinction between the different forms of ownership in China.

Incentives for motivation of the peasants

The Communist parties of the socialist transitional societies did not consider redistribution in the countryside as an end in itself, as did many bourgeois social reformers and populist movements, who had also had a long tradition of radical redistribution demands in Eastern Europe, even before 1945.[103]

The various instruments of land redistribution policy in the countryside were employed to differing degrees as a function of the objectives pursued—by greater emphasis being placed either on efficiency in the development of productive resources or on revolutionization of the superstructure—and as a function of the intensity of more long-standing traditions. The varying class structures in the countryside also determined the nature of redistribution policy.

The instruments primarily employed were:

1. financial incentives;
2. preservation of private plots;
3. control over technical equipment;
4. repression.

1. Financial incentives

In the first period of redistribution in the countryside, many socialist transitional societies worked with *compensation.* In Yugoslavia, compensation consisted more of a nominal consolation payment (59.4 dinars per hectare). In Poland farmers were either granted a fixed pension, regardless of the amount of land expropriated, or offered the chance to take over new land in a different region.[104]

A very cautious approach was adopted in China, too, during the first phase of redistribution. Most of the peasants were allowed to keep enough land to feed themselves. In this phase, a strictly egalitarian redistribution was still avoided, so as not to alienate the rural middle class.[105] As there was no wish to imitate the physical extermination policy that Stalin had earlier adopted for the kulak class in the Soviet Union, the only main concern was to prevent kulaks from becoming too strong, as had happened during the Soviet NEP period. Mao tried above all to prevent middle peasants from taking over management of the cooperatives and only allowed them to join the latter after they had developed sufficient socialist awareness and were prepared to accept leadership by the poor peasants.

The material incentives used in many transitional societies included *smaller compulsory delivery quotas* than those imposed upon private farmers, together with *tax privileges. Production aids* and *cancelation of overdue credit interest* provided further financial incentives for joining the collective farms. In Rumania, for example, a two-year tax exemption was offered, and delivery quotas were cut by 20% compared with those required for the private farmers.

Moreover, legal guarantees for collective *property protection* were often more comprehensive for kolkhoz peasants, and premiums were smaller than those to be paid for private ownership of land and property.

2.   Preservation of private plots

One of the strongest incentives for the peasants was the preservation of private household farms (in Russian: *lichnoe podsobnoe khozyaistvo*) as had developed under the artel' type of Soviet collective farming. At times, private plot farming was interpreted as a continuation of the prerevolutionary institution of family property. Private households were generally limited in the surface area of land and the number of livestock they were allowed to keep—in the German Democratic Republic, for example, this consisted of 0.5 hectares, 2 cows, 2 pigs, 5 sheep, and small domestic animals. In some countries there were even regional differences in these upper limits. In Czechoslovakia, the 0.5 ha limit applied to the Czech part of the country and a 1.2 ha limit to the Slovakian part.[106] Most of these regulations were based on the Soviet model—even in its 1936 Constitution (Art. 7, para. 2), the Soviet Union authorizes private ownership of agricultural means of production up to certain limits. However, the term used here is "personal" property, rather than "private" property, so as to make it clear that this remnant of the private sector falls under the sphere of consumption. Ever since the time of Khrushchev's policy, which was focused precisely on using the countryside to implement the era of intensive construction of socialism, private subsidiary agriculture has always been the object of ideological discrimination. The most convincing explanation put forward was that private farming would have to be tolerated so long as the earnings of collective farmers had not reached the level of the industrial workers' wages.[107] The income differentials between industrial workers and collective farmers could be played down a little by the argument that farmers had the opportunity to earn money on the side, while the remaining differences were minimized by stressing the "deep unity of interest between the peasantry and the working class." This line of argument would have been acceptable had the better-paid sovkhoz workers and even the industrial workers not been allowed to have private plots, thereby again widening the income gap. According to Soviet statistics, the percentage of earnings stemming from private agriculture was 48.3% in 1940 and only 25.2% in 1978.[108] This percentage was admittedly lower in the case of sovkhoz workers, but it was by no means insignificant—in 1964, 22% of earnings were attributable to private subsidiary farming in the RSFSR, as compared to 43% for kolkhoz workers.[109] Although the productivity of these subsidiary activities was lower than that for earnings received for kolkhoz or sovkhoz work, this activity was nonetheless necessary in order to supplement the low level of basic income.[110] The productivity of this subsidiary activity is often overestimated, however, by only considering figures that show that in 1963, for example, kolkhozniks raised more taxes per hectare for produce from private plots than did the kolkhozy[111]—the tax system leads to a certain distortion in proportions here (see Chapter 2, Section 3)—or by only comparing the percentage of subsidiary farming in the net agricultural output of key foodstuffs.

Even though private plots are on the decrease in the Soviet Union (in terms of percentage of total acreage), up to the sixties an increasing tendency could still be observed in terms of absolute acreage and of the number of members of workers' and state employees' families whose main activity was subsidiary farming. In 1965, 30.3% of the aggregate agricultural output and more than half of staple foodstuffs were produced on an acreage accounting for 1.24% of the total agricultural land. When considering such figures, it must be borne in mind, however, that this productivity cannot be attributed to the independent initiative of the plot farmers alone. Not infrequently they would use kolkhoz pasturage for their livestock and part of the remuneration in kind—for example, fodder—in order to obtain such results.[112]

Given these figures, Soviet theory has some difficulty arguing that the phasing out of commodity production is in full swing, and its critics—above all, China—maliciously capitalize on these figures. However, Soviet scholars show that the percentage of income from private plots is constantly diminishing, also in terms of output. In the 1970s output on the private plots rose from 100 to 114, compared to 138 in the whole agriculture[113] (see Table 13).

Chinese critics during the cultural revolution emphasized the "bourgeois instincts" the extension of private plotfarming might cause. Soviet scholars present it, however, as a "useful school for new agricultural techniques." The usefulness of the private plot, it was pointed out, largely outweighs the ideological damage it might cause.[114]

Recent Soviet evaluation is more balanced. "Individualism" and the "rise of market psychology" are mentioned as drawbacks, as well as the conservation of low skills because plot farming tends to decrease the motivation for additional education. On the other

Table 12

Proportion of arable land held by the different categories of farm organizations and the average size of state and collective farms

Country	Year	Collec- tive farms	State farms (sovkhoz, goskhoz)	Private sector	Year	State farms	Coll. farms
						Average size (in 1000 ha)	
Albania	1971	85.3	17.7	3.7	1973		1,081
Bulgaria	1972	65.5	24.0	8.0	1970	936	4,089
	1976	90.7		9.3	1978	5,611	
Cuba					1978		
Czechoslovakia	1976	61.2	30.4	8.3	1978	1,387	4,316
GDR	1976	82.2	8.4	9.4	1978	542	5,106
Hungary	1976	69.5	15.2	15.3	1978	844	4,710
Mongolia					1978	8,862	113,807
Poland	1976	2.0	17.3	80.7	1978	3,255	531
Rumania	1976	54.1	30.1	15.8	1978	2,039	8,123
Soviet Union	1976	33.3	65.3	1.4	1978	359,464	176,108
Yugoslavia	1976	2.6	14.1	83.3	1976	961	440

Sources: Figures until 1976 in: K. E. Waedekin, *Sozialistische Agrarpolitik in Osteuropa* Vol. 2 (Berlin: Duncker & Humblot, 1978), pp. 38ff. Figures for 1978: *Statisticheskii ezhegodnik stran-chlenov SEV 1979* (Moscow: Statistika, 1979), pp. 228f.

hand, the tendency to resist migration and to have a higher level of life satisfaction are classified as the advantages of private plot farming.[115]

Although Maoist criticism of the Soviet Union has always stigmatized this very development with particular vehemence, private plots of land exist in China as well, even on state farms. However, in order to prevent development of market-like adjustment mechanisms such as those prevailing in the Soviet Union—where the kolkhoz market is a place of exchange between town and country on a supply and demand basis—peasants were to some extent not allowed to sell their produce privately, but only to state agencies. In addition, there are also the "agricultural produce and livestock markets" (rural markets) where surplus private agricultural produce is offered at higher prices than in state trade. However, it is estimated that the total turnover of these markets accounted for only 5% or so of Chinese trade turnover as a whole.[116] The private plots that had mostly been restituted during the first wave of enthusiasm when the people's communes began to be set up reappeared after the Great Leap Forward. At the most, they represent 5% of the land farmed by the work teams. But even those who usually admire the People's Republic of China, such as Charles Bettelheim and Joan Robinson, have ascertained that private (nontaxable) incomes amount to between 10 and 30% of the collective income, depending on the location of the communes. The considerable differences between the various estimates of the amount of income originating from private plots are due in part to the limited information we possess in this field of labor policy (which is rather unpleasant for the regime), and partly to the wide regional discrepancies. Estimates for 1957 vary between 33.6% in Southern China and only 18.6% in Northwestern China and Inner Mongolia.[117]

Private plots not only played an important role with regard to the proportion of income they made up, but their production was also of considerable importance as a contribution to China's food supply. According to the estimates of some economists, even during the period of the Great Leap Forward, when private plots were

Table 13

Income of families of kolkhoz peasants

	1940	*1970*	*1978*	*1979*
income from the kolkhoz	39.7	40.3	44.5	43.4
wages of family members	5.8	8.4	8.7	8.8
pensions and scholarships from social funds (including education without payment)	4.9	17.7	20.4	19.3
private plot farming (in the case of workers)	9.2	1.3	0.8	0.8
other income	1.3	1.7	1.2	1.6

Source: *Narodnoe Khozyaistvo SSSR v 1979 g* (Moscow: Statistika, 1979, pp. 392, 391); 1979 (Moscow: Statistika, 1980), p. 411.

subject to heavy ideological discrimination (between 1959 and 1961), commune peasants supplied some 40% of produce from their own plots, such as eggs and pork, to the state.[118]

Consequently, after the Great Leap Forward, politicians reluctantly tolerated the private plots as a "necessary complement to socialist economy." The local cadres who, in 1958, during the communization movement, had been encouraged to absorb private plots into the communes, were then criticized in 1959 and 1961 for having underestimated the importance of private plots for China's food supply and were accused of "subjectivism" and "dogmatism." However, when the ideological struggle against private plots intensified, local cadres did not by any means always seem to have acted as firebrands. Certain researchers have pointed out that since the provinces had a certain degree of autonomy, local cadres tended to ignore and not implement central directives, particularly in this field.[119]

The Chinese never made much of an ideological point of the material incentives of the private plot, and other Asian countries showed much less concern in their approach. Kim il Sung once polemized: "Apparently some comrades feel that the state must buy everything, including the produce of subsidiary farms, and distribute it according to plan, but this is an error and cannot be implemented in practice. The people who produce the products must be given the opportunity to consume them themselves and to bring the remainder to market for sale or barter."[120] This statement might be interpreted as a concealed polemic against the Chinese attitude, which sought to appease the politicans' guilty conscience for tolerating these material incentives by controlling such commodity relations via state purchasing organizations. Although there is a Maoist touch in Kim's political ideas, North Korea's policy on the incentive system comes closer to the Soviet example.[121]

In Cuba, too, the private sector still had a considerable share in agricultural production—as late as 1966, 32% of sugar, 69% of fruit, 83% of coffee, and 90% of tobacco production was still contributed by the private sector.[122] But toward the end of the sixties the percentage of private production was repressed more purposefully than in most Eastern European countries, and from an ideological viewpoint the high percentage was always presented as an unpleasant but necessary "class compromise." Since there was no collectivization, this tolerance of private production did not mark a material incentive to join the collectives, as was the case in Eastern Europe, but instead illustrated the propeasant policy generally adopted by Cuba during the initial phase.[123]

3. Control over technical means of production

As most of the socialist transitional societies were developing countries, redistribution policy could not be conducted simply for its own sake—for establishing social justice—but has always served simultaneously as a lever for developing productive resources in agriculture. In the non-European transitional societies, in particular, the struggle toward mechanization and technicalization of agriculture (contending with what was frequently a hostile attitude on the part of the rural population toward technology) went hand-in-hand with redistribution.

The Machine Tractor Stations (MTS) established in nearly every socialist country along the lines of the Soviet model (although under various names) had a wide range of functions. Through the technical aid supplied, they could serve as an incentive for the peasants, but they could also take on a repressive role by discriminating against the private peasants when it came to utilization of the machines. In addition to these technical development functions, they also had political leadership functions, even in highly developed countries such as the German Democratic Republic, and often included a sophisticated range of cultural, political, and educational facilities as instruments of control. Occasionally, the MTSs were considered to be predominantly instruments of control. In the German Democratic Republic, for example, private farms still accounted for 62% of arable land as late as 1958, but only received 16% of MTS services.[124] Their coercive character could also be inferred from the fact that their abolition in most countries except Albania, Bulgaria, and Rumania was sometimes accompanied by trends toward decollectivization, and later on the authorities themselves sometimes, as in Poland and Yugoslavia, justified the abolition of the MTSs by emphasizing the voluntary character of the collectivization process.[125]

During the transformation of a lower type of collective agriculture into a higher type, the MTSs often played the role of promoters. Yet, the assertion of certain Maoist groups that the abolition of the MTSs in Eastern Europe was a decisive step backwards toward capitalism is a polemical exaggeration, since many countries—particularly the German Democratic Republic and the Soviet Union—did not tolerate a policy of restoration to private ownership in the countryside. Nevertheless, even in the Soviet Union the dissolution of the MTSs, resulting in the sale of over half a million tractors to the kolkhozy, was sometimes regarded as a sort of "downgrading" of the higher form of socialist ownership to a lower form.

Bourgeois economists, on the other hand, tended rather to consider the profitability aspects of this measure and sometimes came to the conclusion that it caused a rise in production costs.[126] A comparison will show that dissolution of the MTSs only delayed or halted the transformation process in the countryside in cases where the party abandoned its objective of redistribution in the agricultural production sphere or did not proceed in resolutely transforming the existing lower-type collective enterprises into higher forms of integration. Even profitability arguments do not come out against dissolution of the MTSs. Once collectivization had been achieved and the collectives intrinsically accepted by the majority of the rural population, the MTSs, as instruments of control, turned out to be rather a hindrance to development, in that they restricted the freedom of enterprises unnecessarily. A certain decline in productivity brought about by dissolution of the MTSs proved to be only transitory.[127]

Nevertheless, all this only holds true in cases where sufficient preparation was made for the dismantling of the MTSs and where distribution of the means of production to kolkhozny did not lead to new forms of injustice. In 1958, weak collective farms with poor soil and faced with rising prices for capital goods were at a distinct disadvantage. It cannot be excluded that the Soviet leadership was indeed aware of this development and had been tolerating it deliberately. It has occasionally been interpreted as a kind of socialist *Bauernlegen* (anomic expropriation of farms on grounds of indebtedness) since this development went on to speed up the rate at which weak kolkhozy agreed to convert to sovkhozy. The Government itself manipulated the terms of trade so ruthlessly that between 1957 and 1960 the sovkhozy were able to increase their investments by a factor many times that of the kolkhozy.

In a developing country such as China the steering of technicalization and mechanization was of even greater importance than in Soviet Russia, where the level of technicalization was higher when collectivization first started. In China, the technical equipment available for agriculture was extremely sparse. There was one draft animal to every two households, one plough to every three, and one waterwheel to every seventeen, so that collectivization appeared to be indispensible, if only for economic reasons and for combating the minifundia.[128] Moreover, some 32% of the tractor fleet was in the hands of state farms. The remaining 68% was controlled by agricultural machinery stations that generally belonged to the state as well and were sometimes set up jointly by the state and the communes. However, Chinese policy on mechanization in the countryside underwent certain fluctuations, as did Soviet policy. Until 1961, there was a tendency to leave more of the machines in the hands of the communes, then up to 1965/66 centralization was pushed forward again, and it was only in the mid-sixties that the communes were encouraged to set up their own machine stations. The trend toward self-contained units never attained the Soviet level, however. In fact, mechanization lagged behind the Soviet Union, which had promoted mechanization at the same time as collectivization, whereas in China mechanization could only be started after a 10-year delay. As late as 1962, a Chinese columnist estimated that only some 10% of land was tilled by machines.[129] Most collectives could not afford machines of their own, nor was there a financial incentive to acquire machines. The state at times provided services from the tractor stations at below-cost price, as an incentive for using the machines at all—the Chinese had much greater reservations about machines than the Soviet peasantry had had during their collectivization campaign. Whereas in the Soviet Union centralized control of machines became more of a hindrance above a certain level of development, it was quite understandable that the Chinese politicians should try to keep control over the MTSs, if only because many of the smaller collectives were lacking in technical skills. The ideological helplessness of village leaders in the face of this dilemma can be illustrated by a statement from a local cadre representative: "When the farmers don't work, we teach them Marxism–Leninism; when the draft animals don't want to draw, we swing the whip, but if the machines don't work, we can't do anything at all."[130] The fact that both political strategies can be justified in the light of respective local circumstances shows once again that in most cases one cannot take sides in the doctrinary controversy between Moscow and Peking. One thing, however, is certain—China's path to mechanization can hardly serve as a model for the conversion of highly industrialized and mechanized systems.

In all socialist countries two promises were made to the peasants as an incentive to collectivization: improvement of their standard of living and a lightening of their burden of work through mechanization. The first promise was achieved in some countries, although this took longest in the Soviet Union. Here, in fact, mechanization of agriculture was only attained via the roundabout way of the MTSs. These were established after the great horse slaughter—one of the negative consequences of forced collectivization—in part so as to provide tractors to fill the gap left by the lost draft animals. But for this forced collectivization, a more gradual mechanization process could probably have been envisaged in the Soviet Union, as was later the case in China. It is questionable whether concentration on mechanization along U.S. lines—which is to be observed, in particular, with Lenin—was the optimal development strategy—unless, that is, we accept the theory that heavy industry must be given priority and that forced mechanization must serve as an expedient to drain a sufficient work force from the countryside.

The second goal, lightening the burden of work for the farmers, was attained most quickly in cases where a rapid technicalization of agricultural work would have come about even without collectivization, such as in the German Democratic Republic and in Czechoslovakia. The extent to which it was necessary to rely on organizational aids such as the MTSs depended largely on the degree of mechanization in agriculture, which is often measured by the tractor fleet per 1,000 hectares (see Table 14).

As late as 1951, China only owned about one tractor per 48,000 hectares, as compared with one per 8,000 hectares in India and one per 154 in the United States. After the Greap Leap Forward, China did not adopt the Western "superstition" that heavy capital input was the best way to develop the mechanization and industrialization of the countryside. Bourgeois economists also frequently expressed the view that if the Soviet MTS model had been forced, this would have produced dysfunctional effects.[131] Instead, the course of development adopted was one that had been repeatedly recommended by Western development theorists such as Gunnar

Table 14
Number of tractors per 1,000 hectares

Country	Year	Tractors
Bulgaria	1977	10.5
Czechoslovakia	1977	20.1
GDR	1977	21.9
Hungary	1977	9.7
Poland	1977	24.4
Rumania	1977	9.3
Soviet Union	1977	4.5
Yugoslavia	1976	18.1

Source: Statistical Surveys. In: *Jahrbuch der Wirtschaft Osteuropas/Yearbook of East-European Economics,* Vol. 8 (Munich: Olzog, 1979), pp. 457ff.

Myrdal, who pleaded against imitation of the Western course.[132] The "middle technology" course, which succeeded through an increase in labor input rather than through the input of capital goods, did not involve the MTSs becoming as important a means of control in China as they did in the Soviet Union. In less mechanized agricultural systems, the control designed to combat resistance to collectivization was exercised less through the provision of tractors and more through control over the irrigation system. This holds true for China as well as for North Korea.[133]

4. Repression

None of the socialist countries flatly offended against Engels' and Lenin's exhortations that peasants should join collectives of their own accord. Ideological indoctrination, the exemplary role of the "mutual aid teams," and mobilization of the masses all played a greater role than did overt repression.

In countries where collectivization did not rank so high as an instrument for the transformation process as in other systems, the class struggle in the countryside turned out to be milder in any case. In the case of Poland, this was explained by the fact that there was no longer an intact bourgeoisie to take over the state, because the party penetrated the country with the Red Army in the leading ranks of the Polish communist soldiers, and the bourgeois government exiled in London could only have returned to government power as a junior partner. The less dictatorial the party's attitude was in conducting the transformation process—in Poland, moreover, the party did not play the same role as in the other countries, not even in the newly gained Western territories[134]—the more majority-based and democratic procedures were respected. In Poland, local preparations for collectivization were sometimes even held back from above and great importance was attached to the fact that the majority of a village population as a whole should be ready to change over to collective farming. By way of comparison, least pressure of all was exerted in the more developed countries of Eastern Europe. Even in the German Democratic Republic, which sometimes employed misleading agitprop, there was no direct pressure exerted—a fact that even critical Western publications admit.[135]

The less developed countries that wanted to achieve rapid and comprehensive collectivization were not able to manage without repressive measures to flank material incentives and mobilization of the masses. However, the degree of voluntary participation in transformation processes in the countryside in these transitional societies depended on various factors:

1. on the *length of experience*—China, for example, had been able to experiment for a long time in the liberated regions and thereby had obtained experience;
2. on the state's ability to provide *technical aid* to the farmers by way of an incentive;
3. on *enterprise structure*—Minifundia promoted readiness for voluntary collectivization;
4. on the extent to which *potential opposition was able to emigrate* —this factor was greatest in Cuba, in the German Democratic Republic, and also in North Korea, where during the Korean war many people left the country with the withdrawing U.N. troops;
5. on *steps taken to prevent farmers from getting used to private ownership*—hence, in China and North Korea the second wave of redistribution was introduced very shortly after the first one.

In most socialist transitional societies, transformation in the countryside was a revolutionary process and not a controlled scientific experiment coupled with precise measurements. In searching ex post facto for indicators as to the extent of voluntariness or repression involved in this transformation process, one can select three:

1. the loss of human life due to violent resistance to collectivization;
2. the loss of livestock and draft animals through slaughtering as a means of expressing opposition;
3. the drop in agricultural production.

1. *Loss of human life*

In no other country did redistribution of the means of production in the countryside claim such a high toll of victims as in the Soviet Union, where, according to estimates, collectivization alone caused 5 million casualties on account of persecution of the kulaks, deportation, assassination of functionaries, government retaliation, and famines, without even considering Naum Jasny's dubious calculations on the drop of the birthrate as an additional factor of human loss.[136] Some authors attribute similar losses to the Chinese land reform. The figures supporting this theory are all rather unreliable and range from a few hundred thousand to between 10 and 15 million casualties.[137]

Undiscriminating admirers of the Chinese model emphasize its complete voluntariness, though it is impossible to obtain a perfectly quietistic image of this transformation process if we merely search Mao's writings for comments on this matter. In 1948, Mao reproached his cadres with the fact that "during the land reform some landlords were unnecessarily executed" and that "wicked elements in the rural areas" exploited the situation for acts of revenge. He recommended the execution of the "worst counterrevolutionaries" but warned the cadres "not to physically maltreat criminals" even then (MSW Vol. 4, p. 244). One thing is certain: in China there was no coldly calculated mass extermination of the kulaks, as in the Soviet Union.

The treatment of resistance in the countryside was based on a four-class model (big landowners, rich peasants, middle peasants, and poor peasants and landless agricultural workers). In the regions dominated by the Communists (before 1945), only the first group was treated with any degree of severity. Even the "kulaks" were treated relatively mildly—as a function of the political situation in the controversy with Japan and the Kuomintang—and this contributed toward mitigating certain elements of opposition in the first phase of redistribution policy.

In the subsequent phases of transition to "higher" forms of collective economy, the number of potential opponents was quite considerable. Mao himself stated at one time that 60 to 70% supported collectivization, although the number of kulaks was reported to total only some 10%. Some of the peasants who had been beneficiaries in the first wave of redistribution policy were apparently considered potential "class enemies" because of their new interests.[138]

Some of the opposition to collectivization, which provoked repression on the part of revolutionary governments, was due to the fact that land had first been split up into minifundia and then at a later stage reamalgamated under pressure, once people had already developed a certain property instinct. Only Cuba, with its extensive plantation farming and Che Guevara's predilection for central control, was spared the error of creating uncertainty in people's expectations through its distribution and subsequent compulsory collectivization policy, since land in Cuba was mostly amalgamated into state enterprises. Nevertheless, the rural population, namely, the social stratum that benefited most from the revolution, strongly backed Castro—very much unlike the situation of war communism in Russia.[139] However, Cuba did have an advantage over Russia and China in that her rural population had not been impoverished by a protracted war.

2.   Loss of draft animals

Another indicator for the extent of repression is the loss of draft animals through slaughtering as a reaction against forced collectivization. When applying this yardstick, even Western economists agree that the losses due to collectivization in China were incomparably smaller than those in the Soviet Union where, according to Soviet statistics, losses must have amounted to some 42% of cattle, 55% of sheep, and 53% of horses.[140]

3.   Economic cost

The economic cost of collectivization cannot be measured easily either. In some countries with serious unemployment in the country-side—China for example—collectivization encountered relatively little resistance because it helped solve the problem of seasonal unemployment in a populous country such as China by organizing the distribution of work. The apprehensions of some cadres who felt that cooperativization might lead to a surplus of labor, as in Poland —an apprehension with which Mao had to deal frequently—proved to be unfounded, since mechanization in China did not go hand-in-hand with cooperativization to the same extent as it did in Eastern Europe. Western economists have calculated that the economic losses suffered by the Soviet Union as a consequence of collectivization had not been fully resorbed by 1938; and in the people's democracies damage was reckoned to be perceptible for 10 to 15 years. In the opinion of certain critics, agricultural output in Czechoslovakia was still below prewar level in 1958.[141] As for China, unkindly disposed observers state that the average annual production figures for 1957 were the first to exceed the production level of the years 1931 to 1937,[142] and this result could have been much better had China not conjured up heavy setbacks again through forced communization. In Cuba, where there was no small-peasant intermediary stage, there was no drop in production; on the contrary, production figures actually increased during the initial years, with stagnation only occurring later on.[143]

A temporary drop in production is often used as a rash argument to question the justification for any redistribution policy at all in the countryside. This reasoning is, however, incorrect, because not all economic losses can be attributed to repression. Some of the losses are due to the fact that, during the first few years after collectivization, investments could not be employed to the full to increase production because it was necessary to create the infrastructure for collective work—stables, barns, administrative buildings, and machine-servicing facilities—and this meant that investments could only yield a medium-term increase in production.[144]

At times, however, production success in the new collective farms did not live up to expectations, even where technicalization had been undeniably successful. This was the case in the German Democratic Republic, where this was due to the fact that the collective farms were usually overstaffed. What was in the starting phase a means to check rural exodus later turned out to be a hindrance to productivity on occasion. Even in the German Democratic Republic, which had a remarkable degree of mechanization, the employment rate in the APCs, that is, 18 persons per 100 hectares, was two-and-a-half times that of the Federal Republic of Germany (7 employees per hectare[145]).

Despite such inevitable economic losses, the attitude of the majority of farmers at the beginning of the collectivization campaign can also not be taken as a yardstick. After a certain number of years, they would generally come to accept inwardly the transformation process directed from above and to recognize its advantages. Even the Soviet kolkhozniks proved to be relatively resistant during the Second World War to the attempts by the German occupation forces to liquidate the kolkhozy.[146] An opinion poll carried out in Czechoslovakia in 1968 revealed, surprisingly, that 61% of those interviewed and 67% of farmers in the sample were in favor of collective agriculture,[147] and during the "Spring of Prague" none of the cooperatives was dissolved.

Nevertheless, experiences of this kind should not be used *ex post* in future transformation processes in order to disregard the will of the majority *ex ante*. The success of transformation depended largely on the balance that the cadres managed to establish between redistribution, efficiency, and voluntary participation. The participation aspect, in particular, has sometimes been neglected in Soviet considerations, and even today the fact that cadres in China are more in touch with the rural world is still qualified as a kind of "populist aberration." However, the party's authoritarian methods of leadership made it very difficult to establish the balance between these socialist target values, and this was bound to lead to prejudicial consequences and fluctuations during later stages of transformation.

In the phase following the completion of redistribution, agriculture, too, experienced a trend toward maximizing efficiency as the foremost target and toward extending the *chozraschet* system, at a time when industry had already slipped into a crisis. Ever since the surplus of labor in socialist agriculture has been on the decrease

—except in populous countries such as China or Poland—and ever since the system of extensive growth coupled with low work productivity has also been abandoned in favor of intensive growth in agriculture, the traditional organizational form of the collective farm has been going through a crisis in a large number of socialist countries and has been losing the historical merit it had gained for achieving initial rationalization and an increase in productivity.[148] Even at this stage it can be predicted that because of their different level of productive resources any highly industrialized systems converting to socialism in future will not employ collectivization coupled with strong repression and forced technicalization to the same extent as have current socialist systems.

2

Redistribution in the distribution sphere

Redistribution of income has repeatedly played an important role in the history of the workers' movement. In the transition to socialism it was frequently easiest for socialist parties to carry along in their wake groups that had not been won over for the revolution— and did not share in redistribution of the means of production— through redistributional measures in incomes policy. In the continuing polemics with the German socialist democrats, however, Marx, in his critique of the concept "undiminished proceeds of labor" in the Gotha Programme, issued a warning against rating distribution so highly at all. He felt that considering distribution independently of the mode of production constituted "vulgar socialism" (MEW, Vol. 19, p. 22). The diminution of the proceeds of labor—for administrative costs, infrastructure costs, social welfare (MEW, Vol. 19, p. 19)—necessary to realize socialist aims is still an unavoidable facet of present-day transitional societies. What Marx failed to foresee was that even in relatively well-developed socialist systems, as we have today, commodity patterns necessarily penetrate distribution patterns, since distribution is not based on a coupon system as Marx believed (ibid., p. 20), but instead on money and wages. From this it could be concluded that Marx rated the status of productive resources in socialist transitional societies considerably higher than has actually been the case since 1917.

Socialist systems would not have been able to concede the right to the "undiminished proceeds of labor" in the accumulation phase even if they had regarded this as theoretically correct. The yardstick for wage developments in socialist systems was not the "undiminished proceeds of labor" but rather the relative proportion of this, measured in terms of the rate of increase in labor productivity. With the exception of the German Democratic Republic, which had artificially low wage levels after the war and had to align upwards, labor productivity in socialist countries increased at two to three times the speed of real wages—a fact that is no longer denied in recent economic literature.[149] (See Table 15.)

At first sight, analysis of incomes in socialist systems would seem to be simpler than in capitalist systems, since income results predominantly from individual labor. Savings, interest from state bonds, licence fee transfers, and patent revenues from abroad scarcely figure in the statistics. On the other hand, however, statistics covering wage developments are very sparse up to the mid-sixties, and, as far as income stratification is concerned, present-day statistics are still at least as discreet as those supplied by capitalist countries. Comparison is further complicated by differing concepts regarding the makeup of statistics, since socialist economics divides national

Table 15

Development of real wages as compared with labor productivity
(in percentages)

	Growth between 1950 and 1965	
Country	Labor productivity	Real wages
Bulgaria	195	60
Czechoslovakia	115	45
GDR	195	268
Hungary	104	65
Poland	130	50
Rumania	200	125
Soviet Union	175	88

Source: *Incomes in Postwar Europe* (Geneva: UN:ECE, 1967), p. 34.

Table 16

Increase in real wages for factory and office workers

Country	(1960 = 100) 1965	1968	1969	(1970 = 100) 1978
Bulgaria	110	131	135	118
Czechoslovakia	106	121	127.4	125
GDR	113.1	125.1	no data	no data
Hungary	109	118	124	126
Poland	108	116	117	146
Rumania	122	133	135	146
Soviet Union	109	123	127	128

Source: Institut ekonomiki mirovoi socialisticheskoi sistemy AN SSSR, *Ekonomika stran socializma 1970 g.* Moscow, 1971, p. 219; for 1978: *Statisticheski ezhegodnik stran-chlenov SEV 1974* (Moscow: Statistika, 1979), p. 53.

income into productive and nonproductive sectors and does not include services in the national product. National income in socialist countries is made up solely of the full range of goods produced. The gross national product in capitalist systems includes amortization of capital and is less adequate as an indicator for social welfare than is the net national product in socialist economics. Socialist economists regard amortization as a type of cost and exclude this from the concept of national income. (See Table 16.)

Redistribution in the distribution sphere figures high on the list of targets drawn up by the Communist party of the Soviet Union. The draft 1961 CPSU party program contains the phrase "and the gap between high and relatively low incomes must thus be gradually reduced." In the definitive version it was duly acknowledged that this did not show evidence of a particularly ambitious striving toward redistribution, and the word "gradually" was replaced by "persever-ingly"—likewise a flexible, step-by-step designation for which no clear-cut implementation measures were specified. Mention was simply made of a number of disparities serving as a yardstick for assessing *present-day* redistribution policy in socialist states. Not a word was said regarding the means of achieving this target. If we attempt to deduce these means from what actually took place, then we find both direct and indirect instruments of redistribution policy. The direct means might be summed up under the heading "wage policy," while the indirect means are to be found in four areas, none of which serves the target of redistribution exclusively, but which nonetheless constitute an important aspect of redistribution:

1. price policy;
2. taxation policy;
3. social policy;
4. education policy.

1. Wage policy

Individual and social consumption

In the concept of socialism, wage labor is a dying phenomenon. Abolition of wage labor cannot, however, be decreed.[150] The decreasing significance of wages as a contribution toward individual consumption is measured in terms of growth in social consumption, although in the Soviet Union in 1972 this was still made up of more than 50% cash payment rather than free social services. In the German Democratic Republic the percentage of payment in kind lagged even further behind the percentage of cash payment. In the Federal Republic of Germany payment in kind increased from 21.1 to 25.4% in the period between 1950 and 1969, whereas in the German Democratic Republic it fell from 30.6 to 27.5% during the same period, although this was nonetheless still above the Federal German level.[151]

The fact that social consum tion should take precedence is largely unchallenged in socialist economics, although, since the reforms, a number of Eastern European economists have been asking quite openly whether an increase in the individual consumption fund is not necessary to bring about the required stimulation expected of the "material lever" system.[152] Even now it is possible to anticipate the Communist principle of "each according to his needs" in the social consumption fund. Thus, insofar as socialist economists do not adopt a completely agnostic attitude toward the long-term objectives of communism, they are reluctant to do without this important indicator. The social consumption fund covers all commodities and services that are not "acquired" but "called upon" and used, such as the infrastructure and social services provided by the state. The term "infrastructure" was at first denounced as a "bourgeois" trick to embellish the social conditions of the working classes, but nowadays it has been accepted as a scientific *terminus technicus*.[153] In the 1950s and 1960s, social consumption grew more rapidly than individual consumption in socialist states (see Table 17). In the Soviet Union the percentage of social consumption in the per capita income of factory and office workers rose from 24.8 to 27.3% during the period between 1950 and 1968.[154] The 1961 Party Program does not set down a precise figure for the social consumption fund, but in view of the rather slow development here the figure of 50% of income-related benefits to be provided free of charge by the state by 1980 can no longer be regarded as realistic. The relative importance of the social consumption fund, however, means that it is not really fair to judge the Soviet standard of living merely on the basis of individual income, as repeatedly occurs in the Western literature.[155] (See Table 18.)

Even though the very extent of the social consumption fund constitutes one of the essential differences between socialist systems

Table 17

Structure of the social consumption funds (1978) as a percentage of the overall social consumption fund

Social Service	Bulgaria	Czecho-slovakia	GDR	Hungary	Mon-golia	Poland	Soviet Union
pensions and allowances	44.4	48.6	36.9	57.4	33.3	42.9	37.1
scholarships	1.0	0.4	1.0	9.2	1.0	1.0	2.3
free medical care and physical education	14.9	15.5	17.1	14.0	19.6	24.3	14.7
free educational and cultural facilities	22.1	20.3	21.7	20.0	21.1	22.5	25.3
expenditure on housing (not included in rent)	—	4.1	10.3	2.0	0.4	7.2	5.7
other services	17.6	11.1	13.0	6.0	16.4	2.1	14.9

Source: *Statisticheskii ezhegodnik stran-chlenov SEV 1978* (Moscow: Statistika, 1979), pp. 49f.

Table 18

Development of individual and social consumption
(annual mean)

		1950– 1955	1956– 1960	1961– 1965
Czechoslovakia	ind.	4.1	6.4	3.0
	soc.	12.2	3.2	5.1
GDR	ind.			2.2
	soc.			2.6
Hungary	ind.		6.4	4.6
	soc.		6.6	4.8
Poland	ind.	5.9	7.4	3.7
	soc.	6.2	4.3	6.8

Source: *Incomes in Postwar Europe. A Study of Policies, Growth and Distribution* (Geneva:
UN:ECE, 1967), pp. 67f.

and capitalism, economists in socialist countries also admit that the
socialist wage is, in its outward appearance, very similar to the
capitalist labor wage. They then, however, hasten to stress the basic
difference between the two, which, as they view the matter, lies in
the fact that the worker is not detached from the means of production and hence wages do not merely represent the value (price) of
labor in modified form.[156]

The socialist wage is two-fold in nature:

1.   Wages are determined firstly by the size of the *consumption fund for the nation as a whole*; this, however, is only manifested
in the state's redistribution activity (via uniform, state-guaranteed
wage rates and national standards for assessment of labor performance).

2.   Secondly, wages are determined by the *percentage value of
a product manufactured by an enterprise*. This means that any wages
over and above the minimum wage guaranteed by the national consumption fund are determined partly by individual performance and
partly through the returns and performance of the enterprise as a
whole.

Marx condemned the performance wage, which still predominates in socialist systems today, as an evil, though as an inevitable
evil "in the first phase of communist society as it is when it has just

emerged after prolonged birth pangs from capitalist society" (MEW, Vol. 19, p. 21). Measurement of this performance is also coming up against growing theoretical difficulties in socialism: factors such as labor expended, result of labor, material incentives, worker qualifications, allowance for the scarcity of certain talents (until such time as the successes of socialist educational policy embrace all spheres), together with the degree of responsibility held by leading cadres all go to make up the socialist concept of performance. As the performance components that can be measured objectively are increasingly supplemented by material incentives, so left-wing criticism of this performance concept[157] becomes all the more vociferous, even though the spread of material incentives can, of course, perfectly well go hand-in-hand with a growing emphasis on collective input (enterprise results instead of individual performance).

In general, conflict is increasing within the socialist camp as to the level of importance of equality policy within the distribution sphere. Followers of the Maoist variant of Marxism tend to brand this strong emphasis on the distribution sphere as marking a step toward its "becoming independent," as was once criticized by Marx in the introduction to his *Critique of Political Economy* (MEW, Vol. 13, p. 627). For the Chinese ideologists, redistribution in the production sphere represented only one of the prerequisites for providing a better solution to the real distribution problems that arose in the creation of equality in the distribution sphere.[158] Soviet countercriticism answered this line of thought with the reproach that "petit-bourgeois egalitarianism" prevailing in China was enforcing equality in the distribution sphere at a much faster pace than was good for it, given the state of productive resources. Ever since Stalin's speech at the Conference of Economists on June 23, 1931, "egalitarianism" (*uravnilovka*) has been a term of abuse that is periodically hurled against left-wing party groups. This reproach does not, however, hold true for the People's Republic of China, since it cannot be maintained that China used incomes policy exclusively for purposes of equality policy, or even that China proceeded to a leveling "downwards" in line with the frugality principle of "petit-bourgeois" ideologists such as Rousseau. First of all, considerable wage disparity still exists in China, and secondly, incomes policy has always been employed to serve other political ends as well. China attempted to freeze wages for long periods at a time, but it would be going too far to say that there had been no wage increases at all since 1956 despite an increase of up to 14.5% in labor productivity.[159]

Wage policy has held different functions in the various transitional societies and cannot thus be measured against the yardstick of

one sole parameter, its redistribution power. At times wage developments lagged behind productivity—fully intentionally on the part of
the leadership—in order to throttle demand for consumption, to
defend priority growth targets in the capital goods industry, and
to ward off potential inflationary trends. Thus at times socialist
developing countries introduced a wage-freeze policy right at the
outset. However, in China, for example, this was by no means
orientated exclusively toward "egalitarianism" but was intended
primarily to further accumulation and the fight against inflation.

Cuba also introduced a wage-freeze policy in 1960. This initially
took the form of a "voluntary agreement" by the trade unions not
to demand further wage increases. Phasing out the "historical wage"
and traditional wage differentials, which, because they constituted a
type of "consolidation of existing wealth patterns," could not be
leveled out voluntarily in socialist systems either, still remains a
problem even today—particularly since Castro confessed to "idealistic
errors" and "revolutionary carelessness" in Cuba's egalitarian policy
at the Thirteenth Trade Union Congress in November 1973, betraying,
moreover, a marked alignment with Eastern bloc terminology.[160] In
Chile, Allende tried in vain to convince the trade unions to accept a
policy of this kind. Wage fixing, however, by no means meant that
there would be no increase in real wages for long periods at a time.
But these increases came about not simply through selective increases
in nominal wages, as has increasingly been the case in the Soviet Union
since 1956, but also through price lowering. Soviet criticism of
China's wage freeze also overlooks the fact that there were as many
as three periods of drastic wage reduction in the Soviet Union (Civil
War, First Five-Year Plan, the Second World War) and in the intervals
between these there were lengthy periods of stagnation in wage
development.[161] Pronounced fluctuations in real wage development
were also to be seen in the more highly developed people's democracies, particularly in small, crisis-prone economies such as Hungary's.
According to Hungarian statistics, the annual increase in real wages
over a five-year period fluctuated from 0.9% (1951-55) to 8% (1956-
60) and then fell again to 1.8% (1961–65) and to 3.5% (1966-60).[162]

In drawing a historical comparison, it cannot be said that
money has played an ever-diminishing role in remuneration. The
marked impetus toward noncash remuneration, which arose under
Soviet war communism, has disappeared. At that time payment in
kind had a widespread leveling effect; at the same time, however,
it undermined motivation in a society where socialist labor discipline
had not yet been brought home, and this had to be counterbalanced
through militarization of the economic leadership. After Stalin's

death material incentives were held to be more effective than this rigid administrative leadership, and the Soviet Union made increasing attempts to stimulate workers through the "money illusion" of rising nominal wages.[163]

Creation of a rational wage class system

Marxist theory works on the basis that the worker who is a joint owner of the means of production develops a completely different attitude from that of the capitalist worker and that material interests and wages occupy a different position in socialist systems. All the same, Lenin did not cherish any illusions during the transitional period and promoted study of the Taylor system, socialist organization of competition and "on the other hand, though, application of compulsion . . . so that the catchphrase of Proletariat Dictatorship will not be tainted by a mushily-organized proletariat power" (LPSS, Vol. 36, p. 190).

With this wide range of means recommended by Lenin for increasing labor productivity, considerable fluctuations in wage policy could perfectly well be justified. The socialist states have been through phases of leveling-out and of accentuating differentials during the course of their history. As long as socialist systems adhered to the performance wage and as long as individual workers or enterprises were able to influence wage structure, there was always the risk of the wage fund expanding too far and overstepping the upper limit, set by the rate of productivity, or falling below the lower limit, set—particularly in the Soviet Union—by the high growth rate in employment.

An important step toward reconciling potential wage equality with the differentials that were still necessary consisted in laying down a series of wage classes based on a rational, centralized performance scale, designed to overcome the "wage anarchy" with which capitalism was reproached.

Despite the credit due to Marxism for its criticism of the irrational, technocratic concept of performance that predominated in capitalist economics,[164] socialist systems had just as much difficulty in working out a rational wage scale as long as the scarcity of talent, the cost of training, and other elitist features of transitional society all had to be assimilated in the wage scale. Nonetheless, it did prove possible to view the wage scale more from a microeconomic than from a macroeconomic angle. One important step was the creation of the eight-wage-class scheme in the Soviet Union, which was adopted by practically all the other socialist states—even by Yugoslavia after the break with the Cominform in 1950. The eight-class scheme was of particular significance in aligning wages in different sectors, although it had the drawback of not giving full consideration to the needs of certain sectors, such as the textile industry. In the Chinese wage reform of 1956, provision was therefore made for the wage scale to be applied less rigidly in certain individual branches than was the case in the Soviet scheme on which the reform had been modeled.[165] A flexible approach was also adopted in the grading of workers into the eight classes. Experience and length of time with the enterprise, skills, and political outlook all came into consideration. The assessment of political outlook was least suited for transparent rules, and it cannot be excluded that this produced majority decisions that, at times, were felt to be unjust. In agriculture too, the rigid wage class system came up against difficulties, and for this reason individual socialist countries, such as Cuba, introduced their own variations here. The bottom wage class for agricultural workers was made equal to the minimum wage for town workers, as set down in 1958, before the revolution.[166]

The theory sometimes put forward by China's admirers, to the effect that the wage classes in themselves were enough to incite competition between workers in the Soviet Union,[167] scarcely holds ground. In an economy with less differentials, a lesser number of wage classes would have been sufficient to produce the same result as in the Soviet Union. In addition, it is not long-term grading in itself that promotes competition but rather the way in which work is assessed and the manner in which individuals are rated. Those who defend complete equality in incomes policy in our pro-Chinese literature also overlook the fact that in China, too, exaggerated talk of wage equality has of late been criticized as deviation on the part of left-wing radicals.[168]

The guarantee of a minimum wage

One consequence of the attempt to set up a rational wage system was the guaranteed minimum wage. Although this was a long-standing socialist requirement, the Soviet Union was only able to start thinking in terms of guaranteeing a minimum wage in the plan era. From March 16, 1934, workers received two-thirds of their wages, regardless of whether production standards had been fulfilled or not. Between 1937 and 1956, the minimum wage of piece-rate workers was set at 110 rubles and for time-rate workers at 115 rubles. In 1956 this amount was increased to 300 to 350 rubles for town workers. Again in 1956, a new protective ruling was introduced, whereby young workers of 16 to 18 years of age, who were only required to work six hours, were to receive the same wages as eight-hour workers. This resulted in an increase in latent unemployment in this group since a large number of enterprises did not wish to employ young people whose labor performance did not correspond to the value of their minimum wage.[169]

In 1956/57, a statutory minimum wage was introduced in most socialist systems. In China the minimum wage amounted to 28 yuan; this was, however, exceeded by a considerable margin in all eight wage classes, varying from branch to branch.[170] Cuba had had a national minimum wage commission even before the revolution. This was dissolved in March 1960, and its competence was transferred to the Council of Ministers.[171]

Even though the majority of socialist states had a guaranteed minimum wage, this was by no means always in line with the subsistence minimum—as it theoretically should have been. With rising consumption costs in a number of countries, minimum wage levels fell behind. According to some Polish authors, roughly one quarter of working-class families have still not come up to the subsistence minimum, and a further 13% of the working population is not very much above it.[172]

The phasing out of payment by the job and piece rates

The leveling effect of incomes policy underwent considerable change with developments in labor productivity. Although Marxists, too, liked to repeat the old saying, *"Akkord ist Mord"* (job-rate work is murder) and regarded piece rates as a specifically capitalist form of exploitation, some two-thirds of workers in socialist countries were pieceworkers in the mid-1950s, compared with one third in the capitalist world.[173]

Soviet economists today express themselves much more cautiously than did former programmatic declarations:

It would be incorrect to assume that time rates must be introduced everywhere instead of piece rates, that collective interests must appear in the place of individual interests or that earnings in communist work brigades must be distributed in a uniform manner. The real job lies in achieving the correct balance between piece work and time work, since it must be realized that with the present state of technology remuneration according to labor performance will continue to occupy an important place in industry, the building trade, agriculture and additional branches of the economy in the near future. The material incentive to work would be undermined if piece rates were to be replaced prematurely by time rates.[174]

One difference between capitalist and socialist wage incentives lies in the emphasis that socialism places on greater reward for group effort, in the form of collective bonuses.[175] Group bonuses are also justified with the argument that this encourages workers to watch over each other's work discipline.[176] Other economists fear, however, that the worker will hardly understand why he should have to pay for the failings of his colleagues out of his own wages. Above all, they feel that this does not fit in with the progressive piece-rate system applied in a number of extractive sectors of industry, where wages increase progressively with output.[177]

This progressive piece-rate system is, however, itself the object of ever-increasing criticism, not so much on humane grounds— though this would be fully in line with the ideals of socialism—but rather on grounds of efficiency. Over short periods the system produced remarkable increases in productivity of up to 200 and 300%. In the long term, however, serious shortcomings emerged in the form of excessive goading of workers, a growing number of accidents at work, and over-high productions costs that in themselves constitute one of the forms of "socialist extravagance." Hence, even in the mid-1950s a number of economists felt that this system was only justified as a temporary measure designed to overcome production bottlenecks.

In the 1956 wage reform China also introduced a piece-rate supplement to the basic time-rate wage.[178] Yet in China piece rates were never used as an incentive to the same extent as in the Soviet Union. In 1956, 77% of those employed in industry and mining in the Soviet Union were paid a piece rate, yet the percentage in China for that same year was only 42%, and even this figure was reduced during the Great Leap Forward.

Ideological egalitarianism was not, however, the sole reason behind this aversion to piece rates. In view of the lower level of productive resources, piece rates would not have had the same stimulating effect in China. In many cases it was difficult, from a purely mathematical angle, to set reasonable standards for piece-work.[179]

Piecework also developed a leveling effect in its own—though not intended—way, since unskilled workers came off well and in some cases even earned more than their skilled counterparts. This, however, simultaneously stifled incentives to obtain higher qualifications, and more emphasis had to be placed on time rates again, if only for reasons of raising the level of vocational training.

New disparity through bonuses and material incentives?

Socialist systems employ material incentives with a guilty conscience, since they are more designed to increase economic efficiency than to promote equality. Lenin justified the bonus system during the transformation period, and over fifty years of experience have not changed matters for the Soviet power; as long as the Soviet Union does not claim to have completed the transition to communism, it can answer the charges leveled against its material incentives by Maoists and Castroites with a reference to Lenin.

Even today, the economies of socialist countries do not speak of profit—and, indeed, the returns of socialist enterprises do play a different role from capitalist profit—yet the moment bonuses ceased to be paid from the wage fund and were financed instead by enterprise returns, there was an immediate turn toward maximizing returns and profitability among management and workers. Individualist modes of thought are also in evidence in the conflicts surrounding labor law, with bonus conflicts ranking as the most frequent and hardest to resolve of legal disputes within the Soviet Union's production sphere.[180]

Yugoslavia was in 1952 the first socialist country to discover the stimulant effect of profit. It has been argued that in the case of Yugoslavia, reintroduction of profit was conditioned in part by extensive cooperation with foreign capital.[181] In the 1960s nearly all Eastern bloc states experimented with various types of bonus systems. Only Albania, following the example of China, implemented a wage reform in 1967 that accentuated the leveling aspects of wage policy. Originally, bonuses in socialist countries only amounted to some 5% of wages. This has risen to roughly 33% in the meantime in the Soviet Union, where for senior workers overall annual bonuses can total up to four months' wages. In exceptional cases an additional bonus of a further two months' wages may be

Table 19

Growing importance of bonuses in the wage structure of socialist countries
(in percentages)

Country	Year	Piece- workers	Time- workers	Employees & engineers
Bulgaria	1965	1.2	11.8	10
	1972	11.9	21.5	18
Czechoslovakia	1965	14.3	14.3	13.8
	1972	20.7	20.9	21.7
GDR	1968	38.6	42.3	
	1972	42.7	46.0	
Hungary	1965	8.1	8.1	
	1972	9.5	9.5	
Soviet Union	1965	7.2	13.0	13.2
	1974	17.9	19.1	27.2

Source: *Oplata truda pri sotsializme* (Moscow: Ekonomika, 1977), pp. 102f.

granted by decision of the Ministry and the Head of the Central Office.[182] (See Table 19.)

Bonuses in agriculture are pitched at a considerably lower level and even in the past constituted more of a quality supplement than was the case in industry. In 1971 the premium for outstanding quality amounted to a mere 10.6% of wages.[183]

In the economic literature of a number of socialist countries, the bonus system is being increasingly justified, and the satisfaction value of material incentives, which benefit the private consumption fund, is discussed without any trace of bad conscience.[184]

The material incentives system has, however, revealed a number of undesirable side effects that have combined unhappily with specific shortcomings in the enterprise planning and supply system:

1. An enterprise working to fulfill its plan cannot switch to a different supply source in the event of its suppliers *breaching their contract*. Manufacturers are not exposed to the same risk of their customers turning elsewhere and thus posing a threat to their very existence, as they are in capitalism, and even the imposition of

sanctions produces no effect since these are set a fairly low level and are generally paid up swiftly by the defaulting enterprise.[185] By taking advantage of the seller's position of power vis-à-vis the buyer and supplying similar but more expensive goods, or goods that bring in greater return, a supplier enterprise can attempt to manipulate its share of material incentives at the cost of other enterprises, which then have to suffer the consequences or make good for production stoppages and unproductive waiting time due to delayed deliveries. A cutting portrayal of ritualistic labor discipline in Yugoslavia reads: "And the workers in their washed-out overalls stand in readiness at their workplace, as though the long-awaited raw materials delivery could appear like a Whitsuntide miracle."[186]

    2.   Since the award of bonuses is conditional upon plans being fulfilled, pressure-groups within socialist enterprise management become more active in a bid to secure *easily fulfillable plans* from the planning authorities.

    3.   The material incentives system revives two practices developed during the period of administrative economy; at the time they served to ward off sanctions imposed for failure to fulfill the plan, whereas today they are used to improve the distribution of bonuses within an individual enterprise. The Russians have the term *blat* (which freely translates as "nepotism") that they use to denote efforts made by management to modify the ministry's set targets for an enterprise or to obtain extra rations of material through bringing personal influence to bear. In sophisticated systems there is even a certain degree of specialization in these activities. A *tolkach* (promoter) is brought in to act as a broker in stimulating the supply of material, thereby improving the enterprise's starting position.[187] Under the new economic systems, the promoter's function has changed somewhat, yet he still lives on—in a new guise—despite the 1940 ban. The state supply system, GOSSNAB, is constantly being undermined by unbureaucratic procurement practices, in which local party and trade union bodies frequently play a role. The limits to corruption on a vast scale—such as when districts or even whole union republics make up target surpluses with produce purchased from private plots[188]—are thus fairly fluid.

    These older forms of corruption were a "market for plan fulfillment," whereas since the reforms of the 1960s a straightforward market-type behavior has been in evidence among management, and this has been unduly stigmatized by left-wing critics as a return to capitalism.

    Khal'tura (which literally translated means slipshod work and when used in the figurative sense denotes easy money earned on the side) is a further dysfunction, and it results firstly from neglect of the services sector and secondly from the excessive production targets set for enterprises with their ensuing work standards for the labor force.[189] The *khal'turishchik* who is keen to make money on the side does not fit in with the official concept of a worker during the communist construction phase, because the worker is systematically taking advantage of shortcomings in the system and in the supply mechanism to improve his individual standard of living. More often than not this spare-time activity requires conservation of the worker's energy during working hours. Dysfunction of this type is frequently put down to insufficient motivation on the part of individual citizens in socialist states. This explanation falls decidedly short of the mark. The Soviet form of corruption is a perfectly functional form for the system. It does not result from corruption in the upper class, as in a large number of capitalist developing countries, but is more of a widespread phenomenon among lower-grade cadres.[190] It is due not only to a lack of motivation in individual citizens, but also to the structural shortcomings in the system, which promote this lack of motivation, since even these forms of "deviant behavior" develop within the ideas of the ruling groups (particularly the planning standards).

It cannot be denied that the bonus system, with the privileges it brings, motivates management to some extent to undermine the regulating mechanism of the central plan system by ordering and collecting excessive quantities of materials. Yet even before incentives came to play such an important role, Soviet versions of white-collar crime were widespread since nonfulfillment of contracts was considered an offence. Ill-meaning controlling authorities could interpret this nonfulfillment as sabotage or as similar offences on the part of an enterprise director. At that time people circumvented the central regulating mechanism in order to retain their positions of power and not, at that stage, to acquire additional earnings.[191] Both types of motivation had similar effects, however. Corrupt practices include incorrect reports and statistics, pressure for easily fulfillable plans, a lowering of quality, pressure for additional material supplies, reserve hoarding, and a resistance to innovation so as not to prejudice short-term plans for obtaining bonuses.[192]

Even drastic threats of punishment for contract violation failed to provide much of a solution, since local authorities not infrequently covered up for enterprises in cases where no enterprises in their own sphere of competence had suffered. The authorities thus repeatedly denounced the localism (*mestnichestvo*) of lower-ranking officials.[193] Investigations into local elite structure have shown that managers and party secretaries—with their similar career patterns and constant, direct contact with one another—not infrequently develop a common front to the outside world and provide each other with mutual support.[194]

For a long time the existence of the "market expert for plan fulfillment," who went under a wide range of legal titles such as "technical agent" or "representative for the exchange of experience," was either denied or associated with Draconian penalties, as was any normal black-market racketeer. Only the more recent reform economy has acknowledged that structural loopholes in the plan system made these functions necessary. What Draconian punishment threats had failed to stamp out was now, in the opinion of the reform economists, to be made superfluous through direct, legalized relationships between supplier enterprises and ordering enterprises.[195]

At first sight this would appear a sensible strategy, yet it involves the risk, firstly, that these legalized trade relations—in conjunction with the bonus scheme—might further strengthen the autonomy of enterprise management and, secondly, that enterprise "profit," while not actually leading to a restoration of private capitalism—as is also feared by a number of Marxists who do not fully support the Maoist restoration theory—might reinforce the link between enterprise and director, thereby weakening worker participation and not exactly offsetting the trend toward "director socialism."

4.   The performance wage is viewed as an inevitable evil of the transitional period. With the bonus system, however, *not even the principle of remuneration according to performance can be put into practice*, because enterprise returns are conditioned by a wide range of factors beyond the worker's control.

Although the Chinese state for a long time sought to play the role of omniscient entrepreneur, leaving very little scope for autonomous decision in the investment sector, there was greater scope for manipulating commodity relations between enterprises.[196] These relations did not, however, have the same negative effect as in the Soviet Union—although even in China corrupt practices did exist— since there were neither bonuses nor excessive plan targets to invite abuse. Chinese planners preferred to put forward moderate levels, which at times were even outbid by enterprise management making higher offers.

5.   With the extension of the bonus system, workers in socialist systems succumb to the *"money illusion,"* and their materialistic interest has to be sustained with rising nominal wages—to some extent through additional bonus payments not included ex ante in the budget.

6.   The growing *surplus in purchasing power* brings additional consequences, since the money illusion alone will not work unless consumers know they can spend their money sensibly. This has therefore led to growing liberalization in the private construction and private welfare scheme sectors (see Chapter 8, Sections 2 and 3).

The effectiveness of the incentive system—which cannot be disputed—is not to be discussed here; instead, we must seek to highlight the antiegalitarian trends in incomes policy. These take four forms:

1.   *The more senior positions in the hierarchy not infrequently bring with them a greater increase in benefit in the form of incentives* —even in the Soviet Union (see Table 19). The same also applies in the Soviet Union (when one considers the special permission referred to above), although one condition laid down in the wage reform was that senior workers were not allowed to receive a bonus greater than the average bonus level throughout the enterprise in terms of the percentage of their remuneration. In view of the cost of living, senior workers come off better under this percentage system, particularly since income tax is not as high in socialist countries as in capitalist countries (see Chapter 2, Section 3).

However, acquisition of higher bonuses must not be regarded as the sole motivating force for socialist enterprise directors. There are other aims apart from maximizing bonuses—prestige, social and political aims, individual promotion opportunities—which, even more than under capitalism where profit is the most important— but increasingly not the only—concern, act as motivation for the directors.[197]

2.   Disparity necessarily develops in cases where *wages are made dependent upon enterprise performance*, as in Hungary, Czechoslovakia (under Dubček), and Yugoslavia, where the state only guarantees a given percentage of wages (in Hungary some 70 to 80%). This is most blatant in Yugoslavia. Trade unions once voiced their criticism in drastic terms: "there can be no talk of self-government or observance of the principle of socialist redistribution whilst a charwoman in one enterprise earns more than an engineer in a neighbor enterprise."[198]

3.   Disparity of this nature threatens to become even more pronounced in cases where workers also *have to bear the brunt of enterprise losses*, and this is most serious in Yugoslavia. (In capitalist systems this threat would only materialize as a result of capital formation schemes.) Attempts are, however, being made to absorb this risk with a "Company Risk Fund."[199]

This type of enterprise risk also exists in Soviet kolkhozy, where the kolkhozniki have to bear losses for which they are not, in the main, responsible—losses resulting from state production or price policy or from weather conditions. The negative consequences of this lack of correlation between work input and increased income have, in the meantime, been the subject of sharp criticism by Soviet economists, who once summed up the long-held and widespread view of economic dogmatics with the cynical remark "that the kolkhoznik receives what he is entitled to and is entitled to precisely as much as he receives."[200]

Even stability funds such as those set up in Yugoslavia still require sacrifices on the part of individual workers, and this leads to discontent when coupled with proposals from company management to cut down wages on account of the enterprise's poor position. The interest rates paid for deposits in the stability fund are not sufficient to offset inflation (see Table 74). Resistance to the scheme, however, is pointless because of socialist work discipline, together with the high rate of unemployment left over from capitalist times (see Chapter 7, Section 1), since in Yugoslavia dismissal is frequently synonymous with unemployment. The seemingly revolutionary principle of profit sharing for all workers doubtlessly has its advantages in Yugoslavia. It increases the workers' sense of responsibility and promotes their interest in the enterprise's position. A survey has shown that 80% of workers take an interest in the enterprise report. Economics teaching has, however, not always proved adequate to satisfy this interest, because almost 44% of workers were unable to understand the report.[201] The drawbacks of the scheme nonetheless outweighed its advantages because of the personal risk involved. In 1968, this affected some 10% of Yugoslav enterprises, which operated at a loss. Performance wages and profit sharing thus work in different directions, and only if sizeable profits were to be recorded could these instruments cancel out the differentials of the performance wage and develop into a "redistribution mechanism in line with socialist thought."[202]

Thus today Yugoslavia is least in a position to implement the principle of "equal wages for equal performance" and has had to intervene with statutory wage limitation in order to put a stop to the runaway wage gap in some branches—such as in 1967 with the "law on the temporary freeze on increases in personal income in the work organizations of certain branches," aimed primarily at banks, commercial enterprises and electric power stations, or in 1969 with the "basic law on fixing and distribution of income in work organizations."[203]

4.   Even where material incentives do not take the form of cash allocations and are based mainly on moral and political qualities, they are frequently regarded as *unjust*. Trade-union-sponsored stays in sanatoria and rest homes play an important role here. Even citizens who are critical of the system rate these facilities as a true achievement.[204] Although as early as the mid-1950s figures showed that 2 to 3 million workers were benefiting from the scheme,[205] this was nonetheless still only a very small minority of Soviet workers, and complaints of favoritism and preferential treatment of officials— and also complaints about stakhanovites, whose exceptional performance was well-arranged in advance by the company and achieved through the concerted action of temporary workers and who then reaped the rich benefits of this surplus effort with lengthy vacations —are not entirely absent from the Soviet discussion. Not infrequently small quasi-material rewards, such as gifts, free tickets, or free shaves at the barber's, were abused as consolation prizes for the mass of workers, while the more lucrative benefits—particularly in view of the inflationary trends in the budget—went more to the privileged status holders.

In China, even before the leveling-out campaigns of 1958 and 1966/68, bonuses for managers did not play as great a role as in the Soviet Union and Eastern bloc countries. Workers received a greater proportion of the bonuses that, up to the cultural revolution, accounted for between 5 and 15% of wage costs, varying from one enterprise to another, than did the managers, and the distribution rules were more democratic than in Eastern bloc countries. In many instances shop-floor meetings decided on the distribution of bonuses. It was not necessarily physical labor that counted here; ideological behavior was also honored. No official data on bonuses has been available since the cultural revolution, although reports of individual cases of bonuses being awarded do appear repeatedly.[206] In 1965 a start was made on phasing out bonuses and incorporating them wholly or in part in workers' wages. The percentage profit— to a maximum of 10%—that enterprises were allowed to keep was largely spent on social amenities or distributed to individuals on criteria other than purely physical work input. Kindly disposed observers of China still put private income from plots, which at most total 5% of the team's cultivated land, at 10 to 30%.[207]

Despite these left-overs from the days of material incentives, enterprise profit does not act as a lever in the same way as it does in other socialist systems. Enterprises strive after efficiency and technical progress, which according to their ideological representation constitute ends in themselves and do not need to be stimulated in a roundabout way by profit. A higher percentage of enterprise profit is transferred to the central office and redistributed centrally than in the Soviet Union. In the Soviet Union, by comparison, it has been calculated that as much as one third of profit is now retained by the enterprise. This is being increasingly passed on to the individual workers, with less money being paid into collective consumption funds.

In Cuba secondary motives were also at play in the renunciation of material incentives. Castro feared that introduction of a bonus scheme could spark off inflation again. Given Cuba's economic difficulties, he frequently had no other choice but to set the printing press rolling again. Nevertheless, Cuba did introduce material incentives, albeit to a lesser extent, at times when the efficiency of the economic system was at stake—such as at the end of 1965, during the sugar and coffee harvest. But by November 1965, Basilo Rodriguez, Minister of Labor, was already dissociating himself again from these material stimuli. He had other rewards in mind, such as prizes and services for particularly active workers.[208] A number of disparities meet the eye in the prize distribution scheme that did actually come into being. On occasion there was criticism that prizes went chiefly to those in the ministries and the army, with not enough going to the sugar workers.

This one-sided decision not to introduce material incentives—not solely for ideological reasons but also conditioned by a shortage of resources—led to a vicious circle of falling productivity, culminating in the *ley contra la vagancia* (law against laziness) on April 1, 1971.[209] The Cuban system's idea of egalitarianism as "immaterial output" not only hampered achievement of other targets, such as efficiency, but also harmed the equality policy itself, since duress created further inequality, which could have been avoided with a higher rate of efficiency.

Developments in Soviet wage policy and the spread of material incentives seemed to confirm the theory held by a number of bourgeois economists that wage disparity develops as a transitional phenomenon in all economies, regardless of the particular system in question, and serves a useful function in all economic development. This is said to be based on three grounds:

1. wage differentials *stimulate unskilled workers to develop their work capacity*;
2. they cause management to *hire more low-cost, unskilled workers* who would otherwise continue their existence as underemployed country proletariat;

3.   they stimulate saving among the higher income brackets at a time when capital is in short supply.[210]

Efforts on the part of trade union representatives such as Tomskii aimed at achieving a leveling wage policy were counteracted by the party relatively early on,[211] and by the time of the Stachanovite movement, at the very latest, wage differentials were being openly used as a stimulus, despite considerable attempts to highlight the idealistic aspect of this new form of competition along the lines of the Subbotniki.

China was the first socialist country to attempt to introduce an equalization policy on repeated occasions—with interruptions—and thus to break out of the vicious circle of economic cause and effect. Whether this has been a definitive success or not will only become apparent when China's productive resources have developed to the same level as those of the Soviet Union.

Except in China, redistribution targets have always clashed with efficiency targets and created new disparity. In the majority of socialist systems the impetus toward an egalitarian, money-free society experienced during the revolution lost its impact in the construction and accumulation phase. Scarcity of talent has become increasingly reflected in remuneration, and only once this has been phased out through a successful socialist education policy will it be possible to use the wage system to new redistributive ends.[212] Difficulty has also been experienced in aligning redistribution policy to the fourth basic objective of socialism—participation. The benefits of a uniform, rational, and transparent state-monitored wage system were often only obtained at the cost of wage earners forsaking their participation. Only with the coming of the economic reforms did the discussion on participation of subsystems come round to the wage question again, and in a number of countries enterprises were granted greater freedom of movement to organize the wage fund.[213] This opportunity, however, mainly opens the way for expert participation at enterprise level.

China has experimented with the possibility of teams fixing their own wage rate—and this to a greater extent than has of late been the case in a number of Eastern bloc countries—in a bid to improve participation in wage matters. Some objection was at times raised to the effect that individual outsiders could come off badly under this system, where wages may be fixed by simple majority. Individuals are protected from excessive group pressure, however, by a "base points system" that allows for the working hours and qualifications of the worker but does not rigorously correlate the basic wage with labor output.[214]

Self-assessment was also introduced in a number of agricultural communes for work that was difficult to quantify. Social monitoring is effective enough to prevent individuals from abusing the qualitative assessment criteria to too great an extent. In the light of experience, however, as the pay gap for different work increases, workers tend to prefer a clear list of quantifiable factors to a majority decision taken by the work teams. Participation in wage formation thus tends to emerge more in the form of cooperation in establishing criteria at enterprise level and above.

2. Reduction of differences between social groups and strata

Wage policy measures in socialist countries are aimed at bringing about an overall reduction in the differences between social groups and strata. Some of these attempts to level out the differences rank high in the hierarchy of long-term targets for the construction of communism. The most important of these are:

1. overcoming the division between town and country;
2. leveling out the differences between mental and physical labor;
3. establishment of equality between men and women;
4. overcoming local differences;
5. alignment of incomes in the different occupational sectors.

All five of these points are closely related to incomes policy, but they are at least as dependent on reeducative and attitude-remolding strategies as they are on state wage and budgetary policy.

Overcoming the division between town and country

The contrast between town and countryside, which Soviet theorists feel will eventually only manifest itself "in a few unessential features" in communism and will even lead to the complete disappearance of the terms "town" and "countryside" in the highest stage of communism,[215] is meant to be steadily reduced in the socialism phase. Soviet policy in the 1920s and 1930s only heeded this point of the program verbally. In fact, it deliberately opted for "a tribute (or sacrifice) from agriculture in favor of industry," as the Trotskyist Preobrazhensky had justified in theoretical terms in the 1920s. Preobrazhensky was also severely criticized by Stalin at the time, but his persecution did not stop Stalin from adopting and concretizing some of Preobrazhensky's ideas—as he so often did in the fight against the opposition. This policy even caused a temporary widening in the gap between town and country. The preferential treatment given by many transitional societies to rapid construction in heavy industry meant that more than half the working population, that is, those working in agriculture (see Table 20) had been reduced to an underprivileged class by the 1950s and 1960s.

China was the only country that, from 1958 onward, made an energetic attempt to counteract this tendency. In 1958 the Government Council decreed that the real wages for unskilled industrial workers should not be noticeably above the income of cooperative farmers. This could not easily be put into practice without considerable interference in the developing communes. However, other extensive control measures—such as steps toward deurbanization—were applied in order to level off the differences between town and country.[216]

By the beginning of the 1960s, average wages in agriculture

Table 20

Average wages in agriculture as compared to industry
(in percentages)

Country	1955	1965
Bulgaria	76	87
Czechoslovakia	70	84
GDR	78	82
Hungary	75	87
Poland	70	77
Soviet Union	68	72
Yugoslavia	82 (1959)	98 (1966)

Sources: V. P. Gruzinov, *Material'noe stimulirovanie truda v stranakh Sotsializma* (Moscow: Mysl', 1968), p. 239; *Statistichki godishniak FNRJ 1960* (Beograd: Savezni zavod za statistiku, 1960), p. 257; (1969), p. 275.

Table 21

Monthly earnings of industrial and sovkhoz workers
(in rubles)

Average monthly earnings	Industrial workers	Kolkhoz workers
1940	32.4	20.7
1960	89.9	51.9
1965	101.7	72.4
1970	130.6	98.5
1975	160.9	126.8
1978	176.0	143.0
1979	180.0	145.2

Source: *SSSR v tsifrakh v 1978* (Moscow: Statistika, 1979), p. 184; *1979* (Moscow, 1980), p. 172.

were being increasingly aligned with industrial wages in all socialist countries. The Soviet Union, by comparison, is in a relatively poor position here as far as her efforts toward alignment are concerned (see the last two lines of Table 31). Apart from the "scissors" between industry and agriculture in general, there were also differences between workers employed under comparable conditions as wage-workers on state farms and as workers in industry. However, according to Soviet statistics, this gap between average monthly earnings in industry and those in state agriculture (sovkhozy) has progressively narrowed (see Table 21).

However, in those countries that would still seem to reflect antiquated agrarian structures in the form of low wages most strongly (chiefly the Soviet Union and Poland), the income of the rural population cannot be measured solely in terms of these figures, because there are all sorts of private, subsidiary sources of income. This holds particularly true for the Soviet kolkhoz peasants, even though their subsidiary incomes have dropped over the last few decades from 48.3% of earnings in 1940 to 27.1% in 1972.[291] Soviet social stratification doctrine no longer denies that the kolkhozniks are still underprivileged in certain respects compared to sovkhoz or industrial workers, but it is pointed out that rapid alignment of these levels is underway.[217]

Over these last few years, socialist countries have made an effort to level out the income differentials that still persist by introducing a system of material incentives also in agriculture.[218] Despite this, the rural population still tend to feel underprivileged in some cases. In Slovakia, an opinion poll conducted in 1968 showed that 50.3% of farmers interviewed and 33% of a representative cross section of the population held the view that the countryside was still making a "tribute" to the town, although the majority of those in the sample had been intrinsically won over to collective farming.[219]

There is increasing insight in Soviet economics into the fact that abolition of the differences between town and country is a problem that cannot be solved by material incentives alone, but one that also calls for the country to be put on a par with the town as far as culture and social security are concerned.[220] This, however, is not yet the case everywhere. As a result, socialist states are also experiencing difficulty in attracting enough doctors to the countryside, despite the substantial wage supplements paid. Moreover, there is criticism of the tendency to send most rural patients to town and district hospitals for their inpatient treatment. In 1964 the Soviet Union admitted that the number of doctors available in towns was nine times greater than that in the country.[221] The rural population is also still underprivileged in the education sector, despite considerable progress made here, and this is particularly evident in the mobility opportunities for leading cadres (see Chapter 2, Section 3).

Leveling out the differences between mental and physical labor

When it comes to leveling out the differentials between mental and physical labor, socialist systems have achieved even less than they have in the field of incomes policy. Although the traditional prerogatives of bureaucracy have been abolished, the distinction between salaried employees and wage earners, and state employees and laborers, has been maintained, even though in many socialist systems their earnings have been increasingly equalized over the last few years.

In general, socialist systems have abolished the status of civil servant and created a uniform type of state employee (*sluzhashchii*), who is compared with the laborer (*rabochii*) for statistical purposes.

In Yugoslavia, the leveling-out of the differences between these two groups (*radnik* and *sluzhbenik*) has, in some respects, been pushed on even more than in the other systems, but there is still a noteworthy difference as far as remuneration is concerned.[222]

In the Soviet Union, despite this alignment, a number of intellectual professions still enjoy certain privileges. Soviet statistics for 1967 put the average industrial wage at 103 rubles per month, whereas the monthly income for a president of the Academy of Science was reported to be 1,200 rubles, for the rector of an important university 1,200 rubles, for a high-ranking government official 600 rubles, and for an army colonel 400 rubles.[223]

Disparities in agriculture had always been much smaller, because the lower degree of mechanization meant there was less skilled technical work to be remunerated. There were, on the other hand, quite considerable local disparities, and in the Soviet Union these served to enhance the strata differences. The southern parts of the Soviet Union were much better off than Byelorussia and the Baltic States, for instance. Stratification of the Soviet rural population takes three different forms, which are also substantiated by income disparities:

1. The *managers of agricultural enterprises* and political cadres in the countryside receive higher remuneration.[224] In the 1960s the pay differential between an average brigade worker and the kolkhoz chairman was slightly above a ratio of 1 to 2.5 (kolkhoz chairman 170 rubles per month, agronomist 116 rubles, veterinarian 69 rubles, brigade worker 70 rubles, head of livestock departments 61 rubles[225]).

2. After liquidation of the MTS the *technical staff of the machine stations* were granted a sort of privilege guarantee. However, their integration into the kolkhozy led to social conflict on account of the privileges they received in terms of remuneration and leave.[226]

3. There are *disparities between kolkhoz and sovkhoz workers* that, according to official doctrine, cannot be explained by differences in productivity since Soviet data show that labor productivity per working day was only 6.5% higher in the sovkhoz than in the kolkhoz. Even the proportionately higher amount of capital expenditure involved (26%) does not justify the disparity in incomes, not to mention the fact that the argumentation about capital input goes against the Marxist labor theory of value. Over the past few years, however, there has been a certain amount of success scored in reducing the disparity between kolkhoz workers and sovkhoz workers. In 1965, the average monthly earnings of a kolkhoz worker amounted

to 68% of a sovkhoz worker's income, whereas by 1971 they had already reached the 75% mark.[227]

Income differences in China, either in the country or in the industrial towns, have never been as high as in the Soviet Union. Following on from the salary reduction for the higher income brackets in 1965, traveling economists established in 1966 that a manager's income was only about two to two-and-a-half times that of a worker.

As far as salary reductions are concerned, an attempt was made to maintain the impression of voluntariness. Employees earning high salaries were urged to ask for a salary reduction from time to time.[228] The rural cadres were paid by the state, and their salaries were only just twice as high as a worker's wage, but from the mid-1960s onward they had to do at least 60 days' field work with the other members of the commune. Recent information still puts the difference between maximum and minimum incomes in Chinese enterprises in the 1 : 3 to 4 : 1 range.[229]

In China the disparity between town and country had its origin in the check on urbanization and in the recruitment of seasonal workers during the "both worker and peasant" campaign, which resulted in lower remuneration and lower social security benefits for this growing group of the population (see Chapter 8, Section 2).

Through the Hsia-fang system, however, which constantly threatens the economic elite with demotion to production level, greater effective alignment has been achieved in psychological terms than has been achieved through the simple alignment of incomes.

4.   In other socialist systems, cadre policy has led to a certain privileging of the economico-bureaucratic *manager elite*, although, contrary to a widespread assertion in literature, those in top management do not earn as much as their counterparts in capitalist systems. In the Soviet Union, managers of the four categories of enterprises earned 350, 400, 200, and 250 rubles respectively, compared with the average worker's wage of 103 rubles.[230] This is not, however, sufficient indication as to the full extent of the privileges that they actually enjoy. These tend to involve special income-equivalent services, ranging from special stores for higher cadres to services provided by the enterprise (with its motor vehicle fleet or its construction brigade), which the managers occasionally make use of. In a bid to do away with privileges of this type, even Cuba has recently started encouraging private purchasing. In the case of cars, as Castro has pointed out, this also saves the provision of a state-salaried driver. The establishment of special stores was quite justifiable in times of stress when one could not afford to have

reliable cadres distracted by standing in queues or side-tracked by the daily struggles about trivialities. In the meantime, however, these stores have become a permanent institution, and this no longer really fits into the modified landscape of the socialist system.

5. Apart from the managers and executives of state enterprises, some of the *intelligentsia* are still favored by incomes policy. The intelligentsia constitute a growing social group; after the 1959 census, when intellectual professions accounted for 19.5% of the working population, their number rose to 27.3% in the 1970 census, and even to 34.4% among the urban working population, as compared to 15.9% in the rural areas.[231] These figures are, however, based on a relatively schematic and broad concept of intelligence which includes all those who have received training at further education level or who hold posts normally requiring this level of educational qualification.

Since the Stalin period there has been talk of the *prosloika* (intermediate stratum), a group that was given increasing encouragement in the light of the growing tasks faced by the Soviet Union. Only part of this intelligentsia is privileged. Certain jobs in the fields of education and public health are even underpaid when compared to skilled workers' wages.[232] In systems that employ material incentives with somewhat more of a guilty conscience than immaterial incentives, privileges are not merely to be found in income disparities. In socialist systems, in particular, we encounter what Kolakowski once called "the qualitative inequality of the privileged"[233]: easier access to housing cooperatives, the opportunity of staying in the popular large cities, higher prestige, and other advantages, which all have positive material effects to some extent.

As far as the few particularly high incomes are concerned, the differences may, at best, be justified by the scarcity of available talent but not by exceptional productivity in terms of the labor theory of value. Some of the top incomes are to be found in occupations considered "unproductive" in the communications and services sectors. On the other hand, considering the esteem in which those engaged in the cultural sector (*tvorcheskaya intelligentsia*) are held and the growing emphasis placed on science as a productive resource, the top incomes of the small cultural-intellectual elite are perfectly justifiable. In 1968 Evtushenko stated that his annual income amounted to some 100,000 rubles, which at that time represented 138 times the minimum wage. While this still bears comparison with similar disparities in capitalist systems, he, at least, is not a parasite living off unearned income.

Income comparisons in socialist countries should not be limited to cross-sectional analyses at a specific point in time but ought to take the chronological evolution of the wage scale into account. Thus it would appear that income disparities are, on the whole, becoming less pronounced. This evolution was, however, forced most in countries that experimented least with material incentives and profit motives, such as Rumania and the German Democratic Republic. If we compare income groups with those during the periods when bourgeois society prevailed in a country, we can then determine the amount of progress achieved through redistribution. The ratio between the five fifths has not been shifted fundamentally. In 1965 we still find the highest incomes in the highest fifth; but the gaps have narrowed and the bulge in income around the middle class has widened somewhat toward the bottom. (See Table 22.)

Up to now the old two-class (plus one stratum = intelligentsia) pattern has not been disavowed. Nevertheless, Soviet sociologists have struggled through to a more detailed differentiation. Thus, social scientists have become increasingly aware of the differences within the classes. Among these, the difference between brainwork and manual work is of decisive importance. This difference is by no means due exclusively to the income gap but, according to Soviet social stratification theory, also stems from:[234]

1. differences in the nature of work;
2. differences in cultural–technical level;
3. remuneration of work;
4. educational differences for the children of those engaged in mental or physical work.

Table 22

Income distribution in Czechoslovakia

Those receiving income	1930	1946	1965
lowest fifth	2.5	3.8	6.3
second fifth	8.5	11.0	14.0
third fifth	16.0	18.0	19.7
fourth fifth	26.0	24.1	25.6
highest fifth	47.0	43.1	34.4

Source: P. Machonin et al., *Československá společnost* (Bratislava: Epocha, 1969), p. 297.

A number of sociologists have divided the working class of the Soviet Union into five groups, generally on the basis of vocational qualification characteristics.[235] Consequently, special store is set by the reduction of intraclass differences, because it is hoped that this will produce a spillover effect into interclass differences.

In spite of the intraclass differences that still prevail with respect to remuneration—and also with respect to educational opportunities—there is a sound basis to the assertion made by Soviet sociologists that this does not bring about the same risks of declassing through horizontal mobility and through job-changing as it does in capitalism.[236]

For a long time neither the analysis of "social stratification" nor the notion of "vertical mobility" has been accepted in Soviet sociology. In the early 1970s, Soviet sociologists spoke of *peremesh-cheniya* (interchanges) between occupational groups. In the meantime the concept of social mobility has been assimilated more and more.[237]

Establishment of equality between men and women

In Marxist doctrine, one of the principal instruments for the emancipation of women was considered to be liberation from "domestic slavery" and integration into the productive process.[238] In all socialist countries—with the exception of Albania—the percentage of women gainfully employed is considerably higher than in most capitalist countries (see Table 23).

Only Japan and Sweden have been able to mobilize comparable percentages of women for gainful employment as the socialist countries.[239] Higher proportions of women are working in socialist countries than in capitalist economies, especially when we compare different age groups. Especially in the age groups 20 to 24 and between 25 and 44, when women frequently take care of children, we find higher proportions of working women in socialist economies (see Table 23). Opinion polls in socialist countries have shown that only a very small percentage of men were still fundamentally opposed to their wives' pursuing a gainful activity (4.2% in Czechoslovakia in 1966 and 25.2% with reservations).[240] The differences in the statistical data from socialist countries cannot, however, be indiscriminately interpreted as reflecting different degrees of women's emancipation. These are due, in part, to a particular scarcity of labor and heavy losses in the male population during the Second World War (USSR,

Table 23

Percentage of employed women of the working population

Country	Year	Percentage of all employed	Percentage of women employed in different age groups (1975)					
			15–19	20–24	15–44	45–54	55–64	over 65
Albania	1967	42.0						
Bulgaria	1975	46.8	34.5	69.4	80.0	74.6	39.4	11.5
Czecho-slovakia	1977	47.9	41.2	80.1	80.9	76.1	30.5	5.1
GDR	1977	49.6	53.2	75.5	80.9	77.7	46.6	7.2
Hungary	1977	43.9	46.3	68.2	70.9	63.3	30.6	4.6
Poland	1977	42.7	25.9	73.6	79.0	78.8	59.5	31.2
Rumania	1975	34.5	53.8	75.9	76.5	75.7	56.7	26.1
Soviet Union	1975	51.5						
Yugo-slavia	1971	31.1						
for comparison:								
FRG			63.3	69.0	49.8	48.5	27.6	5.6
France			34.1	63.9	46.8	48.0	38.9	5.7
Italy			36.7	45.9	32.9	29.2	14.0	3.2
Japan			34.6	73.1	55.7	66.1	50.4	18.3
United States			34.9	58.1	49.8	58.8	43.9	8.9

Sources: Statistical surveys. In: *Yearbook of East-European Economics,* Vol. 8 (Munich: Olzog, 1979), pp. 456ff. For Albania: *Geschichte der Partei der Arbeit Albaniens* (Tirana: Naim Frasheri, 1971), p. 679; For the breakdown of age groups: N. M. Shishkin, *Sotsial-no-ekonomicheskie problemy zhenskogo trud. (Moscow: Ekonomika, 1980),* pp. 30f.

German Democratic Republic). On the other hand, in some socialist countries the percentage of gainfully employed women has not increased in a linear relationship but has been liable to fluctuations with temporary retrograde tendencies. In Hungary, this trend is explained by the argument that many women have turned back to family obligations.[241] This trend is growing even in the Soviet Union. A survey among nonworking women revealed that a good many of these women excused themselves either by the fact that there was no appropriate work near their home or that they had no sufficient specialist's training. About 5% even gave a sufficient income through their husband's wage as a reason.[242]

After 1945, all socialist countries decreed equal pay for men and women.[243] In practice, however, this was only achieved gradually. Even in a highly developed socialist system with a traditionally high degree of women's emancipation, as in Czechoslovakia, the average women's wages in 1966 were still only 66.1% of men's wages. As in western countries, there are few data available on wage differentials broken down according to sex. In general, underpayment of women can only be deduced indirectly from shortages of qualifications and from the high percentage of women working in the worst-paid branches. Discrimination against women was not, however, solely restricted to the field of remuneration. Other variables were just as decisive, particularly:

1. discrimination against women due to their double role in occupational and family life;
2. distribution of the working women over the occupational branches;
3. women's reduced mobility prospects.

1. *Discrimination against women*
    due to their double role in the family and at work

The woman's role was hardest in socialist systems where traditional machismo was as strong as in Cuba. Castro admitted as late as 1973:

> But if someone earned good wages, a young man, and then married a school mistress, he would say: "don't go to work, this is not really necessary" [laughter]. And the country lost the school teacher. And the country lost the nurse. If the country loses the school teacher and the nurse, this is not only so because of the money, but because of backward attitudes, the *machismo* and the superman cult, and all the things that are still clinging to us.[244]

Table 24

Time budget for men and women
(in hours)

	Soviet Union Kostroma (1961)		Czechoslovakia Ostrava (1961)		France (1963/64	
	men	women	men	women	men	women
time related to production (commuting)	1.4	1.4	0.3	0.3	7.5	6.2
housework and toilet, education of children	2.4	5.1	2.0	5.2	2.0	4.5
eating and sleeping	8.2	7.2	8.5	8.1	10.8	10.7
leisure time	3.5	1.5	5.4	3.3	7.4	6.6

Sources: G. S. Petrosyan, *Vnerabochee vremya trudyashchikhsya v SSSR* (Moscow: Mysl', 1965), p. 103; B. Svorenova-Kiralyova, Zena 20, stoleti ve svete prace (Prague: T. Prace, 1968), p. 97. B. Kerblay, *La société soviétique contemporaine* (Paris: Colin, 1977), p. 138.

In these transitional societies, also, traditional patterns of behavior created greater social differences than did the remaining income gaps.

This has been proved again and again by time budget surveys. Although there is no doubt about the difficulties inherent in such time budget surveys, carried out in different countries with varying population structures and different conditions of life, they all reveal that in socialism, too, women are at a disadvantage, especially with regard to the time budget components of leisure time and further education. In a comparative Soviet study that also included capitalist countries, it was the periods indicated as leisure or free time that differed most: USSR (Pskov) 4.9 : 3.0 hours, other socialist countries 4.2 : 2.9 hours, and capitalist countries 4.4 : 3.5 hours per day to the women's disadvantage.[245] Whereas sociologists still frequently attribute the traditional behavior patterns and role separation that produce such results to motivational deficiencies in the minds of men, data on the development of women's emancipation shows that certain structural shortcomings in socialist economies are also responsible for these results as well—in particular the underdevelopment of the services sector and supply difficulties involved in daily chores (standing in line), which are mainly assumed by women.[246] As yet, socialist economy has, in a way, only completed the first step toward emancipation by integrating women into the production process, and this again has been favored by forced industrialization. In a second step, as the primacy of heavy industry and the production of capital goods give way to the development of the services sector and infrastructure, the full emancipation process will be completed.

Socialist literature has come increasingly to recognize that the infrastructural facilities designed to relieve the woman's burden of work still leave much to be desired. Around 1960, Soviet family sociologists were already complaining that only 13% of children aged 1 to 6 years were provided with kindergarten and preschool facilities.[247] Even in the more developed socialist countries the situation in the mid-1960s was not much better—although better than in most capitalist systems. (See Table 25.)

Preschool attendance is growing more-or-less proportionately to the level of productive resources. Between 1960 and 1973, the percentage of preschool registration in the Soviet Union was able to be raised from 12.5 to 35.9%.

2. *Distribution of working women over occupational branches*

This is the field in which socialist emancipation policy has realized its greatest achievements compared with capitalist countries.

Table 25

Number of children of preschool age attending preschool establishments
(per 10,000 schildren)

	1960	1970	1979
Bulgaria	3,296	4,095	5,050
Cuba	no data	1,138	1,784
Czechoslovakia	2,333	3,466	4,637
GDR	3,200	5,045	7,835
Hungary	2,913	3,710	5,685
Mongolia	580	1,425	1,560
Poland	1,033	1,975	2,722 (1978)
Rumania	1,449	1,855	4,183
Soviet Union	1,256	3,185	4,328

Source: *Statisticheskii ezhegodnik stran-chlenov SEV 1979* (Moscow: Statistika, 1980), p. 422.

Table 26

Percentage of women in selected sectors in the Soviet Union and in the German Democratic Republic

Occupational branches	Soviet Union			GDR	
	1965	1972	1974	1967	1977
agriculture	44	44	44	42.9	
industry	44	45	49	28	43.8
building (construction)	30	29	29	4	15.8
education	71	72	73	62	
medical care (health)	86	85	84	81	

Sources: *Narodnoe khozyajstvo SSSR v 1972 g* (Moscow: Statistika, 1973), p. 513. *Zhenshchiny v SSSR. Statisticheskii sbornik* (Moscow: Statistika, 1975), p. 32f. Bundesministerium für innerdeutsche Beziehungen. *DDR Handbuch* (Cologne: Verlag Wissenschaft und Politik, 1979), p. 425.

As a rule, women are less confined to the ghettos of what tend to be considered typically female occupations, although it must be admitted that an even higher percentage of women are employed in the underpaid mass professions (such as medical care and education) than in many capitalist societies. (See Table 26.)

Soviet scientists agree that the employment of women in occupations involving relatively hard physical labor (see "building" in Table 26) is an obstacle to emancipation.[248] In order to help the situation, prohibition lists have been drawn up of certain activities in which women must not be employed. Now that the hectic accumulation phase is nearing its end, the scientific–technical revolution is giving increasing assistance in the emancipation process. Soviet statistics show that during the last few years, the percentage of women in intellectual professions has in some cases exceeded the percentage of men. Even in the 1959 census, 21.1% of women out of the total working population (both urban and rural) were employed in intellectual activities (as compared to 18.1% of men), and this ratio has continued to develop in the women's favor. In 1970, 32.1% of women and only 22.5% of men were working primarily in occupations involving intellectual activity.[249] A comparison of the areas that are considered as predominantly "male" occupations shows that women definitely come off better in socialist countries than under capitalist systems. Even in the early 1960s, one-third of all engineers were women, whereas in the United States women only made up 1% of engineers.[250] On the whole, however, the professional opportunities open to women in socialist countries are not yet as widely developed as are their educational opportunities.

3. *Women's reduced mobility prospects*

Socialist descriptions tend to present mobility prospects in too favorable a light through selective treatment of their data.[251] Frequently, data are taken for a few representative jobs where women appear to be well represented in socialism, compared to capitalist countries. Hence, the percentage of female parliamentary representatives is a favorite subject of comparison. The figures recorded in 1967 were as follows: Soviet Union 29%, GDR (1971) 31.8%, Yugoslavia 20%, Czechoslovakia 20%, Albania, China and Hungary 18%, Rumania and Bulgaria 17%, Finland 16.5%, West Bulgaria 17%, West Germany 6%.[252] Representation is less favorable in bodies having greater importance in political decision making than the national parliaments—for example, the Party's central committees and politbureaus (see Table 27). In key economic positions the balance is no more positive; according to Soviet data, in 1963

Table 27

Women in Soviet politics
(in percentages)

Category	Year	Membership
population	1977	53.5
party		
membership	1977	24.7
Central Committee	1976	4.0
Politburo	1978	0
local Soviets	1977	49.0
Supreme Soviet	1974	31.3
Council of Ministers	1978	1.0

Source: St. White, *Political Culture and Soviet Politics* (London: Macmillan, 1979), p. 156.

women accounted for only 6% of factory managers, 12% of managers of state-owned stores, and 16% of chief engineers. This percentage is higher, however, than in the Federal Republic of Germany.[253]

Particular problems arise when women assume executive jobs in socialist developing countries where women have held even more of a dependent position than in Western Europe. In China, too, complaints are often quoted that female functionaries did not succeed in exerting authority and were made fun of, that women are still too absorbed by housekeeping "so that they cannot fully dedicate themselves to public services," and that married women are not paid the same wages by the collectives because they are withholding part of their working capacity for their families. Hence, it certainly is not pure propaganda if pro-Chinese literature points out that late marriage is advocated not only for demographic reasons but also because of its importance in the emancipation of women.[254]

But for all that, as far as professional structures and systems of education are concerned, socialist systems do have a few good prerequisites enabling them to implement full emancipation of women more rapidly than capitalist systems. The main positive repercussions on women's position within society are expected to originate from three developments:

1. *The scientific-technical revolution*, which is giving women greater opportunity to put in the same performance as men than was the case when hard physical labor predominated;
2. the move away from the efficiency-dominated considerations that prevailed during the accumulation phase when the woman's *professional role* put too much strain on her family role for a while;
3. the rise in the material standard of living and the *improvement in the services system*.

Overcoming local differences through a regional development policy

Regional development policy is the field of redistribution policy that was least able to be controlled by wage policy measures alone. Wage policy used to be an important instrument, however, for regional redistribution, especially in the socialist states covering large surface areas, where redistribution policy had to be applied in order to compensate for climatic and social differences in the standard of living. Moreover, a system of wage zones was needed to adjust price differentials to nominal wages. For a long time, the southern areas of the Soviet Union (Caucasia, the Ukraine, Moldavia) had the lowest retail prices, with the highest retail prices being found in the northern and far eastern regions. The highest wage bonuses were paid to the workers on the Kamchatka peninsula, in the Kuril islands, and in the far North. There is, however, no overall tendency toward alignment in evidence. Whereas in some of the areas with the highest regional bonuses, (such as the East Siberian region) the difference in pay compared with average wage levels in the Soviet Union as a whole did, in fact, decrease, the difference was still on the increase in other regions (such as the Far East) in the 1960s.[255]

If we compare both the differences per branch of activity and the differences in wage bonuses in the various regions, we discover that certain occupations are clearly privileged (for example, coal miners in the Ural) whereas other groups do not come off so well. These regional differences cast doubt upon the assertion that there is no labor market in socialist systems but only a central allocation scheme for labor resources, since individual enterprises are trying to gain advantage on the labor market, within the scope allowed by the Soviet bonus system, through offering additional material incentives. The high emigration rates from unattractive regions, despite bonuses totaling up to a quarter to a third of the Soviet Union's average wage figure, prove that even these regional compensation measures have only been successful in part.[256]

In considering the uncontrolled migration of youth—which is discussed quite openly today—the fear is sometimes expressed in the Soviet literature that there might be limits to the power of material incentives to increase individual motivation. But as far as the future goes, it is hoped that the social consumption fund will play its part in compensating for regional differences in attractiveness and also for migration from the underdeveloped areas of the Soviet Union.[257]

The Soviet Union is the only succession state to an imperial great power that has managed to maintain and integrate former colonial territories, thanks to their geographical proximity. More and more literature is dealing with the economic successes of the Soviet model of development, especially in Central Asia. Comparison of the national incomes of the Soviet Union republics shows that, in absolute figures, the differences in development levels in the north west (Baltic republics) and the southeast (Central Asia and Azerbaydzhan) could not be leveled off. (See Table 28.)

Table 28

National per capita income in the Union republics (1958, 1968)
(in rubles)

1958			1968			1978(1970 = 100)	
1.	Estonia	792	Estonia	1,447	Armenia	178
2.	Latvia	788	Latvia	1,472	Byelorussia	176
3.	RSFSR	666	Lithuania	1,178	Azerbaydzhan	173
4.	Ukraine	614	RSFSR	1,160	Uzbekistan	163
5.	Lithuania	566	Ukraine	1,004	Georgia	160
6.	Turkmenia	509	Moldavia	837	RSFSR	154
7.	Azerbaydzhan	505	Byelorussia	836	Tadzhikistan	148
8.	Moldavia	492	Armenia	753	Estonia	147
9.	Kazakhstan	480	Kazakhstan	721	Latvia	146
10.	Georgie	470	Georgia	668	Lithuania	145
11.	Armenia	453	Kirghizia	639	Moldavia	144
12.	Uzbekistan	423	Azerbaydzhan	628	Ukraine	143
13.	Byelorussia	418	Turkemnia	836	Kirghizia	141
14.	Kirghizia	411	Uzbekistan	567	Turkmenia	138
15.	Tadzhikistan	345	Tadzhikistan	509	Kazakhstan	137

Source: From *Narodnoe khozyaistvo SSSR v. 1959 g.* (Moscow: Statistika, 1958); H. -J. Wagener, *Wirtschaftswachstum in unterentwickelten Gebieten. Ansätze zu einer Regional-analyse der Sowjetunion* (Berlin [West]: Duncker & Humblot, 1972), p. 89. *Narodnoe khozyaistvo SSSR v 1978 g.* (Moscow: Statistika, 1978), p. 386.

The more recent growth figures show that Byelorussia, Lithuania, and Armenia are still holding the lead, but in absolute figures, some of the poorest Soviet Union republics, such as the Kirghiz and Tadzhik Republics, have moved up to the top group. It must be kept in mind, though, that experience has shown that poorer regions typically present higher growth rates. Consequently, although the poor regions are catching up, these growth rates do not indicate any leveling-out of the increasing differences between north and south. (See Table 29.)

The tables show that in socialist states, too, there is a tendency to favor the regions that are already more prosperous. Whereas the top riders of 1958 were able to double their per capita national incomes over a ten-year period, those ranking bottom in the statistics only obtained growth rates of half to a third. However, as is the case in many developing countries, the underdeveloped regions were handicapped in their economic growth by an over-rapid increase in population. Even a system that incorporates comprehensive planning for all production and reproduction conditions is unable to bring this particular variable under control swiftly, since it is deeply rooted in the national and religious *byt* of the peoples of the southeast. Nevertheless, the Soviet Union's redistribution policy at regional level can, on the whole, be rated positively. Regional income differences in the Soviet Union have more-or-less come into line with those in Italy. A good number of indicators prove that, even in absolute figures, the Soviet developing regions are now comparable to east European and southeast European countries, while in the 1920s and 1930s they were still at the level of many Asian countries.[258]

Development differences in Yugoslavia, for example, were hardly any less pronounced right through to the 1960s, despite the versatile

Table 29

Growth rate of national income in the Union republics

(in percentages compared to 1960 and 1970)

	1960	1965	1970	1970	1975	1978
Soviet Union	100	137	199	100	132	153
RSFSR	100	135	198	100	133	154
Ukrainian SSR	100	140	195	100	125	143
Byelorussian SSR	100	141	218	100	149	176
Uzbek SSR	100	145	202	100	139	163
Kazakh SSR	100	131	214	100	122	137
Georgian SSR	100	137	197	100	133	160
Azerbaydzhan SSR	100	125	166	100	139	173
Lithuanian SSR	100	152	238	100	131	145
Moldavian SSR	100	162	223	100	127	144
Latvian SSR	100	141	204	100	133	146
Kirghiz SSR	100	150	218	100	126	141
Tadzhik SSR	100	156	214	100	133	148
Armenian SSR	100	148	234	100	146	178
Turkmen SSR	100	131	173	100	131	138
Estonian SSR	100	143	205	100	131	147

Source: *Narodnoe khozyaistvo SSSR v 1972 g* (Moscow: Statistika, 1973), p. 532; ibid. 1979, p. 386.

Table 30

Per capita income and indices of industrial growth in the Yugoslav republics
(in percentages; 1955 = 100)

	1947	1964	1965	1970	1972
Yugoslavia	100.0	100.0	309	416	498
Bosnia-Herzegovina	79.7	66.2	315	371	442
Croatia	108.0	118.0	283	391	448
Macedonia	68.2	69.3	415	798	909
Montenegro	71.2	63.5	715	910	980
Slovenia	162.5	191.4	251	356	424
Serbia	96.6	94.1	372	494	605

Source: K. Meneghello-Dincic, *Les expériences yougoslaves d'industrialisation et de planification* (Paris: Cuyas, 1971), p. 168; P. Jambrek, *Development and Social Change in Yugoslavia* (Lexington, Mass.: Lexington Books, 1975), p. 262.

development policy also adopted in that country. The relative gap between rich and poor regions in Yugoslavia tended to widen instead, although the absolute growth figures were similar to those of the less developed republics of the Soviet Union. (See Table 30.)

Growth of per capita income is, however, only one development indicator for comparing regional differences, and it is by no means always the best one. Regional development policy in socialist countries must also be measured by its achievements in location policy, its development of industrial complexes, and its ability to prevent developing areas from simply becoming raw-material-supplying appendices to the main areas. The Soviet Union has undeniably recorded great achievements in this domain since its extensive industrial evacuation during the Second World War.[259] If we also take social development indicators and distribution indicators into account, then the Soviet developing areas come off far better than do neighboring regions in capitalist bordering states such as Persia and Turkey.[260]

Those who criticize this type of totting-up of the successes of Soviet developing areas with those of bordering states put forward two main arguments in support of their cautionary reservations. Firstly, they say that the Soviet Union as a whole is more developed than the bordering states, and, secondly, they point out that without the different—capitalist—nature of investment efforts by the neigh-

boring states, it would have been impossible to draw foreign investment into these regions (such as eastern Turkey).[261] In fact, both
arguments come out rather more in favor of the Soviet model, because
otherwise it would also be necessary to explain why the Soviet Union
as a whole is so much better developed than Turkey. In addition, the
advantages of autonomous and autochthonous development (see
Chapter 4, Section 5) would need to be set against the drawbacks
that Turkey, too, has encountered in maintaining independence in its
development, due mainly to foreign aid.

Problems similar to those in the Soviet Union arose in the
People's Republic of China, where the 1956 wage reform was aimed
at reducing regional wage differentials through a policy of redistribution. Bonuses were even paid for developing areas such as Tibet,
Sinkiang, and the Tsaidam Basin in Tsinghai in order to attract
Han-Chinese. For the rest, the country was divided into 11 wage
regions, the highest of which was about 30% above the lowest—
a difference that more or less corresponded to the difference in the
cost of living. In doing this, China was not afraid to attack the
established rights of the developed regions or to implement down-
ward wage adjustments in certain areas.[262] In fact, however, in 1964
there were still some wage differentials that were much greater than
provided for under the wage regions scheme.[263]

Development problems not only occur in the states with large
surface areas (Soviet Union and China) and in the medium-sized
states located on the periphery of Europe (Yugoslavia), but even
small and relatively well-developed states such as Czechoslovakia
have their "mezzogiorno" as well. The high level of productive
resources has meant that development achievements are, by comparison, at their most impressive here. After 1948 Slovakia received
an above-proportionate amount of investment for its population
figure and produced about 80% of the figure that the Czechs contributed to the national income, whereas in 1948 it had only produced
61.2%. Hence, incomes likewise became aligned in the different parts
of the country.[264] Yet, despite the approximation of regional
incomes, differences still persist in the level of modernization.
Traditional behavior patterns are more deeply rooted in Slovakia
than in the other parts of Czechoslovakia. Between 1955 and 1964,
more than half the private houses built were built in Slovakia, even
though income levels were slightly lower there. This shows that home
ownership—as in capitalist countries—is not necessarily a sign of
higher income. On the contrary, it tends rather more to be a status
symbol among lower and less-urbanized income groups.

Approximation of incomes in the different occupational sectors

It was not only the glaring differences in employment between the countryside and the town, but also the income disparities within industrial sectors, that constituted a problem for socialist redistribution policy. In the Soviet Union there are very considerable pay differences, considering that the word-paid sector's wages amount to just over half of the best-paid sector's wages. This pay difference has hardly changed since 1940 (see Table 31).

Most socialist countries follow the Soviet hierarchy of wages: Construction and transport are leading, and science is, in most countries, the third-highest wages group. Only in Poland and Rumania does it rank second before the transportation sector (see Table 31). According to socialist values it is a humiliating fact that the bottom rank in most socialist countries is held by housing services, services for the population, public health, and social welfare. The Soviet Union shows best that the hierarchy of payments has changed since the time of Stalin. If we compare the Soviet figures for 1940, 1960, and 1979, it can be demonstrated that state administration and art have gone down the wage scale, while construction workers and transportation have gone up. In the Soviet Union navigation has remained unchanged at the top of the ranks.

Apart from a few exceptions, such as science and banking, this income scale does not differ much from the income hierarchy in capitalist countries, although the gap was smaller at times than in capitalist economies, provided we ignore income in agriculture, which was greater than in capitalist countries, and if we do not compare the Stalin period, where the income differences in Social Russia were much greater than in capitalist Britain.[265] The disparities are not the same in all socialist systems.

The income gap between a manager and a charwoman varies up to a ratio of 1:6. It must be borne in mind, however, that the standard wages on which these ECE figures are based do not reflect actual incomes, because ever since the bonus system has become more widespread (Table 19), bonuses are often proportionately greater in the higher income brackets than in the lower ones.[266]

For certain countries even greater income gaps were calculated in the 1950s by not restricting the comparison simply to positions in enterprises within one sector. In Czechoslovakia in 1957 the income gap was reported to range from 100 crowns (lowest pension) to 9,000 crowns (editor-in-chief of the Party newspaper *Rudé právo*), that is, a ratio of 1 : 90.[267] This comparison is not quite fair, however,

Table 31 Monthly earnings per sector
(in units of national currency)

Country	Year	Industry	Construction	Agriculture	Transport	Commerce, services	Housing and municipal workers	Science	Education, culture, arts	Public health & social welfare
Bulgaria	1960	80.1	96.2	74.4	89.5	66.8	65.4	72.8	70.3	68.5
	1979	172	190	157	188	147	149	175	148	140
Czechoslovakia	1960	1,442	1,521	1,113	1,457	1,128	960	1,545	1,293	1,183
	1979	2,653	2,875	2,488	3,026	2,204	1,921	2,917	2,917	2,398
Cuba	1970	123	141	108	150	108	n.d.	n.d.	116	118
	1979	151	153	125	179	128	133	171	140	1,141
Hungary	1960	1,604	1,652	1,416	1,482	1,401	n.d.	n.d.	n.d.	n.d.
	1979	3,639	4,025	3,586	3,939	3,237	3,324	3,588	3,655	3,478
Poland	1960	1,708	1,831	1,267	1,533	1,329	1,473	1,846	1,387	1,239
	1979	5,393	5,678	5,290	5,481	4,148	4,867	5,649	4,418	4,234
Rumania	1960	887	877	731	939	724	n.d.	n.d.	n.d.	n.d.
	1979	2,118	2,346	2,060	2,177	1,835	1,844	2,316	2,084	1,958
Soviet Union	1940	32.4	31.2	20.7	34.2	25.0	26.1	47.1	32.3	25.5
	1960	91.6	93.0	55.2	87.0	58.9	57.7	110.7	69.6	58.9
	1979	180.4	196.6	146.0	192.8	128.8	126.7	173	129.6	119.1

Source: *Statisticheskii ezhegodnik stran-chlenov SEV 1980* (Moscow: Statistika, 1980), pp. 415ff.; *SSSR v tsifrakh* (Moscow: Statistika, 1980), pp. 172f.

because the number of very high incomes is lower in socialist countries, where there is no unearned income, than in capialist ones, and
also because it is easy to forget that the differentials would turn out
to be even greater than 1 : 90 in capitalist countries.

China's wage policy also aimed at a systematic leveling-out of
the differentials between sectors. Yet with the introduction of eight
wage brackets in the 1956 wage reform, allowance was made for
certain differences to persist. As the minimum wage of 28 yuan
was fixed at a very low level, de facto wages varied from 123 to
394% above this level, depending on the particular wage bracket in
question.[268] The highest average wages were to be found in mining
(80 yuan) and the lowest in the textile industry (55 yuan). The
difference between unskilled workers (36 yuan) and skilled workers
(120 yuan) was not noticeably smaller than for other socialist
systems. It is estimated that the average industrial wage for a 48-hour
working week was about 55 to 65 yuan. In Cuba, too, there were
differences between the various sectors, albeit smaller than those of
the capitalist Latin American countries; certain branches, such as
oil processing, were, however, highly privileged.[269]

Even in countries with strong egalitarian tendencies, such as
North Korea, there were differences of 1 : 7 among cadres pursuing
the same activity, such as in the party hierarchy.[270] These differences
are often explained by the argument that there is a shortage of reliable
cadres. This explanation may be acceptable for some systems, but for
North Korea, in particular, it is certainly far from convincing: this
is the country with the highest percentage of party membership
among its working population, and hence the argument of a shortage
would not seem to hold ground here (see Chapter 12, Section 1).

Status and occupational prestige

Certain factors would seem to indicate that socialist systems,
too, still have a multidimensional social stratification pattern in
which control over the means of production and the possession of
power and learning are turned into gratifications, although not to
the same extent as the trends that ownership of the means of production is developing in capitalist systems. Furthermore, opinion polls
show that occupational prestige by no means correlates solely with
the income that a job offers; prestige hierarchy to a certain extent
reveals very traditional appraisal patterns (see Table 32). The two
polls are obviously hardly comparable on a number of points. The

Table 32

Occupational prestige in Czechoslovakia and the Soviet Union

Czechoslovakia	*Soviet Union*	*Soviet Union (1973, young specialists)*
1. minister	physicist	physician
2. manager of an industrial enterprise	radio engineer	scholar
3. medical specialist	medical scientist	creative intelligentsia
4. university professor	geological engineer	lawyer
5. chairman of a regional council	mathematician	engineer
6. scientist	chemist	mathematician
7. head of a major department in an enterprise	radio technician	economist
8. writer	pilot	teacher
9. technical supervisor	chemical engineer	agronomist
10. district attorney	biologist	mechanic
11. agronomist	doctor	driver
12. actor	persons working in the fields of art and culture	construction worker

Sources: P. Machonin et al., *Ceskoslovenska spolecnost. Sociologicka analyza socialni stratificace* (Bratislava: Epocha, 1969), p. 386; G. V. Osipov & J. Szczepanski (eds.), *Sotsial'nye problemy truda i proizvodstva* (Moscow: Mysl', 1969), pp. 168ff.; M. Kh. Titma, *Vybor professii kak sotsial'naya problema* (Moscow: Mysl', 1975), p. 144.

Soviet questionnaire was much more unpolitical in its makeup. Political and administrative functions were left out of the catalog of occupations, and, in addition, there was greater differentiation in the list of occupations. This revealed interesting prestige ratings: it is not straightforward medical doctors who enjoy high esteem—the average practitioner in the public health service is not listed in the top group—but rather the doctors who are engaged in scientific work. The Soviet publication lists growth perspectives, income, and opportunities for creativity as the determining factors in the prestige hierarchy. In the Czechoslovakian survey, public opinion seemed to attribute greater importance to the income factor in job ratings, although the nature of the work, social usefulness, and qualifications also played a role. Mere exercise of power, on the other hand, does not translate into equivalent prestige. Party functionaries only rank nineteenth. The surveys have shown that social security is regarded as an important value, and the more the security of elite positions has been threatened through socialist recruitment mechanisms with criticism and self-criticism, rotation, and purges, the less attractive these posts have become in the eyes of the average citizen in socialist countries.

Such findings need not, however—as is the case with comparable Soviet investigations—lead one to the conclusion that there is an invariable prestige hierarchy of occupations in all industrial societies. Striking facts to note here, however, are firstly the persistent trends and secondly the shifts in prestige rating of occupations involving growing technological progress. These trends are still in evidence in the Soviet Union after more than half a century of revolutionary polytechnical education, and they show that equalization policy in socialist states still comes up against strong traditional elements left over in the minds of the population. Nowadays it is even admitted to some extent that new contradictions are arising between the social demand for certain jobs and the prestige that they hold:

> Young people do not generally wish to become laborers or kolkhoz peasants; the prestige of the industrial laborer and the agricultural worker is, to be quite frank, not very high. According to a Novosibirsk sociologist's calculation, a mass worker's job like latheman ranks 39th on the list of occupations that people want to take up, weaver and spinner come 40th, tractor and combine driver 51st and salesclerk 70th, with the first five positions being held by physicists, pilots, radio technicians, mathematicians and geological engineers.[271]

Constant glorification of the laborer and tractor driver in Soviet literature seems only to have had a limited effect on young people.

These embarrassing discrepancies in occupational prestige are put down to specific trends in the atomic and cybernetic age, and Soviet literature is becoming increasingly sceptical about all forms of division of labor, as based on the five disparaties described above, eventually disappearing in communism. It is held that the first three disparities will disappear, and the last two—that is, territorial and occupational division of labor—will remain.[272]

3. Instruments of indirect redistribution policy

Alongside wage policy and the fight against disparity between various groups and social strata, socialist countries have employed four main instruments to promote redistribution policy indirectly:

1. price policy;
2. taxation policy;
3. social policy;
4. education policy.

Price policy

Our analysis of wage policy has already shown that it was the socialist transitional societies with the lowest level of productive resources and the smallest amount to redistribute that were, in the main, the countries that attempted to implement their redistribution policy through price freezing rather than through wage increases.

1. Controversy in Marxist price theory

A major part of the controversy surrounding economic theory in socialist systems has focused on the question of price fixing. Mises, Hayek, and others felt it was impossible for socialist planning authorities to achieve a rational pricing system.[273] One of the arguments put forward here was that the planning authorities were not in a position to work through the hundreds of thousands of equations required for rational price formation. Socialist economists such as

Oscar Lange have pointed out that Hayek himself, as a consumer, did a few hundred equations every day, even if only buying a newspaper or ordering a midday meal.[274] Nowadays it would be more logical to argue that, in this age of the computer, working out hundreds of thousands of equations no longer appears to be as insurmountable a barrier to rational pricing as had been the case before the Second World War, when the controversy was largely "system-ontological" and lacked the benefit of empirical experience as to the functioning of a socialist economy.

Nevertheless, even Marxist economists feel to some extent that a complex production network the size of that in the Soviet Union would not be able to solve the calculation problem, even using data-processing equipment—after narrowing the computer gap—in view of the current level of productive resources. It has been calculated that the Soviet Union would currently need one million computers with a capacity of 30,000 operations per second to work out a model that covered all the data.[275]

Lange's strongest argument at the time was that it was by no means necessary to work out all these calculations: he was thinking in terms of price fixing based on a system of trial-and-error and not implemented arbitrarily by the authorities without the opportunity for ex-post correction. Prices were to have parametric functions.

Free consumer choice and free choice of career were assumed in this model. Market socialism concepts have some of their origins here. Lange did not, however, go as far as Yugoslavia has gone today. In Yugoslavia, prices on the market are fixed in the main by socialist firms, and the market price mechanism is only curbed by factors restraining competition, such as the trend toward concentration and a wide range of individual state price control measures. This was the concept advocated by Dickinson during the former plan-versus-market debate.[276] The greater the emphasis placed on the redistributive nature of price policy in socialist transitional societies, the more Marxist economists in the West, such as Dobb and Sweezy, maintained that central price formation was a vital instrument of central planning.

In socialist systems prices are intended to be "values" expressed in terms of money. This value covers past work in the form of materials and equipment, current work, for which the worker receives the equivalent in the form of wages, and surplus product for which the worker receives nothing in return. The Communist party program stipulates that prices must increasingly reflect the socially necessary labor expenditure. This does not, however, mean that prices are determined on the basis of social labor expenditure alone; they also have to fulfill specific functions laid down in the plan, serve to stimulate the economy, and must not hamper state redistribution policy.

Prices are increasingly coming to reflect relative shortages—this was the case put forward in the early 1960s by the mathematically orientated school of Soviet economists around Nemchinov, Kantorovich, and Novozhilov against the dogmatists.[277] Considerations of this nature still come up against strong scruples on the part of dogmatists, but in general the time is past when the prevailing theory in the Soviet Union was that any price and value calculations at all were superfluous and that economic decisions should be taken without going the roundabout way of economic laws and mathematical calculations. Even Strumilin, a leading figure in Soviet economics, who in 1934 held that the sole law of the economy was "the will to storm on towards communism,"[278] went on to change his views. The radical attitudes adopted during the first plan period are nowadays not infrequently criticized as "Maoist voluntarism" in the Soviet literature.

As the differences in the way economic theory approached price problems in socialist countries became more pronounced, the functions that this price policy had to fulfill became more and more contradictory, and it was increasingly impossible to employ prices exclusively to serve redistribution policy. Three main problems arose:

1. Prices were *overloaded with various functions* that were not always compatible.[279]

2. Even in socialist planned economies, *uniform* price formation could *not always be achieved* on account of the splintering of administrative units and economic competences. The various forms of ownership that live on under socialism also lead to certain contradictions. Prices in the private and cooperative sector play a different role from prices in the state sector. Prices did not just have a function in exchanges between the different sectors—they even appeared on the "plan fulfillment market" within the purely state sector. Even Preobrazhenskii described trends within the Soviet economy toward increasing circulation costs and hence increasing prices:

> Just as the Epicurean Gods made their home in the pores of the universe, so during the initial development of a state trust on the free market, private middlemen attempted to establish themselves not only in private trade channels but also in the nooks and crannies that separated state enterprises from other enterprises and there they cashed in on "circulation costs."[280]

Socialist systems frequently had a two-tier price structure, with one price for the state sector and state-controlled trading and another for what remained of the private economy. China still had three different price levels even after the Great Leap Forward: centrally fixed prices, prices set by political and economic entities, and free prices.[281] The policy of freezing prices in a bid to combat inflationary trends in the bourgeois economies inherited by socialist leadership did, admittedly, have redistributive effects, but this could not— such as in Cuba—lead to a correctly proportioned pricing system.[282] In most cases it was only possible to align a limited number of prices, such as rents, basic foodstuffs, and so forth. At times, though, these price alignments invited abuse, such as when bread prices were kept so low that bread became cheaper than pigswill, or when Castro admitted in 1973 that due to "revolutionary inexperience" an error had been committed in pitching electricity prices at too low a level. This had been done in a bid to portray the new regime in a favorable light, compared with the price policy of the former "Electric Company," which had held a dominant market position, and the state would now have to think in terms of price correction. Deficit prices in the consumption sphere, used by many a revolutionary system for legitimation purposes in the initial stages, are now openly discussed as being intolerable in a large number of socialist countries.[283] Disproportion of this nature in the price system arose when price fixing not only disregarded relative shortages but also the manufacturing costs of products. In the accumulation phase, socialist economies tended as a rule to pitch prices for capital goods too low and prices for consumer goods too high. Only with the coming of price reforms in the 1960s did price formation start to give consideration not only to average costs in the sector—plus a profit margin, generally labeled the "profitability rate"—but also to prices in the other socialist countries and on the world market. This applied least of all in the Soviet Union and was used most extensively in Yugoslavia. In Bulgaria, and for a time in Czechoslovakia, Hungary, and the German Democratic Republic, export enterprises were allowed to keep a certain amount of foreign currency for imports. Detailed export and import controls were phased out most extensively in Czechoslovakia—during the Dubček era—and in Hungary,[284] such that consideration of foreign price levels had the greatest impact here. However, only in Yugoslavia has the world market price become the decisive factor in price formation.

With two theoretical ways open for maintaining development of a flexible price policy—frequent price changes calculated on a central basis or self-regulation through the market—most eastern European systems allowed a mixture of both options, the various effects of which cannot yet be fully measured. In the market socialist systems, which mainly opted for the first course of action, the chief regulating mechanisms have become monetary and financial policy, as in capitalist systems. With a mixed system, however, it will still be possible for individual branches of the economy and individual enterprises to work at a loss in the future, this being based on national economic calculations, although it is sometimes maintained in the Soviet Union that the wholesale price reform of 1967 duly eliminated all branches operating at a loss, according to plan. Soviet data do show that the percentage of enterprises operating at a loss went down. The differences in profit rates between economic sectors were reduced, but not completely eliminated, especially in the coal industry, as optimistic interpretations in the mid 1970s concluded (see Table 33).

Table 33

Profitability as percentage of basic and working capital in Soviet industry

Category	1965	1970	1978
all industry	13.0	21.5	13.5
of which:			
electricity	4.6	10.9	6.4
oil extraction	5.7	27.8	11.9
coal mining	−17.0	7.3	− 3.2
ferrous			
metallurgy	8.6	17.2	10.7
chemical	16.4	20.2	18.4
machinery and			
metalworking	16.7	22.8	15.2
building			
materials	5.4	12.2	6.4
light industry	29.9	42.5	25.3
of which			
textile	23.4	28.4	17.5
food industry	24.4	27.4	20.7

Source: *Narodnoe khozyaistvo v. 1978 g.* (Moscow: Statistika, 1979), p. 518.

Profitability patterns since 1967 were, however, fairly stable. The coal industry is still at the bottom; light industry shows high figures, probably due to undercapitalization.[285]

3.   In conjunction with the shortage of goods, which came about in nearly all socialist transitional societies once the heat of the revolution had abated, price policy became a form of *compulsory saving*, provided that the potential inflationary pressure brought about by a commodity shortage could be kept under control. This did, however, go against efforts to promote redistribution, particularly in countries such as China and Cuba, which did not regard planned consumer asceticism, dictated from above, as a prerequisite for successful socialist accumulation.

The most pronounced redistributive effects were achieved through two measures during the transitional phase:

1.   redistribution in the form of compulsory deliveries;
2.   a price freeze policy.

2.   Compulsory deliveries and price policy

The redistributive power of price policy was used most extensively in revolutionary "war economies," particularly in cases where distribution involved a high percentage of remuneration in kind. In the Soviet Union, the percentage of payment in kind is said to have totaled 64% in 1919 and up to 84% in 1920.[286] Rations were distributed to the workers in the revolutionary centers, in some cases free of charge. Compulsory deliveries had the same effect as taxation in kind since the prices paid by the state were lower than those that enterprises could obtain for their surplus products from the state or on the private markets that remained.

In countries where socialist forces were not yet powerful enough to pass a state decree introducing compulsory delivery quotas, as was the case in Chile between 1970 and 1973, the two-tier state pricing policy system also provided a means of redistribution. This involved distribution of scarce foodstuffs via enterprises at very low prices or even free of charge—in particular before the March 1973 elections. In addition, the state tolerated the "black market," to a far greater extent than states that had gone over to socialism earlier on. The black market developed into an ex-post regulator of the price system, alongside the state-controlled allocations in kind, on the one hand, and the quota system operated through the retail trade, on the other.

Had the Chilean system persevered in this way, the socialist leaders would quite feasibly have been able to increase the satisfaction of the working classes who were upholding the system, despite gigantic price increases, and would have been able to cut the ground from beneath the middle classes and to force them either to emigrate or to accept proletarization and participation in the state-controlled distribution scheme. In revolutionary periods, the two-tier price system was employed for purposes of provisioning those backing the system —workers, intelligentsia, cadres—and for rewarding loyalty to the new regime. The price system also had a further function connected with the "class struggle," namely in the struggle against forces opposed to the regime, who were seeking to undermine state distribution policy through the black market. Price policy was thereby implemented in the struggle against excessively high prices on the black market. In 1948, Czechoslovakia permitted an official "free market," organized in parallel to the ration market, which meant that in some instances prices came into line with those on the black market.[287] At the same time this policy had the advantage of enabling the state to win control over the anomic economic processes. The state-run commission shops still provide a similar safety valve to check the black market today.

3. Price freeze policy and price reforms

Price reductions as an instrument of redistribution policy enjoy high regard in economic theory.[288] In theoretical terms, at least, it is still fascinating to think of continuous price reductions bringing about the demise of the commodity economy and gradually undermining the regulatory function of money, which is nowadays defined as having a "passive" role. Socialist states have employed a selective price-reduction policy for limited periods during the transformation period to serve three ends:

1. Price reductions enabled them to *exert pressure* on the remaining private markets in the economy (such as on the Soviet kolkhoz markets and on private retail trade in the People's Democracies) and encourage them to join in with the cooperative movement.
2. Price reductions contributed toward *redistribution* in the distribution sphere. The People's Democracies in particular experimented with this type of policy.

3. In times of *commodity shortages*, price reduction made it possible to *combat* speculation about rising prices and thereby *combat* the hoarding of wares,[289] where this was felt preferable to the alternative and more repressive administrative approach of direct controls on the cellars and warehouses of shops and small-scale producers.

Although price reductions did indeed stimulate the circulation of manufactured goods, they did not stimulate increased production of new goods. Over the long term, the price freeze policy and price reductions had a further drawback, in that concealed price increases (prices on the free kolkhoz markets were an indicator here) were not immediately apparent. In the Soviet Union, prices on the kolkhoz markets pointed to a concealed inflationary trend for a long time. In the 1950s and 1960s these prices were some 150 to 175% above state retail prices.[290] Hence the planners had a completely ambiguous attitude toward what remained of the free market. In ideological terms the free markets remained a nuisance since they defied ex-ante planning, yet, on the other hand, their function as a safety valve and as an indicator for concealed price movements and consumer desires was duly acknowledged.[291]

Despite these drawbacks encountered with price freeze policies, they nonetheless had marked legitimating effects in psychological terms—particularly in countries that had experienced serious inflation in their former bourgeois economies. However, as things developed further, the consensus of opinion between planners and consumers in matters of price freezing began to wane, with consumers seeing their preferences receiving ever-diminishing consideration in the administrative price system and manufacturers complaining of contradictions in the changing cost structure. One of the advantages of stable prices, namely that of making for easier planning of production processes, threatened to become a drawback—that of inflexible production. For this reason most socialist states permitted an increasingly flexible price policy and in some cases just laid down guide prices, setting fixed prices for a number of commodities. The Hungarian price reform of 1968 and the Czechoslovakian reform in January 1967 probably progressed furthest in this direction, the Czechoslovakian reform going hand-in-hand with extensive redistribution of national income from central funds to enterprise funds. The purpose of this price reform was inter alia to harmonize the tax system, reduce subsidies, and eliminate centrally fixed prices, moving instead to controlled prices, which had to be maintained within certain limits specified by the state. This was intended to give flexibility without the risk of inflation. Only the first objective was fully achieved during the experiment carried out in the Dubček era, while the reform was not able to make its mark on the remaining targets due to the premature and violent ending of the experiment.[292] Only through comprehensive reform of the whole economic system, as implemented in Czechoslovakia, did it prove possible to coordinate sufficiently the various measures.[293]

In a partial reform, which was carried out by the way of experiment in two Soviet enterprises in 1964 (Bol'shevichka in Moscow and Maya in Gorky), profit was taken as the chief indicator for determining the enterprise's success and for calculating the managers' remuneration. In addition, manufacturers and buyers were allowed to conclude direct contracts, so as to provide a basis for planning purposes. Prices and decisions relating to capital investment were, however, still subject to central control. It was not until 1968 that a larger number of enterprises were switched to this new system. A temporary experiment that allowed the two enterprises to fix their own selling prices was broken off,[294] and the idea that price fixing should be left to company management continually came up against sharp ideological criticism.

Reform economists such as E. G. Liberman today regard the extension of direct contractual relationships between suppliers and orderers as an important step toward improving the planning process and eliminating corruption, such as the "grey" dealings between state enterprises.[295]

Although the reforms were, on the whole, regarded as a success, further dysfunctions stemmed from price policy. Since profit orientation meant that managers had little interest in innovation, state price policy had to take on an additional function in the system so as to improve profit prospects on improved goods by means of price supplements. Consumers, however, to a certain extent undermined these measures by preferring to continue buying the old, cheaper products.

In the ideological debate the task of a centralized price policy is frequently regarded as already being a decisive step away from the aims of socialist policy. However, no country—not even China—has been able to escape the trend of necessary price increases. Between 1951 and 1963, the state introduced price increases that were mainly in the form of raised purchase prices (agricultural produce up by 57.4%).[296] On the whole, however, this development was kept under greater control in China. Combating inflation was high on the list of priorities following experiences with the Kuomintang regime, even at the price of temporary, de-facto rationing for key consumer goods.

One advantage of most socialist systems is that they do not need to speculate on the redistributive effects of inflation,[297] since more direct methods of redistribution can be employed. Insofar as a certain inflationary pressure was in evidence in individual socialist systems in the 1960s, this strengthened the groups with the greatest bargaining power—as in capitalist systems—and in a number of countries this was the peasantry.[298] It would, however, be wrong to say that indirect redistribution via inflationary trends became more important for these countries than was the political target of direct redistribution through concerted wage and price policy.

The most serious contradiction within price policy since the economic reforms is the danger of *monopoly positions being abused* with decentralized price formation. This danger is greatest in small countries, where whole branches of the economy are organized along the lines of a state trust, as for example in Hungary.[299] In the German Democratic Republic, too, increasing complaints were voiced at unplanned and unjustified price increases, of which there are said to have been more than 200 in 1970. In many cases cheaper products are no longer supplied, with the more expensive ones being brought onto the market in a bid to increase profits and hence bonus prospects.[300]

One way out of the dilemma for the planners was to prevent unwarranted price increases by having manufacturers and buyers hold each other's profit interests in check through a contractual relationship.[301] It emerged in practice, however, that the producer monopolist generally had greater pull over the buyers and could more readily assert his profit interests. The high degree of monopolization that exists in a number of eastern European economies thus constitutes a tremendous barrier to the development of a market socialist system today—where such is being striven after at all. This is, however, denied on all sides at the present time. Under the current circumstances even Western economists have raised the question as to whether creation of "half a market" could not perhaps entail worse consequences for consumers than having no market at all.[302] If redistribution is to be given due measure in future policy, then it must be said that maintenance of the flexible central price-formation system, with its rapid correction mechanism, is currently preferable to the development of a full market socialist system.

Taxation policy

The socialist states that have come into being to date have, for the most part, developed with a relatively low level of productive resources. The lower the development level of a country, the greater the disparities in the distribution of wealth and income tend to be, and the more there is to be said for using tax policy as an instrument of redistribution.[303]

Tax policy was likewise used for purposes of redistribution during the transformation phase, primarily to bring private owners of the means of production to agree to the formation of mixed state/private enterprises or to join cooperatives (see Chapter 1). In 1925, the Soviet Union introduced a "Kulak tax," and the tax rates for private entrepreneurs went up as high as 81%. Alongside the raising of direct levies from enterprises, tax still maintained a further function that had not actually been provided for in Marxist ideology. In September 1930, trade and consumption taxes were amalgamated into a single-phase turnover tax. Contrary to the case in capitalist systems, prices are not fixed by allowing for the turnover tax component in the price; instead, the amount of tax is determined by prices that have been fixed beforehand. A number of consumer goods, such as foodstuffs sold on kolkhoz markets, are not subject to turnover tax. The state obtains its percentage of the surplus product via income tax.[304]

In socialist tax theory, turnover tax—such as levies on state firms—does not constitute a tax as such but simply a "transfer of that part of the surplus product that society has produced." A number of socialist economists do, however, concede that part of this does represent a kind of indirect taxation.[305] Given the income gap referred to above, this indirect taxation constitutes a relatively heavy burden for the underprivileged income classes in socialist systems. This tax is hidden from the consumer's sight, and in 1955 it still accounted for 40 to 50% of the final price. It is therefore mere propaganda if Soviet scholars sometimes claim that taxes are much higher in the West, ignoring turnover tax, while treating all Western indirect taxes as a "burden on the working classes."[306] (See Table 34.) Socialist states find themselves with two conflicting aims here: on the one hand they want to reduce indirect taxation to promote fair distribution, yet on the other hand this type of taxation is easy to levy and helps to cut down the administrative costs involved in state tax collection. In addition, the flexibility of this instrument

Table 34

State budget revenue
(in percentages)

Country	Year	Turnover taxes	Payments of profits	Personal taxes
Bulgaria	1975	72.9		27.1
Czechoslovakia	1977	82.5		12.4
GDR	1975			4.6
Hungary	1976	78.7		5.3
Poland	1977	35.4	12.8	1.0
Rumania	1977	11.5	22.2	9.7
Soviet Union	1976	30.4	30.4	8.4
Yugoslavia	1975	22.3	9.5	1.5

Source: Statistical surveys. In: *Yearbook of East European Economics,* Vol. 8 (Munich: Olzog, 1979), p. 458ff.

—as compared with income tax—is rated highly for other control functions as well. While tax systems in capitalist countries are generally complex and cumbersome as a result of the repeated introduction of new differentials, socialist countries have developed much greater potential transparency of their tax systems. It is only the secretive attitude of the state that has prevented this from achieving its full legitimating effect. The distributive aspect has, however, come more into the forefront over the past few years.

The tendency in socialist systems is toward allowing consumption taxes to become less significant. In the Soviet Union in the 1930s and in a number of people's democracies in the 1950s these taxes accounted for more than 60% of state revenue. The structure of socialist state revenue has undergone a marked change, as can be illustrated taking the example of the Soviet Union, as shown in Table 35.

Revenue from the surplus product of enterprises constitutes the most important revenue source. Turnover tax is beginning to show a declining trend, although this has for a long time been the most important component of the Soviet tax system in terms of both fiscal and economic policy. State bonds are also losing significance. A number of transitional societies, such as Cuba, did not employ this type of virtual compulsory loan. A short-lived experiment with a public loan of 4% to contribute toward industrialization was terminated with the 1962 tax reform.[307]

Raising of revenue through taxation of the population is on the decrease in all socialist states. This type of taxation has, it is true, increased slightly in percentage terms in the Soviet Union, but this is not due to tax increases but rather to the growth in nominal income. The Cuban budget also illustrates this trend: in 1961, revenue through taxation of the population still made up some 61.6% of the total, whereas by 1963 this had fallen to a mere 18.7%.

In China graduated tax was superseded in 1958 by a system of taxation for the collective units.[308] No precise figures are available for state revenue in China over recent years; during the period between 1955 and 1958, at a time when the economy was being consolidated before the Great Leap Forward, the breakdown of state revenue according to source was as shown in Table 36. The People's Republic of China also preferred to take short measure in equality rather than disturb the efficiency and straightforwardness of the tax system. This was, admittedly, at the price of consumers still having to contribute more than one third of state revenue in one form or another today, as in the Soviet Union; there is, however, one difference between them: with the very slight wage disparity that exists in China, indirect taxes on consumption are not as unjust

Table 35

Structure of USSR state budget revenue (1940-1978)

(in percentages)

Source of revenue	1940	1960	1970	1978
turnover tax	58.7	40.7	31.5	31.6
levies on enterprise profit	12.1	24.2	34.6	29.6
income tax from cooperatives, kolkhozy and enterprises belonging to collective organizations	1.8	2.4	0.8	0.6
state bonds	5.1	0.1	0.3	0.2
individual taxation of population	5.2	7.3	8.1	8.3
state social security	4.8	4.9	5.3	4.9

Source: *Narodnoe khozyaistvo SSSR v 1978* (Moscow: Statistika, 1979), p. 534.

Table 36

Sources of revenue for the Chinese state budget

(in percentages)

Source	Percentage of budget	
Income from		
state enterprises	47	
State debentures	3	
Foreign loans	1.4	
Taxes	47	
comprising		
turnover tax		36
customs levies		2
income tax		9

Source: G. N. Ecklund, *Financing the Chinese Government Budget* (Edinburgh U.P., p. 115.

as they are in the Soviet Union or in those people's democracies where wage disparity is more pronounced.

Income tax policy in socialist countries has changed with the growing level of productive resources. Only at the start of the redistribution period was high direct taxation used as an instrument, as in Cuba in 1962 with the "Nueva ley fiscal." Even then, however, socialist states did not raise the maximum rate of tax significantly above the level introduced in capitalist countries with highly developed welfare systems. In Cuba the maximum rate was 70%. As other means of redistribution became more effective in socialist systems, the authorities became increasingly reluctant to use taxation policy as an instrument of redistribution.

Party leaders subsequently went on to proclaim that personal taxation was soon to be abolished. Albania was, however, the only Eastern European state to carry this through, abolishing income tax in 1967. This measure was probably inspired by the Chinese example. In China not even the 5% paid to the residual national capitalists for their investment in enterprises taken over by the state was subject to tax.[309] Direct taxes for communes were never very high; they have been estimated at 10%. This, too, provided a very considerable incentive for production, since surplus output was not taxed.[310]

The Soviet Union also made repeated efforts to phase out personal taxation. In 1943, the graduated inheritance and gift tax was abolished. In 1960, the Supreme Soviet decided to abolish income tax—a move that Khrushchev celebrated as being to all intents and purposes the abolition of tax. The Presidium of the Supreme Soviet postponed implementation of this measure, however, because of the increased expenditure on defense and construction.

As early as 1960, income tax from the population accounted for only 7.3%, but this rose again gradually to 8.4% by 1978,[311] because the ceiling tax laws (set at 13% ever since the 1960 tax reform) came into play at a monthly income of as low as 100 rubles. The higher income brackets are therefore at an advantage, although personal tax is also the tax that has least impact on the other income brackets. Taking the average budget of a Soviet worker family, these taxes accounted for 4.1% in 1940 and only 8.7% in 1978.[312] It has thus been quite correctly concluded from this tax policy that income tax was maintained for what were predominantly fiscal reasons rather than for distribution reasons.

The socialist state would be able to do without personal taxes if radical redistribution were to be implemented in both the production and the distribution spheres. However, as yet this is not the case. Income tax has maintained its redistributive power in socialist states as far as private income—which, in some cases, is taxed at 80 to 90% —is concerned.

Income tax made little contribution toward redistribution in the wage sector with the bonus system promoting wage disparity, since taxes in socialist countries are at times set at only a quarter of the levels implemented in capitalist countries (in Hungary, for example, it is set at between 3 and 11%). The German Democratic Republic has kept closest to the fiscal traditions of the former German welfare state and has abolished progressive tax scales at a relatively low income level (M 700) incorporating these in a 20% proportional taxation scheme (maximum tax rate 34%). In the Federal Republic of Germany, the lower income groups are taxed to a lesser extent and the higher income groups to a considerably greater extent than in the German Democratic Republic.[313]

Since in socialist countries the essential means of production are in state hands, the tax yield is considerably higher than under capitalist systems. In the Soviet Union, for example, tax yield accounts for twice as much of the gross national product as is the case in the United States, contributing some 50% toward the GNP. In socialist states with a lower level of productive resources, the state's extractive capacity is not so highly refined. In China, tax yield accounted for only 26% of national income.[314] The redistributive power of socialist tax systems is not as great as it could theoretically be. In China, too, experts rate economic efficiency and savings in administration costs above the distributive power of the tax system and above its function of promoting social equality. Only occasionally—as in the case of forced collectivization—did it prove possible to maximize both targets of simplifying the tax system and of rapid redistribution at one and the same time. Hence, in socialist countries greater redistribution potential is to be found, due to the fairly high level of state revenue (compared with the "public poverty" found in capitalist states), which can then be deployed selectively for redistribution purposes, particularly in the field of infrastructure.

Social policy

Social policy in socialist countries is said to be deeply anchored in the core of the anthropologic premises of the theory of socialist society. Marxist scholars therefore refused for quite a time to accept the differentiation of a special field of "social policy" within the general "social nature" of socialist policies on the basis of Marxism-Leninism. "Social policy" in the Soviet Union was long considered a notion coined in capitalist societies to describe the compensations that Western States try to offer to their citizens in order to smooth down the hardships of capitalism. Social security therefore was discussed in a more technical and administrative sense as *sotsial'noe obespechenie*. The first book with the term "social policy" in its title was a translation from Polish in 1977; the first overview of social policies in the COMECON countries was published in 1979.[315] Even the German Democratic Republic, which shared the tradition of the oldest welfare state in the world—the German Empire—and did use the term "social policy," did not give up the generalization until the 1960s that a special social policy in the long run would be unnecessary in a socialist system, being social per se.[316]

These early declarations against a separate field of social policy did not prevent socialist states from adopting social welfare measures in a time of transition in order to further redistribution.[317] This is why social policy—for systematical reasons covered under the heading of protective functions in a socialist state (see Chapter 8, Section 2)—has to be mentioned in a chapter on "redistribution" as well.

The social consumption fund, which, in most socialist countries, provides some 30% of income-related allocations for workers, was said to be more than twice as high as in capitalist countries, where the percentage was estimated at between 5 and 15%, depending on the extent of welfare state development.[318] In the Soviet Union, the Ninth Five-Year Plan even made provision for the proportion of social consumption to rise as high as 40.6% by 1975.[319] The target figure of 50% by 1980 was regarded as somewhat unrealistic by foreign economists, since as people's real income rises they tend to purchase more and more services on a private basis. This tendency can be illustrated with the developments in Hungary. If we take 1970 as 100, then "privately purchased" services in Hungary rose to 107 in 1971, with the social services rising to 106.5.[320] In addition, data on the social consumption fund must always be treated with a degree of caution. At times part of the wage fund is added on here—where payment is made without specific work performance being supplied, such as wage compensation for pregnant women transferred to other jobs.[321]

A number of theorists in comparative economics have argued that in capitalist systems, as in socialist systems, *distribution of risk over time* takes precedence over redistribution of income in the social security system. This generalization seems to take too little account of the historical background. Firstly, it is perfectly clear that in the class struggle phase the social security system is designed to promote redistribution—such as when "enemies of the working class" are deprived of certain benefits from the social consumption fund. As a socialist system becomes more firmly established, however, direct discrimination against individual groups (such as against church employees in the Soviet Union to date) scarcely continues to play a part. Even in later phases, the redistribution aspect constantly comes to the fore again. Income surveys carried out by Soviet economists have shown that the state provides some 46.4% of income for the lower income brackets in the form of subsidies and social benefits, while the figure for the higher income groups is only 11.5%.[322]

It would, however, seem that marked changes are coming about in the orientation of social security systems in socialist countries. With a growing level of productive resources, the efficiency aspect, which was the focal point of the social security system during the accumulation phase, is now fading into the background. Distributive and protective measures were aimed at that time chiefly at maintaining the work force.[323] In the Soviet Union, priority was given to medical welfare services and preventive care in a bid to avoid temporary incapacity to work. As the standard of living rises, the long-term aspects of risk distribution over time—care for the elderly, life assurance, and so forth—are gradually gaining more weight.

The system has always had a source of redistributive power in its social policy, but this has been markedly group-specific and selective:

1. at the level where the distributive power of the system was so little developed that only individual, *privileged groups of workers* were able to benefit from social welfare provisions; Soviet doctrine confirmed during the construction phase that social security was an institution to provide care for the working class; in China this was expressed in less propagandistic terms, yet as late as 1953 and despite considerable effort, worker social security was still limited to enterprises with more than 100 workers, and free medical care was only available to a minority of workers;[324]

2. at the level of *differentiation policy*, where a host of individual protective measures admittedly brought about more tolerable social conditions but at the same time created new disparities and a potential source of discontent through workers comparing their positions and having their expectations raised; nevertheless, steady progress was, in fact, being achieved in absolute terms.

The advantages of a high degree of centralization are partly canceled out by a lack of flexibility and too much bureaucracy when it comes to handling individual cases. The target of social equality begins when a high level of productive resources has been achieved, permitting the transition to communism, although at this point the equality and freedom targets of the social system come again into conflict with each other. Socialist social security systems in the main respond to the increasing social differentiation with a flexible policy of tolerating *insurance* schemes alongside the main organizational principle of *welfare provision*. Their adherence to the concept of a uniform state-monopoly welfare system and the strict ideological emphasis placed on the ruling standards in socialist society, to which each individual is expected to conform, has, however, meant that the *care* aspect of the system, which would react more flexibly in individual and temporary cases of need, has been very much neglected. This even applied in the field of care for deviant behavior groups; despite a number of pioneering sociopedagogical experiments during the early days of the Soviet system, this has been left far too much in the hands of state repression ever since Stalin's time.[325] Anything that social policy in socialist countries was able to gain in terms of redistributive power by emphasis on the welfare principle was then lost again in the distribution sphere through sociopolitical one-sidedness when it came to the state's protective functions (see Chapter 8, Section 2).

Educational policy

Of all the infrastructure measures, education policy was the realm of material policy within socialism where long-term redistribution targets could best be promoted while still keeping closely in line with the target of stabilizing the system. More than just a few socialist leaders set their hopes exclusively on the younger generation and had their doubts as to whether anything more than "good-natured neutrality" toward socialism and its aim of changing mankind could be expected from the majority of those who had lived through a bourgeois socialization process.

The longer it took to implement genuine socialist elements in Soviet Russian transitional society, the greater the emphasis Lenin placed on the necessity of a "Cultural Revolution" in order to achieve socialism in the long run. The most important prerequisites for this were the fight against illiteracy and the creation of a high level of productive resources. The fight against illiteracy in socialist countries was taken up with an unparalleled mobilization of the masses and was at times clearly directed against bourgeois city culture.[326] Nearly all socialist countries head the ranks when it comes to increases in the level of literacy (see Table 37). As for capitalist countries, only a number of small countries, such as Mauritius, the Dominican Republic, Panama, Cyprus, and Trinidad were able to keep pace. The performance of socialist countries would probably be all the more impressive—on a par with the head of the league, Albania—had the dates chosen for purposes of comparison all come after the introduction of socialism. In the case of very large socialist countries, the special regional efforts undertaken must also be taken into consideration to give a fair assessment of performance. According to Soviet data, in the period between 1926 and 1939 the level of literacy in a number of Central Asian Union Republics rose from an average of 12% to some 70%.

Table 37

Literacy levels in socialist countries

(in percentages)

| | | | | Around 1965 | |
Country	Year	Rank out of 118 countries	Percentage of literates	Rank	Percentage of literates
GDR	1950	7	98.5	13	99
Czechoslovakia	1950	17	97.5	13	99
Hungary	1960	19	97	22	98
Poland	1960	23	95	22	98
Soviet Union	1959	23	95	13	99
Rumania	1956	27	89	13	99
Bulgaria	1956	31	85	34	85
Cuba	1950	37	77.5	46	75
Yugoslavia	1961	39	77	43	77
Albania	1950	51	60.0	50	72
Mongolia	1950	55	57.5	50	72
for comparison:					
Italy	1950	28	87.5	28	92
Spain	1960	29	87	31	87
Greece	1961	35	80.0	38	82
India	1951	86	19.3	90	28

Sources: B. M. Russet, op.cit., p.222; Taylor-Hudson, op.cit., pp. 232ff.

The second prerequisite—alongside improving the level of literacy—that Lenin named for a socialist cultural revolution was that of increasing the level of productive resources. Here, too, socialist countries can on the whole point to impressive results. However, it was seen that this prerequisite was in itself dependent upon the existence of a high level of education, and some of the failures experienced in trying to increase industrial output, intensify agriculture, and improve labor productivity can be attributed to the low level of education found in socialist countries (see Chapter 4, Section 3). Only third-world socialist countries have had to contend with literacy problems on the same scale as those that Lenin encountered in Russia. Lenin on several occasions complained at the "semi-Asian lack of culture" among the people.

Soviet interpretation of Chinese statistics would seem to show that the cultural revolution in China actually counteracted the success of previous literacy campaigns to some extent. The illiteracy rate among Chinese workers was estimated at 40% for 1969—a figure that would be higher than in the time before the cultural revolution.

Improving literacy—an area in which socialist countries achieved unparalleled success—was only the prerequisite for an education policy so designed in content that it would develop redistributive trends within society. The requirements as to the content of this education policy were formulated for the first time in March 1919 in the RCP (B) program at the Seventh Party Congress: [327]

1. general polytechnic education, combining instruction with production work;
2. creation of preschool facilities;
3. expansion of vocational training;
4. greater access to institutes of higher education, particularly for the workers.

Developments in the initial years of the Soviet state lagged far behind the set targets, not only in qualitative terms but also in quantitative terms of the requirements as well. It proved impossible to introduce compulsory schooling up to the age of 17. In 1923, many Republics in the Union had to be content with four years' schooling. As late as 1927, only 50% of children in the 8-to-11 age bracket were taken in by the education system, and scarcely one third of all Soviet schools were in line with the four-class standard model set as the target. [328]

At the primary and secondary levels of the education system, differences between capitalist and socialist countries seem to be less serious. The countries that have the highest number of scholars at the secondary level, are, however, clearly ahead of capitalist countries with a comparable level of productive resources, such as Spain or Italy, and can provide a match for highly advanced capitalist nations such as West Germany (see Table 38). The higher rate of schooling for the third level is even more striking. Even Yugoslavia, which falls rather short of average for socialist countries at the first two levels, is approaching the figures for developed capitalist systems here (see Table 38).

The gross schooling rate expresses the number of scholars in a given school grade as a percentage of the age group for which the

Table 38

Percentage of school-age population receiving education

Country	Year	1st level*	2nd level*	3rd level**
Albania	1971	106(6–13)	7(14–17)	16.4
Bulgaria	1974	96(7–14)	87(15–17)	18.7
Cuba	1974	137(7–12)	35(12–18)	9.2
Czechoslovakia	1974	96(6–14)	35(15–18)	11.2
GDR	1975	95(7–16)	90(17–18)	24.5
Hungary	1974	99(6–13)	62(14–17)	11.2
Mongolia	1974	85(8–11)	94(12–17)	6.4 (1970)
Poland	1975	100(7–14)	53(15–18)	15.7
Rumania	1974	109(6–13)	57(14–17)	8.7
Soviet Union	1975	99(7–14)	71(15–17)	21.7
Yugoslavia	1974	97(7–14)	54(15–18)	18.6
for comparison:				
FRG	1975		82(6–18)	20.2
Italy	1975	107(6–10)	71(11–18)	23.9
Sweden	1974	97(7–12)	70(13–19)	21.8
United States	1970	109(6–11)	100(13–17)	49.2

*Age group in brackets.
**20–24 years.

Source: UNESCO, *Statistical Yearbook 1976* (Paris: UNESCO, 1977), pp. 161ff.

school grade is intended (= 100%). Where the percentage rises above 100, then this clearly indicates that there are some children from a different age group in this school grade, that is, there is some discrepancy between the schooling system and the actual schooling situation. This distortion is, moreover, included in the figures up to 100% as well, giving a more favorable impression than is the true situation. We cannot exclude the possibility that this is done deliberately. Only in a few cases are net statistics available for socialist countries as well: Bulgaria = 96%, Yugoslavia = 83%, Poland = 91%, Czechoslovakia = 96%, and Hungary = 95%. Unfortunately these statistics are not available for the very countries where literacy campaigns still have a long way to go. In these cases, especially, it would be particularly valuable to have data on literacy levels in the school grades up to the current school leaving age (see Table 37 for the literacy level of the population as a whole).

Extremely high percentages result from over-age pupils and from early school entry. Although these are chiefly in evidence at the primary level, they do have repercussions on the higher levels as well. The more frequent of the two causes and that which provides more of a key to the success of an education system—as well as being more serious for the national economy—is the over-age pupil problem. In the case of Cuba (137%) this is probably a temporary accompanying facet of the introduction of general education; the high percentage shows that nearly all the children that actually belong into this grade are also receiving education.

In the German Democratic Republic (117%) and in the Federal Republic of Germany (132%), the situation is somewhat different. first of all, these countries are no longer dealing with improving literacy levels but rather with the conserving and overcoming of social handicaps due to education. At first sight, the similar figures would seem to point to similar ratios, particularly in view of the shared tradition of selective schooling. However, since the GDR figure takes in the whole of the schooling system up to the eighth grade and the FRG figure only covers the first to fourth grades, this then brings the GDR figure down again, compared with the FRG figure. Viewed in terms of the other socialist countries where a comparison of gross and net schooling rates is possible, however, the GDR figure would still appear to be relatively high. In Bulgaria, Czechoslovakia, and Hungary the difference varies between 1 and 5%, with Poland and Yugoslavia already at the 11% mark, as compared with the German Democratic Republic's 17%.

The possible causes for over-age pupils are late school entry as a result of insufficient maturity, inadequate performance (being kept down a year), or illness. In countries where the over-age pupils consist primarily of children who have started school late—and this applies to a large proportion of this group in the Federal Republic of Germany—it would imply criticism of preschool educational facilities. In the case of pupils having to repeat a school year—and this is the other main cause in the Federal Republic of Germany— then this points to a difference in basic outlook compared with socialist education systems, since socialist states on the whole try to have as many of their pupils as possible successfully complete their schooling without any time lag, giving coaching where this proves necessary. Keeping a pupil back a year because of below-standard performance is frowned upon as a restrictive bourgeois educational policy measure. This attitude, which also has the effect of bringing pressure to bear on pupils to perform well, leads to a considerable increase in efficiency within the education system, and this, in turn, results in the low drop-out rates in higher education as compared with nonsocialist states. (See Table 39.)

The schooling rate, however, is a very rough guide to the performance of educational systems in socialist systems. It must also be remembered that some of the figures are hardly suitable for comparison because of the differences in the various systems—such as

Table 39

Mobilization for university-level education

Country	Rank out of 121 countries	Students per 10,000 population	
		1965	1978/79
Soviet Union	3	167.4	195.0
Bulgaria	8	122.0	108.0
Czechoslovakia	15	100.0	121.0
Yugoslavia	16	94.8	203.0
Poland	21	80.0	138.0
Mongolia	23	75.6	125.0
Rumania	26	68.6	87.0
Albania	27	68.4	
Hungary	42	50.3	99.0
GDR	45	46.6	76.0
Cuba	49	40.0	139.0
China	75	12.2	
Vietnam			27.0
for comparison:			
United States	1	284.0	269.0
Japan	11	114.0	149.0
France	13	104.2	158.0
FRG	30	63.2	99.0
Italy	35	58.3	131.0
United Kingdom	44	48.5	95.0
India	58	28.4	37.0

Source: Taylor-Hudson, op. cit. p. 229ff.; UNESCO, *Statistical Yearbook 1967* (Paris: UNESCO, 1968). *Narodnoe khozyaistvo SSSR v. 1978 g.* (Moscow: Statistika, 1979), p. 80.

the vast number of US students whose training in numerous colleges is roughly equivalent to the standards at upper-secondary-level education in Europe. The large numbers of correspondence students in the Soviet Union, on the other hand, mean that these figures are not directly comparable with those of the German Democratic Republic, which has retained certain features of the traditional German educational system. Consequently, Soviet figures are even less comparable with those of capitalist systems. Taking figures for the two superpowers in isolation, it is seen that in purely quantitative terms, their performance levels clearly aligned during the 1960s, whereas during the 1950s the United States had still been well and truly ahead of the Soviet Union.

GDR and FRG statistics are of greater value here, since common traditions in their educational systems make their figures more-or-less comparable. The German Democratic Republic overtook the Federal Republic of Germany in educating pupils up to the "Abitur" level (high school diploma) during the 1950s. In 1963, the year in which the campaign against the "education catastrophe" was launched, the percentage of pupils per school year who passed the school-leaving examination was 7% in the Federal Republic of Germany and 11% in the German Democratic Republic. By 1967 the ratio had already changed. The German Democratic Republic had slightly above 7%, the Federal Republic of Germany 9%.[329] Even though it is frequently suggested that the schooling rate is dependent upon the level of productive resources, it is often shown that this does not apply in a comparison with socialist countries. Yugoslavia is the only socialist country that is far ahead of its development level in mobilization of educational reserves, while a large number of capitalist countries fall decidedly below this level. They have also shown a lesser ability to close these gaps through rapid countermeasures, as was at least attempted by the Federal Republic of Germany.

Although the schooling rate for socialist countries is clearly above that of comparable countries, doubts have been arising in educational research in socialist countries, too, as to the value of this rate as an indicator. This is not so much a matter of the quality of studies coming under fire but more an economic viewpoint, following complaints about wasted resources. Criticism is focused, among other things, on the rate at which engineers are being trained, some of whom will subsequently have to be employed in jobs beneath their level, while other fields, which were not so important in ideological terms to begin with—such as chemistry and biology—are being neglected. The fact that altogether too many university graduates are being produced is already leading to complaints: "There is a certain disproportion in the education and further education system for workers in the Soviet Union at present. Whereas there is a surplus of highly qualified experts (in terms of current social requirements) there is a shortage of workers and particularly of skilled workers."[330] Efforts are now being concentrated on vocational training in a bid to resolve this disproportion, as is being done in a number of capitalist countries.

Even in comparative research into education systems carried out in the West, increasing attention is being paid to political factors in the development of education systems. Multivariant analyses of investment in the education sector not only include the level of productive resources but also cover political factors such as the population's *expectations* of its government and the ways in which the government uses its resources and the population's expectations to advantage and makes due allowance for them.[331] In an ideologically molded mobilization regime, however, the expectations of the population are not the independent variables that they are in a number of capitalist systems. Instead, these expectations are pre-shaped by the system's long-term goals in the redistribution and efficiency fields.

In order to judge the quality of educational systems, additional indicators need to be taken into consideration, such as,

1.   number of teachers per pupil;
2.   examination output;
3.   teachers' salaries;
4.   state expenditure on education.

The *number of teachers per pupil* yardstick is, in turn, conditioned by additional indicators. With greater provision of teaching aids and machines and also with more thorough teacher training, a smaller number of teachers per pupil in statistical terms does not necessarily mean a lower quality of education. Taking the teacher: pupil ratio indicator, which is, nonetheless, a valuable guide, it can be shown that the Soviet Union overtook the United States in the 1960s. This also holds true for a number of other socialist countries in relation to comparable capitalist countries.

The degree of structuring and the efficiency of educational systems are also measured in terms of *examination output*, in view of the high *drop-out rate* in capitalist countries. Even statisticians who felt that there were no noteworthy differences between socialist and capitalist education systems when it came to schooling rate had to

Table 40

Graduate students per 1,000 in student age group
(age 20–24)

Country	1956	1962	Number of students	Year
Albania			124.1	1968
Bulgaria	9.2	12.0	236.7	1969
Czechoslovakia	10.6	15.4	164.0	1968
GDR	8.3	12.6	246.5	1970
Hungary			231.5	1969
Poland	10.6	10.2	187.8	1969
Rumania	7.4	7.5	183.1	1970
Soviet Union	14.8	15.9	367.8	1969
Yugoslavia	4.7	14.8		
for comparison:				
FRG	10.0	12.3	259.2	1969
Greece	6.1	8.3	136.1	1969
Italy	5.3	3.7	147.7	1969
United States	35.9	43.5		

Sources: Compiled from National Statistical Yearbooks by F. L. Pryor, *Public Expenditures in Communist and Capitalist Nations* (London: Allen & Unwin, 1968), p. 195; for the third column, UNESCO, *Statistical Yearbook 1972* (Paris: UNESCO, 1973), pp. 424 ff.

admit that socialist educational systems perform better in this area. If a comparison is drawn between countries at a similar stage in development, such as between Italy and Poland, Greece and Bulgaria, and the Federal Republic of Germany and the German Democratic Republic, then this indicator shows the socialist systems to have the higher degree of efficiency. (See Table 40.)

Those who do not set as much store by the qualitative schooling rate as by the quantitative rate, however, do not accept this indicator as proof of greater efficiency and simply regard it as evidence of greater pressure to perform well. Hence, further indicators need to be brought into the comparison.

When comparing *state expenditure on education*, it must be borne in mind that the students and their families bear a greater proportion of the costs in capitalist countries than they do in socialist countries. Even if the fact that the state has taken over a greater portion of this infrastructural investment in socialist systems is regarded as a distinct advantage, one cannot simply take the portion of budget expenditure allocated to education as being representative of overall expenditure on the educational system. When comparing different social systems, consideration must also be given to the percentage of private schools; in a number of countries only the partial subsidies that these receive show up in the state budget. In 1957/58, the number of children attending private schools nonetheless accounted for 13.2% of the total in the United States, 9.5% in Italy, and 7.4% in Greece.[332]

Teachers' salaries in socialist countries tend on average to be rather low and, according to UN statistics, account for some 39 to 55% of current expenditure on education, as compared with 70 to 90% in many capitalist countries.[333] Nevertheless, state expenditure on education was higher in socialist countries in the 1950s and 1960s, and it is the system variable (capitalism or socialism) that is the decisive factor here (see Table 41). Standard cross-country comparisons should, however, be supplemented by time-series comparisons. Expenditure on education is subject to considerable fluctuation in socialist countries, too. After 1958, the Soviet Union, for example, slowed down investment in education in favor of more

Table 41

Proportion of state budget allocated to education and social welfare
(in percentages)

| Country | Year | Expenditure | | |
		Social & cultural	National economy	Defence
Bulgaria	1975	31.3	51.7	15.1
Czechoslovakia	1977	44.7	45.9	7.2
GDR	1975	34.6	n.d	8.4
Hungary	1976	26.8	52.3	3.6
Poland	1976	18.7	44.1	6.4
Rumania	1977	20.9	68.2	3.9
Soviet Union	1976	35.6	52.3	7.7
Yugoslavia	1975	5.2	17.2	27.0

Source: Statistical Surveys. From: *Yearbook of East European Economics,* Vol. 8 (Munich: Olzog, 1979), pp. 458ff.

investment in directly productive activities,[334] whereas in capitalist countries investment increased rapidly in the mid-1960s, when it was realized that there were serious shortcomings in infrastructure. This then reduced the lead held by socialist countries (see Table 42). Since as yet there are no sufficiently comprehensive data available on expenditure on private education, it is not possible to draw comparisons between overall expenditure on education in capitalist and socialist countries for the time being. These comparisons, moreover, are largely superfluous, since even capitalist countries are coming to appreciate that if free use of learning facilities is to become a reality, then all expenditure on education will have to come from the public purse.

For the "cultural revolution" in Lenin's sense of the term it was not the quantitative upswing that was the most important factor, however, as is reflected in these figures. The cultural revolution was much more intended to go hand-in-hand with qualitative changes, such as the expansion of polytechnic education, the promotion of preschool facilities, and vocational training, together with new study material. A number of these qualitative requirements were reflected in quantitative achievements. Since the Soviet Union does not invest proportionately more money in individual students in its schools and institutes of higher education than do the countries that head the ranks among capitalist countries, it has been rightfully concluded that *polytechnic education* and vocational training account for an unproportionately high percentage of expenditure on education. This undoubtably has a redistribution effect in favor of those social classes that have been underprivileged to date. However, polytechnic education in the Soviet Union soon lost its ability to produce an all-round person with multifunctional capacities, as laid down by Marx in the much-quoted claim that it must be made possible for everyone "to do one thing today, another thing tomorrow, to hunt in the mornings, fish in the afternoons, raise cattle in the evenings and criticize after dinner" (MEW, Vol. 3, p. 33).

Polytechnic education was introduced with a strong bias toward production, although there were complaints from the production sector about uneconomic employment of workers who had to train students, which hampered production. In this way, the specialists of the future were able to acquire their vocational skills. Much to the concern of Soviet educational planners, however, they remained dead capital, in part because a large proportion of the trainees did not go in for a career where they could use the skills they had acquired. It was thus logical for Mao to try to stop the trend toward high specialization in China through radicalization of his education

Table 42

Public expenditure on education

Country	Rank out of 131 nations	1965 Per capita in dollars	1965 Percentage of GNP	Percentage of GNP	Year	Percentage of public expenditure	
Cuba	1	29.62	7.5	9.9	1974	no data	
Soviet Union	2	99.13	7.3	7.5	1976	12.7	
North Vietnam	3	6.79	6.8		no data		
GDR	6	79.77	6.3	5.6	1974	7.6	
Poland	15	53.94	5.5	5.0	1970	7.6	1976
Rumania	24	40.21	5.2	no data		8.0	
Czechoslovakia	28	76.77	4.9	4.4	1970	7.0	1970
Hungary	31	51.64	4.7	4.6	1976		
Yugoslavia	31	21.22	4.7	5.4	1976		
Bulgaria	53	31.10	3.7	5.4	1976	8.9	1970
China	53	4.00	3.7		no data		
North Korea	58	7.44	3.6		no data		
Albania						10.6	1971
for comparison:							
Sweden	4	165.24	6.5	7.7	1976	13.3	
Italy	15	60.34	5.5	5.0	1975	11.7	
United States	22	188.50	5.3	6.0	1976	17.7	
Japan	28	41.97	4.9	5.5	1975	22.6	
FRG	66	64.90	3.4	5.2	1976	10.6	
Greece	114	11.69	1.7	1.8	1974	8.0	
Spain	122	7.72	1.4	3.5	1973	15.8	

Sources: For 1965: Taylor-Hudson, idib., pp. 30ff. Later data from: United Nations, *Statistical Yearbook 1978* (New York, UN, 1979), pp. 928ff.; UNESCO, *Statistical Yearbook 1972* (Paris: UNESCO, 1973), pp. 512ff.

policy. Physical labor was no longer just to serve to promote practical specialized knowledge, but was to have as little as possible to do with the pupil's or student's current or future area of study. This seemed best guaranteed through deployment in agriculture, which then also provided further ideological justification for the compulsory "sending-down" to agriculture system.

The chief successes of socialist education policy are to be seen in the resolute way in which countries have striven to fulfill the requirement for *easier access to higher education for the people* (and in particular for the workers). An initial indicator here is the unproportionately high expansion of the third-level educational sector in socialist systems. If we proceed to a class-by-class breakdown of educational opportunities on the basis of Soviet statistics, then this highlights even further the redistributive function of the educational system in socialist countries.

At the start of industrialization and at the end of the NEP period, the nonproletarian classes still accounted for just over half the total number of students. Statistics show, however, that official policy took great pains to improve the situation for the working class. In the years between 1930 and 1932, in particular, decisive progress was made here. In 1935, the number of workers was beginning to fall again, because the social clause relating to admittance to higher education was dropped in December 1935. In 1941 the last worker faculties closed down—these were to be revived again in the German Democratic Republic after the war in the form of worker and peasant faculties. Complaints about inadequate opportunities for worker and peasant students emerged from all socialist countries, however. Even in China, during the cultural revolution, the pressure brought to bear on worker and peasant students to perform well—on the very same students who had, until then, been underprivileged in the educational system—was time and again denounced as "bourgeois arrogance" on the part of the teaching staff.[335]

Similarly, frequent complaints were voiced in Chinese publications about the class breakdown of students. During the 1950s, the number of worker and peasant children continued to rise steadily. In 1951, the figure was 19.1%, in 1958 it had already risen to 48%, and by 1960 it came to 62%.[336] However, after the Great Leap Forward, when Liu Shao-ch'i and the group around him moved into a dominant position, the social origin of students took on less importance as a selection criterion for a while (until the cultural revolution) and more weight was attached to specialist knowledge and performance.

The top positions in socialist countries are not hereditary, despite many hints regarding the closed cast of the *nomenklatura.*[337] Comparisons of three generations in Hungary showed that manual and nonmanual strata of the population in socialist countries reproduced themselves to a large extent. Where the father had a nonmanual position, 56% of the children also had nonmanual positions; where the grandfather was also in a nonmanual job, the share of children in nonmanual jobs increased to 71%.[338] Soviet figures show that there are blatant differences in educational output between the regions and republics,[339] and there are underprivileged groups especially on the collective farms. Recent studies of the agrarian population showed that only 30 to 48% of the kolkhoz population has reached the general aim of a completed middle-school education. In some kolkhozy as many as 12.6% have no more than four years of education.[340] Success in the development of evening schools shows in many respects only the compensatory character of these institutions to improve the redistributive features of the Soviet educational system.[341] Even among those enrolled in middle and higher education, many social differences kept alive: the circa 500 institutions of higher education (*vuzy*) vary greatly in quality, the kind of employment they offer their graduates, and general attractiveness. Students from the more favored families congregate at the better faculties.[342]

Figures (Table 43) show that the proportion of students with working-class background remains below the proportion of workers, despite all efforts of socialist educational policy for the "redistribution of social chances." Part of the students with "working-class background" include children of former workers who have become functionaries. Sometimes the proportion of workers might be even worse than is indicated by the figures. If we compare the figures for Sverdlovsk in 1973 for students in the first and the last classes, then it is clear that the proportion of students with working-class backgrounds declines, and of children of intelligentsia families increases. Soviet sociologists no longer embellish these facts and discuss measures against this "working class erosion."[343]

In all socialist countries, there is a certain period of time that elapses before the redistribution effect of educational policy makes itself felt. This is due not so much to a lack of motivation on the part of individuals or social groups attempting to pass on privilege to their own children (although this does indeed happen—right through to forced private coaching, making use of personal connections, and even corruption[344]) but is rather the result of structural dysfunctions that stem from the very successes of socialist educational policy. The

Table 43

Class origin of students

| | Soviet Union | | | GDR 1966 | Poland 1965 |
	1928	1938	1973 (Sverdlovsk)		
working class	25.4	33	34.3[1]	30.7[2]	39.1	26.3
peasantry	23.9	21.6	1.5	3.8	7.2	18.3
intelligentsia and state employees	50.7	44.6	57.4	63.6	43.2	43.1
self-employed, artisans			6.8	1.9[3]	10.5	7.2
others						4.2

(1) first class; (2) last class; (3) professions.

Sources: N. de Witt, *Education and Professional Employment in the USSR* (Washington, D. C.; National Science Foundation, 1961), p. 72; F. P. Filippov, *Vseobshee srednee obrazovanie v. SSSR* (Moscow: Mysl', 1976), pp. 86f. A. Kruppa, *Wirtschafts- und Bildungsplanung in der DDR* (Hamburg: Hoffmann & Campe, 1976), p. 141. J. R. Fiszman, *"Education and Social Mobility in People's Poland"* in B. L. Faber, ed., *The Social Structure in Eastern Europe* (New York: Praeger, 1976) (83-109), p.88.

Soviet Union lost the balance that it had maintained between the number of secondary school leavers and the number of university places in 1953—somewhat earlier than capitalist countries. This was a result of its target of introducing secondary schooling for everyone. At the end of the 1960s, this goal had been achieved for more than two thirds of pupils in each age group. It thus became necessary to introduce a selection procedure. In practical terms, this selection procedure amounted to a full numerus clausus, although that designation was never accepted. It is, however, being made increasingly plain to Soviet youth that not everyone can go on to the university, and counterpropaganda is emerging in increasingly straightforward terms: "It's not what you are but who you are that counts," or "Better to be a good worker than a bad engineer."[345]

Admittance rates for university places are very low. In the case of China, a figure of 18% was mentioned at one stage,[346] and in the Soviet Union latest statistics put the percentage even lower. Soviet forecasts predict 2.6 million secondary school leavers for 1975 (the figure for 1970 was 2 million). Of these, 400,000 are to go to universities, 300,000 to middle technical colleges, and 250,000 to technical vocational institutes. As for the rest, it is stated tersely that they have gone "to work in the national economy."[347] Compared with other socialist countries, there is considerable discrepancy in the Soviet Union between those who hold formal qualifications entitling them to a university place and those who are actually admitted to the places. The Soviet Union has a particularly ingenious system for giving priority access to university places to individual groups of nationalities, those completing military service, the best students from vocational and evening schools, and those who can show specific professional experience. This then results in lengthy waiting periods for the average student wishing to attend university. Figures of this nature would spark off an explosion in capitalist systems, but in socialist systems they cause less conflict for three reasons:

1.   Secondary technical and *vocational training* is highly developed. This has been the case in the Soviet Union since the introduction in 1969 of secondary vocational schools (providing skilled worker qualifications and a greater opportunity for further education than previously), which the German Democratic Republic in particular had developed along exemplary lines, and also since improvements were made in switch-over arrangements between vocational and university training within the educational system.

2.   University education promises *less material gain*, since a number of the mass subjects (for the welfare and education systems) lead on to professions that appear to be rather underpaid in comparison with qualified skilled workers (see Chapter 2, Section 2).

3.   The *ideological esteem in which manual work is held* means that any insistence on the right to become a university graduate in itself appears as "deviating" and socially damaging behavior and, at very least, as ideologically suspect. Surveys do show, however, that in a large number of socialist systems considerable numbers of young people are striving after a university education, although this wish is not backed up by the additional stimulus of pay and prestige differences between intellectual and manual work, as exists in capitalist systems.

Since the system is dominated by efficiency considerations and labor requirements are calculated on the basis of the *manpower approach*, even socialist educational systems come out against the idea of granting bonuses to classes that have so far been underprivileged. It becomes increasingly difficult to reconcile redistribution considerations with efficiency considerations.[348] Constantly increasing effort is needed in order to bring the worker and peasant children, granted priority access to university under the old 80% clause, through to completion of their university studies.[349] Even Soviet studies reveal that family status and income bracket influence a pupil's success in the higher classes, and hence when pupils are selected for university entrance on the basis of social criteria, new measures are needed to counteract the self-recruiting trends that prevail in the office-worker and intelligentsia strata.[350]

The qualitative achievements of an educational system also have to be measured in terms of the content of subject matter taught. Western educational researchers who rate the quantitative output positively then generally come up with criticism about *overspecialization* and about too much bias toward the work process in education —factors that cannot do much to promote particularly the more humane targets of socialism, such as elimination of the division of labor and alienation.[351] (See Table 44.)

The absence of any classical education (such as predominates in the Anglo-Saxon liberal arts colleges) also gives cause for complaint from time to time (with marked reference to problems in the researcher's own country). On the one hand, this type of belletrist education, composed of a foundation-level course generally followed by a second course of study, is also coming to be seen as outdated in capitalist countries. On the other hand, it is impossible to determine the proportion of artistic and literary education from the structure of schools and their curricula alone. Not even student numbers confirm one-sided statements here. Other indicators, such as the production of books and publication of translations, perhaps give better insight into the actual educational subject matter generally taught in socialist countries. As far as output of art and literature books is concerned, statistics show that the socialist countries, and in particular the Soviet Union, are altogether keeping pace with comparable countries in the capitalist world. Only Spain constitutes an atypical case here, producing an overwhelming proportion of literary works (see Tables 45 and 46). One major difference between capitalist and socialist countries is the high proportion of religious works published in capitalist countries, as opposed to a higher percentage of natural science books—particularly applied natural sciences—in socialist systems.

The proportion of social sciences has been taken as a significant indicator of the intellectual state of the cultural system. Dennis

Table 44

Student numbers and breakdown of subjects

	Albania 1971	Bulgaria 1974	Czecho-slovakia 1974	Rumania 1974	Cuba 1974	FRG 1974	United Kingdom 1974	Spain 1974	Italy 1974
total	28,668	127,319	144,325	152,728	68,051	786,711	650,562	453,389	930,211
humanities	4,407	13,146	10,438	15,985	4,685	49,756	61,490	63,083	179,302
education	5,243	17,039	18,268	7,724	14,667	273,753	139,240	59,058	59,674
fine art	424	3,162	1,999	3,993	1,670	44,571	42,835	31,082	52,071
law	1,050	2,483	8,752	6,402	2,406	46,420	–	38,587	106,941
social sciences	2,173	21,743	13,988	21,864	9,528	119,485	163,766	53,959	120,658
natural sciences	3,291	8,816	6,526	15,961	3,921	67,056	90,104	50,457	99,126
engineering	3,045	47,462	51,974	55,332	15,036	111,862	102,571	67,124	96,358
medicine	1,721	9,479	17,737	14,617	7,252	54,393	44,050	76,496	194,336
agriculture	2,807	3,988	14,643	10,850	7,437	16,025	6,501	11,940	20,579
other	4,507	1	–	–	1,449	3,390	5	1,673	932

Sources: UNESCO, Statistical Yearbook 1976 (Paris: UNESCO, 1977), pp. 390ff.

Table 45 World book production, according to subject (1976)

Country	Titles	Philos- ophy	Religion	Social sciences	Natural sciences	Applied sciences	Arts	Literature	History Geography	Chil- dren's books
Bulgaria	3,813	39	6	998	238	1,039	211	915	248	245
Cuba	726	11	0	256	28	99	8	245	41	54
Czechoslovakia	9,456	119	50	2,145	1,067	2,426	491	2,069	442	488
GDR	5,792	151	271	821	417	911	438	1,545	256	673
Hungary	9,393	109	70	2,338	873	2,980	698	1,595	444	129
Mongolia (1975)	490	10	3	171	27	117	19	118	17	–
Poland	11,418	121	168	2,397	1,030	3,957	703	2,146	673	344
Rumania	6,556	117	28	955	817	2,053	395	1,766	351	163
Soviet Union	84,304	1,298	220	18,913	9,306	35,453	2,342	11,969	2,234	3,215
Yugoslavia	9,054	129	306	3,709	309	1,304	950	1,909	294	408
for comparison:										
FRG	44,477	1,275	2,136	12,372	2,547	4,835	2,722	11,665	3,318	2,815
India	12,708	350	1,025	4,245	532	874	250	337	845	455
Italy	9,463	473	502	2,293	602	1,232	688	2,662	691	571
Japan	36,066	646	739	9,890	1,646	8,422	2,654	890	3,049	2,217
Spain	24,584	1,303	1,394	4,357	1,682	281	1,402	7,105	2,090	2,342
United Kingdom	35,526	1,146	1,180	6,622	3,622	5,694	3,637	9,075	3,744	2,688
United States	85,287	1,419	1,969	8,849	2,845	6,004	3,530	6,961	3,048	2,292

Source: *U.N. Statistical Yearbook, 1978* (New York: U.N., 1979), pp. 938ff.

Table 46
Book translations (1969)

Country	Titles	Philosophy	Religion	Social sciences	Philology	Natural science	Applied natural sciences	Art	Literature	History Geography
Albania	76	–	–	49	–	3	1	–	18	2
Bulgaria	595	17	1	136	3	39	76	53	217	45
Chile	38	6	1	1	–	–	–	–	30	–
Czechoslovakia	1,448	31	3	137	–	123	192	41	815	87
Hungary	960	16	12	133	17	99	161	82	341	88
Poland	821	25	37	133	–	100	138	18	308	54
Rumania	759	9	3	170	2	43	64	71	348	49
Soviet Union	3,851	191	12	551	4	339	367	64	2,075	232
Yugoslavia	1,012	16	39	293	–	36	52	57	482	34
for comparison:										
United Kingdom	3,851	191	12	551	4	339	367	64	2,075	232
France	1,984	74	233	189	10	122	134	110	884	217
FRG	3,541	126	237	264	13	157	188	184	2,040	310
India	824	37	134	110	3	36	39	12	309	140
Italy	2,474	188	371	298	19	100	152	137	867	326
Japan	2,165	122	73	379	15	192	249	79	887	161
United States	2,055	155	258	234	10	224	157	231	532	288

Source: U.N, *Statistical Yearbook 1971* (New York: UN, 1972), pp. 785ff.

C. Pirages has even taken the percentage of students in liberal arts and social sciences as a yardstick for measuring the liberality of a system and has found a considerable shortfall in socialist countries (with the exception of Yugoslavia), which would seem to correlate with the degree of liberality within the system.[352] This indicator seems to have been rather a biased choice, since the proportion of social sciences would seem to correlate more with the development level of a country—unless, of course, further correlation is then made between the level of development and the degree of liberalization and democratization within a society. However, precisely in the case of socialist countries, Pirages was unable to provide any evidence of this, contrary to a number of popular suppositions by convergence and evolution theorists.

It is difficult to pinpoint a satisfactory indicator for measuring the *degree of liberalization* within an educational system. Not even Pirages' highly rated—and initially convincing—indicator of the percentage of foreign students would seem to be reliable. UNESCO statistics on foreign students and student numbers abroad[353] show such small significant differences between the figures for Hungary and Rumania that the real differences highlighted by qualitative analysis do not seem to have been detected.

Furthermore, a comparison of development during the 1960s (see Table 47) shows that even the number of scholarship students studying abroad—the factor that could provide the most valuable indication as to the degree of liberalization—is of little practical use. In general, figures have tended to drop, due in part no doubt to countries expanding their own university systems and hence reducing their need for training abroad.

Correlation between the degree of liberality and the level to which the social sciences have been developed can be seen to be biased in cases where book production as a whole is included in the comparison rather than just the translations from foreign languages (see Table 46) that Pirages used as an indicator. This would then give less of a clearcut picture of the social sciences being neglected, unless, that is, one were to analyze the content of the social science publications available in the various systems and attempt to exclude the purely dogmatic, ideological works, which, experience has shown, account for a high proportion of social science publications in socialist countries.

Although Marxism, in its very essence, is a sociological theory that purports to be the only scientific social theory in existence at all, and despite the fact that Marxist theorists repeatedly polemize

Table 47
Number of scholarship students studying abroad

Country	1963/64	1968/69
Albania	6	—
GDR	319	110
Bulgaria	31	49
North Korea	12	—
Czechoslovakia	296	72
China	26	—
Hungary	154	70
Poland	175	72
Rumania	162	—
USSR	983	712
North Vietnam	3	—
Yugoslavia	8	—

Source: C. P. Roberts & M. Hamour (Publ.), *Cuba 1968. Supplement to the Statistical Abstract of Latin America* (Los Angeles: Latin American Center, University of California, 1970), p. 108.

against the necessarily fragmented and sterile technicoscientific orientation of modern industrial societies, far removed from the life of the people, a marked *neglect of the empirical social sciences* is to be observed in all socialist countries. So long as they were pursued within the framework of dogmatic (and undiscerning) global science, the social sciences tended rather to attract the more mediocre minds of the intelligentsia, whereas the brightest minds simply appeared to flee from the compulsion of belonging to one permanent denomination, taking refuge in the fragmented, esoteric technicoscientific subculture. Over the past few years, the social sciences have undergone a pronounced upswing, which does indeed tally in certain respects with the degree of liberalization—at least in qualitative terms. Empirical studies that did not become worn down into dogmatic typologies first started to emerge in what were, by comparison, the most liberal states, such as Poland and Hungary, appearing subsequently in Czechoslovakia in a brief yet remarkable flourish in 1967/68.[354] This underdevelopment of the social sciences at university level had its repercussions in the schools. Despite the topoi regarding indoctrination in school education, social studies also play an amazingly marginal role in the curricula of most Eastern bloc countries and are generally only taught in the senior classes.[355]

In the eyes of the Bolsheviks, the most important achievement of socialist education systems, viewed in quantitative terms—an achievement that it is impossible to gauge with indicators—was the *democratization of education and science*. Insofar as it is at all possible to measure this against the redistribution of educational opportunities and the facilitated access granted to the previously underprivileged masses, then all socialist countries have to be credited with remarkable achievements here. A truly egalitarian educational policy has still not come about, however; to appreciate this one only has to look at the marked specialization and hierarchization that exist in higher education, together with the persistence of a certain degree of social stratification based on regional, income, and prestige differences.

In Russia the first wave of democratization in the education system was brought to a halt at an early stage after the revolution, in the full exuberance of reform—and not only in its radical form as advocated by theorists such as A. Bogdanov, who were demanding nothing but the democratization, that is, the "socialization," of education through the proletariat's conquest of science. Lenin also took a stand against the *Proletkul't* and against the revolutionary, nihilistic overzealousness of a large number of educational reform groups[356] and made demands for a systematic acquisition of subject matter and the teaching of a certain amount of reliable knowledge. In the spring of 1918, the wave of democratization and decentralization in the Soviet educational system came into conflict with the necessity for centralized, dictatorial measures, in the same way as did syndicalist activities in industry. This produced an educational system that was copied in a large number of people's democracies, but which allowed in particular the humane and democratic impulses behind the Marxist concept of education to be swamped by production-oriented efficiency considerations and constant monitoring of performance. Critical items of knowledge that could prove an embarrassment for the system were not even tolerated to the extent to which educational theory and practice in organized capitalism left scope for a certain latitude of thought and action.

Opportunities for participation—which do, actually, exist—are (just as in participation in the production sphere) oriented 100% toward efficiency, the acquisition of knowledge, skills, and, in socialist systems in particular, toward conviction. The teacher's guiding function is emphasized much more than is student participation.[357]

In China, on the other hand, Mao always polemized against the traditional educational system, complaining at the multitude of books and subjects (referring here to Confucious who, after all, had taught only 6 subjects) and at the inhumaneness of the examination system. When he spoke out in favor of copying and occasional dozing off during lessons in the selective benevolence of his old age in 1964, he touched the heartstrings of millions of schoolchildren throughout the world.[358] He would hardly have done this had there not been serious shortcomings in the system in China, and in a number of instances exaggerated polemics against the performance principle were simply tools in the class struggle and criticism of the continued existence of bourgeois performance concepts among the education cadres. China's unparalleled mobilization of educational reserves also led to the most serious conflicts with the cadres. Under the pretext of having to crush a "bureaucratized education system,"[359] social conflict was waged against the former bourgeoisie classes, which were still at an advantage when it came to education, despite the equality policy, and which, in view of the shortage of good posts, still seemed to be privileged when it came to vertical mobility. In addition to being a weapon in the class struggle against the bourgeoisie, the strategy of replacing quality (intelligentsia) by quantity (the masses) also served labor policy. Since there were so few higher posts, it was impossible to find positions for anything like all the graduates. It was certainly not by coincidence that Mao resolutely fought for short university courses in order to avoid overspecialization, which would have led to increased expectations in subsequent employment. The social tensions that were discharged in the cultural revolution are clearly illustrated by a Chinese newspaper in 1963, which puts the percentage of middle-school graduates allowed to go on to university at 18%. Westernization and the formation of gangs, together with political radicalization, were the consequences, and the system was unable to master these sufficiently through its "sending down" to the countryside under the *Hsia-fang* system. Resistance against the number of politically indoctrinated courses, against manual labor that had nothing to do with students' chosen careers, and against deployment in production campaigns led to a plethora of conflicts in China.

Despite the radical equality policy in the education system since the cultural revolution—with schools run by workers and peasants, which were firstly to serve the systematic elimination of the former teaching cadres and secondly to open up opportunities for underprivileged classes—the primacy of political considerations is constantly being undermined in the cities and in places where advanced technology is needed, with concessions being made to intelligence and expert knowledge.[360]

In a large number of socialist countries, successes in educational policy brought dysfunctional side-effects in their wake, which had not been anticipated despite comprehensive social planning. Almost all socialist countries overmobilized educational reserves and were then unable to satisfy increased job expectations (which were inevitable in what was still a stratified society, despite the constant glorification of manual labor).

The production of ever-higher qualifications became at times so much of a political end in itself that educational output seemed to bear little relationship to social need or the level of productive resources, Castro went furthest here on occasion, such as when he maintained in Chile in 1971 that a person who had only been educated to secondary level should be regarded as an illiterate.[361] In view of the situation in Cuba and the necessities of the labor market following the decision against forced industrialization (and in favor of respecialization in sugar), this has to be seen as rather an unthought-out remark. In countries where the output of intellectuals develops into a status symbol of socialist achievement, there is always the threat of adaptation difficulties exploding in crisis proportions. In the East European uprisings of the 1960s and the Chinese cultural revolution, it was frequently the children of families that had until then been underprivileged that constituted the cadres of the rebellion—these had been mobilized relatively rapidly for education and did, in fact, have cause to be grateful to the state, but they were spurred on in their rebellion through frustration stemming from their aroused expectations.

With its *Nomenklatura*, the party had admittedly created an informal instrument for controlling all the posts and potential candidates for thousands of the most important positions.[362] But this is more a matter of political steering by reliable cadres and does not simply mark an attempt to introduce comprehensive planning for all the more highly qualified manpower.

All these crisis phenomena and shortcomings show that the Eastern bloc countries still have considerable gaps in the comprehensive social planning that socialist systems are endeavoring to achieve. Manpower and education planning, in particular, are lagging far behind the meticulous planning that exists in the production sphere.

3

Redistribution
in the legitimation sphere

A number of privileges in the redistribution sphere were seen to depend less on income differences and more on unequal distribution of power and participation in the lives of the cadres most actively involved in ideological matters. We must, therefore, also investigate redistribution in the political domain.

It is only in socialist countries that any kind of planned redistribution of political opportunities is to be found at all. Contrary to redistributive measures in the spheres of production and distribution, the very act of seizing power is, in itself, the most radical measure for the redistribution of political opportunities. No other change of regime (not even the change from a democratic-pluralist to a fascist regime) would normally entail such an entire replacement of elites. This assertion does, however, need to be modified for certain countries, where the new regime came to power under special circumstances. It is less applicable in systems that were not able to plan in terms of a complete changeover to socialism immediately and had to make allowances for very divergent groups that were not fully won over to socialism, such as in the German Democratic Republic and in Cuba.

Contrary to the case in bourgeois revolutions to date, the distribution of political opportunities in socialism is not merely aimed at straightforward substitution of the elites, but rather at radical equalization of participation opportunities for all those who approve the bases of a socialist constitution. Given the ideological primacy of politics, the political elite takes decisions on all processes, particularly during the first phase, even including the distribution of economic gratifications. Even the administrative elite—who are constantly gaining power also in organized capitalism—consider themselves much more of a political force in the "cadre administration" system than do traditional bureaucracies with their differing rational efficiency criteria, which are to be found most extensively in capitalism in state and industrial administration.[363] With the intertwinement of elites in the administrative, military, political, and economic sectors, this calls for even higher standards in democratic distribution of opportunities than in capitalism, where the "anarchy" of subsystem activities at least produces some rudimentary pluralism of elites capable of generating substantial conflict in all matters other than those affecting the establishment.

Even though the very aim of socialist systems is to achieve nonprofessionalized rule by politically committed amateurs, application of the strict Leninist cadre principle has the paradoxical effect of constantly bringing professionals to rule again. This results in a separation of roles among the population groups, precisely because the separation of competences is supposed to be in the process of being abolished.

Despite the radical redistribution of political opportunities, Leninist Party doctrine recognizes that there are several filters in society that diminish the de facto equality of opportunities:

1.   the filter of party membership;
2.   the filter of party office patronage;
3.   the filter of cooptation of elites.

1.   Filter of party membership

The statement that the majority of party members should be proletarians would be ideologically justifiable if it could be assumed that the overwhelming majority of all nations that have changed over to socialism were made up of "workers." The lower the development level in the first socialist countries, the easier was it to take this statement literally and even to apply it to manual work. However, just as in the field of education, the party could not prevent itself from being flooded with intellectuals, state employees, and employees from the developing services sector, although intense efforts were made to counteract the cleft between brainworkers and manual workers through polytechnical education, mass mobilization, and labor duties.

In none of the Communist parties that are in power in socialist countries does party membership exactly reflect the makeup of social classes and stratifications. However, the extent of the divergence between the stratification structure in the population and the social structure of party membership varies greatly. (See Table 48.)

In none of the three Communist parties that emerged most clearly as exponents of specific directions in Communism, that is, the C.P.S.U., the Communist Party of China, and the Yugoslav League of Communists, were workers' parties in their majority. Only China had a majority of manual workers in the 1950s, even though this was in the form of peasantry. In the Soviet Union, Poland, and Yugoslavia the party has increasingly become a party for the intelligentsia and state employees. In Yugoslavia, the farmers' majority position—similar to that in China—was superseded around 1952 when the employees came into the majority.

This was triggered by the partial reversal of collectivization which, in 1953, led to the exclusion of 39,500 farmers. In Yugoslavia, redistribution of political opportunities was also hampered by the fact that top party cadres were mostly recruited from the highest social strata, and, even among workers, the highly skilled workers dominated the majority of less-qualified workers.

A poll carried out in Croatia during investigations into the decline of farmer membership in Yugoslavia revealed that the farmers, when questioned about the reasons behind the drop in their party membership, felt that the main reason was that party membership had not brought them any benefits. The second reason they mentioned was their disappointment at the Government's agricultural policy.[364]

In Poland, too, the decline in farmer party membership (in 1945: 28.2%; in 1954 only 13.2%) ran parallel to decollectivization.[365]

The growing power of state employees brought on a problem of classification in Soviet sociography, because the intelligentsia and bureaucracy were not considered as a class. An expedient was devised

Table 48

Social structure of Communist parties
(in percentages)

Country	Year	Workers	Peasants	Intelligentsia & public employees	Pensioners	Others
				Social Groups		
Bulgaria	1975	41.1	23.6	30.0		5.0
Czechoslovakia	1975	45.2	5.0	31.0		18.8
Cuba	1972	12.0	28.0	40.0		15.0
GDR	1974	56.0	5.6	18.6		
	1980	56.9	4.7	31.6		6.8
Hungary	1975	58.3	14.2	27.5		
Mongolia	1975	31.3	19.0	49.7		
Poland	1976	40.9	9.3	22.3	7.2	
Rumania	1975	50.0	20.0	22.0		
Soviet Union	1971	40.1	15.1	44.8		
	1977	42.0	13.6	44.0		
Yugoslavia	1973	29.1	5.6	33.0	13.4	13.1

Sources: *Partinoe stroitelsvo,* 63, 4th ed. (Moscow: Mysl', 1971), p. 111; *Kommunisty mira—o svoikh partiyakh* (Prague: Mir i sotsializm, 1976), pp. 93 ff.; *Rocznik statystyczny 1978* (Warsaw: Glowny urzad statystyczny, 1978), p. 22; *DDR. Gesellschaft, Staat, Bürger* (Berlin (East), Staatsverlag der DDR, 1974), p. 18; *Einheit 1980.* No. 10, p. 1021; J. I. Dominguez, *Cuba, Order and Revolution* (Cambridge, Mass.: Belknap, 1978), p. 320.

with the term *prosloika* (intermediate stratum) and later on just *sloi* (stratum). This denoted the stratum that does not actually own a share in the means of production under capitalism either and which, in socialist systems, is involved in collective ownership of the means of production along with workers and peasants. The number of state employees (*sluzhashchie*) rose from 18.8 to 22.6% of the population between the 1959 and 1970 censuses, and these play an important role in the higher ranks of the party hierarchy.

In all other systems, the influence on the party of nonmembers is at most comparable to that of a pressure group, but with the difference that hardly any well-established opinion groups exist at all.

2.   Filter of party office patronage

Apart from the short period when left-wing social revolutionaries participated in the Soviet Government, there were only a
few people's democracies with multiparty block systems that did not
have a party monopoly when it came to the allocation of offices
and only had a strong party influence here. Even on a local level
(*oblast'* and *kraj*), over 99% of the chairmen of the local Soviet
executive Committees were party members as early as the 1930s,
and in the higher offices all were party members.[366] The nonparty
members who always played a certain numerical role in representative assemblies up to the Supreme Soviet (at times holding just
short of one third of the seats) were of no account in the executive.

The small percentage of the population organized in the party
(see Table 107) and the degree of monopolization in office distribution means that there is considerable distortion as far as equality
of opportunities is concerned. The radical redistribution of political
opportunities in favor of a new elite has not been accompanied by
greater scope for the bulk of the population to participate in these
political positions. Even in relatively democratic participation
systems, such as the Yugoslav workers' self-government, the number
of party members increases with the importance of the office, and,
in addition, specific qualifications are required that the average
worker cannot supply (see Chapter 10, Section 3).

A   similar   situation   exists   in   comparatively   unpolitical
hierarchies, such as in the armed forces. Even in Poland, where,
according to some experts, it may be better in career terms to be a
Pax member than a party member, Polish data indicates that almost
100% of the top posts are held by party members and that 72.7%
of all officers and 28.6% of officer cadets in the officers' schools
are party members.[367]

The interlinking of the production and politics spheres, which
is one of the aims of all socialist systems—even though a fully-
fledged system of councils has not developed anywhere—has thus
not led to sufficient political opportunities being kept open for
producers, although this should, in theory, have been possible
through the system.

Allocation of offices by the party to party members is not the
only means of control, however, in addition, there is control even
over the other cadres who are not necessarily obliged to be party
members, through the nomenclature and over the rank-and-file
workers who are not rated as cadres.[368]

Cumulation of party and public offices, which is typical in the top echelon of state leadership in most socialist systems (except in Yugoslavia), gives rise to particular problems when it comes to the succession of top functionaries. In the Soviet Union such struggles for succession among the elites occurred on several occasions, such as after Lenin's and Stalin's deaths, and in China there were even struggles while Mao was still alive. Hardly any fixed democratic rules have been developed for the game of succession in office.[369] It is regarded as sensational progress whenever permanent institutionalization of leadership is rejected, such as when Ceaucescu renounced election as Secretary General for life at the Eleventh Party Congress in November 1974, or again when Mao's name was not mentioned in the redraft of Article 15 of the Chinese constitution of January 1975, such that supreme command of the Army was not associated with him personally but with the function of party chairman instead. In countries where the party occasionally has to compete with other instruments of mobilization, such as in Cuba or China, the problems of succession will probably be even greater in the long run than in the highly institutionalized party systems.

3. Filter of cooptation of elites

A kind of negative theory of convergence has been established for capitalist and socialist systems on the basis of the principle of cooptation of elites, a principle that in socialist systems can be seen to range from sponsorship of new party members and their waiting and probation periods to the candidates in the Central Committee and other controlling bodies. The principle of democratic centralism was developed in the party organization,[370] and although it generally had damaging effects in the participation sector (see Chapter 10, Section 1), it appeared justified in times of struggle within the party. The question still remains, however, as to whether internal party democracy needs to be cut down as far as its present level in order to comply with this principle. Even the most rigid Leninist party principles will hardly suffice to justify why the Chinese Tenth Party Congress at the end of August 1973 took place in almost conspiratorial secrecy, without any announcement or publicity, so that its full outcome, not to mention the actual minutes of the discussions, was never published. It was only the new party statutes that pointed to the fact that significant programmatic changes of line had come about.[371]

Viewed in comparative terms, Western research with its tendency to stress *input* has produced the most quantitative data on recruitment of elites. Owing to a lack of details on decision-making processes, it has had to rely mainly on the *kto-kogo* (who against whom) *approach* when drawing conclusions about possible changes in the decision-making system. The extensive literature on elite recruitment[372] finds that disproportion in the distribution of political opportunities is similar to that in capitalist countries. Some of the disproportion has its origin in the revolutionary seizure of power process, as for example does the biased occupational makeup of the governing assemblies. The majority position occupied by elites who took part in the guerilla fight (in China these still made up 84.5% of the Central Committee in 1965)[373] means that there is a preponderance of men who have hardly received any education other than cadre schools. Despite a number of remarkable exceptions— men such as Chou En-lai, with a very broad education—the educational qualities of Chinese leadership seem to have been rather low compared, for example, with those of the early Soviet elite or the modernization elites found in many developing countries.[374]

During the consolidation period, gerontocratic tendencies develop in the elites of all socialist countries, such that, after a few decades, the generally held view of earlier elite research that revolutionary elites are on the average younger than democratically elected elites[375] undergoes a complete reversal. This, however, also holds true for some of the bourgeois-revolutionary movements. In the United States of America, Van Buren, elected in 1837, was the first President who did not directly belong to the ingroup of revolutionary elite.

Overrepresentation of certain regions that were significant in times of combat (in China, Mao's home province of Hunan[376]), underrepresentation of some nationalities, and underprivileging of women in leading positions (see Chapter 2, Section 2), are further disproportions to be criticized in all the elites of socialist countries.

From the few comparative studies that are available, it is possible to draw a number of conclusions about the general political line. These will not, however, provide more detailed insight into the differences and changes in the individual countries until such time as further data becomes available. Even if additional data was to hand, it is doubtful whether data on social background, for instance, would provide information on the various factions in the parties. Would it, for example, reveal whether the followers of Mao and Liu in China all shared the same social characteristics and career patterns, which were then reflected in their decision to support either the more marked political mobilization approach adopted by Mao or the more administrative-technocratic line of Liu?

Whereas greater correlation exists in socialist systems than in capitalist systems between the post a person holds and his actual power,[377] such that background material on the people in specific posts could potentially provide more information on their actual influence, this information would at best simply enable us to determine their actual behavior through speculation as to the position that certain elite factions hold in the "cryptopolitics" process that is kept from the public eye.[378]

In the initial phases of socialist systems, the nature of career mobility was an indicator of patronage within party groups. However, more recent quantitative studies on career mobility in the Soviet Union have come to the conclusion that the role of patronage in the cooptation of elites is overrated and that, nowadays, mobility decisions in cadre policy are based on efficiency and performance rather than on political criteria.[379]

Despite these three types of selection in the recruitment system (which when measured in terms of individual indicators have even more undemocratic consequences than in capitalist countries), this is less likely to lead to consolidation of the interests of specific groups than would a pluralistic process policy under capitalist conditions. There are a number of reasons for this:

1. *Mobilization and rotation* mean that a larger proportion of the population is involved in political processes than in capitalist systems. Even the Soviet Union with its highly bureaucratized recruitment patterns is, by comparison, a participatory system in many respects.

In top positions there is no more rotation than in capitalist systems, but rotation rates are higher at local level (see Table 49).

2. Socialization of public functions as a start to phasing out the state has not been very effective in any socialist country. Even in Chinese communes, decision-making processes are rarely spontaneous and are virtually always controlled by the party minority (see Chapter 10, Section 2).

In the socialist cadre system, however, there is less *professionalization of executive functions*. Nevertheless, even here complaints are still voiced repeatedly about reprofessionalization in politics, and empirical researchers have also had to confirm a lack of participation among unpaid activists and citizens.[380] Where the degree of profes-

Table 49

Rotation rate in Soviet political institutions, 1966–71
(in percentages)

Position	Rotation rate
CC Members	24
First Party Secretaries of the Union Republics	14
Obkom, First Secretaries	44
Gorkom, First Secretaries of the 50 largest cities	61
Rajkom, First Secretaries (in 10 Republics)	57

Source: J. F. Hough, "The Soviet System. Petrification or Pluralism?" *PoC*, No. 2 (1972),

sionalization is low—as in the local councils—the efficiency level of honorary work, which has to be done without any infrastructural facilities, is generally very low as well.

With the growing differentiation of certain roles, it is becoming increasingly difficult to apply the Chinese rotation system, that is, the "three-thirds system." Under this system, one third of functionaries work in production, one third are engaged in inspection and control work, and the other third do office work. All the same, the bonus on multifunctionality of executive functions is greater than in nonsocialist systems. This, however, is countered to some extent by one-sided specialist training—except where training in political work is concerned. In addition, the threat of demotion and transfer and, at very least, the constant ideological confrontation with an exaggerated glorification of manual work does present a check on any tendency toward professionalization.

3.   The interlinking of politics and economics means that the tendency toward cumulating gratifications is even greater in socialism than in capitalism. This holds true in particular for post-revolutionary periods that are marked by a serious scarcity of commodities and where privileges such as special stores for functionaries already produce disproportionately high privileging effects. This vertical privilege structure nonetheless leads to a lesser horizontal concentration of role interlinking and cumulation of privileges (a typical facet of class societies) than in most capitalist countries.[381] Even highly paid cadres are constantly menaced by purges and rotation. Moreover, they have no recourse to any pawns in the form

of ownership of means of production, no matter how great their power in controlling access to the means of production in monopolistic state socialism may be.

This insecurity factor was certainly strongest in China, where the "sending down" (*hsia fang*) system has taken on considerable proportions. At times this has still been aggravated by transitory concealed unemployment and by the difficulty of accommodating the surplus of university graduates (see Chapter 2, Section 3). "Sending down" is only offset to a small extent by "sending up" (*shang-fang*), and the disproportion will presumably grow greater as the level of special skills required for the higher jobs in technology, economics, and administration rises.

Even in the more complex systems, in which cadres are tending to become increasingly specialized and thus less interchangeable, the state's protective function does not extend to the protection of personally acquired rewards and to the maintenance of possessions, as is the case in capitalist democracy.

The problem of redistribution in the sphere of legitimation may be summarized as follows: despite the considerable success that socialist redistribution policy has scored, society still remains stratified in terms of status, income, and prestige hierarchies. Although the party is constantly working toward changing this,[382] society has repeatedly put its stratifying mark on many evident features of the party and its recruitment policy, even though the party's intention is to have a much more egalitarian structure.

II

EFFICIENCY

4

Efficiency
in the production sphere

Since the socialist countries have centrally planned and state-administered economies, the instruments available to them for achieving a deliberate increase in economic efficiency are quite different from those available to capitalist systems. The example of Cuba (that is, the expenditure breakdown of the Cuban state budget) shows most clearly how quickly economic development can become a central concern of national policy. The most important shift in state expenditure policy during Cuba's years of revolutionary change is the substitution of a government economic development policy to replace private investment (see Table 50).

Can this unparalleled concentration of effort toward increasing economic efficiency be set on a par with success in actually increasing efficiency in this field, however? This question calls for a certain consensus regarding efficiency criteria.

Whereas the distributive and redistributive capacity of socialism has always been greatly emphasized in the production sphere and has only recently been brought forward for the distribution sphere (along with the increase in the level of productive resources), efficiency has always been a point of controversy in systems comparison and in the rivalry between the different social formations.

Table 50

Expenditure breakdown of the Cuban state budget

(in percentages)

Category	1957-58	1963
development of the economy	—	41.6
municipal services and housing construction	12.4	4.6
culture, health, and social services	27.0	29.1
state administration	22.6	6.9
defense and security	25.7	10.2
public debt	10.7	6.1
reserves and other expenditures	1.4	1.5

Source: E. Strnad; *Der kubanische Staatshaushalt (vor und nach der Revolution)*. Ph.D. dissertation (Rostock: 1968), p. 110.

The toughest theoretical conflicts, however, are no longer found within the East–West systems controversy but rather within the socialist camp itself. In China, at the Tenth Party Congress held in 1973, Chou En-lai denounced the view that the country's main task consisted in developing production as a "heresy of the Lin Piao clique" and a "revised version of the absurd revisionist tattle that Lui Shao-ch'i and Chen Boda had smuggled into the resolution of the Eighth Party Congress."[383] This view certainly is no longer held by the Chinese party leaders.

Although capitalist and socialist economists agree that economic efficiency must be a major concern of state policy, the possibilities for measuring efficiency are still disputed. Efficiency comparisons mostly relate to the production sphere, even though capitalist economists also point out nowadays that the "welfare" of a country does not depend on economic variables alone but also on extra-economic indicators and a number of other social indicators, such as income distribution, which are frequently neglected in statistics.[384]

When it comes to the number of chief criteria for measuring success and efficiency, there is no consensus to be found on this in comparative economics. The indicators used most frequently are *static* efficiency (in the allocation of resources), *dynamic* efficiency (growth potential), and growth. The addition of income distribution as a fourth indicator from the distribution sphere is also accepted by socialist economists, but once we come on to the fifth indicator, that is, consumer satisfaction, agreement would seem to be diffi-cult,[385] particularly since the normative, subjective elements of assessment reduce the chances of achieving a consensus across the spectrum of social systems.[386]

Even if agreement is reached on the most important criteria, indicators, or indices, complex problems of methodology still arise when comparing efficiency. Customary index comparisons call for simplifications, and the selection of price levels means that the relative productivity coefficient of one country may appear advan-tageous when compared with another if the prices taken are those of the second country. This phenomenon, named after its discoverer, is called the Gerschenkron bias. The Gerschenkron bias results from a negative correlation between the production quantities being compared and their respective prices. It has its most marked effect in countries that have concentrated on producing goods at the lowest possible cost, such that when their aggregate output is converted into the higher prices of a second country it appears to be greater than when expressed in the country's own currency. For this reason, socialist economists also intend to use the international standard prices worked out by the United Nations as well.[387] Once these technically resolvable problems of comparison are overcome, there are still the problems of evaluation to be tackled. Even Soviet economists occasionally criticize the exaggerated statistics given for the national income growth index, and they are moving increasingly away from the "purely quantitative indices" used previously, search-ing for indices that also contain qualitative elements (such as national wealth, gross product, national income etc.). To avoid developing a fetish about statistical comparisons, however, it pays to keep Sherman's remarks in mind, when he stated that all comparisons of efficiency have to work with a "some heroic assumptions to reach any conclusions."[388]

Performance analysis in economics is taking an increasing number of indicators designed to measure both efficiency, in the strictest sense of the word, and the distributive and even partici-patory and protective capacities of a system. The systematic arrange-ment of this study is such that the distributive criteria of efficiency, such as income distribution, consumption distribution, and invest-ment (Chapter 2), the protective criteria of efficiency, such as job protection, health care, job alienation (Chapter 7), and the partici-patory criteria of efficiency, such as codetermination, freedom of job choice, and choice of place of work (Chapter 10) are dealt with in other chapters. This leaves us with the following most frequently used efficiency criteria in the production sphere:[389]

1.   growth;
2.   industrial output;
3.   labor productivity;
4.   growth, employment, and price stability;
5.   innovative capacity of the economic subsystem;
6.   occasionally the balance of payments, but the small volume of foreign trade in socialist economies means that this does not play as great a role as it does in capitalism.

1.   Growth

The most approximate, though most frequently used, indicator of economic efficiency is gross national product. Socialist states, however, use national income here (*nacional'nyi dochod*), which comes closest to the Western concept of national income, with the difference that it includes the indirect taxes levied by the state and does not include a large proportion of the services that are included in the capitalist concept of national income. Comparative studies have frequently committed the error of ignoring this difference. Comparisons of capitalist and socialist national incomes often come up against obstacles such as an insufficient allowance for depreciation in socialist countries, distortion in price structure through public subsidies, and the problems of converting the respective national currencies. Not even the socialist systems apply uniform calculation methods here.

Services account for about one quarter of the national income in capitalist systems, and these are growing faster than material production, such that in the past, statistical comparisons have often given capitalism an arithmetical advantage. The accuracy of statistics from socialist countries is questionable, on the other hand, since enterprises tend to magnify their production successes. Recently the bonus system has meant that enterprises are tempted to conceal the quality shortfall in many production sectors by the growth shown in their figures. In addition, even taking the usual growth indicators, the low level of development results in higher percentage growth rates. It is not by chance that Albania comes off rather well in growth comparisons of this type. Even Western economists differ in their estimates here, but their figures are generally below those given by socialist countries. One method that critics use to reduce the growth rates of socialist countries is to compare the goals set by the Plan with the figures actually achieved. This kind of comparison was useful in the time of Stalin, when the plans normally envisaged higher goals than were achieved.[390] This method is useful in tracing certain forms of socialist "wastage," and it shows that high rates of growth are not necessarily tantamount to economic efficiency of the system, as we also know from the experience of capitalist developing countries.

Even drawing a comparison with the Soviet Union after 1928, China demonstrates fairly rapid rates of growth. Since 1957, the GNP has had to be reconstructed by rather crude methods, since there were no sufficient data. One of the reasons for this may be the enormous fluctuations in GNP. During the Great Leap Forward between 1959 and 1961, the GNP fell by about 20%; the 1959 level was reached only in 1965. Though there are different estimations, most scholars agree that the average annual growth rate was about 6%. In the middle of the 1970s there was a downturn of economic performance as a result of political disruptions in 1974 and 1976, the Hopei earthquake in 1976, and poor weather in 1976 and 1977, rather than because of long-term structural causes such as misallocated investment resources, the burden of agriculture on the rest of the economy, and declining labor productivity.[391] Comparisons with OECD countries in their take-off phase are favorable for China but may be not quite fair for the other countries. In some respects (for instance GNP per capita), China seems to be a developing country; in other respects, China in the 1970s is remarkably modern; for instance, less than one quarter of China's GDP is derived from agriculture. Also, technology transfer makes comparisons with other systems in the nineteenth century not very telling.

Even drawing a comparison with the Soviet Union after 1928 would not be quite fair to China, because the Soviet Union was in some respects at a much higher level of development at the start of her intensified industrialization. The Soviet Union does not come off too badly in comparison of the take-off phases of the respective economies either (see Table 51). On the other hand, China's performance is considered more favorably when regional and sectoral development—especially the balance between agriculture and industry—is taken into consideration.[392] A comparison with Asian countries of a similar size and with similar climatic difficulties and population numbers may be informative here, such as a comparison with India. China is far ahead of India when it comes to absolute GNP figures as well as in terms of per capita national product, despite its higher population figures (see Table 52). Many Western economists believe

Table 51

Comparison between the development levels of the Soviet Union and the Reople's Republic of China

	Soviet Union		China	
	1928	1932	1952	1957
urban population (in millions)	28	36	67	91
labor force (in millions)	86	90	338	380
industrial workers (in millions)	10	19	19	25
per capita output of cereals (kg per person)	566	458	311	290
woollen clothing (m per person)	17.7	17.0	7.3	8.0
electricity (kw per 1000 industrial workers)	190	250	100	180
arable land per capita of the rural population (acre per person)	2.3	2.7	0.7	0.7

Source: K. C. Yeh, Soviet and Chinese Industrialization Stages. In: D. W. Treadgold (ed.), *Soviet and Chinese Communism. Similarities and Differences* (Seattle: University of Washington Press, 1970), p. 343.

that the prospects for rapid development are better for China than for India, where more traditional economic and cultural structures are being preserved.

Recent comparisons by Bergson suggest that the COMECON countries have neither surpassed nor lagged behind OECD countries but simply matched them. Comparisons of countries on both sides of the iron curtain that once were part of one state, such as the two German states and Austria on the one hand and Czechoslovakia and Hungary on the other, especially in productivity growth, are not too favorable for the socialist systems, and even the investment rates are not as superior in socialist countries as sometimes claimed[393] (see Table 56).

The capitalist countries that achieved growth rates that were as high as those of the socialist countries can be roughly divided into two groups:

1.   prosperous islands in the third world (Israel, Taiwan, etc.);

2.   defeated capitalist nations during the reconstruction phase after the Second World War (Japan, West Germany, Italy).

Growth rates of above 8% were obtained over comparable periods only by Japan (8.8%) and by a number of prosperous islands of capitalism in the third world such as Israel (10.1%) and Taiwan (1960-65: 9.6%). The oldest socialist industrial state, the Soviet Union, on the other hand, reached a respectable but not unmatched growth level of 6.2% between 1953 and 1964 (as compared with the Federal Republic of Germany 1950-65: 6.6%). Since Russia had already undergone a rapid capitalist development before the October revolution (Russia was, after all, the fifth-strongest industrial power in the world as early as 1913), a comparison can be made with the growth rates of the bourgeois period. Between 1917 and 1967, the Soviet national product increased by a factor of more than 50. Despite this, a number of economists in capitalist countries, such as Nutter, have come to the conclusion that growth rates during the Soviet era have, during certain periods, been below those achieved in Tsarist Russia,[394] even if the setbacks of the postrevolutionary period are left out of account. The Soviet Union regained its prewar output level in 1927/28. Nutter's views were harshly contradicted by Soviet economists[395] and statistics (see Table 53). Their arguments were based on the premise that Russia lagged relatively far behind, and to support this they frequently quote Lenin's paper on "How to Increase Per Capita Consumption in Russia?" in which he asks the question, "Why do we lag increasingly further behind?" It is not easy to resolve this controversy, since Nutter and the Soviet economists based their arguments mostly on different periods of time. Nutter extended his trend extrapolations over far longer periods than did his opponents. The basic assumption nevertheless remains hypothetical, even though, given Russia's raw-material and human resources, it cannot be completely excluded that under capitalist conditions Russia might have experienced as rapid a development as Japan.

Comparisons of Soviet growth with the growth of highly developed capitalist countries, which still tend to be rather popular in system comparisons today, are even more pointless. Comparing USSR and U.S. growth rates over identical periods of time is not very meaningful, because the two countries are at completely different stages of development. Any effort to make a historically fair comparison of the "contemporary in noncontemporaneity" will always involve certain arbitrary basic assumptions. To begin with, no consensus exists as to the indicators to be applied in measuring

Table 52

China's GNP and the growth of population

Year	GNP in billions of dollars	Percentage of change	Population (estimation) (1)	Population (estimation) (2)	Increase of population (1)	Increase of population (2)	GNP per capita in dollars (1)	GNP per capita in dollars (2)	Rate of change in BSP per capita in percentages (1)	Rate of change in BSP per capita in percentages (2)
1949	54.37		538		1.20		101.08			
1950	66.83	22.9	547		1.35		122.08		20.78	
1951	77.83	16.5	558		1.51		139.45		14.23	
1952	92.34	18.6	570		1.80		162.03		16.19	
1953	98.06	6.2	583		2.25		168.32		3.88	
1954	102.23	4.3	596	588	2.31		171.52	173.86	1.90	
1955	111.68	9.2	610	601	2.39	2.21	183.02	185.82	6.70	6.88
1956	120.75	8.1	625	614	2.43	2.16	193.16	196.66	5.54	5.83
1957	128.44	6.4	640	627	2.36	2.12	200.63	204.85	3.87	4.16
1958	152.98	19.1	655	642	2.26	2.39	233.49	238.29	16.38	16.32
1959	145.07	- 5.2	670	655	2.14	2.02	216.61	221.48	- 7.32	- 7.05
1960	141.02	- 2.8	683	667	1.82	1.83	206.44	211.42	- 4.70	- 4.54

Year										
1961	111.73	-20.8	695	679	1.53	1.80	160.85	164.55	-22.08	-22.17
1962	124.15	11.1	707	692	2.01	1.91	175.61	179.41	9.18	9.03
1963	139.42	12.3	722	705	2.12	1.87	193.15	197.80	9.99	10.25
1964	156.54	12.3	737	718	2.17	1.84	212.25	218.02	9.89	10.22
1965	174.28	11.3	754	732	2.26	1.95	231.14	238.09	8.90	9.21
1966	195.64	12.3	771	746	2.22	1.91	253.71	262.25	9.77	10.15
1967	187.67	- 4.1	789	759	2.30	1.74	237.95	247.26	- 6.21	- 5.72
1968	189.19	0.8	807	773	2.35	1.84	234.35	244.75	- 1.51	- 1.02
1969	210.07	11.0	827	787	2.39	1.81	254.14	266.93	8.44	9.06
1970	244.05	16.2	847	801	2.38	1.78	288.27	304.68	13.43	14.14
1971	260.90	6.9	867	815	2.31	1.75	301.02	320.12	4.42	5.07
1972	273.04	4.7	886	828	2.20	1.60	308.03	329.76	2.33	3.01
1973	308.14	12.9	906	841	2.10	1.57	340.22	366.40	10.45	11.11
1974	319.62	3.7	924	855	2.00	1.66	345.76	373.22	1.63	2.03
1975	341.54	6.9	943	869	1.98	1.64	362.18	393.03	4.75	5.14
1976	341.92	0.1	962	883	1.98	1.61	355.31	387.23	- 1.90	- 1.48
1977	372.80	9.0	983	896	2.26	1.47	379.44	416.07	6.79	7.45
1978	413.80	11.0	1,004	909	2.04	1.45	412.15	455.23	8.62	9.41

Sources: (1) A. G. Ashbrook, *Chinese Economy Post-Mao* (Washington: GOP 1978), p. 208.

((2) L. A. Orleans, "China's Population Growth. Current Scene." *Developments in Mainland China*, No 2/30 (1978), pp. 1–24.

W. Kraus, *Wirtschaftliche Entwicklung und sozialer Wandel in der Volksrepublik China* (Berlin [West]) : Springer, 1979), p. 527.

Table 53

Indices for the economic development of the Soviet Union compared to Czarist Russia
(1913 = 1)

	1913	1917	1940	1945	1950	1965	1970	1975	1979
national income	1	0.7	5.1	4.2	8.2	29	41	56	67
industrial production	1	0.7	7.7	7.1	13	61	92	131	157
"A"	1	0.8	13	15	27	142	214	311	378
"B" consumer goods	1	0.7	4.6	2.7	5.7	20	30	42	49
agricultural production	1	0.9	1.4	0.9	1.4	2.5	3.1	3.2	3.5
transport	1	0.8	3.9	3.0	5.7	22	30	41	47
railways	1	0.96	5.5	4.1	7.9	26	33	42	44
investment	1	–	5.7	5.3	11	50	72	100	116
employment	1	–	2.6	2.2	3.1	6.0	7.0	7.9	8.6
labor productivity	1	–	4.9	5.0	8.4	26	36	45	52
manufacturing	1	–	3.8	4.3	5.5	14.0	18.5	24.7	28.1
agriculture	1	0.9	1.9	1.3	2.1	4.0	5.3	5.7	6.5

Source: *SSSR v tsifrakh v 1979 godu* (Moscow: Statistika, 1980), pp. 40f.

the level of development, which is then to be divided up into its historical phases. Western economists generally consider per capita income, growth rate of per capita income, the share of the GNP allocated to investments, and the percentages of primary, secondary, and tertiary employment rates when determining development levels. But even a pioneer in the field of intersystem economic comparison, such as Simon Kuznets, has become increasingly sceptical about the serviceability of these indicators.[396] Supposing that the indicators are accepted, however, it then turns out that in certain sectors the Soviet Union has not yet reached the development level of the developed capitalist systems. If we include such an important factor as labor productivity—socialist economics attaches great importance to this indicator (see Chapter 4, Section 3)—then the Soviet Union's level of development comes out more-or-less equal to that of Italy and thus cannot be reasonably compared with the Federal Republic of Germany. This kind of comparison of indicators is inadequate for intersystem comparisons, even if only because certain factors are assumed to have the same impact on both social systems, even though it has been ascertained that the Soviet Union's impressive growth is due less to the increase of labor productivity—on which much verbal emphasis is placed—and more to the mobilizing power of the socialist system.

Occasionally the socialist systems derive a mathematical advantage because their planned population policy gives them better control than capitalist systems over population growth. Comparisons of the Soviet Union and the United States showed a more rapid population growth in the latter than in the former, which meant that per capita growth calculations turned out more favorably for the Soviet Union. On the other hand, since mobilization of the work force was more intense in the Soviet Union, the United States came off better in the growth-per-worker comparison and in the comparison of labor and capital factors, except during the periods between 1928 and 1937 and between 1950 and 1955.[397] (See Table 54.)

If despite these reservations we attempt to interpret figures for specifically delimited, comparable phases of development, Soviet performance still appears remarkable. However, it is not unique, because a number of capitalist countries reached similar growth rates (such as the United States and Australia at the end of the nineteenth century and Japan in the 1920s and 1930s). This growth was, however, accompanied by such a rapid increase in population that it would not turn out so favorably if converted into per capita growth rates.

Table 54

Gross national product

	Rank out of 135	GNP in $1,000,000	Growth rate 1960-65	Growth rate 1950-65
Soviet Union	2	313,000	6.4	6.2
China	7	76,000		
Poland	11	30,800	6.0	6.6
Czechoslovakia	13	22,100	2.0	5.1
GDR	15	21,546		
Rumania	22	14,800	8.5	9.5
Hungary	25	11,100	4.4	5.7
Yugoslavia	30	8,800	8.3	8.9
Bulgaria	35	6,800		
Cuba	49	3,000		
North Korea	56	2,500		
North Vietnam	60	1,900	2.7	4.3
Albania	88	700	7.0	6.9
Mongolia	103	500		
for comparison:				
United States	1	695,500	4.6	3.7
FRG	2	112,232	4.7	6.6
Japan	6	84,347	9.2	8.8
Italy	8	56,947	5.0	5.4
India	9	49,220	3.0	3.7
Brazil	14	21,970	4.3	5.2
Sweden	16	19,714	4.9	3.8
Mexico	17	19,432	5.8	5.9
Spain	19	17,743	8.0	6.0

Sources: Taylor-Hudson, op. cit, p. 306 ff.: for Cuba: *Cuba 1968. Supplement to the Statistical Abstract of Latin America* (Los Angeles, Latin American Center, University of California 1970).

There are only a few countries (such as South Africa and Japan) that could stand up to comparison with the Soviet Union here, and in the case of a number of smaller countries (such as Sweden), the growth rates appear in a particularly favorable light when converted into per capita growth.[398] The human costs expended to achieve this good result during certain periods in the development of Japan and South Africa cannot, however, be rated so much more positively than the costs of the Stalinist development. (See Table 55.)

Comparisons of the growth rates attained during the socialist era and those obtained during bourgeois eras in Eastern European countries turn out only in part in favor of the socialist system, although the socialist lead is not spectacular everywhere. In Hungary, for instance, annual growth in national income rose from 4.8% under the bourgeois regime (1933/34, 1937/38) to 6.8% (1966-70) and 5.8% (1971/72).[399] In recent times a certain slackening of the growth rate is to be observed in nearly all Eastern European countries. This is especially true for the German Democratic Republic, which, when compared with the other people's republics severely affected by the War, such as Poland and Czechoslovakia, clearly lagged behind initially in terms of investment and had not recovered its prewar level of national income by 1950, as had the others. One burden was that of the occupation costs in the German Democratic Republic, which were much higher than those of any other country and which meant that one fifth of the net national product still went as factor costs in the early 1950s, accounting for some 26.1% of production in 1946/47, before the foundation of the state, as compared to 15.9% and 12.7% in the American and British zones.[400]

Per capita investment in socialist countries has, on the whole, remained constantly proportional to the countries' development level. Apart from per capita investment, the aggregate mass of investment plays a role as well, and in big states such as the Soviet Union and China, this intervenes as an important variable even when per capita investment appears to be relatively below that of smaller countries.

Consequently, there is no clear-cut causal relationship between political regime and economic growth. Even highly reactionary systems such as Spain have reached growth rates similar to those of the socialist countries (1960-65: 8%). Here, of course, the particular advantages of Spain's tourist boom need to be taken into account. Moreover, there is not much point in referring to isolated spectacular successes in capitalist regimes, because there will always be plenty of deviant examples to hand proving the very opposite. This is very different from the socialist camp, where average growth rates are

Table 55

Per capita gross national product

Country	Rank out of 135 countries	Per capita GNP in dollars	Growth 1960–65	Growth 1950–65	Growth 1970–75
Czechoslovakia	17	1561	1.1	4.2	
Soviet Union	20	1357	5.0	4.9	3.1
GDR	22	1260			
Hungary	25	1094	4.0	5.3	
Poland	27	978	4.8	5.1	
Bulgaria	30	829	7.7	8.4	
Rumania	31	778	1.7	1.3	
Mongolia	46	453			2.3
Yugoslavia	47	451	5.9	7.2	
Cuba	52	393			
Albania	55	366	4.0	3.8	
North Korea	82	207			0.9
China	98	109			5.3
North Vietnam	103	100			
for comparison:					
United States	1	3575	3.2	2.0	1.6
Sweden	3	2549	4.2	3.1	
FRG	12	1901	3.4	5.5	
Austria	21	1278	3.5	4.7	
Italy	24	1104	4.2	4.7	
Japan	28	861	8.2	7.8	4.0
Spain	39	561	7.2	5.1	
Mexico	45	455	1.8	2.4	
Portugal	51	406	5.5	4.2	
Taiwan	73	227	6.4	4.5	
South Vietnam	91	150	2.2	2.2	
South Korea	100	105	4.7	2.9	
India	101	101	0.6	1.7	

Source: Taylor-Hudson, op. cit., pp. 314 f. *World Bank Atlas,* 1977, p. 6.

high for all countries in the group. This holds true even for such highly developed countries as Czechoslovakia, which experienced periods of stagnation, like its capitalist neighbors (1960-1965: 2%) but nevertheless attained a long-term growth rate of 5.1% (1953-1965) (see Table 53).

It must, however, be pointed out that socialist countries were at a serious disadvantage compared with their capitalist neighbors, because they had:

1.   no starting-up aid from the Marshall plan;
2.   no capital investment from financially powerful states;
3.   high destruction rates during the war;
4.   the capitalist states' embargo policy toward the Warsaw Pact.

Even when these disadvantages are taken into account, the theory put forward in socialist economies to the effect that socialism, by its very nature, creates higher growth rates,[401] is untenable. Even if this were true, it could not be automatically assumed that a higher growth rate means higher efficiency, because efficiency assessments have to be based on far more sophisticated calculations than do simple comparisons of growth rate.

In order to improve the value of the growth rate as an indicator, it needs to be set against the *investment rate*, and in this respect socialist countries—with a few exceptions, such as the Federal Republic of Germany—have been well ahead of most capitalist countries since the Second World War.

Only the German Democratic Republic remained below the level of the Federal Republic of Germany's investment figures. On the whole, it can be said that socialist countries not only managed to mobilize a greater labor force but also spent a greater proportion of their national income on investment. However, the sharp reduction in consumption can hardly be explained simply through the different degrees of accumulation in socialist states (see Chapter 2). Where a higher degree of efficiency seems to be achieved on average by socialist countries compared to capitalist countries (measured solely in terms of "growth rate"), this has, in fact taken a high toll in economic and social costs—as was the case in the accumulation phase of early capitalism. (See Table 56.)

In the production sphere, these costs consisted in:

1.   *misallocation of resources* and forms of "socialist wastage of capital," due to a somewhat one-sided interpretation of the labor theory of value—capital goods did not have a "value"

Table 56

Gross investment as a percentage of the GNP
(accumulation fund—1979—in percentage of the national income)

Country	1950–54	1955–59	1960–63	1955–66	1970	1979
Bulgaria	23.7	27.7	41.5	34.0	29.2	22.8
Czechoslovakia	23.5	27.3	27.7	25.2	27.0	24.6
GDR	14.5	19.4	23.6	20.7	24.4	20.1
Hungary	25.9	24.2	27.2	23.9	24.9	25.6
Mongolia					32.7	38.6
Poland	21.1	25.1	28.1	25.5	25.1	25.1
Soviet Union				26.6	29.5	24.9
Eastern Europe (average)	21.7	24.7	29.6	26.0		
for comparison:						
FRG	21.1	24.3	26.4	24.6		
France	18.1	20.3	21.7	20.5		
Italy	19.7	22.4	25.6	20.8		
Western Europe (average)	19.1	21.2	24.1	21.1		

Sources: M. Ernst, Postwar Economic Growth. In: US Congress Joint Economic Committee, *New Directions in the Soviet Economy* (Washington, D.C.: G.O.P., 1966) (873–916), p. 890; figures for 1979: *Statistichestkii ezhegodnik stran-chlenov SEV 1980* (Moscow: Statistika, 1980), p. 46, colums 5 and 6; A. Bergson, *Productivity and the Social System. The USSR and the West* (Cambridge, Mass.: Harvard U.P., 1978), p. 207 (column 4).

that could be calculated in money terms, interest-like surcharges for capital goods were tabooed as being "capitalist"; only with the "flowback time"—that is, the time required for an investment to show a saving in labor—did Soviet planners conduct what were at least indirect interest calculations; Yugoslavia was the first socialist country to introduce a 6% charge on capital goods in 1954, and in the 1960s all Eastern European countries except Albania and Rumania went on to follow this example;

2. *overstraining the workers* through all-too-frequent mobilization of the masses (see Chapter 12, Section 2);
3. *underdevelopment of the management sciences* and the temptation for people to avoid taking on responsibility, as a result of the overcentralization of the decision-making process, to "commandism," and to the neglect of modern methods in the training of economic management executives (input-output calculation, and similar); however, as these deficiencies have gradually been made up by strengthening the autonomy of the subsystems and improving managerial training, socialist systems have come to overtax their managers with mental and physical stress in the same way as seen in capitalist systems;[402]
4. *intensified urbanization* (except in China and Cuba);
5. new forms of *damage to the environment* (see Chapter 8, Section 4);
6. *neglect of consumption* during the accumulation phase—it has become evident, however, that this is not a permanent evil of socialism (see Chapter 5): in the early 1970s the Soviet Union planned for the first time to allow the consumption fund to grow faster than the accumulation fund;
7. *neglect of the other* (protective, participatory, and redistributive) *goals of socialism* and too great a subordination of these to efficiency-minded reasoning based on quantitative performance concepts.

2. Industrial and agricultural output

Through its planning socialism is said to have a greater capacity for keeping the various sectors of the economy in balance. Socialist planners, however, have been anything but adherents to the theory of balanced growth, and only in more recent publications by Eastern European socialist economists has this theory come to be given greater credit at all.[403] The promotion of heavy industry has been given top priority, with a "tribute" being placed on agriculture or the consumers in varying patterns, except in Cuba and China after Soviet influence had been phased out. When it comes to comparisons of industrial output, socialist countries generally come off very well in terms of world standards. Comparisons with the industrial output of capitalist countries, however, are even more problematical than comparisons of gross national product. An additional difficulty encountered in calculation stems from the fact that socialist statistics do not usually include the building sector (see Chapter 8, Section 3).

Hence, the usual industrial output figures quoted for agitatorial purposes (such as 1961 to 1972: 9.9% annual growth in industrial production in the Soviet Union as opposed to 5.2% in the developed capitalist countries[404]) need to be examined very cautiously. The statistics of socialist countries, with their emphasis on gross industrial output (especially when expressed in domestic currency prices), tend to make performance appear higher than it actually is. There has even been talk of a "gross-gross output concept" in socialist countries, because calculation factors are frequently duplicated by the fact that at each production stage the input value taken over by other enterprises is included in the statistical calculation of industrial output. Capitalist countries, on the other hand, try to take only the value added at each stage and to exclude internal transactions within enterprises. Consequently, comparisons of output statistics will give socialist economies certain mathematical advantages that do not exist as far as the consumer of the finished product is concerned. Only in recent Soviet statistical works have attempts been made to avoid the distortion effect of output calculations in socialist countries and to give enterprises plan targets based on the volume and quality of production achieved, instead of on gross production figures.

Socialist statisticians developed a certain preference for the gross production index earlier on for three reasons:

1.   These statistics *profit from a certain form of "socialist extravagance,"* since the extent of what is often excessive capital input is not taken into account and the question as to whether goods produced are actually used or not does not arise because of the extremely limited degree of consumer freedom.[405]

2.   The *calculation of materials twice over* in different units is generally not eliminated.

3.   The *agricultural activities* in the economy, which show a considerably slower growth rate than the industrial activities, are not taken into account.[406]

In the first phase after the Revolution there was a significant drop in the output figures. The gross output of industry in the Soviet Union had only reached one third of its prewar level by 1923 (see Table 52). Hence, opponents of socialism had an easy job when it came to comparing efficiency in the revolutionary period with systems that had not experienced such political breaks. These initial losses were smaller in the case of the people's democracies that turned to socialism after the Second World War. According to data supplied by statistical offices and according to Western economists' own calculations, Czechoslovakia and Poland reached their prewar output at around 1948/49, and even the German Democratic Republic, with its handicaps in the start-up period, attained its 1936 output level by 1950 and its peak pre-1945 output in 1944 by 1955.

The industrial output growth rates were most impressive, however, in the least developed countries such as China, Albania, Rumania, and Mongolia. The data widely used for propaganda purposes are less when they are confronted with the average annual growth rates of industrial production in capitalist countries (see Table 57, last columns).

The Comecon figures also show that the annual growth rate for gross industrial production is slowing down with the increasing level of development. Poland and Czechoslovakia constitute a temporary exception to this rule in the Comecon statistics. (See Table 58.)

The growth rates in the individual branches of industry are on average considerably less uniform and subject to greater chronological fluctuation than in capitalism. This results in part from the political setting of priorities, with the exception of a number of fluctuations in agriculture.

Hirschman's thesis that developing countries lack the ability to make decisions and the ability to invest cannot be applied to socialist developing countries such as the Soviet Union and China during the transformation phase. All socialist countries show a tendency toward overinvestment in certain sectors, particularly in machine building, which threatens to create unpredicted disparities.[407] (See Table 59).

The late industrializers, and especially the socialist countries with a planned development strategy at their disposal, generally have the advantage of being able to adopt superior technologies. As a rule, this is reflected in an acceleration of output in the machine-building sector as compared with other industrial output. Despite particularly harsh starting conditions, China also achieved better results over certain periods than did countries at a comparable level of development at an earlier stage, both under capitalist and socialist systems.

However, not all sectoral disparities and fluctuations are the result of judicious setting of priorities by the political leadership. Some of them stem instead from mobilizational self-hypnosis. In Cuba too, intensified industrialization trends were in evidence to start with, but these were checked again in the 1960s, as can be seen

Table 57

Average annual growth rates of gross industrial production
(in percentages) (1950 = 1)

Country	1950–57	1961–65	1966–70	1971–75	1976–78	1979
Albania	20.4					29
Bulgaria	14.3	11.7	10.9	9.1	6.8	23
China	26.9					31
Cuba				8.5	4.7	2.0[1]
Czechoslovakia	10.8	5.2	6.7	6.7	6.2	8.2
GDR	11.8	5.8	6.5	6.5	5.1	8.9
Hungary	12.5	7.5	6.2	6.2	5.5	8.6
Mongolia		9.8	9.9	9.2	6.1	15
Poland	14.8	8.4	8.3	10.4	7.0	15
Rumania	13.5	13.8	11.9	12.9	11.1	31
Soviet Union		8.6	8.5	7.4	5.1	12

for comparison:

France						3.9
GFR						5.2
Italy						6.2
Japan						3.9
United Kingdom						2.1
United States						3.4

(1) 1955 = 1

Sources: *Der okonomische Wettbewerb zwischen der UdSSR und den USA* (Berlin (East): Die Wirtschaft, 1961), p. 117. *Statisticheskii ezhegodnik stran chlenov SEV 1979* (Moscow: Statistika, 1979), p. 67; *SSSR v tsifrakh v 1979 g* (Moscow: Statistika, 1980), p. 63.

from the distribution of investment. Whereas Castro avoided a bias in favor of industry, he did tend to exaggerate his agricultural goals (see Table 60).

Mobilization regimes that wanted to incite their populations to put in a special effort at times even set themselves unrealistic targets for propaganda purposes. The most spectacular case of this is probably the magically exaggerated 10-million-ton limit that Castro endeavored to attain in 1970, in an unparalleled mobilization campaign. The target could not be reached, and all other sectors of the economy suffered repercussions. Only in 1971 did Cuba learn from its mistake and come up with the slogan: *"La zafra y todo lo demás"* ("harvest sugar and do everything else as well"), a slogan inciting overwork that can only lead to short-term success, all the same. These one-sided attempts to maximize a single target are, in fact, due in part to the pressure from the capitalist world system. This certainly holds true in the case of Cuba, where the United States' embargo was a hindrance to a more reasonably balanced policy and to the efforts to achieve economic diversification.

These unrealistic output targets occurred not only in the agricultural sector where forecasts are problematical at all times. Some socialist countries also misallocated their resources through investments in costly industrial projects based on coal and steel. Planners such as Ernö Gerö in Hungary and Hilary Minc in Poland were the most ambitious when it came to creating costly iron and steel collective combines. Some of these plants, such as Nowa Huta in Poland, the Klement Gottwald combine near Moravská Ostrava

Table 58

Index numbers of industrial production
(1970 = 100)

Country	1960	1970	1977
Bulgaria	34	100	175
Czechoslovakia	56	100	154
GDR	55	100	116
Hungary	51	100	150
Poland	44	100	193
Romania	30	100	230
Soviet Union	44	100	159
Yugoslavia	45	100	167
for comparison:			
France	59	100	126
FRG	59	100	116
Italy	50	100	123
United Kingdom	77	100	106
United States	61	100	129

Source: United Nations, *Statistical Yearbook 1978* (New York: UN, 1979), 162ff.

in Czechoslovakia, and the Stalinváros combine (later called the Dunaujváros combine) in Hungary were initially low-profit prestige developments that were later criticized increasingly openly even within the people's democracies as "monuments" of a misconceived form of industrialization following the Soviet model.[408] According to critics, the Bulgarian combine of Kremikovtsi is even said to have been fitted with relatively outdated equipment by the Soviets. Only its Rumanian counterpart in Galati, which was equipped with the most advanced Western machinery, developed rapidly into a profitable business.[409]

When comparing output indicators, we are faced with the difficulty of measuring the quality of production. Western economists rated quality as rather mediocre in the 1950s, and not without good reason. The Eastern bloc economists, on the other hand, who were

Table 59

Growth rates in machine building
(in percentages)

Country	Years	Growth rate
China	1952–57	31.1
	1957–66	12.3
	1952–66	18.6
Soviet Union	1927/28–37	26.0
	1952–58	11.0
	1937–58	8.0
India	1951–66	17.6
	1956–67	14.7
	1951–67	15.6
Japan	1946–51	30.8
	1952–60	20.5
	1960–66	10.1
	1953–66	15.1

Source: Ch. -Y. Cheng, *The Machine Building Industry in Communist China* (New York: Aldine, 1971), p. 228.

Table 60

Distribution of Cuba's investment by sectors
(in percentages)

Sectors	1963	1964
agriculture	32.6	36.0
industry	29.4	26.0
transport and communications	5.5	7.5
building	11.2	7.5
education and culture	7.7	5.5

Source: E. Strnad, *Der kubanische Staatshaushalt. (vor und nach der Revolution)*. Ph. D. dissertation (Rostock: 1968), p. 116.

still caught up in their tonnage ideology, were at first delighted by simple increases in quantity. The number of awards won at world exhibitions can hardly be accepted as counterevidence in the day-to-day production for the domestic market in the 1950s.

Social consequences are of even greater importance than the mere level of output. Socialist economy prides itself on not even knowing surplus production crises. This sort of sweeping statement has been modified in the meantime. As even Marxists admit, there may indeed be overproduction of unsaleable consumer goods in socialist systems, but not overproduction of capital goods.[410] Thus, the fault is again put down to the purely motivational aspect. But could not this misdirected motivation on the part of socialist planners also lead to overproduction of capital goods, or at least to misallocated investments? This doubtlessly happened when giganto-mania led to the construction of the first rolling mills and other industrial objects of prestige. These could only be converted into more profitable operations at the cost of additional investments later on.

Even though socialist countries are to some extent faced with problems of overproduction (though not nearly to the same extent as capitalist economies), there is no overproduction as yet in the agriculture and food sector—in marked contrast to the experiences of the EEC countries in the West. As far as agriculture is concerned, the socialist countries have had to contend with the very opposite problem, namely, with undersupply and insufficient productivity. Whereas the socialist countries' industrial balance can clearly be rated positively, the same cannot be said for agriculture. In eight European socialist systems the national income, at 8%, was 3% above the world average, and the industrial income, at 10%, was 4% above this average. The agricultural output of 4%, on the other hand, reflected the world average. Set against important comparable countries, this tends to give rather an unfavorable picture of socialist agriculture. Consequently, allowance must be made for the share of agriculture in the GNP before generalizing about growth in socialist countries, because agriculture makes up a much bigger share in many of these than in the capitalist system that is used as comparison. This should not, however, lead to the mistake of considering a high share of agriculture as being identical with underdevelopment. The cases of New Zealand, Denmark, or the Netherlands would immediately shatter such an overhasty conclusion.

The role of agriculture in socialist systems is also important to some extent because it had to pay a "tribute" to intensified industrialization, which meant that it made a much greater contribution to growth than is reflected in its sectoral growth rates, particularly since agriculture was the sector that benefited least from the stimulating linkage-effect of the rapidly growing machine industry. Even in China, where agriculture accounted for a major part of the national product at the end of the first plan in 1957, 70% of machinery output was absorbed by the industrial sector and by the defense system.[411]

In the Soviet Union, for example, the increase in agricultural output was not attained by intensification, but by "extensification" and expansion of arable land. None of the other socialist countries could have imitated this strategy, because all of them—with the exception of China—already possessed a considerably greater portion of arable land, which could not be expanded without involving even more disproportionate investment than in the Soviet Union. (See Table 61.)

Of all the countries that became socialist after the Second World War, the People's Republic of China was keenest on reclaiming land, but even so it was only able to increase its percentage of arable land from 10.2 to 11.2% between 1949 and 1958.

Even though land reclamation schemes initially seemed to be a success, the socialist developing countries, especially, found that their capacity to reclaim land with *shturmovshchina* and special operations exceeded their subsequent capacity, and hence part of the reclaimed land returned to decay.

None of the younger socialist countries has neglected agriculture in favor of industry to the same extent or placed as high a

Table 61

Land utilization (1966)

| | Utilized surface area | | Surface | Permanent |
	1,000 hectares	Percentage surface area	area ploughed	pastures & grassland
Albania	1.230	42.8	40.7	59.3
Bulgaria	5.802	52.3	78.7	21.3
Czechoslovakia	7.144	55.9	75.2	24.8
GDR	6.423	59.5	77.6	22.4
Hungary	6.927	74.4	81.5	18.5
Yugoslavia	14.716	57.5	56.2	43.8
Poland	19.947	63.8	78.6	21.4
Rumania	19.335	81.5	77.6	22.4
Soviet Union	614.100	27.4	39.2	60.8
China (1958)		15.28	11.4	27.78
for comparison:				
United States	440.201	47.0	40.9	59.1
Great Britain	19.587	80.3	38.2	61.8

Sources: *FAO Production Yearbook 1967;* G. Schöpflin (ed.), *The Soviet Union and Eastern Europe* (London: Blond, 1970), p. 24; L. T. C. Kuo, *The Technical Transformation of Agriculture in Communist China* (New York: Praeger, 1972), p. 34.

tribute on the peasants as did the Soviet Union. But China again only adopted the slogan of "walking on two legs" and providing for symmetrical development of agriculture and industry after she had experienced various adjustment difficulties. Up to the point of the Great Leap Forward, a comparison of Chinese and Soviet investments at the beginning of industrialization reveals a similar pattern in both countries. (See Tables 62 and 63.)

China also had to pay for her one-sided preference for heavy industry during certain periods of the accumulation phase. In the First Five-Year Plan, investment in heavy industry represented 49%, light industry 7%, transportation and communication 18.7%, and other sectors 17.1%, whereas agriculture only made up 8.2%.[412] As a consequence, mechanization progressed rather slowly. As late as 1960, only some 5% of the land was cultivated by machines and 15% by semimechanical methods. (See Table 64.)

Table 62

Agricultural and industrial shares in gross domestic product in a cross-systemic comparison (around 1965) and in national income of socialist countries in 1979
(in percentages)

Country	Rank out of 106 around 1965	Agri- culture	Indus- try	The whole economy		Industry & construction		Agriculture		Transport & communication		Non- production basic funds	
				1960	1978	1960	1978	1960	1978	1960	1978	1960	1978
North Vietnam	9	57											
Albania	20	43											
China	23	40	18										
Bulgaria	31	34	45	52.2	67.6	20.6	37.5	13.8	11.6	16.8	15.3	47.8	32.4
Rumania	43	30	48	58.3	74.8	29.3	47.1	14.9	11.1	12.0	12.6	41.7	25.2
Yugoslavia	45	29	38										
Poland	61	23	51	48.8	64.1	17.1	32.5	17.1	15.9	10.1	10.3	51.2	35.9

Soviet Union	66	22	52	57.0	65.3	26.6	34.2	13.8	13.7	13.4	13.6	43.0	34.7
Hungary	72	20	58	53.8	62.3	19.6	29.4	7.7	11.9	19.1	16.0	46.2	37.7
Czechoslovakia	82	13	65	63.7	66.2	33.6	37.2	7.0	8.5	19.1	15.5	36.3	33.8
GDR	82	13	74	49.9	65.9	30.2	44.1	6.1	8.2	10.2	9.7	50.1	34.1
Mongolia				74.3	68.4	15.8	26.9	28.9	23.5	27.2	13.5	25.7	31.6
for comparison:													
India	12	51	18										
Spain	70	21	30										
Japan	85	12	29										
FRG	103	5	45										
United States	105	4	34										
Great Britain	106	3	41										

Sources: Ch. L. Taylor & M. C. Hudson (ed.), *World Handbook of Political and Social Indicators* (New Haven: Yale U.P., 1972), pp. 338 ff.; *Statisticheskii ezhegodnik stran-chlenov SEV 1979* (Moscow: Statistika 1979), pp. 52f.

Table 63

Land distribution in China
(in percentages)

Type of land	Percentage	
arable land	15.3	
cultivated		11.4
uncultivated		3.8
forests	7.9	
land fit for afforestation	31.2	
grassland	27.8	
deserts and wasteland	17.8	

Source: L. T. C. Kuo, *The Technical Transformation of Agriculture in Communist China* (New York: Praeger, 1972), pp. 34 and 229.

In socialist countries with a low level of productive resources, governments had great trouble in getting their populations to accept technology, not only by reason of the scarcity of means, but also because of the motivational idiosyncrasies of some of the peasants. Although the Great Leap Forward is presented as a campaign that familiarized the masses with technology (even if the utility effect of the small blast furnaces was admittedly not very high), it also gave rise to a new wave of hostility toward technology in agriculture. Local cadres frequently stigmatized mechanization as a "Western capitalist superstition," and agricultural "prophets" appeared as defenders of traditional farming methods. Some economists have concluded from these difficulties in international comparison that even if China were measured against a number of capitalist developing countries (such as the Philippines, Pakistan, and Thailand), the efficiency increase in Chinese agriculture would not be particularly impressive because of the frequent zig-zag course adopted.[413]

Output comparisons of Chinese and Soviet agriculture—which have been carried out more frequently—must not overlook the fact that in 1949, at the end of the Revolution, China had a much lower percentage of workers employed in big industry than the Soviet Union had had before starting industrialization. In 1926, the figure was 1.9% of the population in the Soviet Union, as against 0.2 to 0.55% in China in 1949.[414]

Expressed in absolute figures, China had more factories in the 1950s than the Soviet Union had had around 1928, and China achieved remarkable results by concentrating temporarily on her coastal regions, with a less well developed transport system and a poorer raw-material situation than the Soviet Union had had.[415]

Social scientists analyzing the efficiency of systems have kept searching for further indicators that would allow rapid measurement of growth and efficiency and eliminate the problems of data collection, together with errors that inevitably occur when several indicators are combined. This search resulted in the discovery that, according to calculations effected by McClelland, the quantity of electrical energy consumed correlates with a large number of other factors and even with performance indicators measured by data drawn from a textbook analysis.[416] Marxists ought to have no objection to this method, which is in line with Lenin's dictum that "socialism = Soviet power plus electricity." Today, of course, overall energy consumption would be a more useful indicator: firstly, because taking electricity production alone would favor certain countries such as Austria and Italy that have coal and hydroelectric power, and secondly, because other sources of energy are gaining more and more importance.

Table 64

Breakdown of public capital investment by sectors in the Soviet Union (1928/29–37) and in China (1953–57)

(in percentages)

	Soviet Union		China
	1928–32	*1953–57*	*1953–57*
industry	40.9	39.3	47.9
agriculture	19.2	15.5	14.9
transport and			
communications	18.4	16.7	15.1
other	21.5	28.6	22.1
housing construction	9.0	8.7	7.3

Source: K. C. Yeh: "Soviet and Chinese Industrialization Strategies." In: D. W. Treadgold (Edit.): *Soviet and Chinese Communism. Similarities and Differences* (Seattle: University of Washington Press. 1970), p. 334.

If socialist systems are measured by this indicator, which is surely more informative than the output growth indices for a large number of other production sectors, then two socialist countries (Czechoslovakia and the German Democratic Republic) are found to rank among the five top nations of the world with respect to per capita energy consumption. Other systems in the socialist camp, like Bulgaria with 14.3% per capita growth in energy consumption from 1950 to 1965, recorded the highest growth rates in the world. This group includes China, which, despite a setback after the Great Leap Forward, had an average growth rate of 10.6% between 1950 and 1965. (See Table 65.)

One should not, however, be overhasty and conclude that a high per capita energy consumption necessarily implies a high level of efficiency. During the transitional period, a number of socialist economies were characterized by high energy consumption as a form of "socialist extravagant waste," while consumption in private households was low (as there was an insufficient number of kitchen appliances). Hence, other indicators also need to be taken into consideration in order to measure efficiency.

To sum up, it can be said that the growth of industrial output alone is not very informative as an efficiency criterion. This is due to the fact that:

1. the usual index figures do not reflect the *level of investment* or the labor input—forms of socialist extravagance often constitute the reverse side of the coin;
2. social systems, despite their disdain for the dominant exchange value factor in capitalism, have also been guilty in their own way of *neglecting the question of the utility value* of goods produced.

During periods when labor productivity was on the increase in the Soviet Union, capital productivity was far from keeping pace. Consequently, critics of socialist planned economy have attributed a good number of growth successes to the regime's dictatorial power to mobilize capital at the expense of consumption and to use inexhausted labor reserves, rather than to the virtues of the system. This verdict, however, is very much conditioned by the Western approach of separating out the economic and political subsystems. One of the alleged qualities of the socialist system does lie, however, precisely in the fact that this schematic separation is abolished and that socialist governments possess a higher mobilizing power than do capitalist governments.

Table 65

Energy consumption

Country	Rank out of 129 countries	Per capita consumption 1976	Per capita in kilograms (1965)	Per capita growth rates 1960–65	Per capita growth rates 1950–65
Czechoslovakia	4	7,397	5,676	3.5	4.3
GDR	5	6,789	5,460	3.2	3.4
Soviet Union	14	5,259	3,611	4.9	4.9
Poland	16	5,253	3,504	2.5	2.3
Hungary	21	3,553	2,812	6.0	7.0
Bulgaria	26	4,710	2,571	13.7	14.3
Rumania	31	4,036	2,035	7.4	9.9
Yugoslavia	36	2,016	1,192	6.2	7.1
Cuba	40	1,225	950	2.3	4.6
Mongolia		1,166			
Albania	63	867	347	2.6	8.0
China	57	706	461	6.1	10.6
for comparison:					
United States	2	11,544	9,201	2.7	1.7
FRG	11	5,396	4,234	2.8	3.1
India	—	218	172	4.1	3.6

Sources: For 1976: *UN Statistical Yearbook,* 1978 (New York: UN, 1979), pp. 390ff.; for 1960–65: Ch. L. Taylor & M. C. Hudson (ed.), *World Handbook of Political and Social Indicators* (New Haven: Yale U.P., 1972), pp. 326f. More detailed figures broken down according to economic sectors are to be found in: *Statisticheskij ezhegodnik stran-chlenov SEV 1978* (Moscow: Statistika, 1979), p. 54.

3.   Labor productivity

Social scientists who wish to go beyond a rough appraisal of efficiency using output data on material goods, and who see efficiency as being linked to the mental state of development of a society, generally hold the indicator of labor productivity to be a better instrument for measuring the efficiency of a system than the data on economic growth and the ways in which income is generated and utilized.

Evaluating the "labor productivity" indicator is also an approach that should satisfy Marxist scientists, since they hold the view that socialism develops the mental capacities of the working individual without exploiting him. Lenin (LW, Vol. 27, p. 247 ff.) considered labor productivity to be "the most important thing in the last resort" for implementing socialism. It was to be achieved by "people working voluntarily and consciously together." Western economists also consider the increase in labor productivity to be the most relevant growth indicator.[417]

In theory, according to its own ideological claims, the socialist system ought to achieve higher labor productivity than capitalism, for the three following reasons:

1. the equality and *social security* policy for workers enhances their capacities and willingness to work;
2. the development of a *socialist consciousness* stimulates the worker's enthusiasm to a greater extent than is the case with the alienated worker in capitalism;
3. in socialism, *infrastructural and educational policies* rapidly satisfy the preconditions for productive work with technical know-how and an improvement in the level of education.

Earlier Soviet statistics on the growth of labor productivity in industry, which generally only set their own growth rates against those of capitalist countries, seemed to indicate that it was only a matter of time before the socialist countries would catch up with the capitalist economies and overtake them (taking an index of 100 = 1913, an increase of 950 was shown for the Soviet Union in 1957, as against 228 in the United States).[418] The growth rates indicated for the Comecon countries are, however, of little informative value as such and ought to be considered in comparison with the data for Western countries at a comparable development level. Thus, the ILO values are more expressive here (see Table 66). It must also be noted that only the productivity of industrial work can be compared from the data available, since socialist countries do not include nonproductive sectors in their national income calculation.

Moreover, data on labor productivity ought always to be compared with data on *capital productivity*. Chronological analyses for the Soviet Union revealed that growth in labor productivity (1951 to 1969: 5.7% per year) was coupled with a drop in capital productivity, with the effect that the Soviet Union came to rank among the most backward of the developed industrial countries in terms of this factor.[419] Figures on the share of labor productivity in national income growth (Table 67) provide a better guide than do the general labor productivity growth rates; the more developed the socialist economy, the higher the share. Hence, Czechoslovakia and the German Democratic Republic hold the top ranks. The 1971-1975 plan shows, however, that the German Democratic Republic is expected to move into the first place in Comecon, before Czechoslovakia.

Although labor productivity in socialist countries has constantly increased, it has so far tended to be lower on average than in comparable capitalist countries. Taking the approach adopted by McClelland and other U.S. social scientists, which consisted in calculating a few correlations between individual output indicators (such as energy production) and the motivation for working people to perform, then the intersystem differences hardly seem to be worth mentioning. It is, however, seen that specific indicators correlate to a marked extent right across the different systems. Correlation, however, does not explain the causes, and when searching for the underlying reasons we must look out for the variables that come into play and which have meant that, so far, socialist countries, despite their ideological claims, have not been able to come up with the successes in labor productivity that the theorists had once forecast.

The only explanation for the higher labor productivity found in a large number of capitalist countries (and the explanation that even a number of GDR economists use in their enlightened literature on system comparison) is in the various shortcomings of capitalism. These lie in the fact that capitalism scores its success through "imperialist exploitation" of developing countries, through the brutal pressure placed on workers to compete and perform, and through pushing on ruinous labor productivity at the expense of social consumption.[420] This then also leaves the question as to why, despite strong ideological and sometimes even repressive pressure to perform in initial phases of socialist systems, these systems do not achieve similar successes with their comparable means. One of the most far-reaching explanations that leftist critics of the Soviet Union give is that this over-low labor productivity in the Eastern bloc reflects the "worker's resistance."[421] There is a good deal of

Table 66

Increase in labor productivity (1963 = 100)

1. **aggregate national economy**

Country	1964	1965	1966	1967	1968	1969	1970	1971	1972
Czechoslovakia	101	104	112	117	124	130	134	139	
Poland	106	109	115	119	127	129	136	144	153
Rumania	111	122	133	143	153	165	179	198	218
Soviet Union	108	112	120	129	138	143	154	161	166
for comparison:									
FRG	106	111	114	116	124	132	138	141	145
Italy	103	109	117	124	132	138	145	148	155
United States	103	107	112	113	118	118	117	120	

2. industrial sector (gross production per worker)

Country	1964	1965	1966	1967	1968	1969	1970	1971	1972
Bulgaria	107	115	119	128	140	150	160	170	182
Czechoslovakia	104	110	115	121	126	132	142	151	160
GDR	107	113	120	128	134	143	151	159	165
Hungary	105	110	116	122	123	122	132	141	151
Poland	107	111	115	119	126	132	141	148	157
Rumania	110	118	128	139	149	156	167	175	185
Soviet Union	104	109	114	122	128	135	144	153	161
Yugoslavia	107	111	117	118	126	135	143	150	155
for comparison: (net production per employee)									
FRG	108	112	114	119	133	143	146	150	158
Italy	102	110	121	129	139	146	153	153	162
Spain	109	122	138	146	156	176	186		

Source: ILO, *Yearbook of Labour Statistics, 1973* (Geneva: ILO, 1973), pp. 546 ff.

Table 67

Share of labor productivity in the growth of the national income
(in percentages)

Country	1966–1970	1971–1975
Bulgaria	51	70
Czechoslovakia	78	95
GDR	70	100
Hungary	48	68
Mongolia	9	66
Poland	48	75
USSR	68	80–85
Comecon altogether	60	75

Source: A. Keck, *Leistung, Wachstum, Wohlstand. Unser Nationaleinkommen—Quelle des gesellschaftlichen Reichtums* (Berlin (East): Verlag die Wirtschaft, 1972), p. 59.

wishful thinking in this judgment. Surveys among Soviet workers, which included possible conflicts at the workplace, showed, however, that Soviet workers are aware of certain factors that may cause conflicts and have a negative effect on work productivity. In Sverdlovsk, 35.9% of those interviewed mentioned deadlocks in supplies, which later have to be caught up with by *shturmovshchina*, and 27.3% mentioned insufficient supplies of tools in the factories.[422]

1.   The lower labor productivity of socialist countries is not so much due to a fundamental structural shortcoming of their socialist economies, but rather to the fact that the Soviet Union is compared with most capitalist countries from a *lower level* and has developed less technological know-how. The two World Wars and the wars of intervention are also rated as attenuating factors. The most striking structural shortcoming may perhaps be the wastage of labor that came about during the accumulation phase, in addition to the wastage of capital. This, however, applies much more to the Soviet Union than to China, where labor productivity could be rated comparatively higher, because this system could not employ any means to waste capital.

2.   The prevailing development strategy during the accumulation period was *mobilization of the labor reserves*, and this led to a drop in labor productivity. With instruments ranging from the

mobilization of women to the sometimes repressive implementation of the principle "those who do not work need not eat either," considerable success was achieved in recruiting additional labor. China, on the other hand, with its labor surplus, adopted a much more liberal attitude at first in labor policy. There were even cases of students refusing the jobs allocated to them and then remaining unemployed for a fairly long stretch of time.[423] Only the Soviet Union adopted the course of forced labor to mobilize its work force during the accumulation phase to an extent that did not exactly contribute to a rise in labor productivity.

Forced labor was, however, not the only factor to reduce labor productivity. The more-or-less voluntary work in some socialist countries of students, school children, and office workers also brought labor productivity down. This was so not only in land reclamation programs conducted under harsh climatic conditions in the Soviet Union, but also in Cuba's sugar harvests, where compulsory participation was introduced by a decree from the Ministry of Education in 1964.[424] Whereas a good sugar worker can harvest 3 to 4 tons a day, even agricultural students with technical training can only manage 1.5 to 1.8 tons, an ordinary citizen about 500 kilos, and the remaining bureaucrats and intellectuals that are called upon, a possible 250 to 300 kilos.[425]

3. It is not only campaigns with unskilled and semivoluntary workers that force down productivity; even when workers were employed in their own trades, labor productivity did not rise in the proportions that had been hoped for with the growing of socialist awareness. The renowned national economist Wassily Leontief once even tried to prove from the case of Cuba that labor productivity was not decreasing despite socialism, but was, on the contrary, falling precisely on account of the blessings of socialism, because the *fear of losing one's job* no longer existed *as a stimulus*, and the lack of attractive goods meant that the incentive to consume did not provide any motivation either.[426]

With this policy, there was hardly any risk of unemployment. In case of doubt, enterprises and public authorities were overstaffed rather than having labor laid off. Only in countries with such a rapid population increase as China and Poland was there the problem of open and latent unemployment.

In the Soviet Union, however, this was of less importance. Between 1928 and 1940, the number of workers grew by 3.7% per year, whereas the population had only grown by 1.2%. It was only between 1950 and 1958 that this trend was reversed, and the population came to grow faster than new labor could be mobilized.

This capacity to mobilize labor partly explains the Soviet Union's impressive growth.

Even in the German Democratic Republic, which had no trouble in employing all workers in suitable jobs and up to 1961 even experienced a notorious labor shortage owing to the refugee movement, labor productivity did not reach the level of comparable capitalist countries, such as the Federal Republic of Germany. At the Sixth SED (Socialist Unity Party of Germany) Party Congress in 1963, Walter Ulbricht admitted that the German Democratic Republic's productivity lagged behind that of the Federal Republic of Germany by some 25%. Western estimates indicate an even greater lag.

4.   Despite a successful *educational system*, labor productivity did not even increase to the same extent as in countries that were notoriously behind in developing their educational systems, such as Spain. In the Soviet Union in particular, mobilization of labor overtook the rate at which skilled workers could be trained as technicians and experts, such that in the 1950s labor productivity was still only 40% of the United States' labor productivity.[566] Even in the 1960s, the share of professionals and technical "brain" occupations was still low, but data is only available here for a number of the socialist countries (see Table 68). The quality of technical education often lies below Western standards, and, despite the socialist ideal of nonspecialized polytechnical training, high-grade specialists tend to be even more specialized than in capitalist systems; this may lead in cases of a change in the production to "technological unemployment," since the management is reluctant to dismiss displaced workers.[427]

In socialist countries, too, there is no clear-cut relationship between the educational system and growth of labor productivity. It has been found in the Soviet Union that automation by no means produces a higher level of qualification in all jobs and tends instead to bring about a polarization of the qualification structure, in that it creates a multitude of jobs with low qualificational requirements in the services sector, where skilled workers are frequently employed below their training level. The danger of skills being wasted is to be found above all in socialist systems, where, for ideological reasons, the output of skills has been inadequately matched to demand (see Chapter 2, Section 3). In socialist systems, too, overqualification has negative consequences on work satisfaction.

Even though socialist economy, with its forms of participation (see Part IV), is described by its defenders as being particularly innovative, this is difficult to prove with figures. Replacement of industrial equipment destroyed in the war has not triggered the same innovative impetus in the Soviet Union as it did in Japan or Western Europe, even though the view that Soviet technology in 1950 (at the end of the reconstruction period) was still at its 1940 level must be considered as being rather exaggerated.[428]

There are a few other reasons for the lack of technical innovation, despite the growing emphasis placed on the productive resource "science" ever since Stalin:

a. Ideological blinkers meant that certain innovations in fields ranging from economic planning methods to chemistry or computer technology were only taken up after a certain delay. The computer gap between socialist countries and capitalist systems had not been fully overcome by the early 1970s, even though the Soviet Union was already registering a higher growth rate in the number of computers than the United States of America (see Tables 69, 70, 71).

A further indicator is provided by the number of inventions registered per 100,000 inhabitants. Socialist countries do not come

Table 68

Scientific and technical manpower

Country	Year	Total in 1,000	1978
Bulgaria	1966	400	800
Czechoslovakia	1970	1,119	1,824
GDR	1970	717	1,318
Hungary	1970	711	560 (1971)
Poland	1970	1,781	3,088
Rumania	1968	900	n.d.
Soviet Union	1970	16,841	26,400
Yugoslavia	1969	827	
for comparison:			
France	1969	1,702	
Great Britain	1968	833	
Greece	1969	263	

Sources: UNESCO, *Statistical Yearbook 1971* (Geneva: UNESCO, 1972). *Statisticheskii ezhegodnik stran-chlenov SEV 1979* (Moscow: Statistika, 1979), p. 452.

Table 69

Computers in use per million inhabitants (1970)

Socialist countries	19	Capitalist countries	
Bulgaria	5	Austria	64
Czechoslovakia	16	FRG	109
GDR	21	Japan	56
Hungary	8	Sweden	86
Poland	6	United States	344
Rumania	2		
Soviet Union	23		

Sources: J. Slama & H. Vogel, "Die Verbreitung neuer Technologien in der UdSSR." *Fallstudie 1, EDV. Forschungsberichte des Osteuropa-Instituts* (Munich: Osteuropa Institut, 1973), p. 144. J. Wilczynski, "Cybernetics. Automation and the Transition to Communism." In: C. Mesa-Lago & C. Beck (eds.), *Comparative Socialist Systems* (Pittsburgh: University of Pittsburgh, Center for International Studies, 1975) (397–417), p. 402.

Table 70

Comparison of the production of computers and data-processing equipment, Soviet Union and United States (1958–65) (in millions of dollars)

Year	United States	Soviet Union
1958	410	35
1959	490	45
1960	630	55
1961	895	70
1962	1,965	95
1963	1,240	120
1964	1,375	140
1965	1,585	200
annual growth	21.3	29.3

Source: K. Miller: "Computers in the Soviet Economy." In: *US Congress Joint Economic Committee: New Directions in the Soviet Economy* (Washington: 1966) (327–337), p. 333.

Table 71

Number of inventions per 100,000 inhabitants (1964)

Country	Number of inventions
Belgium	164
Austria	147
Denmark	131
Norway	121
Czechoslovakia	52
Hungary	20
Poland	10
Rumania	7

Sources: *UN Demographic Yearbook 1964* (New York: UN 1964), pp. 126ff.; R. V. Burks, "Technology and Political Change." In: Ch. Johnson (ed.), *Change in Communist Systems* (Stanford: Stanford U.P., 1970) (265–311), p. 272. Further data in : J. Osers, *Forschung und Entwicklung in sozialistischen Staaten Osteuropas* (Berlin (West): Duncker & Humblot, 1974), p. 205.

off very well in this comparison either, even if compared with systems that are not spectacularly innovative (such as Austria).

b. Despite the planned organization of innovator movements, *incentives for inventive work are not very high.* Although all important research work is carried on in state institutes, the number of inventions by private hobby researchers is still remarkably high compared with organized innovation.[429]

Surveys have demonstrated that workers make suggestions very much with a view to improving their own situation, but certainly not through any basically greater level of commitment to their enterprise than is the case in many capitalist countries. Whereas skilled workers mostly rated the feasibility of their improvement suggestions correctly, unskilled workers were found to make numerous utopian recommendations that were due, in part, to ignorance of the necessary technology.[430]

However, in view of socialist countries' high level of investment in education, the correlation between level of education and feasibility of suggestions must, in the long term, give rise to a greater number of feasible suggestions being made. Innovation only ever marks potential technical progress, however, and whether or not it is applied, depends in part on the organization and steering system of the socialist economy and, in particular, on an economic system's capacity to assimilate innovations rapidly into the production process. The excessive steering in socialist countries has often proved to be prejudicial in this respect, because it has frequently constricted research and creativity.

c.   The *bonus system, coupled with plan fulfilment*, did not promote technical innovation in times of "command" planning, because innovation suggestions could sometimes lead to a fall in remuneration.

d.   The *contract system* applied in socialist economic systems favors the supplier rather than the purchaser. The customer service and maintenance system involves much less obligation on the part of the supplier than in capitalist systems, since supplier firms usually assume no further responsibility for their products once they have provided the initial servicing instructions. Extension of the direct contractual relationship between customer and supplier, as propagated by reform economists, is to combat these shortcomings in the future.

Despite the successes of education policy, *technical know-how* was scarce, to judge by international comparisons of the "persons employed in technical occupations" indicator. Owing to this scarcity, technical know-how often had to be deployed very selectively. A high level of mechanization often went hand-in-hand with a surprisingly low level of mechanization in auxiliary and feeder services, such as, for example, in the coal industry in the 1920s.[431] Even today, this discrepancy will occasionally strike the passing visitor to high-standard industrial plants in the Soviet Union.

In the 1960s, however, a new handicap developed before the first one had been overcome, namely, the growing importance of the "productive resource, science," which also had its repercussions on labor productivity. Ever since the 1950s, growth theory has repeatedly asserted that technical progress is more important for increasing output than is a quantitative increase in the production factors of capital and labor. In the United States, E. Boretzky and others developed sophisticated formulae for measuring technical progress that involved calculating the total cost saving for the economy for each additional unit of innovation applied. System comparisons, however, usually work only with selected indicators, and these are generally relatively selective, such as the number of contributions to international scientific periodicals and the number of domestic scientific periodicals taken as a measure of scientific capacity. The highly developed countries such as the German Democratic Republic, Czechoslovakia, and the Soviet Union show remarkable achievements when measured in terms of the second indicator, but still lag far behind when it comes to international cooperation on a world-wide scale, which is becoming increasingly important, particularly for small countries. This indicator is only of limited informative value, however, because international communication within the socialist camp has not yet been examined in sufficient depth; this, on the other hand, leaves much to be desired, by reason of the mistrust of the socialist countries, anxious to safeguard their sovereignty. (See Table 72.)

In the Comecon countries, as compared with the European Economic Community, we see the negative effects that development

Table 72

Scientific capacity

Country	Rank out of 113 nations	Contributions to world scientific authorship 1967–69	Scientific journals
Soviet Union	5	82,000	2,100
Poland	10	9,500	750
China	13	290	660
GDR	16		550
Czechoslovakia	20	12,900	420
Yugoslavia	22	5,700	400
Hungary	27	2,300	250
Rumania	32	4,400	170
Bulgaria	34	2,700	150
Cuba	39	40	100
North Korea	48		60
for comparison:			
United States	1	417,000	6,000
Japan	2	42,200	2,820
FRG	4	68,900	2,560
Italy	7	19,800	1,530
India	12	22,600	670

Source: Taylor-Hudson (edit.), op.cit., p. 322 f.

of joint steering institutions without full consensus among the countries involved has on economic integration.

5. In a number of socialist developing countries, *rapid population growth* and the ensuing *urbanization* came as additional intervening factors.

China had problems similar to those of the other countries, but labor productivity was even lower there because of her lower level of mechanization after the Revolution, and because her rapid population increase meant that she had greater problems of latent unemployment during the accumulation phase than did the Soviet Union. The problem was temporarily solved by overstaffing, which, after 1959, led on to the *hsia-fang* movement, with much of the redundant labor being sent back from the town to the country. Thus, according to a survey carried out in 15 large cities, 60% of the population was classified as unproductive in July 1957.[432]

At the same time, China's course was less set on obsessive capital-intensive growth; despite a slower mechanization movement, capital intensity and the development of labor productivity were kept better in balance through China's "medium-range technology." In the Soviet Union, the industrial labor force rose from 3.1 to 8 million between 1926 and 1932, and two thirds of this came from the countryside. Between 1926 and 1939, the percentage of urban population nearly doubled, with an increase from 17.9 to 32.8%. China deliberately attempted to avoid this kind of development and adopted the course of deurbanization. Cuba, too, is one of the few countries that tried to prevent further extension of the "top-heavy" capital by a deliberate location and labor deployment policy.

To sum up, it can be said that the theory that socialist economy ipso facto guarantees higher labor productivity is untenable. The comparatively good results of the developed capitalist countries, however, cannot simply be interpreted as resulting from "higher efficiency." Capitalist systems doubtlessly owe part of their successes in labor productivity to the less positive side of the system: to the latent risk of unemployment and the "reserve army" that this provides. In times of full employment, positive material incentives alone can serve to replace this stick with a carrot.

In fixing its priorities as security and full employment, socialism created new contradictions, which had repercussions on the system's efficiency. The economies of socialist countries are paying increasing attention to the lag in labor productivity and are no longer trying to ignore or talk away misappraisals, as happened during the phase of revolutionary passion. A number of Eastern European socialist countries have started research into the conditions of labor productivity with capitalist economists and have submitted their results in the context of the ILO.[433] In doing this, they have not adopted the convergence theory viewpoint that the level of labor productivity depends on asystemic factors and correlates with indicators such as output level and per capita income, as has been upheld in Western economics at times.[434]

4. Growth, employment, and price stability

For a long time the economic theory of socialist countries fostered an artificial contradiction between the Marxist theory of reproduction and the "bourgeois" theory of growth, even though both theories dealt with same questions. This changed first in Polish and Hungarian economic theory, with the pioneering works of Oscar Lange and Kalecki. In the meantime, however, a large part of the growth theory terminology has slipped into the accumulation debate and even into the vocabulary of economists who verbally dissociated themselves from the Polish economists.

Although the economic literature of socialist countries points out that only socialism facilitates "proportional growth," this is by no means the same as the theory of "balanced growth" put forward by Scitovsky, Rosenstein-Rodan, and Nurske. In the very first debate on growth in a concrete socialist experiment, namely, in the debate on Soviet industrialization between 1924 and 1928, the "right-wing" opposition, including Bukharin, admitted the necessity of discontinued, unbalanced growth, whereas the left-wing opposition, which included Preobrazhensky, fell in with the new general course to some extent, broke with Trotsky, and only took offence at the unparalleled brutality of the experiment, which, they feared, would bring about heavy social upheavals. Now that the experiment is considered to have been a success on the whole, despite the unnecessarily high costs involved, socialist economists, even after the Second World War, are still tending toward a "chain of imbalances" theory, while occasionally borrowing from Soviet shock strategy, so that, despite a number of superficial similarities, this theory still differs widely from Hirschman's concept. Even though this strategy had nothing in common with balanced growth, it nevertheless made for remarkable uniformity of growth.

The People's Republic of China professed adhesion to balanced growth to a greater extent than did the Soviet Union, although, up to the Great Leap Forward, she tended rather to practice a *big-push* strategy in developing certain selected branches of industry. However, the "walking on two legs" theory seemed in some respects to be a retroactive change. Under Soviet influence, heavy industry was initially, up to 1959, given priority, and it was only after the agricultural crisis around 1960 that the priorities were changed. A general economic theory of balance can certainly not be deduced from Mao's teachings either. The theory of prevailing imbalance resulted, as it were, from application of the theory of contradiction to China's economic development.

Mao defended unbalanced development in 1958 in the light of the Great Leap Forward: "Disequilibrium is a general, objective rule. The cycle, which is endless, evolves from disequilibrium to equilibrium and then to disequilibrium again. Each cycle, however, brings us to a higher level of development. Disequilibrium is normal and absolute whereas equilibrium is temporary and relative." Mao even rejected Lenin's one-sided formula that socialism equals "Soviet power plus electrification."[435]

In May 1958, Liu Shao-Ch'i varied the idea that consumption and production and accumulation could be increased symmetrically, by sharply criticizing those who considered that the contradiction between consumption and investment meant that they were mutually exclusive opposites. There were also several economic theorists in China who developed a theory of balanced growth on the basis of Mao's theory of contradiction. Ma Yin-Ch'u advocated balanced growth even at the cost of a lower growth rate.[436]

Irrespective of theoretical attitudes toward the question of "balanced" or "unbalanced growth," however, socialist developing countries were also marked by imbalance because of their *dual technology*, that is, the coexistence of advanced and archaic technologies. This became all the more pronounced where foreign aid in advanced technologies widened the gap between these and the other sectors of the economy.

Unlike fascist or authoritarian dictatorships, which, at times, also seemed to reach a high level of efficiency, the socialist course is a long-lasting succession of growth processes. Growth in socialist countries has, on the whole, tended to be more stable than in capitalism, although the very countries that have the highest development level, namely the German Democratic Republic and Czechoslovakia, witnessed a stagnation in the early 1960s that made drastic economic reforms necessary.

These developments meant that the economies of socialist countries were faced with facts that had so far had no place in the prevailing doctrine. Cyclical crises were considered to be incompatible with socialism—at most, there could be some cyclical fluctuation perhaps—since there were no trade cycles and no fluctuations stemming from the market mechanism, as in capitalist systems. The economists of socialist countries held fast to the opinion that there might perhaps be "waste of utility values" through realization crises, but certainly not a "surplus of exchange values," as in capitalism. Moreover, Marx's law on the cyclical drop of the profit rate was considered not to apply to socialist economies. At very most, reference was sometimes made to the cyclical drop in the accumulation rate. The occasional realization crises were seen as being limited to the consumer goods sector, and surplus production of capital goods was usually denied as being a possible cause, although there was in fact evidence of this in the form of misallocation of resources by the central planning authorities (Chapter 4, Section 3).

In the light of the temporary stagnation experienced by socialist countries, socialist economists had to concern themselves with "cyclical fluctuations" and develop a sort of crisis theory of socialism. Polish and Czech economists played a pioneering role here. In 1969, Goldman and K. Kouba even spoke about "quasi-cycles" in socialism without, however, falling victim to the "wave fetishism" found in the economic cycle doctrine of the critics of bourgeois economy.[437]

Socialist economists now also recognize that their high initial growth rates are tending to drop with increasing development, but they believe that with appropriate organization of the socialist conditions of production it will be possible to prevent a drop down to the growth rate level found in developed capitalist countries.

Socialist analysis of crisis-like output fluctuations is based on the following six explanatory patterns:

1. influence of climatic fluctuations in agriculture on overall development;
2. influence of external economies on small socialist countries;
3. fluctuations in population growth and their influence on labor mobilization;
4. apathy of the masses due to political errors committed by the leadership;
5. contradictions in steering the plan system;
6. political zig-zag course.

    1. The influence of *climatic fluctuations in agriculture* on

overall economic development was one of the explanations given. To begin with, preference was given to the explanatory patterns that put the blame on factors beyond the planners' control, and one of these was the weather. This explanation was not merely a pretext. As long as the socialist countries had a predominantly agrarian structure, climatic fluctuations inevitably led to output fluctuations, even though this cause was at times overrated. Thus, for example, when explaining the drop in production during the Great Leap Forward, Chinese leaders put more weight on flood catastrophes than they did on the erroneous decision making, which led to over-high targets being set during the communization movement. All the Eastern European socialist countries show strikingly similar development in growth of agricultural output in specific years (1952, 1956, 1962). But even in the case of Cuba, well-meaning observers largely attribute the fall in production between 1964 and 1966 to external, climatic conditions.[438] (See Table 73.)

2.   The *influence of external economies* on small socialist countries, through bottlenecks in the supply of raw materials and imported goods, has been put forward by the Czech crisis theorists, in particular, to explain the fall in production in Eastern Europe in the early 1960s. This theory becomes all the more credible if we consider that the Soviet Union has been much less afflicted by such fluctuations than have the people's democracies. This phenomenon has in particular led Comecon to speed up economic coordination within the socialist camp. Since the oil crisis and the price increase in the raw materials that the Soviet Union supplies to the Comecon countries, this theory has gained additional value as an explanation.

3.   *Fluctuations in population growth* and their influence on labor mobilization, on the other hand, was an explanation closer to the hearts of Soviet economists. This explanation was still supported quite recently by V. F. Terechov, along with the labor-absorbing influence of nonproductive sectors.[439] Although the growth rates in the German Democractic Republic underwent greater flucuation after 1961—the year of the building of the wall—than they had done prior to that date, the explanation that these fluctuations were due to an "exodus of qualified labor to the West" still prevails among GDR scientists.

4.   *The apathy of the masses*, resulting from excessive bureaucratization in Eastern European systems, was an explanation expressed mainly by left-wing critics outside the Eastern bloc.

5.   *Contradictions in the plan system* and the need for liberalization marked the counterpart to the fourth theory, and it was one

Table 73

Fluctuations in agricultural output (1951-1969)

Year	Bul-garia	Czecho-slovakia	GDR	Hun-gary	Poland	Ru-mania	Soviet Union	Yugo-slavia
1951	40	1	19	n.d.	- 7	25	- 7	45
1952	-16	- 3	3	n.d.	2	- 7	9	-34
1953	22	0	8	18	3	17	3	44
1954	-12	- 1	4	2	6	1	5	-12
1955	9	11	1	13	3	18	11	14
1956	- 7	4	- 3	-12	7	-19	13	-13
1957	17	- 1	7	13	4	24	3	14
1958	- 1	3	4	4	3	-13	11	-18
1959	18	- 1	- 3	5	- 1	19	0	33
1960	3	6	9	- 6	5	2	2	-12
1961	- 3	0	-11	0	10	5	3	- 6
1962	4	- 7	- 1	3	- 8	- 8	1	5
1963	2	7	8	5	4	4	- 7	10
1964	12	3	4	4	1	6	14	3
1965	2	- 4	8	- 4	8	6	2	- 6
1966	15	11	3	8	5	14	9	24
1967	3	5	5	4	3	1	1	- 5
1968	- 8	6	1	1	4	- 3	5	- 4
1969	2	1	- 7	6	- 5	5	- 3	10
1951-69	6	2	4	4	3	5	5	5

Official rates on constant prices. The comparability between the years and the countries is limited. The table is only meant to illustrate the possible scope of fluctuations.

Source: J. Wilczynski, *Socialist Economic Development and Reforms* (London: Macmillan, 1972), p. 12.

that most of the bourgeois economists were willing to accept. Marxist critics on the left, however, consider the decentralizing economic reforms to be a means of driving out the "devil of stagnation" with the "Beelzebub of economic levers." It has rightfully been asked whether the peculiar blend of market and planned steering elements that at times prevailed in Eastern Europe did not necessarily mean that instability was bound to become even greater for a time because of this structural incompatibility.[440]

6.   Even in a logical centralistic planning system, however, large-scale fluctuation can arise precisely through the constant *political reshuffles* that result from internal faction struggles within the party. In addition to the first-mentioned cause, this sixth cause probably had the greatest influence on output fluctuations in China. The conflicts between the groups around Liu and Mao from the Great Leap Forward to the Cultural Revolution created this type of fluctuation. According to certain revelations published on wall newspapers during the Cultural Revolution, Liu had canvassed for his concept in the Party by threats of a crisis. Liu is said to have repeatedly claimed that nearly all government departments were working "in the red" and that an economic crisis, "as is common in capitalism," was imminent.[441] Alternatives such as those proposed by the Maoist line of Marxism in order to rekindle the class struggle —that is, cultural revolution or restoration of capitalism—are presumably intended to accentuate the zig-zag course, while further repercussions on economic efficiency are consciously accepted as side effects.

Although the existence in socialist countries of crisis-like fluctuations can no longer be denied, one should not jump to conclusions in line with the convergence theory. Fluctuations in socialist economies do not have the same effects as the crisis cycles in capitalist economies:

1.   *Fluctuations* are usually on a *smaller scale*, and, provided that early warning systems are sufficiently well developed, the socialist system with its centralized planning is able to *counteract* these fluctuations more rapidly than the crisis management in capitalist countries. Where supply bottlenecks and price increases were involved, however—as in Poland, for instance—countersteering measures were applied only after a fierce protest and strike movement in the country.

2.   Fluctuations are *not accompanied by the same stagflation trends* as those characteristic of recent trends in capitalism. The inflationary trends in particular are much smaller. This does not, of course, mean that there are no inflationary trends in socialism (as is still occasionally put forward in apologetic texts). These appear in various symptoms:

a.   They become evident as *latent inflation* in the difference between free prices (as, for instance, on the kolkhoz market) and the state retail prices. In the 1950s and 1960s, free prices were some 50 to 70% above the state prices.[442]

When comparing the UN statistics, Poland and Yugoslavia seem to have been the only countries in the socialist camp to have experienced noteworthy inflationary trends in the 1960s (see Table 74). If we go back to the 1940s and 1950s, similar price rises can be seen in Czechoslovakia and Bulgaria in the early 1950s, but most countries and halted this trend by the mid-1950s. The upward trend was most marked in countries where the abolition of the rationing systems was not coupled with monetary reform—for example, 1951 in Hungary and 1953 in Poland.[443] In 1974 and 1975, inflation rates must have been higher (they were estimated at 3.6% in Hungary and at some 5% in Poland). The early appeasing declarations from the GDR government, to the effect that rising raw material prices would not affect consumer prices, can scarcely be upheld after 1975.

    b.   Unlike capitalist economies, where inflation generally originates in monetary inflation, the plan system creates *real inflation* when output targets exceed the resources actually available for achieving them. Socialist planners, however, even prefer monetary inflationary pressure to deflation, which involves the threat of unemployment.[444] Following the lifting of rationing after the Second World War, the governments of socialist countries as a rule tolerated an excess demand for goods, with the effect that queues formed in front of stores and long waiting lists developed for larger consumer goods.

    c.   With the development of material levers, the *money illusion* came to be used increasingly in wage policy; but its stimulus faded away after some time due to the rising prices, and hence other consumption facilities had to be found—particularly in the protective sphere of state functions (see Chapter 8, Section 2).

    d.   *Expansion of foreign trade based on credit* and opening up of the socialist economies to the world market have contributed to inflation. Despite these inflationary trends in socialist economies, the socialist state is in a position to take more effective countermeasures. Placing inflationary phenomena in capitalism and socialism on an equal footing and virtually disregarding worldwide inflation in the capitalist system, as was still found in system comparisons of the 1960s,[445] is now no longer possible in the light of the experience in the 1970s.

    3.   The cyclical fluctuations in socialist economies only have a *limited effect on the labor market* and certainly do not result in mass unemployment (see Chapter 7, Section 1).

226

Table 74

Inflationary trends according to consumer price indices
(1970 = 100)

Country	1971	1972	1973	1974	1975	1976	1977	1978
Bulgaria	100.2	100.2	101.1	102.2	102.8	103.3	103.5	104.7
Czechoslovakia	96.6	99.4	99.5	99.7	99.6	100.8	102.2	104.1
GDR	100.6	99.6	98.2	98.6	99.7	99.7	99.7	99.7
Hungary	102.0	103.1	107.9	108.4	109.7	120.9	127.5	132.1
Poland	101.9	101.8	102.8	113.1	114.1	118.0	124.0	136.8
Rumania	101.5	102.1	103.3	105.1	105.5	106.1	107.1	108.1
Soviet Union	100.3	100.3	100.5	100.8	100.9	100.9	100.9	101.9
Yugoslavia	116.6	138.8	161.1	195.9	278.3	329.5	385.7	481.0
for comparison:								
FRG	103.8	109.7	118.0	123.6	130.1	136.8	143.7	145.2
Italy	104.0	110.6	123.9	145.9	172.2	201.6	240.5	271.6
Japan	105.9	110.1	124.4	158.9	179.5	195.5	209.0	216.3
Switzerland	106.6	113.7	123.6	135.7	144.8	147.3	149.2	150.8
United States	103.0	107.5	123.1	140.7	152.7	157.4	167.3	179.5

Source: UN, *Statistical Yearbook 1971* (New York: UN, 1972); ILO, *Yearbook of Labour Statistics 1979* (Geneva: ILO, 1979), pp. 549ff.

5.   Autonomy and innovative capacity
of the economic system

At the time of the Cold War, it was sometimes asserted that socialist systems were, on the whole, incapable of innovation because their excessive bureaucratization killed off any individual initiative.[446]

However, the start of every socialist transformation was marked by extensive innovation, if we accept Alexander Gerschenkron's typology of the industrialization process. In this typology, autonomous and autochthonous development is one of the most desirable features of modernization.[447] Only the socialist systems have been able to liberate themselves sufficiently from the dominant capitalist world system to be able to talk of autonomous development, and, being late developers, they have had the advantage of profiting from some of the experiences—positive as well as negative—of capitalist development. The building of an ex ante planned economy was probably the greatest innovation that any single country had tried to achieve in economic history. The transitional societies emphasized their autonomic development to varying degrees. The bigger the country, the easier it seemed to be to choose an autonomous and autochthonous course of development. But smaller countries also attempted to develop their own concepts, as for instance did Kim il Sung in North Korea with his *dshuche* concept.

His definition ran: "Developing the dshuche means abiding by the principle of solving all questions relating to the revolution and construction independently, in harmony with the reality of the country, and essentially by using our own strength."[448] *Dshuche* was not to mean complete autarky (as was the case with a number of radical Maoists), and indeed could not be in such a small country as Korea. The principle was, however, directed against the danger of forming new dependent relationships, created under the "pretext of economic cooperation and international division of labor." Like the Chinese, North Koreans thus became somewhat imprisoned in a theory of imperialism narrowly based on economic dependence. Ideological and political dependence, on the other hand, was only recognized to a lesser degree, although Kim il Sung had also referred to a "dshuche in ideology." But he simultaneously pleaded for a practical contribution from the country in protecting the purity of Marxism–Leninism and in strengthening the unity of the communist world movement. He did not, however, realize that these two aims might conflict and that in her foreign relations a small country such as North Korea could hardly enforce her definition of "pure

Marxism," which could have been totally independent of the powers that dominated the communist world movement.

However, none of the socialist countries—not even the first, the Soviet Union—has managed its economic development in complete independence of other countries. In the 1920s in particular, the Soviet Union issued licences in many sectors of the economy, and up to 1932 there were some 4,140 foreign specialists working in the country. At the same time, trade relations with the Soviet Union's major partners, Germany and the United States, were showing a growing deficit.[449] Nevertheless, when the Soviet Union became the protective power of the new socialist states created after the Second World War, she proved to be very sensitive whenever a people's democracy expressed a desire to take up economic aid from the West. In the case of Czechoslovakia, pressure was applied to prevent acceptance of Marshall plan funds.

Occasionally the theory is put forward that *dshuche* is only conceivable for large, virtually self-sufficient socialist countries. It has, however, been seen that relatively independent development is possible where the protective power is not in the immediate vicinity of the country in question, such as in the case of Albania in relation to China and of Cuba in relation to the Soviet Union. But even in these two cases, ideological dependence reflects a certain degree of economic dependence. The Albanian leadership admitted quite frankly in its Fourth Five-Year Plan: "The deficit was to be covered by the generous international aid from the PR of China. . . ."[450]

Development aid

Yugoslavia is the only socialist country to have accepted aid from capitalist foreign countries on a large scale, and this has not been without effect on the revival of market relations within the country and on the country's orientation toward the world market. All other socialist states owe the major part of their development aid to the Soviet Union. On the whole, socialist states rank very low on the world list of countries with the highest per capita development aid (see Table 75), which would imply a high level of autonomous and autochthonous development. Viewed on a world scale, the United States has granted far more money to its preferred beneficiaries. A skillful selection and cumulation policy, however, has meant that the Soviet Union's contributions to certain socialist countries were large enough to at least give rise to sectoral depen-

Table 75

Foreign aid

	Soviet Union		United States	
	Aid in $1,000,000 (1954–65)	Aid per capita in $	Economic & military aid (1958–65)	Aid per capita in $
Yugoslavia	232	11.19	951	48.74
Poland	2,986	9.48	76	2.43
Cuba	1,226	16.07	21	2.80
Albania	293	15.76	–	–
Bulgaria	5,197	63.39	–	–
China	16,242	2.32	–	–
Czechoslovakia	552	3.90	–	–
GDR	763	4.46	–	–
Hungary	1,214	11.97	–	–
Mongolia	1,836	166.34	–	–
North Korea	752	6.22	–	–
North Vietnam	1,123	5.91	–	–
Rumania	2,181	11.46	–	–
for comparison:				
South Vietnam	–	–	905	105.68
South Korea	–	–	3,331	117.39
Greece	84	9.82	1,058	123.75
Spain	–	–	1,053	33.30
India	1,022	2.10	4,893	10.05

Source: Taylor-Hudson (ed.), op.cit.,pp. 360 ff.

dencies. Now that some of the countries are aiming at a greater economic independence from the Eastern bloc, capital import from capitalist foreign countries is playing an increasing role, as for instance in Rumania. Left-wing critics are watching this evolution with growing uneasiness. However, the arguments advanced in ideological debates are mostly beside the point. The Chinese line criticizes the Soviet Union for having made the people's democracies economically dependent through capital aid. The Soviet Union, in turn condemns the fact that ever since the breach with Moscow in 1960,

China's trade relations have mainly been directed toward the capitalist countries and brands this as antisocialist behavior.[451] This criticism overlooks the fact, however, that in all countries except Yugoslavia development aid and capital aid is subject to the priorities laid down in the national plans. Foreign capitalists cannot act as pressure groups on the planning bodies. In the case of the Soviet Union, they sometimes do not even know the location of the plant or the equipment to be constructed when they sign the contract.

Dependence through foreign trade relations?

Since capital aid does not play the same role in socialist countries as its does in capitalist developing countries, autonomy in development can also be affected by foreign trade relations. This risk is especially prevalent in countries whose economic structure has meant that they have been largely dependent—like Cuba and Chile —on the export of a few specific goods or—like Czechoslovakia and the German Democratic Republic—on the export of a wide range of goods. Perhaps it is not merely by chance that the three countries with the highest degree of concentration as regards orientation of their exports to one country—namely, Bulgaria, Cuba, and the German Democratic Republic—have also become very dependent in their development process. This holds particularly true for a country such as Cuba, where export and import account for a high percentage of national income, or Bulgaria, which as late as the 1960s still had to rely upon extensive loans from the Soviet Union, thus creating an additional dependence toward her, which was also confirmed by the fact that Bulgaria was the only country in the Eastern bloc to go along with the Soviet monetary reform in 1961. (See Table 76.)

Since 1975, the share of Comecon member states' trade which is conducted within the bloc is very high (see Table 77). However, as far as imports are concerned, a slightly decreasing tendency was to be observed around 1970. The conducting of trade mainly within an organized group is a phenomenon common to the EEC as well, but here none of the individual countries holds such a predominant position in the foreign trade of member states as does the Soviet Union in Comecon, where some 75% of aggregate intra-Comecon trade is realized with the Soviet Union.

The predominant position of the Soviet Union in the foreign trade of socialist countries meant that dependences could be created

Table 76 Import and export (value in 1,000,000 dollars)

Country	Import					Export				
	1938	1948	1958	1970	1977	1938	1948	1958	1970	1977
Albania	7	n.d.	79	n.d.	n.d.	3	n.d.	29	n.d.	n.d.
Bulgaria	60	n.d.	367	1,831	6,329	68	n.d.	373	2,004	6,329
China	187	140	n.d.	n.d.	7,395	170	104	n.d.	n.d.	7,180
Cuba	106	547	777	1,311	4,066	145	724	763	1,046	3,573
Czechoslovakia	239	681	1,357	3,695	11,149	295	753	1,513	3,792	10,818
GDR	–	–	1,511	4,332	14,344	–	–	1,704	4,132	12,024
Hungary	123	167	631	2,506	6,522	155	166	684	2,317	5,832
Mongolia	n.d.	34	77	116	375	n.d.	36	55	84	232
Poland	248	516	1,227	3,608	14,674	225	533	1,060	3,548	12,336
Rumania	137	n.d.	482	1,960	6,095	157	n.d.	468	1,581	6,138
Soviet Union	273	1,224	4,350	11,732	40,817	255	1,308	4,298	12,800	45,161
Yugoslavia	115	368	685	2,874	9,634	117	304	441	1,679	5,254
for comparison:										
FRG	–	1,690	7,730	29,814	100,672	–	780	9,220	34,189	117,895
Greece	132	365	565	1,958	6,778	90	94	232	643	2,724
India	576	1,725	1,844	2,124	6,593	614	1,387	1,222	2,026	6,222
Italy	593	1,539	3,216	14,970	47,580	553	1,077	2,577	13,206	45,063
Spain	152	482	872	4,715	17,846	98	373	486	2,387	10,230

Source: *UN Statistical Yearbook 1973* (New York, UN, 1974), p. 394ff; (1979), pp. 442ff.

Table 77

Share of intra-Comecon trade (1979)

Countries	Turnover	Export	Import
Bulgaria	78.4	76.7	80.1
Cuba	78.9	81.4	76.4
Czechoslovakia	68.5	69.0	68.0
GDR	68.8	71.0	66.7
Hungary	52.1	55.3	49.5
Mongolia	96.8	96.0	97.3
Poland	54.7	58.0	51.9
Rumania	39.7	41.9	37.7
Soviet Union	55.7	55.5	55.8
Yugoslavia		38.9 (1977)	31.8

Sources: *Statisticheskii ezhegodnik stran-chlenov SEV. 1980* (Moscow: Statistika, 1980), p. 373. Yugoslavia: *Jahrbuch der Wirtschaft/Osteuropas Yearbook of East-European Economics* Vol. 8 (Munich: Olzog, 1979), p. 494.

through price discrimination. It has been claimed that between 1955 and 1964, the Soviet Union charged prices 31.2% higher, and paid prices 16.3% lower, than those applied in comparable trade with capitalist countries.[452] Today, even Western literature assumes that the tendency toward price discrimination is not just to be found on the Soviet side alone, but that there is a general trend toward mutual price discrimination that is not due to evil intentions but to the lack of a uniform "socialist" pricing system.[453]

Pricing systems in the Eastern bloc have become increasingly divergent, particularly since the time when Poland and Hungary carried out price reforms in order to get rid of deficient prices for raw materials, while in other Comecon countries raw material prices scarcely covered cost prices in some cases.

In most of the socialist countries, Soviet aid did not have the same impact as American aid had in many capitalist developing countries. Nevertheless, it cannot be denied that China in particular owes a good deal of the remarkable results in her industrialization policy—especially in machine building—to Soviet assistance in the form of technical know-how and financial aid (see Table 78). In no case did the Soviet Union give free grants to China.[454] Considering the volume of this Soviet aid, it has occasionally been inferred that a dependence relationship existed between them. At first sight, figures would seem to confirm this hypothesis, but in terms of the amount of technical aid provided financial aid was relatively insignificant. It is reckoned that only 20% of the financial aid was destined to enable China to purchase machines and industrial equipment. The remaining 80% covered war debts and military aid.[455] For 1955, the deficit in the trade balance that had accumulated was estimated at 1.4 billion.[456]

Soviet deliveries were of great importance for the first phase of China's industrialization. Up to 1959, one sixth of Soviet machine exports and three quarters of equipment for complete plants were sent to the People's Republic of China. Any dependence could only have originated after spring, 1958, when the Soviet Union showed unwillingness to grant long-term credits, thereby forcing the Chinese government to increase its exports in order to pay for the imported Soviet machines.[457] As far as the production of spare parts was concerned, China is said to have tried to become independent from Soviet deliveries as early as 1956.[458]

Table 78 shows that losses due to the sudden decrease in deliveries from 1960 onward were considerable, even though the Soviet Union was quite generous as regards her claims for repayment after the 1960 crop failure.[459] China changed her policy, and in 1963 her trade with the West exceeded her trade with socialist countries for the first time since 1951. In the 1970s (except 1976), trade with the Soviet Union was increasing again.[460]

Until the end of the autarky period (around 1956), all the socialist countries endeavored to reduce their dependence on foreign trade, a trend that occasionally led to unwise investment in low-profit sectors of industry solely for purposes of meeting this political target. Only later on was it discovered once again that certain countries have a comparative cost advantage in specific branches of the economy, and so attempts were made to avoid the cost disadvantages that inevitably arose for other countries on the world market. So far, the call for world market price orientation to be replaced by "socialist foreign trade prices," based on coordinated Comecon production costs, has not been followed up.

Virtually no other country pushed the concept of autarky as far as China did following her disappointment at the Soviet sanctions. A number of statements made by Chinese politicians and by Maoist ideologists outside China even went so far as to regard any acceptance of financial aid in the exchange of capital or commercial goods as a potential infiltration attempt, bringing the danger of nonequivalent exchange and political dependence in its wake.

This outlook, however, disregards the fact that

Table 78

Soviet machinery and equipment exports to China
(in 1,000 rubles)

Year	Exports	Year	Exports
1949	17,373	1944	51,944
1950	37,208	1965	69,296
1951	98,833	1966	77,596
1952	140,896	1967	22,178
1953	145,217	1968	13,409
1954	178,964	1969	19,422
1955	206,615	1970	13,581
1956	274,274	1971	49,175
1957	244,401	1972	75,830
1958	286,165	1973	74,918
1959	537,768	1974	80,517
1960	453,527	1975	69,617
1961	97,281	1976	122,849
1962	24,594	1977	64,194
1963	37,969	1978	95,864

Sources: *Vneshnyaya torgovlya SSSR 1918-1966* (Moscow: Statistika, 1967), p. 208f.; *Vneshnyaya torgovlya SSSR v 1978 g.* (Moscow: Statistika, 1969-1978), p. 231, and earlier issues.

1. the concept of autarky can only be envisaged seriously by *states with a large surface area* such as the Soviet Union, China, or Brazil, and cannot be transposed to smaller countries;
2. forced autarky, which, in the case of China, was also rational on the basis of *strategical considerations*,[461] could scarcely make such rational considerations appear rational to smaller states in a less threatened positon;
3. this all-inclusive apology of the autarky concept disregards the fact that the *foreign trade monopoly* and the integration of foreign trade policy into the central planning system covering all economic processes make the danger of foreign dependence and internal disproportion arising appear less grave than in the capitalist world;[462] this has led to the somewhat exaggerated assumption that the central plan and the foreign trade monopoly must already have been undermined by the recent economic

reforms carried out in Eastern European socialist countries, but this is not the case.

Hence, since it appears that China's emphasis on autonomy and independence in a socialist economy cannot simply be transposed to other socialist countries, we must even ask ourselves whether China's autonomous development has ever been jeopardized by foreign trade. I feel that it was not, for the following reasons:

1. *Foreign trade* only ever *played a minor role* in the People's Republic of China. China made no effort to reconquer her former leading position in the export of individual crops (soybeans, tea). Even though China accounted for one quarter of the world population, her share in world trade was still below 2% in the best periods, and her trade with the West was less than that of the tiny territory of Hong Kong. During the Great Leap Forward, China's exports fell to such an extent that the losses had not been made up by 1965. (See Table 79.) Despite the burden of the extensive loans from the Soviet Union, these only represented between 0.3 and 0.4% of China's estimated gross domestic product for the years 1950 to 1957 and only accounted for approximately 1% of China's savings.

2. As early as the start of 1956, China's role of capital importer changed into the role of capital exporter with repayments and the provision of development aid.[463] From 1956 to 1962, China paid back $1116 million to the Soviet Union and even achieved a positive balance.

Even during the construction phase, China's balance of payments was relatively favorable, despite import surpluses in trade with the socialist countries, on account of payments from Chinese abroad and export surpluses in trade with the West. With expanding trade with the West, however, the Chinese trade balance showed a major deficit for the first time in 1973. Chinese financial policies remained, however, rather conservative. There were no direct loans or buyer credits and no long-term borrowing. About 1979, China started to liberalize these policies.

3. Despite strong Chinese criticism of the Soviet Union, the reproach of *nonequivalent exchange* in trade among socialist states was only voiced rather late and then only very cautiously, similar to Che Guevara's criticism with regard to Cuba.[464] However, there was no foreign trade theory available to the socialist countries after the Second World War, since "socialism in one country," that is, the Soviet Union, had long stayed away from the capitalist world market. Because of the labor theory of value, socialist economy is also faced with a number of theoretical problems when it comes to

Table 79

China's foreign trade with selected countries (1971-1975)
(in 1,000,000 dollars)

	1971	1972	1973	1974	1975
Import					
Australia, New Zealand	33	50	167	385	343
FRG	160	190	357	421	523
France	125	67	103	161	374
United Kingdom	92	90	238	168	180
Honkong, Macao	5	5	10	59	34
Italy	71	88	84	105	145
Japan	607	640	1,093	1,988	2,259
Canada	213	296	356	446	371
Malaysia, Singapore	35	45	135	147	88
Soviet Union	80	120	135	143	129
United States	0	79	812	788	304
Export					
Australia, New Zealand	43	62	97	143	102
FRG	89	92	130	193	224
France	67	91	128	184	174
United Kingdom	69	77	102	157	135
Hongkong, Macao	445	535	825	1190	1372
Italy	56	73	112	117	126
Japan	322	468	928	1305	1531
Canada	28	49	53	62	55
Malaysia, Singapore	170	190	325	484	433
Soviet Union	75	135	135	139	150
United States	5	32	64	116	158

Sources: *China; A Reassessment of the Economy* (Washington: GOP, 1975), pp. 468ff.
W. Kraus: *Wirtschaftliche Entwicklung und sozialer Wandel in der Volksrepublik China*
(Heidelberg: Springer, 1979), p. 424.

drawing up criteria of fair exchange. This emerged again and again in concrete conflicts, such as when Castro, in 1966, after the suspension of Chinese rice deliveries, proposed an agreement whereby one ton of rice would be exchanged for one ton of sugar. He argued that sugar was 4 to 5 times as expensive as rice in China, while rice was 2 to 3 times as expensive as sugar in Cuba. China entered this agreement but canceled it at the end of the same year.[465]

Whereas in the 1950s China was very reticent with recrimination about nonequivalent trade, bourgeois economists following foreign trade in the Eastern bloc had long been pointing to the nonequivalent terms of trade in the Soviet Union's relations with her socialist allies.[466]

Many Western economists felt that China was at a disadvantage when it came to prices, and it has been maintained that in the late 1950s some Soviet prices were above those of the Western trade partners.[467] Nevertheless, in studies carried out after the Cold War had died down, economists have come to realize that the importance of Soviet aid and trade for China cannot be measured simply by the terms of trade. The usefulness of the Soviet goods, the credit facilities that would scarcely have been conceded by capitalist countries, and the advantage of trade between planned economies are certainly positive factors, despite certain disadvantages in pricing.

4.   Even though the Soviet Union sanctioned China in 1960 by withdrawing specialists and limiting deliveries, *the USSR adopted a rather generous approach in her repayment claims* after the 1960 crop failure. The Soviet Union had learned a lesson from earlier failures in economic warfare with Yugoslavia, and, having realized that the Chinese could not be distracted from their course by sanctions either, she showed growing readiness to compromise in subsequent disagreements with Cuba and Rumania.[468]

Despite China's negative experience with one-sidedness in her economic relations with one single country and the resulting vulnerability of some of her plans, China did not shrink from applying repressive measures similar to those that the Soviet Union had formerly applied to China. China's rapidly expanding trade with Cuba was abruptly cut back in 1966, not only because of differences of opinion about terms of trade referred to above, but also for what were chiefly political motives. Castro accused the People's Republic of China of wanting to make political capital out of the rice deliveries and criticized the intense propaganda put out by the Chinese Embassy, aimed at winning the population over to its viewpoint in the conflict between Peking and Moscow. The Soviets had admittedly lost political credit with the increasing economic credit they granted to the island, but Castro could neither afford to nor wished to risk an open breach with Moscow. Che Guevara was much more critical about Cuba's pro-Soviet policy, even though, in his own State Department, he still defended the idea of intensified industrialization —an idea that China had partially revised by then, following the Great Leap Forward.[469]

Whereas Cuba stressed the domestic aspect of autonomy through planning even more than did the Chinese leadership, Cuba's exposed geographical situation and its economy, which could not be rapidly diversified, forced the country to make considerable departures from the autarky concept that had also been propagated at times in the early days of the regime. Integration into the socialist division of labor and the danger of new dependence as a result of long-term trade agreements with the Eastern bloc countries cannot be overlooked. The forced reorientation in Cuba's foreign trade was already a problem in itself. Before the Revolution, 70 to 75% of Cuba's trade was with the United States, and in 1957/58 her trade with the East only accounted for 0.3%, including such insignificant goods as Christmas decorations from Czechoslovakia. In the early 1960s, Cuba reoriented her foreign trade, and within two years 80% of her trade was with the Eastern bloc countries—a development that did not go without frictional losses (Table 77).[470]

Nevertheless, one cannot speak of dependence in the case of Cuba and draw a parallel with "imperialistic" relations of dependence, because plan priority means that the internal repercussions differ from those experienced in some capitalist developing countries.

Ideological relations of dependence

Even where no direct economic dependence developed, milder forms of dependence can certainly not be excluded, as Galtung has shown in the communications sector. A new form of dependence in the communications sector may be seen in the dependence of revolutionary ideology, which can also influence the innovative capacity of an economic system. Many developing countries miss out on radical reforms and redistributive measures because of foreign development aid, and in the long term this can be detrimental to the efficiency of an economic system. Slavish imitation of the Soviet Union meant that some of the socialist states, and particularly those that had been at a higher level of development than the Soviet Union, became more hostile to innovation. It was only with the economic reforms of the 1960s that they gradually began to recover from the consequences of this attitude. The socialist countries have to some extent gambled away the advantages derived from autonomous development in that they have increasingly come to regard plan fulfilment as the most important efficiency criterion. Soviet scholars increasingly emphasize the variety of "socialist models," that is, different economic and political institutions and in some cases a multiparty system. But they normally stress that independent organizations, especially trade unions, are not compatible with "the socialist system."[471] This applies especially to Czechoslovakia in 1968 and recently to the Polish events in 1980.

After the War ideological dependence was expressed particularly in:

1. the *imitation of gigantic projects* constructed by the Soviet Union in the early accumulation phase;
2. *integration into a socialist division of labor system within Comecon*, which was not always in line with the countries' own interest—such as the German Democratic Republic building up a low-profit shipbuilding industry when the country had no tradition of this.

Whenever Comecon industrial states exported goods to the Soviet Union, without their own demand being met first, it can be said that ideological dependence, at the very least, was at play here.

6. Comparative appraisal of efficiency

If we attempt to make a final judgment on the efficiency of the socialist economies using the five major criteria, we once again come up against the problem of appraisal. Socialist planners tend to identify high plan fulfilment or even overfulfilment with high efficiency. Measured by this criterion, calculations for the 1971-to-1975 plan period published in "The Economist" showed that the countries with what were by comparison the most stringent plans, such as the Soviet Union, Bulgaria, and Rumania, came off less favorably than countries with a more flexible planning and administration system, such as Poland and Hungary, who headed the race for plan fulfilment in Comecon in 1972, although this does not necessarily imply that they had the highest economic efficiency. A Polish scholar remarked correctly that Polish decentralized planning institutions seem to be far superior to those of the German Democratic Republic, which nevertheless has higher economic efficiency explained in terms of "political culture" and working morale.

Plan targets are, however, generally no longer compared with potential alternatives and until now have not been open to public discussion—that is, a discussion that is not directed from the top— with the possibility of alternative planning. Whereas capitalist economists mainly measure efficiency with the criterion of the least expensive combination of input (labor and capital),[472] socialist planners tend rather to go by what they think is the optimal combination of results (output). Consequently, most efficiency comparisons have not paid sufficient attention to the differences in economic ideology that underlie the systems.

Here, however, we must take account of the differences between the leading elites and the bulk of the citizens in socialist states. Not all citizens have fully absorbed the values of the almost "puritanic efficiency mentality" that the ideology propagates.[473] Questionable surveys by Radio Free Europe among West German and Polish citizens have shown that West Germans rate efficiency criteria higher in the evaluation of success in life than do the Poles.[474] The socialist values of the elite can be enforced more effectively, however, through the concentrated application of instruments ranging from enlightenment to repression than is possible in fragmented capitalist systems.

In the light of those systemic divergences, it is not possible to make global pronouncements about efficiency, because political targets, such as "reeducation of man," cannot be assessed in terms of economic efficiency criteria. Schemes that appeared to be economic, such as land reclamation programs and a large number of other campaigns, always pursued political objectives as well, and these occasionally defeated economic efficiency. Hence, efficiency comparisons will always be partial. Even when it comes to efficiency that is measurable in economic terms, conclusive appraisals will in the last instance depend on the level of comparison. Prosocialist economists even certify that U.S. capitalism is more efficient on a microeconomic level, although this is achieved at the price of negative repercussions on income distribution, on the securing of world peace, and on the rationality of the system in terms of society as a whole.

Hence, even though purely quantitative efficiency comparisons can no longer be used for an uncritical apology of capitalism today, the comparison of individual indicators in the efficiency field is not nearly as superfluous as some system ontologists in socialist systems would at times have had it be. All the same, overall efficiency must be viewed in conjunction with other goals, such as redistribution and participation. Only in cases where there were lengthy periods of misalignments, policy fluctuation due to the repeated introduction of new campaigns, and concessions to individual groups, which triggered off increased expectations in other groups and infringed the Pareto optimum, did the efficiency problem also develop into a legitimation crisis for socialist systems as well. However, this only affected the respective elite and its heads (Rákosi, Novotny, Gomulka, Gierek), and has so far never jeopardized the socialist system, contrary to the crisislike phenomena that have developed in a number of capitalist economies.

5

Efficiency
in the distribution sphere

In all transitional societies, socialist policy can point to considerable success in redistribution (see Chapter 2). As yet this cannot be equated, however, with efficiency in the distribution sphere—in fact precisely the contrary is the case, because a radical redistribution policy can temporarily hamper production to such an extent that distribution also suffers indirect repercussions. Redistribution, coupled with efforts to maximize the "accumulation" target (that is, to increase efficiency in the production sphere), tends to mean that the consumption opportunities created for citizens in socialist states are subjected to drastic temporary cutbacks. Whereas redistribution and expropriation policy were chiefly accepted and supported by the unpropertied masses, transitional societies could generally not legitimate themselves so rapidly in the distribution sphere. Creating a consumer and producer identity proved to be a longer job than the ideological postulation had been.

1.   Distributive efficiency, consumption, and advertising

Marx stated that in capitalist societies "production thus creates the consumers."[475] In socialist systems, on the other hand, producer and consumer were theoretically identical. It was only "occasional incorrect leadership methods," cedes a GDR economist, that made it difficult for the worker to appreciate fully this coincidence of interests, and a Soviet economist points to the "existence of contradictions between production and consumption," criticizing the fact that these are merely reduced to the difference between supply and solvent demand.[476]

It would, however, be questionable methodology to use the comparable facts available to draw general conclusions as to the inevitable victims in the distribution sphere in all socialist transformation processes, since nearly all systems started off under the restrictive conditions of one variant or another of "war communism." Only a country such as Cuba, which appeared privileged because its socialist government did not inherit an economy ruined by long wars or civil war, would be of interest for revolution research as marking a deviant case. Even here, it was seen that some of the shortcomings of forced expropriation policy had negative repercussions on the distribution sphere—albeit with the difference that during the revolutionary "honeymoon" the position of consumers was noticeably improved. This improvement proved to be short-lived, however, because the increased consumption of meat, for example—which the revolutionary government at first paraded as proof of an improved supply situation—did not all stem from increased production but rather from a redistribution of reserves and from excessive slaughtering, which were the first consequences of redistribution, as they had been in China and in the Soviet Union (see Chapter 1, Section 3).[477]

Although in terms of comparative economics she was in a better starting position for rapid development than many other developing countries, the Soviet Union in particular developed an exaggerated anticonsumption ideology, of which Joan Robinson once said cuttingly: "ideology taught that consumer goods are not essential. Queues in front of shops, poor quality overcrowded housing and ill manners were part of the sacrifice for socialism."[478]

Scarcity of commodities leads to particular forms of control over the consumer. Lines in front of stalls and counters threaten to develop into status symbols for the state trading functionaries. Where no lines formed, there were obviously no "sought-after goods," and the mere fact that lines did build up at certain stalls developed into a type of functional equivalent for capitalist advertising in the socialiist consumption sphere. The Ninth USSR Five-Year Plan up to 1975 provided for notable improvements in the consumer's position.[479] The Eastern European people's democracies, however, show considerable fluctuation in the growth of private consumption, and during the accumulation phase there is evidence that the percentage of private consumption in the gross national product clearly fell (Czechoslovakia from 76.3% in 1948 to 57.7% in 1970; German Democratic Republic from 82.9% in 1950 to 76.7% in 1970).[480]

The Chinese leaders are acknowledged to have been less opposed to consumption, and all travelers bring back reports that the arrogant, bureaucratic type of customer service, which makes life difficult in the Soviet Union, is nowhere to be found in China. Despite the relatively low level of industrial development, management experts credit Chinese enterprise management with the fact that their range of goods does not constitute the same extravagant waste as found in capitalist countries yet does not reveal the same drab monotony as goods found in former Soviet stores. In addition, despite the fact that Chinese managers' level of training and know-how in marketing is below the Soviet average, they nonetheless show more interest in looking after consumers' needs than do their Soviet counterparts. This greater degree of liberality toward consumption has, however, been subject to fluctuation. In 1958 Mao defended drastic cutbacks in consumption in favor of accumulation when preparing for the Great Leap Forward. Then, during the cultural revolution, the extravagant waste originating in Liu Shao-chi's efforts to "preach a bourgeois kaleidoscopic colorfulness" was denounced.

The very fact that agriculture was underprivileged in the Soviet Union set a vicious circle in motion, which held the level of consumption down at too low a level, compared with growth rates. Since income differentials were small by comparison, this did not generate any feelings of hate despite the general frugality that prevailed.

If we compare consumption structure in terms of the minimum subsistence level, then all socialist systems provide ample data here (see Table 80). The UN statistics—which go by the rough yardstick of calories and protein content of food—show that on average there is no deficit, although the proportion of animal foodstuffs—taken by many statisticians as an indicator of food quality—does reveal noticeable differences. North Korea and North Vietnam (and also China) then lagged far behind, although no further behind comparable countries such as South Korea, South Vietnam, or India. On the other hand, however, these figures give a poor country such as Mongolia, which still has large numbers of nomadic shepherds, a consumption level otherwise only found in the chart leader, the German Democratic Republic.

These figures might at best be informative in comparisons with nonsocialist developing countries, since they supply a yardstick by which to measure whether the minimum per capita subsistence level is guaranteed and exceeded. It would, in fact, be interesting to know the actual distribution pattern of consumer goods, but no figures are available here. China and Cuba's achievement lies less in their level of mean consumption and more in the simple fact that, despite shortages, no one in either country needs any longer to starve to death or consume food unfit for human consumption, as still happens in many parts of the Third World. The figures are less significant when it comes to comparing the Soviet Union and the People's Democracies with the United States and Western Europe, since they provide little information on the quality of foods and on the lack of choice and variation, which is constantly coming under fire in socialist countries.[481]

If we take the statistics on consumption outside the food sector, then we see that socialist citizens spend a higher proportion of their income on food, drink, and clothes than do their capitalist counterparts. These commodities accounted for some 70% of the family budget in the Soviet Union in 1965, while in Great Britain the same commodities claimed only 40%.[482]

These differences correlate to some extent with the level of development. The number of children and the age structure of the population have considerable bearing on certain differences in food patterns, which cannot always be sufficiently well interpreted through a simple comparison of statistics.[483] Exaggerated criticism from Western economists, asserting that, according to a comparison of family budgets in the United States and the Soviet Union, the latter in 1950 was still lagging behind the US standard of 1890,[484] was, even at the time, only due to inadequate consideration of the level of social consumption, and today this has no foundation whatsoever in the statistics.

These comparative figures for family budgets should not lead to the immediate conclusion that the standard of living is much lower. Statistics of this type need to be correlated with the share of agriculture in the national income. Socialist countries would seem to be somewhat behind here, since they have tended in the main to overburden agriculture in favor of promoting industrialization. It must also be considered that citizens in socialist states need to set aside

Table 80

Net food consumption

Country	Year	Cereal	Potato	Sugar	Vegetables	Meat	Milk	Fats	Daily calories Total	Animal %
Albania	1964/66	435	38	48	25	84	255	14	2,370	14
Bulgaria	1964/66	534	62	64	19	109	236	35	3,070	13
Cuba	1964/66	297	214	135	37	111	216	14	2,500	16
China	1964/66	387	247	10	39	47	9	7	2,050	9
Czechoslovakia	1964/66	348	295	103	8	167	356	44	3,030	27
GDR	1964/66	270	383	88	6	171	316	67	3,040	37
Hungary	1963/65	374	241	81	11	140	268	58	3,050	32
North Korea	1964/66	469	211	5	75	21	1	1	2,270	4
Poland	1964/66	383	347	98	10	138	552	40	3,140	30

Rumania	1964/66	500	182	48	24	105	319	26	3,010	18
Soviet Union	1964/66	428	378	106	19	106	476	33	3,180	21
North Vietnam	1964/66	411	181	3	11	40	24	4	2,000	9
Yugoslavia	1963/65	534	176	57	27	74	281	36	3,130	18
Mongolia	1964/66	374	50	46	–	302	237	8	2,540	37
for comparison:										
FRG	1963/65	203	322	94	12	179	546	73	2,950	37
South Korea	1963/65	515	233	4	17	15	3	1	2,270	3
South Vietnam	1964/66	486	70	16	11	27	13	6	2,200	7
Japan	1963/65	404	181	48	45	28	96	18	2,410	11
India	1963/65	381	35	54	55	4	118	10	2,000	6
Spain	1963/65	279	308	57	33	73	238	63	2,790	18
Sweden	1963/65	190	264	114	9	141	714	61	2,950	42
United States	1963/65	178	127	131	22	276	672	58	3,140	41

Source: UN, *Statistical Yearbook 1971.* (New York: UN, 1972), pp. 508ff.

considerably less of their budget for other purposes—rents account for only 5 to 10%, which is less than half the amount required in most capitalist countries, even though this has admittedly not been able to make up for the marked dissatisfaction with undersupply in the housing system (see Chapter 8, Section 3).

As long as stratification still exists in socialist systems, the stratification factor also has to be taken into consideration. Sociological surveys conducted in the Soviet Union repeatedly revealed that the budget of a working class family divided up as shown in Table 81.

The lower price level is particularly evident in the *services* area and also in a number of consumer goods such as medicine, although outside the state hospital system princely sums are also still demanded for medicine in socialist countries. In the German Democratic Republic, expenditure on comparable services in the energy, transport, communications, laundry, and hairdressing sectors is roughly half that in West Germany.[485]

Table 81

Budget of Soviet working class family in historical perspective
(expenses in percentages)

Years	1940	1965	1970	1975	1979
food	53.8	37.9	35.7	32.9	31.8
clothing	11.1	13.9	15.5	15.4	15.6
furniture and equipments (including motorcycles)	1.7	6.1	5.8	6.5	6.6
construction	n.d.	0.4	0.4	0.3	0.4
heating	1.2	0.4	0.3	0.2	0.1
education, health, and services from the social funds	9.0	13.8	13.9	13.8	14.2
rent and municipal services	2.9	2.7	2.7	2.7	2.7
savings	4.7	2.8	4.1	6.3	6.6
taxes	4.1	7.2	7.9	8.5	8.7
other expenses	5.8	7.0	6.8	6.8	6.6

Source: *Narodnoe khozyaistvo SSSR v 1979 g* (Moscow: Statistika, 1980), p. 410.

The importance of services with the increasing standard of consumption is more adequately measured by the labor employed in this sector rather than by the expenditure of individual families, although admittedly it is difficult to draw the distinction between services supplied to individuals (such as repair work) and services supplied within the social security system and by way of infra-structural expenditure. With the exception of Bulgaria and Hungary, there has been a slow—though steady—rise in the proportion of people employed not in production but primarily in the services sector.[486]

Socialist countries are increasingly acknowledging the fact that an improvement in the services will be necessary if some of the more humane goals of socialism are to be achieved; this would allow more rational use of leisure time than is possible today in the light of current supply levels.[487] In addition, the socialist countries are coming to realize that "reality" forbids them to do what economic theory has for so long allowed them to do—namely, to lump together all the services as an unproductive area of labor."[488] All the same, this low regard for the services is still reflected in the low wages paid in the service sector today (see Table 29).

On the other hand, since the services sector is still highly under-developed, *chal'tura*, or working on the side, occupies an important role; it is reluctantly tolerated by the state, even though these side jobs do border on corruption (see Chapter 2, Section 1).

As the level of productive resources increases, the consumption structure undergoes shifts similar to those experienced in capitalist systems. Services start to account for a higher percentage, while food drops to a lesser rank. The fact that food still accounts for an over-proportionate part of the family budget in the German Democratic Republic and Czechoslovakia, in relation to these countries' level of development, stems in part from the high taxes levied on food, which cannot be compensated by the low price level for basic foods such as bread and potatoes. (See Table 82.)

The marked shifts that have come about in consumption struc-ture over the past few years mean that earlier generalizations about hostility toward consumption are becoming increasingly untenable. These generalizations are based on a short period in the accumula-tion phase, when there were indeed sharp cutbacks in consumption, though the global figures of the development of the consumption fund do not show an increase in all of the socialist countries. (See Table 83.)

Only during the accumulation phase are socialist countries on the whole inclined to spend a much higher proportion of their gross

Table 82

Comparison of the expenditure structure in four-person households of employees in West Germany, the German Democratic Republic and the Soviet Union

Expenditure	West Germany 1968	GDR 1968	Soviet Union (as far as comparable)		
			1940	1965	1979
food	31.8	36.7	67.3	45.2	35.7
clothing	11.7	16.3	10.9	13.7	15.6
furniture and living requirements	3.8	4.0	1.1	4.2	6.2
rents and communal services (electricity, gas, etc.)	20.1	5.8	3.8	2.0	1.6
travel and communication	3.5	2.3			
culture and recreation	3.8	2.9	4.8	14.0	14.5
other services (repairs, hairdresser, etc.)	6.9	6.6			
savings			6.3	8.0	8.9
taxes			1.4	1.4	1.4
others			4.1	8.9	14.0

Sources: *Bericht der Bundesregierung u. Materialien zur Lage der Nation. 1971* (Bonn: Bundesministerium für innerdeutsche Beziehungen, 1971), p. 141; G. S. Sarkisyan & N. P. Kuznecova, *Potrebnosti i dochod semi* (Moscow: Ekonomika, 1967), p. 65; *Narodnoe chozyaystvo SSSR v. g.* (Moscow, 1980), p. 411. *Statistisches Jahrbuch der DDR* (Berlin (East): Staatsverlag der DDR, 1973), p. 338.

Table 83

Share of the consumption fund in the national product

Country	1960	1970	1979
Bulgaria	72.6	70.8	77.2
Czechoslovakia	82.3	73.0	75.4
GDR	81.8	75.6	79.9
Hungary	76.9	75.1	74.4
Poland	76.0	74.9	74.9
Rumania	n.d	n.d	63.1 (1977)
Soviet Union	73.2	70.5	75.1

Source: Statistics from: *Jahrbuch der Wirtschaft Osteuropas /Yearbook of East European Economics,* Vol. 4 (Munich: Olzog, 1973), p. 481ff. *Statisticheskii ezhegodnik stran-chlenov SEV. 1980* (Moscow: Statistika, 1980), p. 46.

national product on investment rather than on consumption. During the 1950s, which marked a construction or reconstruction phase in all socialist systems, the Soviet Union, Yugoslavia, and the German Democratic Republic were among the seven countries in the world that spent the lowest proportion of their GNP on private consumption.

The general sacrifices demanded of consumers during the socialist accumulation phase are temporarily justified, provided that no large-scale disparities are maintained at the same time. These shortcomings in distribution policy have not, however, been permanently eliminated in all socialist systems. There are still three factors that diminish equality in the consumption sphere in a number of socialist systems today:

1. The *existence of a black market* favors the ex-middle classes and those who have the time to stand and queue and who can then sell their place on the waiting list at a profit (such as with the order lists for cars in a number of systems). Trends such as these become even more antiegalitarian where countries are unable to check inflation, as China was able to do, and where inflation heightens the discrepancies still further, as wage increases cannot be directly translated into consumer benefits for the workers through the surplus of purchasing power and the shortage of goods, as happened in Cuba and in Chile up to 1973.

2. The *anticonsumption ideology* propagated by the bureaucracies of a number of socialist systems was in itself antiegalitarian,

in that it temporarily benefited the cadres upholding the system, however unavoidable this may have been from an efficiency angle.

Special privileges introduced for the workers during the initial phase of the changeover to socialism can be a sensible instrument of redistribution (such as the "people's shops" of the "Instituto Nacional de Reforma Agraria" (INRA), which sold goods cheaply to Cuba's agricultural population), but later on these can threaten to develop into unjustified privileges for individual groups of the population.

3.   *Shortages* in the consumption sphere during the accumulation phase and, in particular, in the housing system, have a markedly *restrictive* effect on *horizontal mobility and hence on vertical mobility as well at times.* Some people have to turn down good posts because they are unable to find accommodation in their new location, and in other cases state-subsidized housing entices people to immobility.

All three factors would suggest that the transition to socialism should be carried out in such a way as to avoid large-scale economic setbacks, since excessive scarcity has a stratifying effect, unless a country relentlessly employs a "sending down" system (such as the Chinese *Hsia fang* system) in cases where upward alignment is impossible because of the level of productive resources. Maximization of well-being in the distribution sphere calls for a compromise of several goals and cannot be read off from a system of equations, as was sometimes assumed during the "storm and stress" phase of planning.

The reform economists of the socialist camp did not, however, turn back to promoting consumption again solely on grounds of protective and distributive policy; they also realized that in the long term their true goal, that is, efficiency, simply could not be furthered through asceticism of consumption. Soviet economists thus worked on the basis of Liberman's realization that "at a certain stage, restrictions on consumption start becoming an obstacle to effective accumulation."[489]

The planned combination of an increase in consumption with a rise in the level of productive resources, however, conjured up a spirit of consumerism that a number of planners feared they would never be rid of again.

Party leaders who take the quest to the building-up of communism very seriously show concern at consumers' growing self-awareness and at the increasing differentiation of their needs. Some of the concern of socialist politicians, who fear that "consumer sovereignty" could undermine the priorities set out in the plan through market mechanisms, is as yet unfounded. According to socialist economists, under socialist planning consumer sovereignty —

or at least a wider range of options open to the consumer—does not have to produce the same irrational decisions as occur in capitalism, because there is no permanent consumer brainwashing through irrational advertising, and socialist governments' enlightenment policy can bring about much more rational decisions.[490] Even in this field, however, left-wing criticism is already troubled by the consumer friendliness revealed in the politics of some socialist countries. The *advertising* of socialist planners still comprises a tight knit of political enlightenment and economic promotion. This can bring about an indirect incentive to purchase because the desire to purchase is somehow linked to the consumer's affirmation of the achievements of socialism and is anchored to the consumer's political loyalty. In addition to this, the functions of advertising—with chief stress placed on the function of plan fulfilment[491]—are repeatedly used as grounds for justifying sales promotion for goods that are difficult to sell. A discontinuous sequence of advertising campaigns, producing anything but consumer enlightenment, serves to compensate for planning errors. On the other hand, however, socialist economic policy can better monitor the factual content of advertising and provide more comprehensive consumer protection against underhand practices than has so far been possible in capitalist countries. Nevertheless, socialist systems, too, have now seen the danger of advertising reducing people's tendency to save by arousing latent needs and thereby enticing consumers to obtain extra income for themselves. This would mean that the ex-ante regulation of needs, which marks one of the prerequisites of a planned economy, could one day become increasingly difficult.

There are, however, other features of the system that place certain limits on the dysfunctions of socialist advertising. Labor law generally has a much wider scope of application in socialist systems than in capitalist economies: labor law not only governs the quantitative interrelationship between work time and leisure time, but also reduces potential for unwise use of leisure time. As a rule, it is not permitted to use time set aside for rest to earn extra money. The repressive and regulatory side to the labor law (see Chapter 7, Section 4) on the one hand has a markedly protective function when it comes to the consumption sphere, though the importance of this for family life and the nation's health is difficult to quantify.

The growing proportion of social consumption in workers' incomes also means that individual consumers are left with less scope for setting their priorities wrongly. While even under the conditions of a socialist society this cannot always be excluded entirely, it is argued that it does not tend to involve the same consequences for the individual in question and for his family as it would under a capitalist system, where "fictitious consumer" sovereignty even gives people the freedom to ruin themselves, undermine their health, and deprive their families through luxury consumption.

A further advantage of socialism is said to lie in the fact that distribution and redistribution rank among the chief tasks of the system, except that is, where the ruling beaurocratic party elite, spurred on by great power motivations, has highhandedly set priorities in a different order. In capitalist systems, on the other hand, for a long time workers and their unions had to wrestle every little improvement in their living conditions out of the system's ruling powers through wage conflicts and class struggles.[492]

6

Efficiency
in the legitimation sphere

Modernization theory has worked out a number of indicators for the efficiency of a system, which include "functional specialization of government activities," professionalization of bureaucracy, elimination of corruption, and expansion of participation,[493] but these cannot be used for a comparison of socialist systems. Specialization of government activities and standards of participation are ipso facto much greater in socialist than in capitalist systems, and socialist systems are also aiming precisely at not having a professionalized bureaucracy, even if this has not been completely avoided over the long term.

The primacy of politics, which is the ideological requirement underlying the actions of socialist elites, calls for a different classification of the instruments available for increasing a system's political efficiency. There are basically four steering instruments open to socialist systems:[494]

1.   ideology and socialization;
2.   organization and planning;
3.   force;
4.   gratifications.

All four of these instruments also exist in capitalist systems, but in a somewhat different rank order. Indirect steering with gratifications, which, in theory, ranks last in socialist systems, still marks the most important steering instrument in capitalist systems. Quantifiable indicators are difficult to find for any of the four instruments and for the instrument of "force" in particular. Thus this chapter can essentially only consist in a verbal description of the problems involved.

1.   Ideology and socialization

In view of the effectiveness of capitalist "remnants" and the persistence of presocialist attitudes, the instrument of socialization appeared to be the most efficient and most promising in the long term. Valuable indicators as to the effectiveness of ideological schooling can be found by using indicators related to the educational system. This is particularly so if the data available (see Chapter 2, Section 3) is supplemented by a breakdown of the study material taught. Quantitative data on study material is quite rare and the information available is mostly descriptive. The focal points in study subject programs and in book production could provide a certain guide as to differences in socialist systems here. This information would need to be backed up by information on the effectiveness of other means of indoctrination outside the socialization system, in the strict sense of the term.

Statistics on the *mass media* would mark an initial step here. The earlier modernization literature attached a relatively high level of importance to the "mass communications media" indicator for analyzing development levels. This approach becomes absurd, however, when used by Lipset[495] to compare socialist developing countries with capitalist developing countries, without any allowance being made for the eminently political variable of "media policy" that socialist countries deliberately employ for ideological schooling and socialization purposes. This is why in relation to their level of development socialist countries have an overproportionately high number of newspapers, radios, and televisions (even in the sphere of personal consumption). Hence, in mobilization systems of this type the mass media can at best be taken as an indicator for the level of ideological steering (see Table 84).

An even more informative indicator would be the *material communicated by the mass media* in socialist countries. Virtually no quantitative surveys have been carried out here. One can simply venture the theory that the stringency of the ideological steering system as reflected in the mass media correlates with the length of the struggle preceding the takeover of power. The values of the partisans and underground fighters are not the sole acting force, although the socialist systems in developing countries could well lead one to suppose this. In Yugoslavia, for example, despite the partisan myth, rational bureaucratic values from presocialist and extrasocialist political cultures very soon gained ground again. The detotalization of socialist elites' expectations and the demarginalization of these groups generally seems to progress more rapidly in countries with a high level of productive resources, however, and, as can be seen from the development of communist party elites in Western Europe, this can take place well before the seizure of power.

Even in a country like the Soviet Union, however, which during the first few decades of her existence had to try to offset a shortfall in efficiency in the production sphere with an increase in efficiency in the legitimation sphere, growing successes in the military, industrial, and scientific spheres were seen to lead to rapid erosion of symbolic, ideological output in favor of successes in the production and distribution spheres, which could be measured more precisely. As a consequence, socialist countries seeking a model for the chiliastic elements of symbolic output had to orient themselves more toward Mao, Castro, or Ho Chi Minh than toward the dark-suited revolutionaries with their silver-grey ties, such as Brezhnev or Kosygin.

Taking Alex Inkeles' distinction between "agitation" and "propaganda," it could be generalized that the socialist regimes of developing countries now work more with action-oriented agitation, whereas the more sophisticated Eastern European systems are increasingly inclined to content themselves with propaganda that is not specifically action-oriented and is aimed at a general strengthening of loyalties.[496]

As the level of productive resources and the level of education increases, the requirements placed on the agitators also undergo change as well. The nonspecific, all-round doctrinarian with limited specialist knowledge is sharply criticized in the Soviet Union, which aims instead at the well-educated political informer.[497] As symbolic

Table 84

Mass media and communications indicators

Country	Rank out of 25 countries	Yearly Newspaper number circulation of copies per 1,000 per person		Radio receivers per 1,000		Television receivers per 1,000 population		Tele-phones per 1,000	Per number of calls	Lettermail per capita		Per 100
		1973	1978	1973	1978	1973	1978	1973	1978	1973	1973	1978
GDR	6	421	177	337	375	188	330	97.0	3736	75	9	7.4
Czechoslovakia	19	280	93.4	263	248	149	266	105.3	1812			8.3
Soviet Union	21	264	148	320	246	68	237	13.3	406			3.6
Hungary	28	178	98	245	239	82	246	55.8	n.d.	51	n.d.	8.2
Bulgaria	33	172	98	219	142	24	183	34.0	482			3.2
Poland	36	167	76	179	232	66	213	41.1	1549	30	2	4.2
Cuba (1961)	41	181	37	74	n.d.	42	n.d.	30.3	5.2			0.7

Rumania	44	157	58	147	110	26	156	n.d.	24.9			3.8
Yugo-slavia	50	90	n.d.	154	n.d.	30	n.d.	n.d.	21.2	53	7	n.d.
Mongolia (1963)	51	88	60	n.d.	89	n.d.	25	203	12.3			0.8
Albania	71	47	n.d.	70	n.d.	1	n.d.	n.d.	n.d.			
for comparison:												
United States	1	310		1234		362			481.4	347	14	
Sweden	2	505		382		270			437.9	172	20	
FRG	5	326		440		193			149.1	146	18	
Japan	10	451		209		183			125.1	95	2	
Italy	34	113		208		117			116.0	101	14	
Spain (1963)	39	153		144		55			87.7	77	18	
Greece (1959)	42	121		106		n.d.			59.4	30	n.d.	

Source: Taylor-Hudson, op.cit., pp. 236ff.; figures for 1978 from: *Statisticheskii ezhegodnik stran-chlenov SEV 1979* (Moscow, Statistika, 1979), p. 333.

output becomes progressively rationalized, so the repressive components of ideological indoctrination and socialization are cut back as well. At the time of the four clean-ups in China, for instance, these still bore marked repressive and disciplinary traits.[498]

Even in more developed socialist systems where open terror is virtually a thing of the past, as in Poland, the appeal to fear still remains an ideological steering instrument as well as the "Gulag Archipelago which has crept into the mind," as Milovan Djilas once put it—methods unworthy of the humane goals of socialism.[499]

Socialist systems have so far had the advantage of not experiencing an increase in expectations in the same proportions as capitalist countries, because they held back conspicuous consumption in favor of conspicuous production (see Chapter 4, Section 2). The increased yield is more collective in nature and there are no interest groups to stir up expectations or take sanctions. Hence, even though stratification through gratifications and rewards is avoided to the extent that prevails under capitalism, there is still evidence of a certain ideologically-based stratification if we accept Siegfried Bernfeld's view that *penalties* can also have a stratifying effect. Thus, the more a system renounces material gratification and employs a mix of rewards and penalties in a gigantic national reeducation scheme, the greater the accompanying repressive component will be.

Negative gratifications have a much stronger tendency to accumulate than positive gratifications here, because behavior in one sphere is taken as an indication of behavior in other spheres as well. The simple fact of being drunk at work can be blown up to indicate a lack of conscience and, under some circumstances, may lead to sanctions being taken on a number of levels. Contrary to the case under capitalism, however, this more frequent use of sanctions is accompanied by the opportunity for individuals to prove themselves through "work probation" or, in the case of more serious sanctions, through "probation on the production line." Thus people have the chance to free themselves from the negative gratifications they have accumulated in the ideologically steered system. Even the consequences of a prison sentence are generally not so serious as under capitalism because the released convict does not seem to be cast so much onto the margin of society or to be so stigmatized.

Most socialist countries have not as yet been aiming for non-controlled socialization and communication, although as the arts and media have become more differentiated, and, as international arts and science communication has increased, the control, which has been exercised ever since the agitprop department of the Central Committee was set up in 1920, has come a long way from the totalitarian models. This often gives rise to that blend of open criticism, stemming from the awareness that in the 1970s a well-known intellectual can no longer simply disappear as used to happen during the Stalin era. There is also a loyal "submission to the communist world movement," leading, in many cases, to resistance against the temptations of emigration, which the regime would quite welcome, despite persecution and job bans.

Despite the *samizdat* and underground literature that at times is tolerated as a safety valve, the scarcely fragmented and multi-dimensional type of proletarian public opinion, which should theoretically develop if work ceases to be solely a commodity, has not come about. Critical theories are scarcely admitted in socialist countries, apart from episodes in Cuba, Poland, Czechoslovakia, and Yugoslavia. This has disadvantages when it comes to the innovative capacity of the system, however, and these have made it extraordinarily difficult for the system to take in new problems not anticipated in the ideology, such as crime, neglected youth, dissatisfaction in the army, signs of mental illness. Hence, when critics attempt to test the actual substance of what, in quantitative terms, seem to be impressive successes in the educational system, they then come up with a less positive assessment.

The development of socialist systems is marked by the old "intellectual aristocratism versus Machaevshchina" faction struggles (named after the Polish-Russian social democrat, J. Machajski, who wanted to leave the replacement of intellectual leadership by a proletariat leadership to come about by itself). Even Castro, who perhaps created the most vivid image of an intellectual revolutionary for himself and who was not by chance the idol of left-wing intellectuals in the West during the late 1960s, started pursuing the intellectuals increasingly after 1968, and, with his repression of the renowned Cuban lyricist, Herberto Padilla, he gambled away part of the worldwide credit he had earned for critical socialism. In the case of Mao, his mistrust of the intellectuals was apparent right from the start. He himself did not hesitate to criticize his own behavior during his younger years. This mistrust of intellectuals still penetrates today deep into the subject-matter taught in the education system, right down to the content of children's books.[500]

Short experiments with tolerance, such as the "hundred flowers" campaign and the lull after the Great Leap Forward, had to be speedily broken off due to the excessive criticism.[501]

The movements against the intelligentsia simultaneously constituted a measure against specialization trends within the elites. Mao repeatedly feared that even though the party would still continue to control ideology, the intelligentsia could take over the reins of technology. As a preventive measure, differences of opinion between "reds" and "experts" were therefore frequently leveled out.

The reverse side of this mistrust of intellectuals, which has constantly kept flaring up, is the nondiscriminating glorification of work, which no longer allows the difference between alienated work and nonalienated work to be perceived under socialist systems. Even Marxist theorists, are, however, ever more prepared to admit that, for the moment, alienated work is on the increase in socialism.[502]

Ideological oversteering not only results in signs of intellectual paralysis but can also constitute a heavy financial burden for a developing socialist system, as a result of the overstaffing of unproductive propagandist jobs. Capitalist countries have no right to reproach socialist systems here, however. Statisticians have worked out that "spiritual welfare expenditure" on clergymen in the United States accounts for the same level of national income, with about 0.1% of the population, as do party functionaries and propagandists in the Soviet Union.[503]

At times of crisis, ideological oversteering of a system threatens to produce markedly dysfunctional consequences. These consequences include:

1.   *Overstraining of the principle of criticism and self-criticism*, with consequences reminiscent of witch trials in the Middle Ages, when innocent virgins confessed to having wantonly cavorted with the devil on top of the church spire. Monstrous plots were "uncovered," whereby as early as 1918 Bukharin and Trotsky reputedly wanted to have Lenin murdered, and Trotsky had supposedly been an agent of the German secret service since 1921.[504] The very fact that these confessions could at times be obtained without torture shows that the reproaches were unfounded, because they were obtained by appeals to revolutionary honor. Even the defendants felt the primacy of party discipline so strongly that they disregarded their subjective feelings of innocence and confessed to deeds that they had never committed. One of the most blatant reports of self-incrimination came from Vyshinski with an interrogation of Kamenev:

> Vyshinski: "How are the articles and explanations that you wrote in 1933 and in which you expressed your devotion to the party to be assessed? Was it deceit?"
> Kamenev: "No, worse than deceit!"
> Vyshinski: "Breach of loyalty?"
> Kamenev: "Worse."

Vyshinski: "Worse than deceit, worse than breach of loyalty—can
you find the word?—Betrayal?"
Kamenev: "You've found it!"[505]

In China, spy hysteria did not reach the same excesses as that
experienced during the Soviet clean-up campaigns. Yet even during
the cultural revolution, Mao's wife, Chiang Ching, gave public
warnings about the U.S. and Chiang-Kai-Shek agents who were
reputed to be in the country.[506] The exaggerated battle ideology not
infrequently leads to fictitious enemies from outside being suspected,
and the incapacity of an overideologized system to admit to structural shortcomings in the socialist system, attributing all these
defects instead to a lack of motivation on the part of individual
functionaries, has repeatedly set scape-goat mechanisms in motion
in domestic politics, which have degenerated into a type of "leftist
McCarthyism."

The new constitution of the Communist Party of China adopted
at the Tenth National Congress in 1973 does, indeed, categorically
state in Article 5 that "it is absolutely inadmissible to stifle criticism
and take retaliatory measures." Nonetheless, the indiscriminate
criticism of Liu Shao-ch'i and Lin Piao, in the small amount of
Congress material made public, shows that the freedom to criticize
is a long way from including all the Marxist positions long discussed
in China.

2. In cases where socialist systems in developing countries
have indulged temporarily in a frugality ideal because their level of
productive resources was not sufficient to permit rapid redistribution by redistributing the annual increase in growth, there have been
signs of *collective masochism* in socialist countries at times. One
example here is Cuba, when the ecstasy of privations went so far that
spontaneous voices rang out at mass meetings with "let us tighten
our belts even further." In China and Cuba, the "new socialist man"
bore many of the traits of a well-disciplined soldier who maintains
conflict-free human relations. At times of a rapid change, of course,
an appeal to voluntariness can in some cases prove more effective in
terms of ideological steering than does bureaucratic organization,
but psychologists feel that this does not produce a lasting change
of attitude in the long term. Manipulated voluntariness cannot serve
to make unpopular moves popular, although it can numb active
resistance for a time with the fear of sanctions,[507] and in critical
transitional periods this may be a decisive factor for the survival
of a system established through revolution. This type of ideological
steering does, however, also bring the danger of socialist leaders

overestimating the degree of consensus already achieved—as happened to Mao in the "hundred flowers" campaign, which brought out a level of dissent that the leaders had obviously not reckoned with.

3. The most serious consequence for socialism, which sees itself as a scientifically based system, was the *stagnation of a number of sciences* due to ideological rigidity. These consequences can still be seen today if we take individual indicators such as book production or the distribution of students and output of graduates (see Tables 44 to 46). Not even the natural sciences were spared this undesirable trend—as is shown by the grotesque consequences of Lysenko's theory for Soviet agriculture.[508]

In most of the natural sciences these undesirable trends were rapidly overcome after Stalin, but a taboo still lives on in the social sciences today, so that considerable ideological barriers lie in the path of any specialization of the empirical social sciences (such as sociology, social psychology, political science, and so forth) and the closed ideological system of Marxism–Leninism sees itself threatened by any attempt at specialization, even though statements from Marx as to the impossibility of understanding the legal system and political circumstances by oneself (MEW, Vol. 13, p. 8) do not provide sufficient legitimation for this.

With Mao, too, there is evidence of a marked aversion to specialized science as a breeding ground for the pragmatic thinking of intellectuals. Insofar as he made any concrete reference to the various subjects at all, it can be seen that his attention was focused chiefly on sport and physical training on the one hand and on relatively traditional educational subjects such as Chinese history, literature, and philosophy on the other.

The specialist social sciences are only encouraged to a relatively limited degree in all socialist countries, and if they are taught at all then they are used exclusively for purposes of stabilizing the system. Even today they do not do justice to the view that ever since Stalin, science has been acknowledged as a "direct productive resource" (to use Marx's expression). Today, however, the demand for more training of sociologists is brought up quite openly: "The training of both broadly specialized and narrowly specialized sociologists has not been organized to date. Without sociologists it is difficult to compile social plans for the development of collectives and to ensure that the right 'social climate' develops in these collectives for them to operate successfully and fulfill their social function."[509]

Ideological mobilization generally requires that people produce positive evidence of their support for the ideology. Only in later times were socialist systems prepared to content themselves with passive acceptance of the system, taking Kádár's view in Hungary: "Those who are not against us are for us." This causes a shift in the degree of commitment required—the indifference zones grow greater, and ideological adherence to many of the aims of socialist states that are compatible with traditional nationalism would seem to be sufficient in order to prove oneself a loyal citizen. At the same time, however, mobilization for the further-reaching targets in the "goal culture" of communism, and, more especially, arousal of efforts for the transition to communism, is becoming increasingly difficult. There is a growing tendency to let socialist citizens become consumers of services offered by their leaders along the path to communism.

2. Organization and planning

Marx and Engels may have only outlined the goals vaguely because of their dialectical concern not to indulge in unacceptable concretization, but when it comes to the instruments to be employed, these were explored even less in their rudimentary allusions to dictatorship of the proletariat. Engels' comments on the progressive role of force could be taken as a basis for the use of repression, but as far as organizing planning is concerned, there was virtually no backup material available at all. Lenin (LPSS, Vol. 35, p. 147) complained that no one could compile a plan for organizing economic life. He envisaged the plan being worked out by concerted action of the masses and the party avant-garde: "Only the masses can do this from below, on the basis of their experience. Obviously, instructions will be issued and the general directions outlined but a start must be made from both above and below at the same time."

Ideologists of fully comprehensive ex-ante planning generally overlook the fact that Lenin was not only rather helpless in matters of planning but also made some surprising theoretical statements here, such as toward the end of 1917 when he explained to a social revolutionary in the Central Executive Committee: "May the workers proceed to organize worker control in the factories and plants, may they supply the country with finished products and trade them for bread. For each product made and for each pound of bread, accounts must be kept because socialism is above all a matter of accounting" (LPSS, Vol. 35, p. 57). The subsequent drawing-up of accounts for what had been spontaneous market processes constituted at best ex-post steered barter trade and has very little in common with the planned economy of a socialist system. It was only in the heat of a political battle that Lenin could fall victim to this short-sighted view of a socialist transitional economy.

Whereas directly after the revolution Lenin frequently invoked the creative initiative of the masses, his adoption of a state-capitalist strategy, which produced sharp criticism from left-wing communists, made it effectively impossible for him to develop a system of planning involving participation of the masses. Due to a tightening up of work discipline and the disciplining of the labor force and its trade unions (see Chapter 7, Section 5) successful initiatives from below were not forthcoming, and comprehensive planning from above initially had to be renounced in the NEP period. Only at the end of the 1920s did forced industrialization and collectivization come to serve as a background for what was, in fact, anything but a thorough planning system. It became evident that it was not sufficient to plan the allocation of resources and leave the labor market free, and this led to a further disciplining of the labor force in the early 1930s.

Since this time, the principles of planning and participation have come increasingly into conflict. Planning was seen as being linked to the primacy of politics, but as forms of consultative participation and enterprise autonomy became more widespread, economic interests began to surface again despite the many attempts made to keep the minds of socialist citizens free from economic considerations.

The greater the emphasis placed on the need for centralized planning—as in Cuba—in the early 1960s, the less effective participation of those concerned tended to be in the planning, particularly since manipulated participation, steered from above, concentrated chiefly on fulfillment of predetermined plan targets in critical areas.

Left-wing critics who view the Cuban or Chinese way as the only correct one of steering a socialist system at times see the primacy of politics—which presupposes effective planning—threatened by the very fact that the Eastern European countries tolerate "material levers" and a certain subsystem autonomy. Defendants of Eastern European policy point out, and quite rightly so,[510] that the primacy of politics can be overdone, such as at the time of the personality cult, when Stalin replaced material stimuli with "bare administration." It does not, however, run contrary to planning as a structural principle of socialism to view the organizational side of system steering in terms of instruments. Instrumentalization is vital in order to operationalize what planning actually means in the concrete context of a system. Nor does it go against the target of participation to measure this by the yardstick of concrete mobilization processes. Without this type of instrumentalization, neither planning nor participation could be analyzed as to their "class content." In each individual case it must be possible to work out scientifically whom planning serves, the details of the instruments it employs, and how far it has a negative bearing on other structural principles (such as participation), which share an equally high rating.

Viewed from the angle of maximizing efficiency in the legitimation sphere, it is a typical feature of socialist countries that planning, in terms of instruments, in theory goes hand in hand with organization as target-oriented participation. It turns out to be very difficult to draw the line deliberately between socialist organization and socialist planning in a typology. J. M. Montias attempted to make a clear-cut distinction between mobilization systems, centralized administration systems, decentralized administration systems, and market socialist systems. Even the assurance that these are simply ideals that are scarcely found in reality[511] cannot hide the fact that all four elements are built to varying degrees into most system planning in socialist countries. At best one can separate out different phases when one or another of these elements predominated. A high degree of centralization, which was originally taken as a straightforward indicator of centralized administration systems, is seen to be dependent upon a series of other variables, such as "level of development," extent of "shortage of resources" due to the destruction wrought by civil or other wars, "size of country," and "degree of segmentation of territorial or functional units." This is why any attempt to deduce in the abstract the level of efficiency that an organizational system has attained from its particular blend of elements is bound to fail. A high degree of centralization can be less damaging for a small country like Cuba than for a highly segmented land like Yugoslavia, and a high level of mass mobilization can be used more effectively to solve problems in a basically agricultural country like China, where the rice harvest is the main factor, than in a second basically agricultural country, where the sugar cane harvest calling for greater manual skills is the main factor. Only by taking a whole series of indicators such as labor productivity, innovative capacity, and contribution toward maintaining the system's autonomy and the number of accidents at work does it

268   *Efficiency*

become possible to draw conclusions as to the planning and organization system's contribution toward efficiency (see Chapter 4, Sections 3 to 5).

The fact that planning has come to be regarded as the most important means of securing efficiency throughout the whole of society in the system has meant that in the Eastern bloc countries' debate, efficiency—and not simply economic efficiency—is deduced directly from organization of the planning system and from the central allocation mechanism,[512] and that "centralization" is considered as an efficiency criterion in itself. Some of the new leftist criticism of Eastern European planning and leadership systems is also marked by an unspoken nostalgia of war communism, which is, by the way, even ahistorical as well.

No transitional society has ever known comprehensive planning in its initial stages; at most, societies have had nationalized, controlled, and free sectors existing side by side, with partial planning being the only target attainable in the short term, marking a transitional step toward overall planning. The last two sectors were still organized along such antiquated economic lines that they could only be abolished and not effectively steered. The delegates at the Ninth RCP (B) Party Congress in early 1920 were being optimistic when they adopted a 4-stage plan.[513] Economic setbacks and political pressure through repeated intervention from outside forced them to reduce their planned projects. The state electrification committee (GOELRO) was only a rudiment of overall planning. Even after Lenin had signed the GOSPLAN degree on February 22, 1921, there were still only annual plans for individual branches of the economy to begin with.

Even when comprehensive economic planning was introduced, it could not do justice to the postulate of "comprehensive planning for all the conditions of production and reproduction"—as is still set down in the leftist literature today. On the labor market planning was slow to take a hold, and even today it frequently only takes in the higher cadres. For a long time, manpower planning was insufficiently coordinated with educational planning, and in fields such as science, planning has still not reached the level of economic calculation. The errors of quantitative planning based on a "tonnage ideology" inevitably produced even more disastrous consequences in the field of education and science than in the field of industrial output.

The question then arose in planning theory as to whether one could perhaps only speak of really effective steering once a high level of productive resources had been attained. During the initial years (from the period of war communism in Russia in 1920 to the Chilean system in 1972/73), when any fluctuation in course brought the regime to the verge of collapse, steering remained highly restricted and arbitrary.

The comprehensiveness and scope of planning do not, however, increase linearly with the development of productive resources. Even in socialist systems, the demand for total steering wanes once higher levels of economic efficiency are attained, and yet steering becomes increasingly more efficient and comprehensive, embracing all the fields that were barely covered in the beginning, from education output to population growth.

The "plan-versus-market" debate that was fought out between the two World Wars by market socialists and capitalist economists (particularly in the price discussion) (see Chapter 2) and which, after the Second World War, went on to develop into a true trench war between "leftist critics" and those economists branded as "revisionist" economists by established socialist economies, lost part of its schematic, abstract nature as more experience was gained of real socialist transformation processes. The front lines are also no longer as clear as they used to be. Even a number of leftist critics warn against schematic comparisons of plan and market today. Charles Bettelheim, for example, was cured of his mystification of the plan through disappointment at Che Guevara and Fidel Castro. Once he had overcome his uncritical enthusiasm for Cuba, he even went on to reproach the Cuban leadership with "ideological obscurantism."[514] For Bettelheim, the ideological commitment to planning is no longer a decisive social principle—this, after all, also exists verbally in the People's Democracies and in the cases of Cuba and China would need to be compared more closely with the realities of planning—but rather the question as to which class holds power. All leftist critics of planning start from one variant or another of bureaucracy rule, though to date the concrete power held by state bureaucracies has been more the subject of lump-sum criticism than proper investigation.

Even when analyzing rule structures in socialist countries, however, it is seen that comparison with capitalist rule mechanisms is more of a hindrance than a help. As a rule, planning as a social principle tends to be conceived of too narrowly, when only rigorous and comprehensive ex-ante regulation is awarded the title of "planning"—like a socialist plaque of honor. There are several reasons for this:

1.   The small, *non-self-sufficient* socialist countries cannot live up to this rigorous demand as can the large countries. On the

one hand they are more dependent on the socialist division of labor, and on the other because of their expanding grade on the capitalist world market they have to take more notice of world market prices. This can even produce crisis phenomena at times.

World powers are really the only countries that can achieve prerequisite-free ex-ante planning—even the larger and virtually self-sufficient socialist countries are coming to be increasingly guided by parameters laid down by the predominantly capitalist *world market system* as they expand their international trade relations. Contrary to Maoist denunciation of this orientation data, however —which could even take effect in China in a few years' time—this does not mean that centralized planning is becoming fully dependent on world market price considerations. The ship's wake of the capitalist world market, which Marx described for the presocialist world, is beginning to take increasing effect on the socialist world now. Critics, not incorrectly, see a connection between market-economy regulatory mechanisms taking hold and the expanding links with the world market. As long as the plan still exists, and foreign investors are fully subjected to it (as is still the case in all Eastern European countries), these adaptations do not undermine ex-ante planning, however. One may complain at this alignment to the capitalist world market system, but basically a socialist world market system would not function any differently as long as there was no uniform socialist world planning system. However, in the light of the growing ideological conflict in the socialist camp and the growing number of socialist countries, this will remain but a dream— and probably not even a pleasant dream at that.

2.   The principle of ex-ante planning cannot exclude *feedback and correction to planning* following *ex-post in part.* The early market socialists such as Oscar Lange were not the only ones to make provision for ex-post regulation in their models (see Chapter 2, Section 3a); modern cybernetic planning theory also works on the basis that part of the regulation will always follow afterwards through feedback processes, and the idea that ex-ante planning runs automatically like clockwork comes under attack in the present-day literature of socialist countries.[515]

The ex-post assessment of intended and implemented policies, which even supporters of ex-ante planning regard as necessary, always contains a certain element of ex-post coordination, because information flows back to the steering centers in a decentralized fashion, and even socialist systems cannot avoid cross-cutting pressures.

Soviet planners have also recognized the dilemma of plans

developing into self-fulfilling prophecies, and in retrospect it is frequently assumed that a plan that was fulfilled must have been the optimum plan. In a bid to avoid this Oedipus effect, there has now been a call, in theory at least, for some degree of ex-post discussion of plans and alternative plans.[516] The numerous sudden changes of course in the Soviet Union (land reclamation, "leap forward in chemistry") and in China (Great Leap Forward, cultural revolution) have usually been lacking an impartial comparison with the results of the course adopted beforehand.

There is no point in schematic comparisons of ex-ante and ex-post regulation, if only because the most rigid form of centralized planning, which, *in structural terms*, is based completely on ex-ante regulation, needs all the more ex-post coordination when it comes to the *motivational* aspect. In a rigid ex-ante planned system, all the shortcomings of plan fulfilment and coordination have to be attributed to motivational shortcomings, which then need to be corrected subsequently through criticism, compulsion to self-criticism, purges, sending down, and other means. This has at times led to the grotesque dysfunctional consequence of whole armies of "agents, saboteurs, and defeatists" needing to be found in order to compensate for the shortfall in ex-ante planning. Though the political course fluctuations that result from this can, in fact, be excused on the basis of the "primacy of politics," they nonetheless, as crisis phenomena, impede realization of the goals of socialism in a large number of fields and at times take on proportions similar to capitalist crises, resulting from blind trust in market regulation (see Part V, Section 4).

Whether the chosen blend of ex-ante and ex-post regulatory mechanisms is an appropriate blend or not cannot be measured with abstract models but only from output indicators on the one hand and from the level of decision-making costs incurred in processing social input on the other. If ex-ante regulation is too rigid, then experience has shown this to lead to an enormous increase in decision costs. The number of planning bureaucrats can be taken as an indicator here. According to Soviet data, 1.3 million people were already employed in economic administration in the early 1960s.[517] A number of publicists set the de facto figure considerably higher. The Soviet cyberneticist, V. M. Gluzhkov, extrapolated the prevailing growth trend in planning and economic administration cadres for a joke and calculated that, by 1980, the whole of the Soviet working population would be engaged in administration if the trend kept up.[518] Even if computer aid meant that the "perfect plan" was not as unrealistic as was once the perfect market of nineteenth-century bourgeois economics, there would still be the problem that even the most mathematicized of planning centers could not make the exchanges between economic subjects disappear and could at best help toward shortening the adaptation process in these exchange processes.

This growing and increasingly differentiated machine with its special skills can no longer be directed along the archaic lines of the Stalin era, and its involvement does at least provide expert participation. But even this development does not solve the dilemma, because the whole of the planning elite can distance itself from the needs of the masses and become increasingly independent—"planners prefer to be able to prefer,"[519] it has been not incorrectly ascertained. Where the maintenance of one's own scope for action becomes an important target of activity, then the danger is rife for ex-ante planning becoming a fetish.

3.   Overemphasis on ex-ante regulation threatens to promote the very same *bureaucratic manipulation* that it claims to be fighting and in addition reduces society to the level of a single subject. Marx held this to be wrong and speculative (MEW, Vol. 13, p. 625). Moreover, this threatens to aggravate an evil of capitalist society, of which Marx once said: "Whereas bureaucracy constitutes gross materialism on the one hand, its gross spiritualism, on the other hand, is revealed by the fact that it wants to do everything, i.e., in that it makes the will the causa prima, because bureaucracy is merely an active existence which receives its substance from outside and can thus only prove its existence through shaping or limiting this substance. The bureaucrat regards the world as a mere object of his dealings" (MEW, Vol. 1, p. 250). One of the origins of the voluntarism that lies in overemphasis on the primacy of politics is this "spiritualism" of planning bureaucracies that "want to do everything."

One of the concrete consequences of this expansion of direct competences in the Soviet Union was inflation in the production directly allocated by the central planning authorities. Even Soviet authors—who saw the list of such goods swell from 13,000 to 18,000 between 1960 and 1962 alone—wondered just how far this process could contrinue.[520] Paradoxically, it was seen afterwards that just before the more pronounced market elements were introduced, the market of intermediaries and agents acting between firms had developed precisely on account of the excess of ex-ante planning and not in spite of it. The Soviet Union, in particular, has always had a "plan fulfilment market" (see Chapter 4).

To counteract the tendency to independence of technocratic planners, socialist systems have repeatedly gone through phases when the enforcement of ideological postulates has been given primacy.

But even if faction struggles of this type did not lead to harmful policy fluctuations, they were still not without dysfunctional consequences when it came to ex-ante planning. Planned systems, coupled with markedly ideological one-party rule, tend to aim for excessive plan targets. It has, however, been rightly said against this process that the principle of "it is necessary to aim for the impossible to achieve the possible" does not apply here because the nonfulfilment of individual plan elements set at too high a level can also have harmful repercussions on other plan components connected with them. It also hampers the formation of reserves, which could be used more appropriately than other measures to balance out planning errors.

4.   "Parametric planning" and "comprehensive planning of all conditions of production and reproduction" *have not so far proved to be 100% mutually exclusive in empirical terms.* No socialist system to date has developed a fully comprehensive, macroscopic, cross-government goal system. No system as yet satisfies the scientific requirement for ex-ante analysis of intended policies and ex-post evaluation of these after implementation. Nevertheless, steering in socialist systems is more effective than in capitalist systems, and a number of built-in parametric steering processes certainly provide an effective safeguard against oversteering. A number of socialist systems suffered from oversteering in that they obtained their high steering capacity at the price of exaggeratedly regimented management from above and inadequate mobilization of voluntary consensus from below. The main criterion when drawing up pragmatic classificaton of concrete socialist steering systems into types must be the question as to *direct calculation—* calculation that does not follow the roundabout way of *indirect market mechanisms* and that is marked by the overall economic and longterm nature of planning. Subsidiary consideration of indirect calculation and decentralization must be a question of appropriateness at each particular concrete point in the development of a socialist society and must be made a function of the complexity of the economy, the extent of class resistance, and a number of other factors. People rightly speak of a "recognition function" for the socialist market that has to be fulfilled at the plan compilation stage.[521]

Leftist critics of the Eastern European systems, such as Bettelheim, tend toward the view, however, that even plans that seem to be characterized by a marked degree of central control only just accompany commodity relations, and they regard the plan simply as an "artificial market" or "ex-post overall steering."

Planning theory in developed socialist systems has had to deal increasingly with the parametric steering elements in the socialist system in the light of the continued existence of commodity production and the theory of value in socialism. A number of Marxist authors have ascribed the plan and market with complementary regulatory functions:[522]

Plan	*Market*
governs the main lines of the economy	governs the details
shapes the material side of the reproduction process	the theory of value governs the value side of the reproduction process
fixes the targets	stimulates achievement of these targets.

Marxist economics, attempting to protect itself from the reproach of revisionism, rejected all these interpretations, since in the last instance they point to the plan as a subjective, derived regulator of less importance than the objective theory of value. The GDR economy tried to solve the dilemma with a fourth interpretation dichotomy, which declared the alternatives of plan and market as invalid and postulated:

production (and not planning) to be set against the market	the market relates only to a specific phase in the reproduction process, namely to the circulation phase.

According to this idea, part of socialist planning consists in an active market policy. Socialist economy is a planned economy of socialist commodity production. For GDR economists this means, inter alia, that socialist commodity production does not share certain features of capitalist commodity production (such as competition), despite the fact that enterprises do have a certain degree of autonomy. Obviously this cannot apply to those socialist systems that, like Czechoslovakia in 1968, spoke out in favor of a limited degree of competition between enterprises so as to improve "consumer sovereignty" through competition in supply.

The prevailing economics in the Soviet Union and the German Democratic Republic thus rightly refutes the suggestion that they are aiming at implementing a market socialist model, which even reform economists such as Liberman could at best regard as "guild socialism" or "anarcho-syndicalism."[523] Even in a market socialist system such as Yugoslavia's—which also provides the opportunity for true participation (see Chapter 10, Section 3)—simple decentralization alone does not produce solely positive consequences. The banks have to some extent filled in the gaps left in centralized steering by the state when it gave up imperative planning with the 1965 economic reform, or where state influence appeared in what was a fragmented fashion but no longer controllable by the self-government organs.

Since planning is a constitutional principle (since the Soviet Constitution of 1936, Art. 11), each individual plan is accorded greater dignity by being declared a law, and this then marks an important difference in all socialist countries from the indicative planning of capitalist states.[524]

But even the cautious and to some extent convincing GDR interpretation cannot explain away one dilemma of socialist commodity production: namely, that during the very period of "comprehensive construction of socialism," the money–commodity relations that ought to disappear completely in communism are on the increase. The complete belittlement of commodity production and theory of value even leads to inconsistency at times. It is no longer clear why socialist doctrine still insists on phasing out commodity production and the theory of value at all, and the verbal demand for transition to communism no longer sounds very convincing to a number of theorists in the light of this long-term reconcilement to commodity relations.

Fortunately, the fronts between the different positions in the Eastern European states are increasingly breaking down. Ideological compromise formulae for uniting dissimilar steering elements should not be viewed statically, however. These are only ever formula compromises between political groups that are still fighting each other more and more vigorously. The lines of conflict do, however, overlap to some extent:

1. The *"over-industrializers,"* who were persecuted in the Soviet Union to begin with—although this did not lead to their rehabilitation in most cases—and who then gained de facto acceptance in the Stalin line, stood against those economists who were prepared to make concessions to a mixed economy and balanced growth. The overindustrializers gained acceptance in a number of

people's democracies for a while, although not in China (against Soviet advice) or in Cuba (more under Soviet influence).

2.   The *Libermanists* and those who advocated material incentives were up against the *Guevarists*, who placed emphasis on immaterial incentives; the latter had the upper hand almost constantly in Cuba and with interruptions in China.

3.   The *centralists* were up against the *decentralists*. The decentralists won temporary victory in the Soviet Union under the Sovnarkhoz system, during the period when centralized ministerial administration from above was phased out, and also during the economic reforms of the 1960s. In the German Democratic Republic, the recentralization trend gained ground again in 1970 after a fairly abrupt change of course.

Central planning can only ever mean centralized decisions being taken about fundamental priorities. The three lines of conflict in the organization debate are thus overshadowed today by the real question of relevance, namely the extent of participation that the masses and the groups into which they are organized have in decisions about priority-fixing. Viewed from this angle, we see increasingly marked shortcomings in the participation structure of all socialist systems (see Chapter 10).

3.   Repression

At the time when totalitarianism theories, with their one-sided analysis of input phenomena, predominated for explaining socialist policy, the function of terror for modernization was generally not fully appreciated. More recent theories, however, point to a parallel with the use of coercion in absolutism and also during phases of dictatorial renewal in European history as well. They see socialist repression as being a virtual functional equivalent of these early phenomena in the bourgeois state.[525]

Repression in socialist states must, however, be regarded as more than Karl Deutsch's "damage control mechanism." This was only conceived of as a type of power-politics acid-test, applied solely to demonstrate the system's capacity to maintain itself. In socialist ideology, however, repression is a means of achieving modifications in the system. Repression is limited in time and clearly calculated in terms of its human cost. The longer the struggle of socialist systems in establishing themselves in the face of what is still an all-powerful capitalist world system, the more they used repression simply in order to maintain their systems. In this way systems at the start of their development used repression to defend themselves on the basis of their future potential against systems in other social formations (capitalism), which seemed to be superior at the time. Frequently this repression was employed without any calculation of the human costs it would involve. During the socialist transformation phase, repression had to help bridge the gaps in organization and in socialization. At the time when redistribution policy stands at the forefront for motivating the population, repression of the "class enemy" has a decisive role to play, even if this is by no means the only instrument used (see Chapter 1, Section 3).

In a second phase, when the goal is increased efficiency in view of a ruined economy, and when systems attempt to maximize efficiency at the expense of other targets, repression likewise develops new repercussions (for which no provision at all is made in Marxist theory). This time, the effects of repression are not directed against the "class enemy" but chiefly against the system's own followers, and participation is down-graded from one of the most important socialist goals to a mere instrument. The overdose of repression in this phase leads to a "dictatorship within a dictatorship."

The concept of "national bourgeoisie" embodied a degree of tolerance toward that part of the bourgeoisie that was not counter-revolutionary-minded. Some foreign socialists regarded this as dangerous, but Liu Shao-ch'i in particular defended this step as being one of the necessary gradualistic measures.[526]

Despite the marked emphasis placed on the need to continue the class struggle, highlighted more clearly by Mao's contradiction theory than by the Soviet doctrine of that time, which spoke of the dying out of the state and the emergence of the "state of the whole people," the repression measures employed against individual strata were always very carefully measured out and were marked less by open terror than by the terror of psychic reeducation.

Mao rejected oppression measures and force "within the people"—"the atmosphere here must be free." On the other hand, however, he did approve of oppression being applied against counter-revolutionaries. As for who could be termed a "counter-revolutionary," this varied greatly depending on which particular faction held the upper hand. Frequently the mass mobilization method meant that China repeatedly lapsed back into this type of "revolutionary popular action" instead of developing a rudimentary socialist legality (see Chapter 12, Section 2). The *Hsia Fang* system is a milder instrument of force, which was nonetheless repeatedly employed against specific groups and in particular against intellectuals. Even Mao did not speak of voluntariness here—his words are "let us drive opera singers, poets, playwrights, and men of letters out of the cities, and drive all of them to the countryside. Send them down to villages and factories in groups and at different times. Do not let them stay in offices all the time; they cannot write anything there. If you do not go down, no meals will be served to you. . . ."[527] Again this raises the question as to the protective function of the socialist state: who decides whether the work of an intellectual still counts as productive work or not? Who makes sure that hardship is avoided—the hardship that must arise when people are torn from their personal circle of family and friends in this countrywide horizontal rotation system? Instruments such as criticism and self-criticism, the coercive instruments in mobilization of the masses (see Chapter 12, Section 2), constitute the milder form of repression not intended to claim any victims, although these are frequently accepted as being one of the consequences—the number of fatalities during the cultural revolution is estimated at one hundred thousand. Only occasionally are official figures given on repression, such as that 4.5% of all state officials have been penalized in some way through the Sanfan movement.[528]

North Korea is a special case when it comes to repression, since it was the only country to be temporarily occupied by Western troops once socialism had been introduced. The numerous collaborators were penalized (insofar as they had not fled to South Korea) and in the countryside, according to questionable estimate from emigrants, this accounted for 30 to 40% of the population.[529]

The Soviet Union employed the instrument of forced labor on a large scale under Stalin. These measures were at times motivated not only on political grounds but on economic grounds as well. However, these attempts at maximizing efficiency proved to be a failure (see Chapter 7, Section 4).

Not all systems employed terror to the same extent. The German Democratic Republic and Czechoslovakia applied much less terror during the mobilization phase than did the other systems. Consideration of the strength of the remaining bourgeois forces, the danger of intervention of nonsocialist countries in countries situated on the edge of the Soviet sphere of influence, and a number of other factors all contributed toward this.[530]

Political rights and civil liberties have been measured (see Table 85). Most of the socialist countries with the exception of Poland and Hungary received the worst marks available. All of

Table 85

Comparative measures of freedom

Countries	Political rights	Civil liberties	Status of freedom
Albania	7	7	not free
China	6	6	not free
Cuba	6	6	not free
Czechoslovakia	7	6	not free
GDR	7	7	not free
Hungary	6	5	not free
North Korea	7	7	not free
Mongolia	7	7	not free
Poland	6	5	not free
Romania	7	6	not free
Soviet Union	7	6	not free
Yugoslavia	6	5	not free
for comparison:			
Finland	2	2	free
France	1	2	free
FRG	1	2	free
Japan	2	1	free
South Korea	5	5	partly free
Switzerland	1	1	free
Sweden	1	1	free
Turkey	2	3	free (?)
United States	1	1	free
United Kingdom	1	1	free

Source: R. D. Gastil ed.: *Freedom in the World. Political Rights and Civil Liberties 1978* (Boston: G. K. Hall, 1978), pp. 10ff.

(The scales use the numbers 1–7, with 1 comparatively offering the highest level of political or civil rights, and 7 the lowest).

them rank in the hierarchy of the status of freedom among those countries considered "not free." If we want to measure the differences and details in a country that is not free, compared to Western democracies, we have to look for further indicators that are more easily accessible than the amount of social control, supervision by secret service, or censorship. Some relevant data are available for the following indicators:

1. number of deaths due to political class struggles (see Chapter 1, Section 3);
2. number of political prisoners and political trials;
3. strength of security forces and organs of repression;
4. number of emigrants.

The number of *political prisoners* and inmates of labor camps is frequently taken as an indicator of the amount of repression applied. The reliability of available data varies greatly from one system to another, however. Only a number of leaders in socialist systems have spoken so openly about this as Castro did when in an interview he put the number of political prisoners in Cuba at 20,000.[531]

In the Soviet Union there has been a sharp drop in the number of political prisoners since the peak of repression experienced during collectivization and during the clean-up campaigns. Yet even at the start of the 1970s, more than 200 labor camps were known by name, and the true figure is estimated to be even higher. A number of authors believe there to be some 1 million inmates today. No information whatsoever is available on the number of political prisoners in psychiatric clinics.[532]

Whereas repression is employed fairly openly during the transformation phase, this changes as the need for legal security becomes more pronounced. During Lenin's time, open repression and terror served specific functions, intended only to be temporary functions for purposes of securing the revolutionary regime. Not once did Lenin attempt to cover these measures with the cloak of "socialist legality," however.[533] Even if "socialist legality" was initially only a means of ideological justification under Stalin, after his time it developed into more in all socialist countries. Repression had to be increasingly camouflaged, because open mass repression obviously lacked legitimation in the eyes of the population. There was an increasing tendency not to liquidate or arrest opponents but to condemn them instead to the margin of society as mentally ill during the Brezhnev/Kosygin era. This was also reported to have been used as a means of control by the group around Liu Shao Ch'i prior to the cultural revolution.[534]

In a large number of socialist systems it is impossible to put figures on the phase sequence of open mass terror, the cloaking of terror as "socialist legality," and the phase of potential conceal- ment of terror. This is the very field where socialist systems are reluctant to publish data. Nevertheless, it can be seen from the Yugoslav statistics, for example, that political conflicts (measured in terms of political sentencing) develop in inverse proportion to economic conflicts (measured in terms of trials in the labor courts). In Yugoslavia, the numbers sentenced for political crimes "against the people and the state" fell from 10,211 in 1947 to 92 in 1967. Since then there has been a slightly increasing trend (1968: 174, 1969: 284, 1970: 203), which can presumably be explained by the unrest experienced since the end of the 1960s.[535]

Since it is difficult to calculate the repression balance using the first two indicators, attempts have been made to assess the significance of the instrument of "repression" during socialist transformation through the *strength of security organs*. There are, after all, discussible figures for certain periods in the Soviet Union, though none at all exist for the numerous Chinese clean- up campaigns. Even Soviet criticism and those of the people's democracies (which at times have good information and do not even hold it back) seem to be groping in the dark in this respect. The cultural revolution was to involve "political and probably also physical destruction" of certain leadership groups.[536]

Both for China and for the Soviet Union we have to rely on pure estimates when it comes to the strength of the security organs. Figures on military and paramilitary organizations (which always take on domestic policy functions as well in the struggle against the "class enemy") permit us at most to draw indirect conclusions here (see Table 86, last row). However, this calls for a certain amount of caution. In view of the dominance of the capitalist world system, the foreign policy function of the security forces takes precedence, a fact that has indeed been rated as one of the essential features of socialism. Since the difference in foreign policy threat to individual socialist states is not so great as the difference in the number of their armed forces, it has been concluded that domestic policy considera- tions are the decisive factor and that the party elites feel threatened from inside—a feeling that correlates negatively with the degree of liberalization.[537] This view is at best defendable in countries with a

Table 86

Comparison of data on military expenditure and manpower (1979–1980)

	Military expenditure (in billions of $)			Military expenditure ($ per head)		Military expenditure as % of GNP/GDP		Military expenditure as % of government spending	Expenditure per soldier in	Military manpower in 1,000	Est. reservists in 1,000	Para-military in 1,000
	IISS 1980[a]	SIPRI 1979[b]	SIVARD 1977[c]	IISS 1980[a]	SIVARD 1977[e]	IISS 1979[a]	SIPRI 1976[g]	IISS 1980	SIVARD 1977[e]	IISS 1980[a]	IISS 1980[a]	IISS 1980[a]
Socialist countries												
Warsaw Treaty Organization												
	1.14	0.666	0.599	128	68	2.1	2.7	6.0	4,020	149.0	240.0	189.0
Czecho-slovakia	3.52	(2.16)	1.895	229	126	2.8	3.8	7.6	10,470	195.0	350.0	133.5
GDR	4.79	4.38	3.179	285	190	6.3	4.4	7.5	20,248	162.0	305.0	571.5
Hungary	1.08	0.791	0.738	101	69	2.1	2.3	3.8	7,165	93.0	143.0	75.0
Poland	4.67	3.195	3.746	131	108	2.4	3.0	6.0	12,202	317.5	605.0	445.0

Romania	1.47	*1.064*	0.972	66	45	1.4	1.7	4.0	5,400	184.5	502.0	737.0
Soviet Union	124.0	*(105.70)*	90.000	490[d]	348[f]	11–13	*(9.9)*	n.a.	24,490	3,568.0	5,000.0	460.0
Other												
China	56.941	*(44.20)*	22.000	56	22	9.0		18.0	5,570	4,450.0	—	9,000.0
Cuba	1.126	1.065	0.430	114	45	n.a.	6.9[h]	8.[i]	2,275	206.0	90.0	0
Yugo-slavia	3.634	*2.416*	2.097	164	96	5.6[d]	5.6	56.9	8,065	264.0	500.0	1,016.0

(continued)

Table 86 (continued)

	Military expenditure (in billions of $)			Military expenditure ($ per head)		Military expenditure as % of GNP/GDP		Military expenditure as % government spending	Expenditure per soldier in	Military manpower in 1,000	Est. reservists in 1,000	Para-military in 1,000
	IISS 1980[a]	SIPRI 1979[b]	SIVARD 1977[c]	IISS 1980[a]	SIVARD 1977[e]	IISS 1979[g]	SIPRI 1980	IISS 1977[e]	SIVARD 1977[e]	IISS 1980[a]	IISS 1980[a]	IISS 1980[a]
for comparison:												
Western (capitalist) countries												
Nato and other countries												
Great Britain	24.448	15.536	11.890	437	213	4.9	4.9	10.7	35,074	329.2	265.5	—
Canada	4.240	3.877	3.881	177	167	1.7	1.8	8.6[l]	48,513	78.6	29.8	—
France	20.220	18.993	14.912	374	281	3.9	4.0	17.5	29,705	494.7	342.0	85.5
FRG	25.120	21.636	17.319	410	282	3.3	3.3	22.2	35,417	495.0	750.0	—
Italy	6.580	6.283	4.986	124[j]	88	2.4	2.3	8.2[l]	15,109	366.0	738.0	201.0
Netherlands	5.239	4.434	3.778	374	273	3.4	3.3	7.3	34,346	115.0	171.0	8.1
United States	142.700	110.145	100.928	644	465	5.2	5.2	23.3	48,337	2,050.0	817.9	n.a.

Neutral countries

Austria	0.915	0.762	0.551	122	73	1.3	1.3^k	4.1	14,892	50.3	870.0	11.3
Sweden	3.588	3.066	2.679	432	325	3.3	3.4	7.7	38,826	66.1	656.5	—
Switzer-land	1.830	1.790	1.300	292	206	1.9	2.1^k	18.9	68,421	18.5	621.5	—

Sources:

(1) The International Institute for Strategic Studies (IISS), *The Military Balance 1980–1981* (London: The International Institute for Strategic Studies, 1980).

(2) Stockholm International Peace Research Institute (SIPRI), "World Armaments and Disarmament," *SIPRI Yearbook 1980* (London: Taylor & Francis, 1980).

(3) Ruth Leger Sivard (SIVARD), *World Military and Social Expenditures 1980* (Leesburg, Virginia: World Priorities, 1980).

(a) IISS, pp. 96–97. The difficulty of calculating suitable exchange rates makes conversion to dollars imprecise.

(b) SIPRI, pp. 20–23. Figures are in US $ billion, at 1978 prices and 1978 exchange rates (Table 1A.2. World military expenditure, in constant price figures).

(c) SIVARD, pp. 21–23. Table II: "Comparative Resources, 140 Countries, 1977."

(d) IISS, p. 96, data for Soviet Union from 1975. IISS provides no data for 1979 and 1980.

(e) SIVARD, pp. 24–29. Table III: "Ranking of Countries, Military and Social Indicators, 140 Countries, 1977."

(f) SIVARD, pp. 32–33: "Estimating Military Expenditures of the USSR and its Warsaw Pact Allies."

(g) SIPRI, pp. 29–33, Table 1A.4. "World Military expenditure as a percentage of gross domestic product

Italics: uncertain data or SIPRI estimates of military expenditure. *(Parentheses)*: rough estimate.

(h) SIPRI, p. 31. Data for Cuba from 1970.

(i) IISS, p. 97. Data for China from 1979.

(j) IISS, p. 96. Data for Italy from 1979.

(k) SIPRI, p. 29. Data for Austria, Sweden, and Switzerland from 1978.

(l) IISS, p. 96. Data for Canada, France, and Italy from 1979.

high percentage of paramilitary mobilization (the highest percentages being in the German Democratic Republic and Albania). Yet even these paramilitary organizations are not oriented 100% toward domestic policy (particularly in China and Albania). After all, even authors outside the ranks of the blanket criticizers of China fear that the militia, which for a time became a formal counterforce to the army, is used more to maintain the status quo than to achieve revolutionary change, although it is not necessary to go as far as the current exaggeratedly sharp Soviet criticism of Chinese "barrack communism."[538]

Even just a fleeting comparison of this rank order of figures from the early 1960s shows that the divided nations belong among those with the highest level of military mobilization. In addition come the supreme power of the Soviet Union and also Albania, which, in its exposed geographical position, is endeavoring to follow an independent course from the Eastern bloc. It is unlikely that the correlation between the degree of military mobilization and the degree of illiberality in a system can also be interpreted as a causal relationship, particularly since the reverse conclusion is unlikely— namely, that China and Rumania can be ranked among the most liberal states because their level of military organization is smaller by comparison than in most other socialist systems.

If the figures for capitalist states are also included in the comparison, then this shows how useful a comparison of different social formations is as well. The level of military strength is obviously less dependent on the extent of repressiveness and illiberality of the system than on a series of other factors, such as:

1. geographical exposure (Albania, Israel, Taiwan);
2. degree of manifest and latent conflict (the divided states— Korea, Vietnam, Germany);
3. level of development (China, India);
4. the leadership position a country holds in the bloc system (Soviet Union, United States).

The extent of repression employed can obviously not be deduced from the size of potentially repressive institutions. By way of control figures—apart from the mainly incomplete repression balances based on deaths and political prisoners—one could take the *emigration statistics*, which are nonetheless a sign that the class struggle is not aimed at physically destroying opponents but is intended to make them politically harmless. Here, however, it is virtually impossible to compare systems that experienced a long civil war coupled with a high level of emigration (such as Russia and China) with countries that had no civil war or bloodshed.

A series of socialist systems have tried to minimize the repression balance by allowing opponents to the regime to emigrate. Castro declared that if necessary, a million people could emigrate so that Cuba could abide by the ideal of a society of free people. But even Castro was not able to keep to this, despite a liberal emigration policy in the initial years. From 1968 onwards, the restrictions were tightened, when about one-half million Cubans had left the country. This 6% emigration from Cuba is thus the second-highest emigration figure, after the German Democratic Republic, which 3.5 million citizens had left up to 1961.

Emigration can, however, become an instrument of repression at times, where it is applied selectively to individuals uncomfortable for the regime, such as in the early 1970s in the Soviet Union, when undesirable intellectuals whose high international esteem prevented the State from taking any action against them were stripped of their citizenship during trips abroad and were not allowed to reenter their homeland.

Socialist governments in the main recognize this overdose of repression as being a problem after the consolidation phase. Growing anomic participation (see Chapter 12, Section 3) draws attention to the problem. This also reawakens the ideological requirement for the dying-out of the state (used as a metaphor for the phasing out of the repressive functions of the system). It is not by chance that China took a sharp stand against the idea of the dying-out of the state or even of the party and against proclamation of the "state of the whole people" at a different stage in development from the Soviet Union. The transfer of individual sovereign functions to social organizations is generally held up as evidence that the state is increasingly pushing back the system's repressive functions. It was seen, however, that citizens did not always find the transfer of protective functions in the field of social security to the trade union and in the field of justice to comrade-administered justice as being any less repressive than when the state organs exercised these same sovereign functions. In addition, even apologists of socialist systems who have kept a certain critical distance admit that this process does not fully release the transferred functions from their connection with the state, because people are still living in a state-organized society in which all relationships are indirectly affected by the state power.

4.   Gratifications

Gratifications are beyond doubt the instrument that gives rise to the most contention in socialist systems. Radical communists felt that force was more compatible with the aims of communism than were *material gratifications*. Ideological purists have always had a virtual phobia about material incentives. The elites of socialist countries do not possess any material pawns for their power. Insofar as they do derive material advantage from it, then they indulge in the very opposite of conspicuous consumption, namely in concealed consumption, so as not to offend the puritanical morale of public opinion that is geared to totalities. With the income differentials that still persist, however, *immaterial gratifications* alone are not sufficient in socialist systems. Even here, equality has not yet been achieved, because manual laborers would seem to be somewhat underrepresented when it comes to the distribution of these. Immaterial gratifications were used most in Cuba. Cuban workers are, however, showing a declining interest in socialist competition and are less and less willing to let themselves be fed off with symbolic gratifications instead of material benefits.[539] Immaterial gratifications are closely linked to the symbolic output of the socialist system. The longer socialist systems exist, the more difficult it becomes to maintain the fiction that there are only motivational shortcomings in socialism and no structural shortcomings. So long as this fiction still holds, the principle of "criticism and self-criticism" seems to be sufficient to eliminate motivational shortcomings in those living in socialist countries. Shortcomings or even sabotage on the part of opponents to socialism are countered with more stringent means, such as repression or reeducation. The principle of self-criticism is perhaps the most abstract expression of the use of symbolic gratifications in politics. It absorbs a large proportion of oppositional energy through passionate identification with abstract and removed symbols. The less social processes are able to be steered through mobilization of the masses (as seems possible during the transformation phase), the more the abstract gratifications dealt out by the system, which produce a proliferation of orders and honorary titles such as "work hero" and "meritorius sportsman of the people," fade into the background.

In the developed socialist countries, Marxist theory has adapted itself to the requirements of a differentiated society that can no longer achieve progress through the heave-ho process of mass campaigns. This has provoked the Maoist reproach that the increased use of material interests and economic levers has led to the primacy of politics being abandoned. This reproach is rightly countered with the argument that the primacy of politics principle may not be used to neglect all the specific interests of groups, because the stage of communism cannot be reached forcefully, and this stage has not even been touched upon so long as

1. all the economic processes are still deliberately shaped politically;
2. material interestedness goes hand-in-hand with the development of political awareness;
3. no one group is able to establish itself over and above all other groups.[540]

Material stimulation in developed socialist countries is said to have nothing in common with the wild growth of profit interests in capitalist systems. Instead, it is planned and calculated rationally, and rational indicators are coming to be applied increasingly to gauge the effect of the stimuli.[541]

The economic levers do not serve "to stimulate the fulfilment of random tasks" without the social utility of this material interest being rationally established beforehand. As the "ideology of tons" is increasingly overcome, the overall social rationality of the economic lever system also increases in some respects, although ex-ante planning seems to have slackened somewhat.

Material interest in socialism can also not be simply equated with egoistic self-interest. Of the three types of material interest—social, company, and personal—the last type does not necessarily have to be the only type that is used as a lever, and even this is more collective in nature than under capitalism (such as brigade competition, collective wages: see Chapter 5). The ideologists of material incentives among economists in socialist countries repeatedly stress that material incentives are ineffective if not coupled to moral stimuli. The dangers of routine bureaucratic bonuses "garnished with indifference" have, in the meantime, come to be recognized.[542]

Western economists view the ideological downgrading of material gratifications in some countries that have not yet completed the socialist accumulation phase with a fair amount of scepticism. They put forward two arguments in particular:

1. So long as moral stimulation only produces relatively curtailed success in raising labor productivity (see Chapter 4, Section 3) repeated attempts will be made to compensate the shortfall in

labor productivity by pumping in capital and installing complex technical equipment, following the Soviet example. Because of the very shortcomings of immaterial gratifications, however, the servicing of this equipment is by no means guaranteed. China and Cuba have not yet pumped in capital and technology to the same extent as did the Soviet Union. Hence, it is difficult to say whether the return to material stimulation will go *hand-in-hand with technicalization of the economy* to the same extent as it did in the Soviet Union.

2.   A certain *demonstration effect* is assumed to emanate from the developed capitalist and socialist economies, which, due to the expansion in worldwide trade relations in the capitalist world system, could even become more marked in China. A number of well-wishing Western observers of the Chinese experiment do, however, feel on the contrary that China, with her new economic orientation and her focus on moral stimulation, could exercise more influence on the world than the world on China.[543]

Hopes of this type can scarcely be backed up by experience of influence processes on a world scale. The pronounced fluctuations in Chinese policy, coupled with waves of cultural revolutionary denigration of all things economic, make predictions of this type problematical because no socialist country has brought about greater change in its priority rating of economic and extraeconomic goals than has China. It was only in 1965 that the Chinese economy finally recovered from the first antieconomic act of power, namely the Great Leap Forward—a recovery that went fastest in heavy industry —albeit with the additional burden that an extra 75 million Chinese mouths had to be fed in the meantime. Despite these encumbrances, a new course was adopted the very same year, which proved to have (presumably unintended) negative consequences on output that can still be felt today.[544] It is, however, difficult to decide whether Mao really launched the cultural revolution according to a plan whereby the economy could serve as the basis for a second political mobilization campaign.[545]

Management specialists feel it is possible that material incentives will become less important in socialist countries as the standard of living increases, particularly in the Soviet Union.[546] If this forecast proves correct, then the right tactics would be not to do away with material stimuli at a low level of productive resources but rather to "drive out the devil with Beelzebub," phasing out material incentives through a rapid increase in prosperity. For complex industrial societies under socialism, the middle course of humane socialism, as proclaimed by the Yugoslav Practice Groups, is presumably acceptable: "Experience has shown that we cannot build up socialist society as primitive utopian communism would have had it, without the back-up of interests, including material interests. But making material interests absolute is no more acceptable than is ascetic obsession with moral stimulation. Developed communism overcomes revolutionary asceticism not by vulgar hedonism but by humanistic hedonism instead.[547]

All four instruments employed to increase the efficiency in socialist systems differ fundamentally from ruling and legitimation techniques used in bourgeois systems.

Ever since capitalism lost the innovational impetus of its early phase, the mobilization function of the *ideology* has declined, and ideology is increasingly masked by necessity-orientated thinking. Socialist ideology, on the other hand, develops the opposite trend of spoiling any success it might score through its mountain-moving nature by too careless a disregard of certain constraints, which even in socialism cannot be done away with by voluntaristic decision.

Organization, signifying the comprehensive planning of all production and reproduction conditions, occupies a completely different position from the organization found in organized state-interventionist capitalism.

During the transformation period, *force* is feared less than in the constitutionally-based thought of bourgeois democracies. It is frequently assumed that force will be of a transitory nature, however, and in the initial impetus of the revolution the fact that a repression policy once started tends to be of a lasting nature is generally overlooked.

Socialism also has an ambivalent attitude toward *gratifications.* The intention is for immaterial gratifications to predominate. But material gratifications, on which capitalist systems generally rely, take on a growing importance as long as socialist society is still marked by a shortage of commodities.

The better organized the efficiency of a socialist economic system becomes, the more precisely that socialist system needs to calculate the benefit derived from moral stimulation in mobilization campaigns. It can be seen from growth rates that the economic benefit derived from stimulation is not very high, and if excessive use is made of stimulation in campaigns then this can even produce dysfunctional effects (see Chapter 12, Section 2). This does not, of course, mean that immaterial stimuli, too, are of unlimited benefit to the system. This benefit lies mainly in their leveling effect, which must be taken into account as immaterial output from the system if one is to arrive at a fair judgment of the instruments employed in socialist regimes.

III

PROTECTION

The protective functions of socialist states are quite different from those of capitalist societies:

1. Owing to the policy of redistribution in all spheres (see Part I) protective policy in the socialist *state respects the social status quo to a much lesser degree* than protective policy in capitalist systems.

2. Socialist social security systems are based to a greater extent on the realities of class, strata, and *large, collective groups.* The protective function of the state is less orientated toward the individual, with his increasingly refined needs, in the initial stage. Only as the level of productive resources increases are individual needs for protection in the social sphere allowed scope to develop, always provided that they do not openly counteract redistribution policy.

3. Bourgeois systems have traditionally considered the state's protective function as residing in the spheres of legitimation and security. So far, powerful forces have always regarded extension of the state's protective functions to all sectors of economy and society with unconcealed mistrust. During the transformation phase, at least, the protective activity of the socialist state is mainly *concentrated on the production sphere.*

7

Protection
in the production sphere

1. Elimination of unemployment

The construction of socialist systems was coupled with an unparalleled mobilization of labor, so that socialism in itself often appeared to be the most radical cure for the hereditary capitalist ills of unemployment. International statistics only indicate unemployment now in Yugoslavia (on a large scale) and until 1970 in Poland (on a small scale) (see Table 87). However, this is one field where statistics call for interpretation. They only cover those without jobs who register as unemployed. And since no unemployment benefit is paid in socialist states, there is no incentive for the workers affected by frictional unemployment to register.

In addition to temporary *frictional unemployment*, which is tending to increase rather than decrease in many socialist states, with the migration and job-changing that is resulting from liberalization of the employment contract, there has always been *latent unemployment* as well, which is not included in the statistics. The Soviet Union also had a high percentage of unemployment in the

Table 87

Unemployment
(percentage of active population)

Country	1965	1970	1975	1977
Poland	0.7	0.7	—	—
Yugoslavia	6.1	7.7	10.2	11.9
for comparison:				
Italy	3.6	3.2	3.3	7.2
Japan	0.8	1.2	1.9	2.0
Spain	3.0	1.1	1.9	4.1
United Kingdom	2.5	2.6	4.2	6.2
United States	4.5	4.9	8.5	7.0

Sources: UN: *Statistical Yearbook 1978* (New York: UN, 1979), pp. 92f. ILO: *Yearbook of Labour Statistics 1979* (Geneva: ILO, 1979), pp. 288ff.

1920s, accounting for 0.9 million in 1925 and rising to 1.4 million in 1927.[548] In addition to this came seasonal unemployment in agriculture, with up to 40% of kolkhoz peasants admittedly not "unemployed" but "underemployed" at certain times—chiefly during the winter months. In Poland and Czechoslovakia, as well as in other countries, "concealed unemployment" was also encountered again and again, and part of this shifted from agriculture to industry with expanding industrialization. There is disagreement, however, as to the methodology to apply in determining latent unemployment. Today, this is generally attempted through comparisons of labor productivity.[549]

China, too, had to contend with the problem of unemployment. As she did not go in for intensified industrialization, unemployment repeatedly developed in the cities, even after some of the 4 million jobless inherited from the capitalist system had been found jobs for a while. Unemployment was combated with the radical cure of "sending down" to the country. Whereas a good number of socialist countries tried to check latent unemployment by over-staffing bureaucracy, China took a different course with clean-ups in her over-heavy state apparatus. This also contributed to temporary unemployment of workers living in the cities. The Great Leap

Forward and other mobilization campaigns were intended as a renewed attempt to solve the problem of unemployment through "political" measures.

In the event of conflict, socialist governments would rather put up with inflationary pressure than with deflationary trends and the ensuing increase of unemployment.[550] This illustrates the high priority given to workers' security in the production sphere in socialist society. Being aware of this priority, enterprise management generally tended to hoard labor in periods of labor shortage. This, of course, was very detrimental to labor productivity.

It is a new development of recent years that these problems are now openly discussed in the literature of socialist countries. It is even admitted today that latent labor surpluses still exist in some Comecon countries, and that these must be redeployed within Comecon, for example by employing Polish and Hungarian workers in the German Democratic Republic and Czechoslovakia, or Bulgarian workers in the Soviet Union.[551]

Frictional unemployment is also discussed openly today. It is a problem that arises when kolkhozes are converted into sovkhozes, because usually not all the former kolkhoz peasants can be reemployed (see Chapter 1, Section 3). Economic reforms have also led to new, unexpected dysfunctions. Many enterprise managers no longer tend to hoard labor, as in the early days of the accumulation phase, but have tried to keep the number of workers down, ever since the "number of workers" index has come to be left increasingly in the hands of the enterprises and since the bonus system makes it seem more profitable for an enterprise to achieve its performance with the lowest possible number of workers.

Two measures have become common practice in a bid to alleviate the hardships of frictional unemployment:

1. Enterprises seek to prevent social hardship by paying generous redundancy money to workers laid off, although this is no equivalent for formal unemployment benefit.

2. The workers themselves are already beginning to make private provisions for redundancy and other risks, and this is reflected in an increase in voluntary savings and insurance schemes[552] (see Chapter 8, Section 2). The abolition of unemployment insurance (in the Soviet Union as early as 1930) can at very least be regarded as a hasty step, considering that temporary unemployment still exists and bearing in mind the social hardship that can arise even in short periods of unemployment, until a new job is found. Only very few

systems, such as the German Democratic Republic, have provided for alleviation of the consequences of this temporary joblessness, even if only through scanty benefits.

2.   Development of health protection in the plants

All the socialist countries come up with positive results in the development of health protection. However, comparable statistical data is only available for a few of them. In comparison with capitalist countries, the socialist systems come off better, although in this particular field doubts are raised again and again as to the reliability of statistics. The cover-up rate in this field is doubtlessly high in capitalist systems as well.

In the German Democratic Republic, for instance, accidents at work are recorded only from the third day onward and are therefore not fully comparable with our figures. However, the necessity of having accurate statistics for prevention of accidents at work is being emphasized in the German Democratic Republic too. During the transformation period, protective provisions were developed only slowly, and where they did exist they were not always complied with because of economic shortcomings. It was only after the Twentieth Party Congress that promotion of safety at work was treated as a separate sector of labor law in the Soviet Union again. (See Table 88.)

Legal protection in the event of an accident has also improved in the Soviet Union. Trade unions, in the form of a commission appointed by the *fabkom* (works committee) or the trade union's technical inspector, have to take part in investigations into the accompanying circumstances, and the employee may bring his case before the fabkom—an important factor when it comes to making his insurance claims.

The idea of preventive protection has not been given its due so far, and even in political theory, industrial safety has been linked to ex post facto measures, such as with the right to recuperation.[553] Forced mechanization and intensification of work, together with new forms of remuneration, particularly piece-rate work (see Chapter 2, Section 1), have temporarily led to a marked increase in the number of industrial accidents. In the mining sector the figure rose from 1,095 per 10,000 workers in 1923/24 to 1,524 in 1925/26. These figures were recognized as being alarming at the Fourteenth

Table 88

Industrial accident rates (mining and quarrying)
(Rates per 1,000; years of 300 days each)

Country	1969	1970	1971	1972	1973	1974	1975	1976	1977	1978
Czechoslovakia	0.47	0.43	0.35	0.47	0.35	0.31	0.36	0.54	0.56	0.34
Hungary	0.48	0.32	0.45	0.45	0.44	0.36	0.33	0.36	0.30	0.62
Yugoslavia	0.24	0.50	0.39	0.19	0.18	0.20	0.19	0.32	0.22	n.d.
for comparison:										
FRG	0.71	0.68	0.71	0.62	0.69	0.56	0.46	0.49	0.52	0.56
Italy	0.47	0.43	0.33	0.35	0.26	0.41	0.34	n.d.	n.d.	n.d.
United Kingdom	0.44	0.45	0.36	0.39	0.47	0.29	0.36	0.32	0.24	0.40
United States	0.48	0.53	0.42	0.53	0.42	0.38	0.33	0.28	0.30	0.27

Source: ILO, *Yearbook of Labour Statistics 1979* (Geneva: ILO, 1979), pp. 573ff.

299

Party Congress and at the Seventh Trade Union Congress and were openly discussed.

Although the balance is positive over the long term, the assertion encountered in socialist economics textbooks to the effect that socialism ipso facto brings about a drop in industrial accidents is not tenable as a generalization. Occasionally the number of accidents at work will rise under circumstances such as campaigns with inexperienced labor and so-called *shturmovshchina* (plan fulfilment campaigns). Not only forced labor, but also the work of enthusiastic volunteers, such as subbotniki and stakhanovists, results in an increase in the accident rate.[554]

The socialist states themselves are evidently not yet satisfied with their success in checking the accident rate, to judge, for example, by the fact that the German Democratic Republic, in her New Economic System, even envisaged extending material incentives to accident insurance, by graduating accident contributions according to risk classes on the basis of the actual accident rates in enterprises.

In the long term, however, preventive health protection is better developed, and not only in the field of epidemics control where socialist countries like the German Democratic Republic definitely come up with better and faster successes, as a rule, than do capitalist countries with their generally individual and isolated quarantine measures. Moreover, the enterprise, as an entity, plays an incomparably greater role in the field of health care, rehabilitation, and social hygiene than in capitalism. As early as 1968, there were only half as many industrial accidents in the German Democratic Republic as in the Federal Republic of Germany. The increase in overall life expectancy is a further indicator for the protective successes of a system, especially in the production sphere (see Table 89).

The advantages of socialist systems have an even greater impetus in underdeveloped countries such as China. Even those who voiced rather sharp criticism at the economic and human costs involved in forced communization during the Great Leap Forward have seen the true success of the commune system as lying in work safety and health protection.[555]

Western scholars are still occasionally rather sceptical about preventive health planning. They reproach socialist countries with trying to plan the sickness rate just as exactly as gross production or profits.[556] Now, however, Western welfare state theorists have also come to recognize that the ex-post regulation of health problems in capitalist systems is an even more inhumane laissez-faire approach that puts the socially weak at an even greater disadvantage.

Table 89

Life expectancy and population growth

Country	Year	Divorce rate	Population growth per 1,000	Year	Life expectancy	
					Men	Women
Albania	1971	0.8	25.2	1965–66	64.9	67.0
Bulgaria	1977	1.5	5.4	1974–76	68.7	73.9
China	1970–75	n.d.	16.6	1970–75	59.9	63.3
Cuba	1976	2.4	14.2	1970	68.5	71.8
Czechoslovakia	1977	2.1	7.2	1978	66.9	73.7
GDR	1977	2.6	−0.1	1977	69.0	74.9
Hungary	1977	2.6	4.3	1974	66.5	72.4
Mongolia	1970–75	n.d.	29.5	1970–75	59.1	62.3
North Korea	1970–75	n.d.	26.3	1970–75	58.8	62.5
Poland	1977	1.3	10.1	1976	66.9	74.5
Rumania	1977	1.2	10.0	1975–77	67.5	72.1
Soviet Union	1977	3.5	8.5	1971–72	64.0	74.0
Vietnam	1970–75	n.d.	21.0	1970–75	43.2	46.0
for comparison:						
FRG	1977	1.8	−2.0	1974–76	68.3	74.8
Italy	1977	0.2	3.6	1970–72	68.9	74.8
Spain	1977	–	10.3	1970	69.6	74.9
United Kingdom	1977	2.6	−0.1	1974–76	69.6	75.8
United States	1977	5.1	6.5	1975	68.7	76.5

Source: UN: *Statistical Yearbook 1978* (New York: UN, 1979), pp. 76ff. *Statisticheskii ezhegodnik stran-chlenov SEV. 1980* (Moscow: Statistika, 1980), p. 10.

3. Reduction of working hours and humanization of leisure time

Part of the great humane potential of socialism lies in its potential to reduce working hours. Marx's statement in "The German Ideology," which is frequently regarded unbelievingly as a communist poetic idyll, reads as follows:

whereas in communist society, where no-one has an exclusive field of activity but where everyone may train in any branch of his choice, it is society that regulates general production and thus makes it possible for me to do this today and that tomorrow, to hunt in the morning and fish in the afternoon, to breed cattle in the evening, and criticize after dinner, just as I please, without ever becoming a huntsman, fisherman, herdsman or critic (MEW, Vol. 3, p. 33).

According to Marx, two preconditions were essential in order to create this type of society:

1.   further reduction of the division of labor;
2.   development of productive resources.

Considering the level of development required to achieve this, it seems unlikely that the agrarian activities mentioned by Marx will still play an important role for the majority of individuals.

The above quotation was not a utopian statement of the "preeconomic" Marx, as has sometimes been assumed. In his economic writings we can also read: "Beyond this [the realm of necessity—author] man starts to develop his strength, an end in itself, the true realm of liberty that can only blossom on the basis of the realm of necessity. The shortening of the working day is the basic precondition" (MEW, Vol. 25, p. 828). To counteract tendencies toward antiauthoritarian, lazy socialism, however, Engels later pointed out in his argument with anarchists and "antiauthoritarians," as he called them, that there could be no workers' autonomy in the question of determining working time: "The mechanical apparatus of a large factory is far more tyrannical than any of the small capitalists who employed workers have ever been. As far as working hours are concerned at least, one could inscribe above the factory gates: 'You who enter here, give full rein to autonomy'" (MEW, Vol. 18, p. 306).

Such statements have served as ideological justification for the fact that, for many decades, the Soviet Union never seriously pursued the basic condition of moving away from the realm of necessity, as put forward by Marx. Even before the invasion of the Soviet Union in the Second World War, pressure at work was intensified as a result of the abolition of the free employment relationship in 1940 (see Chapter 7, Section 4), and this often resulted in 10- to 11-hour working days. It was only in mid-1945 that prewar conditions were rapidly restored.

However, implementation of theoretical requirements was dependent upon the development of labor productivity. This explains why this target has also not yet been attained to the desired extent in socialist systems, since socialist systems have not so far been able to catch up with the most developed capitalist countries in terms of labor productivity (see Chapter 4, Section 3). Whereas the rate of increase in labor productivity is slowing down with the increasing level of development, every additional hour subtracted from the working day requires an increase in the labor productivity rate. The textbook *Politische Ökonomie. Sozialismus* indicates that a 12.5% increase in labor productivity was required in order to cut the working day from 8 to 7 hours. For the reduction from 7 to 6 hours (which, according to this source, was already achieved in the fourth quarter of 1956 to 1960 for some 60 million employees in the Soviet Union), a 17% increase of labor productivity is required. A further reduction from 6 to 5 hours will then call for as much as a 20% increase in labor productivity.[557]

This shows once more that the targets of socialism are inter-dependent. Not only is high efficiency a prerequisite for this target of protection, but fair distribution and participation are indispensable as well. Income disparities and divergent rights threaten to grow worse when a goal such as the reduction of working hours is pursued. Office employees and teachers who worked an average 39.4 hours a week were slightly ahead of the workers' average of 40 hours. To a certain extent, the tendency toward a reduction in working hours is stronger in the unproductive spheres (including military service) than in the productive ones. It did, however, cover some 15% of the working population in the 1960s, which is nevertheless a lower percentage than in capitalist countries, where it has been estimated to cover 33%.[558] However, such overall figures would no longer be tenable if we did not include the large number of agricultural workers in socialist countries (especially in China) in the quantitative comparison. In agriculture, working hours tend as a rule to be longer than in industry. However, if we just look at the pacemakers of development, then an international comparison with capitalist countries, on the basis of UN statistics, shows that the Soviet Union has led the way, compared with the higher developed capitalist countries such as Great Britain and West Germany, as far as the reduction of working hours is concerned. In both systems there are fluctuations in the continuity of the process. In capitalism, occasional increases in working hours are caused by booms, whereas in the socialist countries this seems to occur rather in times of temporary bottlenecks and crises. (See Table 90.)

Table 90

Working hours in manufacturing

Country	1969	1970	1971	1972	1973	1974	1975	1976	1977	1978
Czechoslovakia (weekly)	43.9	43.8	43.8	43.7	43.6	43.6	43.6	43.6	43.7	43.5
Hungary (monthly)	n.d.	165.0	165.4	163.8	162.3	161.3	161.9	164.5	163.8	162.4
Poland (monthly)	173.0	172.0	171.0	169.0	168.0	166.0	164.0	165.0	163.0	n.d.
Soviet Union (weekly)	40.5	40.6	40.5	40.7	40.9	40.6	40.7	40.7	40.6	
Yugoslavia (monthly)	188.0	184.0	182.0	181.0	181.0	181.0	182.0	185.0	185.0	185.0
for comparison:										
FRG (weekly)	43.8	43.8	43.0	42.7	42.8	41.9	40.4	41.4	41.7	41.6
Japan (weekly)	43.9	43.3	42.6	42.3	42.0	40.0	38.8	40.2	40.3	40.6
United Kingdom (weekly, male)	45.7	44.9	43.6	44.1	44.7	44.0	42.7	43.5	43.6	43.5
United States (weekly)	40.6	39.8	39.9	40.5	40.7	40.0	39.5	40.1	40.3	40.4

Sources: ILO, *Yearbook of Labour Statistics 1979* (Geneva: ILO, 1979), pp. 301ff.; UN, *Statistical Yearbook 1978* (New York: UN, 1979), pp. 95f.

Although socialist states were generally not able to reach the targets set in the field of working hours, even their critics agree that they are tackling their policy of shortening working hours with increasing determination, despite the labor shortage in the Soviet Union.

Today, reducing working hours has become a sort of stimulus for mobilizing the very last reserves (especially housewives), so that more of them remain within the productive process than before. Another explanation is the government's idea of satisfying consumers by giving them more leisure time instead of the consumer goods that are unavailable for the time being[559] and increasing true "leisure time" as opposed to "time outside work," which, in Soviet literature, is partly considered as being dedicated to "social activities.[560]

Should this, indeed, be the calculation of socialist planners, then it is not quite right, because increased leisure time usually also increases the demand for the consumer goods required for recreational activities. Hence, leisure time cannot simply serve as a substitute for lacking consumer goods.

A conclusive evaluation of success in the protective field of reducing working hours will only be possible when *leisure time* is included to a greater extent in considerations of the working day— unlike in capitalist economy, where organization of leisure time is left mainly up to the individual on the grounds of an ancient liberal concept of personal freedom. The humane goals of socialism are seen to lie primarily in the field of *leisure time organization.* Apart from some unnecessarily repressive aspects (such as keeping a tight rein on the arts), socialism is clearly ahead of capitalism in this field, right through from the promotion of sports and culture to assistance in leisure time organization and further education.

Comparative time budget research[561] shows that the Soviet Union has been very successful in the creation of leisure time. With 4.9 hours a day for men (women come off less favorably in the Soviet Union by comparison—see Chapter 2, Section 2), the Soviet Union holds top position of the sample of countries, together with the United States and the Federal Republic of Germany (see Table 92). However, the Soviet study reveals that the findings are not quite so clear-cut in other socialist countries. The countries with the lowest daily leisure times include both capitalist countries like France and socialist countries like Bulgaria and Hungary (in the case of France, however, the 10.7 hours for the satisfaction of physiological needs, such as sleeping and eating, which ranks top of the sample, probably also contains a certain amount of leisure time).

On the whole, time budget patterns seem to be coming more

Table 91

The time budget structure of the male working population in system comparison
(daily average hours of a seven-day week)

	Working hrs. (incl. overtime, compl. works)	Total	Time related to work	Travel to and from work	House-work	Physiological needs (incl. 7.4–8.1 hrs. of sleep)	Leisure time	Misc. activities
Soviet Union, Pskov	6.2	17.8	1.4	0.7	1.4	9.3	4.9	0.8
Bulgaria, kazanlik	6.7	17.3	1.7	0.8	1.7	9.8	3.5	0.6
Hungary, Győr	7.2	16.8	1.6	1.0	1.6	9.4	3.8	0.4
GDR, Hoyerswerda	6.1	17.9	1.5	0.9	2.0	9.4	4.5	0.5
Poland, Toruń	6.7	17.3	1.3	0.9	1.4	9.3	4.8	0.5

Yugoslavia,							
Kragujevac	6.5	17.5	1.4	0.8	1.1	9.6	4.7	0.7
Maribor	6.7	17.3	1.2	0.7	2.1	9.5	4.0	0.5
Czechoslovakia,							
Olomouc	5.8	18.2	0.9	0.7	2.0	10.0	4.8	0.5
for comparison:							
Belgium	6.8	17.2	0.9	0.6	0.8	10.4	4.7	0.4
United States							
national							
average	6.3	17.7	1.3	0.7	1.1	9.7	4.8	0.8
Jackson	6.3	17.7	1.1	0.5	1.1	9.7	5.0	0.8
France	6.6	17.4	0.9	0.6	1.5	10.7	3.8	0.5
FRG							
national							
average	6.6	17.4	1.01	0.5	1.3	10.4	4.4	0.3
Osnabrück	6.5	17.5	0.8	0.4	1.1	10.2	4.9	0.5

Source: V. D. Patrušev, "Das Zeitbudget der städtischen Bevölkerung in sozialistischen und kapitalistischen Ländern," in R. Ahlberg (ed.), *Soziologie in der Sowjetunion* (Freiburg: Rombach, 1969) (199–213), p. 201.

and more into line in the industrialized countries. Soviet scientists feel, however, that these converging time budget patterns are only comparable in quantitative terms and not in qualitative terms, since the use of leisure time differs greatly, at least as far as the Soviet Union is concerned.

Even though it is true that the time dedicated to belletristic literature is gradually shifting toward television, just as in capitalism, socialist countries still claim to have a qualitative advance through the different substance of their television programs.

Table 92

Use of leisure time
(hours per day)

	Soviet Union (Pskov)		Other socialist countries		Capitalist countries	
	men	women	men	women	men	women
study, private study	0.7	0.5	0.3	0.2	0.1	0.1
social activity	0.1	0.1	0.1	0.1	0.1	0.1
reading of belletristic literature, periodicals and newspapers	2.4	1.5	1.9	1.2	2.1	1.5
television	0.8	0.5	0.8	0.7	1.3	0.9

Source: Patrushev, ibid., p. 206.

4.   Freedom of choice of career and of choice of job

The first restrictions in the labor sphere were introduced at the beginning of 1918, when the Soviet Union gradually abandoned the concept of comprehensive socialization of all the means of production and management by workers' councils. Lenin had to contend with the left-wing communists' argument that labor discipline, coupled with the reappointment of former capitalists to production management, would not bring about a worthwhile increase in productivity but would weaken the proletariat (LPSS, Vol. 36, p. 260ff). Trotsky—whose supporters today often claim that he was the chief approver of genuinely democratic workers' self-management through Soviets—expressed even stronger feelings than did Lenin in favor of rigorous restriction of the freedom of choice of career: "Implementation of the duty to work is inconceivable without militarization of work to a greater or lesser degree. Expressing this view immediately takes us into the field of utmost superstition and woeful cries from the opposition."[562]

Workers' self-management and collective management fell victim to the concept of state capitalism. Since, however, no comprehensive plan existed for organizaing the economy as a whole, and since, according to Lenin (LPSS, Vol. 35, p. 147), a plan of this type could only be drawn up progressively through the system of initiatives from below and from above, no planning existed on the labor market either, and even during the plan periods labor planning always lagged behind the allocation of resources and investments, as it still does today.

So, despite the restrictions placed on the labor market since 1930, the scope for choice of employment was at first larger than the planners had intended it to be, owing to the lack of central planning for all the country's labor resources. There were two exceptions to this:

1. The first was *the attraction of kolkhoz workers into industry*, which encountered crafty resistance from the kolkhozes. The Council of People's Commissars tried to break this resistance by their explicit ban, dated March 16, 1931, on the setting up of obstacles in the path of peasants' migration. Sometimes kolkhoz workers were hired only for specific seasonal jobs, and sometimes they were granted the right to claim part of the wages (about 10%) of the higher-earning kolkhoz members during their time in industry.

2. From the fact that industrialization coincided with the introduction of mass *forced labor* in the Soviet Union, even predominantly well-meaning observers of socialist politics have inferred that forced labor was motivated more by economic than by political considerations, although the profitability of forced labor was found to be undeniably negative.[563] In fact, it was not during the time of civil war and class struggle after the Revolution that the number of forced laborers was highest. According to estimates, they numbered only 140,000 in 1927, as opposed to a maximum estimate of some 13,500,000 in 1941.[564]

However, the benefit of forced labor for economic efficiency was only ever of marginal significance for the overall economy, even when unfree labor reached its peak. According to the plan for 1941, which was found by the German troops and came into the hands of the allied authorities after the war, the Department of the Interior, which was in charge of the forced labor camps, contributed only 1.21% to the total industrial output.[565] Freedom of career and job choice was phased out in several stages: by mobilizing women and young people, by campaigns for voluntary attachment to enterprises, and by making employment relationships more difficult to get out of, right up to progressive introduction of the employee's record book—a development that culminated in the abolition of the free employment relationship in 1940. It was only toward the end of the Stalin era and with the revival of the trade unions that greater contractual freedom was restored on the labor market. After Stalin's death, labor legislation was gradually liberalized. An important step here was the decree of March 8, 1956, abolishing criminal prosecution in the case of unauthorized absence from work and conceding the workers the right to change jobs without the consent of the works management, at two weeks' notice. A decree issued on March 18, 1955, had already abolished the recruitment of young people in commercial schools and railway schools.

However, the growing liberalization in choice of job did not result in greater job satisfaction. In a sample taken in the early 1960s, 15.7% declared themselves dissatisfied and 43% as indifferent with regard to their current job. The method of seconding workers to less attractive careers and sectors is no longer used today, but the orientation prescribed at the start of university studies and professional life is defined as "an insight into necessity."[566] Earlier on, a worker in the Soviet Union had no guarantee that he would not be put into a job other than that for which he was qualified, even once he had chosen his career. Now, however, Soviet labor law has also come to provide actionable protection against these cases. A worker's transfer to another enterprise is contingent upon the consent of the worker concerned and is linked to payment of compensation guaranteed by law, similar to that granted in the case of temporary business trips or limited *komandirovka.*[567]

Nowadays, East European socialist states steer their work force chiefly by indirect means. Instead of coercion and detachment to jobs, they create motivation particularly in the choice of education and training, and later through material incentives (see Chapter 6, Section 4). The old *orgnabor* system of labor control turned out to be no longer efficient with an increasingly differentiated employment structure. Even in the early 1960s, only some 4% of employment contracts were still concluded through state intervention, 6% were based on obligations of school and university graduates, whereas 90% were concluded on a free basis. Toward the end of 1966, State Committees were established in the Ministers' Councils of the Union Republics, but it was only in the big cities that these were to act as a sort of placement office. Coordination councils are being established to provide vocational guidance for scholars, thereby promoting ex-ante (non-coercive) steering in a bid to combat errors in choice of career, which, in turn, lead to fluctuations within the cadres.

It is openly admitted today that labor organization involves processes beyond the control of the planning authorities. The migration currents among Soviet youth (60% of the migrants are aged 16 to 24) are causing the planners serious trouble. Today, in many cases, these currents can only be controlled by material incentives. However, the varying levels of professional prestige make indirect steering through restricted access to higher education, provision of information, and vocational guidance rather difficult. Planners are coming to realize that the methods of psychology, long denounced as being subjective, need to be applied to a greater extent in socialist countries as well.[568] So far, it is still possible for secondary-school graduates to content themselves with a medium-grade technical education in technical colleges or with skilled worker training.[569]

This has not as yet been challenged in the Soviet Union. If the growing demand for university education keeps up, however (see Chapter 2, Section 3), it will be sowing the seeds for conflict, which could lead to an increasing demand for more freedom in the choice of career. Indirect steering through material incentives is being constantly extended and employed with success. When it comes to material incentives, the wage motive should not be the only factor considered, as applies in the choice of career as well. However, the wage motive does seem to be gaining growing importance in socialist countries again, to judge by the surveys on labor fluctuation. In a Soviet survey of 1966, wages only ranked fifth of the reasons given by the sample for leaving their enterprise. At the same time, they ranked at the top of the reasons for fluctuation in the German Democratic Republic. Consequently, the Soviet survey explained the high fluctuation by neglect of the social and cultural aspects of work.[570]

The results obtained in the Soviet Union and in the German Democratic Republic cannot be compared undiscerningly. Whereas the reason "home location" ranked first in the Soviet Union, it only played a minor role in the German Democratic Republic, coming at the bottom of the list of motives. The Soviet surveys do not provide a clear picture, because very different questions were asked, and even where the questions were the same, the answers given varied widely from region to region. In big cities, such as Leningrad, the wage motive seems to play a greater role than in the country.

The motivational structure is expected to become even more complicated in the future, with the growing differentiation in living conditions, such that monocausal explanatory patterns will no longer suffice as a basis for indirect labor policy.[571]

Socialist developing countries inevitably had to fall back on methods of labor steering, even if only to combat traditional unemployment. The People's Republic of China did this both to ensure the work output of the communes and to check overurbanization. Nevertheless, it proved difficult to control the labor market fully in such a huge country. Official recruitment mechanisms were bypassed again and again. In China, enterprises had less freedom to hire and fire than in the Soviet Union.[572] On the other hand, there was no country-wide labor distribution system, although—contrary to the case in the Soviet Union—the majority of jobs had been assigned via state labor offices since the 1960s. The workers at times regard the resulting restrictions in choice of career and job as outside interference—despite a delegation system through work collectives and through certain participatory facilities for the workers. In addition, certain courses of study give rise to increasing expectations that cannot be satisfied.

When undesired developments in labor policy could not be prevented, the government tried to correct these with the hsia-fang system in 1956/57, that is, by sending workers down to the country. This sending-down movement was designed to pursue a number of goals:

1. to reverse partially the exodus to the towns;
2. to reduce overstaffing in administrative authorities;
3. to absorb the excess of students and graduates;
4. to fight the trend toward autonomy within the intelligentsia and the urban elites.

With Mao, the hsia-fang system was aimed expressly at the intellectuals. The very fact that Mao speaks of "driving out" in itself indicates that this process was not always accepted inwardly, as the system's apologists like to claim. Chinese newspapers and pamphlets reported numerous complaints about nonsensical waste of labor and arbitrary selection of the people sent down. Therefore, many of them—some 40 millions, according to estimates—took advantage of the general travel boom during the Cultural Revolution and returned to the cities.[573]

For a long time, Cuba had the most liberal labor legislation of socialist transitional societies. With increasing economic setbacks and the failure of moral gratification, labor legislation was tightened up in 1971 with the "law against absenteeism." The argument advanced by apologists that this disciplining has to be viewed differently in the light of the constant growth of the social consumption fund does not provide sufficient justification, however—even less so if we consider that in 1971 there was no drastic increase in the social consumption fund to compensate for this sudden intensification in repression.

The severe temporary restrictions in choice of career and job that are in evidence in most socialist systems are not, however, a necessary facet of socialism. In the discussions of the older generation of economic scientists, in which much emphasis was placed on theoretical models, Oscar Lange had provided both for a broad measure of consumer freedom and for freedom in choice of job, so that the random central pricing policy of the planning authorities could be corrected ex post through trial and error. The advocates of market socialism have helped to lend theoretical credit to the right to freedom in this field of the production sphere again.

Yugoslavia has proved that socialist economy is perfectly compatible with extensive freedom of movement, as is to be found in capitalist countries. She has, however, had to accept a number of social consequences, such as unemployment and works egotism in recruitment policy.

5. The protective function of the trade unions and the right to strike

In theoretical terms, trade unions could become superfluous in a system of self-managing producers, as has only formally existed in Yugoslavia up to now. A prerequisite for this would be a multi-party system or the possibility of factions being created within a unified workers' party, to assume the organizational function of the self-management bodies.

During the transformation period it was undisputed that the trade unions would have to preserve their protective function in transitional society as well—if only because of the coexistence of various forms of ownership. It was mainly after Lenin's death that the protective functions degenerated into repressive functions.

Since the end of the NEP period, trade unions have been increasingly oriented exclusively toward production policy and have been used as a lever for raising economic efficiency. This has sometimes led to the paradoxical situation of the works managements being more receptive to workers' demands than were their trade unions. The Soviet trade unions took their "slave-driving" attitude quite a long way, even in official statements, such as at the Special Wage Policy Conference in January 1933: "We must take the same severe action against those trade unionists who allow misrepresentation of the Party's directive in wage matters as the Party takes in its own ranks against those opportunists who interfere with cereal supplies or with other fronts of socialist construction.[574]

On September 28, 1929, the labor contract was declared an instrument of state wage policy. Since then, collective bargaining has been phased out de facto, although it has not been abolished de jure. It developed into nothing more than a "declaration of obligations." It is only in recent times that the protective functions of collective agreements have come to be stressed again.[575] For a long time, the worker was in an extremely dependent and vulnerable position vis-à-vis the state monopolies.

The function of the trade unions was reduced to such an extent that during the 17 years between 1932 and 1949, no trade union congress was convened. Even in 1949, no spectacular move was made to change the trade unions' role, except for an attempt to comply to a greater extent with the formal principles of democracy. No new policy was proclaimed, and representation was as undemocratic as ever, with only 23.5% consisting of worker officials and the large majority of professional trade union officials.[576] From 1952 onward, the trade unions were given a greater propaganda function, as more emphasis was placed on qualitative production targets, and in 1953, after Stalin's death, the stakhanov system was phased out by a less pressuring wage system with real collective agreements.

Even where trade unions always represented a factor of organizational power, they had little opportunity to strengthen the protective function of the socialist state, because they lacked the instruments for imposing sanctions. Above all, they lacked the most important sanction, namely the *right to strike*. In the penal code of a number of socialist countries, the mere attempt to organize a strike carries drastic penalties.

The fictitious identity of employees with works management has led to the argument that the worker cannot strike "against himself" in socialist systems. In Soviet Russia, however, there was dispute about the point from which this identity could be assumed to exist. In 1922, Lenin still felt the Central Committee's resolution "On the role and functions of the trade unions under the conditions of the New Economic Period" to be necessary, in the light of the continued existence of class society in the NEP period and the protective function of the state and trade unions, with the right to strike providing a means of taking sanctions. However, this protective function was already thought of as coupled to a repressive function, since, apart from representing the interests of employees, trade unions "as participants in the state power and builders of the overall national economy" could "not do without instruments of pressure" (LPSS, Vol. 44, p. 348). Lenin thus took a stand against Trotsky, who wanted to limit the trade unions' role to the disciplining of the working class for purposes of production, and more on the side of Tomskii, for many years chairman of the Central Council of Trade Unions, who defended the trade unions' protective interests against certain party ideologists. Lenin formulated a compromise between the two positions. Consequently, his attitude toward the right to strike turned out to be somewhat tortuous. The resolution did not mention the right to strike, and the trade unions were charged with the task "of contributing toward the quickest possible settlement of the conflicts" should a strike occur (LPSS, Vol. 44, p. 344).

The idea of recognizing strikes in a situation where capitalist remnants still existed in the economic system was realistic. Between the trade union congresses of 1921 and 1922, 102 strikes involving 43,000 workers were reported to have taken place, as well as 4,156 labor disputes, most of which were settled by conciliation. In 1921–22, the right to strike was widely claimed and exercised. In 1922, a political change came about. The right to strike in private industry was not affected, but in state industry a two-stage *compulsory dispute settlement procedure* was to become the only right of the trade unions (the conciliation court, and if no agreement was achieved there, the arbitration tribunal). It was only in February 1926 that the government granted economic organs of state the right to demand compulsory conciliation on the interpretation of collective agreements. After that there were practically no trade-union-backed strikes in the state sector, although there was a growing number of "wild-cat strikes" up to 1929.[577] Workers' opposition, by way of a counterpole to the mere transmission-belt function of the trade unions, was crushed. The differences of opinion between Lenin and Trotsky on this point were more of a tactical nature. For both of them, the party's priority was unquestioned, however. Trotsky put more emphasis on the party, whereas Lenin stressed the educational function of the trade unions instead. In practice, they were in agreement. Trotsky's concept of "state trade unions" without a protective function gained acceptance once Tomsky had been eliminated from trade union leadership following a party resolution of the Central Committee.[578]

When sporadic opposition began to be voiced in the Soviet Union in the 1960s and occasional strikes became more frequent again, a passage was inserted into the RSFSR Penal Code by virtue of a decree of September 16, 1965, stating that the "organization of, or participation in group activity . . . involving interruption of work in the enterprise" was punishable with one year of reform labor or a fine of 100 rubles.

Following the Soviet model, the right to strike was abolished in all the people's democracies. This did not, however, lead to a complete extinction of strike activity, and occasional wild-cat strikes still occurred, although these were not infrequently qualified as "counterrevolutionary." Extensive strikes occurred in the German Democratic Republic in 1953, in Poland and Hungary in 1956, and in Czechoslovakia the trade unions even called out a short-term general strike in 1968 in reply to the military intervention of the Warsaw Pact states.

The most extensive strike activity in an Eastern European socialist country developed in Yugoslavia in the 1960s. The first strike in January 1958 in Trbovlje still came as a shock to the party. The press hushed it up. In 1960 there were 60 strikes, in 1961 as many as 130, and in 1962 the number rose to 225. However, the party's apprehension that toleration of the strikes would result in a further increase in their number proved unfounded. The number of strikes even dropped after 1964 (271), whereas the number of strikers per strike tended to increase.

Strikes remained isolated events, without country-wide coordination and generally without participation of white-collar workers. Unlike in capitalist systems, action is relatively short in the main—often lasting only one day—and is directed against the management organs, though at times against decisions of the workers' self-management as well. The principal issues are questions of income distribution.[579]

Although no provision exists for these strikes in the constitution or the legislation, Yugoslav dogmatics deal much more openly with the workers' latent need for conflict than do the parties of the other socialist countries, and Yugoslav publications are even discussing the possible legalization of strikes.

But Yugoslavia also had ideological difficulties in recognizing the legitimacy of strikes. On the one hand, strikes were justified as a means of counteracting the etatism that is widely denounced in Yugoslav Marxist doctrine. On the other hand, however, strikes did not quite fit into the system of self-management and the more extensive participation rights granted to the Yugoslav workers. Even though official doctrine contested the sense of the right to strike in a self-management socialist system, the number of strikes increased, and these could no longer be played down as "walkouts," since the strikers virtually enjoyed the tacit approval of the local party and trade union organs. The reason given for this is the traditions of the labor movement and the fact that older workers in particular regard the strike as the most effective means of pressure for safeguarding their interests. In addition, strikes are attributed to certain errors committed by the party in mobilization. However, even those who are very outspoken in their criticism of the shortcomings of their own system rightfully maintain that in a system where self-management has been fully achieved (and where workers have a greater opportunity to participate at a macroeconomic level as well), the right to strike will no longer have the same significance as today. For the transitional phase of "monopoly socialism," however, the guaranteed right to strike is being increasingly claimed in the people's democracies as well. In Poland it was used in 1980 for the first time so vigorously and so cautiously at the same time, that the new independent trade union movement has changed the whole system. The Soviet orthodoxy, however, has not changed its verdict against independent labor unions formulated after the Dubček era.[580]

The only country where the right to strike remained authorized by law was the People's Republic of China. This right was even incorporated in the new constitution approved by the Fourth People's Congress on January 17, 1975 (Art. 28). Reporter Chang pointed out that it was Mao himself who had written the right to strike into the constitution. It has been inferred from this statement that there must have been opposition within the Chinese Communist party as well, which made it necessary to call upon Mao's authority. The Soviet Union voiced severe criticism against this particular passage. Here, too, it was emphasized that it did not make much sense for workers to strike "against themselves." The function of the strike has a truly protective aspect here, although not so much with regard to the economic and social rights of the workers. Mao's theory does not consider strikes to be class struggles but justifies them as "contradictions within the people" and as a means to fight the abuses of bureaucracy. As far as this second justification is concerned, Mao can refer to Lenin. But, similarly to Lenin, Mao also went on to narrow substantially his declaration of principle that strikes were permitted. In 1957 he warned the cadres: "When some of our local-level comrades have gone back home they should not say that a congress was held in Peking, which decided that big strikes could be organized all over the country (laughter), and that workers and schools could come out on strike. The comrades might possibly say that I said so, but that is not quite right either."[581]

There were repeated reports of strikes occurring in China. To some extent, these were political strikes, such as during the Cultural Revolution, when workers came out on strike without the backing of their trade union leaders and tended to fight on the side of the management against the extremists and Red Guards rather than against their works management.

The Maoists' predilection for mass mobilization strategies resulted in implicit justification for political strikes, whereas their contempt of material incentives led to economically motivated strikes receiving seemingly more disapproval than in any other socialist system. In the mass-mobilizational variants of Marxism, strikes are especially tolerated in cases where they are used not to enforce individual interests but as a means of contributing toward construction of the system and fighting bureaucratic abuses.

The *compulsory settlement of disputes* that developed after abolition of the right to strike (by virtue of the Supreme Soviet's decree of January 1957) is implemented by the Conciliation Commission for Labor Disputes (KTS = *Komissii pro trudovym sporam*), which is made up of an equal number of representatives from the administration and from the enterprise trade union committee. The second instance of conciliation is the enterprise trade union committee itself, and the third the ordinary law courts. The dispute commissions in socialist systems have a much wider scope of competence, a larger circle of potential applicants, and more flexible rules of procedure. One advantage of this system is the decriminalization of minor economic offenses. Encroachment of the public into the private sphere, as well as the somewhat vague nature of some offenses such as "work-shy behavior," have to be rated as disadvantages, however. The citizens of socialist states do not seem to regard enterprise justice as containing solely advantages.

To judge by the number of cases that are taken to court, it would seem that the protective function of the trade unions, which could develop most effectively at the second instance, is not used to the full. It can be assumed from Soviet information that the courts are more inclined to rule in favor of the worker (particularly in cases of dismissal) and that, as a result, workers have greater confidence in the independent courts than in their trade union representations. The literature shows that this protective function of the courts is considered to be insufficiently developed as yet in the production sphere. There are occasional complaints that the courts do not penalize the managements with a sufficient degree of conviction. A growing tendency to bring labor conflicts before the courts can be detected especially in Yugoslavia, which publishes reliable data on the matter. Here, the increase in the number of labor court proceedings is inversely proportional to the phase-out of the political judiciary.[582]

The shortcomings of the trade unions' protective function are compensated to some extent by the many different controlling bodies. Since the trade unions lack truly independent competences, however, the wide range of conflicting control functions meant that these often failed to produce the desired effect of strengthening the protective function of the state. Nothing can be changed here so long as the ideology continues to stress that the protective function is superfluous and only aims at maximizing the organizational efficiency of the trade unions for purposes of plan fulfilment. Only in the Yugoslav literature has the protective function of collective workers' control been duly appreciated again as a means of compensating for defects in the participatory and planning apparatus.

It will only be possible to take this approach further when socialist systems recognize that although socialism can indeed have fewer structural shortcomings than capitalism when it comes to realizing this protective function, the shortfalls in the planning and participatory systems of socialist states cannot be ascribed to motivational shortcomings alone.

In those socialist systems that take the final goals of their ideology very seriously, such as the People's Republic of China, the protective function of the trade unions has occasionally come into conflict with the forms of mass participation. The repeated attempts made to liberate the trade unions to some extent from their transmission-belt function vis-à-vis the party caused the Chinese trade unions to wage war on two fronts, that is, against the party and against the mass movements, such as during the Cultural Revolution. Since membership of China's Communist party was relatively low (see Table 105), trade unions played an important role as a filter in the recruitment of party members. The trade unions' moves toward autonomy were frequently combated by the party. During the Cultural Revolution in particular, the insistence on the protective function of the workers' mass organizations was branded as "economistic aberration" in China, so that trade unions became the target of attacks from the Red Guards during that period.[583] Even in countries where the party does not have an important role to play, such as in Cuba, the party usually has its say in trade union matters, or, as Castro put it at the Thirteenth Trade Union Congress in 1973: "The party was not uninvolved in the choice of candidates [for leadership of the CTC—author]. But the party did not intervene by asking the top leaders of the labor movement about the viewpoint of the worker masses. . . ."[584]

Hence, exaggeration of the primacy of politics does not seem to further the development of the protective function in the production sphere. The ways open for extending the trade unions' protective functions vary according to the branch of industry and the enterprise in question. Whenever management and plant management are working together on good terms, and this is quite frequently the case, the trade union leadership usually has a weak position in the triumvirate. This holds true particularly when plant management succeeds in securing the support of a large part of the work force by obtaining the highest possible allocations and plan targets that are most likely to be fulfilled. We would, however, be judging the function of the trade unions in socialism incorrectly if we merely transposed the dualistic conflict pattern of capitalism, where both sides of industry are autonomous, to the different conditions prevailing in the socialist systems. Critics of socialist trade union policy are right, however, when they point out that the bargaining scope for trade unions in socialist systems is considerably curtailed because wage policy and working condition guidelines (working hours, leave) are regulated entirely by governmental decrees. However, this is a development that is also beginning to emerge in organized capitalism, and it is quite indispensable in socialism if redistribution policy and protection policy are to be taken seriously in the socialist state. The real shortcoming that exists in socialist systems might possibly lie in the hypocritical statement that conflict is no longer conceivable between the bodies representing the workers' interests and the centralized decisions of the politicians, within the scope for manoeuver left for the social organizations. In socialist countries there is a stronger tendency than in capitalist pacification strategies to implement the protective function of the system solely in the form of the pursuit of individual rights and not through the collective action of organized workers.

8

Protection
in the distribution sphere

1.   Development of the Health System

Apart from those achievements of socialist systems in their health
sectors that have already been covered in the sphere of production
(see Chapter 7, Section 2), socialist systems can be shown to have
achieved clear success in health care, which is reflected primarily
by indicators such as the population per doctor and hospital beds
per 10,000 population (see Table 93). Global figures of this type
cannot hide the fact that disparities exist in health care in socialist
systems as well (mainly regional disparities, but some strata-based
disparities too) but the degree of disparity is less than that found in
capitalist countries (see Chapter 2, Section 2).

The protective function of the socialist state is not only evident
in the minimal amount of positive advertising for products that come
onto the market but also in the extent of negative advertising. State
advertisements give greater warning about the consequences of
alcohol and nicotine consumption than in any capitalist country,

Table 93

Health systems

Country	Rank out of 135 nations	Physicians per 10,000 population		Hospital beds per 10,000 population		Population per physician 1976
		1963/ 65	1978	1963/ 65	1979	
Soviet Union	2	20.5	35.4	109	123	299
Hungary	3	17.9	26.6	82	82.1	439
Czechoslovakia	5	17.5	30.1	124	77.7	404
Bulgaria	7	16.2	28.3	92	90.3	453
Rumania	15	13.8	16.8	82	89.5	750
Poland	21	12.1		62	72.2	615
GDR	24	11.4	24.6	111	105.0	523
North Korea	27	11.0				
Mongolia	32	10.3	20.9		105.0	4,931
Yugoslavia	35	8.3			60.0[1]	792
Cuba	37	8.0	18.2		44.7	1,121[2]
Albania	55	4.3				159[3]
China						26,960[4]
						2,870[5]
for comparison:						
FRG	11	14.45				506
United States	12	14.35				617
United Kingdom	23	12.00				524
Japan	29	10.82				845
India	77	1.73				3,961

(1) 1975; (2) 1974; (3) 1977; (4) 1971; (5) 1978.

Sources: Ch. L. Taylor & M. C. Hudson, *World Handbook of Political and Social Indicators* (New Haven, London: Yale U.P., 1972), pp. 260f. 3rd column: Statistische Übersichten From: *Yearbook of East European Economics,* Vol. 8, (Munich: Olzog, 1979), p. 493; *Statisticheskii ezhegodnik stran-chlenov SEV. 1980* (Moscow: Statistika, 1980), p. 443; last column: UN: *Statistical Yearbook. 1978* (New York: UN, 1979), pp. 893ff. On China: W. Kraus, *Wirtschaftliche Entwicklung und sozialer Wandel in der VR China* (Berlin: Springer, 1979), p. 531.

though at times with limited success. A socialist country (Hungary) ranks second in the world in terms of per capita cigarette consumption (1970), with Poland, Bulgaria, and Rumania following in sixth, eighth, and tenth places.[585] Large-scale abuse of medicaments and drugs, as occurs in capitalist systems, can be more readily eliminated in socialist economies with their state-owned pharmaceutical industries.

Preventive health care comes up against less of a restrictive, old-fashioned liberal concept of freedom than it does in Western democracies. U.S. economists admitted in the 1960s that the Soviet Union had caught up with and even overtaken the highly developed countries of the West including the United States, and in recent comparative literature the system is evaluated[586] favorably in the light of a number of indicators.

Certain shortcomings in socialist health systems, on the other hand, are virtually impossible to express by means of quantitative indicators, namely the many complaints about the impersonal nature of care and various qualitative shortfalls, for which perhaps the low pay of nursing staff provides an indirect indicator—pay for nursing staff ranks bottom of the branches of the economy listed in Table 31—and the uneven quality of the medical staff, which is indirectly admitted by Soviet publications. The marked concentration of health care in regional hospitals (see Table 93, 3rd column), which was necessary in order to bridge the pronounced difference in health care standards between town and country,[587] leads to discrepancies between outpatient medical treatment and inpatient facilities, even in highly developed countries such as the German Democratic Republic. These discrepancies are attributed in the literature to "a conservative attitude toward the function of the hospital in socialist health systems."[588]

Compared with China, the Eastern European health scene seems to be a deadly bore.[589] The mobilization of paramedical personnel ("barefoot doctors"), the official support of traditional Chinese medicine, the closing of medical schools during the cultural revolution, the efforts of periodic "patriotic" health campaigns to eradicate certain diseases, such as malaria, and the emphasis on health in the countryside versus the deemphasis on hospitals in urban centers has attracted a good deal of enthusiasm in the West as well, but it is considered more critical in the light of recent events, since the rule of the "Gang of Four" has come to an end.

2.   The Social Security System

Efforts toward building up protection in the distribution sphere were focused first and foremost on the social security system. Socialist countries were under a certain pressure of competition here, because the capitalist countries, who emphasized the distribution sphere in order to ward off socialist transformation (and thus experienced problems in the production sphere) achieved undeniable success in legitimating their system through the redistributive power of politics.

It has already been seen in Chapter 1 on Redistribution that the low level of productive resources only permitted limited efforts initially and that the preventive measures were largely "Tayloristic" in nature, that is, designed to maintain the labor force. The "social lag" in socialist countries, which were caught up in transformation difficulties, emerges clearly from the slow-moving development of social legislation in the Soviet Union.

The economic and planning difficulties experienced after 1917 made a uniform social security scheme in the hands of the state unfeasible. The first measures introduced were unemployment insurance and health insurance, which provided all wage-earners and their dependents with insurance cover. In 1919, the trade unions tried to gain a greater say in social policy. However, since they lost the political battle within the party, they simply became lay members in Soviet Russia's social security system. In 1920, a People's Commissariat was set up for social welfare. During the NEP period, the social security system was expanded primarily on an insurance basis, as was the case in capitalist countries. In the plan era, from 1929 onwards, the insurance system came to be subject to economic efficiency criteria. After a campaign against alleged class enemies, who were abusing the insurance schemes, individual professional groups, such as doctors and workers in a number of key industries, were given privileges, and a benefit and pension scale was introduced, graduated according to the importance of the branch of industry.

In the 1930s, too, the individual measures tended in the main to be rather isolated. One contested step was the abolition of unemployment insurance in 1930, despite the fact that admirable success had been achieved in finding employment for the full labor force. Even once free labor contracts had been abolished by a decree from the Presidium of the Supreme Soviet on June 26, 1940, under the euphemistic title: "On the change-over to the 8-hour day and the

7-day week and on the ban of workers and employees unilaterally withdrawing from their enterprises," consequences of migration and fluctuation were still to be felt, although these could have fallen under the protective function of the socialist state (see Chapter 7, Section 4). China also followed this example and abolished unemployment benefits with the provisional law of July 1, 1950, before the full employment that had already been postulated had, in fact, been achieved.[590]

All socialist countries focused their social security systems sharply on production during the accumulation phase. The systems were rather selective with protective benefits and did not cover the whole of the population, as they should have. In general, it was the peasants who were particularly disadvantaged. Even in the Soviet Union, a generally binding social insurance fund was only introduced for the kolkhoz peasants in 1965, and the "Law on Pensions and Benefits for Kolkhoz Members" brought about an essential improvement in assistance for the elderly. In the German Democratic Republic, on the other hand, the LPG peasants were included in the public social security system right from the start.[591] In China, too, the masses were mainly excluded from the central security system, in particular the commune peasants and craftsmen in the cooperatives. They were catered for in very different forms and with very different levels of efficiency by the welfare funds of their organizations. Without any great material outlay, these schemes created a model with their "Five Guarantees System" (assistance for the elderly and handicapped, orphans, guarantee of basic foodstuffs, clothing, and heating, education), which at first was able to compensate for the lack of a centralized social security system for everyone. Developing countries such as China, which were basically agrarian in structure, were not, however, able to eliminate social hardship entirely. The antiurbanization policy and the privileging of industrial workers put those who were neither integrated in a commune nor permanently employed in a factory at a disadvantage. Grey areas with inferior social security provision developed between the town and the countryside. The ideological ecstasy of the "both worker and peasant" movement cannot hide the fact that the group of seasonal workers served the system as a source of cheap labor and at the same time did not benefit from the social security schemes in factories and communes. In the Soviet Union, too, seasonal workers have posed legal and social problems.[592] Not even all the workers were able to be covered in the initial stages. In China, only 14 million workers out of 45 million, that is, barely one third of the total, were in the system by 1958, although even this was better than the situation in Taiwan at the same time (see Table 94). The egalitarian policies of the tumultuous 1967–76 decade by no means eliminated disparities in material welfare between the units at all levels in rural society.[593] The highest-developed countries also had the highest degree of social security coverage during their transformation phase. These countries were, however, also the ones that retained traditional concepts of contribution financing the longest, that is, a system orientated toward cost-covering. In the Soviet Union, on the other hand, the security system receives 63% of its funding from the state budget, and the remainder is levied on enterprises, kolkhozes, and social organizations.[594] In the German Democratic Republic, state subsidies for the social insurance system rose from 3.5% in 1955 to 43% in 1974.[595]

Social policy in socialist countries is based on principles different from those in market societies:

1.   One of the goals is to *substitute services and material aid for monetary benefits* in the long run, and this is frequently taken as proof of the construction of communism. There is little proof that monetary benefits on the whole are decreasing in socialist countries. Only health protection is an exception to this rule. But the two German states show that in this issue area, both capitalist and socialist societies tend to favor material benefits and social services (compared

Table 94

Percentage of workers covered by old-age insurance

Country	Year of survey	Percentage
Yugoslavia	1953	44
Poland	1950	63
Hungary	1960	59
Czechoslovakia	1950	100
for comparison		
Taiwan	1956	16
FRG	1960	89
Sweden	1950	100

Source: From *The Yearbook of Labour Statistics;* D. Zöllner, *Öffentliche Sozialleistungen und wirtschaftliche Entwicklung. Ein zeitlicher und internationaler Vergleich* (Berlin (West): Duncker & Humblot, 1963), p. 118.

to monetary benefits) in a ratio of 4:1. On the whole, monetary benefits exceed the 50% mark[596] in the Soviet Union as well. Despite a higher proportion of pensioners in the German Democratic Republic than in West Germany, the cash flow (in absolute figures) of social benefits to the citizens seems to be lower than in the Federal Republic. But we have deducted from this amount certain benefits that rarely occur in socialist countries, such as allowances for the unemployed or rebates for the poorer strata, on account of increasing housing rents.[597] In West Germany, services and nonmonetary benefits are growing; in the German Democratic Republic, there is a tendency toward increasing monetary distribution.

2.   The main difference between capitalist and socialist social policy is the emphasis on collective or *social consumption*. The global figures for this are not easy to compare across the systems. There are many governmental expenses listed under "social consumption," which in Western budgets would be found in the rubrics of "education," "sponsoring of sports," and other items. In earlier comparisons, the social consumption funds in the 1960s were calculated to amount to roughly 30% of all the relevant benefits for individual family incomes. In capitalist countries, the proportion was about 5 to 15%.[598] In the Soviet Union a proportion of 40.6% was envisaged for social consumption by the time the ninth Five-Year-Plan ended in 1975. This goal was almost reached if we compare the figures for 1975.[599] But it is still unlikely that social consumption can be used as a proof that "communism" is being built—as Suzlov tried to do at the Twenty-Fourth Party Convention. In some socialist countries—such as in Hungary—the social consumption funds even underwent a slight setback compared with individual consumption funds and wages.[600] The data for social consumption have to be taken with a pinch of salt. Sometimes parts of the wage funds are included, as far as these are independent of certain work achievements (such as allowances for the transfer of pregnant women).[601]

3.   The *production-orientated nature of social security systems* in socialist states is also evident from the relatively late development of protection in areas that were not directly productive (such as maternity grants in the Soviet Union as of June 27, 1936) and also from the fact that *old-age* pensions remained at the bare subsistence level for a long time. Pensions developed more rapidly in the highly developed capitalist countries. Whereas a pensioner in West Germany in 1971 received an amount equivalent to some 52% of his gross wage from the social security, the percentage in the German Democratic Republic was only 41%.

The social benefit ratio, that is, the ratio of public social benefits to the social product, is also lower in the German Democratic Republic than in the Federal Republic of Germany, even though one would expect higher social benefits in the former on account of its higher percentage of working population and its less favorable age structure (percentage of elderly people, that is, men over 65 and women over 60: German Democratic Republic, 19.2%; Federal Republic of Germany, 17.7%). The social benefit ratio in the Federal Republic of Germany increased from 17.0 to 19.5% in the period between 1950 and 1969 and stagnated between 14.4% and 13.6% in the German Democratic Republic over the same period. These differences result in part from a more rapid increase in social security contribution rates (20%) and in the assessment limit for contributions (600 Marks) which, in the German Democratic Republic, were kept at a constant level for a long time. This cost advantage for the individual was achieved at the expense of pensions keeping up less with price developments than in the capitalist welfare state, although price developments were also admittedly on a lesser scale (see Chapter 4, Section 3).

A comparison of the two German states does not, however, seem quite fair if this is to be used to draw conclusions for the comparison of capitalist and socialist systems as a whole. For purposes of its own legitimation, the Federal Republic of Germany took on many of the costs of the war on behalf of the whole German population within its sphere of influence, including more than 3 million GDR refugees. FRG social benefits thus come out atypically high for a capitalist country in an international comparison. In addition, allowance must be made for the German Democratic Republic's difficult economic starting conditions.

Another indicator for the production-oriented social policy system of socialist countries is the encouragement for pensioners to continue to work. Continued integration into the labor market is highly emphasized by socialist systems even after retirement age has been reached. This is in striking contrast to Western countries governed by labor parties, and there are rather coincident views held by politicians of socialist countries and politicians of conservative groups in market societies (such as the Liberals and the Christian Democrats in West Germany). Both favor different motives for the continuation of work and offer material stimuli by guaranteeing only small deductions from retirement allowances for pensioners who continue to work. A Soviet law from 1970 to 1975 led to the case where, of the 29.7 million pensioners (in 1976), about 17 million continued to work after reaching retirement age, in less-developed socialist countries in particular. Women in the age groups

between 55 and 64 and above 65 also work in much higher proportions than in Western democracies (see Table 23 last column).[602]
Whereas pensioners working in capitalist societies are considered as
"exploited" it is held to be "all-round development and integration
of the aged" under socialist conditions.

4.   The literature on social policy in socialist countries sometimes claims higher benefits for retired people than in most capitalist
countries. In this respect, *performance* in most socialist countries is
inferior to the developed capitalist systems. Soviet scholars boast of
retirement allowances of 60% of the wage.[603] The figure is not easy
to scrutinize, since the Soviet law on retirement allowances contains
exact indications of the ratio of allowances to average wages, but we
are not told what percentage of the workers is in the different
categories. Western economists have calculated that the average
retirement allowance is 75 rubels per month.[604] There is no doubt
that allowances compared to wages seem to be higher in the Soviet
Union than in the German Democratic Republic. But this does not
indicate any superiority of the former over the latter, since the
overall level of wages is considerably lower in the Soviet Union.
The Soviet Union cannot afford to go much below the minimum
wage, since it would then reach the minimum level necessary for
survival. Therefore, Soviet pride at superiority in the social security
system, in terms of the wages-to-retirement allowance ratio, is hardly
justified, even compared to capitalist systems. But socialist systems
admit considerable time lags in the adjustment of minimum pensions
to the development of minimum wages—the ratios were 100% in
1960, 75% in 1965, 50% in 1970, 64.2% in 1975).[605]

5.   Socialist systems promote the principle of *social maintenance*. The insurance principle, where it is still strong in socialist
countries such as in the German Democratic Republic, is frozen in,
since the contributions from the individual citizens have been kept
constant over the years. Nevertheless, the individual insurance
principle is gaining ground. In the Soviet Union, life insurance has
been readmitted, after being abolished in 1919 as a bourgeois
remainder of individual social care. Most of the benefits are still used
for saving for long-life consumer goods. But sometimes they are also
used for protection against risks, which is not provided for by the
Soviet system, such as unemployment. The Soviet Union prematurely
abolished unemployment insurance in 1930, and even today there
are remainders of frictional unemployment—sometimes several
months are needed before a worker is settled in a new job. The
German Democratic Republic introduced a voluntary additional
insurance in 1971, with features of individual additional protection

against the risks of life, which in some respects threatens to increase social disparities in retirement that have been avoided during the years of enrollment in the labor market.[606]

6. The *redistributive capacity* of social policy is emphasized in socialist systems. In socialist countries, vertical redistribution among the classes and strata of societies is more emphasized than among Western societies. In the first years of the Soviet system, the social security system was deliberately used as an additional instrument of social redistribution. The "class enemy" was disowned to no less an extent in the social security system than he was expropriated in his capital ownership. With growing stabilization of the socialist systems, no groups are discriminated against any longer—with one notable exception in the Soviet Union: the employees of the churches. Soviet studies in income distribution in the 1960s showed that the state allocates by subsidies and social allowances 46.4% of the income of low-income groups, but only 11.5% of the higher-income strata.[607] At first glance, the redistributive power of socialist systems would seem to exceed that of market societies. Comparative studies have shown, however, that the Soviet Union is most egalitarian when it comes to ideology and one of the least egalitarian in practice.[608] Privileges for the top bureaucrats on the one hand, and the continuing existence of underprivileged groups on the other (kolkhoz farmers, women, marginal groups, retired people) contradict the egalitarian self-image.[609]

7. *Social welfare measures for special emergency cases* are thought to be unnecessary. Capitalist countries have always taken cognizance of their own shortcomings and have admitted private and state activities to take care of all those cases of individual social need that were not regulated in advance by insurance and income maintenance measures of the welfare state. The socialist systems disliked the individual approach, which differed from their collectivist conceptions. Socialist systems boast of having no physical poverty left and normally underrate the impact of "psychological poverty" and alienation in modern society. Maybe certain forms of social work in socialist countries are less urgent, since the system of social security is more extended and social control of all possible cases of needs is more highly developed. The increasing need for emergency measures of social work in capitalist societies, such as special homes for deviants or special treatment for those addicted to drugs, are certainly not proof of a harmonious social system. In other fields, such as creche and preschool institutions, socialist countries mostly show an advantage over capitalist countries. The reintegration of criminals into the labor market and into social life is also usually

easier under the conditions of a planned society. But the under-development of individual help, without bureaucratic routines, which is more likely to happen in private and public institutions for emergency help in Western societies, is not justified under socialist conditions, even if some authors argue that individual emergency help is not advisable since it is usually looked upon as being discriminating and even stigmatic by the recipients. But even this can be mitigated by creating more legal entitlements and by liberating emergency social work from the traits of "charity." Moreover, the discriminating practices of individual treatment are not unknown to socialist societies, especially as "antisocial elements," "hooligans," and other deviants concerned are usually treated as "social prophylaxis" in order to prevent crime.[610]

Another type of comparison works with indicators in cross-national perspective. The indicator used most frequently in international comparisons is the social consumption ratio. Measured in terms of this indicator, the performance of socialist states is not as spectacularly high as some apologists would have it be. (See Table 95.)

Economists have concluded from comparisons of this kind that it is not the nature of the social system but rather the level of productive resources that is the decisive factor in determining the level of social expenditure.[611] Factors such as the employment rate, shortage of manpower, drop in labor employed in agriculture, differentiation in the employment structure, and a number of other factors do

Table 95

Share of public welfare expenditure
(at the GNP factor price in 1956 and 1962)

Country	1956	1962	Country	1956	1962
United States	4.8	6.7	Czechoslovakia	11.9	13.7
FRG	13.5	15.0	GDR	10.7	13.1
Austria	15.6	17.8	Soviet Union	6.4	8.1
Ireland	9.5	7.6	Hungary	5.6	5.4
Italy	10.7	11.7	Poland	6.5	6.6
Greece	5.9	8.1	Rumania	3.8	5.6
Yugoslavia	7.4	7.7	Bulgaria	5.5	6.2

Source: F. L. Pryor, *Public Expenditures in Communist and Capitalist Nations* (London: Allen & Unwin, 1968), p. 145.

indeed seem to exercise a certain influence on the development of a social security system, independently of the social formation. A mere comparison of expenditure will lead to erroneous conclusions, unless allowance is made for a number of factors:

1. *distribution* of the population over *town and country* and distribution of the forms of ownership;
2. the *age structure* of the population—it has been seen that as per capita income increases, the number of over-65s also increases, which in turn brings a growing need for social expenditure; the differences between the socialist countries are considerable (see Table 96)—the more developed a country, the higher its proportion of retired people;
3. the extent to which a country was *affected by the war*—the most affected countries in East and West had for quite a time the highest burdens in certain sectors of social welfare.

The impact of ideology—which was found relevant when comparing socialist and conservative governments in the West—seems to be less important. The age of a social security system and the amount of reliance of a state on indirect taxes proved to be important intervening variables that explain the performance of social security systems in the socialist world as well.[612]

Table 96
Proportion of pensioners (1979)
(in percentages)

Country	Pensioners
Bulgaria	21.7
Czechoslovakia	21.3
Cuba	6.9
GDR	21.5
Hungary	18.8
Mongolia	3.9
Poland	11.7
Soviet Union	18.3

Source: Calculated from the figures in: *Statisticheskii ezhegodnik stran-chlenov SEV 1980* (Moscow: Statistika, 1980), pp. 7, 448.

3.   Housing construction policy

According to Engels in his paper "On the housing question," to speculate about the distribution of living space in a future society leads one straight into the realms of utopia. There was thus no uniform theory as to how to deal with the housing problem in socialist countries during the transformation period. Since the socialist systems mainly grew from wars or civil wars, resulting in widespread destruction, living space was in particularly short supply.

In the years following on from war and revolution, redistribution of living space was the focal point of government activity in all socialist countries. A number of countries introduced administrative control over living space, and others preferred instead to have indirect means of social control for promoting a redistribution of living space. Mass mobilization in China not infrequently led the rich to make part of their living space "voluntarily" available to the local housing authorities under "gentle pressure."[613] Cuba worked on the basis of a drastic reduction in rents. This lessened the attraction of constructing new housing through private initiative, which had to be compensated for through further measures such as the compulsory purchase of non-built-up plots of land and a higher level of state housing construction.[614] Redistribution in the housing system was pushed ahead with the "reforma urbana" of 1960, which declared all previous tenancies null and void. In the first stage of redistribution of living space, each family was to be able to pay a certain sum, over 5 to 20 years, which would then give them the chartered right to their own up-to-standard apartment.[615] Although housing conditions were precisely one of the factors that could play an important part in developing the new socialist, the qualitative aspect of housing was very rapidly neglected in the face of physical need. Revolutionary experiments with housing communes in the period after 1917 were soon forgotten, although isolated theorists such as the economist Strumilin propagated the idea of housing communes (*domkommuna*) again in the 1960s. As for the quality of human relations, even the cooperatives have not progressed noticeably beyond the each-family-for-itself attitude of capitalist cooperative building societies.

Even in quantitative terms, however, the protective function of the socialist state has not been sufficiently developed in the housing sector. It is not untypical for housing construction to be excluded from industrial output. During the transformation period, housing construction figures were far behind those of the highly developed capitalist nations.

Two important indicators for measuring the housing situation are the average number of square meters per person and the average number of persons per room. In the Soviet Union, it is admitted that the revolutionary government's target of 9 square meters of living space per person as the minimum for a dignified existence has still not been achieved, more than half a century later. In 1965, the average was 6.5 square meters, or roughly half the average in the Federal Republic of Germany and Central Europe.

In the rural areas, where the housing situation seemed more favorable for a time as a result of forced industrialization and urbanization, the situation became worse. In the Soviet Union, there were 2.6 persons to a room in 1923, 3.9 in 1940, 4.02 in 1950, and 2.78 in 1960. Only in the mid-1960s did any improvement come about.[616] The situation in the towns also improved. In 1968, each urban dweller had 10.5 square meters of living space, although there were very pronounced regional discrepancies.[617] In China, the housing situation in the towns was even worse than in the Soviet Union. A Chinese survey of 1956 revealed that only 3.6 square meters living space per person was available to industrial workers and their families.[618]

In addition to the quantitative indicators, qualitative indicators are repeatedly applied in international comparisons. Defenders of the socialist planned economy praise the fact that by choice of location and investment policy the economy is in a position to implement a more rational housing construction policy and *prevent conurbations from growing any further.* Construction of new industrial plants was forbidden in Moscow and Leningrad. In 1939, the Eighteenth Party Congress asked for this ban to be extended to Kiev, Char'kov, Rostov, Gorky, and Sverdlovsk.[619] In the developing areas of Central Asia, despite the efforts of Soviet planners to achieve decentralization of investment, it is only during the Soviet era that "top-heavy" capitals have come to develop at all. Around 1970, between 11 and 15% of the population of each of the Central Asian Union Republics lived in the capital.[620] Since infrastructural investments are particularly expensive in these regions, the planners, against their better judgment, continued to invest in the conurbations. One positive feature here is that *no slum areas have formed* in the developing regions of socialist countries, even though there are barrack settlements with inadequate sanitation. (See Tables 97 and 98.)

Socialist housing construction policy comes off badly if the comparison of the German states is taken as a point of reference. Whereas the comparison between the Federal Republic of Germany

Table 97

Number of apartments constructed per 10,000 population

Country	1960	1965	1970	1975	1978	1979
Bulgaria	63	55	54	66	77	75
Cuba	n.d.	6.3	4.6	19.8	17.3	14.9
Czechoslovakia	54.1	54.9	78.2	99.6	85.2	81.1
GDR	46.7	40.1	44.6	83.6	100	97.2
Hungary	58.4	53.9	77.8	94.5	82.5	82.4
Mongolia	22.1	9.5	10.0	28	30	28
Poland	48	54.1	59.7	77.6	83.4	80.5
Rumania	137	101	78.6	77.9	76.3	87.1
Soviet Union	121	97	93	88	80	73

Source: *Statisticheskii ezhegodnik stran-chlenov SEV 1980* (Moscow: Statistika, 1980), p. 185.

and the German Democratic Republic is problematical in many cases because of the former's greater starting aid, this is less so when it comes to the housing system. Measured in terms of two indicators, the German Democratic Republic even had an advantage over the Federal Republic of Germany after 1949. One the one hand, the former had a lesser occupant density over her territory: in 1939 the occupant density was 3.7 persons per apartment, for what was to become Federal territory, and only 3.3 persons per apartment for what was to become GDR territory. On the other hand, Federal

Table 98

Living conditions (occupants per apartment), 1977

Country	Occupants
Bulgaria	3.4
Czechoslovakia	3.0
GDR	2.5
Hungary	2.9
Poland	3.6
Yugoslavia	3.7

Source: "Statistische Übersichten." In: *Jahrbuch der Wirtschaft Osteuropas/Yearbook of East-European Economics,* Vol. 7 (Munich: Olzog, 1979), pp. 481ff.

Germany territory had suffered considerably greater destruction of living space through bombing during the war than GDR territory. Nevertheless, the German Democratic Republic fell rapidly behind in terms of living conditions, with an average living space of more than 20% per apartment below that in the Federal Republic of Germany. In the latter, more than 50% of building capacity was used for housing construction, whereas in the former the percentage was only 35 to 40%.[621] Although they had both started out from the same initial position, the German Democratic Republic fell back to the level of Italy in its housing system, especially if amenities are included as well. (See Table 99.) The second most highly developed country in the Eastern bloc, Czechoslovakia, also experienced a

Table 99

Completed apartments per 1,000 population

Country	m^2 per new apartment	1955	1956	1958	1959	1960	1971
Bulgaria	64.6			6.1	6.4	6.3	5.7
Czechoslovakia	69.5	3.9	4.8	4.0	5.0	5.6	7.6
GDR	57.8	1.7	1.7	2.8	3.5	2.9	4.5
Poland	56.7	3.4	3.4	4.5	4.7	4.2	5.8
Rumania	47.5						7.3
Soviet Union	47.1	7.6	8.2	13.0	14.5	14.0	9.4
Yugoslavia	60.4	1.7	2.1	3.4	3.3	4.0	6.1
for comparison:							
FRG	87.0	10.6	12.0	9.4	10.6	10.5	
France		4.9	5.5	6.5	7.1	7.0	
England		6.4	6.1	5.4	5.5	5.9	
Italy		4.5	4.8	5.7	6.0	6.0	
Spain		3.9	4.2	3.4	3.8	4.3	
Greece		6.7	6.0	n.d.	6.7	6.5	
United States				n.d.	8.8	7.1	

Source: Economic Commission for Europe, *Housing Trends and Policies. 1956* (Geneva, 1957), p. 2; idem, 1960 (Geneva 1961), p. 2; for 1971: M. E. Ruban, "Wohnungsbau und Wohnungswirtschaft in den RGW-Ländern," *DA,* Vol. 12 (1973), p. 1313. More detailed data in absolute figures in: *UN Yearbook of Construction Statistics 1963-1972* (New York: UN, 1972).

marked fall-back in her housing system during the initial years of socialism, although war damage was less here than in other countries and the expulsion of Germans meant that the living-space situation improved in statistical terms (occupants per room in 1930: 1.40; in 1946: 1.36 (after the expulsion of the Germans); in 1950: 1.45 (the situation had deteriorated to below the 1930 level); in 1955: 1.48).[622]

The very impressive performance scored by a number of socialist countries in housing construction is seen to give the wrong picture if we then compare the construction figures with the size of the apartments constructed and their amenities. In the Soviet Union, the average size of apartments is still very small. A large number of small units had to be built to begin with in order to give each family a self-contained apartment: at the start of the 1960s only 60% of families in a city such as Leningrad had an apartment to themselves.[623] Housing amenities (Table 100) likewise remained below Western standards for many years, although they are beginning to catch up at present.

The comparatively low-level realization of protective functions was made even worse by certain disparities in the distribution of apartments. Even today, the privileged groups have easier access to good apartments. Shortage of housing to some extent hinders horizontal and vertical mobility within socialist societies in that some people do not take up better posts because living conditions would be worse at their new location. Waiting lists for state apartments are often still endless, and even a Soviet propaganda publication concedes that "someone who is allocated a state apartment should not be too choosy. If he refuses the apartment allocated when his turn comes up, because he does not like the area in which it is located, for example, then he must continue to wait until a new offer is made to him. It is the same as having lunch at home: you don't have to pay the bill after the dessert, but you have to eat the starting course and main dish that your wife puts before you."[624] As for this somewhat ironical, scanty regard of consumer wishes, it should be noted that the danger of an apartment hunter disliking a particular district is less great than in capitalist systems. There are, of course, more attractive and less attractive residential areas in socialist countries, too, and one's place of work automatically leads to certain preferences, but there are not the class and strata-based differences between neighborhoods that generally develop in towns in capitalist countries (with the exception of a few districts where the state functionaries live).

Table 100

Housing conditions

Country	Year	Owner occu-piers	Percen-tage tenants	Average no. of persons		Amenities		
				Per room	Per house-hold	Running water indoors	WC	Electric lighting
Bulgaria	1965	71.0	17.1	1.2	3.2	28.2	11.8	94.8
Cuba	1953	37.2	36.5	n.d.	n.d.	38.9	40.4	55.6
Czecho-slovakia	1961	50.4	42.0	1.3	3.1	49.1	39.5	97.3
GDR	1971	23.0	69.3	1.2^1	2.6	82.1	56.6	100.0
Poland	1970	n.d.	n.d.	1.4	3.4	47.3	33.4	96.2
Rumania	1966	n.d.	n.d.	1.4	3.2	12.3	12.2	48.6
Soviet Union	1965	n.d.	n.d.	1.5	3.7	n.d.	n.d.	n.d.
Yugoslavia	1971	70.7	29.3	1.5	4.0^2	34.0	26.5	87.9
for comparison:								
FRG	1968	34.3	65.7	0.7	2.9	99.7	87.7	99.9
Greece	1971	70.6	25.1	1.5	3.0	65.0	45.0	88.3
Italy	1961	45.8	46.8	1.1	3.6	62.3	n.d.	95.9
Spain	1960	n.d.	n.d.	n.d.	4.0	45.0	n.d.	89.3
Sweden	1970	35.2	51.6	0.7	2.6	96.5	90.1	n.d.
United States	1970	62.9	37.1	0.6	3.2	97.5	96.0	n.d.

(1) Figure for 1960. For 1970 the figure 1.1 was given. See M. E. Ruban, "Wohnungsbau und Wohnungswirtschaft in den RGW-Ländern," *DA* No. 12 (1973), p. 1313.
(2) 1961

Source: *UN Statistical Yearbook 1973* (New York: UN, 1974), p. 728ff.

The housing shortage has, on the other hand, developed increasingly into a material lever with which companies can attract labor. According to a Soviet survey carried out in 1966, shortage of housing was rated as the prime reason for fluctuation at work. In the German Democratic Republic and in other, better-provided-for socialist countries, this reason does not carry the same weight as in the Soviet Union,[625] although here, too, cooperative housing construction is being used more and more to tie workers to their enterprise.

A survey in 1976 showed that 89% of persons interviewed gave housing construction priority before all other projects in the construction area.[626]

The comparative lack of success in housing construction can be traced to five causes, which are to some extent incorporated into the very structure of the socialist system, as it has functioned to date, and are not just motivational shortcomings due to the failure of individual planners:

1.   Despite the emphasis placed on planning, this was more-or-less restricted to industrial output, and housing construction was not considered as industrial output. *Town planning* was only developed to a limited extent after a number of model town experiments during the postrevolutionary phase. Only in the 1950s did a number of large cities, including Moscow and Leningrad, compile long-term development and space utilization plans.[627]

2.   *Industrial construction* had clear priority during the transformation period. It was not until 1969 that the percentage of housing construction came more into line in the two German states (Federal Republic of Germany, 40%, German Democratic Republic, 24%), though the German Democratic Republic's housing stock was very old by comparison. Whereas in the Federal Republic of Germany, in 1968, 46.7% of housing dated from 1948 onwards, a survey carried out in the Germany Democratic Republic in 1971 showed that only 15.6% of housing had been built after 1946; for 1980 a percentage of 40% was projected.[628]

3.   Overcentralization resulted in *local authorities becoming powerless*, and this proved an extraordinary handicap in housing construction. From the planning system right through to the tax system, the communes were at a much greater disadvantage, compared with the state territories, than in capitalist countries.

4.   The *advantage of lower rents* brought the simultaneous drawback that rent levels were not high enough to provide for the necessary maintenance to apartments.

Low rents mean that the individual makes a lesser contribution toward the upkeep of housing (although his indirect contribution is nonetheless still high through the high turnover tax levied on any goods). As a rule, rents cover only half the upkeep.

Western economists who work on the cost coverage principle have repeatedly let themselves be carried away with global pronouncements as to the irrationality of prices in socialist systems, particularly with regard to rents. This would appear to be unfair, however, if housing construction is taken to be a social service, as part of the state's protective function. Unfortunately, socialist systems have not taken this protective function seriously enough. The growing flood of applications for building permission and requests to join housing construction cooperatives, which are by no means all granted, are a sign that the Soviet citizen would even agree to a higher level of private financing if this meant that demand could be met. Private building is becoming less widespread (see Table 101). Private investment, on the other hand, is, according to Soviet forecasts, still a significant factor in the Five-Year Plans.

The services, which were treated in the output statistics with as much disdain as housing construction, are of particular importance in this field, however. Cooperativization and nationalization of trade and industry had brought about a marked cutback in the repair trade, even though, into the 1960s, half of all repair services were provided by private individuals.[629] A large percentage of the work was done by mechanics moonlighting. The state frequently turned a blind eye and as a rule refrained from applying the sanctions provided for in the law for earning on the side through fear that the bottleneck in the repairs sector would become even worse.

5.   The *quality of building workers* is inadequate, and the quantity-based ideology of the construction phase reduced the quality of apartments built even further. Fulfilment of plan targets and the assignment of funds on the basis of the number of apartments allocated repeatedly led to new buildings being allocated to people before they had actually been completed.[630] The high number of defects that come to light in new buildings after a short time is criticized again and again in the Soviet Union. The figure of 60% was once quoted for Leningrad. This dilemma cannot be explained through poor pay in the building sector, as has been done at times. Wages in the building sector certainly come out top of the list (see Table 31). The real reason lies in inadequate training and the employment of comparatively unskilled labor. China, as an even less developed country, has to contend with these same problems on an even larger scale.[631]

This relatively gloomy appraisal would, however, be seriously prejudiced against socialist systems if a number of clearcut advantages of the housing system in socialist countries were not given due praise:

1.   The percentage of *owner occupiers* is greater than in most capitalist countries, with the exception of the United States (see Table 101, column 2). During the transformation period some tenancies were converted into ownership. Whereas in most capitalist states (with the exception of the United States) just under half of apartment occupiers are owner-occupiers, the figure for socialist states is (insofar as figures are available) over two thirds in some cases. In 1960/1961, owner occupiers accounted for just over 50% in Czechoslovakia and Poland, for 62% in Hungary, for over 78% in Yugoslavia and, even in the Soviet Union, with 39% in the towns, the figure is above the average of capitalist countries.[632] A warning must, however, be given against rating private ownership of apartments as an unequivocally positive indicator in socialist states. The countries that have the highest development level, such as Czechoslovakia and the German Democratic Republic, or which place a great deal of emphasis on public ownership, such as the Soviet Union, also have the highest growth rates in state housing. Even within these countries it can be seen that the districts that have the highest level of private housing construction are, by comparison, the least developed districts, and those that have retained the most of their traditional social structure, such as Slovakia in Czechoslovakia, where more than half the private dwellings in the whole country were constructed in the period between 1955 and 1964.[633] (See Table 101.) Socialist forms of ownership are being promoted more strongly in the housing sector, too, and the "grandfather principle" of "saved for myself, bought myself, built myself, and live in myself" is mocked in official Soviet publications.[634] Private building still played an important role in the Soviet Union's Seven-Year Plan between 1959 and 1965, but its share fell from 33.7% in 1959 to 26.8% in 1965. Discrimination in supplies of materials, together with administrative difficulties, is increasingly acting against private housing construction in the Soviet Union.

The cooperative sector of the building industry, on the other hand, is being keenly promoted, primarily through three measures:

1.   granting of credit;
2.   aid from state organizations in planning projects;
3.   more generous cooperation in the creation of infrastructure (schools, restaurants, baths, and so forth) than is the case in most capitalist countries.

In the German Democratic Republic, cooperative housing experienced a decline for a number of years, only to be keenly

Table 101

Share of investors in housing construction

Country	State communes	Cooperatives	Factories	Private	Private subsidized	nonsubsidized
Bulgaria	20.5	0.7		78.8		
Czechoslovakia	58.5	11.6	6.4	23.5	6.5	17.0
GDR (1958)	53.7	30.7			15.6	
Hungary	42.1	46.8		69.4	29.3	40.1
Yugoslavia	46.8			53.2		
Soviet (1950)	50.9	24.5[1]		24.5		
Union (1968)	67.9	18.2		13.9		
for comparison:						
France	34.6			65.4	55.1	10.3
Netherlands	23.6	26.2[2]		50.2		
FRG	2.4	26.1[2]	3.5	68.0		

(1) including kolkhozes; (2) housing construction companies.

Sources: Secretariat of the Economic Commission for Europe, *European Housing Trends and Policies in 1960* (Geneva: 1961), pp. 16–19; Soviet Union: E. Mickiewicz (publ.), *Handbook of Soviet Social Science Data* (New York and London: Free Press, 1973), p. 129. A more detailed list (but with a typology of investors that is not comparable with other countries) for the period 1918–72 in: K. Zhukov & V. Fyodorov, *Housing Construction in the Soviet Union* (Moscow: Progress, 1974), pp. 65f.

promoted at the start of the 1970s, reaching a level of 45% by 1975. At the end of 1971, private housing construction was also promoted more vigorously in the German Democratic Republic, following an initial check on private building in 1970/71 due to the shortage of building materials and the repercussions this was having on the state building industry. The ideological foundation put forward for this ran: "As private property acquired through the work of family members, a private house does not constitute a contradiction to socialist forms of acquisition in the field of private consumption";[635] 10% and more every year are built by private initiative.[636] This was such a straightforward explanation, and one that fitted so well into the context of Marxism, that people are wondering why private housing construction was the subject of discrimination for so long, like the Proudhonist aberrations that Engels had criticized in his paper on the housing question. The change of attitude on the part of the GDR leadership appears to have come about inter alia in conjunction with the wage and bonus system,[637] and it cannot be excluded that the surplus of purchasing power, which still prevails in a number of socialist countries despite a growing supply of consumer goods, will find itself an outlet in the private construction sector.

2. In addition, those who live in rented accommodation enjoy much greater *security of tenure* than in capitalist countries (a factor that leads to exaggerated efforts to build one's own house and overmortgage oneself in capitalist countries). Giving Soviet tenants notice to vacate their apartment is exceedingly difficult, even where the apartment is provided free of charge by the state. Criminality is one of the few grounds permitted. In this respect, the protective function of the state in the socialist system is clearly greater than in the capitalist system, despite all the attempts toward better tenant's rights legislation.

3. *Rents are extremely low.* They account for something over 5% of a worker's income, as opposed to 20 to 30% in most capitalist countries. In the German Democratic Republic, the percentage rent that an employee household has to pay out of its budget is only one third of that in the Federal Republic of Germany.[638] Inequality in allocation and supply have not yet fully disappeared in socialism either. They do not so much stem from differences in income but rather from the status advantage that the ruling elite holds. Completely free-of-charge housing, which the Soviet Union set itself as a target in 1961, has not yet been achieved and would also not produce solely positive effects, so long as income differences persist.

4. Socialist countries have generally had more success in phasing out *class-based separation of residential areas.* But this does not mean that there are no class privileges in housing, such as lower rents for important workers and functionaries.[639] One part of the population benefits from low rents in state-owned dwellings, while others must pay "economic" rents and thus indirectly contribute to financing the losses in the state-owned housing. Only a part of the beneficiaries of low rents are low-income groups, as has been proved for Czechoslovakia[640] or Hungary. It has even been found out that the class of tenants subsidized by the state to the highest degree are those earning the highest incomes.[641]

The humane and innovative possibilities of modern building and new forms of communal living are scarcely used in socialist countries—not even in China. Leftist groups in capitalist systems, whose ideas are gradually being assimilated in a wider circle of liberal public opinion as a genuine part of the cultural heritage, are at present able to generate greater innovative impulses than are the reformers in the housing systems of most socialist countries. This shows once again that socialism can only develop the full beneficial potential it is claimed to possess on condition of remaining open to the variations of a pluralistic society.

The attitude of socialist countries to housing construction is in the course of modification. Apartments can no longer be classified along with consumer goods, as is the case for other items. Their importance to social hygiene, labor productivity, legal security, and study success at school is coming to be increasingly appreciated by the socialist countries as their level of productive resources increases and the protective function of the housing system is emphasized more strongly than its mere distributive function.

4.   Environmental policy

Marx pointed out in a letter as early as 1869 (MEW, Vol. 32, p. 53) that even preindustrialized systems, which had not actually "consciously controlled culture" and had let it take its "natural" course, still transformed their environments into deserts. He also saw industrialized capitalism as being in constant danger of destroying the environment through the "anarchy of production." Only socialism, in the socialist countries' own appreciation, is capable of consciously mastering technicocultural progress without destroying the environment.

Environmental damage in capitalist systems, on the other hand, is considered to be "class-conditioned." Socialism was seen to develop "social optimism" against Western ecological pessimism. Recently the ecologization of economy was hailed as another proof for the construction of communism in the Soviet Union.[642] Even though the ideologists of socialist countries consider the capitalist system to be incapable of environmental protection, the socialist countries are increasingly prepared to cooperate with capitalist systems in this field.[643]

The potential impact on the environment in socialist and capitalist countries correlates with the *degree of urbanization* and the *traffic level.* Especially the demographic aspects of ecological problems—more-or-less independent of the political nature of the system—are more and more accepted in recent literature.[644] The socialist countries made enormous progress on both these counts

Table 102

Urbanization
(in percentages)

Country	Rank out of 135 countries	Population in cities of 100,000 or more[1]		Urban population[2]	
		1950	1960	1960	1978
Cuba	25	24.2	27.5	54.9	64.4
Poland	29	23.1	26.6	48.3	57.5
Soviet Union	36	20.9	24.8	49.9	62.0
GDR	47	20.2	21.3	72.0	76.0
Yugoslavia	53	11.7	16.0		
Mongolia	57	0	17.2	40.2	51.0
Rumania	60	10.0	16.2	32.4	49.0
North Korea	61	10.6	16.0		
Czechoslovakia	64	13.9	14.4	57.4	67.5
Bulgaria	66	9.1	14.0	38.0	61.2
China	76	7.2	10.6		
Albania	83	0	8.4		
North Vietnam	89	3.7	6.3		
for comparison:					
United Kingdom	3	70.6	71.6		
FRG	7	48.4	51.5		
United States	8	43.9	50.5		
Japan	10	26.7	41.9		
South Korea	43	15.2	22.8		
South Vietnam	77	8.1	10.5		
India	109	8.1	9.0		

Sources: (1) Taylor-Hudson, op. cit., pp. 219ff; (2) *Ezhegodnik stran-chlenov SEV* (Moscow: Statistika, 1979), p. 14.

during the 1950s and 1960s (Tables 102 and 103), although, in so doing, they failed to pay sufficient attention to the external effects.

The level of industrialization and urbanization is not, however, sufficient an indicator for measuring the impact on the environment. The key factor here is to find out which *branches* of the industry *have the highest emission levels* (energy and basic materials industry, transport). According to U.S. calculations,[645] *export* activity has a particularly high impact on the environment, which affects the German Democratic Republic and Czechoslovakia in particular in the socialist camp.

Since methods for measuring pollution of the environment in capitalist countries are still very much at an initial development phase, it cannot be expected that indicators of this nature will be available in the near future for measuring well-being in the protection sphere. Even if more than isolated data were available for countries with capitalist and socialist systems, this would have to be correlated with the *availability of certain natural resources*, and the situation in socialist countries varies a great deal here. In 1970, for example, 12,250 cubic metres of water per annum were available for each person in Yugoslavia, 10,400 in Rumania, 8,700 in Albania, and only 2,340 in Bulgaria. The German Democratic Republic likewise ranks among the countries with a poor water supply.[646]

The percentage of emission-intensive, two-stroke engines in road traffic, the concentration of industry (and the opportunities available for evacuation to less populated areas), the percentage of lignite used for heating fuel, and many other factors would have to

Table 103

Transport (1977)

	Billion tons/km /year	Billion persons /km	Of these in percentages	
			rail- roads	cars
Bulgaria	76.4	23.9	31.3	59.6
Czechoslovakia	99.4	47.6	37.5	59.1
GDR	149.5	54.4	41.1	41.2
Poland	457.0	95.3	46.5	51.0
Rumania	148.6	44.9	51.6	44.7
Soviet Union	5432.0 (1976)	802.0	40.2	42.9

Source: *Yearbook of East European Economics,* Vol. 8 (Munich: Olzog, 1979), pp. 457ff.

be taken into account in a quantitative comparison of impact on the environment.

Despite the system's claim to planning for all conditions of production and reproduction (see Chapter 6, Section 3), socialist systems have not published any specialized environment statistics to date, either. But the compilation of indices for the quality of the environment is regarded as a desideratum. Soviet authors admit that perspective planning for the quality of the environment has still not been integrated into overall economic planning and that the measures taken by socialist states to date have only been interventionist and defensive measures, without any ex-ante planning of the "results of the measures." The primacy of prevention proclaimed by the Comecon countries--as opposed to the capitalist approach of making good damage to the environment after it has occurred—has by and large failed to materialize. Recently the external costs in calculating prices are stressed in Soviet literature.[647]

Socialist countries had a severe handicap when it came to identifying environmental problems, namely, the socialist system's claim to perfection. Even today, Soviet industrialization is still presented as having always taken care to preserve a harmonious relationship between man, machines, and nature,[648] ever since Lenin's Goelro plan. Yet Lenin's decree "on the protection of natural monuments" (1921) cannot be interpreted as anything more than isolated protection for certain areas—a practice that has become standard in capitalist countries. For a long time it was only the literary intelligentsia who brought up the subject of environmental policy in public, such as Sholokhov's famous appeal for conservation of Lake Baikal. In the 1950s and 1960s, literary magazines such as *Novii Mir* and *Literaturnaya Gazeta* discussed the problem. It was not until 1970, however, that the periodical *Ekologiya* provided environmental problems with their own organ.[649] Even in the 1970s, however, the concept of *"preobrazovanie prirody"* was taken primarily in a technocratic sense, as a hydrotechnical problem, and as a necessary cost calculation for scarce natural goods, which until then had been included in planning calculations without any monetary value.[650]

If we go beyond the level of ideological self-satisfaction, then a number of environmental problems in socialist countries are very similar to those found in capitalist countries—without this implying straightforward negative environmental convergence:

1. through the effects of the *population explosion* and the mass migration of labor, which, it is admitted, can no longer be controlled;

2.   through the *growth fetishism* in the accumulation phase and through overemphasis on heavy industry (see Chapter 4, Section 1). Even in Western countries, economic crisis brought a setback for ecological concern, and the OECD has even recommended a less restrictive use of environmental laws; in most socialist countries the primacy of production remained unchallenged;[651]

3.   through unforeseen *consequences of technical progress*—along with the United States, the Soviet Union and even China[652] are the countries that have carried out the most extensive experiments into warding off meteorological influences (regulation of precipitation, breaking up hail clouds, and so forth), though present-day literature still admits that "undesirable climatic changes, independent of our will" cannot be entirely excluded in the future through environmental planning;[653] some of the side effects are nonanticipated dysfunctions of positive measures taken by the socialist state, such as the consequences of diverting water courses in Siberia, with the ensuing climatic changes: the drying-up of a number of areas and salt deposits resulting from excessive evaporation of newly-brought-in water in other areas.

Alongside these factors come a number of causes that rank differently within the system context of socialism from within capitalism:

1.   *Plan fulfilment pressure* and subsequently the possibility of obtaining greater premiums through *increasing enterprise profit* led enterprise management to act inconsiderately toward the environment.

2.   The *excessive centralization* of economic administration led to local pecularities being neglected when environmental measures were taken. Though Soviet sources boast of a number of central institutions dealing with environmental protection,[654] critics argue that the most eminent polluters are huge industrial plants for which there is only competence at the Union's level, whereas all environmental laws are in the hands of the Union Republics.[655] Local initiatives were not encouraged. Local decentralization under Khrushchev with the people's economic councils (sovnarckhoz) would perhaps have had a more positive environmental impact in the long term, because most people first become aware of environmental problems as they emerge as local and regional phenomena. Mere centralization of environmental protection, as an offshoot of centralization of the economic administration, is not much better a solution for the external effects than is the price mechanism of the market

economy, because of the generally arbitrary nature of the central planners' assessments of social problems. Only nonmanipulated participation of the masses could perhaps produce a centrally planned environment policy with positive effects. The nonexistence of "public interest groups" is perhaps the greatest disadvantages of the socialist countries in the field of environmental protection.[656]

3. *State ownership of land* repeatedly led to wastage. The extractive industry in the Soviet Union not infrequently caused considerable destruction, until 1967 when lease charges were introduced for prospecting for mineral resources; the gravel industry on the Crimean quarried gravel without consideration of the consequences until these began to show in the form of subsidence and deterioration of the beaches.[657]

4. *Neglect of the services sector* also had a negative impact on the environment. Public services such as refuse collection were technically far behind those in the highly developed capitalist nations. Expansion of bulky refuse collection, refuse incineration, and composting are to prevent the self-help methods consisting of random dumping of refuse. The purification and filter units that are needed today are not always available in the optimum quality owing to the shortage of foreign currency resources. Thus it is openly admitted that the technical know-how of capitalist countries is still needed in this field.

Despite these system-specific factors, which are hazardous for the environment, socialist countries still persist with the explanation that only motivational shortcomings and not structural ones are responsible for damage to the environment in socialist systems. These motivational shortcomings are put down to the inheritance from capitalism (as a result of the capitalist "exploitation" of nature prior to the change to socialism) or as the failure of individuals. This would seem to be a weak explanation particularly for those areas in which many of the location decisions and the choice of production technologies were made after the capitalist era—such as in Central Asia.

If we pinpoint a number of structural shortcomings that can lead to the environment being particularly endangered in socialist systems (and this does not mean that we can belittle the shortcomings of capitalism in this field in any way!), then we must also recognize a number of advantages that the socialist system has when it comes to tackling environmental problems:

1. Through their late industrialization, socialist systems were able to benefit from the experience of other industrial states and were better informed about the external effects of industrialization strategies than were the early capitalists. A certain measure of this

advantage was, however, gambled away again through the forced system competition and the campaigns for "catching up with and overtaking" the most highly developed countries, because one-sided maximization of efficiency had a negative effect on the environment.

2.   In the socialist transformation period, wages were generally lower than the cost of goods produced. This did not incite socialist countries to copy the same planned waste as occurred in capitalist systems. Superfluous luxury packaging was avoided. Waste and scrap products were valued more highly than in capitalist systems and were reprocessed more frequently. Nevertheless, domestic waste in a country such as the German Democratic Republic has already reached $11,500,000m^3$ and the figure for 1980 was set at some $17,000,000m^3$.[658]

3.   *Planning in the housing construction sector* led to a reduction in the number of sources of pollution by cutting down the number of private fireplaces and replacing these by central heating systems with easy-to-monitor emission levels. Since private initiative has again come to be increasingly tolerated in home building, a grey area of illegal construction has developed on private plots and allotments in the form of disguised weekend houses, and this is threatening to lead to the same destruction of natural areas as has been achieved in capitalist systems with the uncontrolled building-up of the countryside.

4.   Socialist countries *did not follow the path of forced automobilization*, and even though this may not have been prompted by environmental policy motivations (as has been assumed for Cuba), it did, until recently, have positive repercussions for the environment. Only of late has the antiautomobile effect begun to be phased out, with the same external consequences as in capitalism. This even applies to Cuba. Castro put the following rhetorical question to the masses at a trade union congress: "The country is going to import a number of rented cars, a very expensive undertaking, to replace the pile of scrap that is cluttering up the streets in our towns. A number of cars will also be bought for technicians in a bid to increase their productivity. Will you be in agreement with this? (Shouts of 'yes' and applause)."[659]

5.   The *wider powers held by the socialist state* make protective measures in the environmental field more rapid to implement than in capitalist countries, where every meaningful measure is threatened with delay through extensive counter-lobbying by industrial interests or even with sabotage. Socialist systems were not tied to such complex expropriation processes in their land policy as were capitalist systems. This was also an advantage when it came to

taking rapid action to protect the environment. However, this factor should not be rated too highly. The planning authorities of socialist states often had to conduct long-drawn-out negotiations in order to convince those involved to incorporate environmental protection measures in their planning and to win over plant management to their measures.[660] In the jumbled competences of the economic administration, the culprits of damage to the environment are often more difficult to track down than in a capitalist enterprise, and hence the "cause" principle comes up against considerable bureaucratic obstacles when put into practice.

The measures employed to prevent destruction of the environment are the same as those used in capitalism, though in somewhat different proportions:

1.   Socialist mobilization systems have a clear advantage over capitalist countries in *spreading information and in mass mobilization.*

2.   The socialist countries are also ahead of capitalist economies when it comes to *improving planning,* because they already have a comprehensive planning system.

3.   The proposal for an *environmental levy,* as spread by Federenko and Gofman in the Soviet Union,[661] comes closest to certain proposed solutions in capitalist systems, even if socialist states seem to act less on the principle of the individual responsible if the environment levy takes on the nature of a special tax.

4.   *Increased investment* for protection of the environment is likewise easier to realize in a state-owned industry.

5.   *Repression* is called for in particular in areas where the idea still lives on that only motivational shortcomings are answerable for damage to the environment in socialist systems. Very frequently the moral appeal to the population is still tied to the call for more draconian penalties.

6.   *Increased participation of free local and citizen's action groups* has not been encouraged much to date. Direct action by the masses is also regarded as a means of solving environmental problems in capitalist systems. With the growing readiness to accept non-manipulated participation, free initiative from below could develop into a considerable counterforce against destruction of the environment in future. The protective angle and participatory angle of socialist policy's target package are still poles apart on this particular point, however.

9

Protection
in the legitimation sphere

1. The protective function of law in the legal doctrine of socialist countries

The protective function of the early liberal bourgeois state was confined almost exclusively to the spheres of legitimation and security, even though the caricature of the "night-watchman's state," which relieved citizens of almost all their duties, has never existed, or only existed for a short time in history. In the tradition of cameralistics and police science, the state had always been conceived of as being complemented by other social protective functions as well. The strong emphasis placed on fundamental rights as the most important area of protective function during the bourgeois struggle against absolutism has been retained to the present day, and fundamental rights have come to be greatly stressed again in bourgeois jurisprudence, following the experience of totalitarian dictatorships. Whereas, before the Second World War, a more-or-less functionalist-sociological interpretation had begun to emerge in parts of positive law schools, the theory that inviolable fundamental rights are firmly anchored in neonatural law began to gain ground again after the fascist experience.

New attempts at a functional interpretation, such as that presented by Luhmann in 1965, are still far from becoming ruling doctrine. Luhmann himself was perfectly aware of the fact that "a levelling-out of the divergences between sociological research and dogmatic interpretation was not within sight."[662] The state's protective function in the sphere of fundamental rights is of a different nature from all the other protective functions. More than in the production and distribution spheres, it is a subjective right that the citizen is entitled to claim and the state is committed to provide. Fundamental rights imply a frontier between the state and the private sphere of the individual.

Marxist doctrine, which provides the basis for the formulation of the protective functions of the socialist state in the legitimation and security spheres, departs from the theory of "civil liberty" on at least a number of points:

1. Once the class aspect of society has been phased out, it is *no longer accepted* that a potential *conflict of interests* could occur between the individual and society.

2. The individual, as the *subject* of civil liberty, is considered more from a *collectivist* angle. The protection provided by fundamental rights is destined more for "man" as a generic term than for man as an individual. Only after the Stalin era did individual philosophers in Poland, such as Kolakowski and Schaff, underline again the necessity of protecting the individual. In the Soviet Union, too, the recognition of subjective rights is gaining ground in discussions on constitutional law.[663]

3. The Marxist line of thought does not consider fundamental rights as belonging to a prestate sphere of values, unaffected by social change, but as *historical phenomena* dependent on the will of the state to set standards and on the objective law established by the state—marking the expression of the will of the ruling class. Consequently, owing the the supremacy of the working class, fundamental rights during the dictatorship of the proletariat stage are subject to a *constitutional reservation* (Article 39 of the USSR constitution of 1977; No's. 55 and 56 of the Hungarian constitution; Article 72 of the Polish constitution, and Article 86 of the Rumanian constitution). According to these provisions, the limit to each fundamental right is "the interests of the workers and the interests of the citizens," as expressed by the leading bodies of the party. For this reason, a number of Western lawyers are unwilling to accept the idea that

genuine fundamental rights exist in socialist states.[664] This attitude probably goes too far, since it denies any fundamental rights concept that is not embodied in natural law the status of fundamental rights. It would also strike against sociological-functionalist theories and be incompatible with contemporary social requirements, because a rational consensus would be difficult to reach on a question such as whether ownership rights are to be rated as fundamental rights derived from natural law. Moreover, there is a growing consensus today that ownership rights should be regarded as being tied to social obligations.

4.   The *character of repression and punishment* was given a new interpretation in socialism. Although the notion of punishment (*nakazanie*) still existed in the Soviet Union to begin with, it was referred to (even in law codes, for example, in Article 26 of the penal code of 1922) as a "measure of social defense" or as a "social protective measure.[665]

2.   Fundamental rights

Considerable differences between the protective function of fundamental rights in capitalist countries and in socialist countries lie in the differently conceived hierarchy that underlies the fundamental rights guaranteed in socialist constitutions.

1.   The *socioeconomic fundamental rights*—such as the right to work, recreation, material welfare, and education (in certain people's democracies also the right to health protection by the state, protection of youth, and so forth—are emphasized to a greater extent than in the constitutions of capitalist democracies. Ownership rights were not listed among the fundamental rights in the Soviet constitution but were dealt with in a different, less important part of the text (Article 7, Par. II; Article 10). Only recently has the *right of ownership* been included under socioeconomic fundamental rights in the legal dogmatics of socialist countries.

As a logical consequence of the discrimination against the right of ownership, the *right of inheritance* was abolished in 1918 by the decree of April 27. But even by 1922 it was being introduced again to a limited degree. In the meantime, Marxist legal doctrine in socialist countries has adopted a rather relaxed attitude toward the right of inheritance. It is rightfully argued that that part of the juridical superstructure that relates to the right of inheritance in the law of socialist states has had a different meaning ever since its economic basis changed. Marx had already pointed out in the Report of the General Council on the Law of Inheritance of 1869 that the right of inheritance was "not a cause, but the effect, that is, the juridical consequence of the existing economic organization of society" (MEW, Vol. 16, p. 367). Since no ownership of means of production can be inherited, the right of inheritance plays the role of an "anachronistic stimulus" for socialist societies.[666] It is said to contribute to the strengthening of the sense for social property and to bringing about "a harmonious concordance of personal and collective interests."

The implementation of the state's protective tasks, however, which the state has fixed for itself in its socialist constitution, can hardly be read off from the mere wording of the norms. Empirical examination of the production and distribution spheres has shown again and again that the gap that exists in all states between constitutional norm and social reality is particularly wide in some fields of socioeconomic fundamental rights in socialist states, as may be demonstrated by the example of the right to strike (see Chapter 7, Section 5).

2.   A further peculiarity of the socialist system is the stronger emphasis placed on *equality rights*, which are an essential prerequisite for socialist redistribution policy. In this field, more progress has been achieved in equality in law than in most capitalist democracies, even though the implementation of these equality rights in the distribution of income and opportunity still leaves a good deal to be desired (see Chapter 2, Section 2).

3.   The *political rights* are listed very much as in bourgeois constitutions (freedom of thought, freedom of speech, right of assembly, freedom of association). The *right to vote* is usually listed outside the fundamental rights catalog. The German Democratic Republic moved away from the Soviet model in 1968 by coherently incorporating the right to vote within the fundamental rights.

4.   *Freedom of the press* was an obvious necessity for Marx, so as to permit the people to confront and monitor themselves as they developed within society and the state (MEW, Vol. 1, p. 152 ff).[667] In socialist countries, the freedom of the press was only regarded as restricted for opponents of the system, and capitalist systems cannot be too critical here since they also apply restrictions

of this type. Here again, the main problem is the lack of a *due process* for determining hostility toward the system. Mao sought to prevent his thesis of the 100 flowers that were to blossom from being misunderstood by polemizing against an "allowing to blossom" that would signify "bourgeois liberalization."[668] The qualification of "bourgeois" was, however, extended to positions such as that held by Liu Shao-ch'i, when it proved necessary.

In defense of its own viewpoint, Soviet doctrine asserts that bourgeois ideologists were trying to force an opposition system upon socialist systems in the name of political fundamental rights, which they had previously defined as the main feature of democracy. Attempts of this type do indeed occur, owing to the bias in favor of a parliamentary system with alternating governments. Thought-out functionalist approaches would possibly look for initial signs of pluralism and opposition worthy of protection, which could, if necessary, be reconciled once and for all with the single-party state that has become established. These, however, are already strongly discriminated against on an ideological basis as being *krugovchina* and parliamentary group activity, even though a system with intra-party competition could perfectly well develop into a functional equivalent for the multiparty system.

Among rights with political implications, the *freedom of religion* is the most severely affected by the ideological and constitutional reservations that socialist systems make against fundamental rights. It is not only constantly menaced because of the deliberately party-oriented ideology of the state and the promotion of atheist research, but it is considerably limited in other respects as well, contrary to the case in laical democracies. Only the People's Republic of China is considered to have learned from the Soviet errors in religious persecution and has not only avoided creating martyrs, but has even "courted" the followers of certain religions—particularly of buddhism. On the other hand, the fight against "imperialistic elements" in China also provided pretexts for special treatment of certain religions. The Christian churches had made themselves particularly suspect in China. A pamphlet published in Spanish by the Foreign Language Publishing House in Peking even provided instructions for Cubans on purging the Catholic Church of antipatriotic and criminal elements; this included ways of getting religiously-minded persons to seek martyrdom through protest and opposition, by compromising themselves as antipatriots.[669] By prohibiting missionary activity and by prescribing a language and liturgy adapted to China, it was possible to subject the undesired Christian religions to special treatment, in spite of the freedom of religion guaranteed by the Chinese constitution.

As far as the Eastern European socialist countries are concerned, Albania came closest to the Chinese model in applying differentiated treatment to the various religious creeds. The most repressive policy was adopted against Catholicism. the Orthodox Church was treated with a greater amount of tolerance, and Islam was almost looked upon benevolently at times. In official Albanian statements referring to religious class enemies, the "mosques" are always mentioned after the "churches."[670] In the German Democratic Republic the new 1968 constitution contains a more restrictive version of the religious freedom granted earlier, which is limited to the right "to profess a religious faith and to exercise religious acts," whereas the existence and confirmation guarantees for the church have been dropped.

4.   The *rights of personal freedom* (such as the inviolability of the person and of the home and the secrecy of correspondence) to which citizens of capitalist states are very sensitive, as seen in the reactions to restrictions introduced by emergency legislation and the constantly recurring phone-tapping scandals, are indeed mentioned in the constitutions, but cut down by ideological reservations with in some cases excessive restrictions imposed on them through penal laws and decrees. The *right of free movement* was only set down in the constitution in countries that were most strongly committed to long-standing liberal-democratic traditions, such as the German Democratic Republic and Czechoslovakia. In the new GDR constitution of 1968 the former Article 10, Par. 2, providing for a *right to emigrate*, was dropped again in the light of the role of the Berlin wall. The right of free movement was restricted to the territory of the Germany Democratic Republic (Article 32).

The *right of asylum* is usually granted in socialist constitutions. In the Germany Democratic Republic this right was restricted in the 1968 constitution (Article 23, Par. 3), following the Soviet model, to the cases of "defense of peace, of democracy, of the interests of the working people," and of "participation in struggles for social and national independence." The inviolability of the home and the secrecy of correspondence are not actually guaranteed, but they are declared to be protected by law. Basically, this means nothing more, in the wording of Article 128 of the Soviet constitution, than a reference to the relevant extraconstitutional standards. The seizure of mail is subject to authorization by a public prosecutor or to an order of court, but the conditions to be fulfilled are rather flexible, as in the case of house searches.

3. Fundamental duties

It is a special feature of socialist constitutions that they list fundamental duties in addition to fundamental rights, and although these are not given the same weight as fundamental rights in dogmatics, it is recognized that they may restrict fundamental rights in case of conflict.

The fundamental duties include respect of the law, discipline at work, compliance with the rules of socialist community life, defense of socialist property, payment of taxes, and defense of the homeland. For a long time, offenses against *work discipline* were threatened with the most severe punishments. According to Article 74 of the RSFSR criminal code of 1940, "hooligan activity" in enterprises, which even included being more than 20 minutes late, was punishable with one year of imprisonment in the Soviet Union. It was only by decree of April 25, 1956, that disciplining by penal law was abolished and replaced by disciplinary measures. Article 7 of this decree makes provision for idleness at work (*progul*) to be punished by dismissal and an entry in the work book, as well as for the case to be brought before a "comradeship court." Offenses against *socialist property* are subject to even more drastic punishment today.

Thus, viewed from a functional angle, the legal dispositions for ensuring that fundamental duties are carried out have, to some extent, become further restrictions on the fundamental rights.

4. Institutions for legal protection and the protection of fundamental rights

Some of the socialist countries are lacking sufficient institutional facilities for implementing fundamental rights. Only in Yugoslavia has it been possible, since 1964, to bring a case of breach of fundamental rights before the courts through a complaint of unconstitutionality. Yugoslavia has *constitutional jurisdiction*, which does not exist in any other socialist country as yet. But even so, the Yugoslav system still contains institutional loopholes when it comes to implementing the protective functions of the state in the legitimation sphere.

Essential rights, such as the right of participation in the workers' self-management system, could not, however, be protected by the constitutional court, despite thousands of cases of flagrant violation, because the court had to declare itself incompetent, as its competence only covers matters that cannot be ruled on by other courts.[671]

However, in capitalist countries *administrative jurisdiction* has also been regarded as an equivalent in the development of the constitutional state's protective function, so that a lack of constitutional jurisdiction does not necessarily imply that legal protection in general is inadequate. The rules of administrative procedure in most Eastern European countries in the socialist camp allow action for annulment of acts of administration to be brought only in a few specific cases provided for by law. This is not really fundamental rights protection, in fact, because it is not the fundamental rights but other norms that grant the right of protection. There is no such fully-fledged administrative jurisdiction as that which exists in capitalist states, but definite legal protection is certainly assured via the ordinary courts.

The protective function is best able to be realized through the institution of the *prokuratura*, whose protective function (which it assumes alongside a number of important functions) have occasionally been compared with those of the ombudsman in Western states.[672]

The establishment of the prokuratura in 1922 constituted a revival of a former institution of the absolutist state, created by Peter the Great in 1722 as "the Tsar's eye." Since Soviet dogmatics rejected constitutional controls along the lines of the Western capitalist model, it was only logical to fall back on absolutist control bodies. This institution of public prosecution (or *prokuratura*), however, marked the first important step toward greater legal security after a period of "revolutionary legality," where the Institute of Popular Complaint gave every "worker entitled to vote" the right to bring charges, which amounted to legalizing a system of mass denunciation.[673] Admittedly, at the climax of political terror, even the by no means inconsiderable protective function of the prokuratura was no longer effective. In the late 1930s, even the Prosecutor General, Andrei Vyshinskiy, who had played an extremely repressive role in the Stalinist purge trials, was unable to protect his own people when they protested against the excesses of the secret police in the course of exercising their functions. Some 90% of provincial prosecutors are said to have lost their jobs during this period.

Even today it would be unwise to place excessive hopes on the autonomous function of the prokuratura for developing the protective function:

1.   The prokuratura is still more *centralistic* in its setup than are other state organs, and it is subject to instructions.

2.   The *prokurory* (or prosecutors) are *not independent of the party.* They are usually party members or have been approved by the party prior to their appointment. Moreover, practice has shown that bureaucrats and party members tend to seek protection for their decisions in advance from the prokuror, through a sort of preventive control of norms, so that complaints are voiced again and again that the prokuror do not sufficiently assume their supervisory and protective functions.[674]

The smaller the degree of institutionalization of the state functions, the less the legal system of socialist countries is able to assume its protective function. In small countries such as Cuba, where the *máximo lider* favors a very personalistic style of rule, there is frequent evidence of a rather cynical approach to law and certain state-protected freedoms, and Castro has made no secret about this. Asked about the autonomy of the University of Cuba during his 1971 visit to Chile, he replied: "I don't know whether, legally speaking, the autonomy of the University of Cuba exists or not (laughter). I know this is a problem I haven't heard of for ten years (laughter)." He motivated his lack of interest in this legal aspect by the rather unsatisfactory explanation that the students were "almost the masters of the Cuban state."[675]

The less the charisma of individual leaders or of the party as a whole, the more the legal system prompts an interest in realization of the protective function and in the articulation of even latent interests (which, according to Castro were not being articulated).

Recent moves toward increased institutionalization of legal protection are to be seen in the tendency to incorporate further political rights in the constitution, such as the *right of petition* and *officials' liability* (in the Albanian, Bulgarian, and Rumanian constitutions). With the strengthening of legal security, the right of petition has indeed gained growing importance in most of the socialist states. It serves as a functional equivalent for defending specific interests that cannot be easily articulated. The dogmatic statement on this claims that the petition systems of capitalist societies and socialist societies are incomparable right from the start because of the differing class content of these formal institutions. This does not appear justified, considering the assertion that the petition in capitalist states is nothing but "a petition of a subject"—addressed to an unknown and hostile state power—whereas in socialism it is the expression of a citizen assuming his coresponsibility.[676] In the socialist legal system we come across similar shortcomings, such as formal replies and subjective decisions (owing to a lack of supervision over resolutions taken and to bureaucratic behavior), as those that are rightfully criticized in capitalist systems. From a functional viewpoint, the petition system will only ever be a safety valve for shortcomings in the participation system, leading to the articulation of requests that have fallen through the net of the protective system. Therefore, sophisticated systems have little to reproach themselves with when they stress the necessity of this relic. In general, however, it may be said that a well-run ombudsman's office or a comparable prokuror's office—provided that the prokuror is not absorbed too much by his other supervisory functions—works more efficiently and more independently than a committee, which enjoys little parliamentary prestige and receives only marginal attention in both capitalism and socialism, on account of its insignificant role in political recruitment. However, petitions in socialist systems are gradually turning into an equivalent to *shot-gun pressure* and mass letter campaigns.

As soon as the petition system took on a mass character, however, the Soviet authorities reacted with repression, and most strongly so when the representatives of the Crimean Tartar people, who had been deported in 1944, attempted to obtain authorization for their people to return to the Crimea by way of mass petitions.[677]

A further attempt to extend legal protection are the *appeals committees* established in the German Democratic Republic. Dogmatics claim that these are a form of legal protection that is superior to the administrative jurisdiction of capitalist states,[678] precisely because, unlike administrative courts, they do not make decisions on the case at issue, since this is considered incompatible with socialist executive activity.

In addition to these trends toward an extension of political rights, socialist constitutions also reveal certain *retrograde tendencies.* This is due to the fact that the first constitutions in the transitional periods still had to make a number of concessions to the bourgeois concept of law, which were dropped later on when a new constitution was drawn up for socialism, as for example were the right to resist (Article 4, Par. 1), the press censorship ban (Article 9, Par. 2), the right to strike (Article 14, Par. 2), the freedom of art, science, and teaching (Article 34, Par. 1), and even the right to free choice of career (Article 35, Par. 1) in the GDR constitution of 1968.[679] Non-European socialist countries cannot be expected simply to reproduce the traditions of the European constitutional state. In the case of China, especially, it would be naive to expect a move toward what is sometimes mockingly qualified by the Chinese as "the primitive stage of what you call the rule of law."[680] But even in China we can see that after the turbulent years of anomic movement (Great Leap Forward, Cultural Revolution), forms of socialist legality that are in line with the Chinese legal tradition are increasingly gaining ground again as a means of creating greater security for the citizens' expectations.

During this period of revolutionary transformation, the protective function in the legitimation and security spheres was bound to be disadvantaged in the face of the necessity of maintaining the power of the state, of redistribution policy, and of increasing efficiency. However, only inhumane dogmatism could provide an uncritical justification for the fact that the protective function in the fundamental rights area is still underdeveloped, even after 60 years' socialist construction. Violation of a large number of fundamental rights is not an indispensable feature of socialism, but at most an expression of the hybris of power of what has become an arbitrary cadre party.

Moreover, it appears to be undialectical to think that all the achievements of bourgeois society (such as constitutionality and protection of fundamental rights) must be negated and eradicated in the new synthesis. On the contrary, the dogmatic statement that fundamental rights can indeed only develop their real substance under socialism is a correct assumption. However, this will remain but a cynical concealment not only as long as these advantages of socialism remain unutilized, but also as long as socialist states that have established their power sufficiently well continue to curtail fundamental rights more than is necessary for achieving the goals of socialism. In so doing they not only offend against the ontological concept of fundamental rights protection, which they reject, but also against the sociological–functionalist ideas that underlie the treatment of fundamental rights in socialism. Only by developing a non-repressive Marxist conflict doctrine will it be possible to create the preconditions for allowing the protective function of socialism to regain its due place among the objectives to be achieved.

Development of the protective function also needs to cover a good many rights in the private sphere of the individual, which are frequently associated with considerable individual hardship because of a carefully watched-over pruderie in all socialist states. Only in China was the strong discrimination against marriage for men under 30 and women under 25 motivated on protective grounds as well.

It was argued that this policy was not adopted for reasons of efficiency considerations for production, or of the housing shortage, but in order to protect women's emancipation and allow women freedom to develop their personalities during their time in production, rather than have them moving from the repressive structure of their families straight to new dependencies with their husbands through early marriage.

This move would, however, seem rather to be based on rationalization, and there is insufficient evidence to suggest that the citizens also view the state's dirigism in this sphere as a form of protection. Apart from these specifically Chinese problems, systems that make intensive use of campaigns, labor market steering, and cadre policy create a host of problems in the sphere of the individual's family and community life, which have not been able to be settled to the satisfaction of citizens in other socialist states either.

IV

PARTICIPATION

It is in the target concept of "participation" that the greatest differences between capitalist and socialist countries' concepts of democracy are to be found today. These differences are based on a number of dissimilar conceptions:

1. The closer *association of the three spheres of society*—and, ideologically speaking, the tendency for these to merge together completely—means that democrats in socialist countries do not conceive of participation as being chiefly restricted to the sphere of legitimation and the political superstructure. Participation at the place of work is more closely linked with the *other* spheres and, in terms of the ideology of the council system, may even be seen as a functionally graded system of opinion-moulding, extending right through from the enterprise brigade to the highest organs of state.

2. Participation is coupled to a long-drawn-out *socialization process* designed to form a socialist awareness.[681] This potentially marks one of the most important targets when it comes to the realization of man and the phasing out of rulership. Western democracies, on the other hand, place their emphasis on the instrumental nature of participation, and their elite-based democracy concepts regard participation almost as a sign of crisis. In systems where the

idea of "permanent revolution" has become established, albeit in a watered-down form, participation appears in the form of *permanent mobilization*. Apathy—and even the concept of apathy acting as a stabilizer for the system, which forms the basis of a number of bourgeois concepts of democracy—finds no justification and remains politically suspect. The level of organization in the mass organizations is correspondingly high. In the Soviet Union, the organization level of the "potential group" (workers and white-collar workers) in trade unions grew from 9.5% in 1917 to 97.6% in 1973, and the organization level among the 15- to 24-year-olds in Komsomol rose from 24.1% in 1950 to 71.3% in 1966.[682]

This high level of organization cannot, however, be directly equated with true participation. Social organizations outside the party repeatedly complain about the spread of new forms of apathy and about the fact that so-called members of the FDGB (Free German Trade Unions Association) or the "Germano–Soviet Friendly Society" soon fall into arrears with their membership fees and stop attending meetings. The "Society for Sport and Technology" in the German Democratic Republic is not infrequently used solely for the apolitical promotion of hobby interests.

3.   The close association with socialization and education concepts leads on further to the idea that participation *does not arise spontaneously*, as a number of spontaneistic variants of Marxism assumed, but comes about instead through an avant-garde of the working class, which needs to be steered by the party, thereby increasing the danger of manipulated pseudoparticipation.

Since participation, in particular, is firmly anchored in the anthropological core of Marxist thought, it is here that the decisive differences between the different variants of socialism have developed. Today only very limited consensus is to be found among various forms of bureaucratic cadre rule in the Soviet Union and the people's democracies, the forms of mass mobilization (if necessary both without and beyond the party) in China and Cuba, the Yugoslav concept of workers' councils, and the different attempts at reviving the council concept in the people's democracies.

Now that capitalist systems are increasingly coming into line with the socialist systems in the efficiency and distribution spheres, the greatest future potential of the socialist system lies in its expansion of participation. It has been rightly pointed out that socialist systems cannot really expect to sell themselves on the basis of their economic efficiency. A changeover to socialism can, however, be motivated in highly developed countries in protest against human poverty and not so much in protest against material poverty.

10

Participation
in the production sphere

1. Leninist theory of participation

One of socialism's greatest innovations lay in the expansion of participation in the production sphere. One of the first measures introduced by the Soviet government was the "Decree on Worker Control" dated November 14, 1917. This granted access to all business procedures, revoked business secrecy, and gave works councils the right to take binding decisions. According to Lenin's "Draft Provisions for Worker Control," only trade union associations and congresses should have the right to revoke decisions taken by the works councils. The derived power of this higher instance, however, was brought out in Article 6, which placed the implementation of worker control in the context of "responsibility toward the state" and threatened accountability or, in the event of offense, even sanctions against the offenders (confiscation of their entire assets and up to five years' imprisonment) (LPSS Vol. 35, p. 31). These claims had previously been listed in "The threatened catastrophe and how it should be tackled" (LPSS, Vol. 34, p. 161). In this way, the dual-track rule that at times existed between the works council and enterprise management during the revolution period was phased out, in favor of sole rule by the councils. It soon became apparent, however, that there was a danger of the old capitalism being superseded by a kind of "producer capitalism," with the scarcity of goods in war communism prompting enterprises to gear their production solely to the needs of the production team or to requirements for the necessary exchange dealings. During the civil war, worker self-management thus became irreconcilable with the self-preservation interests of the proletarian state, and the functions of the workers' councils were taken over first by the trade unions and shortly afterwards by the state. The dissatisfaction of large sectors of the working population at this withdrawal of power was expressed through the Kronstadt uprising and on other occasions. It came, at best, to a kind of triumvirate, consisting of the state director, the party representative, and the trade union's man of confidence, bringing all the frictional loss that secondary governments of this type entailed in NEP enterprises. It was the Soviet Union that first created the model of usurpation of workers' power that was later to be copied by almost all socialist countries. The works councils were absorbed by the trade union committee, and this, in turn, was incorporated into the central directive-issuing apparatus. Thus "control from above" came increasingly to replace "control from below."

In the German Democratic Republic, dissolution of the works councils was definitively completed in 1948, with the "Bitterfeld resolutions." Enterprise trade union leadership became an executive organ of the FDGB machine, could be dismissed by the FDGB, and was bound to FDGB decisions. The number of trade union leaders who also held posts in the party (some 50%) highlighted even further the dependence of the trade union leadership on party resolutions, as compared with the works councils that had previously been elected from below.[683]

Although the chief prerequisite for self-determination (and not simply codetermination) is fulfilled in socialism, namely socialization of the means of production, participation in the production sphere has not progressed beyond a considerably limited level of codetermination. The very fact that the tell-tale prefix "co-" still lives on in GDR usage, in the words "cooperation" and "codetermination," in itself offends against the spirit of socialist worker control. These are concepts that have developed in capitalism, which still works on the basis of the dualism of capital and labor.

Distinctions do, however, need to be drawn when assessing the extent of participation in relation to the question of forms of owner-ship. In periods of revolutionary transformation, participation in the state sector is rated differently from participation in the private sector. In the state sector, participation does not have the same pro-tective angle as in the private sector. In the private sector, mass participation is generally employed deliberately for purposes of speeding up redistribution policy (see Chapter 1, Section 3). As for the competence left to capitalist entrepreneurs, not even Chile attempted to achieve codetermination in the sense of coresponsibility for all management decisions here. Instead, the sole demand was for worker control—a strategy similar to that adopted by a number of European trade unions.[684] Codetermination in Chile scarcely pro-gressed beyond the German model of codetermination based on a fifty–fifty representation of both sides of industry, since an agree-ment between the CUT and the government provided for the ad-ministrative councils of industrial enterprises to be made up of 5 worker representatives, 5 technicians appointed by the government, and one representative from the state, appointed by the President of the Republic, who was to chair the council. Strong criticism was voiced at this arrangement, whereby only 3 of the 5 worker repre-sentatives were true "proletarians," since 2 representatives from the administration sector were included in the 5-man contingent.

Once the private sector is fully expropriated or has virtually no more role to play, the concept of worker control becomes superfluous and has at times been regarded by the parties as suspect and counter-revolutionary.

Participation in the production sphere has been decisively weakened by the transfer from the political sphere to the economic sphere of two organizational principles:

1. through the principle of "democratic centralism";
2. through the principle of one-man leadership (*edinonachalie*).

1. The stunted growth of the participation function in socialist states began with the transfer of the organizational principle of *"democratic centralism,"* which may have seemed necessary to the party during the conspiracy period, to all spheres and subsystems of the proletarian state once the takeover of power was complete. Even if it is true that "broad democratism" is "only empty and harmful fooling-around in the gloominess of autocracy, where it is the gen-darmes who make the selection" (LPSS, Vol. 6, p. 140), there was still no need after the revolution for democratic elements to be

absorbed by centralistic elements—not even for purposes of maintaining the system. This development had already been prepared in ideological terms after the Third Party Congress, however, at which the newly-coined, paradoxical phrase of "democratic centralism" was interpreted as meaning that centralism was the chief form of organization and the actual forms of democratism that developed in each particular case were conditioned by the local circumstances and action methods.

In view of the centrifugal tendencies within Soviet society, Lenin also made it clear during the NEP period—a period in which certain concessions had to be made to the groups that had not been fully won over to participation within the context of socialism—that discussion on all sides could not mean participation in decision making at the same time: "Hold meetings but rule without the slightest waver, rule with a strong hand, just like the capitalist ruled before you" (LPSS, Vol. 4, p. 166). And he declared himself ready to employ iron discipline and, if necessary, executions in order to implement this principle. Changes in medium and long-term targets could thus no longer be truly influenced from below. A lack of unmanipulated participation left the fixing of priorities for maximization of the three other target packages—redistribution, efficiency, and protection—to a minority.

The principle of "democratic centralism" has also been upheld in China, in theory, and even during periods of decentralized policy the principle of democracy was never propagated at the expense of the principle of centralism. The compromise formula of "centralized policy, shared management" was frequently called upon for propaganda purposes.[685]

The organizational principle of democratic centralism is based on the separation of decision making, through discussion, from implementation of the decisions taken. Criticism from Western systems theorists and cyberneticists has led to the defendants of democratic centralism adopting cybernetic metaphors. Georg Klaus in the German Democratic Republic felt that the distinguishing feature of democratic centralism lay in the fact that "it is not a pure control system but a regulatory system. It does not simply pour a flow of orders from above to below (as would a control system) but involves regulation at all levels of the system hierarchy, i.e., the successes or failures of actions serve as feedback impulses on decisions and future actions."[686]

Expressed in this general way, defense such as this is not completely wrong. Even the darkest Stalinism did not get by without a certain degree of feedback, even if this was only via information from the security organs. The real opportunities for participation in socialist systems cannot, however, be deduced from this abstract model and need to be measured empirically from the degree of truly nonmanipulated participation. It is not enough for social research to be told "that an optimum relationship between action and reaction" can only be achieved in a system of democratic centralism, because this assumes a common interest between the hierarchy and the basic units of organization,[687] and it is precisely this common interest that is disputed. An optimum relationship can only reveal itself in the analysis of real conflicts and should not be ontologized as constituting a premise of the whole model.

2.   The second ideological change of course came with the abandoning of the principle of collective leadership in the economy and its replacement with *one-man leadership* (*edinonachalie*). After Stalin's economic reform of 1934, the territorial concept was abandoned, and the principle of one-man leadership established itself in the place of collective leadership throughout the whole of the economy. This was accompanied by an unparalleled sector concentration.

It was difficult to justify this one-sided development with statements from the classicists. Engels had indeed stated in his conflict with the anarchists that the questions of work organization "are to be solved authoritatively." He left open the question, however, as to whether these should be "solved by the decision of a delegate at the head of the branch or, if possible, by a majority decision" (MEW Vol. 18, p. 306).

In the wake of economic reform, a number of socialist states experimented with collegial forms of leadership in state enterprises and put forward proposals suggesting that the concept of a uniform socialist property fund be modified to a concept of operatively administered enterprise property for the particular portion of state property in question. In the terms of this concept, the state would only retain the right to decide upon the field of activity, location, and liquidation of the enterprise.[688] These tendencies toward shifting state ownership toward cooperative forms of ownership were always regarded as "anarchosyndicalist deviation" and as being politically suspect.

In the People's Republic of China the principle of one-man leadership underwent decline as of 1955. The party attacked it among other reasons because it feared the development of independent centers of power outside the party and because it was generally suspicious of the middle-level cadres who were threatening to push in-between the party leadership and the masses. China accepted a two-fold drawback when she introduced collective leadership into the economy. Firstly, this innovation contributed toward the developing conflicts with the Soviets, and, secondly, it reduced the potential for implementing the central plan.[689] The Chinese literature itself not infrequently warned against the excesses of meeting democracy, which was set against the Soviet model of one-man leadership.

This two-fold narrowing of the concept of participation in the production sphere paved the way for the subsequent reduced form of participation that went on to develop.

2. Participation opportunities in the enterprise and workers' production consultations

The reduction in participation opportunities became evident at several points.

Participation and plant management

Participation scarcely has any bearing on plant management in socialist enterprises, since this is organized along different collective, participatory lines.

Comparisons with capitalist participation models often come out biased, if only because the enterprise, as a relatively independent unit in the socialist countries (with the exception of Yugoslavia), plays a completely different role from the enterprise in capitalist systems. Enterprise directors are not elected by the labor force but are appointed by a "higher body, insofar as the Minister has not retained this right for himself."

Since large enterprise concerns do not have Boards of Directors in socialist countries but only their individual management—the General Directors of the VVBs (Administration of a state-owned enterprise) and the Directors of the VEBs in the German Democratic

Republic—codetermination at top management level is hindered right from the start. The social councils (of the VVBs) and the production committees of the VEBs form the equivalent of the West German supervisory boards (*Aufsichtsräte*). The trade unions do have a say here, but the party plays the more decisive role. The production consultations tended to provide an opportunity for participation for workers not wishing to take the roundabout way via the party. In 1958, the standing production conferences were set up in order to watch over plan fulfilment, competition, innovation, the fight against slipshod work, "unrhythmical" production, and security measures.

To begin with, there was conflict in the enterprises as the initial enthusiasm for the new participation opportunities opened up by the production conferences led to the conference overstepping its competences and going over the heads of the plant management to take up contact with higher-ranking bodies (at that time with the *Sovnarckhoz*) to request material supplies and allocations. Later on came complaints about the lack of independence vis-à-vis the management, because management representatives frequently dominated the standing production conferences.[690]

Other socialist states—in particular the German Democratic Republic—adopted the new Soviet institution shortly afterwards. Here, an initial measure was introduced with the "Law on improvement and simplification of the work of the state apparatus in the GDR" of February 11, 1958, and this was followed in June by the "Directive of the Presidium of the Association Board of the FDGB on the execution of production consultations in socialist enterprises and on the election of committees for production consultations." At the beginning of 1958, so-called production consultative committees were set up as executive and supervisory bodies for the production consultations. Their chief functions include participation in the compilation of enterprise plans, improvement of work organization, and the consolidation of labor discipline—all aims serving to increase efficiency. The fact that the production consultative committees also frequently assumed the protective function that had been insufficiently developed at plant level came under fire as being "petty trade unionism," in that the committees concerned themselves with working conditions rather than with higher-ranking tasks. This may have contributed toward the need for a coordinating body, which was set up in the form of a production committee. After a number of experiments, the production committee was firmly anchored in the "Labor Code" with the insertion of a paragraph 10a.

The production committees had 25 members (corresponding roughly to the earlier committees) and were intended to create an institution that could meet more frequently and carry out more relevant work. It has also been assumed that a secondary intention was at play here as well, namely the intensification of party control. The production committees could carry out checks and submit objections and complaints to the plant director. The principle of democratic centralism, with its separation of consultation and decision making, remained intact, however. The resolutions only have the force of recommendations, and all decisions are taken by the plant manager alone. The production committee's function was not to represent the labor force vis-à-vis plant management, but to represent the plan and the state and party's interest instead. In 1971, the production committees were again transformed into central production consultations. Until 1976/77, the members were elected in all plants with more than 50 workers (in the Soviet Union with more than 300 workers). Since that time they are selected by the Trade Union Committee in the plants.[691] Nevertheless, despite its overwhelmingly passive nature, this form of participation did open up a number of possibilities in that the production conferences provided a means of making enterprise plans and measures transparent and gave the workers insight into the function of their own individual cogwheels within the whole economic apparatus.

As a rule, capitalist systems make no attempt to arouse this kind of interest. It would seem that a certain degree of mistrust of the trade unions by the party was at play here. The production committees were elected by the labor force as a whole, but the right of nomination lay with the social organizations, which proved particularly favorable for the party. Contrary to the case with other elections (such as for the plant trade union leadership or the dispute committees) an open vote was obligatory, and this strengthened the control potential open to the party. In addition, the Chairman was to be the Secretary of the SED party organization and his deputy the Chairman of the plant trade union leadership. A further loss of power for the enterprise trade union leadership has thus far been inferred from this.[692] Nonetheless, in terms of organization theory, these new bodies did mark progress, in that they were capable of potentially securing a greater degree of participation in plant management. They were, however, abolished again in 1971.

Management experts report from a number of Chinese firms that the enterprise directors are elected annually. Richman found that this was the case for 40% of enterprises he visited.[693] In China, too, the party has a 99-to-100% guarantee of retaining control and having its candidate elected, however. Nearly all the managers are party members, and in the management typology they tend to be classified as "reds" rather than as "experts." Also, contrary to the case in the Soviet Union, they received no more money than the highest-ranking party official in the enterprises. Over and above this, a number of original methods were developed for destabilizing power within the enterprise:

1. the *obligation for leading cadres to carry out physical work*, even if this was at times only of symbolic significance;
2. *campaigns against the power of plant management*, such as were introduced into the enterprises by the Red Guards—at times, however, this prompted countermobilization by the workers, who took the side of the management;
3. *alignment of income and the elimination of special privileges through the bonus system* (see Chapter 2).

Travelers to China reported already in 1974 that the principle of free elections for plant management had been widely undermined. The Red Guards, who were not always very popular, were squeezed out of management, and the plant directors, whom they had previously removed from office, were reelected to their old posts. It is difficult to predict the future, despite a number of indications reminiscent of the cultural revolution. At all events, the Soviet criticism that the revolution committees were pursuing an adventurer's policy as organs of the war-bureaucratic dictatorship is polemically exaggerated as far as the situation in the cultural revolution was concerned.[694]

All in all, industrial democracy scores less highly than the agrarian communes. The masses, or in some cases just the Red Guards, were indeed allowed continuous participation in plant management, but these participation trends were regarded as suspect and "anarcho-syndicalist." The anomic activities during the cultural revolution, however, were aimed more at the destruction of established groups and bureaucracies than at participation in decision making.[695] The compulsion for managers to return to work in production was more an attempt at leveling down the opportunities for participation than an upward drive aiming at development of a lasting industrial democracy, with the workers themselves shaping the decision-making process.

Trade union dependence
and subjection of plant trade union leadership
to orders from above

The dogmatic literature of the Soviet Union lists four functions as the most important participation functions of the trade unions:

1.   preparation of plant plans;
2.   leadership of the production conferences;
3.   conclusion of collective agreements;
4.   organization of socialist competition.[696]

On points (1) and (3) in particular, however, the plants themselves are left with relatively little room for maneuver.

The plant trade union leadership (Fabkom in the Soviet Union) is also handicapped in the implementation of its participation functions through the fact of its being bound to orders from above. The trade unions achieved their greatest measure of success not in participation in plant management but—as is the case in capitalist systems—through participation in personnel matters. Even this is not enough, however. Plant trade union leadership generally has no influence on appointments, only limited influence on transfers or repostings, and only when it comes to formal notice of dismissal do they have full participation rights (in the Soviet Union, since the Supreme Soviet's Decree of July 15, 1958).

In practice, however, it has been seen that loopholes do exist in these participation rights, because the plant management can avoid giving notice of dismissal by issuing cancelation agreements; and in the case of cancelation agreements the trade unions are only entitled to subsequent information. The cadre record (personnel record) in which all modifications pertaining to the worker's labor situation are entered has supplied the plant management with a disciplinary weapon, making it possible for the dissolution of a labor relationship to be made to appear as though it had been "voluntary," so as to spare the worker concerned any drawbacks and to allow plant management to avoid having to seek the consent of the trade union.

The trade unions in most socialist countries have held the function of a transmission belt for the party and have remained relatively powerless vis-à-vis the party cell in the enterprise as well. In countries that did not enjoy an old syndicalist tradition, such as China, the trade unions virtually assumed a feeder function for the party in that there was frequently a kind of preselection of potential party candidates within the trade unions.[697] The limited empirical information available from interview studies conducted in Yugoslavia and the German Democratic Republic shows that the majority of workers scarcely rate the role of the trade union in the enterprise any higher than that of the party.[698]

The jumbled competences
of the participation institutions

The jumble of competences across a multitude of participation institutions has led to high frictional loss. The participation institutions work partly on a representative basis and partly on plebiscitarian, acclamatory basis. They can be divided into three groups according to their durability and representativeness:

1. collective agreements;
2. collective, consultative participation bodies—standing production initiatives (socialist competition, innovator movement);
3. meetings democracy—labor force meetings, trade union members' meetings, and so forth.

The vast number of institutions for potential participation can be illustrated by taking the example of the German Democratic Republic, the literature of which lists the following[699] :

1. the basic organization of the SED with its elected leadership;

2. the trade union organization, with its elected leadership and other bodies:
    members' meeting,
    consultants' meeting,
    standing production consultations at plant and departmental level,
    innovator activists group,
    work and wages committee,
    competition committee,
    worker support committee,
    honorary work safety inspectorate,
    culture and education committee,
    schooling committee,

youth committee,
legal committee,
women's committee,
dispute committee,
standing workers' control supervisory groups,
social insurance council,
mass sport committee,
committee for the socialist upbringing of children;

3.   the basic organization of the FDJ (Free German Youth), the
Germano-Soviet Friendship Society, the Society for Sport and
Technology, and the German Gymnastics and Sports Associ-
ation, with the following bodies:
FDJ control posts,
young technicians' club,
MMM working group,
Germano-Soviet Friendship Circle for the evaluation of
Soviet experience;

4.   social bodies to support the state leadership:
parliamentary representatives' activist group,
socialist study group,
enterprise committee of the Worker and Peasant Inspec-
torate,
housing committe;

5.   the organs of the Chamber of Technology:
enterprise section;
technical section.

A number of these "social organs of the labor force," such as
the production committees, were no longer mentioned in the "Decree
on the functions, rights and obligations of state-owned enterprises,
collective combines and VVR," which came into force on May 1,
1973.

The tendency to oversteer social processes is very evident in
the case of the participation function, and this has in the main led to
two drawbacks:

1.   The greater the number of people mobilized, the more
rapidly their activity degenerated into mere *ritualism*. Such strong
complaints were voiced in the Soviet Union about the production
conferences and their inactivity (they frequently passed virtually

identically-worded resolutions and in many cases ceased to meet at all) that a new institution was set up—the production activists' group. Not infrequently, these new institutions, under pressure to prove themselves, counteracted the efforts of older organizations. This was the case with the Soviet Inventor and Rationaliser Groups, which developed into an obstacle to innovation after a certain period of time, since each new idea then needed the approval of these groups as well as that of the plant management.[700]

Soviet listings report increasing success in innovation as a result of suggestions made by the workers. The number of innovations rose from 591,000 in 1940 to 3,300,000 in 1959, with a saving of 90,400,000 and 1,100,000,000 rubles respectively for Soviet industry.[701] Five percent of workers are said to have participated in the innovations. Between 1956 and 1959, the bonuses for these innovations accounted for 4.1 to 4.8% of the enterprises' annual savings.

Even in cases where participation of innovators and rationalizers was actively encouraged, this did not produce the desired results, owing to the economic background. Stimulation of intellectual innovation only proved successful in cases where management was prepared to take the risk of trying out new production methods. As a rule, however, innovations called for additional capital and only led to the hoped-for increase in production after a certain lean period. A system that strongly emphasized the rotation of elites and control was asking the plant manager to take on too great a career risk here, because even short-lived falls in production generally led to managers losing their jobs.

2.   The new institutions set up to replace older ones were frequently *more elite in their makeup*. This was true of the production activist groups, which were set up alongside the inefficient production conferences in 1941, comprising young management staff, engineers, technicians, and Stakhanovites, and which reinforced the trend toward expert democracy. Theorists in socialist countries did not fail to recognize this danger either.[702] Claims on leisure time and a certain apprehension about taking on additional responsibility are the reasons given in the literature for the apathy associated with participation opportunities.[703]

Complaints were even voiced about the Chinese commune organs, about whose internal workings relatively little is known. These complaints were due less to the party's attempts at manipulating preselection (such as in Eastern European systems) and more to the lack of counter candidates and the lack of rules for improving participatory competition.[704] In addition, the lack of influence of the masses and the irregularity with which the commune and brigade congresses meet also comes under fire.

Subordination of participation to the target of economic efficiency

With the development of planning, participation in the production sphere came to be increasingly subordinated to economic efficiency criteria and the fact that even participation develops more and more into productive resource was not sufficiently appreciated.

China was the only country that did not set so much store by efficiency at the cost of participation as did the Eastern European states—at least, this was true during her great campaigns (Great Leap Forward, Cultural Revolution).

Recent publications quite openly list plan fulfilment, rationalization, and implementation of social control as the most important functions. Protective functions are hardly mentioned at all. Even self-disciplining methods, such as the Seifert method, which marks a preliminary step toward the standardization of work and aims at minimizing lost time and waiting time for materials, are in themselves regarded as positive participation functions, and the organization of competition is also proclaimed as a great achievement. Organization of socialist competition has, however, frequently led to manipulated pseudoparticipation, and the workers have frequently regarded this as a kind of slave-driving to which they reacted with scepticism or even obstruction.

Manipulated pseudoparticipation in the production sphere reached its peak with the creation of the Stakhanov movement on August 30, 1935. This movement was set up by a foreman in the coal-mining industry who mined 102 tons of coal with his team instead of the 7-ton standard. Even critical bourgeois economists do not dispute the spontaneous nature of the movement. This applies in particular to the mobilized second generation of young people, who wished to make a contribution toward the building of socialism that was comparable with that made by the first generation. All in all, however, the spontaneity was subject to much steering, and the workers' feelings against this slave-driving are evident from countless sources. The fear of an increase in plan standards and annoyance at the well-coordinated actions of those who benefitted through special vacations and other gratifications, raising them above the level of the masses to the realm of a worker aristocracy, also figure in the criticism.[705]

A paramilitary trait came to be introduced into participation in the production sphere in this way. Warlike expressions such as "production battle" predominated in the language of the work campaigns, and in the countries that glorified the revolutionary guerrilla spirit (such as China and Cuba) the "fight" in the production sphere is a concept of central importance. Fights are fought against accidents at work, against absenteeism, and against low productivity in the same breath as the fight against imperialism, exploitation, and counter-revolution.

The socialist countries do thus offer a wide range of participation opportunities, although coresponsibility tends to outweigh the de facto possibilities for participation in the decision-making process. In addition, there is not a proper balance of power, because the labor force has been stripped of all means of sanction taking. The socialist enterprise statutes on the other hand, which also reject the principle of power sharing in the production sphere, do assume a certain degree of mutual control. The trade union leadership acts as a counter-force to the plant directors. At times, the third force in the enterprise, the party, acts as a countermobilization force to both forces through looser forms of participation, but these, too, rarely show signs of spontaneity.

High-level participation

Trade unions in socialist countries generally point to the greater opportunities open to them for participation at above-enterprise level, compared with those that exist in capitalist systems. In socialist countries the trade unions (like other mass organizations) have some of their own representatives in parliament and on the councils (FDGB faction in the Volkskammer with 68 seats) and have representatives in the planning and supervisory organs. Since, however, the trade unions accept the unconditional leadership of the party at this level, their participation rights are scarcely any more effective than those that the party could organize itself. Even admirers of socialist systems express regret that participation rights cannot be rated as "democracy from below" and that the extension of consultative rights is in danger of developing into a purely elite expert democracy.

In countries where the plan is rated particularly highly in ideological terms—such as in Cuba at the time when Che Guevara was Minister for Industry and mystic qualities were attributed to participation of the masses—foreign economists have assessed effective participation in plan compilation to be at a very low level.[706] After the failure of the 10-million campaign in the 1970 "sugar battle," the leadership drew a number of consequences and announced greater opportunities for participation of the masses.[707] A new participation model has, however, not been worked out to date.

Even a more decentralized system such as China did not necessarily create better participation at above-enterprise level. Participation in plan compilation at this level tended to be rather insignificant in that since the Great Leap Forward the plan had ceased to enjoy the importance that it had previously held. Plans are no longer published, and long-term planning has undergone a decline. The annual plans were compiled on a relatively elite basis, even if reports that Chou-En-Lai commissioned a 50-man committee of experts to draw up the 1968 economic plan prove to be an exaggeration. During the Cultural Revolution the central trade union apparatus was practically destroyed, since it developed into a focal point of the antibureaucratic hate of the extremists, and only at the start of 1973 were large trade union congresses held in Shanghai and Peking again.

Participation at enterprise level, on the other hand, was strongly emphasized. The three "participate in's" mean that cadres and management have to do their share of physical work, that workers participate in management, and that consumers are involved in the variation and quality determination of their products. This form of participation marks an improvement on the Soviet hostility toward consumers. However, it is only really conceivable in a non-too-complex, small-scale production system that is in close contact with its consumers. The Chinese model has by no means proved its universal applicability in a highly sophisticated mechanized industry where part of production is intended for export.

Even observers who wish the Chinese experiment well yet attempt to keep an ironical distance confirm that the somewhat childish slogans calling for participation (such as "dare to think, dare to create, dare to do") do indeed contain motivating power that seems to be geared to the intellectual level of the labor force and against which any atlantic presumption is misplaced. These somewhat blunt forms of enlightenment only become "childish" when Maoists transpose them to the complex society of highly industrialized countries. And it should not be forgotten that in these highly industrialized countries, they radiate more than just an exotic charm to little-motivated and highly alienated young people and develop a consoling and group-consolidating power.

Integration of the production and legitimation sphere

None of the participation models to date has succeeded in its target of an optimum integration of these two spheres—a target that presumably cannot be achieved without an authentic council system. In the Soviet Union, a repeated attempt was made at the Seventeenth Party Congress in 1934 to bring together factory work and political activity in state administrative organizations. The experiment did not meet with much success, and even the Yugoslav model that comes closest to a system of councils likewise leaves much to be desired when it comes to the integration of these two spheres (see Chapter 10, Section 3). Only under the condition of a predominantly agrarian society did the Chinese communes succeed in bracketing the spheres together, insofar as the communes merged with the former local administration units. As the communes became larger, and decentralization tendencies began to develop again, the greater degree of decision-making autonomy given to the brigades and teams brought a decline in the tendency for territorial administration organs to be amalgamated with the economic participation institutions. It can be provisionally concluded from this, taking all the due precautions, that even a system that had attempted to put a radical stop to the separation of economics and politics found that an increasingly sophisticated society and production units caused a fairly wide separation of functions to develop again.

Furthermore, the very efforts made to link productive work with participatory-political activity create certain shortcomings in themselves. Local peoples' deputies in the Soviet Union, asked about the amount of time they spend on their representation activity, replied that they only spent about 10 hours per month.[708] The desire to avoid professionalization has led to the peoples' deputies being given even fewer infrastructural facilities for their work than in capitalist systems, and it is to be feared that on the basis of this concept their role will always remain rudimentary.

3. Workers' councils (the Yugoslav model)

Since 1917, the principle of "democratic centralism" and the fundamental concept of rigid party leadership have overridden the spontaneous participatory basis of pluralistic council-democratic groups in the Soviet Union. These have at best been able to express themselves as opposition from time to time, from Kronstadt to Prague. The Czechoslovakian experiment in 1968 had definite promise of developing into a democratic participation system for the production sphere, but this was not destined to last for long.[709] Spontaneous workers' councils were also set up during the unrest in Poland and Hungary in 1956. In Hungary they were dissolved again between April and August 1957, and in Poland they were prevented at national level from establishing themselves. The councils were left to dry out so that they developed into nothing more than "instances of complaint."

Only in Yugoslavia did the party build up a system of self-management, although even here there were forces within the party that viewed the experiment with mistrust and tried to bring about delays, such as the secret police under Ranković up to 1966.

Participation is achieved via several organs. Originally, the labor collective in enterprises with a labor force of 30 or more elected the workers' council (in enterprises with a labor force of 30 to 70 the council was optional). The system showed the need for improvement, and with constitutional amendment No. 15, in 1968, the organizational form was made more flexible and the labor collectives were given a greater say in its determination. Term of office and composition were no longer laid down as binding, and even the administrative committee no longer formed an obligatory component of the representative system. This could be replaced by a business committee, comprising management representatives together with representatives from the workers' council, and could delegate a number of functions to the workers' council.

Despite these modifications, the number of complaints about the "management's usurpation of participation rights" and about "separation of the leading cadres from the masses" continued to grow, and in 1971 the "Basic Organization of United Labor" was set up to reinforce the masses' organization and to include more workers directly in the rota of offices.

An attempt was made to counteract the danger of an anarchistic splintering of opinion-moulding processes within the workers' units by the simultaneous introduction of "self-management arrangements" and "social contracts" aimed at improving interenterprise coordination. The managerial functions are assumed by professional management cadres who are elected directly by the workers and can be dismissed from their posts. Prior to the constitutional amendments of the 1970s, the posts were publicly advertised and applications processed by a 6-man committee, 3 of whom were appointed by the workers' council and 3 by the local municipal assembly. As a rule, more than 90% of applicants and committee members are party members.[710] In the past, there has seldom been real competition against established managers. The job requirements are already tailored to the special knowledge and career specifications of the management in office to such an extent that other applicants rarely give themselves a chance. In 1972, less than one fifth of the new applicants were recruited. There are repeated complaints that the system does not produce enough qualified and pretrained enterprise managers. Comparing the qualifications of the new recruits with those of the reappointed managers, Yugoslav statistics have shown for 1972 that 48% of the newly appointed managers and only 34% of reappointed managers had reached the highest qualification level, which serves to confirm the trend toward selection on the basis of educational and performance criteria.

Participation is achieved in part on a representative basis and in part on a plebiscitarian basis. Emphasis on the representative component has frequently been criticized by the orthodox as being ideological deviation, yet it seems to be gaining ground in the Yugoslav literature. Enterprise management has frequently shied away from the plebiscitarian instrument of the referendum,[711] and attempts have been made to specify the justifying initiative for a referendum as restrictively as possible.

The Yugoslav self-management system has a number of advantages compared with the participation models of the other socialist countries:

1. The trade unions have recognized and *asserted* their *protective function* to a greater extent. At times, the primacy of the party is even regarded as superfluous when it comes to expansion of the system. The trade unions also have a greater capacity for conflict than in other countries, as the fairly high number of walk-outs shows (1964: 273; 1965: 231; 1966: 134).[712]

2. The Yugoslav model goes further than other participation models in its attempt *to link functional representation* of the workers with *territorial self-management.*

3. The increasing expansion of the self-management system *is reinforcing the tendency towards nationalization*, even though, in terms of the percentage of nationalized enterprises, Yugoslavia is experiencing a retrograde trend in some sectors. Even the private sector, however, is indirectly being brought to "nationalization" to a greater extent through self-management. The participation function is seriously accepted as a basic target of socialism. Steps are taken to counteract the tendency toward simply regarding self-management as

a means of increasing economic efficiency. Yugoslavia is not giving way to the argument that greater success could be achieved at the current stage of development by using authoritarian leadership methods for the sake of the longer-term and all-round targets of socialism.

The original self-management system has, however, not achieved the desired effects, and this for several reasons:

1. *The constitutional reforms were too unstable*, and the experiments carried out were too short-lived. Each experiment was always replaced by an increasingly complex construction instead of the country following the logical course of yielding the centers of power to the workers' desire for participation.

The attempt to integrate the industrial microlevel and the political macrolevel of decision making to a greater degree led to particular policy fluctuations. The local municipal assembly was a kind of two-house system, comprising the municipal council and the workers' collective council (the latter being elected by those employed in the labor and state organizations, cooperatives, and social organizations). In 1953, the central state organization was also brought into line with this model, and the traditional two-house system was abolished. The old council of nationalities was incorporated into the Upper House, the Federal Council. Its place was taken by the producers' council.

The constitutional reform of 1963 marked the end of the attempt to establish a type of class system of franchise for the producers' council based on work performance, which involved a certain injustice in representation between town and country and between individual regions. The reforms divided the Federal Assembly into five councils (Federal Council, Economic Council, Education and Cultural Council, Social and Health Council, Sociopolitical Council). The following constitutional reform, which was intended to strengthen the nationalities in the light of the growing unrest, reduced the different bodies to three houses, with the three workers' collective councils being merged. From then onwards, the representatives on the sociopolitical council were elected directly by the citizens of the municipality and no longer by the municipal assembly.

Conflicts outside the production sphere—that is, conflicts between nationalities and cultural groups—which the dogmatists merely classified as "left-overs" and which first came to be regarded as legitimate by the critical Marxist theory in Yugoslavia,[713] overshadowed the conflict of interests in the self-management system, and there was constant reorganization of the institutional sphere in a vain bid to alleviate the conflicts. The effects of the spring, 1974, constitutional reform on the self-management system still have to be seen.

Despite the pronounced political fluctuations resulting from the steady flow of constitutional modifications and a somewhat jumpy reform policy, it nonetheless remains remarkable that Yugoslavia is the first socialist system to experiment constantly with new forms of participation and to attempt to monitor these in the light of actual developments instead of simply claiming for propagandist purposes that they will be a success, right from the start.

2. The complexity of the institutional system became increasingly incompatible with the *dominating role of the party*, which was no longer able to fill the wide range of institutions with life without undermining its monolothic claim to leadership. The party still played the decisive role, even at enterprise level. Nearly all plant managers are party members and are filtered by the party through preselection. Empirical studies have shown that participation correlates with the hierarchical position within the enterprise and in particular with party membership.

3. Despite the successes in education policy, the socialist state has not yet been in existence long enough to smooth out the *educational and qualification differences* that influence participation opportunities in the self-management system.

Yugoslav statistics show that the more highly skilled in the labor force in general, and the workers among them in particular, have achieved greater representation over the years (see Table 104). These objective findings are confirmed by studies on the subjective feelings of Yugoslav workers. Surveys show that the skilled labor force has more influence than do the rest of the workers. Opinion polls carried out in a number of Zagreb enterprises do, indeed, show that the majority of workers—85%—feel participation to be an achievement worthy of defending,[714] and this presumably represents a higher degree of legitimation than that achieved by the participation opportunities offered in countries with a more markedly bureaucratic socialist system. Nevertheless, only very few of those questioned —4%—felt that the workers' councils were an essential body, and, in the eyes of Yugoslav workers, it is the manager who holds the greater power, as in other systems. At times there is criticism that the plant manager holds too weak a position compared with the case in other countries, this being on account of the rather vague delimitation of competences within the self-management bodies. A recent opinion poll showed that only 19% of workers felt their interests to be adequately represented through the self-management bodies, as compared with 65% of management staff and 69% of party officials.[715]

Table 104

Social composition of the workers' councils and administrative committees in Yugoslavia

	Workers' councils		Administrative committees	
	1960	1970	1960	1970
total membership	156,300	135,204	51,261	46,994
	(percentages)			
total workers	76.2	67.6	67.2	44.2
highly skilled	15.1	17.2	19.3	18.2
skilled	40.5	33.7	34.8	20.4
semiskilled	13.4	9.0	8.9	3.4
unskilled	7.2	7.4	4.2	2.2
other employees				
with higher vocational training	4.2	10.1	11.0	27.8
with middle vocational training	12.0	15.9	15.0	22.0
with low-level vocational training	7.6	6.4	6.8	5.6

Source: N. Jovanov, "Streik und Selbstverwaltung in Jugoslavien." *Gewerkschaftl. Monatshefte,* H. 6 (1973), (355–364), pp. 357ff.

There is even a great deal of scepticism about the trade unions, and the majority of this same sample felt that they were comparatively powerless in all decisive questions.

The role of the manager and an expert elite is still considerable but has not remained unchallenged. The right of recall does exist but has played a comparatively small role. In 1956, only 8.8% of workers' council members were recalled and 1.2% of administrative committee members. The reasons were primarily economic offenses and serious breaches of discipline. Scarcely any of the recalls were founded on economic inefficiency of the management or directed against a whole council. In the case of managers, there was a greater turnover. In

1968, 2727 managers were reappointed, 421 were first-time appointments, and 421 failed to be reappointed.[716] New forms of consolidation of power thus developed in the enterprise, despite the fact that these were supposed to be eliminated through a system of deliberate deprofessionalization of functions.

Doubt is expressed at times in the literature as to whether the workers' councils possess the necessary specialist knowledge and information to exercise more effectively their control in the complex economics of large enterprises. Only a full-time control body is believed capable of providing a counterbalance to the management.

4.   Despite the battle against alienation on grounds of bureaucratic–etatist organization, *new forms of alienation* have emerged in the Yugoslav system as well. This is particularly the case where the egoism of self-management groups only made it possible for a type of collective "producer capitalism" to develop. These tended to exploit the other groups and members of society for purposes of maximizing their own enterprise profits in the same way as the individual entrepreneur would do in capitalism. Excessive decentralization repeatedly threatened to undermine the state's equalization and redistribution policy, although countless decisions relating to enterprise policy (such as price formation and investment policy) were—at least until 1965—subject to central state control.

Some of the complaints are due not so much to the self-management system itself but are the expression of certain distortions that stem from other areas of economic policy (involving inflation and unemployment). These complaints should not be misused for purposes of declaring the self-management system itself unworkable. The chief problem of the self-management system is still that the self-management bodies have no influence on certain processes such as the market situation or bank investment decisions, yet they nonetheless have to bear the consequences of them, even if this is in the form of "collective entrepreneurship." A number of decentralized decisional powers enhance these negative tendencies in the economic subsystem. Thus the system offers little incentive for employment of the unemployed, and the relatively highly skilled workers all strive to work in the most prosperous enterprises.[717]

It still remains disputed whether a fundamental anarcho-liberal trend can be said to be inherent in the Yugoslav system—as Soviet and more particularly Chinese polemics maintain—or whether this is simply the consequence of certain exogenic factors, such as Yugoslavia's break with the socialist camp, the penetration of capitalist powers, or the size of the private sector. Yugoslav theorists, however, generally work on the basis that the anarcho-liberal tendency, which camouflages itself under socialist collective ownership, does indeed constitute a real danger for the system but is not an inevitable consequence of the move away from an etatist-bureaucratic type of socialism. The Yugoslav theorists must be credited with the fact that self-management does not need to be synonymous with the disintegrating decentralism of a number of phases during Yugoslavia's development. The continued existence of commodity production, the use of material stimuli, and other leftovers from presocialist times have not been able to solve all the problems in Yugoslavia that the other socialist systems have in the main been able to overcome (such as elimination of unemployment). In addition, the distribution forms have created new problems that are not even found in capitalism (the collective entrepreneur's risk that has to be borne by the workers), such that the Yugoslav participation model has not yet produced the successes that are theoretically possible.

This explains why, when a large sample (2,060) was questioned, 42.7% were of the opinion that the economic units had been given greater rights, but that the system as a whole has not created sufficient prerequisites for these rights to be implemented.[718] Nevertheless, the openness with which such shortcomings were discussed in Yugoslav publications at the end of the 1960s appears to provide a better starting point for extending participation than do the "tasteless apologies for socialist democracy" that the Yugoslav theorists rightly reject as not being worthy of the cause.

Participation in the production sphere of socialist countries cannot be viewed in isolation. Of the four great functions, participation is the target that has been developed least. Some of the reasons for this lie in the prevailing ideologies. The first "sin" lies in the transfer of the principles of "democratic centralism" and one-man leadership to all spheres of society. The second lies in the degradation of the trade unions to transmission belts and in the reduction of their conflict potential.

Although in a large number of countries the gradual rigidification of the participation opportunities for the trade unions led to the creation of new, spontaneous forms of participation, such as the production conferences and production committees, the fact that the trade unions' protective function was underdeveloped meant that these new participation forms either developed into pseudo-participation controlled by the works management, or made themselves suspect of "trade unionism" because they were concerned primarily with plan fulfilment and not with the situation at the workplace. Even in a system such as Chile's, which had fully taken over the bourgeois concept of freedom to form a coalition, the production committees developed into a kind of "secondary trade union."[719]

The participation function proved itself to be not only dependent on the extent to which the production function of the workers' representation had been developed but also on the quality of redistribution policy (see Part I). Not only the well-meaning Yugoslav model suffered from the relics of unjust distribution. Nonmanipulated participation is virtually inconceivable without more-or-less equitable distribution, particularly in the educational sector. This has lasting influence on the quality of participation, in phasing out the information lead held by enterprise management and skilled workers and technicians—a lead that has only led to a kind of consultative, expert democracy developing in all socialist countries to date.

11

Participation
in the distribution sphere

As a rule, socialist states have entrusted the trade unions with the administration of the social security system. This does not constitute participation as such, but involves the execution of instructions from state authorities, with limited possibilities open for participation via the lobby channels of the trade union apparatus. Even in the field of wage policy—the area of distribution policy that most directly concerns the worker—there is virtually no participation of the workers' representations on an overall economic basis. Trade unions are generally unable to proceed to wage corrections, even in cases where manifest errors have been made by the planning authorities. Furthermore, the state and party were caught up in their own constraints when they linked the wage level to the increase in labor productivity without always being in a position to give a rational explanation for the growing disparities in development of these two variables.

Greater participation in wage fixing has so far only prevailed in predominantly agrarian socialist societies (with the exception of Cuba). Here, the production teams were given greater opportunities for self-assessment again—following a period of overcentralization in this field, as well. This was only possible, however, because there were not so many state-paid bonuses and material benefits to be distributed as there have been since the mid-1960s in Eastern European systems (see Chapter 2, Section 1).

In Cuba, on the other hand, Castro systematically rejected all the workers' claims for higher wages for large-scale increases in production, branding them as "antisocial speculation."[720]

The forms of participation that are open to social organizations precisely in the distribution sphere are often rated as a step forward along the path toward communism and toward the realization of the communist principle of needs.[721] Nevertheless, it must be realized that genuine participation opportunities have been developed to a greater degree in the production and legitimation spheres than in the distribution sphere. At any rate, participation is at its most "anomic" here, to judge by the experience of the Polish cities in 1970 and 1980/81. Only with the growing development of indirect lobbying, in the crypto-pluralism of socialist systems, does a change seem to be coming about.

12

Participation in the legitimation sphere

According to socialist ideology's own portrayal of itself, there are several possibilities for participation in the legitimation sphere:[722]

1. election of the organs of power;
2. accountability of the people's representatives;
3. participation in social organizations;
4. proposal and petition rights;
5. expression of the will of the people by referendum.

There are two further forms of participation that are not mentioned in bureaucratic socialism:

6. mass campaigns;
7. anomic participation.

1.   Degree of organization

In the first five forms of participation, socialist countries are able to report clear-cut success, viewed in purely numerical terms. The election and accountability of the people's representatives seems to be more democratic in socialist systems, because imperative mandates and the right to recall are guaranteed. Until now, however, it has been disputed as to whether the Soviet law of 1959 on the recall of deputies, which marked the first step toward positivizing the recall facility that had been announced earlier, can, indeed, be considered a genuine right to recall. It is not the electorate who are entitled to submit requests for recall, but only the social organizations, and it is the Presidium of the Supreme Soviet who decide whether a recall procedure should be set in motion.

In the other socialist countries, there are no facilities for recall on the basis of spontaneous expression of the majority will of the electorate either. In fact, recalls are even rarer than for representatives in the production sphere, and when they do occur they tend to be prompted by a wink from the Party from above rather than by spontaneous discontent.

Recalls play a very small role in the central institutions of socialist countries.[723] They are employed more widely in the local representative organs. According to a Soviet survey, 541 deputies were recalled in 1968.[724] In the Yugoslav workers' self-management institutions, the right to recall does have a certain significance (see Chapter 10, Section 3), but in cases involving top positions (such as plant managers), which require approval by state instances, the majority of recalled managers were removed from office on the initiative of state organs and not through action within the enterprise. As far as the lower levels are concerned (recalls from the management committee, for example, the mass organizations, that is, the party and the trade unions, have generally played their part in Yugoslavia as well in prestructuring genuine recalls from below.

Outside these mass organizations there is little scope for participation, even in the production sphere. How wide is the participation in the social mass organizations, however? In purely numerical terms, the participation level is impressive. Measured by the membership figures for parties, trade unions, and youth organizations, socialist countries generally come out at the top of the world scale.

In all socialist countries, the social organization that carries the state is the Communist party. The very level of organization within the Party, however, highlights differences in the extent of ruling isolation indulged in by the party elites. Ever since the first Communist party seized power in Russia in 1917, organizational policy has gone through phases of changing orientation. The opposition around Trotsky, Zinov'ev, and Bukharin involved different recruitment policy concepts each time. The periods of liberal recruitment policy were followed by elitist waves, such as at the time of Shdanov, who had a very marked influence in the 1940s even on the internal life of the Party. It was seen that the concepts of an elitist cadre party and a proletarian mass party could not always be reconciled. Lipset's attempt to establish a negative correlation between Communist party membership and the level of development has frequently been considered as untenable.[725] If we classify the Communist parties according to their increase in membership over periods for which exact data are available, we then obtain a more differentiated picture (see Table 105).

It has been deduced from these figures that the growth in membership correlated with the system's degree of liberalization. The period chosen for the quantitative analysis is probably too short to permit such a sweeping conclusion. If we were to take a different period—around 1949—the German Democratic Republic would come out with one of the most impressive growth rates, since party membership rose from 1,200,000 in 1946, after the unification of the SPD and KPD in the SED, to 1,770,000 members in 1949. This figure had dropped to 1,230,000 by 1953, stabilized between 1954 and 1957 at 1,400,000, and then gradually increased to reach the 1,700,000 mark again in 1966.[726]

The initial increase in membership could not automatically be taken as signifying growing liberalization, however, despite speculation about the impact of the 52% SPD members that were absorbed into the SED in 1946. On this point, as well as on many others, the German Democratic Republic marks a deviant case, but even if we exclude this country, the liberalization hypothesis is untenable in the light of membership increase in a number of other countries—such as Rumania—as well.

Membership increases must also always be viewed in relation to trends in the opposite direction, that is, to membership drops due to clean-ups. All Communist parties have experienced radical purges on repeated occasions. However, none of them insisted as much as did the Chinese Communist party on the need for even party members to be submitted to tests to prove their loyalty time and again. This may also be a contributory factor to the relatively low percentage of the population that is organized in the Communist party.[727]

Table 105

Membership of Communist parties

Country	Party members	Year	Percen-tage of popula-tion	Members 1968	1976
Albania	53,000	1962	3.2	66,327	n.d.
Bulgaria	528,674	1965	6.3	613,393	789,796
China	18,000,000	1965	2.5	27,000,000*	27,000,000*
Cuba			3.9	60,000	202,807
Czechoslovakia	1,676,509	1964	11.6	1,700,000	1,382,860
GDR	1,610,679	1963	9.9	1,769,912	1,914,382
Hungary	520,000	1963	4.8	600,000	754,353
Mongolia	46,000	1963	4.5	48,570	64,713
North Korea	1,300,000	1964	15.5	1,600,000	
Poland	1,614,237	1965	4.3	2,030,065	2,359,000
Rumania	1,240,000	1965	4.7	1,800,000	2,547,434
Soviet Union	12,000,000	1965	4.2	13,500,000	15,694,187
Vietnam	570,000	1963	3.6	766,000	1,100,000
Yugoslavia	1,030,041	1964	5.4	1,013,500	1,076,711

*1973

Sources: *Kommunisty mira—o svoikh partiyakh* (Prague: Mir i sotsializm, 1976), pp. 92ff; 1968: E. Mickiewicz (ed.), *Handbook of Soviet Social Science Data* (New York: Free Press, 1973), pp. 219ff.

The degree of organization within the parties is dependent upon a number of variables, which only have a rather indirect relationship to the degree of liberalization:

1.   The first of these is the extent of the *feeling of a national threat* and the communist government's ability to legitimate itself in the eyes of the citizens as a guarantor of national independence and to mobilize active support (for example, in Rumania, Yugoslavia, and North Vietnam). In North Korea, the claim for reunification had a strong mobilizing impact. North Korea holds the top rank in terms of the population's affiliation to the party organization: more than one quarter of the aggregate working population are in the organization. Kim il-sung has always taken the entire population of

40 million as a yardstick for the party's strength, and he thus forced the multiplication in the number of cadres on the basis of responsibility for Korea as a whole.[728]

2.   The second variable is the *party's position* in the system. In cases where the party was temporarily supplanted by other forms of mobilization, as in China and Cuba, membership rates stay surprisingly low, although this does not point to a particularly elitist form of rule.

Despite relatively low membership rates in the parties, even the countries with the highest degrees of decentralization in decisional powers, such as China and Yugoslavia, have a relatively high level of control. The Chinese Commune Committees were controlled by the party right down to brigade and team,[729] even though party membership was disproportionately low in the countryside. In the Yugoslav workers' self-management organs, party membership clearly correlates with the importance of the functions held. Whereas about 12% of the overall labor force were party members, the percentage in the Councils was 31% and in the Management Committees 41.5%.[730] Among the managers, there was such a comfortable majority of party members that, despite all the decentralized initiatives, the party was, in fact, effectively able to steer the work of the self-management organs. Only in a country such as Cuba, which is distinguished by its very low degree of institutionalization (Cuba until 1976 had no constitution and not even a party program), is the usual model of cooptation for recruitment not applied. In Cuba, the decision as to who should be delegated to the party is taken by the production unit, including nonparty members.[731]

3.   The mobilizational power of the party also depends on the socioeconomic problems with which the party leadership is confronted, leading to an increase in target group work in a bid to solve them (farmers, intelligentsia, young people, national bourgeoisie).

A number of parties were, however, by no means aiming to swell their membership. They were content with mass campaigns to mobilize the masses on an ad hoc basis whenever necessary.

2.   Mass campaigns

Socialist transformation processes are inconceivable without mass participation. The organization of mass participation is one of the foremost aims of all Communist parties, and this has sometimes yielded unparalleled successes during the transformation period and even afterwards.

As a rule, mass participation requires little stimulation in the *redistribution process*, because the immediate interests of the majority can be realized directly through participation. The second major form of mass participation, however, aimed at restoring *efficiency*, is less spontaneous in nature. Efficiency in the economic sphere in particular is impaired to such an extent by revolutionary transformation processes that particular effort is called for in mastering the economic problems. This by no means applies solely to post-revolutionary periods. Even during attempts to achieve a peaceful transition to socialism, such severe distribution problems will arise that mass participation needs to be organized in order to ensure that even the most elementary protective and distributive functions of the state are assumed. Allende expressed this in a talk with Debray: "This is active participation; they will help with the distribution of milk, in the fight against garbage, in instructing mothers on how to prevent infantile diarrhea, and in this case, for example, in controlling the price and quality of bread."[732]

In the early periods of planning, mass campaigns were still an indispensable instrument for achieving plan fulfilment, a factor that was to become the system's topmost criterion of efficiency. However, the Soviet *shturmovshchina* method (fire-brigade method) for plan fulfilment had the drawback that it created new bottlenecks, due precisely to the withdrawal of resources and labor whenever Soviet resources were all assigned to one specific short-term objective in a bid to combat a particular bottleneck.

In the socialist developing countries, the periodical mass mobilizations had a far less dysfunctional effect on the system. On the one hand, the systems were less sophisticated, and, on the other, they contained even fewer elements of a formalized democratic process than did those of the Eastern European countries. Discussions and indoctrination took place to a greater extent in face-to-face groups or in functional working and living units than was the case in the more complex mobilization societies. China, in particular, favored a consistent approach, seeking to change personal relationships as well—partly by destroying the bonds of the traditional extended family, and partly by using these bonds to stir up agitation. Agitators thus came mainly from within these groups and not from outside them.

It is doubtful, however, whether these methods, which are successful in agrarian societies, would also be successful with a growing level of urbanization. In most cases to date it is only the agricultural communes and mobilization processes in the countryside that are put forward as model cases. The urban communes, on the other hand, have remained at a rather rudimentary stage.[733] Mao also did not fail to see that there was stronger resistance to these mobilizational forms in industry than in the countryside. From time to time he would polemize against the cadres who sneered at mass movements as being in "rural working style" or dismissed them as "practices of partisan warfare." Soviet analysts of the Chinese transformation process are likewise sceptical about the Chinese method of mass mobilization today. The "all hands on deck" method is now being criticized as though it had never been used in the Soviet Union at all.[734]

In this connection, it is of less interest to us whether the method is efficient under industrial conditions. Our main concern is whether the method, under Chinese conditions, leads to manipulated participation or not. If we take the writings of the Chinese leaders seriously, then this, indeed, gives rise to doubt. Mao at times pre-programmed the campaigns into the annual plans as if they were compulsory training periods.

In no other country has the change in the people's conscious-ness, even before the change in social and ownership conditions, been as significant as in China—even in land reform (see Chapter 1, Section 3). "Fight—criticism—transformation" was praised as an ubiquitous instrument of change. Reeducation, commonly referred to as "brain-washing," was an experiment in group dynamics, with precisely coordinated phases of group identification achieved through conveying a feeling of solidarity, through the development of self-criticism, the dissolution of ties with former reference groups, and finally through submission and "rebirth."[735] This sets psychic processes in motion that run completely counter to the traditional Chinese values (such as disavowal of the family). The father's re-education does not always run as smoothly as that described in the touching reports of certain issues of the Peking Review. One ques-tionable matter is the "compulsion of losing one's face," which is practiced quite frequently despite Mao's warning against the opposite extreme of self-abasement in his 1963 directive on overcoming self-complacency.[736] This perhaps also helps to explain why the success scored through carefully dispensed enlightenment and psychical pressure on the Chinese intelligentsia (particularly in the school and university system) has obviously not always resulted in lasting changes of attitude. It is questionable whether reeducation, guided by external objectives, is ever likely to become the object of non-manipulated participation.

Surveys on the publicity background music accompanying mass campaigns have also contributed to raise doubts about nonsteered mass participation. The Chinese campaigns have usually been started off by a contrived letter campaign to the newspapers. The programmed spontaneity was then interpreted as the will of the masses, and only after this was the actual campaign launched.

Although the reeducation and class struggle campaigns were mainly based on steered pseudoparticipation, the socialist developing countries were nevertheless successful in organizing campaigns destined to solve specific problems, which received majority approval, such as in the "Year of Education" or in the "Schools of Revolutionary Instruction" in Cuba.[737] Here, too, the clash with urban, bourgeois culture was just as evident as in the Chinese education campaigns.

Western critics have occasionally rated these campaigns according to their technical success and questioned the exaggerated reports of success by pointing out that in the literacy campaigns, for example, a good part of the newly literate population had only been instructed superficially and a regression became apparent very soon as a result of the lack of reading material and the lack of opportunity to apply newly acquired knowledge at work.

The intrinsic success of the campaigns cannot be expressed in traditional terms of efficiency; it consists in the breaking down of resistance within society, in the mobilization of loyalties, and in giving the individual the impression that he or she is a subject of history, albeit only in the cogs of a mass campaign.

Experience has shown, however, that the policy of mass participation—which again and again fascinates young people in oversaturated late capitalist societies—does not work as a lasting solution.

1. The very fact of socialist systems' longer-term *successes* in many fields, such as social welfare and the educational system, means that there is soon little scope left for the legitimizing power of special campaigns in these particular fields.

2. Mass mobilization tends to have a *disintegrating effect*, unless it leads to the creation of new institutions, even though the neo-institutionalists may indeed have occasionally overemphasized the need for the rapid creation of institutions. In China, Mao was able to employ mass mobilization only at the price of serious damage to the party's organizational steering capacity. The Maoist theory of contradiction also applied to the party, and during the Cultural

Revolution (when sharp criticism was voiced at the "independent kingdom" of the City of Peking's Party Committee), Mao made it clear in a conversation with Prime Minister Chou En-lai about the struggle for power that he considered this struggle for power within the party as having absolute priority over economic efficiency considerations:

> I support the power struggle. After it we must get down to revolution and encourage production.[738]

This struggle for power, however, was no longer a "controlled social experiment," as it had sometimes been called, and Mao himself was plagued at times by apprehension that it would not be possible to score lasting success in the fight between the right- and left-wing factions. He even thought it possible that after his death the right wing might take over power and only hoped that a new counter-initiative would develop "after seven or eight years."[739] The struggle for power finally turned against the party itself and virtually undermined the central planning system, that is, the system's two foremost institutions. Although Mao had never regarded the party as an "eternal institution," he had nevertheless hoped that its end would "come neither too late, nor too soon," and, in this sense, the party's temporary agony seems to have come "too soon."[740]

Although China and Yugoslavia stand at the extremes of a wide range of concepts regarding the socialist transformation process, they do have one thing in common, namely an occasional questioning of the party monopoly. Ever since the dissolution of Cominform, the Eastern bloc countries have repeatedly reproached Yugoslavia with drowning the party in the big sociopolitical mass organizations, thereby undermining the "dictatorship of the proletariat."

Only toward the end of the 1960s did it become apparent that the sclerosis of Marxist thought and the centrifugal efforts of groups and nationalities had led to a situation where the party was, in fact, no longer able to control all the processes and had increasingly turned into a recipient of group pressure in what was a relatively pluralistic society.

In China, the consolidated structure within the party was eroded in a quite different manner, not through a slow process of development, as in Yugoslavia, but by questioning the party itself, or at least a good number of its suborganizations, on a cultural-revolutionary basis. The result was dysfunctional in two respects: on the one hand, it became necessary to tolerate the military as a factor of order for a time, whereas in all other variants of Marxist theory the military only has a service function.[741] On the other hand, the institutional vacuum produced the very contrary of what the Cultural Revolutionaries had been aiming for. Since the laboriously established institutions of organized mass communication had been shattered, once the situation had normalized and a certain apathy had settled in, the leadership found itself further away from the masses than ever. Now that the first timid attempts have been made at reviving country-wide institutionalization of representation (Tenth Party Congress 1973, Trade Union Congresses), it still has to be seen whether this structured communication can be rapidly restored.

The Chinese leadership does, however, seem to have learned from its experience. During the most recent mobilization campaign (the anti-Confucius campaign of 1974) the movement was subject to severe control and the formation of new "Red Guards" was banned.

The flood of partial protest expressed by the masses in 1974 in wall newspapers, the so-called *dazibao*, seems to mark an attempt at an original compromise between controlled development from above and free initiative from the masses from below. Whereas Soviet protest had to take the channel of total opposition in the *Samizdat* movement, it seems that in China there is a way of channeling protest within the system without basically jeopardizing the system. Whereas in the Soviet Union the principle of "criticism and self-criticism" scarcely succeeded in rousing spontaneous impulses from society, the new statutes of China's Communist party (Article 5) seek to provide increased protection for criticism under the protection of minorities:

> Party members have the right to criticize the party organization and the leading functionaries at all levels and to submit suggestions to them. If a party member has a different opinion on the resolutions or instructions of the party organization, he is entitled to maintain his opinion and to appeal directly to any higher organ, up to the Central Committee and the Chairman of the Central Committee. It is absolutely inadmissible to stifle criticism and to inflict repressive measures."[742]

Marxist theorists, too, have not failed to recognize the fact that revolutionary movements become subject to erosive processes, particularly once the integrating effect produced by the class enemy both from within and from outside has worn off. This occurs with the elimination of the bourgeoisie within the country and the extension of coexistence with the bourgeoisie outside the socialist camp.

The high degree of social mobilization, which cannot be converted into an institutionalized system of roles, then even constitutes a danger to the system. A powerful mobile mass will increasingly come into conflict with a revolutionary elite, which has difficulties in deciding whether it should have the role of "reds" or "experts," and the mass will usually be unwilling to reintegrate itself in the former traditional milieu from which it was uprooted.

3. Permanent mobilization favors *personality cults*, even though socialist leaders deny this theory. In relatively unstructured situations of permanent mobilization socialist leaders cannot prevent their followers from calling them "great chairman" or "máximo lider," even if they seriously want to, for the priority role is indeed very much contested in certain systems. This applies in particular to China, where in times of "de-Maoization" there have been countercults against Mao, such as those around Marshall P'eng and Te-huai and around Liu Shao-ch'i. Defenders of Maoism even deny the existence of a personality cult over here, with the argument that there is no "commodity fetishism" such as that of the Western souvenir hunters.

But the sources show that Maoism is not exactly an iconoclastic movement if we consider a quotation from the same author in a report on the No. 3 Shanghai Coal and Steel Works: "Before the pictures of Chairman Mao, the workers in the different workshops swore to drive forward the revolution and to promote production, to defy the high temperatures and to achieve high production figures, to do away with old habits and to break new ground, and in doing so, to prove their loyalty to Chairman Mao."[743] Even when personality cult does not take on religious traits, there is the danger of a paternalistic policy developing, with the initiative coming solely from above, as once expressed by Che Guevara: "The initiative usually comes from Fidel or from the Supreme Command of the Revolution and is explained to the people, who then take it up as their own."[744]

4. In the economic sphere, permanent mobilization proved to be detrimental to labor productivity, and in groups that made genuine efforts but overstrained themselves, in particular, it resulted in a *rise in accidents at work*, due to lapses of attention caused by overtiredness (see Chapter 7, Section 2). Even apart from the numerous special campaigns in economy, socialist states have also occasionally run counter to another goal of socialism through overmobilization, namely the assumption of their protective function, especially with regard to young people. Again and again, warning

voices came up in Chinese newspapers, requesting more leisure and spare time for young people and criticizing the fact that permanent mobilization overstrained their health.[745] Sometimes school students' delegations had to put in a claim for such self evident rights as the right to eight hours' sleep.

5. A negative effect of the overstraining caused by mass mobilization is the development of ever *new forms of apathy*. The nuclear physicist, Andrei Sakharov, mentioned in an interview in 1973 that "exhaustion, apathy and cynicism" were spreading in the Soviet Union. This is not merely an assertion from an opponent to the system. Soviet sociology, too, has tried to investigate nonparticipation. When asked about the reasons for nonparticipation in social actions, 48% of the sample stated that they had not been requested to participate, and 44% answered that they had not been prepared for participation.[746] Even at the climax of mass campaigns large sectors of the population keep away from the hectic events in the streets. Critical eyewitnesses of the Chinese events have also pointed to the "bourgeois normalcy of life" on Sundays and after working hours, even during the Cultural Revolution.[747]

People who are mobilized for a limited period will also easily fall back into apathy, particularly when frequent changes of course, such as those resulting from the Chinese "policy of leaps," make overcommitment even appear dangerous in the light of the uncertain future. However, not only the fear of a change of course, but also a physical weariness is reflected in the numerous requests from Chinese workers, students, and school children that Sundays and evenings should be free from mass events. Even in the high-circulation literature of a number of authors, such as Feng Ting, "the right to private happiness" has been propagated as a claim compatible with socialism. The stagnating or decreasing membership rates of some youth associations, such as the Communist League of China, were a reaction to overmobilization. Young people are becoming more and more resourceful in finding ways of placing the minimum commitment required of them in the most unpolitical organizations (such as in the "Society for Sports and Technology" in the German Democratic Republic). It seems that some forms of partial apathy are the very result of overmobilization, because, in the light of the unstructured campaigns, the family and small groups are again gaining a greater integration value for the individual.

After years of overheated mobilization, organizational forms such as the family, nationality, and religious communities, which Marxist ideology regards as leftovers, are experiencing an unforeseeable revival. The increasing importance of sects in the Soviet Union and the growing self-awareness of nationalities in all Eastern European states are signs of this evolution. The social organizations, which are thus gaining greater popularity, can occasionally act as outspoken advocators of the right to relaxation. Cardinal Wyszyński, for example, compared "Sunday shifts" with "Egyptian slave labor" in a public sermon.[748] Even in countries like North Korea and North Vietnam, which had distinguished themselves by their unflagging fighting spirit, signs of exhaustion and the wish for more rest periods were observed on repeated occasions, and these created an immunizing effect against renewed attempts at mobilization.

The more complex a transformation society becomes, the less successful the stop-and-go methods of the struggle period appear, and the less willing the population becomes to mobilize. In a relatively highly developed country like Poland, it took only 10 years for a poem like the one by Adam Wazyk to circulate all over Poland, and later over the whole world.[749]

> *Fourier, the dreamer had so prettily predicted*
> *that lemonade would flow in the seas.*
> *Does it flow?*
> *They drink sea water and scream:*
> *Lemonade!*
> *Back at home they vomit discreetly. . . .*
> *They ran to us shouting:*
> *"Under socialism a cut finger does not hurt."*
> *They felt the pain.*
> *They lost faith.*

6.   The ideal type of *cadre administration* would seem to correspond to a system of mass mobilization and could be a functional equivalent of the rationally standardized administration that has developed in capitalism. During the transformation period, most socialist countries developed a type of cadre administration without rigid frontiers between cadres and noncadres. These were management administrations without elites or specialization, without full-time attributions, and without prespecified job descriptions laid down in regulations for the administration offices. As the political system became more sophisticated, however, this type of administration gave way to a bureaucracy in Weber's sense of the term, even though China for a while obstinately refused to accept this evidence and was seeking to counteract the development with the hsia-fang system.[750]

7.   As the dull monotony of everyday life sets in more and more in a socialist system, once the first wave of revolutionary enthusiasm has died down (a GDR poet has called his state "the most boring state in the world," although he basically approved the system), so mass participation threatens to degenerate into nothing but an *instrument of faction struggles.* This was the case with some of the campaigns in the struggle for power between Liu and Mao, where mass mobilization developed from a means to an end, even prior to the Thermidor. In the Politbureau's discussions on communization other factional lines seem to have existed earlier as well, with Chou En-lai, backed by the military, seemingly holding a different position from that of Mao and Liu.

During long crises, these political faction fights run the risk of developing into the functional equivalent of system irrationalities in capitalism. Material expectations are also used in mobilization and countermobilization on frequent occasions. During the Cultural Revolution, Mao was able to employ frustrated students who felt their mobility chances threatened by a rigidified party bureaucracy with a heavy preponderance of former bourgeois and intellectual classes. The puritanical words ought not to obscure insight into the actual interests involved. On the other hand, however, the Liu group had also promised gratifications and had even used material stimuli in the form of back payment of wages during the Cultural Revolution, in order to win the workers over to their side. Although the "tactics of constant manoeuvering and balancing" between the groups do not necessarily result in a "military-bureaucratic dictatorship," as Soviet criticism occasionally claims, it does lead to a zig-zag course that makes it very difficult to establish long-term priorities and repeatedly leads to hasty concessions being made to specific groups.[751]

8.   The arousal of strong *aggression*, which constitutes a central factor of Maoist mass mobilization, seems to give rise to further dysfunctions. These are due in particular to the tendency for people to work off their aggression spontaneously in anomic actions (a tendency that is more marked in China than in other socialist countries), such that these actions can no longer be sufficiently controlled even by the mobilizers.

Revolutionary zeal, kindled through permanent depiction of the enemy image, can even turn against the organization itself, if the enemy fails to materialize due to a lack of resistance. In the second phase of the Chinese Cultural Revolution, activities were partly directed at the country itself, after a number of bureaucracies had been crushed. The fiercest radicals began to attack the "Committee of the Cultural Revolution" within the Central Committee, whose first deputy was Mao's wife, Chiang Ching, and the Red Guards carried out "internal purges" and "rectification campaigns" within their own ranks. It is difficult as yet to assess the long-term consequence of the Chinese campaign policy. In the early 1970s, the exuberance that accompanied the Cultural Revolution was considerably dammed up in China, and today even Western European admirers of the People's Republic of China point out (obviously in disagreement with Maoist groups in Europe) that excessively fierce attacks and self-purges lead to "petit-bourgeois personalization." Discipline instead of spontaneity, theoretical preparation instead of *action directe*, and the collective knowledge of scientists instead of *connaissance directe* are being upheld again as the features of a fighter with the right attitude.[752]

Considering the fluctuations within the Chinese educational system, it would seem that this style of reeducation and mobilization is not in line with Western concepts of emancipated education based on discursive communication, and that, in the long run, it is likely to be detrimental to the continuous passing down of the socialist ideological heritage.

3. Anomic participation

The mobilization figures of socialist systems are certainly impressive at all levels, but they cannot hide the fact that a good deal of manipulated pseudoparticipation exists, which, even in severely controlled socialist societies, is counteracted by frequent anomic participation. Even though the data is incomplete, the figures for anomic participation seem, on the average, to be higher in socialist countries than in comparable capitalist systems. (See Table 106.) The reasons for this are:

1. insufficient consideration of conflict in the theory of socialist states;
2. abolition of institutionalized channels for conflict;
3. the new trend of cadres becoming alienated from the masses, in spite of the permanent rotation of elites and mobilization of nonelites.

Table 106

Anomic participation (deaths from domestic political violence)

Country	1948-67	Peak			
Hungary	40,000	1956	20,000	1957	20,000
North Vietnam	28,000	1954	28,000		
Cuba	4,200	1958	2,500		
GDR	140	1953	79		
Soviet Union	399	1956	100	1962	287
Poland	553	1956	536		
Albania	782	1956	778		
North Korea	82	1954	70		
Czechoslovakia	74	1951	60		
Yugoslavia	28	1953	21		
Bulgaria	1				
for comparison:					
United States	320	1965	105	1967	99
France	112	1962	81		
Italy	109				
Japan	28	1954	16		
Spain	55	1948	39		
FRG	10	1967	4		

Source: Taylor-Hudson, op. cit. pp. 110 ff.

CONCLUSION

TOWARD A THEORY
OF SOCIALIST SOCIETIES

1. Contradictions in the system policy of socialism

Socialist policy is *output* orientated. It serves the realization of goals that are ranked according to a relatively consistent system of ideological pronouncements and postulations and which, over the long term, are operationalized into material policy guidelines by Communist parties and planning elites. Thus, if it is to do justice to the subject, comparative research into socialism cannot simply stop at the "inputism" of most earlier theories. The latter concentrated primarily on the decision input of socialist states and did not look into the consequences of these decisions for the individual citizen.

A comparison of material output as it appears in the form of policies within socialist countries shows, however, that *policies* are frequently more contradictory than the forces that act in the decision-making process. The system's input is more consistent than its output. Socialist countries attempt to analyze inconsistencies with the term *contradictions*, and it is in contradiction theory that the greatest ideological changes are coming about in socialist systems today.

Over the past few years, social science in socialist countries has moved considerably away from abstract scholastics in the direction of concrete research into social processes, particularly as far as the theory of contradictions in socialism is concerned. Earlier Soviet literature still explained contradictions as stemming from "violation of the objective laws of the development of socialist society." According to this theory, "abstract conflict potential" would also disappear with the transition from socialism to communism. More recently, in the confrontation with socialist pluralists, it has been stressed that central planning prevents existing contradictions from developing to their full centrifugal potential.[753] At the beginning of the 1970s it was realized that although the majority of contradictions were linked to the continued existence of the capitalist world system, there were, in fact, certain contradictions that were seen for the first time to be reinforced by the very spread of socialism itself. In GDR ideology this more favorable attitude toward conflict was reflected in the euphemistic term "socialist human community," in Ulbricht's bid to play down contradictions.[754]

The Soviet literature still tends to classify contradictions in capitalism as a zero-sum game that has to end with the annihilation of one of the parties to the dispute, whereas in socialism the common fundamental interests provide a basis for the successful resolution of contradictions.

Linguistic sophistications, such as the distinction between "fundamental contradiction" and "chief contradiction," or "contradiction" and "antagonism,"[755] have been abandoned. In 1972, Jürgen Kuczynski introduced a new turn into the debate with the theory that antagonistic contradictions could indeed exist in a socialist system, even though the chief reason for antagonistic contradictions of this type (namely the contradiction between capital and labor) was no longer present.[756] Kuczynski sees the chief criterion of an antagonistic contradiction not so much in the class content of the contradiction but rather in its potential for resolution—as the guardians of orthodoxy critically noted. Kuczynski's idea that the conflicts end through a type of zero-sum game, that is, with the annihilation of one of the parties to the conflict (in the case of the class struggle, the bourgeoisie), is derived from the traditional concept of the class conflict. Liquidation of the "imperialist conflict party," which is Kuczynski's concern, is all the more important for his theory in that a large number of the contradictions in socialism are explained either through *genetic causes* (development of socialism out of capitalism) or through *outside historical causes* (contradictions brought into socialism from outside). This theory certainly contributes toward positivizing the contradiction debate that has been conducted mainly in abstract terms to date.

The system requirement calls for a scientifically founded system policy, which, in turn, presupposes a planned effort to overcome those contradictions that still exist in socialism.

Despite this requirement, the contradictions that do arise are generally put down to *motivational weakness on the part of individuals* rather than to *structural shortcomings on the part of the system.* During the Stalin era, in particular, whole armies of "saboteurs and defeatists" had to be found. Even in China, where Mao's contradiction theory would allow the real contradictions to be analyzed without embarrassment, the Chinese still tend to concentrate on individuals and their shortcomings. At the Tenth Party Congress of the Communist Party of China, the jubilation at the "crushing of the Lin-Piao Clique" took up half the space of the sparse declarations published. The "extreme proletarian indignation" at their goings-on was expressed solely in the denunciation of motivational shortcomings on the part of certain "bourgeois careerists," "conspirators," "two-faced rogues," "renegades," "swindlers," and "traitors," just to quote the more frequently used designations.[757]

This type of hunting out of shortcomings is detrimental to the scientific claim of socialism. It is even doubtful whether the hunt for ever new "revisionists," who are then found guilty, has a legitimating effect on the population in the long term. There are no signs as yet that the process of forming a "socialist consciousness" can be conducted outside the framework of the general principles of the psychology of learning and motivation. This psychology would certainly not view the permanent hunt for scapegoats as a factor serving to increase the educational effect of transformation processes. In a large number of countries, socialism is sufficiently legitimated today through majority approval and objective success for the leaderships of socialist transitional societies to be able to afford to adopt a relaxed and scientific method when it comes to tracking down shortcomings and dysfunctions.

If we attempt to classify the indicators used to measure the "achievements" of socialist systems and list the reinforcement variables and interference variables against each of these so as to clarify relationships within the system, we arrive at an initial typology of contradictions and dysfunctions. Contrary to contradiction theory, however, an objective classification cannot restrict itself to the genetic or external reasons behind contradictions, but must include certain contradictions that are acknowledged to stem from the very dynamics of the socialist system, that is, which constitute the reverse side of the advantages of the system. Some of the contradictions in the output sphere of the system are due to the incompatibility of different goals at particular development stages, or to the incompatibility of goals and political instruments or even just to dysfunctional effects of incompatible instruments at times when the set goals are basically within reach. These contradictions can be attributed in part to motivational causes and in part to structural ones.

Socialist theory started out as criticism of capitalism. Only a small amount of preliminary theoretical work was conducted on the theory of socialism in the time from Marx to Lenin. In view of the theoretical cleft between general *goal culture* and postrevolutionary *policy analysis*, it was not surprising that people worked on the erroneous assumption that a whole series of problems would be overcome through abolition of the greatest obstacle to change in capitalist systems, namely, private ownership of the means of production. Socialist systems did indeed succeed in removing a large number of obstacles to radical innovation that continued to live on in capitalist systems. There were thus structural *reinforcement variables* for each of the individual goals, which can be appropriately classified. These should, in principle, have led to socialist systems performing better than capitalist systems. Alongside these *reinforcement variables*, however, came an even greater number of *interference variables* in the socialist transformation process. These robbed socialism as a social formation of part of its potential success and had not been sufficiently anticipated by socialist theory.

Interference variables and dysfunctions occurred on both structural and motivational grounds. The *structural grounds* can be listed as follows:

1. partial incompatibility of *goal packages*;
2. a number of cases where the goals of socialism are incompatible with the particular *instruments* employed to achieve them;
3. incompatibility of *different instruments* employed, which produce the need to choose the lesser evil wherever possible.

The separation of goals from instruments—which brings a dichotomy of *policy* and *operations* in its wake at the practical administration level—has been disputed in recent organizational sociology. This dichotomy has even been criticized by Max Weber. Socialist countries have discussed similar problems, although under different terminologies. China's *"Reds" approach* works on the basis of an organizational model that sees the goals of organization as only being attainable through improvement of human communication structures. The *expert approach*, on the other hand, presumes that application of division of labor and modern technology is the best instrument for realizing the goals.

While the theory generally does not acknowledge structural dysfunctions, the first two forms of *motivational* dysfunction, at least, frequently have to answer for the whole range of shortcomings, in socialist systems. Once again, there are three such forms:

4. motivational interference variables due to the *continued existence of the dominant capitalist system*;
5. motivational errors due to *bourgeois relics in the thinking* of socialist populations;
6. erroneous motivational development on grounds of *socialist ideology itself* at times when the ideology or a part of it becomes incompatible with certain realities in the development of socialist states.

These six types of contradiction can be traced in all four goal areas of socialism.

1. *a*. For most socialist movements, *redistribution* in the production sphere was not conceived of as an end in itself but as an instrument for creating the basis of a more efficient and more democratic economy. All socialist systems adopted the view that the gradual approach via factory legislation, expansion of codetermination, and central state control of the economy could not produce the same success as a fully-fledged socialization of ownership of the means of production. Social democrat Eduard Bernstein's tenet that "there can be more socialism in a good factory law than in the nationalization of hundreds of enterprises and works" was rejected by all the Communist parties that proceeded to radical redistribution.

The redistribution measures taken by socialist states must be seen in conjunction with other goal concepts and especially with:

1. the goal of economic *efficiency* as a prerequisite for the construction of communism;
2. the goal of *participation* for the development of a democratic economy.

The guidance that Marx gives on the organizational form of a socialized economy in his description of the "Commune" (MEW, Vol. 17, p. 339f) was not sufficient to allow an analysis of the consequences of different organizational models, implemented under a system of giant monopolies with a vast bureaucratic machinery. Karl Korsch was the Marxist theorist who after Marx and Engels recognized most clearly that mere nationalization still did not necessarily imply true socialist socialization. He tried to steer a theoretical course between the two extremes of a merely nationalized, functionary-administered industry and a syndicalist cooperative model with group ownership. On the one hand, he wanted to avoid the "bureaucratic schematization and rigidification" that kills off "private initiative," and on the other hand he wanted to prevent the sought-after "industrial autonomy" from being understood in such a way that only a type of consumer capitalism or producer capitalism developed, based on special ownership for a specific group.[758] A *consumer capitalism*, which Korsch did not exclude, even with predominant nationalization of ownership of the means of production, has not developed anywhere. No socialist country has evolved a system where the consumers' interests predominate and producers can only assert their interests indirectly. A type of *producer capitalism*, in which the interests of those involved in group ownership predominate is, however, to be seen in the Yugoslav model. In this model, the industrial autonomy of the individual plants has strongly hampered the steering capacity of the state planning authorities as far as the interests of society as a whole are concerned. It is of secondary importance here that no provision has been made for the ownership rights of socialized means of production to be allocated to the workers' collectives. According to Marxist theory (and contrary to a number of anarchosyndicalist proposals) this would be irreconcilable with socialism.

In most socialist systems, redistribution policy became a more-or-less independent factor during the initial revolutionary phase and had to violate the goal of optimization of all the fundamental goals of socialism, in order to first create the preconditions for a new social formation.

Once the redistribution phase had been completed, all effort then had to be concentrated just as one-sidedly on maximizing efficiency, as a medium-term goal, in order to restore the economy and consolidate the socialist countries' existence in world society. This took place during the NEP period in the Soviet Union (particularly after the 1923/24 scissors crisis) and during the 1950s in the Eastern European people's democracies.

The "excessive redistribution" generally associated with socialism has in the main been measured by Western critics on the basis of the values of Western society.[759] A more objective yardstick for measuring excessive redistribution would be the extent to which redistribution threatens to become incompatible with the other goal concepts of socialism. It is seen that redistribution is tremendously popular to begin with and proceeds with the unprecedented spontaneous participation of the masses. As soon as the second redistribution phase commences, however, which involves the expropriation of small farmers and proprietors in trade and industry as well, this marks the start of one-sided goal maximization coupled with waning participation on the part of the masses.

A further criterion could be the justification of most of the excessive measures on grounds of the need to break "bourgeois resistance." Not infrequently, however, this target has been overshot, and the remaining bourgeoisie have been made answerable for all the shortcomings of imperfect control of the economy and inequality of distribution. At times, this leads on to the search for ever more scapegoats. In the case of Cuba, which started off with an unparalleled participation of the masses, the measures taken against absenteeism and lack of work discipline since 1971 have revealed the masses themselves as being to blame, as a result of insufficient socialist motivation. It is at this point that substitution of the Communist leadership for the masses, on whose behalf they claim to speak, is completed.

The development of socialist countries shows that socialism is clearly superior in terms of the will and capacity to effect redistribution (see Part I). The serious disparities that it has still been impossible to eliminate do not have the same impact as in capitalist systems because fragmentation of groups and interests is not so far advanced, even if a rudimentary pluralism does develop again after an initial totalitarian phase.

Ideological steering in capitalism leads to a situation where, even with much and varied agitation by socialist groups, the underprivileged still compare themselves more with those in the same situation and with their own past situation when setting their expectations than with better-off groups.[760] In socialist countries, on the other hand, equalization propaganda has on the whole led to a more equal level of aspiration, and socialist policy must do justice to this. Despite all the left-over privileges for individual groups—particularly for the leading cadres—the differences are less marked in everyday life than in capitalist systems. Where they do start to spark off conflict, the ideology of equality has a greater chance of closing the gap again between the target situation and the actual situation. This gap is obscured, however, to such an extent—not so much by the relative increase in the usefulness of certain groups or the diverging of interests but through selective allowances—that it does not lead to open conflict in the same way as in highly developed capitalist systems.

b. The fact that no socialist country to date has come anywhere near achieving a balance in the realization of the four basic goals of socialist societies is due not least to the low starting level of productive resources.

Premature socialist revolution in a developing country with a low level of productive resources has meant that *efficiency*, in particular, has been a weak link in the chain right from the start. It can even be disputed whether initial accumulation does not need to be complete before a socialist system can be successfully established. There is something to be said for Marx having viewed economic efficiency as a precondition for the realization of the other three goal values rather than as an equally-ranking goal in itself. In the "German ideology," a high level of development of production resources was shown to be a precondition for the fight against alienation, because, in Marx's opinion, without "this practical prerequisite" "shortages would only become more generalized and pressing needs would set off the fight for bare necessities and the whole mess would start all over again" (MEW, Vol. 3, p. 34f).

The fight against alienation was obviously aimed at higher goals than just the self-evident efficiency of the system. Even the level of productive resources in the highest-developed capitalist countries today is not such as to allow all regulation in the distribution sphere to be abandoned, even if a transition to socialism nowadays could be guaranteed with a lower drop in productivity, thanks to larger majorities in the socialist transformation phase.

Problems also arose for socialist states from the fact that, despite warnings from Marx and Engels, the distribution sphere repeatedly threatened to become an independent factor within the medium-term goal schedule of socialist systems and to the fact that the rapid growth that was made possible by socialist development of productive resources developed dysfunctions that had not been foreseen in Marxist theory. The socialist elites—similarly to elites in capitalist systems—tended increasingly to regard growth and economic efficiency per se as having a legitimating effect.

In the Marxist goal concept, efficiency was to be of an instrumental nature, designed to master the realm of necessity. With increasing prosperity, however, came the danger that the maximization of prosperity would develop from an instrument into a goal and would maintain its instrumental nature at best by way of justification ideology for the state bureaucracy (as in organized capitalist societies). Further parallels were seen in the claim of the "objective character" of the individual developments in socialist countries. The requirement for scientific findings to be expressed in terms of objective laws came to be extended to ever more questions of detail as the political economy of socialism applied itself in an increasingly sophisticated manner to the empirical study of problems and conflicts in society. Parallels with "bourgeois" technocrat positivism also meet the eye, albeit with the difference that recent positivists formulate their pronouncements very carefully, as statements of trends or hypotheses, whereas recent Marxist justification ideologies, with their determination to formulate social laws with the precision of scientific findings, have more in common with the earlier positivism of the nineteenth century.

Apologists assume that despite these parallels between socialism and organized capitalism the consequences of the particular developments are not identical. In theoretical terms, rapid growth could have less negative consequences in a comprehensively planned system than in capitalism. Nevertheless, there are a series of disproportionate developments here, too, which show that the claim to system planning is not yet completely fulfilled and that planning is still predominantly orientated toward hard output data, giving too little consideration to all the other social processes.

Even within the purely economic developments there have, however, been marked disproportions. Those that developed between agriculture and industry and between the individual industrial sectors would have been less serious had the distribution functions of the socialist state been sufficiently well developed. This was not the case, however. Thus a number of destabilizing effects of rapid economic growth came about, similar to those also found in capitalist growth processes. Despite the absolute growth rates in the utility of all groups of society, the share received by individual groups—and consumers as a whole—seemed to be too small, and this, in turn, led to the "revolution of rising expectations." Rapid urbanization and forced mobilization of people for education, who were later unable to find jobs that fitted their newly raised requirements, constituted further results of growth processes whose consequences had not been sufficiently well thought out beforehand. Finally, certain strata of the "first hour revolutionaries," such as children of the technical intelligentsia with a certain lead in education and mobility opportunities, showed tendencies of becoming independent. This led to discontent and at times to claims against the bureaucratized cadre rule, ranging from the Hungarian revolution in 1956 to the Chinese cultural revolution. In the cultural revolution it was precisely this underprivileging of those who had only recently been mobilized for education which constituted a triggering factor in the recruitment of Red Guards.[761] Contrary to similar experiences in twentieth-century capitalist systems, anomic outbursts of protest have never, however, led to a fundamental theoretic questioning of the socialist system.

c. Some of the contradictions in the field of the *protective functions* of the socialist state likewise result from the temporary incompatibility of socialist goals. Protection was raised out of the individualistic, group-bound concept of bourgeois states, in which the formal, statutory aspect of equality and the need for the protection for group interests predominated. Protection policy has, however, lost part of its social impetus through the tenacity of the dominant capitalist world system. In the light of the long-drawn-out competition between the systems, the protective function of the socialist state shifted increasingly toward stabilization of its outer borders. It is with the growing development of the system's economic efficiency and the increasing success in the distribution sphere that the greatest change in the protective function has come about, however. The protective function derived advantage from socialist system policy in that it did not simply conceive of itself as a statutory regulator of the particular position of a specific group in the distribution struggle—as is by and large the case in capitalist systems. Protection was never just the "maintenance of property levels" under conditions of inequality but was closely woven in with the other goal of redistribution.

Nevertheless, as development progressed, precisely these two interdependent goals came partly to contradict each other. Since new incentives had to be constantly found to increase efficiency and since the surplus of purchasing power meant that increases in nominal wages could not fulfill the lever and stimulation function alone in the long term, the more highly developed socialist states have taken recourse to allowing individual groups and interests collective (and also individual) protection and welfare facilities. The price that had to be paid for this development was the partial intensification of the inequalities that had recently arisen in a large number of sectors, namely housing construction, savings, life assurance, additional old-age and risk insurance (see Chapter 8).

d. It was the goal of *participation* that underwent the greatest deformation. During the phase when redistribution was at the forefront, transformation proceeded with a great deal of organized and spontaneous participation of the masses (see Chapters 1 and 12). As soon as the second phase had begun, however, where the prime concern was to increase economic efficiency (except in China as of 1958), manipulated pseudoparticipation began to predominate. This was perpetuated and ideologically secured through the transfer of organization models such as "democratic centralism" and "one-man leadership," which may have seemed essential during the revolutionary fight for power, to all areas of the economy and society.

The requirement for symmetrical optimization of the four basic goals of socialism should, however, be accompanied by a warning that it is all too easy to know better after the event. Schematic symmetry would be just as difficult to achieve as would a strictly planned transformation process that abides by an ex-ante schedule. There are several reasons for this:

a. The socialist transitional societies to date have been a *minority in the dominant capitalist world system.* Since there have only been a few autonomous and autochthonous transformation processes (see Chapter 5, Section 5), the socialist countries have had to take account of a wide range of unforeseen internal and external policy difficulties, due to the fact that world revolution has not come about. Leftist criticism, adopting a know-all attitude subsequent to the event, today even goes as far as reproaching Lenin with having got caught up in the concessions of the NEP period and having failed to carry out a systematic planning and nationalization policy in all fields. This criticism, however, overlooks the fact that in foreign policy terms this would presumably have marked the end of the first socialist experiment. Even Yugoslavia, China, and Cuba, the only three systems with anything resembling the opportunity to conduct an autonomous socialist development, had to accept a wide range of inconsistencies on foreign and domestic policy counts. Only future transformation processes—particularly those that are not pursued by a single country in isolation, such as Chile—will be able to do greater justice to the claim to comprehensive system planning during the transformation phase as well.

b. It is impossible to conceive of a socialist-democratic transformation process in which the status-threatened owners of the means of production will not try to stop, or at least to slow down, the modification process through *obstruction* or sabotage (even in cases where the transformation process has majority support). The ordeal of Chilean socialism up to 1973 supplied a wealth of observation material on this. Depending on the strength of these powers of resistance, short-term concessions or lapses into repression will not be completely unavoidable. Socialist-minded scientists, such as Sweezy, Huberman, and Baran, who obtained their first opportunity to advise revolutionaries in action during the Cuban revolution (while all earlier leaderships had believed they could master the situation in theoretical terms on the basis of the classicists or their own ad-hoc theories) have thus rightly put forward the case for not stopping at the half-way stage. Semisocialist solutions in the question of ownership become all the more problematical the more systematically the bourgeois direct their obstruction policy against the majority and the more support they receive from abroad. It should not be forgotten that Castro's nationalization policy initially constituted a response to North America's obstruction policy (see Chapter 1).

c. An inwardly consistent system policy is difficult enough in times of peace, without foreign threats of intervention. During times of stress it is made all the more difficult by *differences of opinion in the leading socialist party.* Bourgeois pluralists in the main work on the assumption that any projections that are made with respect to the public interest and which form the basis of a goal catalog (such as that postulated here) will only ever represent the opinions of a few groups. It is, however, seen that certain concepts of "public interest" do develop a capacity to attract general consensus and do not necessarily just have to represent the opinions of the cadres in authority (provided that the "participation" goal is not dictatorially trimmed down). This was, in fact, shown by opinion polls carried out during the first phase in Cuba.[762] An attempt to press on ahead too rapidly in optimizing a goal value also frequently has the function of reinforcing a majority opinion within the party, of creating "faits accomplis," and of carrying along the still "stunned" and straggling majority in their wake. In their initial phase, socialist societies are generally confronted with the paradox that the necessary knowledge and time required for comprehensive, all-round participation is only available in a socially satisfied, affluent society. In times of revolutionary change, where an extreme scarcity of commodities prevails, the temptation for the leadership to substitute itself for the masses becomes particularly great. In this way socialist revolutionary elites repeatedly violate the view that "shock tactics" are only to be applied for short innovation periods[763] and attempt to apply them over longer periods of time in order to achieve different goals, thereby overstraining the majority of the population.

2. Even more frequently than incompatibility of the overall goals themselves, during the transformation phase we see *incompatibility between goals and the instruments* used to achieve them. The repressive instruments, which are applied, firstly, for redistribution and subsequently for restoring the efficiency of the economic system, have dysfunctional consequences for the other chief goals, namely for expansion of the state's protective function and for expansion of participation opportunities for the population. Permanent mass mobilization serves at best to increase efficiency for the short term. Over the long term it generally has an unfavorable effect on the protection sphere (health policy, prevention of accidents at work) and on the efficiency sphere (on an increase in labor productivity). Doctrinarian restriction to immaterial gratifications results in a fall

in efficiency in the same way as too much emphasis on material gratifications threatens to cancel out some of the achievements in the distribution and redistribution sphere again. Planning and organization are vital for the comprehensive system planning of socialism, but oversteering and overstaffing, new privileges for the cadres, and other phenomena are harmful to the participation sector in particular, and tend instead to lead to the consolidation of bureaucratic rule.

Individual operationalized goals (such as growth, or output of people with higher education) repeatedly threaten to become independent factors. Socialist countries at times tend to allow themselves to plan further than their actual needs in matters of higher education —even more so than for their growth targets (see Chapter 1, Section 3).

3. The most frequent contradictions that occur are the *contradictions between different instruments employed for achieving different goals.* This is the field where the problems are most similar in capitalist and socialist systems. There is, however, one difference in that capitalist systems—provided they keep to a pluralist system— are frequently incapable of concentrating their instruments on one specific objective and of appropriately counteracting the deployment of instruments in other spheres. On this plane of conflict it is the socialist politicians who are most flexible when it comes to choosing the lesser evil. It has been seen that in the event of conflict they prefer to opt for inflationary pressure rather than for deflation and unemployment (in the same way as capitalist welfare states) and to opt for an increase in the accident rate at work and a reduction in labor productivity rather than run the risk of a fall in output. They will adopt a flexible pricing policy rather than force redistribution on further at stages in development where the increase of efficiency has priority (see Chapter 2, Section 3) and will neglect the equality of the tax system rather than touch upon the efficiency of the extractive capacity of the tax system.

The insistence on planning cannot hide the fact that in a large number of socialist systems it is only economic planning that is truly comprehensive at best, while other areas (population policy, environment planning, land utilization, educational policy) still suffer extensively from the "anarchy of production," as in organized capitalism.

4. Motivational interference variables *resulting from the continued existence of the capitalist system* have a particular influence in the field of "efficiency in the production sphere" since socialist countries did not receive Marshall aid or development aid, did not permit any foreign capital investment (partly so as to retain their independence and partly because they were boycotted by capitalist

countries), or were subjected to embargo policies or specific types of economic warfare by capitalist countries (see Chapter 4, Section 5).

5. Erroneous motivational development also came about throughout the *"bourgeois" relics in the attitudes and thinking* of the populations of socialist states. Some of these dysfunctional interference factors for the socialist policy of simultaneous maximization of several target packages were even due to socialist policy itself. Land distribution during the initial expropriation phase, for example, marked the first move to create a large number of potential opponents to the subsequent collectivization phase (see Chapter 1, Section 3). And again, once the initial enthusiasm had died down, new forms of absenteeism and "passivism" developed as a result of the state's distribution policy, whereby a surplus of money remains set against a shortage of the commodities in demand. On the other hand, however, facets such as black markets, discrimination against women, and the maintenance of prestige hierarchies in the structure of trade and industry (which have much in common with capitalist societies— Chapter 2, Section 2) came about without necessarily being caused by specific measures taken by the socialist state. In these areas, socialist politicians can in any case be reproached with the fact that they did not take more energetic countermeasures or did not reckon sufficiently with the population's ideological inertia. It would seem, however, that once the dominant class conflict has died down in socialist systems, a whole series of problems that had virtually been considered eliminated as dying relics—namely nationalism, religion, individualism in leisure time, and so forth—comes to the surface again.

6. Apart from these interference variables, for which the socialist system is not always fully responsible, there are a number of interference variables that *develop precisely from socialist ideology itself* and tend to be all the more intense, the more the cadres have internalized the value scale of Marxist ideology. Interenterprise trade (see Chapter 4), with its specific socialist corruption phenomena such as *blat* and *tolkach*, is not prompted by a capitalist mentality but through the very fact of business managers taking the trouble to abide by the rules of the planned economy and fulfill their targets. Given the organizational and material bottlenecks, they would not always be able to do this without an unforeseen and even unlawful measure of their own initiative. The forcing of frugality ideals, the overzealousness of the cadres in redistribution, and the application of repression could perhaps be avoided with improved ideological and organizational steering. These are nonetheless generally features of the initial years of socialist transformation processes. More difficult

Figure 4

Schedule of a number of frequently occurring contradictions in the goal and instrument field of socialist policy

	Production	Distribution	Legitimation
REDISTRIBUTION	collectivization agriculture private plots mechanization nationalization of industry urbani- concen- zation tration	wage policy individual social consumption consumption phasing out of strata system town/ men/ branch of country women industry man. regional status/ brainwork diffs. prestige indirect redistribution price tax social edu- policy policy policy cation policy	party oligarchy office patronage cooptation of elites
EFFICIENCY	growth output labor productivity stability growth employ- prices ment autonomy and innovation	consumption	ideology planning repression material gratifications
PROTECTION	unemployment accidents at work work time/ leisure time choice of career and job trade union functions	health policy social policy housing policy environment policy	legal policy
PARTICIPATION	one-man leadership participation at the workplace	participation	organization mass campaigns anomic participation

425

to combat are the motivational interference variables that repeatedly occur at subsequent stages due to certain biases in ideology, such as "growth fetishism," "ton ideology," the neglect of certain sciences, neglect of management training, some forms of socialist wastage of material and energy, and conspicuous production (see Chapter 4).

In the light of the experiences of socialist countries to date, it is possible to highlight the factors that accompany the successes and failures of socialist policy in the form of reinforcement or interference variables as types of *secondary social indicators*[764] during past development. Their potential future effects can also be predicted with a relatively high degree of reliability. As far as contradiction doctrine is concerned, it is the interference variables that are of greatest interest.

Whereas the structural interference variables could be avoided, particularly in the second field, during future democratic transformation processes to socialism by means of greater emphasis on participation and pluralism and less recourse to repression, the motivational interference variables could be elimited first and foremost by a less dogmatic handling of socialist ideology. Some of these variables will also become less marked if there is less pressure from the capitalist system, which appears to be more successful in the economic efficiency sphere. It is difficult to say, however, how many more countries will have to convert to socialism before the actual and imagined "system pressure" is alleviated.

2. Modernization theory and indicator research in the comparison of socialist systems

The mere typology of potential contradictions (even when these are expressed in relative chronological terms for individual systems) has not yet satisfied quantitatively orientated social researchers. Correlations were thus sought between interference and reinforcement variables in a bid to develop the wealth of statements on details of socialist systems into broader pronouncements. The attempts of Western social scientists to date are, however, unsatisfactory precisely when it comes to the socialist systems, because they do not take the countries' own goal prerequisites into consideration. There have been three main attempts at correlation analysis:

1. the search for modernization variables and their threshold values;

2.   the search for democratization factors;
3.   the search for liberalization factors.

   1.   Traditional *modernization indicators* proved themselves to be of little value in comparative research into socialist systems. If we take, for example, the modernization threshold values proposed by Karl W. Deutsch (90% elementary education, over 50% of population urbanized and industrialized, per capita product of 500 dollars, franchise for all male citizens over the age of 25) then these prove to be more problematical for socialist countries than for capitalist countries.
   It has, in fact, been shown that capitalist countries have exceeded these threshold values at greatly differing points in time and that the period of time between a country reaching the first threshold value and having all five indicators at the threshold value varies greatly as well—between 140 years in England and 50 years in the United States and Japan. By way of a truism, one could probably ascertain that this period of time is very much shorter for socialist countries. But it is, nonetheless, advisable to take different indicators here. A general franchise, for example, goes without saying in a socialist country and yet is still relatively meaningless. In addition, the different goal-setting configurations adopted by the individual systems mean that the fact of the other four indicators all being at the same level does not say a great deal. Urbanization and industrialization do not play the same forced role in China's list of priorities as they once did in the Soviet Union. And periods of forced urbanization (such as the agrotown experiment) were not attributable to a continuous development process that interacted with other factors. It is seen that only in capitalist systems, where the economic sphere is largely independent, does this have a determining effect on a large number of aspects in the political subsystem. Hence correlations between socioeconomic indicators and political indicators can be sought more meaningfully in capitalist systems than in socialist economies that operate under the primacy of politics.
   Even if one were able to find a more suitable catalog of indicators for measuring threshold values for socialist systems (this could perhaps be based on the criteria that Marxist theorists name as the preconditions for the transition from socialism to communism) a mere comparison of absolute figures in time sequences would still not constitute a suitable procedure. The advantage of socialism is not just that it reaches the threshold values calculated for capitalist modernization processes in a shorter time; a number of capitalist late-industrializers can point to this advantage as well, and the

general acceleration of modernization processes has already worked to the benefit of the late-developing nations in the capitalist system (such as Germany and Japan as against England and France). Even if the development process measured in terms of specific indicators (labor productivity, agricultural output, output of certain branches of industry, uniformity of dynamic growth) is not very impressive compared with the latecomers in capitalist modernization, the more uniform distribution of that which has been achieved speaks out in favor of socialist countries at present. Even if India were ahead of China in terms of all the indicators—which is not the case—the Chinese path would be seen as the superior path at this stage because, despite all the open repression, it is marked by a lesser measure of *structural power* that keeps large numbers of the population in conditions unworthy of them and exposes no less a number to the daily threat of starvation to death. Development indicators alone are thus of no value in an overall assessment of system performance if no allowance is made for structural indicators (see Chapter 4).

The overall assessment of a system like Cuba, which has a much greater lead at the outset than China, would come out the same. A critical admirer summed things up as follows: "A socialist revolution like the one in Cuba cannot achieve any faster an economic growth than capitalist liberalism. A socialist revolution, on the other hand, can give all the country's population enough to eat, enough clothes to wear and enough health care."[765] The first sentence is untenable in its generalized form and also cannot be concluded from the isolated example of Cuba. But even if it could count as proved that capitalist developing countries generally have greater growth than socialist countries—which at best only applies to a few "islands of prosperity" in the Third World—the potential for future growth and uniform distribution is greater in socialist systems (see Chapter 4, Section 5).

When the measure of direct revolutionary power applied and the measure of *open dictatorial* power and *structural power*, which is fairly high in capitalist developing countries, is included in the comparison of developing countries, this will generally come out in favor of the socialist countries. The assessment becomes more complex, however, when systems that have already completed the initial accumulation phase are brought into the comparison.

2.   It is even more evident in the light of the system comparison that the search for *democratization factors*, as undertaken by S. M. Lipset, for example,[766] will inevitably lead to meaningless results in a comparison with socialist countries. There is not much point in taking the high level of literacy in socialist countries (see Table 37)

or the state-promoted spread of mass media (see Table 84) and drawing conclusions as to the level of democratization. In mobilized, one-
party systems this scarcely correlates at all with the socioeconomic
indicators taken by Lipset (see Table 107).

    3. The search for *determining factors in the liberalization
process* in the Western literature is also guilty of a similar inadmissible
transposition of correlations, which are only of any informative value
in capitalist systems. The very concept of "liberalization" is questionable in itself. In socialist systems democratization and pluralization
do not necessarily imply a development toward liberal bourgeois
principles, as the expression would seem to suggest, even if in a
number of fields—such as in the protective field in the legitimation
sphere (see Chapter 9)—processes do take place that seem to resemble
bourgeois constitutionality.

    One of the basic assumptions of Western research into socialism
(insofar as it has moved away from the totalitarianism hypothesis)
works on the basis of an increasing "liberalization" process that is
presumed to correlate with a number of socioeconomic indicators.

Table 107

Scaled scores summarizing developmental level

	Communi-cation	Education	Wealth	Average
East Germany	89	44	71	68
Czechoslovakia	66	64	68	66
Hungary	56	40	41	46
Soviet Union	33	43	54	43
Bulgaria	36	55	29	40
Poland	27	45	41	38
Mongolia	16	38	35	30
Rumania	26	29	27	27
Yugoslavia	21	36	09	22
North Korea	13	—	00	07
Albania	06	05	04	05
North Vietnam	—	—	00	00
China	00	00	00	00

Source: D. C. Pirages, "Socioeconomic development and political access in the Communist
Party-States," in J. Triska, ed., *Communist Party-States* (Indianapolis: Bobbs-Merrill,
1969) (249–281), p. 261.

If, however, one attempts to correlate development level with the level of political liberty and tolerance, using a set of indicators from the communication, education, and economic growth sphere, the results will be disappointing. Socialist countries' rank order of development does not correspond to an equivalent degree of liberalization. Those ranking at the top of this indicator comparison, namely, the German Democratic Republic and Czechoslovakia, are by no means the most liberal, and a number of the most "liberal" socialist states, such as Yugoslavia, rank along with some of the most illiberal, such as Rumania and Albania, right at the bottom of the indicator listing.

After this failure of correlation analysis, Pirages tried to track down other correlations. He only succeeded, however, in establishing a link between a number of truisms and the degree of liberalization. The size of the armed forces, the number of students studying in the West, and the extent of press suppression can immediately be seen to be interdependent without the need for a quantitative survey. Of greater interest are the correlations between illiberality, the low average increase in wages, and the low growth rate of party membership, since from these it can be concluded that the Communist party is pursuing its political goals without much consideration for the requirements of the masses and is fairly set apart from the masses within its power system, encapsuled in its elite cadre party.

Correlation calculations based on the data available to date can only lead to a superficially impressive pseudo-accuracy. The data base is too varied and in some cases not comparable, and even the published material is too fragmentary. So far it has really only been possible to attempt a classification of indicators and to formulate hypotheses as to which correlate with which.

In capitalist systems it has been found that there is a very high degree of correlation between a large number of social and economic sectors, although it is impossible to pinpoint one specific field as a focal point. Instead, the centers of gravity of state activity lie in different sectors such as nutrition, education, housing construction, or the communication system.[767] This is generally not so in socialist systems. The figures listed show that educational systems and ideologically influenced communication systems have for the most part been built up to above the general level of development. Housing construction and other fields, on the other hand, tend to lie below the average level of productive resources. Correlation calculations here would at best reveal what descriptive analysis already presupposes, namely, that these phenomena are by and large the result of deliberate priority fixing, which can certainly be criticized but which does not stem from the anarchy of production. Whereas indicator researchers are thus unwilling to draw conclusions as to casual relationships from correlations as far as capitalist systems are concerned, they could get away with this much more easily in the case of socialist policy, providing that the socialist leaderships do really control all the social processes to the extent that they claim they do. This assumption does not even always apply to the economy, however, let alone to all the other social spheres.

Insofar as correlation analysis does reveal system-neutral interdependences between indicators in the comparison of socialist and capitalist countries, these nonetheless sometimes have to be interpreted differently. The impact of the growth of individual indicators on the development process will not necessarily be the same at all stages of development, as has been shown in the case of urbanization and the birth rate. Indicator growth that is creative and *innovative* at one stage may be *parasitic* at another. Hence the difference in development level must always be kept in mind at the same time. In all socialist countries, with the exception of the German Democratic Republic and Czechoslovakia, this is on the average below that of most comparable Western European countries.

When it comes to comparative analysis of socialist systems, too, one should only make limited claims as to the significance of the interrelationships substantiated by figures in the descriptive analysis. One can speak at best of *correspondences*, since the term "correlation" has to be abandoned, and, even in a planned socialist system, clear-cut cause-and-effect relationships can only rarely be established. This does not imply that correlation analyses are superfluous in the comparison of socialist systems. In the light of the incomplete data available at present and the small number of autonomous socialist transformation processes they are, however, somewhat premature.

3.   Social input and political output in socialist systems

Socialist systems have two advantages over capitalist systems when it comes to implementing a system of properly concerted policies:

1.   They have succeeded in *reducing group fights* for shares in the surplus product to a minimum and have even succeeded in fully neutralizing the most powerful of these groups, which always managed

to take the lion's share in capitalist systems. An iron law of pluralism cannot be sustained in the light of recent findings.[768]

2. They have a *steering system* available that is less exposed to pressure from residual specific interests and organized groups than is the case for even the most highly developed of capitalist planning systems.

Whereas output in capitalist countries was so very much a mere fraction of the input of dominating social desires and interests for a long time that only the input mechanism needed to be studied, this approach is far less successful in the case of socialist systems. It is true that at the time when totalitarian models prevailed the bias toward input structures had also been adopted by socialist systems, but ever since policy output has taken on a greater importance than it had enjoyed during the frugal years of Stalin's rule policy output has been studied with increased attention. As a first step, an interest group model was transposed to socialist systems.[769]

This, however, called for a different group configuration from that applied in capitalist countries. Thus, Skilling distinguished between the following groups: leadership groups or factions, bureaucratic groups, intellectual groups, broad social groups such as peasants, workers, and opinion groups that are generally only loosely associated. Despite all the results obtained from detailed group analysis—especially in individual decision-making processes—it proved impossible to derive *policy output* directly from *group input* to the same extent as in capitalist systems, except by applying one of the numerous class theories, which simply defined the Soviet elite as a bureaucratic class with a clear-cut class interest. As of the late 1960s these theories were made popular again by Neomarxists.

The demand for empirical examination of group conflicts, based on the Marxist principle that contradictions can "never exist as such" but only in concrete processes, was put forward with growing insistence in Poland and Czechoslovakia in the 1960s.[770] This demand remained at the program stage for the most part, however, inasfar as the theory of socialist countries, which believed that the "fundamental contradiction" should be resolved via the class conflict, considered the redistribution effort put in by the system to be great enough for significant distribution conflicts to be regarded as nonexistent under socialist conditions. Only when it was realized that the second major goal of socialism after the redistribution wave, that is, increasing economic efficiency, had not been achieved to a sufficient extent for the term "mature socialism" to be applied, did questions start to be raised about the conflict effects of unequal distribution in socialism.

Inequality in qualification and remuneration (see Chapter 2) has repercussions on unequal distribution in all fields where gratifications are distributed, even where these are only seemingly immaterial gratifications such as predominate in Chinese and Cuban socialism.

Even where these disparities are acknowledged to exist in a large number of fields, socialism is still credited—and to some extent rightly so—with the advantage that gratifications, such as income, power, education, and prestige (to take the typology of the system theorists who have adopted Parsons' AGIL-system), do not tend to cumulate so much and instead are distributed more independently of each other.[771] *Vertical distribution of gratifications* does not produce the same *horizontal concentration of positions* as that found in capitalism, which is a typical feature of class society.

This viewpoint is on the verge of becoming increasingly correct. The more the primacy of politics is undermined by certain tendencies toward autonomy within the economic substratum, and the more the political leadership has to take domestic commodity production processes and its trade partners in world-wide foreign trade into consideration, the stronger becomes the trend toward a separating-out of roles and gratifications. In periods after revolutions, the scarcity of goods to be distributed in particular has meant that gratifications have tended to be more concentrated than in capitalism because virtually no means other than political were available for obtaining property, education, or prestige.

The distribution approach that was heeded in Polish sociology in particular has a disadvantage for socialist countries, however, in that it followed Western models but restricted their scope to the distribution sphere. Latent conflicts within the production sphere, which are due to a lack of democratization, despite nominal socialization of all the means of production, also have to be included in an empirical conflict analysis of socialist systems.

The assertion that tendencies for gratifications to cumulate are inherent in industrial society itself is just as one-sided as the restriction to the distribution sphere. Gerhard Lenski, who professed this view,[772] obviously assumed that his distribution laws also applied to socialist societies. According to these laws, people are prepared to share the products of their labor insofar as these are necessary for the survival of society. It is power, however, and thus the predominance of those groups who profit from unequitable distribution of gratifications, that decides about the distribution of the total surplus produced by society. The pessimistic view on redistribution that emerges from these laws is unnecessary in the case of socialist systems. It would even be possible to draw up a counterhypothesis for the initial violent phase of redistribution: in socialism, some members of society are refused subsistence, if need be, so that more than just the surplus product of society can be made available for redistribution.

In socialist systems the correlations between the four gratifications are quite different from those prevailing in capitalism:

1.   Under the primacy of politics, it is easier for the gratification "political *power*" to be converted into economic power. Even declining power is generally still transformed into economic power, to a greater extent than in capitalist systems, because politicians who are ousted from power are often entrusted with leading economic posts (such as Molotov, Malenkov, Dubček, for example).

On the other hand, the relationship does not work in the reverse direction as easily as in capitalism. Since the economic elites do not own the means of production that are at their command, they lack a "material pawn" to ensure permanent political power, such as that held by the big proprietors of capital goods in capitalism.

2.   In revolutionary phases, the gratification *"education"* is more difficult to transform into other gratifications in the power and economic spheres, except in cases where certain charismatic revolutionary leadership qualities are set on a par with education.

3.   The gratification *"prestige"* may appear to be widely dissociated from the political sphere, and has in some cases resulted in surprisingly high economic privileges and gratifications (such as preferential treatment in taking foreign exchange out of the country and in the import of goods, in travel facilities, in preferential consumer goods allocations). Yet, on the whole, it does tend to be dependent on politicoeconomic activity.

Even social strata that do not belong to the leading elite have a share in these gratifications through ideological training and the abundance of distinctions (work hero, Lenin medal) that are shared out to society year by year, and people are more inclined to take these gratifications in the form of "status allocated" by the party and as being an appreciation by the majority of the population than they are in capitalist societies.

If we bring the gratifications in the four subsystems of a social system into relation with the three spheres of society as well, we might risk the following generalizations:

1.   Gratifications in the *production sphere* can be converted relatively easily into educational advantages. Owing to the regulated access to higher qualifications and the planned restrictions on admission to university, "probation through production" is an important vehicle for promotion via "release for further education." The cumu-

lation of offices, particularly at the lower level of territorial and functional units, means that power in the production sphere is also coupled with political power, because decisions taken in the production sphere concerning a specific individual have greater impact than they would usually have in capitalism, insofar as there is near-on full employment. When it comes to repostings, entries into the cadre record, allocation of factory apartments, or the building of a dacha by the works' own construction brigade, the position of the individual worker in the production process is decisive.

The stronger the emphasis on material interests, the greater the tendency will be for conflicting interests in the production sphere of socialist countries to be depoliticized and economic in nature.

2. Gratifications in the *distribution sphere* are more likely to be linked with positions of power in the economy, the party, and the state than is the case in the sophisticated societies of late capitalism. This is due to the fact that, whereas the scarcity of commodities and the largely centralized allocation of a large number of commodities through infrastructural measures ensures that there is plenty of money available for additional distribution, this is not then generally matched by an equivalent supply of goods. In extreme cases, such as in Cuba, economists have calculated that there are some 3 billion Pesos circulating in the country without commodity coverage. Thus, every person has some 400 Pesos, roughly equivalent to the average annual consumption, which there is nothing to spend on, and this in turn has had detrimental repercussions on labor productivity.[773] As long as there are stores that sell scarce goods to privileged specialists, or simply to those with Western currency, the trend toward cumulation of gratifications in the various spheres of society will still live on. This is certainly not the intention of socialism, however, which is aiming to free precisely the distribution sphere from the influence of power gained in other spheres.

Even more than in capitalism, the private consumption of the ruling groups in transitional societies does not account for a particularly large share of the surplus. Their true unproductive extravagance lies in what critics have branded "the auxiliaries of monopoly bureaucracy", that is, the armies of functionaries, security agents, and propagandists whose unproductive work is destined to safeguard the established rule.

3. Gratifications in the *legitimation sphere* are relatively easy to acquire in the initial phase of revolutionary transformation but become increasingly tied to additional qualifications in other areas (education, leadership activity, technical skills) as development progresses.

Redistribution in the distribution sphere has been designed by the socialist state to alleviate conflict, particularly if productive resources develop at the rate envisaged, such that the amount of goods available for distribution (after deduction of the resources required for socialist accumulation) is constantly on the increase.

It would be ahistorical to construct a socialist model with strict dividing lines between the three social spheres and then to assert that certain tendencies are inherent in the distribution sphere in socialist systems. Certain reservations must therefore be placed on these statements, which only take account of past developments. It looks here as though only the most recent attempts at socialist transformation have produced completely new problems that neither the Soviet Union nor the people's democracies had to contend with, when they constructed socialism on the ruins of their war-worn countries and consequently had no surplus product worthy of mention available for distribution. Recent attempts, and even attempts in countries that are not as highly developed as the European countries, such as Cuba and Chile, are, however, showing noteworthy effects, which seem to originate precisely in the distribution sphere today. Both Castro and Allende implemented drastic wage increases and froze prices or even reduced prices in certain social fields, such as rents. The positive impact on the legitimation sphere was rather short-lived, however, since the excess of money and the growing scarcity of goods in these countries meant there was no interest in further distribution. The ensuing negative consequences for labor productivity then had to be compensated for by expanding the repressive element in the legitimation sphere. Cuba had to resort to increased coercion (similarly to the bureaucratic socialist systems with their antiparasite laws) because the alternative solution of material incentives was still rejected by ideology. So far, the "ley contra la vagancia" (law against laziness) of April 1, 1971, with its measures against refusals to work and absenteeism, has marked the culminating point of this reorientation. This was a reorientation that had not been allowed for in the original concept of Castroism, with its theory of moral incentives.

Paradoxically, moves toward socialism in higher-developed countries today must try to do without cheap redistribution demagogy, and these very experiences ought to be taken to heart by Western European nations. Calls for this imposed discipline (which is difficult to achieve unless trade unions are simply held on a leash by the communist parties, as is the case in bureaucratic socialism) will only be credible if drastic measures are simultaneously taken to align incomes. Attempts to opt for the most popular method of short-term upward alignment have so far invariably ended up in the banknote printing press and led to long-term uncompetitiveness for every single socialist economy.

The input by groups and strata into the political system and the political output, in terms of decisions, have as a rule been quantified separately. Input-output analyses based on overall economic calculations have only been carried out on rare occasions.

In Western elite research, correlation analyses of elite recruitment input and political decision output have generally proved to be costly and not very elucidating. In socialist countries, an input–output analysis of this type would be even more likely to fail. According to the party's concept of representation, the elite input into a number of decision-making bodies is shaped beforehand (such as with a given percentage of workers, women, young people, and so forth), such that this manipulated input does not in any case have any corresponding output proceeding autonomously from conflicts between these groups. Marxist sociologists' refusal to adopt the pluralistic interests model from Western democracies is justified even in the case of those who, like J. Wiatr in Poland, themselves allow for a certain pluralism in socialist society and constantly analyze this pluralism in their works.[774]

Contradictions in socialism originate to a lesser extent in interest and group differences and to a greater extent in the material policy output, as shown above. This does not, however, exclude the possibility that, in the long run, certain contradictions, such as a weakening of the effects of redistribution and the creation of new disparities, will bring about a growing amount of organized group conflict in socialism, too. However, a mere comparison in the literature of a socialist system tending toward liberalization and pluralization with a virtually one-party system—such as in Mexico—that allows for limited group pluralism[775] tends to be misleading. It is not so much the differences in political culture, but the goal concepts of the political elites that are diametrically opposed.

Even in countries with a rudimentary multiparty system, genuine political pluralism is unlikely to develop. Five socialist countries had a nominal "multiparty system"—Bulgaria, China (in the early phase), Czechoslovakia, the German Democratic Republic, Poland—with the other parties being largely reduced to pressure-group status. Under the leadership of the Communist parties they are permitted to articulate ideological needs, provided that they do not interfere with the claim to leadership of the workers' party. Although much has been written—openly and in secret—in socialist countries on socialist pluralism, there is little empirical material available on this subject. An opinion poll carried out in Czechoslovakia in 1968 revealed, however, that 81% of the sample would have preferred the non-communist parties to be partners of equal rank to the Communist party, and that as many as one quarter of the Communist party members in the sample did not approve of the hegemonic position of their party.[776] It may be that these results cannot be straightforwardly transposed to the other rudimentary multiparty systems, since, in some cases, these only had a very weak tradition of a democratic system prior to the socialist era. However, opinion polls are also available from Yugoslavia and the German Democratic Republic, reflecting so much latent discontent with the party that this could lead to a call for greater pluralism.

Despite these parallels, analogies on the surface of authoritarian systems are not much help to research. The bourgeois authoritarian systems running from Spain to South America are characterized primarily by the lack of a uniform ideology, by the lack of a unity party with effective steering capacity, and by a certain elite pluralism of military and civil elites. None of these characteristics applies to the changing socialist systems. Contrary to the bourgeois authoritarian systems, they are characterized by the following features:

1.   the *leadership role of the Communist party*;
2.   the strong preshaping power of an *ideology*, which is more than glorification of the particular national course adopted, with the addition of a few populist theories;
3.   the use of *mass mobilization*;
4.   the characteristic *blend of political instruments employed* (see Chapter 6), with repression being less predominant than in the authoritarian dictatorships of the capitalist world.

The political systems of socialist countries are less complex than their environment, to a far greater degree than in capitalist countries. They therefore generally compensate for the excess complexity caused by permanent mass mobilization through a reduction in the decision-making mechanism. Comprehensive discussion in connection with central decision making, however, is only possible as long as the decisions are in the main accepted unquestioningly. Ideological legitimation considerably facilitates the development of a consensus, as compared with capitalist systems, and is only questioned when the legitimation forms of "ideology" and "system efficiency" (particularly in the distribution sphere) start to clash with each other. The greater selection capacity of the socialist system then threatens to become lost. Growing group struggles and intraparty factionalization are starting to produce equivalents of the diffuse articulating power of capitalist-pluralist systems.

The process of differentiation within society is advancing in socialist countries, too, as a result of the world-wide interdependence of problems, ranging from the protection of the environment to the threat of nuclear extinction for the whole of mankind, even though the socialist countries' ideology is opposed to differentiation. This opposition is legitimate in all cases where differentiation is abused for purposes of justification of classes or domination but becomes less plausible where differentiation is based on an "equal grounding," such as through growing social pluralism on the basis of socialized means of production.

4. Crisis management and steering capacity in socialist systems

A typology of contradictions such as offered here cannot be applied to support the theory that socialist systems develop the "same" or "similar" contradictions to those in capitalist systems. Instead, we must highlight the concrete historical situations that have given rise to the individual dysfunctions and specify the conditions under which they could be eliminated and avoided in future socialist transformation processes.

The most serious dysfunctions, such as corrupt market steering for purposes of plan fulfillment, do not stem automatically from socialist planned economy, as is at times maintained, but are the result of efficiency being increased on the basis of plan organization without simultaneous maximization of the level of participation. Balanced maximization of the four basic target values and realization of this in material policy would probably serve to correct a large number of the contradictions that arise in socialist systems, although this, of course, should not leave us with the illusion that no new forms of dysfunctions will emerge. Conservative critics of planning have, however, used this argument at times to declare all efforts at planning to be in vain.[777]

Without permanent correction of these dysfunctions through planning it would not even be possible to maintain the status quo as far as goal achievement is concerned for the people—not even under capitalist conditions. The growing problems of an increasingly complex industrial society call for an increasingly comprehensive planning system simply to satisfy the ordinary needs of the moment.

The anxious question repeatedly asked by disconcerted political scientists "does politics matter?" can be answered in a much clearer "yes" for socialist than for capitalist systems. Although the debate on "organized capitalism" has increasingly shown that the hypotheses developed in particular in the United States for earlier stages of capitalism, asserting that socioeconomic variables had a far greater impact on policy output than did political variables, can now no longer be maintained without reservation on account of the growing organization of capitalism.[778] Research has nevertheless applied similar hypotheses to socialist countries and simply attributed fluctuations in policy output to a number of socioeconomic variables. Despite these fluctuations, crises in socialist countries have been less frequent—a fact that has led apologists of socialist countries to present crises as being a feature of capitalism. Even if this is a biased view, crises do nonetheless have a different significance in socialist systems, and this for several reasons:

1.   Crises in capitalist systems result chiefly from contradictions in the production sphere. In socialist systems, on the other hand, crisis symptoms tend to develop in the *legitimation sphere*. As the system becomes more abundant and more successful, achievements that once had to be fought hard for become increasingly taken for granted. Furthermore, socialist systems have not been spared the temptation to achieve legitimation via the distribution sphere ("catch up with and overtake the United States"). However, as distribution conflicts fade into the background in socialist systems, so the emergence of value conflicts becomes all the more striking, both among Marxists and in the form of non-Marxist ideologies. The groups start to ask fundamental questions of essence that can no longer be settled through bargaining, as could distribution conflicts.

Marxist patterns of interpretation are either enriched in their utopian core with new substance or are replaced by other patterns of interpretation, thereby reviving conflicts between nationalities, religions, and groups that had been deemed definitively resolved during periods of optimism in inter-system competition. In a number of socialist countries, such as Yugoslavia and Poland, there has been open discussion since the end of the 1960s about the delegitimizing tendencies resulting from the sclerosis of Marxist thought. The decline in social activity by the masses has been matched by an increase in institutional activity, whereas enthusiasm potential is threatening to shift to the archetypes of the family, folklore, religion, and national culture.

Even if the crisis symptoms simply appear to be the outcome of "secondary contradictions" (since the "chief contradiction" between labor and capital has been resolved), it would seem that a number of those secondary contradictions can come together in an unfortunate combination, such that they are perceived by those involved as a chief contradiction. This was the case in Yugoslavia when the Croats' national, social, religious, and cultural conflict motives overlapped to such an extent that they plunged the state into a serious crisis in 1969/70.

2.   Crisis phenomena in socialist systems are conditioned less by economic factors and more by *political* factors. They result more from political reshuffles than from shifts of power among the groups in the decision-making process. The degree to which the fluctuations in expenditures for different policies are due to succession, especially in investments, has sometimes been overrated.[779] It is not necessary in this context to ascertain to what extent recent findings about intervening variables such as decentralization, modifications in statistical reporting, and other more political factors are more important in the explanation of these variations than is leadership succession.[780] For this reason I do not reproduce the tables in more recent studies but prefer Hutchings' (Table 108) very simple evidence (which has the advantage of including more recent data, although the article is older), since it is sufficient to demonstrate that these fluctuations exist. They are comparable in scope to those of capitalist output fluctuations, which result in the latter case from an insufficient level of steering. If we take as an indicator the changes in estimates for the Soviet budget with its three main expenditure groups (financing the economy, defense, social and cultural facilities), then this gives such considerable fluctuations from one year to the next that one is quite justified in asking how rational planning is possible in the longer term with this zig-zag policy. It has to be concluded from this that there is at least a certain amount of disagreement about distribution among the sectors and groups in the leadership, which cannot be seen immediately from an analysis of the surface processes.

Although socialist systems are not usually orientated toward a theory of balanced growth (see Chapter 4, Section 4), "maintenance of the correct proportions" is repeatedly stressed for program purposes such as in the Soviet Communist Party program. When it comes to the assessment of plan fulfilment, the leaders are also conducting increasingly realistic analyses of the cases where the correct proportions have not been observed, such as Ulbricht did during preparation for the Eighth SED Party Congress.[781] These fluctuations do not undermine the primacy of politics; on the contrary, they are in fact

Table 108

Fluctuations in estimates of Soviet budget expenditure

Year	Economy	Defense	Social and cultural facilities
1945/46	+ 37.5	− 65.7	+ 17.1
1946/47	+ 29.6	− 5.2	+ 23.9
1947/48	+ 17.2	− 0.9	+ 9.2
1948/49	+ 3.5	+ 13.0	+ 2.9
1949/50	+ 11.9	+ 0.3	+ 1.5
1950/51	+ 14.1	+ 17.0	+ 0.1
1951/52	+ 1.9	+ 17.4	+ 4.0
1952/53	+ 12.1	− 3.6	+ 5.0
1953/54	+ 23.8	− 9.9	+ 11.5
1954/55	+ 6.0	+ 11.8	+ 5.7
1955/56	+ 14.9	− 9.6	+ 14.5
1956/57	+ 7.5	− 4.8	+ 26.9
1957/58	+ 12.5	− 1.4	+ 23.8
1958/59	+ 51.7	− 0.2	+ 20.0
1959/60	+ 19.6	+ 0.0	+ 15.6
1960/61	+ 10.6	− 3.6	+ 24.2
1961/62	− 14.4	+ 41.6	+ 14.5
1962/63	+ 20.7	+ 4.8	+ 22.5
1963/64	+ 42.1	− 6.0	+ 18.0
1964/65	+ 36.1	− 5.0	+ 46.5
1965/66	+ 14.9	+ 6.4	+ 29.3
1966/67	+ 30.7	+ 10.7	+ 25.4
1967/68	+ 32.7	+ 22.0	+ 28.9
1968/69	+ 81.3	+ 10.0	+ 53.1
1969/70	+ 51.6	+ 1.5	+ 37.3
1970/71	+ 135.5	+ 0.0	+ 36.7
1971/72	+ 56.0	+ 0.5	+ 44.2

Source: R. Hutchings, "Fluctuation and Interaction in Estimates of Soviet Budget Expenditure." *Osteuropa Wirtschaft,* No. 1 (1973), (57–59), p. 62.

more an expression of it. Nevertheless, certain changes are coming about in the way politics is conceived. It is becoming formalized, much to the regret of the Marxists, who would like to preserve the "pure flame of the revolutionary will" to change.

The more the needs within a socialist society become differentiated, the more demands will be put to the political leadership. Shortcomings in distribution in the socialist system are blamed more directly on the state than in capitalist systems, where the political leadership can still use the capitalist class as a buffer between it and the demands of the masses and can pick out scapegoats from among the capitalists (such as during the oil crisis). Legitimacy is perceived by the citizens to be based more narrowly upon "performance" than in Western democracies.[782] There are no such buffer zones in socialist systems. The leadership is obliged to look for the guilty parties in its own ranks, and this again can have delegitimating effects. The more ready the political elites are to admit that the system's achievements are not yet fully satisfactory and the more they are forced to the defensive by society's claims, the greater the tendency becomes for formal rationalization of the political process, with bargaining strategies and hearing and participation rights. This process also involves a change in the instruments employed for realizing goals in socialism. Violence fades into the background, and material incentives and indirect steering methods come to the fore again.

Neomarxist "system ontologists" often see the only choice as being between "restoration of capitalism" or "cultural revolution." It is, however, more likely that intermediate courses will be adopted for further development in the future, and Eastern European systems will probably attempt to chase out the "devil" with "Beelzebub" (in the eyes of the ideological purists). Although pluralistic bargaining strategies will indeed slow down the transformation process, they will also reduce the social and economic cost of course changes and centralized decisionmaking, because as society becomes more complex it becomes increasingly risky to try to save on legitimation costs.

3. Although the "systemic character" of socialism and the deliberate ex-ante planning of all conditions of production and reproduction are being upheld, there is plenty of evidence in the empiric literature to show that *nonanticipated social processes* occur again and again and that these may lead to crisis symptoms. A typical feature here is seen in the nonpolitical usage of the revolution concept in socialist literature when mention is made of revolutions as "running their own course" in the sphere of demographic development, the migration of labor, or destruction and protection of the environment.[783] For many social scientists who are optimistic about progress,

it is only a matter of time before these processes will be brought under control. Scientifically-minded Soviet scientists are still hoping for sociological forecasts that have the same level of accuracy as those for natural science with its controlled experiments. However, social scientists have also come increasingly to warn against placing exaggerated hopes in forecasts that "cannot work miracles." The belief in the possibility of future "conflict-free" problem solving (the use of the term is quite new in itself) has also been partially abandoned.[784] There is empirical proof of the fact that the number of processes that cannot be fully controlled is on the increase in the social and economic spheres, such that the systemic character of the political measures taken in a number of areas such as social policy has even been doubted at times (see Chapter 2, Section 3). Originally the parties of socialist states conceived themselves as being universal conflict parties that brought together and resolved by force all the social conflicts that would be mitigated through pluralism in the bourgeois state. This ran very much counter to other dictatorial systems, such as the fascist systems, which sought to appease internal conflict through ideology and repression and to direct social aggression past them toward the outside. As productive resources expand, however, the Party tends to withdraw itself increasingly from certain conflict areas. Even at a foreign policy level, the scope for passing on the blame for aggression to the class enemy "abroad" is diminishing, since the policy of co-existence will allow nothing more than verbal aggression. The socialist state is increasingly coming to operate on an ex-post basis in a number of fields and is no longer taking the ex-ante approach of deliberately stepping up conflicts, as it did during the first revolutionary phase of redistribution.

The supporters of comprehensive system planning will be more inclined than any material policy analyst to adopt too rationalistic and deterministic an attitude. This applies even more to socialism than to capitalism in the light of the socialist system's strict claim to rationality. Ever since Max Weber, a sort of negative theory of convergence has been in subliminal existence, fostered by scepticism about the feasibility of completely rationalizing society, and in particular the economic subsystem. Max Weber once maintained rather pithily that "material and formal rationality (in the sense of exact *calculation*) will inevitably diverge to a large extent; this fundamental and ultimately ineluctible irrationality of economics is one of the sources of all 'social' problems and particularly those of socialist systems."[785] Hence it has always been a tempting approach to prove quantitatively the common cultural tradition—and the increasing ideological alignment in basic attitude toward the technological potential of the world—by means of indicators as well, and to attribute a number of the differences between capitalist and socialist systems not so much to the different nature of the systems but to their different developmental stages instead. This method leaves certain decisive differences between the two social formations uncovered, however. These lie not only in the origin of crises, which is different from that in capitalism, but also in differences in the crisis-resolving capacity of the political systems. Socialist systems have a range of means at their disposal for keeping crises latent or for mitigating them, which are different from the instruments available to capitalist crisis management:

    1.   The *primacy of politics* makes for a speedier response to crisis symptoms and for changeovers with less decisional costs than in capitalistic democracies—albeit with its own particular dangers for the participation and protection function within the system, as outlined above. Just how rapid fluctuations can be is to be seen at times from the way in which opposition within the party is handled. Not infrequently "deviations" are denounced loudly, only then to be implemented quietly at a subsequent stage. This was the case with Preobrazhensky's concept of the "tribute" to be imposed on agriculture, that was ideologically contested by Stalin but was then put into practice as of 1928 without any reference to the theorist behind the policy. In China the same thing happened with the concepts of Hu Geng, who had been branded as a "rightist deviationist," but whose ideas were then largely put into practice later on, without Hu Geng himself being rehabilitated into society. The socialist system's rapid reaction capacity does, however, have its price: socialist planners are constantly losing the "battle against time," insofar as the rapidity of the response to crisis symptoms breaches the postulate of simultaneity of measures and unity of material policies. This experience has frequently prompted the planners to act less rapidly than would have been theoretically possible. In such cases, a counterpart to the "muddling through" that goes on in capitalist systems develops. This tendency becomes all the greater as the degree of dissent between the party wings grows and as the degree of consideration that the leadership majority has to pay to the other groups in the party increases.

    2.   Whereas certain authoritarian capitalist systems are striving to imitate the concentration of power found in socialist countries so as to be able to react more swiftly to crisis phenomena, they are not succeeding in imitating the *mobilizational aspect of socialist politics.* Despite the possibility of the repeatedly renewed mobilization of mass participation, socialist planners must come to realize, with the increasing sophistication of planning instruments, that perfectionist,

total rationalization can never be possible. The channeled forms of mass participation are no longer sufficient in the case of serious crisis symptoms, since the citizens of socialist states, as they are gaining greater maturity, are making their leaders much more directly responsible than in capitalist systems for the system's defects. Consequently, anomic forms of participation are on the increase in many socialist countries (Czechoslovakia, Poland, Hungary).

It is becoming increasingly impossible to avoid structural ruptures that disturb the harmony of coordinated material policies simply by extending subsystem autonomy in the enterprises, as was tried in the economic reforms. The economic reforms of a number of Eastern European countries show that the reforms were so eclectic that they gave rise to new contradictions and that administrative orders from above frequently clashed with the economic parameters that the expansion of enterprise autonomy had introduced into decentralized decision-making processes. Decentralization and autonomy in decision making for the enterprises brought to some extent the danger of a cut-back in expert participation (see Chapter 10, Section 2). The feedback of information was indeed improved, but the value of this information was at times reduced by the bonus-winning motives behind the enterprise reports. The Eastern European planners' reaction to this experience was a partial return to greater centralization. But even recentralization is no way out of the dilemma.

Decentralized participation alone is of no advantage unless conflicts regarding alternative planning can be fought out with open participation at the highest level. Mere decentralization can also lead to anarcho-syndicalist isolation of local and sectoral opinion-formation processes, and this conflicts with the principle of socialist ex-ante planning. Even when subsystem autonomy and participation are extended, the central planning level should still be maintained. Alternative planning concepts must be discussed democratically, and, once the plan periods have run their term, these must be assessed ex-post and corrected where necessary. The plain recentralization model brings the danger of plan forecasts developing into a type of self-fulfilling prophecy. Soviet planners, too, have recognized the dilemma whereby planners are inclined to take plan fulfillment as proof of the fact that the implemented plan was indeed the optimum plan variant, not considering the "Oedipus effect" of plan forecasts or the self-fulfilling tendencies of social forecasting.[786] If this were to be fully appreciated, it would result in a greater degree of pluralism and extended participation in the decision-making process of the central authority. The price that would have to be paid for this would be tolerance of factions forming within the party, so as to allow organized discussion about alternative planning configurations to develop. Planners mostly tend to shy away from this consequence, however, because the "bourgeois anarchy of intellectual production" of which every organization and planning theorist has his own individual concept, not recognizing a common platform with his colleagues, still remains a trauma for socialist organization theory.[787]

3. The strongest plus point of socialist countries when it comes to crisis management is still the consistency of their ideological basis and the *regenerative capacity of Marxist doctrine*. Although a certain agnosticism may develop regarding the final goals of communism, as productive resources increase and as a greater degree of differentiation grows in society and its groups, it cannot be denied that socialist systems have repeatedly developed innovation and further development prospects for their system, even after signs of bureaucratic degeneration have appeared. Admittedly, the bourgeois democracies have also shown evidence of innovative forces at times, which many felt they were no longer capable of showing, but these sometimes took the form of borrowing from socialism—the welfare state, democratization of the masses, system planning, and so on.

Socialist oppositions operate on the same ideological foundation, and in a number of countries their demands are being increasingly incorporated into the concrete political decision-making process. The socialist system has tried harder than any other to date to reconcile the necessities of the age of technology and the rational organization for the promotion of productive resources with the fight against the "demystification of the world" that Max Weber once bemoaned. This is what makes this basic attitude so fascinating for large numbers of young people even outside the socialist countries, although the phasing-out of alienation, the fight against the constraints of the age of technology, and the harmonious interplay of human roles from the production sphere right through to the legitimation sphere are admittedly no longer a monopoly of Marxist thought today.

ABBREVIATIONS

APSR	*American Political Science Review*
BdBfouiSt	*Berichte des Bundesinstituts für ostwissenschaftliche und internationale Studien,* Cologne
CHQU	*China Quarterly*
DA	*Deutschland Archiv*
DZfPh	*Deutsche Zeitschrift für Philosophie*
LPSS	Lenin. *Polnoe sobranie sochinenii*
MEW	Marx/Engels. *Werke*
OE	*Osteuropa*
OE/W	*Osteuropa/Wirtschaft*
PCh	*Planovoe khozyaistvo*
PoC	*Problems of Communism*
PVS	*Politische Vierteljahresschrift*
SGiP	*Sovetskoe gosudarstvo i pravo*
SI	*Sotsialogicheskie issledovaniya*
StiCC	*Studies in Comparative Communism*
SW/GesWB	*Sowjetwissenschaft/Gesellschaftswissenschaftliche Beiträge*
VE	*Voprosy ekonomiki*
VF	*Voprosy filosofii*

NOTES

Introduction

1. J. N. Rosenau, "Comparison as a State of Mind," *StiCC*, No. 1/2 (1975), pp. 57-61.

2. G. Marchais, *Le défi démocratique* (Paris: Grasset, 1973), p. 158.

3. J. Zelt & W. Morgenstern, in *Deutsche Außenpolitik (GDR)*, No. 12 (1976), pp. 1891-1897.

4. F. J. Strauss in the German Federal Diet, Protokoll der 240. Sitzung, May 11, 1976, p. 16, 838 on Peter Ch. Ludz and the author.

5. I. Sieńko, "Klausa von Beymego model spoleczenstwa socjalistycznego." *Studia nauk politycznych*, No. 4 (1976), pp. 143-151.

6. Cf. R. Dutschke & B. Rabehl (eds.), *Die Sowjetunion, Solschenizyn und die westliche Linke* (Reinbek: Rowohlt, 1975).

7. C. J. Friedrich & Z. K. Brzezinski, *Totalitarian Dictatorship and Autocracy* (Cambridge, Mass.: Harvard U.P., 1965), pp. 367ff.; for a more balanced view of the second author, see: Z. Brzezinski, "Dysfunctional

Totalitarianism," in K. von Beyme (ed.), *Theory and Politics. Festschrift zum 70. Geburtstag für C. J. Friedrich* (The Hague: Nijhoff, 1971), pp. 375-389.

8. J. Tinbergen, *Central Planning* (New Haven: Yale U.P., 1964).

9. See N. Luhmann, "Sociology of Political Systems," in K. von Beyme (ed.), *German Political Studies*, Vol. 1 (London, Beverly Hills: Sage, 1974), pp. 3-29.

10. The functional approach in research of socialist systems proved sometimes to be not at all culture-free and quite frequently stuck to a biased perception of the "normal" political system, the United States. See A. H. Brown, *Soviet Politics and Political Science* (London: Macmillan, 1974), p. 14f. Most traditional-minded: G. Ionescu, *Comparative Communist Politics* (London: Macmillan, 1972), p. 11. Sceptical about the whole comparative impetus is still: R. L. Tökés, "Comparative Communism. The Elusive Target," *StiCC* (1975), pp. 211-229.

11. P. M. Johnson, "Modernization as an Explanation of Political Change in East European States," in J. E. Triska & P. M. Cocks (eds.), *Political Development in Eastern Europe* (New York: Praeger, 1977) [30-50], p. 34. A. Jones, "Modernization and Socialist Development," in M. G. Field (ed.), *Social Consequences of Modernization in Communist Societies* (Baltimore: Johns Hopkins, 1976), pp. 19-49.

12. W. Gellhorn, *Ombudsmen and Others. Citizens' protectors in Nine Countries* (Cambridge, Mass.: Harvard U.P., 1966), pp. 336ff.

13. *Razvitoe sotsialisticheskoe obshestvo* (Moscow: Mysl', 1973), p. 38, contains a more economy-centered definition. For a discussion of the "mature socialism" model see G. Meyer, *Sozialistische Systeme* (Opladen: Leske, 1979), pp. 26ff.

14. Ibid., p. 288.

15. B. N. Topornin, *Politicheskaya sistema sotsializma* (Moscow: Mezhdunarodnye otnosheniya, 1972).

16. *Partiya i gosudarstvo v stranakh sotsialisticheskoi orientatsii* (Moscow: Nauka, 1973). Cf. K. von Beyme, "Soviet Foreign Policy in Asia," *Journal of National Security (Seoul)*, Vol. 9 (1979), pp. 109-126.

17. *Kraje socjalistyczne po drugiej wojnie światowej 1944-1974* (Warsaw: PWE, 1977), p. 10.

18. A. Brown & J. Gray (eds.), *Political Culture and Political Change in Communist States* (London: Macmillan, 1977), p. 14. H. Nick, *Gesellschaft und Betrieb im Sozialismus. Zur zentralen Idee des ökonomischen Systems des Sozialismus* (Berlin [East]: Verlag die Wirtschaft, 1970), p. 136.

19. R. Furtak, *Die politischen Systeme der sozialistischen Staaten* (Munich: DTV, 1979), p. 7.

20. W. D. Narr & C. Offe (eds.), *Wohlfahrtsstaat und Massenloyalität* (Cologne: Kiepenheuer & Witsch, 1975), p. 10.

21. P. Shoup, "Comparing Communist Nations. Prospects for an Empirical Approach," in R. E. Kanet (ed.), *The Behavioral Revolution and Communist Studies* (New York: Free Press, 1971) [15–47], p. 16f. For the planning systems: A. Eckstein (ed.), *Comparison of Economic Systems* (Berkeley, Los Angeles: University of California Press, 1971), p. 159f. J. M. Montias, "A Classification of Communist Economic Systems," in C. Mesa-Lago & C. Beck (eds.), *Comparative Socialist Systems* (Pittsburgh: University of Pittsburgh Center for International Studies, 1975), [39–51], p. 40f. For a classification that tries to overcome the absence of attention to time series data see: W. A. Welsh, "Towards an Empirical Typology of Socialist Systems," ibid., [52–91], p. 66.

22. F. Pryor, *Public Expenditures in Communist and Capitalist Nations* (London: Allen & Unwin, 1968), p. 31.

23. S. N. Grigoryan & V. Georgiev (ed.), *Kritika teoreticheskikh osnov Maoizma* (Moscow: Nauka, 1973), p. 65.

24. A. Meyer, "Legitimacy of Power in East Central Europe," in S. Sinanian et al. (eds.), *Eastern Europe in the 1980s* (New York: Praeger, 1972) [45–86], p. 56.

25. *Annuarul statistic al republii socialiste România* (Bukarest, 1978).

26. I. P. Suslov, *Teoriia statisticheskikh pokazatelei* (Moscow: Statistika, 1975), p. 113. J. St. Mill: *A System of Logic*, New Impression, Book III, Chapter VIII, 1–2 (London: Longmans, 1959), pp. 253ff.

27. *Materialy XXV S"ezda KPSS* (Moscow: Izpolit, 1976), pp. 1–20. I. V. Bestuzhev-Lada, "Opyt tipologii sotsial'nykh pokazatelei obraza zhisni obshchestva," *SI*, No. 2 (1980), pp. 34–42.

28. Quoted in: A. Nove, *The Soviet Economic System* (London: Allen & Unwin, 1978), p. 367.

29. M. A. Sivertsev: *Problemy tipologii v mezhdunarodnoi statistike zanyatosti* (Moscow: Nauka, 1975), p. 204.

30. A problem in the West criticized by O. Morgenstern, *The Accuracy of Economic Observations* (Princeton, N.J.: Princeton U.P., 1963), pp. 13f.

31. K. S. Karol, *Guerilleros in Power* (London: Cape, 1971), p. 34. On early problems of statistics: C. Mesa-Lago, "Availability and Reliability of Statistics in Socialist Cuba," *Latin American Research Review*, No. 1 (1969), pp. 53-91, No. 2 (1969), pp. 47-81.

32. For example, the indicators for the proportion of children in pre-school institutions. In 1973 Cuba and Mongolia were mentioned, in 1974 these countries were excluded altogether from the statistics. *Statistisheskii ezhegodnik* (Moscow: Statistika, 1973), p. 470 (1974), p. 466.

33. A. Eckstein, *Communist China's Economic Growth and Foreign Trade* (New York: McGraw Hill, 1966), p. 276; T. Ch. Liu, "Quantitative Trends in the Economy," in A. Eckstein et al. (eds.), *Economic Trends in Communist China* (Chicago: Aldine, 1968) [87-182], p. 88.

34. M. I. Sladkovskii (ed.), *Promyshlennost' KNR* (Moscow: Nauka, 1979), pp. 30ff. The Soviet statistical yearbook as far as it compares Soviet output with other nations reports "China does not publish data since 1960," *Narodnoe Khozyaistvo SSSR v 1978 g* (Moscow: Statistica, 1979), p. 53.

35. St. E. Schattman, "Dogma vs. Science in Soviet Statistics," *PoC.*, No. 1 (1956), pp. 30-36; H.-J. Wagener, "Zur sowjetischen Statistik der industriellen inputs und outputs," *Jahrbuch der Wirtschaft Europas/Yearbook of East European Economics*, Vol. 4 (Munich: Olzog, 1973), pp. 439-479. A. Zauberman, *Mathematical Theory in Soviet Planning* (London: Oxford U.P., 1976).

36. Cho-Ming Li, *The Statistical System of Communist China* (Berkeley: University of California Press, 1962), p. 120. Cf. also: Nai Ruenn Chen, *Chinese Economic Statistics. A Handbook for Mainland China* (Chicago: Aldine, 1967).

37. A. Nove, *The Soviet Economic System*, 2nd ed. (London: Allen & Unwin, 1978), pp. 350ff.

38. H.-D. Schulz, "Statistisches Jahrbuch der DDR ein teilweise blinder Spiegel," *DA*, No. 11 (1973) [1022-1025], p. 1023.

39. R. Emde, *Sozialindikatoren und Systemvergleich* (Frankfurt: Campus, 1979), p. 107.

40. B. M. Gross, in R. Bauer (ed.), *Social Indicators* (Cambridge, Mass.: M.I.T.

Press, 1966), p. 221. More optimistic: N. M. Bradburn, *The Structure of Psychological Well-Being* (Chicago: Aldine, 1969), p. 233.

41. R. A. Bauer et al., *How the Soviet System Works* (Cambridge, Mass.: Harvard U.P., 1953); J. A. Ross, "The Composition and Structure of Alienation of Jewish Emigrants from the Soviet Union," *StiCC*, No. 1/2 (1974), pp. 107-118.

42. M. Zeitlin, *Politics and the Cuban Working Class* (Princeton: Princeton U.P., 1970). W. Soergel, *Arbeiterselbstverwaltung oder Managersozialismus. Eine empirische Untersuchung in jugoslawischen Industriebetrieben* (Munich: Oldenbourg, 1979). P. Jambrek, *Development and Social Change in Yugoslavia* (Lexington, Ky.: Lexington Books, 1975).

43. J. A. Piekalkiewicz, *Public Opinion in Czechoslovakia 1968/69. Results and Analysis of Surveys conducted during the Dubcek-Era* (New York: Praeger, 1972); D. Voigt, *Montagearbeiter in der DDR* (Darmstadt/Neuwied: Luchterhand, 1973).

44. For this distinction see: A. Wallace, *Culture and Personality* (New York: Random House, 1961), p. 148. Ch. Johnson (ed.), *Change in Communist Nations* (Stanford: Stanford U.P., 1970), p. 7.

45. M. P. Gehlen, *The Communist Party of the Soviet Union. A Functional Analysis* (Bloomington: Indiana U.P., 1969), pp. 103-108.

46. Th. J. Lowi, "American Business. Case Studies and Political Theory," *World Politics* (1963/64) [667-715], pp. 690f.

Part I

Chapter 1

47. J. S. Berliner, *Economy, Society and Welfare. A Study in Social Economics* (New York: Praeger, 1972), p. 67.

48. R. Lorenz, *Anfänge der bolschewistischen Industriepolitik* (Cologne: Wissenschaft und Politik, 1965), p. 109.

49. V. I. Vanin, *Gosudarstvennyi kapitalizm v KNR* (Moscow: Nauka, 1974), pp. 304ff.

50. These four stages are, however, not so easily squeezed into four periods of time such as 1944-1947, 1947-1949, 1949-1953, 1958-1962, as it has been attempted in Soviet literature; cf. K. I. Mikul'skii, *Klassovaya struktura obshchestva v stranakh sotsializma* (Moscow: Nauka, 1976), p. 40.

454 *Notes*

51. A. Zauberman, *Industrial Progress in Poland, Czechoslovakia and East Germany 1937-1962* (London: Oxford U.P., 1964).

52. M. Haendcke-Hoppe, "Die Vergesellschaftungsaktion im Frühjahr 1972," *DA*, No. 3 (1973) [37-41], p. 38.

53. N. Brunner, *China's Economy* (London: Anglo-Chinese Educational Institute, 1969), p. 24.

54. D. Nohlen, *Chile. Das sozialistische Experiment* (Hamburg: Hoffmann & Campe, 1973), p. 187.

55. T. Suranyi-Unger, *Studien zum Wirtschaftswachstum Südosteuropas* (Stuttgart: G. Fischer, 1964), p. 137.

56. F. Fejtö, *Die Geschichte der Volksdemokratie*, Vol. 1 (Graz: Styria, 1972), p. 319.

57. H. Conert, "Gibt es einen jugoslawischen Sozialismus?" *Das Argument*, No. 82 (1973) [735-767], p. 756. R. K. Furtak, *Jugoslawien. Politik, Gesellschaft, Wirtschaft* (Hamburg: Hoffmann & Campe, 1975), pp. 36ff.

58. A. Labrousse, *L'expérience chilienne. Réformisme ou révolution?* (Paris: Editions du Seuil, 1972), pp. 309ff.

59. Uri, *Communist China 1949-1959*, Vol. 1 (Hongkong: Hongkong U.P., 1961), p. 157.

60. B. Richman, *Industrial Society in Communist China* (New York: Vintage Books, 1969), p. 901.

61. G. Leptin, *Die Deutsche Wirtschaft nach 1945. Ein Ost-West-Vergleich* (Opladen: Leske, 1971), p. 23.

62. Nohlen, op. cit. (note 54), pp. 188f.

63. *ODEPLAN: Informe Económico anual 1971* (Santiago de Chile), p. 135.

64. F. L. Pryor, *Property and Industrial Organization in Communist and Capitalist Nations* (Bloomington: Indiana U.P., 1973), p. 165. Less systematic nationalization in capitalist systems is according to Soviet assessments: *Gosudarstvennaya sobstvennost' i antimonopolisticheskaya bor'ba v stranakh razvitogo kapitalizma* (Moscow: Nauka, 1973), pp. 231ff.

65. D. W. Douglas, *Transnational Economic Systems. The Polish-Czech Example* (New York: Monthly Review Press, 1972), pp. 332f.

66. *Jugoslavija 1945-1964. Statisticki pregled* (Beograd, 1965), p. 158.

67. *Statistisches Jahrbuch der DDR 1969* (Staatsverlag der DDR), pp. 266ff.

68. *Granma*, March 31, 1968.

69. H. Nick: *Gesellschaft und Betrieb im Sozialismus* (Berlin [East]: Verlag Die Wirtschaft, 1970), p. 141.

70. R. P. Rochlin & E. Hagemann, *Die Kollektivierung der Landwirtschaft in der Sowjetunion und der Volksrepublik China. Eine vergleichende Studie* (Berlin [West]: Duncker & Humblot, 1971), pp. 37f.

71. A discussion with Ruth Fischer reported in: R. Fischer, *Stalin und der deutsche Kommunismus* (Frankfurt: Verlag der Frankfurter Hefte, 1949), p. 662.

72. I. T. Sanders (ed.), *Collectivization of Agriculture in Eastern Europe* (Lexington, Ky.: Lexington Books, 1958), p. 70.

73. A. Woś, *Proces socjalistycznej rekonstrukcji rolnictwa polskiego* (Warsaw: Ksiazka i Wiedza, 1976), pp. 18ff.; H. Slabek, *Polityka Agrarna PPR* (Warsaw: Ksiazka i Wiedza, 1978), pp. 246ff.

74. D. Keese, "Beschäftigungsprobleme in Polen," *OE/W* (1966) [115-130], p. 120.

75. Douglas, op. cit. (note 65), p. 343.

76. J. I. Dominguez, *Cuba. Order and Revolution* (Cambridge, Mass.: Belknap, 1978), pp. 147ff.

77. Sanders, op. cit. (note 72), pp. 144, 148.

78. J. Krejci, *Social Change and Stratification in Postwar Czechoslovakia* (London: Macmillan, 1972), p. 16.

79. G. J. Conrad, *Die Wirtschaft Rumäniens von 1945 bis 1952* (Berlin [West], Duncker & Humblot, 1952), p. 28.

80. N. Spulber, "Uneasy Symbiosis in Land Tenancy," in idem, *Socialist Management and Planning* (Bloomington: Indiana U.P., 1971) [80-101], p. 89.

81. Chao Kuo-Chuen, *Agrarian Policy of the Chinese Communist Party 1921-1959* (Bombay, 1960), pp. 96f.

82. Law in: *Collection of Selected Laws of the Chinese People's Republic* (Peking, 1957), pp. 127ff. P. Schran, *The Development of Chinese Agriculture 1950–1959* (Urbana, Ill.: University of Illinois Press, 1969), p. 27.

83. N. Brunner, *China's Economy* (London, Anglo-Chinese Educational Institute, 1969), p. 15.

84. I. J. & D. Crook, *Revolution in a Chinese Village. Ten Mile Inn* (London: Routledge & Kegan Paul, 1959), pp. 160ff.

85. Mao Tse-Tung, *Selected Works*, Vol. 4 (Peking, 1969), p. 251.

86. Ho Chi Minh, *Selected Speeches and Writings* (New York: Praeger, 1967), pp. 308ff.

87. K. R. Walker, *Planning in Chinese Agriculture. Socialisation and the Private Sector* (London: F. Cass, 1965), p. 7.

88. M. P. Canapa, "Réforme économique et socialisation agraire en Yougoslavie," *Revue de l'est*, No. 1 (1971) [69–94], pp. 72ff.

89. L. T. C. Kuo, *The Technical Transformation of Agriculture in Communist China* (New York: Praeger, 1972), p. VI.

90. F. Schurmann, *Ideology and Organization in Communist China* (Berkeley: University of California Press, 1966), p. 483.

91. H. J. Lethbridge, *The Peasant and the Communes* (Hongkong: Dragon Fly Books, 1963), p. 167.

92. J. R. Townsend, "Democratic Management in the Rural Communes," *China Quarterly*, No. 16 (1963) [137–150], p. 138.

93. Sh. J. Burki, *A Study of Chinese Communes* (Cambridge, Mass.: Harvard U.P., 1965), pp. 8ff.

94. H. E. Salisbury, "The Asian Hartland: A Non-Marxist View on the Mongolian People's Republic," in H. G. Shaffer (ed.), *The Communist World. Marxist and Non-Marxist Views* (New York: Appleton-Century-Crofts, 1967) [405–412], p. 408.

95. L. Volin, "Agrarian Policy in the Soviet Union," in M. Bornstein (ed.), *Comparative Economic Systems. Models and Cases* (Homewood, Ill.: University of Illinois Press, 1965) [310–343], p. 317.

96. Grigoryan, op. cit. (note 23), p. 175.

97. Ch. Bouvier, *La collectivisation de l'agriculture: URSS, Chine et démocraties populaires* (Paris: Colin, 1958), p. 72f.; Sanders, op. cit. (note 72), p. 144.

98. K.-E. Waedekin, *Sozialistische Agrarpolitik in Osteuropa*, Vol. 2 (Berlin [West]: Duncker & Humblot, 1978), pp. 30ff.

99. M. Lavigne, *Les économies socialistes soviétique et européennes* (Paris: PUF, 1970), pp. 42f.

100. K. Pankova, "K voprosu o perevode sovkhozov na polnyi khozyaistvennyi raschet," *VE*, No. 11 (1966) [34-44], p. 35.

101. K.-E. Waedekin, *Die sowjetischen Staatsgüter. Expansion und Wandlungen des Sovchossektors* (Wiesbaden: Harrassowitz, 1969), p. 22.

102. A. Donnithorne, *China's Economic System* (London: Allen & Unwin, 1967), p. 97; Rochlin-Hagemann, op. cit. (note 70), pp. 100ff.

103. G. D. Jackson, *Comintern and Peasant in Eastern Europe. 1919-1930* (New York: Columbia U.P., 1966). G. Ionescu & E. Gellner (eds.), *Populism. Its Meanings and National Characteristics* (London: Weidenfeld & Nicolson, 1969), pp. 97-121.

104. Sanders, op. cit. (note 72), p. 180f. Lavigne, op. cit. (note 99), p. 41.

105. E. L. Wheelwright & B. McFarlane, *The Chinese Road to Socialism* (New York: Monthly Review Press, 1970), p. 33.

106. Krejci, op. cit. (note 78), p. 20.

107. W. Cesarz, *Die persönlichen Hauswirtschaften in der LPG Typ III* (Berlin [East]: Deutscher Landwirtschaftsverlag, 1960), p. 51.

108. *Narodnoe Khozyaistvo SSSR v 1978 g* (Moscow: Statistika, 1979), p. 392.

109. V. A. Peshekhonov, *Rol' tovarno-denezhnykh otnoshenii planovom rukovodstve kolkhoznym proizvodstvom* (Leningrad: 1967), p. 184.

110. K.-E. Waedekin, *Die Bezahlung der Arbeit in der sowjetischen Landwirtschaft* (Berlin [West]: Duncker & Humblot, 1972), p. 247.

111. A. M. Emel'yanov, *Metodologicheskie problemy nakopleniya i rentabel' nosti v kolkhozakh* (Moscow: 1965), p. 309.

112. H. Schweitzer, *Sozialistische Agrartheorie und Praxis in China und der Sowjetunion: ein Modell für Entwicklungsländer?* (Berne: Lang, 1972), p. 162.

113. I. F. Suslov, *Ekonomicheskie interesy sotsial'noe razvitie kolkhoznogo krest'yanstva* (Moscow: Mysl', 1973), p. 178. P. I. Simush, *Sotsial'nyi portret sovetskogo krest'yanstva* (Moscow: Politizdat, 1976), pp. 106ff.

114. L. Kalinin, "O lichnom podsobnom khozyaistve pri sotsializme," *VE*, No. 11 (1968) [52-63], p. 55.

115. V. I. Staróverov, *Sotsial'naya struktura sel'skogo naseleniya SSSR na etape razvitogo sotsializma* (Moscow: Nauka, 1978), p. 181.

116. Donnithorne, op. cit. (note 102), pp. 110f.

117. Walker, op. cit. (note 87), p. 34.

118. Ch. Hoffmann, *Work Incentive Practices and Policies in the People's Republic of China 1953-1965* (Albany: State of New York U.P., 1967), p. 54.

119. P. Chang, "Peking and the Provinces. Decentralization of Power," *PoC*, No. 4 (1972) [67-75], p. 73.

120. Kim il Song, *Speeches*, Vol. 2. Pyöng Yang, 1971, p. 453.

121. R. A. Scalapino & Ch.-S. Lee, *Communism in Korea*, Vol. 2 (Berkeley: University of California Press, 1972), p. 1154.

122. P. Sweezy & L. Huberman, *Socialism in Cuba* (New York: Monthly Review Press, 1969), Chapter 7.

123. R. Dumont, *Cuba. Socialisme et développement* (Paris: Éditions du Seuil, 1964), p. 42.

124. Leptin, op. cit. (note 61), p. 19.

125. A. Korbonski, "Peasant Agriculture in Socialist Poland since 1956. An Alternative to Collectivization," in J. F. Karcz (ed.), *Soviet and East European Agriculture* (Berkeley: University of California Press, 1967) [411-431], p. 412.

126. H. E. Walters & R. W. Judy, "Soviet Agricultural Output by 1970 in Karcz," op. cit. (note 125) [306-355], p. 321.

127. D. B. Diamond, "Trends in Outputs, Inputs, and Factor Productivity in Soviet Agriculture," in US Congress Joint Economic Committee (ed.), *New Directions in the Soviet Economy* (Washington, D.C., G.O.P., 1966) [299-381], p. 364.

128. M. R. Larsen, "China's Agriculture under Communism," in Joint Economic Committee of the US Congress (ed.), *An Economic Profile of Mainland China* (New York: Praeger, 1968) [197-295], p. 214.

129. Renmin Ribao, No. 9, 1962, quoted in Donnithorne, op. cit. (note 102), p. 119.

130. Renmin Ribao, Oct. 25, 1957, quoted in Donnithorne, op. cit. (note 102), p. 119.

131. L. Sirc, "Economics of Collectivization," *Soviet Studies* (1966/67) [362-370], p. 366. D. H. Perkins, "Centralization and Decentralization in Mainland China's Agriculture," *Quarterly Journal of Economics* (1964) [208-237], p. 221.

132. U. Menzel, *Theorie und Praxis des chinesischen Entwicklungsmodells* (Opladen: Westdeutscher Verlag, 1978).

133. Scalapino & Lee, op. cit. (note 121), p. 1057.

134. Z. A. Kruszewski, *The Oder-Neisse-Boundary and Poland's Modernization* (New York: Praeger, 1972), p. 165.

135. *Die Zwangskollektivierung des selbständigen Bauernstandes in Mitteldeutschland* (Bonn: Gesamtdeutsches Ministerium, 1960), pp. 16ff.

136. Ch. K. Wilber, *The Soviet Model and Underdeveloped Countries* (Chapel Hill: University of North Carolina Press, 1969), p. 115; N. Jasny, *The Socialized Agriculture in the USSR* (Stanford: Stanford U.P., 1949), pp. 322ff.

137. Lethbridge, op. cit. (note 91), p. 198. J. Domes, *Die Ära Mao Tse-Tung* (Stuttgart: Kohlhammer, 1971), p. 46. Scalapino & Lee, op. cit. (note 121), p. 1042.

138. T.-L. Tung, *Agricultural Cooperation in China* (Peking: Foreign Languages Press, 1959), p. 28. A. Hsia, *Die chinesische Kulturrevolution* (Neuwied: Luchterhand, 1971), p. 127.

139. R. M. Bernardo, *The Theory of Moral Incentives in Cuba* (Tuscaloosa: University of Alabama Press, 1971), p. 128.

140. K. C. Yeh, "Soviet and Chinese Industrialization Strategies," in D. W. Treadgold (ed.), *Soviet and Chinese Communism. Similarities and Differences* (Seattle: University of Washington Press, 1970) [327-363], p. 336. For the following see: N. Jasny, *The Socialized Agriculture*, op. cit. (note 136), p. 61.

141. J. M. Michal, *Central Planning in Czechoslovakia* (Stanford: Stanford U.P., 1960), p. 90.

142. Domes, op. cit. (note 137), p. 50.

143. W. M. Breuer, *Sozialismus in Kuba* (Cologne: Pahl-Rugenstein, 1973), pp. 94f.

144. J. F. Brown, *Bulgaria under Communist Rule* (London: Pall Mall, 1970), p. 42.

145. E. Tümmler et al., *Die Agrarpolitik in Mitteldeutschland* (Berlin [West]: Duncker & Humblot, 1969), p. 152.

146. N. J. Sinizina & W. R. Tomin, "Das Scheitern der faschistischen Agrarpolitik in den okkupierten Gebieten der UdSSR. 1941-1944," *SW/Ges. WB* (1966), pp. 1190-1199.

147. Piekalkiewicz, op. cit. (note 43), p. 309.

148. R. C. Stuart, *The Collective Farm in Soviet Agriculture* (Lexington: (Lexington Books, 1972), pp. 194ff.

Chapter 2

149. E. G. Liberman, *Ökonomische Methoden zur Effizienzsteigerung der gesellschaftlichen Produktion* (Berlin [East]: Akademischer Verlag, 1973), pp. 31f.

150. P. Naville, *Le salaire socialiste*, Vol. 1 (Paris: Anthropos, 1970), p. 324.

151. *Narodnoe khozyaistvo SSSR v 1972 g* (Moscow: Statistika, 1973), p. 535. *Materialien zum Bericht zur Lage der Nation 1974* (Bonn: Bundesminister für innerdeutsche Beziehungen, 1974), p. 454.

152. J. Wilczynski, *Socialist Economic Development and Reforms* (London: Macmillan, 1972), p. 121.

153. K. Podolski (ed.), *Infrastruktura spoleczna w Polsce* (Warsaw: PWE, 1978); V. I. Drits (ed.), *Sotsial'naya infrastruktura—rezultat i faktor effektivnosti proizvodstva* (Minsk: Nauka i tekhnika, 1980).

154. H. Vogel, *Der gesellschaftliche Konsumtionsfonds als Instrument der sowjetischen Wirtschaftspolitik* (Berlin [West]: Duncker & Humblot, 1971), p. 101.

155. N. Jasny, *Essays on the Soviet Economy* (Munich, 1962). P. Wiles, *Distribution of Income. East and West* (Amsterdam: North-Holland Publishing Comp./New York: Elsevier, 1974), pp. 91ff.

156. *Lehrbuch Politische Ökonomie. Sozialismus* (Berlin [East]: Westgerman edition Frankfurt, Marxistische Blätter, 1972), p. 318.

157. Ph. Neumann, *Zurück zum Profit. Zur Entwicklung des Revisionismus in der DDR* (Berlin [West]: Oberbaum, 1973), pp. 220ff.

158. E. L. Wheelwright & B. MacFarlane, *The Chinese Road to Socialism* (New York: Monthly Review Press, 1970), p. 221.

159. Donnithorne, op. cit. (note 102), p. 208.

160. C. Mesa-Lago, *The Labor Sector and Socialist Distribution in Cuba* (New York: Praeger, 1968), p. 81.

161. R. Becker, *Sowjetische Lohnpolitik zwischen Ideologie und Wirtschaftsgesetz* (Berlin [West]: Duncker & Humblot, 1965), p. 55.

162. *Statistisches Jahrbuch Ungarns* (Budapest, 1973), p. 271.

163. J. G. Gliksman et al., *The Control of Industrial Labor and the Soviet Union* (Santa Monica, Calif.: Rand Corporation, 1960), p. 6.

164. C. Offe, *Leistungsprinzip und industrielle Arbeit* (Frankfurt: Suhrkamp, 1970).

165. Ch.-J. Chen, *Die Lohnstruktur ver VR China* (Berne: SOI, 1972), p. 49.

166. J. Talavera & J. Herrera, "La organización del trabajo y el salario en la agricultura," *Cuba socialista*, No. 5 (1965), p. 70.

167. P. Kuntze, *China, die konkrete Utopie* (Munich: Nymphenburger, 1973), p. 219.

168. Ch. Bettelheim, *Révolution culturelle et organisation industrielle en Chine* (Paris: F. Maspero, 1973), pp. 134f.

169. A. A. Maxwell, "Juvenile Unemployment in the USSR," *Soviet Survey* (Oct./Dec. 1958), p. 63; Gliksman, op. cit. (note 163), p. 20.

170. J. Wilczynski, *The Economics of Socialism* (London: Allen & Unwin, 1970), p. 105; Chen, op. cit. (note 165), p. 60.

171. Mesa-Lago, op. cit. (note 160), pp. 81f.

172. J. Kuroń & K. Modzelewski, *Monopolsozialismus* (Hamburg: Hoffmann & Campe, 1969), p. 21.

173. Wilczynski, op. cit. (note 152), p. 122.

174. *Lehrbuch*, op. cit. (note 156), pp. 545f.

175. N. S. Maslov, "O nekotorykh voprosakh organizatsii zarabotnoi platy v promyshlennosti," *VE*, No. 8 (1955), pp. 293f.

176. A. Zvorkin & D. Kirzhner, "Nekotorye voprosy organizatsii zarabotnoi platy v ugol'noi promyshlennosti. Sotsialisticheskie oplaty truda vo promyshlennosti," *SGiP*, No. 6 (1956), p. 31.

178. Chen, op. cit. (note 165), pp. 50f.

179. D. H. Perkins, "Incentives and Profits in Chinese Industry," in K. I. Chen & J. S. Uppal (eds.), *Comparative Development of India and China* (New York: Macmillan, 1971) [133-143], p. 137).

180. M. McAuley, *Labour Disputes in Soviet Russia. 1957-1965* (Oxford: Clarendon Press, 1969), p. 180.

181. G. Lemân, "Neue Entwicklungen im jugoslawischen System der Einkommensverteilung," *OE/W* (1969) [262-276], p. 276; idem, *Stellung und Aufgaben der ökonomischen Einheiten in den jugoslawischen Unternehmungen* (Berlin [West]: Duncker & Humblot, 1967), pp. 126ff.

182. *Lehrbuch*, op. cit. (note 156), p. 547. J. Wilczynski, "Differentiation of Income under Modern Socialism," *Jahrbuch der Wirtschaft Osteuropas* (Munich: Olzog, 1972) [467-488], p. 477.

183. Suslov, op. cit. (note 113), p. 73.

184. R. Krzyżewski, *Konsumpcja spoleczna w gospodarce socjalistycznej* (Warsaw: PWE, 1968), p. 15.

185. G. Fink, *Gossnab SSSR. Planung und Planungsprobleme der Produktionsmittelverteilung in der UdSSR* (Berlin [West]: Duncker & Humblot, 1972), p. 61.

186. P. Brügge, "Samstags ohne Bezahlung ins Werk," *Der Spiegel*, No. 14 (1973) [134-142], p. 135.

187. J. S. Berliner, *Factory and Manager in the USSR* (Cambridge, Mass.: Harvard U.P., 1957), pp. 182ff., 306ff.

188. B. Lewytzkyi, *Die Kommunistische Partei der Sowjetunion* (Stuttgart: Kohlhammer, 1967), p. 87.

189. P. Osten & F. Kantowski, "'Chal'tura'—ein sozial-ökonomisches Phänomen," *OE*, No. 2 (1972), pp. 99-114.

190. St. J. Staats, "Corruption in the Soviet System," *PoC*, No. 1 (1972) [40-47], p. 46.

191. J. S. Berliner, "Managerial Incentives and Decision Making. A Comparison of the United States and the Soviet Union," in M. Bornstein (ed.), *Comparative Economic Systems. Models and Cases* (Homewood, Ill.: University of Illinois Press, 1965) [386-417], p. 409.

192. H. J. Sherman, *The Soviet Economy* (Boston: Little, Brown, 1969), pp. 151ff.

193. B. Richman, *Soviet Management. With Significant American Comparisons* (Englewood Cliffs, N.J.: Prentice Hall, 1965), p. 109.

194. J. F. Hough, *The Soviet Prefects. The Local Party Organs in Industrial Decision-Making* (Cambridge, Mass.: Harvard U.P., 1969), pp. 257ff.

195. Liberman, op. cit. (note 149), p. 61.

196. B. M. Richman, *A Firsthand Study of Industrial Management in Communist China* (Los Angeles: University of California Press, 1967), p. 17.

197. B. A. Balassa, *The Hungarian Experience in Economic Planning* (New Haven: Yale U.P., 1959), p. 133.

198. *Borba*, February 26, 1969.

199. Wilczynski, op. cit. (note 182), p. 479.

200. Emel'yanov, op. cit. (note 111), p. 79.

201. *Radnicko samoupravljanje* (Beograd, 1961), p. 59.

202. *Borba*, February 10, 1969.

203. Lemân, op. cit. (note 181), pp. 262, 266.

204. Gliksman, op. cit. (note 163), pp. 68f.

205. *Trud*, February 26, 1953; Sovetskii soyuz, May, 1950, p. 23.

206. A. Eber, "Die Entwicklung der materiellen Lage der chinesischen Arbeiterklasse," in *Klassen- und Klassenbeziehungen in der VR China* (Dresden: Verlag Zeit im Bild, 1973) [115-123], p. 119.

207. H. Marchisio, in Ch. Bettelheim et al., *Der Aufbau des Sozialismus in China* (Munich: Trikont, 1969), p. 96f.

208. *El Mundo*, November 27, 1965; *Granma*, December 12, 1965.

209. *Granma*, March 17, 1971.

210. L. G. Reynolds & C. H. Taft, *The Evolution of Wages Structures* (New Haven: Yale U.P., 1956), p. 373.

211. A. Bergson, *The Structure of Soviet Wages* (Cambridge, Mass.: Harvard U.P., 1946), p. 187.

212. A. J. Pietsch, "Differenzierung der Arbeitslöhne in der UdSSR und der BRD," *OE/W*, No. 3 (1972), pp. 183-196.

213. F. L. Pryor, "Barriers to Market Socialism in Eastern Europe in the Mid 1960s," *StiCC*, No. 2 (1970) [31-64], p. 38.

214. D. H. Perkins, *Market Control and Planning in Communist China* (Cambridge, Mass.: Harvard U.P., 1966), p. 93f.

215. V. I. Staroverov, *Sovetskaya derevnya na etape razvitogo sotsializma* (Moscow: Politizdat, 1976), pp. 46ff.

216. Donnithorne, op. cit. (note 102), p. 204.

217. A. A. Ambrosov, *Ot klassovoi differentsiatsii k sotsial'noi odnorodnsti obshchestva* (Moscow: Mysl', 1972), p. 165. V. P. Zenin, *Rabochii klass i kolkhoznoe krest' yanstvo* (Kiev: Naukova dumka, 1976).

218. A. Rudakov, "Sovershestvovanie oplaty truda v kooperativakh evropeiskikh stran-chlenov SEV," *VE*, No. 1 (1970) [104-112], p. 112.

219. Piekalkiewicz, op. cit. (note 43), p. 317.

220. A. Barkauskas, "O preodelenii kul'turno-bytovykh razlichii mezhdu gorodom i derevnei," *Kommunist*, No. 8 (1973), pp. 55-66.

221. G. Sarkisian, "Sblizhenie urovnei zhizni rabochikh i kolkhoznikov," *VE*, No. 6, p. 79.

222. H. Roggemann, *Das Modell der Arbeiterselbstverwaltung in Jugoslawien* (Frankfurt: *EVA*, 1970), p. 65.

223. M. Matthews, *Class and Society in Soviet Russia* (London: Allen Lane, 1972), p. 89.

224. K.-E. Waedekin, *Führungskräfte im sowjetischen Dorf* (Berlin [West]: Duncker & Humblot, 1969), pp. 115ff.

225. K.-E. Waedekin, *Die Bezahlung der Arbeit in der sowjetischen Landwirt- schaft* (Berlin [West]: Duncker & Humblot, 1972), p. 264.

226. A. Nove, "Incentives for Peasants and Administrators," *Was Stalin Really Necessary?* (London: Allen & Unwin, 1964) [186-205], p. 191.

227. Suslov, op. cit. (note 113), p. 64.

228. E. F. Vogel, "Voluntarism and Social Control," in Treadgold, op. cit. (note 140), (168-184), p. 175.

229. J. S. Burki, "A Study of Chinese Communes," in Chen & Uppal, op. cit. (note 179), (169-182), p. 173.

230. L. Kostin, *Wages in the USSR* (Moscow: Mysl', 1960), p. 60; Matthews, op. cit. (note 223), p. 92.

231. *Itogi vsesoyuznoi perepisi naselenia 1970 g,* Vol. 6 (Moscow: Statistika), p. 6f.

232. L. G. Churchward, *The Soviet Intelligentsia* (London: Routledge & Kegan Paul, 1973), p. 79.

233. L. Kolakowski, "The Fate of Marxism in Eastern-Europe," *Slavic Review* (1970 [175-181, 201-202], p. 202.

234. Ambrosov, op. cit. (note 217), pp. 177f.

235. G. I. Pivatsaikin, *Obshchestvennye otnoshenia razvitogo sotsializma* (Minsk: Nauka i tekhnika, 1973), pp. 112f.

236. M. N. Rutkevich & F. P. Filippov, *Sotsial'nye peremesheniya* (Moscow: Mysl', 1970), p. 88.

237. M. N. Rutkevich, "O poniatii sotsial'noi struktury," *SI*, No. 4 (1978), pp. 29-41. M. N. Rutkevich & F. R. Filippov (ed.), *Sotsial'naya struktura razvitogo sotsialisticheskogo obshchestva v SSSR* (Moscow: Nauka, 1976). There is a growing interest in Western sociology in the analysis of social

structure: D. Lane, *The Socialist Industrial State. Towards a Political Sociology of State Socialism* (London: Allen & Unwin, 1976), pp. 197ff.; B. Kerblay, *La société soviétique contemporaine* (Paris: Colin, 1977), pp. 199ff.; G. Brunner, *Politische Soziologie der UdSSR* (Wiesbaden: Akademische Verlagsanstalt, 1977), 2 vols.; M. Yanowitch, *Social and Economic Inequality in the Soviet Union* (London: Martin Robertson, 1977); W. Teckenberg, *Die soziale Struktur der sowjetischen Arbeiterklasse im internationalen Vergleich. Auf dem Wege zur industrialisierten Ständegesellschaft?* (Munich: Oldenburg, 1977); J. Brockmann, *Die Differenzierung der sowjetischen Sozialstruktur* (Wiesbaden: Harrassowitz, 1978), pp. 1ff.

238. For the early Women's Liberation Movement see: R. Stites, *The Women's Liberation Movement in Russia. Feminism, Nihilism, and Bolshevism, 1860-1930* (Princeton, N.J.: Princeton U.P., 1978).

239. *Yearbook of Labor Statistics* (Geneva: ILO, 1979), pp. 26ff.

240. S. Köhler-Wagnerová, *Die Frau im Sozialismus. Beispiel CSSR* (Hamburg: Hoffmann & Campe, 1974), p. 71.

241. E. Szabady, "Emanzipation und Erwerbstätigkeit der Frau in Ungarn," *OE* (1971) [A 780-784], p. A 781.

242. *Demograficheskie aspekty zanyastosti* (Moscow: Statistika, 1975), p. 48.

243. For the Soviet Union cf.: *Zakonodatel'stvo o pravakh zhenshchin v SSSR* (Moscow: Yuridicheskaya Literatura, 1975).

244. Quoted: G. Maschke, "Cubanischer Taschenkalender," *Kursbuch 30* (1973), p. 143.

245. V. D. Patrushev, "Das Zeitbudget der städtischen Bevölkerung in sozialistischen und kapitalistischen Ländern," in R. Ahlberg (ed.), *Soziologie in der Sowjetunion* (Freiburg: Rombach, 1969) [199-213], p. 206; N. P. Pishchulin, *Proizvodstvennyi kollektiv, chelovek i svobodnoe vremya* (Moscow: Profizdat, 1976).

246. L. Lennon, "Women in the USSR," *PoC*, No. 4 (1971) [47-58], p. 56; A. Heitlinger, *Women and State Socialism* (London: Macmillan, 1979).

247. A. G. Kharchev, *Brak i semya v SSSR* (Moscow: Mysl', 1964), pp. 274f.; 2nd edition 1979.

248. E. S. Danilova, *Sotsial'nye problemy truda zhenshchinycrabotnitsy* (Moscow: Mysl', 1968).

249. Itogi, op. cit. (note 231), Vol. 6, p. 7.

250. B. Lewytzkyj, *Die Gewerkschaften in der Sowjetunion* (Frankfurt: EVA, 1970), p. 93.

251. United Nations, *Participation of Women in the Economic and Social Development of their Countries* (New York: UN, 1970), p. 9.

252. K. Wrochno, *Problemy pracy kobiet* (Warsaw: PWE, 1971), p. 92; *Geschichte der Partei der Arbeit Albaniens* (Tirana: Institut für Marxistisch-leninistische Studien beim ZK der Paa, 1971), p. 679.

253. *Zhenshchiny i deti v SSSR* (Moscow: Statistika, 1969), p. 102.

254. C. Broyelle, *La moitié du ciel* (Paris: Denoel & Gonthier, 1973).

255. Figures in: A. Teriaeva, "Zonal'nye problemy vosproizvodstva rabochei sily i oplata truda v sel'skom khozyaistve," *VE*, No. 11 (1968) [41-51], p. 45.

256. V. Pereventsev, "Migratsiia naseleniia i ispol'zovanie trudovykh resursov," *VE*, No. 9 (1970), pp. 34-43; cf. H. Carrère d'Encausse, *L'empire éclaté* (Paris: Flammarion, 1978), pp. 117f.

257. V. M. Rakitskii, *Obshchestvennye fondy potrebleniya kak ekonomicheskaya kategoriya* (Moscow: Ekonomika, 1966), p. 161.

258. H. J. Wagener, *Wirtschaftswachstum in unterentwickelten Gebieten. Ansätze zu einer Regionalanalyse der Sowjetunion* (Berlin [West]: Duncker & Humblot, 1972), p. 92; A. Inkeles, "The Soviet Social System: Model for Asia?" in idem, *Social Change in Soviet Russia* (Cambridge, Mass.: Harvard U.P., 1968), pp. 383-398; Wilber, op. cit. (note 136).

259. H. Chambre, *Union soviétique et développement économique* (Paris: Aubier-Montagne, 1967), pp. 364ff.

260. A. Nove & J. A. Newth, *The Soviet Middle East: A Model for Development?* (London: Allen & Unwin, 1967), pp. 105ff.

261. W. Gumpel, "Etatismus oder Sozialismus? Eine Untersuchung über Prinzipien und Effizienz der Entwicklungspolitik in der Türkei und in Sowjetmittelasien," in W. Gumpel & D. Keese (eds.), *Probleme des Industrialismus in Ost und West. Festschrift für Hans Raupach* (Munich: Olzog, 1973) [45-76], pp. 74f.

262. Donnithorne, op. cit. (note 102), p. 208.

263. Burki, op. cit. (note 229), p. 181.

264. Krejci, op. cit. (note 78), pp. 30ff.

265. Pryor, op. cit. (note 64), pp. 88f.; Wiles, op. cit. (note 155), pp. 91ff.; P. Wiles & S. Markowski, "Income Distribution under Communism and Capitalism," *Soviet Studies* (1970) [344-369, 497-511], p. 497, 500.

266. J. Kosta et al., *Warenproduktion im Sozialismus* (Frankfurt, Fischer, 1973), p. 175.

267. Michal, op. cit. (note 141), p. 193.

268. Chen, op. cit. (note 165), p. 60f.

269. Bernardo, op. cit. (note 139), p. 94.

270. Scalapino & Lee, op. cit. (note 121), p. 772.

271. A. Inkeles & P. H. Rossi, "National Comparisons of Occupational Prestige," in A. Inkeles, *Social Change in Soviet Russia* (Cambridge, Mass.: Harvard U.P., 1968) [175-191], p. 190.

272. Cf. M. M. Kucherenko, *Molodoe pokolenie rabochego klassa SSSR* (Moscow: Mysl', 1979).

273. F. A. Hayek (ed.), *Collectivist Economic Planning* (London: G. Routledge & Sons, 1935), pp. 87ff.

274. O. Lange, "On the Economic Theory of Socialism," in B. E. Lippincott (ed.), *On the Economic Theory of Socialism* (Minneapolis: The University of Minnesota Press, 1948) [57-143], p. 88.

275. A. Carlo, *Politische und ökonomische Struktur der UdSSR, 1917-1975* (Berlin [West]: Wagenbach, 1972), p. 67.

276. H. D. Dickinson, *Economics of Socialism* (London: Oxford U.P., 1939), pp. 104f.

277. Debate in *VE*, No. 3 (1964).

278. *Planovoe khozyaistvo*, No. 8/9 (1934), p. 200.

279. F. Haffner, *Das sowjetische Preissystem* (Berlin [West]: Duncker &

Humblot, 1968), p. 316; J. Popkiewicz, "The Price System in Socialist Economy," *Revue de l'est*, No. 3 (1973), pp. 49-64.

280. E. Preobrazenskij, *Die neue Ökonomik (1926)* (Berlin [West]: Verlag Neuer Kurs, 1971), pp. 127f.

281. Ch.-Y. Cheng, *Communist China's Economy 1949-1962* (South Orange, N.J.: Seton Hall U.P., 1963), p. 95; F. Schurmann, "Politics and Economics in Russia and China," in Treadgold, op. cit. (note 140) [297-326], p. 309; S. H. Chou, "Prices in Communist China," *The Journal of Asian Studies* (1966), pp. 645-663.

282. C. Mesa-Lago (ed.), *Revolutionary Change in Cuba* (Pittsburgh, Pa.: Pittsburgh U.P., 1971), p. 176.

283. R. V. Greenslade, "The Soviet Economic System in Transition," in *New Directions*, op. cit. (note 127) [1-17], p. 15.

284. F. L. Pryor, "Barriers to Market Socialism in Eastern Europe in the Mid 1960s," *StiCC*, No. 2 (1970) [31-64], p. 47.

285. Nove, op. cit. (note 28), p. 180.

286. A. N. Malafaev, *Istoriia tseno-obrazovaniya v SSSR 1917-1963* (Moscow: Ekonomika, 1964), p. 24; A. Agocs, *Preisbildung und Preisentwicklung in der Sowjetunion* (Zürich: Juris-Verlag, 1971), pp. 13ff.

287. Michal, op. cit. (note 141), p. 159.

288. *Lehrbuch*, op. cit. (note 156), pp. 509, 557f.

289. L. Turgeon, "Overall Price Movements and Price Policies," in idem, *The Contrasting Economies* (Boston: Allyn & Bacon, 1963) [177-209], p. 207.

290. *New Directions*, op. cit. (note 127).

291. B. H. Kerblay, *Les marchés paysans en U.R.S.S.* (Paris, The Hague: Mouton, 1968), pp. 347ff.

292. O. Kýn, "Market and Price Mechanism in Socialist Countries. The Rise and Fall of Economic Reform in Czechoslovakia," *The American Economic Review*, No. 2 (1970) [300-306], p. 303.

293. O. Kýn, "Die tschechoslowakische Wirtschaftsreform und ihr Ende," in H. H. Höhmann et al. (eds.), *Die Wirtschaftsordnungen Osteuropas im Wandel* (Freiburg: Rombach, 1972), Vol. 1 [139-180], p. 159.

294. *Pravda*, May 17, 1964; *Pravda*, February 4, 1971; *Izvestiya*, September 23, 1965.

295. Liberman, op. cit. (note 149), p. 23.

296. A. Eckstein, *China's Economic Revolution* (Cambridge: Cambridge U.P., 1978), pp. 114ff., 145ff.

297. J. Lipinski, "The Correct Relation between Prices of Producer Goods and Wage Costs in a Socialist Economy," in D. C. Hague (ed.), *Price Formation in Various Economies* (London: St. Martin's Press, 1967), pp. 107-125.

298. A. Brzeski, "Finance and Inflation under Central Planning," Part II, *OE/W* (1967) [278-297], p. 294.

299. J. Nagy, "Das Monopolproblem in Ungarn," *OE/W*, No. 4 (1972), pp. 221-240.

300. W. Hössler, "Preisdisziplin gehört zur politischen Verantwortung von Industrie und Handel," *Die Wirtschaft (GDR)*, No. 15 (1971), p. 20.

301. R. Damus, *Entscheidungstrukturen und Funktionsprobleme der DDR-Wirtschaft* (Frankfurt: Suhrkamp, 1973), p. 228.

302. Pryor, op. cit. (note 284), p. 31.

303. F. Neumark, *Grundsätze gerechter und ökonomisch rationaler Steuer-politik* (Tübingen: Mohr, 1970), p. 199f.

304. R. W. Davies, *The Development of the Soviet Budgetary System* (Cambridge: Cambridge U.P., 1958), p. 211.

305. M. V. Kolganov, *Natsional'nyi dokhod* (Moscow: Finansy, 1959), p. 285; Z. Kh. Rusin & L. L. Eidinova (ed.), *Gosudarstvennyi byudzhet SSSR* (Moscow: Finansy, 1975), pp. 45ff.; V. V. Lavrov & K. N. Plotnikov (ed.), *Gosudarstvennyi byudzhet SSSR* (Moscow: Finansy, 1975), p. 68; *Spravochnik po nalogam i sboram s naseleniya* (Moscow: Finansy, 1973).

306. Nove, op. cit. (note 28), p. 232.

307. E. Strnad, "Der kubanische Staatshaushalt," *Diss. Rostock (GDR)* (1968), p. 106.

308. T. H. Tsien, *La république populaire de Chine; droit constitutionnel et institutions* (Paris: Librairie générale de droit et de jurisprudence, 1970), p. 441.

309. Wheelwright & McFarlane, op. cit. (note 158), p. 138.

310. Hoffmann, op. cit. (note 118), p. 56.

311. *Narodnoe Khozyaistvo SSSR v 1972 g* (Moscow: Statistika, 1973), p. 725, (1978), p. 533.

312. *Narodnoe Khozyaistvo*, op. cit. (1978), p. 391.

313. *Bericht der Bundesregierung und Materialien zur Lage der Nation* (Bonn: Bundesministerium fur innerdeutsche Beziehungen, 1971), p. 134.

314. G. N. Ecklung, *Financing the Chinese Government* (Edinburgh: Edinburgh U.P., 1966), p. 115.

315. A. Rajkiewicz (ed.), *Sotsial'naya politika* (Moscow: Progress, 1977); M. P. Mchedlov & Ju E. Volkov (ed.), *Sotsial'naya politika kommunisticheskikh i rabochikh partii v sotsialisticheskom obshchestve* (Moscow: Politizdat, 1979).

316. A turning point was the work by Helga Ulbricht, "Aufgaben der sozialistischen Sozialpolitik bei der Gestaltung der sozialen Sicherheit in der DDR," *Habilitationsschrift* (Leipzig: 1965). The leading compendium is *Theorie und Praxis der Sozialpolitik in der DDR* (Berlin [East]: Akademie-Verlag, 1979).

317. M. S. Lantsev, *The Economic Aspects of Social Security in the USSR* (Moscow: Progress, 1979), p. 11.

318. R. Krzyżewski, op. cit. (note 184), p. 115.

319. *Gosudarstvennyi pyatiletnyi plan razvitiya narodnogo khozyaistva SSSR za 1971-1975 gody* (Moscow: Politizdat, 1972), p. 290.

320. *Statistisches Jahrbuch Ungarns* (Budapest: Statistischer Verlag, 1973), p. 277.

321. Cf. L. Tulchinskii, "O metodologii ischisleniya obshchestvennykh fondov protebleniya," *Vestnik statistiki*, No. 5 (1966), pp. 39f.

322. Matthews, op. cit. (note 223), p. 78.

323. W.-R. Leenen, *Zur Frage der Wachstumsorientierung der marxistisch-leninistischen Sozialpolitik in der DDR* (Berlin [West]: Duncker & Humblot, 1977).

324. Donnithorne, op. cit. (note 102), p. 213; D. M. Lampton, "New 'Revolution' in China's Social Policy," *PoC*, No. 5/6 (1979), pp. 16-33.

325. Cf. K. von Beyme, *Sozialismus oder Wohlfahrtsstaat? Sozialpolitik und Sozialstruktur der Sowjetunion im Systemvergleich* (Munich: Piper, 1977), pp. 77ff.; D. Connor, *Deviance in Soviet Society* (New York: Columbia U.P., 1972); P. H. Solomon, *Soviet Criminologists and Criminal Policy* (New York, Columbia U.P., 1978).

326. R. R. Fagen, *The Transformation of Political Culture in Cuba* (Stanford: Stanford U.P., 1969), pp. 138ff. R. F. Price, *Education in Communist China* (London: Routledge & Kegan Paul, 1970), pp. 27ff.

327. *Narodnoe obrazovanie v SSSR. Sbornik dokumentov 1917-1973 gg* (Moscow: Pedagogika, 1974), pp. 18f.

328. O. Anweiler & K.-H. Ruffmann (eds.), *Kulturpolitik der Sowjetunion* (Stuttgart: Kröner, 1973), p. 23.

329. A. Hearnden, *Bildungspolitik in der BRD und DDR* (Düsseldorf: Bertelsmann, 1973), p. 269.

330. V. G. Afanasev, *Nauchno-teknicheskaya revolyutsia, upravlenie, obrazovanie* (Moscow: Politizdat, 1972), Chapter 11.

331. W. I. Garms, "The Correlates of Educational Efforts: A Multivariate Analysis," *Comparative Education Review* (1968) [281-299], p. 282.

332. Pryor, op. cit. (note 22), p. 207.

333. United Nations, *UN Statistical Yearbook 1978* (New York: UN, 1979), pp. 928ff.

334. St. H. Cohn, "Soviet Growth Retardation," in *New Directions*, op. cit. (note 127) [99-132], p. 102.

335. F. R. Scheck, *Chinas sozialistischer Weg. Berichte und Analysen der Peking Rundschau* (Frankfurt: Fischer, 1971), p. 205.

336. Klassen, op. cit. (note 206), p. 201. For 1958 higher figures have been mentioned (1958: 62%). Renmin Ribao, Oct. 8, 1959, quoted in Hsia, op. cit. (note 138), p. 69.

337. M. S. Voslensky, *Nomenklatura. Die herrschende Klasse der Sowjetunion* (Vienna: Molden, 1980), p. 195.

338. Lane, op. cit. (note 237), p. 204.

339. Figures in *Narodnoe khozyaistvo* (1978), p. 482; E. K. Vassil'eva, *Sotsial'no-ekonomicheskaya struktura naseleniya SSSR* (Moscow: Statistika, 1978), p. 46; *Narodnoe obrazovanie a nauka i kul'tura v SSSR. Statisticheskii sbornik* (Moscow: Statistika, 1977), pp. 93ff.

340. V. I. Staroverov, op. cit. (note 115), p. 190.

341. E. V. Klopov et al. (ed.), *Sotsial'noe razvitie rabochego klassa SSSR* (Moscow: Nauka, 1977), p. 107.

342. M. Matthews, "Educational Growth and the Social Structure in the USSR," in M. G. Field (ed.), *Social Consequences of Modernization in Communist Societies* (Baltimore: Johns Hopkins U.P., 1976) [121-145], p. 141.

343. F. P. Filippov, *Vseobshchee srednee obrazovanie v SSSR* (Moscow: Mysl', 1976), pp. 86ff.

344. *Izvestiya*, September 12, 1969.

345. D. Glowka, "Numerus Clausus. Darstellung eines Problems am sowjetischen Beispiel," *OE*, No. 11 (1970) [751-775], p. 761.

346. Hsia, op. cit. (note 138), p. 76.

347. Gosudarstvennyi, op. cit. (note 319), p. 309.

348. M. Yanovitch & N. Dodge, "Social Class and Education. Soviet Findings and Reactions," *Comparative Education Review* (1968) [248-267], p. 254.

349. Cf. L. Liegle, "Soziale Schichtung, Familienerziehung und Schulerfolg in der Sowjetunion," in O. Anweiler (ed.), *Bildungsreformen in Osteuropa* (Stuttgart: Kohlhammer, 1969), pp. 56-72.

350. Engl. translation of an article by F. L. Liss, in M. Yanowitch & W. A. Fisher (eds.), *Social Stratification and Mobility in the USSR* (White Plains: International Arts and Sciences Press, 1973), pp. 275-288.

351. N. de Witt, *High-Level Manpower in the USSR* in *New Directions*, op. cit. (note 127) [789-816], p. 816.

352. D. C. Pirages, *Socio-Economic Development and Political Access in the Communist Party States* in J. F. Triska (ed.), *Communist Party States* (Indianapolis: Bobbs-Merrill, 1969) [249-281], p. 267.

353. UNESCO, *UNESCO Statistical Yearbook 1971* (Paris: UNESCO, 1972), pp. 462ff.

354. G. Kiss, *Marxismus als Soziologie. Theorie und Empirie in den Sozialwissenschaften der DDR, UdSSR, Polen, der CSSR, Ungarns, Bulgariens und Rumäniens* (Reinbek: Rowohlt, 1971); J. J. Wiatr (ed.), *The State of Sociology in Eastern Europe Today* (Carbondale and Edwardsville, Ill.: Southern Illinois U.P., 1971); V. Léon, "Les sciences sociales en Europe de l'est," *Revue de l'est,* No. 3 (1971), pp. 155-171; E. A. Weinberg, *The Development of Sociology in the Soviet Union* (London: Routledge & Kegan Paul, 1974); R. Scharff, "Organisation von Forschung und Lehre in der sowjetischen Soziologie," *Berichte des Bundesinstituts für ostwissenschaftliche und internationale Studien, Cologne,* No. 3 (1980).

355. N. Grant (ed.), *Society, Schools, and Progress in Eastern Europe* (Oxford: Pergamon Press, 1969), p. 91.

356. On the early Soviet educational policy: Sh. Fitzpatrick, *The Commissariat of Enlightenment; Soviet Organization of Education and the Arts under Lunacharsky, October 1917-1921* (Cambridge: Cambridge U.P., 1970), pp. 89ff.

357. O. Anweiler, "Gesellschaftliche Mitwirkung und Schulverfassung in Bildungssystemen staatssozialistischer Prägung," *Bildung und Erziehung,* No. 4 (1973) [260-272], p. 270.

358. *Mao Papers* (London: Oxford U.P., 1970), p. 95f.

359. R. F. Price, *Education in Communist China* (London: Routledge & Kegan Paul, 1970), pp. 266ff.

360. E. K. Ong, "Education in China since the Cultural Revolution," *StiCC,* No. 3/4 (1970) [158-176], p. 165.

361. *Chile 1971: Habla Fidel Castro* (Santiago de Chile: Ed. Universitaria, 1971), p. 29.

362. M. S. Voslensky, op. cit. (note 337); R. E. Blackwell, Jr., "Cadres Policy in the Brezhnev Era," *PoC,* No. 2 (1979), pp. 29-42; R. Schwarzenbach, *Die Kaderpolitik der SED in der Staatsverwaltung* (Cologne: Wissenschaft und Politik, 1976); G.-J. Glaessner, *Herrschaft durch Kader. Leitung der Gesellschaft und Kaderpolitik in der DDR* (Opladen: Westdeutscher Verlag, 1977); G.-J. Glaessner & I. Rudolph, *Macht durch Wissen. Zum Zusammenhang von Bildungspolitik, Bildungssystem und Kaderqualifizierung in der DDR* (Opladen, Westdeutscher Verlag, 1978).

Chapter 3

363. B. Balla, *Kaderverwaltung. Versuch zur Idealtypisierung der "Bürokratie" sowjetisch-volksdemokratischen Typs* (Stuttgart: Enke, 1972), pp. 176ff.

364. M.-P. Canapa, "Réforme économique et socialisation agraire en Yougo-slavie," *Revue de l'est*, No. 1 (1971) [69-94], p. 89.

365. M. Sadowski, *Przemiany spoleczne a system partyjny PRL* (Warsaw: PWN, 1969), pp. 202ff.

366. T. H. Rigby, *Communist Party Membership in the USSR. 1917-1967* (Princeton: Princeton U.P., 1968), p. 418.

367. J. J. Wiatr, "Military Professionalism and Transformations of Class Structure in Poland," in J. van Doorn (ed.), *Armed Forces and Society* (The Hague & Paris: Mouton, 1968), pp. 229-239.

368. Voigt, op. cit. (note 43), p. 134.

369. M. Rush, *Political Succession in the USSR* (New York: Columbia U.P., 1968).

370. K. von Beyme, "A Comparative View of Democratic Centralism," *Government and Opposition* (1975), pp. 259-277.

371. *The Xth Party Meeting of the Communist Party of China. Documents* (Peking: Foreign Languages Press, 1973).

372. M. C. Lodge, *Soviet Elite Attitudes since Stalin* (Columbus, Ohio: Charles E. Merrill, 1969); R. B. Farrell (ed.), *Political Leadership in Eastern Europe and the Soviet Union* (Chicago: Aldine, 1970); F. J. Fleron, "Cooptation as a Mechanism of Adaptation to Change: The Soviet Leadership," in R. E. Kanet (ed.), *The Behavioral Revolution and Communist Studies* (New York: Free Press, 1971), pp. 125-150; T. H. Rigby, "The Soviet Leadership: Towards a Self-stabilizing Oligarchy?" *Soviet Studies* (1970), pp. 167-191; C. Beck et al., *Comparative Communist Political Leadership* (New York: McKay, 1973); R. J. Hill, *Soviet Political Elites* (London: Martin Robertson, 1977); K. E. Bailes, *Technical Elites and Soviet Society under Lenin and Stalin* (Princeton: Princeton U.P., 1978).

373. D. J. Waller, "Evolution of the Chinese Communist Political Elite 1931-1965," in R. A. Scalapino (ed.), *Elites in the People's Republic of China* (Seattle: University of Washington Press, 1972) [41-66], p. 55.

374. D. J. Waller, *Status and Change in Revolutionary Elite: A Comparison of the 1956 Party Central Committees in China and the USSR* (Beverly Hills:

Sage, 1970), p. 657; J. W. Lewis (ed.), *Party Leadership and Power in China* (Cambridge: Cambridge U.P., 1970).

375. H. D. Lasswell & D. Lerner (eds.), *World Revolutionary Elites* (Cambridge, Mass.: MIT Press, 1965).

376. Waller, op. cit. (note 373), p. 57.

377. P. Ch. Ludz, *The Changing Party Elite in East Germany* (Cambridge, Mass.: Mit Press, 1972), pp. 35ff.

378. T. H. Rigby, "Crypto-Politics," in J. F. Fleron (ed.), *Communist Studies and the Social Sciences* (Chicago: Rand McNally, 1969) [116–128], p. 119.

379. Ph. D. Stewart et al., "Political Mobility and the Soviet Political Process," *APSR* (1972) [1269–1290], pp. 1284f.

380. J. J. Wiatr & K. Ostrowski, "Political Leadership: What Kind of Professionalism," in J. J. Wiatr & J. Tarkowski (eds.), *Studies in Polish Political System* (Warsaw: PWN, 1967) [140–155], p. 145.

381. Cf. F. Parkin, *Class Inequality and Political Order* (London: Paladin, 1971), p. 138.

382. Cf. D. Lane, *The End of Inequality? Stratification under State Socialism* (Middlesex: Penguin Books, 1971).

Part II

Chapter 4

383. *The Xth Party Convention of the Communist Party of China. Documents* (Peking: Foreign Languages Publishing House, 1973), p. 5.

384. E. D. Domar, "On the Measurement of Comparative Efficiency," in A. Eckstein (ed.), *Comparison of Economic Systems. Theoretical and Methodological Approaches* (Berkeley: University of California Press, 1971) [219–240], p. 228.

385. B. A. Balassa, "Success Criteria for Economic Systems," in M. Bornstein, op. cit. (note 191), pp. 2–18.

386. For Soviet view see: L. M. Konstantinova & Z. V. Sokolinskii, *Ekonomicheskaya effektivnost' obshchestvennogo proizvodstva. Analiz statisticheskikh pokazatelei* (Moscow: Statistika, 1974).

38'. A. Gerschenkron, *A Dollar Index of Soviet Machinery Output* (Santa Monica: Rand Corporation, 1951); J. M. Montias, "A Note on Gerschenkron Biases," in *YoEC*, Vol. 3 (Munich: 1972), pp. 153–166.

388. H. J. Sherman, *The Soviet Economy* (Boston: Little Brown, 1969), p. 114.

389. Bornstein, in Eckstein, op. cit. (note 384), pp. 347f.

390. A. Erlich, *The Soviet Industrialization Debate, 1924–1928* (Cambridge, Mass.: Harvard U.P., 1967), Chapter IX.

391. Eckstein, op. cit. (note 296), p. 224; A. G. Ashbrook, in *Chinese Economy Post-Mao. A Compendium of Papers Submitted to the Joint Economic Committee Congress of the United States* (Washington, D.C.: GOP, 1978), pp. 204ff.: L. A. Orleans, "China's Population Growth. Another Perspective," *CS*, No. 2/3 (1978) [1–24], p. 22; W. Kraus, *Wirtschaftliche Entwicklung und sozialer Wandel in der Volksrepublik China* (Berlin: Springer, 1979), pp. 437ff.; *Promyshlennost' KNR* (Moscow: Nauka, 1979), pp. 53ff.; N. R. Lardy, in *Chinese Economy Post-Mao*, pp. 52ff.

392. U. Menzel, *Theorie und Praxis des chinesischen Entwicklungsmodells* (Opladen: Westdeutscher Verlag, 1978), p. 611.

393. A. Bergson, *Productivity and the Social System. The USSR and the West* (Cambridge, Mass.: Harvard U.P., 1978), pp. 193ff.

394. G. W. Nutter, *Growth of Industrial Production in the Soviet Union* (Princeton: Princeton U.P., 1962), p. 285.

395. *Der ökonomische Wettbewerb zwischen der UdSSR und den USA* (Berlin [East], 1971), pp. 77ff.

396. S. Kuznets, *Economic Growth of Nations. Total Output and Production Structure* (Cambridge, Mass.: Harvard U.P., 1971), p. 19.

397. Nutter, op. cit. (note 394), p. 289.

398. S. Kuznets, in A. Bergson & S. Kuznets (eds.), *Economic Trends in the Soviet Union* (Cambridge, Mass.: Harvard U.P., 1963), pp. 336f.

399. B. A. Balassa, *The Hungarian Experience in Economic Planning* (New Haven: Yale U.P., 1959), p. 233. Later figures in *Statistisches Jahrbuch Ungarns 1979* (Budapest, 1979).

400. "Aufwendungen für die Besatzungsmächte, öffentliche Haushalte und Sozialprodukt in den einzelnen Zonen," in *Wirtschaftsprobleme der*

Besatzungszonen (Berlin [West]: Duncker & Humblot, 1948), p. 120, 136; A. Zauberman, *Industrial Progress in Poland, Czechoslovakia and East Germany 1937-1962* (London: Oxford U.P., 1964), p. 43.

401. *Lehrbuch*, op. cit. (note 156), p. 606.

402. F. Graetz, "Probleme der Arbeitsbelastung von Führungskräften in Ost und West," *DA*, No. 9 (1972), pp. 942-946.

403. I. Friss, *Economic Laws, Policy, Planning* (Budapest: Akadémiai Kiadó, 1971), p. 26.

404. L. Albalkin, "Ekonomicheskii rost SSSR i problemy upravleniya proizvodstvom," *Kommunist*, No. 13 (1973) [39-51], pp. 39; I. I. Kuz'minov et al. (ed.), *Ekonomicheskie problemy razvitogo sotsializma i ego pererastaniya v kommunizm* (Moscow: Mysl', 1977), pp. 82ff.

405. A. Nove, "Economic Irrationality and Irrational Statistics," in idem, *Was Stalin really necessary?* (London: Allen & Unwin, 1964) [172-185], p. 173.

406. L. Turgeon, "Comparative Economic Statistics," in idem, *The Contrasting Economies* (Boston: Little Brown, 1964) [25-43], p. 30.

407. Ch.-Y. Chêng, *The Machine Building Industry in Communist China* (Chicago: Chicago U.P., 1971), p. 233.

408. F. Fejtö, *Die Geschichte der Volksdemokratien*, Vol. 1 (Graz: Styria, 1972), p. 322.

409. Brown, op. cit. (note 144), p. 159.

410. E. M. Kanevskii, *Effekt reklamy* (Moscow: Ekonomika, 1980), pp. 169ff.

411. Chêng, op. cit. (note 407), p. 236.

412. L. T. C. Kuo, *The Technical Transformation of Agriculture in Communist China* (New York: Praeger, 1972), p. 233.

413. O. L. Dawson, *Communist China's Agriculture* (New York: Praeger, 1970), pp. 135ff.; Eckstein, op. cit. (note 296), p. 231.

414. *Ten Great Years* (Peking: Foreign Languages Press, 1960), p. 183; Ch. Howe, *Employment and Economic Growth in Urban China, 1949-1957* (Cambridge: Cambridge U.P., , 1971), p. 108.

415. G. Jahn (ed.), *Die Wirtschaftssyteme der Staaten Osteuropas und der VR China* (Berlin [West], Duncker & Humblot, 1962), pp. 500ff.

416. D. C. McClelland, *The Achieving Society* (Princeton: Van Nostrand, 1961), Chapter 3.

417. P. Wiles, "Growth versus Choice," in Bornstein, op. cit. (note 191) [19-31], p. 21; Bergson, op. cit. (note 393), pp. 199ff.

418. *Der ökonomische Wettbewerb*, op. cit. (note 395), p. 180.

419. M. L. Weitzman, "Soviet Postwar Economic Growth and Capital Labor Substitution," *The American Economic Review* (1970), pp. 676ff.; capital productivity of the GDR is far below the West German level: W. Obst, *DDR-Wirtschaft. Modell und Wirklichkeit* (Hamburg: Hoffmann & Campe, 1973), p. 34; M. Schnitzer, *East and West Germany. A Comparative Economic Analysis* (New York: Praeger, 1972), p. 364.

420. D. Klein, "Systemauseinandersetzung. Zur Theorie des Klassenkampfes zwischen Sozialismus und Kapitalismus," *Forum*, No. 15 (1972), p. 9, col. 2.

421. Carlo, op. cit. (note 275), p. 73. Similarly negative: R. di Leo, *Occupazione e salari nell'URSS 1950-77* (Milan: Etas Libri, 1980).

422. M. T. Iovchuk & Ln. N. Kogan et al., *Sotsialisticheski rabochii kollektiv— problemy dukhovnoi zhizni* (Moscow: Nauka, 1978), p. 255; cf. W. Teckenberg, "Arbeitsbeziehungen, informelle Kontakte und Produktivität in sowjetischen Betrieben. Neuere Umfrageergebnisse," *Berichte des Bundesinstituts für ostwissenchaftliche und internationale Studien*, 19/1980, Cologne.

423. Donnithorne, op. cit. (note 102), p. 178.

424. Mesa-Lago, op. cit. (note 160), p. 168; Bernardo, op. cit. (note 139), pp. 76ff.

425. R. Dumont, *Cuba, est-il socialiste?* (Paris: Éditions du Seuil, 1970), p. 96.

426. W. Leontief, "The Trouble with Cuban Socialism," *The New York Review* (January 7, 1971) [19-23], p. 21, col. 2.

427. J. S. Berliner, *The Innovation Decision in Soviet Industry* (Cambridge, Mass.: MIT Press, 1978) (Paperback edition), p. 158.

428. M. Boretzky, in *New Directions*, op. cit. (note 127), p. 149.

429. E. Zaleski et al., *Science Policy in the USSR* (Paris: OECD, 1969), p. 415.

430. Voigt, op. cit. (note 42), p. 120.

431. R. W. Davies, "Aspects of Soviet Investment Policy in the 1920s," in C. H. Feinstein (ed.), *Socialism, Capitalism, and Economic Growth. Essays presented to Maurice Dobb* (Cambridge: Cambridge U.P., 1967) [285-307], p. 301.

432. Donnithorne, op. cit. (note 102), p. 185; Howe, op. cit. (note 414), p. 132; R. M. Field, in Eckstein, op. cit. (note 33), p. 637.

433. ILO, *Measuring Labor Productivity* (Geneva: ILO, 1969), pp. 95ff.

434. B. Balassa, "Growth Performance of the East European and Comparable West European Countries," *American Economic Review/Proceedings* (May 1970), pp. 314-320.

435. *Mao Papers* (London: Oxford U.P., 1970), p. 66.

436. K. R. Walker, "A Chinese Discussion on Planning for Balanced Growth," in C. D. Cowan (ed.), *The Economic Development of China and Japan* (New York: Praeger, 1964), pp. 160-191; Menzel, op. cit. (note 392), pp. 348ff.

437. J. Goldman & K. Kouba, *Hospodársky rost CSSR* (Prague: 1969), pp. 46ff.; R. Hutings, "Periodic Fluctuations in Soviet Industrial Growth Rates," *Soviet Studies* (January 1969), pp. 331-352.

438. W. M. Breuer, *Sozialismus in Kuba* (Cologne: Pahl-Rugenstein, 1973), p. 124.

439. W. F. Terechow, *Die Effektivität der sozialistischen Wirtschaft (am Beispiel der RGW-Länder)* (Moscow: APN, 1973), pp. 68, 71.

440. P. Hennicke (ed.), Probleme des Sozialismus und der Übergangsgesellschaften (Frankfurt: Suhrkamp, 1973), p. 106; J. G. Zielinski, *Economic Reforms in Polish Industry* (London: Oxford U.P., 1973), pp. 297ff.

441. L. Schapiro & J. W. Lewis, "The Role of the Monolithic Party under the Totalitarian Leader," *CO*, No. 40 (1969) [39-64], p. 61.

442. F. D. Holzman, "Soviet Inflationary Pressure 1928-1957. Causes and Cures," *Quarterly Journal of Economics* (May 1960) [167-188], p. 170.

443. Th. Wilson, *Inflation* (London: Oxford U.P., 1961), p. 127.

444. A. R. Oxenfeldt & E. Van den Haag, "Unemployment in Planned and Capitalist Economies," *The Quarterly Journal of Economics* (1954) [43-60], p. 54.

445. Turgeon, op. cit. (406), pp. 202f.

446. L. M. Herman, "The Limits of Forced Economic Growth in the USSR," *World Politics* (1963/64) [407-417], pp. 414f.

447. A. Gerschenkron, *Continuity in History and other Essays* (Cambridge, Mass.: Harvard U.P., 1968), p. 80.

448. Kim il Sung, *Selected Works*, Vol. 1 (Pyöng Yang: Foreign Languages Publishing House, 1971), p. 281f.

449. A. C. Sutton, *Western Technology and Soviet Economic Development*, Vol. 1 (1917/1930) (Stanford: Stanford U.P., 1968), pp. 344ff.

450. Geschichte, op. cit. (note 252), p. 643.

451. M. Sladkovskii, "Maoistskii kurs na militarizatsiyu i ego posledstviya dlya ekonomiki KNR," *VE*, No. 11 (1971) [71-83], p. 83.

452. J. Wilczynski, *The Economics and Politics of East-West Trade* (London: Macmillan, 1969), p. 337.

453. W. Meissner & P. Farkas, "Preisdiskriminierung innerhalb des RGW?" *Yearbook of East-European Economics*, Vol. 4 (1973) [295-318], p. 316.

454. J. Sigurdson, *Technology and Science in the People's Republic of China* (Oxford: Pergamon Press, 1980), pp. 4ff.

455. Ch. Y. Cheng, *Economic Relations between Peking and Moscow, 1949-1963* (New York: Praeger, 1964), p. 103.

456. A. Eckstein, "Foreign Trade of China," in A. A. Brown & E. Neuberger (eds.), *International Trade and Central Planning* (Berkeley: University of California Press, 1968) [246-252], p. 246.

457. R. O. Freedman, *Economic Warfare in the Communist Bloc. A Study of Soviet Economic Pressure against Yugoslavia, Albania and Communist China* (New York: Praeger, 1970), p. 115.

458. Schurmann, op. cit. (note 90), p. 241.

459. P. J. D. Wiles, *Communist International Economics* (Oxford: Blackwell, 1968), p. 513.

460. F. H. Mah, *The Foreign Trade of Mainland China* (Edinburgh: University Press, 1972), p. 180; R. E. Batsavage & J. L. Davie, "China's International Trade and Finance," in *Chinese Economy,* op. cit. (note 391), pp. 707-741.

461. D. H. Perkins, "International Impact on Chinese Central Planning," in Brown & Neuberger, op. cit. (note 456) [177-201], p. 177.

462. A. L. Levin, *Sotsialisticheskii vnutrennii rynok* (Moscow: Ekonomika, 1973), pp. 123ff.

463. Ph. Richer, *La Chine et le Tiers Monde (1949-1969)* (Paris: Payot, 1971); U. E. Simonis, *Die, Entwicklungspolitik der VR China 1949-1962* (Berlin [West]: Duncker & Humblot, 1968).

464. *Peking Review,* May 8, 1964, and Nov. 17, 1964; *Hoy,* February 26, 1963.

465. R. F. Darnberger, "Prices, the Exchange Rate, and Economic Efficiency for Foreign Trade of Communist China," in Brown & Neuberger, op. cit. (note 456), (202-236), p. 202.

466. F. D. Holzman, "Soviet Foreign Trade Pricing and the Question of Discrimination," *Review of Economics and Statistics* (May 1962), pp. 134-147; idem, "More on Soviet Bloc Trade Discrimination," *Soviet Studies* (July 1965), pp. 129-161.

467. Mah, op. cit. (note 460), p. 111.

468. Freedman, op. cit. (note 457), p. 173.

469. K. S. Karol, *Guerillas in Power* (London: Cape, 1971), p. 323.

470. E. Bornstein, *The Economic Transformation of Cuba* (New York: Praeger, 1968), p. 62f.

471. B. N. Topornin, *Politicheskaya sistema sotsializma* (Moscow: Mezhdunarodnye otnosheniya, 1972), pp. 12f, 192, 175.

472. J. Berliner, *Economy, Society, and Welfare. A Study in Social Economics* (New York: Praeger, 1972), p. 51.

473. H. C. F. Mansilla, *Systembedürfnis und Anpassung* (Frankfurt: Athenäum, 1973), pp. 249ff.

474. RFE, Audience and Public Opinion Research Department, *Preconditions for Success in Life in Poland and West Germany* (Munich: 1971); J. M. Montias, "Modernization in Communist Countries. Some Questions of Methodology," *StiCC*, No. 4 (1972), pp. 413-427.

Chapter 5

475. K. Marx, *Grundrisse der Kritik der politischen Ökonomie* (Frankfurt: EVA, 1970), p. 13.

476. A. Keck, *Leistung, Wachstum, Wohlstand* (Berlin [East]: Verlag Die Wirtschaft, 1973), p. 21.

477. Leontief, op. cit. (note 426), p. 19, col. 3.

478. In Charles Bettelheim et al., *Zur Kritik der Sowjetökonomie* (Berlin [West]: Rotbuch Verlag, 1969), p. 146.

479. *Gosudastvennyi pyatiletnii plan razvitiya narodnogo khozyaystva SSSR na 1971-1975 gg* (Moscow: Statistika, 1972), passim.

480. F. L. Altmann & J. Slama, "Wirtschaftliches Wachstum und privater Verbrauch in der Tschechoslowakei," in Gumpel & Keese, op. cit. (note 261), p. 226.

481. D. W. Bronson & B. S. Severin, "Recent Trends in Consumption and Disposable Money in Income in the USSR," in *New Directions*, op. cit. (note 127) [495-553], p. 550.

482. P. Hanson, *The Consumer in the Soviet Economy* (London: Macmillan, 1968), p. 86.

483. Cf. D. V. McGranahan et al., *Contents and Measurement of Socioeconomic Development* (New York: Praeger, 1972), pp. 20ff.

484. J. G. Chapman, *Consumption*, in A. Bergson & S. Kuznets (eds.), *Economic Trends in the Soviet Union* (Cambridge, Mass.: Harvard U.P., 1963) [234-282], p. 264.

485. Ch. Otto-Arnold, "Die Kosten der Lebenshaltung in der DDR im Vergleich zur Bundesrepublik an der Jahreswende 1972/73," *DA*, No. 8 (1973) [851-855], p. 853.

486. Figures: E. Yakovleva, "Izmenie struktury zanyatosti v stranakh SEV," *VE*, No. 4 (1970) [109-115], p. 112.

487. V. Kostakov et al., "Sfera uslug i zanyatost' naseleniya," *VE* (1971), No. 8.

488. The Comecon statistical yearbook however continues to do this: *Statisticheskii ezhegodnik stran chlenov SEV. 1979* (Moscow: Statistika, 1979), pp. 441ff.

489. Liberman, op. cit. (note 149), p. 80.

490. M. Dobb, *Welfare Economics and the Economics of Socialism* (Cambridge: Cambridge U.P., 1969), p. 214.

491. E. M. Kanevskii, *Effekt reklamy* (Moscow: Ekonomika, 1980), pp. 144ff.

492. K. K. Waltuch, *Entwicklungsproportionen und Befriedigung der Bedürfnisse* (Berlin [East]: Verlag Die Wirtschaft, 1972), p. 26.

Chapter 6

493. Montias, op. cit. (note 474), p. 418.

494. A. Meyer, *Legitimacy of Power in East Central Europe*, in S. Sinanian et al. (eds.), *Eastern Europe in the 1970s* (New York: Praeger, 1972) [45-86], p. 56.

495. S. M. Lipset, *Political Man* (London: Mercury Books, 1963), pp. 52ff.

496. A. Inkeles, *Public Opinion in Soviet Russia* (Cambridge, Mass.: Harvard U.P., 1950), p. 41.

497. I. Volyges, "Political Socialization in Eastern Europe," *PoC*, No. 1 (1974), pp. 46-55.

498. R. Baum, "Revolution and Reaction in the Chinese Countryside. The Socialist Education Movement in Cultural Revolutionary Perspective," *CHQU*, No. 38 (1969) [92-119], p. 94.

499. D. C. Pirages, *Modernization and Political Tension-Management. A Socialist Society in Perspective. Case Study of Poland* (New York: Praeger, 1972), p. 21.

500. Ch. P. Ridley et al., *The Making of a Model Citizen in Communist China* (Stanford: Stanford U.P., 1971), p. 6.

501. M. Goldman, "The Unique 'Blooming and Contending' of 1961-62," *CHQU*, No. 37 (1969), pp. 54-83.

502. E. Mandel, *Entstehung und Entwicklung der ökonomischen Lehre von Karl Marx* (Frankfurt: EVA, 1968), p. 189.

503. G. Fischer, "The Number of Soviet Party Executives," *Soviet Studies* (January 1965), pp. 330-333; Pryor, op. cit. (note 22), p. 131.

504. R. C. Tucker, "Stalin, Bukharin and History as Conspiracy," in idem, *Stalinism and Post-Stalin Change* (London: Pall Mall Press, 1971) [49-86], p. 60.

505. A. J. Wyschinski, *Gerichtsreden* (Berlin [East]: Dietz, 1951), p. 515.

506. E. Gordon, *Freedom is a Word* (London: Hodder & Stoughton, 1971), p. 101.

507. E. F. Vogel, "Voluntarism and Social Control," in Treadgold, op. cit. (note 140) [168-184], p. 184.

508. D. Joravski, *The Lysenko Affair* (Cambridge, Mass.: Harvard U.P., 1970).

509. W. G. Afanasjew, *Wissenschaftlich-technische Revolution, Leitung, Bildung* (Berlin [East]: Staatsverlag der DDR, 1974), p. 420.

510. U. J. Heuer, *Demokratie und Recht im neuen ökonomischen System* (Berlin [East]: Staatsverlag der DDR, 1965), p. 155.

511. J. M. Montias, "Types of Economic Systems," in Johnson, op. cit. (note 44) [117-134], pp. 118ff.

512. L. Abalkin, "Ekonomicheskii rost SSSR i problemy upravleniya proizvodstvom," *Kommunist*, No. 13 (1973), pp. 39-51.

513. *Devyatyi s"ezd RKP (b) mart-aprel 1920 g. Protokoly* (Moscow, 1960), pp. 405ff.

514. G. Bettelheim, *Zur Kritik der Sowjetökonomie* (Berlin: Rotbuchverlag, 1969), p. 116.

515. G. Klaus, "Der Plan als kybernetische Kategorie," in idem, *Kybernetik und Gesellschaft* (Berlin [East]: Staatsverlag der DDR, 1973), p. 266; Heuer, op. cit. (note 510), p. 163.

516. A. M. Gendin, "'Effekt Edipa' i metodologicheskie problemy sotsial'nogo prognozirovaniya," *VF*, No. 5 (1970) [80-89], pp. 86ff.

517. *Narodnoe Khozyaistvo SSSR v 1954 g* (Moscow: Statistika, 1955), p. 547.

518. *Literaturnaya gazeta*, September 25, 1962.

519. A. Nove, "Planners, Preferences, Priorities and Reform," in G. Feiwel (ed.), *New Currents in Soviet Type Economics* (Scranton, Pa.: International Textbook Co., 1968), p. 286.

520. *Ekonomicheskaya gazeta*, No. 13 (1963), p. 7.

521. *Lehrbuch*, op. cit. (note 156), p. 273.

522. H. Nick, *Gesellschaft und Betrieb im Sozialismus* (Berlin [East]: Verlag Die Wirtschaft, 1970), p. 146f., 150.

523. Liberman, op. cit. (note 149), p. 53.

524. J. N. Hazard, *Communists and Their Law* (Chicago: University of Chicago Press, 1969), p. 346.

525. A. Meyer, "Theories of Convergence," in Johnson, op. cit. (note 44) (313-341), p. 332.

526. Liu Shao-chi, "The Victory of Marxism-Leninism in China," in *Ten Glorious Years* (Peking: Foreign Languages Publishing House, 1960) [1-34], p. 13.

527. *Mao Papers* (London: Oxford U.P., 1970), p. 95.

528. Schurmann, op. cit. (note 90), p. 318.

529. Scalapino & Lee, op. cit. (note 121), p. 832.

530. G. W. Breslauer, *Political Terror in Communist Systems* (Stanford: Hoover, 1970), pp. 136ff.

531. L. Lockwood, "Castros Cuba, Kubas Fidel," in G. Feltrinelli (ed.), *Lateinamerika, ein zweites Vietnam* (Reinbek: Rowohlt, 1968), [17-64], p. 59.

532. P. Reddaway, *Uncensored Russia. The Human Rights Movement in the Soviet Union* (London: Cape, 1972), p. 205.

533. B. Lewytzkyj, *Vom Roten Terror zur sozialistischen Gesetzlichkeit* (Munich: Nymphenburger, 1961), p. 253.

534. W. Bukowskij, *UdSSR. Opposition eine neue Geisteskrankheit in der Sowjetunion* (Munich: Piper, 1971); Gordon, op. cit. (note 506), p. 205.

535. Cf. Z. Mlinar, "Les conflits sociaux et le developpement social en Yougo-slavie," *Revue de l'est*, No. 2 (1972) [5-39], p. 9.

536. *Kritika teorii i praktiki Maoizma* (Moscow: Mysl, 1973), p. 153.

537. Pirages, op. cit. (note 352), p. 267.

538. *Kritika*, op. cit. (note 536), passim; A. P. Pamor, "Stellung und Rolle der Armee in der sozialen Struktur Chinas," in *Klassen und Klassenbeziehungen in der VR China* (Berlin [East]: Deutscher Verlag der Wissenschaften, 1973) [209-224], p. 223.

539. Mesa-Lago, op. cit. (note 160), pp. 145ff.

540. Heuer, op. cit. (note 510), p. 128.

541. L. M. Gatovsky, "Some Problems of the Use of Material Incentives in Industrial Enterprises," in M. C. Kaser (ed.), *Economic Development for Eastern Europe* (London: Proceedings of a Conference held by the International Economic Association [Plovdiv 1964], 1968) [219-234], p. 223.

542. K. Fomin, "Premiya s garnirom," *Pravda*, February 15, 1969; Liberman, op. cit. (note 149), pp. 39f.

543. Wheelwright & McFarlane, op. cit. (note 105), p. 210.

544. Hoffmann, op. cit. (note 118).

545. D. H. Perkins, "Economic Growth in China and the Cultural Revolution." *CHQU*, No. 30 (1967), pp. 33-48. "Critique of these Hypotheses Klett," ibidem, No. 31 (1967) [151-159], p. 158.

546. Richman, op. cit. (note 196), p. 215.

547. S. Stojanovic, *Kritik und Zukunft des Sozialismus* (Munich: Hanser, 1970), p. 217.

Part III

Chapter 7

548. P. Naville, *Le salaire socialiste* Vol. 1 (Paris: Anthropos, 1970), p. 279.

549. P. Wiles, "A Note on Soviet Unemployment by US definitions," *Soviet Studies* (1971/72), pp. 619-628; ILO, *Measurement of Underemployment* (Geneva: ILO, 1957), pp. 24f., 86f.

550. A. R. Oxenfeldt & E. van den Haag, "Unemployment in Planned and Capitalist Economies," *The Quarterly Journal of Economics* (1954) [43-60], p. 45.

551. Terechow, op. cit. (note 439).

552. D. Keese, "Freiwillige Ersparnis in der Sowjetunion," *OE/W*, No. 2 (1968) [141-146], p. 142.

553. V. I. Semenkov, *Okhrana truda v SSSR* (Minsk: Nauka i tekhnika, 1976), pp. 10ff.

554. M. Tchimichkian, "La protection et la sécurité du travail dans les entreprises industrielles soviétiques," *Revue de l'est*, No. 1 (1972) [69-136], p. 126.

555. Th. Hughes, *The Chinese Communes* (London: 1960), p. 70f.

556. K. Pleyer & J. Lieser (eds.), *Zentralplanung und Recht* (Stuttgart: G. Fischer, 1969), p. 190.

557. *Lehrbuch*, op. cit. (note 156), p. 163.

558. Wilczynski, op. cit. (note 152), p. 27.

559. St. H. Cohn, "Soviet Growth Retardation," in *New Directions*, op. cit. (note 127) [99-132], p. 102.

560. N. P. Pishchulin, *Proizvodstvennyi kollektiv, chelovek i svobodnoe vremya* (Moscow: Profizdat, 1976), p. 198.

561. K. Pütz, *Zeitbudgetforschung der Sowjetunion* (Meisenheim: Hain, 1970), pp. 26ff.

562. L. Trockij, *Terrorismus und Kommunismus* (Hamburg: Hoym, 1920), p. 113.

563. W. Hofmann, *Die Arbeitsverfassung der Sowjetunion* (Berlin [West]: Duncker & Humblot, 1956), p. 268, 275.

564. S. Swianiewicz, *Forced Labour and Economic Development* (London: Oxford U.P., 1965), pp. 25ff.; D. J. Dallin & B. Nicolaevsky, *Arbeiter oder*

Ausgebeutete? Das System der Arbeitslager in Sowjetrußland (Munich: 1948).

565. Hofmann, op. cit. (note 563), p. 269.

566. Nazhimov, "Chelovek i ego professiya," *Voprosy psikhologii*, No. 5 (1967), p. 185.

567. *Trudovoe zakonodatel'stvo* (Minsk: Nauka i tekhnika, 1974), p. 19f.

568. A. N. Leontev, "Vtoroe dukhanie psikhologii," *Pravda*, February 22, 1968; Th. Kussmann, "Berufslenkung, Berufswahl und Berufsberatung in der UdSSR," *OE/W* (1968), pp. 296-310.

569. V. V. Krevnevich, "Ekonomicheskie osnovy professional'noi orientatsii molodezhi," *Sovetskaya pedagogika*, No. 2 (1968) [44-54], p. 44.

570. I. D. Jermolajew, *Objektive Gesetze und wissenschaftliche Leitung der Gesellschaft* (Berlin [East]: Staatsverlag der DDR, 1973), p. 166f.

571. Cf. M. Kh. Titma, *Vybor professii kak sotsial'naya problema* (Moscow: Mysl', 1975), pp. 109ff.

572. B. M. Richman, *A Firsthand Study of Industrial Management in Communist China* (Los Angeles: Division of Research, University of California, 1967), p. 18.

573. Hsia, op. cit. (note 138), p. 79, 190.

574. *Trud*, January 24, 1933.

575. *Materialy XV s"ezda professionalnykh soyuzov SSSR* (Moscow: 1972), p. 68.

576. I. Deutscher, *Die sowjetischen Gewerkschaften* (Frankfurt: EVA, 1969), p. 148.

577. McAuley, op. cit. (note 180), p. 15.

578. Sources in F. Kool & E. Oberländer (eds.), *Arbeiterdemokratie oder Parteidiktatur* (Olten: Walter, 1967), pp. 164ff.

579. H. Roggemann, *Das Modell der Arbeiterselbstverwaltung in Jugoslawien* (Frankfurt: EVA, 1970), p. 196; N. Jovanov, "Streik und Selbstverwaltung in Jugoslawien," *Gewerkschaftliche Monatshefte*, No. 6 (1973), pp. 355-364.

580. Cf. B. N. Topornin, *Politicheskaya sistema sotsializma* (Moscow: Mezhdunarodnye otnosheniya, 1972), p. 175.

581. *Mao Intern* (Munich: Hanser, 1974), p. 102.

582. Z. Mlinar, "Les conflits sociaux et le développement social en Yougoslavie," *Revue de l'est*, No. 2 (1972) [5-39], p. 9.

583. P. Harper, "The Party and the Unions in China," *China Quarterly*, No. 37 (1969) [84-119], pp. 111ff.

584. F. Castro, "Rede vor dem XIII. Gewerkschaftskongress," *Das Argument*, 85 (1974) [241-272], p. 269.

Chapter 8

585. G. Liebscher et al., *Gewerkschaften, Gesundheitsschutz, Arbeitsschutz, Sozialversicherung* (Berlin [East], Volk und Gesundheit, 1964), pp. 953ff.

586. J. Fry, *Medicine in Three Societies* (New York: Elsevier, 1970); R. L. Siegel & L. B. Weinberg, *Comparing Public Policies* (Homewood, Ill.: Dorsey Press, 1977), p. 211; A. McAuley, *Economic Welfare in the Soviet Union* (London: Allen & Unwin, 1979), p. 234.

587. G. A. Popov, *Ekonomika i planirovanie zdravookhraneniya* (Moscow: Izdatel'stvo Moskovoskogo universiteta, 1976), p. 272.

588. L. Mecklinger et al., *Gesundheitsschutz und soziale Betreuung der Bürger* (Berlin [East], Staatsverlag der DDR, 1974), p. 28. Recent emphasis on out-patient clinics in: N. Shesternya, *Health Protection* (Moscow: Novosti, 1976), p. 17.

589. J. S. Horn, *Away with All Pests* (Feltham: Hamlyn, 1969). M. Oksenberg, "The Chinese Polica Process and the Public Health Issue: An Arena Approach," *StiCC*, No. 4 (1974), pp. 375-408; Kraus, op. cit. (note 437), pp. 316ff.

590. Tsien Tche-hao, *La république populaire de Chine. Droit constitutionnel et institutions* (Paris: Librairie générale de droit et de jurisprudence, 1970), p. 62.

591. G. Manz & G. Winkler (eds.), *Theorie und Praxis der Sozialpolitik in der DDR* (Berlin [East], Akademie-Verlag, 1979), pp. 162ff.; W.-R. Leenen, *Zur Frage der Wachstumsorientierung der marxistisch-leninistischen Sozialpolitik in der DDR* (Berlin [West], Duncker & Humblot, 1977).

592. *Klassen und Klassenbeziehungen in der VR China* (Dresden (GDR): Verlag Zeit im Bild, 1973), p. 173; D. N. Shinik, *Pravovye regulirovanie trudovykh otnoshenii sezonnykh rabochikh i sluzhashchikh* (Kishinev: Stiinca, 1975), pp. 34ff.

593. D. M. Lampton, "New 'Revolution' in China's Social Policy," *PoC*, (1979), No. 5-6 (16–33), p. 18.

594. Sources in: *Sotsial'noe obespechenie i strakhovanie v SSSR* (Moscow: Yurlit, 1979).

595. P. Stiller, "Die sowjetische Rentenversicherung 1917–1977," *BdBfowiSt*, 42 (1979), p. 93.

596. Sources in: Klaus von Beyme, *Sozialismus oder Wohlfahrtsstaat? Sozialpolitik und Sozialstruktur der Sowjetunion im Systemvergleich* (Munich: Piper, 1977), p. 73f.

597. H. Rolf, *Sozialversicherung oder staatlicher Gesundheitsdienst? Ökonomischer Effizienzvergleich der Gesundheitssicherungssysteme der BRD und der DDR* (Berlin [West]: Duncker & Humblot, 1975), p. 31; *Wohlstand des Volkes* (Moscow, APN-Verlag, 1976), p. 10.

598. *Materialien zum Bericht zur Lage der Nation. 1974* (Bonn: Bundesministerium für innerdeutsche Beziehungen, 1974), p. 454, para. 851.

599. R. Krzyzewski, *Konsumpcja spoleczna w gospodarce socjalistycznej* (Warsaw: PWE, 1968), p. 115.

600. *Gosudarstvennyi pyatiletnyi plan razvitiya narodnogo khozyaistva SSSR na 1971-75 gody* (Moscow: Politizdat, 1972), p. 280; *SSSR v tsifrakh 1975* (Moscow: Statistika, 1976), p. 178.

601. *Statistisches Jahrbuch Ungarns* (Budapest, 1973), p. 277.

602. L. Tulchinskii, "O metodologii ischisleniya obshchestvennykh fondov potrebleniya," *Vestnik statistiki*, No. 5 (1966), p. 39f.

603. *SSSR v tsifrakh 1976*, p. 209; V. P. Barybin & K. V. Protsenko, *Sotsial'noe obespechenie* in *Trud i zarabotnaya plata v SSSR* (Moscow: Ekonomika, 1975) [333–357], p. 353.

604. Ju L. Dostovalov, *Kritika burzhuaznikh i revizionistskikh teorii sotsialisticheskogo razpredeleniya* (Moscow: Vysshaya shkola, 1975), p. 71.

605. M. S. Lantsev, *The Economic Aspects of Social Security in the USSR* (Moscow: Progress, 1979), p. 72.

606. D. Keese, "Freiwillige Ersparnis in der Sowjetunion," *OE/W*, No. 2 (1968) [142-146], p. 143; H. Vortmann, "Einkommensverteilung in der DDR," *DA*, No. 3 (1974) [271-277], p. 273.

607. S. G. Figurnov, *Stroitel'stvo kommunizma i rost blagosostoyaniya naroda* (Moscow: Nauka, 1962), p. 158.

608. H. W. Wilensky, *The Welfare State and Equality* (Berkeley: University of Chicago Press, 1975), p. 39; cf. also: P. Wiles, *Distribution of Income. East and West* (Amsterdam: North Holland Publishing Co.; New York: Elsevier, 1974), pp. 91ff.

609. For details see: K. von Beyme, "Soviet Social Policy in Comparative Perspective," *IPSR*, No. 1 (1981), pp. 73-94.

610. D. A. Kerimov et al. (ed.), *Sotsial'naya profilaktika pravonarushenii v sotsialisticheskom obshchestve* (Moscow: Mysl', 1979), pp. 29ff. On deviance: W. D. Connor, *Deviance in Soviet Society* (New York: Columbia U.P., 1972); v. Beyme, op. cit. (note 596), Chapter 6, pp. 77ff.

611. M. S. Gordon, *The Economics of Welfare Policies*, (New York: Columbia U.P., 1963), p. 20; Pryor, op. cit. (note 22), p. 139ff.

612. B. Scharf, "Correlates of social security policy in East and West Europe," *IPSR*, No. 1 (1981), pp. 57-72.

613. Vogel, op. cit. (note 228), p. 176.

614. R. Furtak, *Kuba und der Weltkommunismus* (Cologne: Westdeutscher Verlag, 1967), pp. 31ff.

615. Text in: *Ley de reforma agraria* (Bogotà, n. d.), pp. 48ff.

616. T. Sosnovy, *The Housing Problem in the Soviet Union* (New York: Research Program on the U.S.S.R., 1954), p. 276.

617. *Narodnoe khozyaistvo SSSR v 1968g* (Moscow: Statistika, 1969), p. 580.

618. Klassen, op. cit. (note 592), p. 117.

619. *KPSS v rezolytsiakh i resheniyakh s"ezdov, konferentsii i plenumov TsK* (Moscow, Politizdat, 1954), Vol. 3, p. 123.

620. *Problemy razvitiya vostochnykh rayonov SSSR* (Moscow: Ekonomika, 1971), p. 153.

621. *Bericht der Bundesregierung und Materialien zur Lage der Nation. 1971* (Bonn: 1971), p. 119.

622. Michal, op. cit. (note 141), p. 61.

623. M. E. Ruban, "Wohnungsbau und Wohnungswirtschaft in den RGW-Ländern," *DA*, No. 12 (1973), p. 1313, 1315.

624. *Stroitel'stvo i arkhitektura Leningrada 1967*, No. 2, p. 25 quoted in: D. Cattell, "The Problems of Soviet Housing," *Yearbook*, op. cit., vol. 3 [231-250], p. 231.

625. Jermolajew, op. cit. (note 570), p. 167; Voigt, op. cit. (note 43), p. 148, 150.

626. V. P. Kochikyan, *Planirovanie sotsial'nogo razvitiya kollektivov predpriyatii v otraslyakh mashinostroeniya* (Moscow: Ekonomika, 1976), p. 26.

627. K. Zhukov & V. Fyodorov, *Housing Construction in the Soviet Union* (Moscow: Progress, 1974).

628. *Bericht*, op. cit. (note 621), p. 120; Manz & Winkler, op. cit. (note 591), p. 306.

629. Sh. Turetskii, "Tseny na uslugi," *Planovoe khozyaistvo*, No. 10 (1965), p. 11.

630. G. Seidenstecher, "Zur Wohnungsraumversorgung in der UdSSR," *OE/W* (1971) [125-142], p. 134.

631. Kang Chao: *The Construction Industry in Communist China* (Edinburgh U.P., (1968), p. 189.

632. D. V. Donnison, *Housing*, in G. Schoepflin (ed.), *The Soviet Union and Eastern Europe* (London: Blond, 1970) [447-453], p. 448; idem, *Government of Housing* (Harmondsworth: Penguin, 1967).

633. Krejci, op. cit. (note 78), p. 86.

634. *Zhilishchnoe stroitel'stvo* (Moscow, 1971), p. 18.

635. L. Penig, *Der komplexe Wohnungsbau als staatliche Aufgabe* (Berlin [East]: Staatsverlag der DDR, 1973), p. 34.

636. Manz & Winkler, op. cit. (note 591), p. 315.

637. H. Buck, "Lockerungen für den privaten Wohnungsbau," *DA*, No. 5 (1972), [509-515], p. 513.

638. *Bericht*, op. cit. (note 621), p. 121.

639. *Zhilishchnoe zakonodatel'stvo* (Kiev: Politizdat Ukrainy, 1975), p. 174.

640. J. Adam, "Housing Policy in European Socialist Countries: The Czechoslovak Experience," *Yearbook*, op. cit., vol. 6 (1975) [231-250], p. 250.

641. I. Szelenyi, "The Housing System and Social Structure in Hungary," in B. L. Faber (ed.) *The Social Structure of Eastern Europe* (New York: Praeger, 1976) [301-329], p. 314; O. S. Kolbasov (ed.), *Sotsializm i okhrana okruzhayushchei sredy* (Moscow: Yurlit, 1979), pp. 15ff.

642. A. A. Pavel'ev, *Sotsial'nyi optimizm i ekologicheskii pessimizm* (Moscow: Mysl', 1977), p. 79; Yu. M. Manin, *NTR i ekologizatsiya prozvodstva* (Minsk: Nauka i tekhnika, 1979), p. 121; N. N. Kiselev, *Ob"ekt ekologii i ego evolyutsiya* (Kiev: Naukova Dumka, 1979).

643. V. Vasil'ev et al., *Ekologiya i mezhdunarodnye otnosheniya* (Moscow: Mezhdunarodnye otnosheniya, 1978), pp. 95ff.

644. *Naselenie i okruzhayushchaya sreda* (Moscow: Statistika, 1979), pp. 13ff.

645. W. Leontief & D. Ford, *Air Pollution and the Economic Structure: Empirical Results of Input-Output Computations* (Cambridge, Mass.: MIT Press, 1971).

646. W. Oschlies, "Umweltschutz in Bulgarien," *OE*, No. 3 (1974) [213-224], p. 213; H.-H. Höhmann et al., *Umweltschutz und ökonomisches System in Osteuropa* (Stuttgart: Kohlhammer, 1973), p. 85f.

647. P. G. Oldak, *Sokhranenie okruzhayushchei sredy i razvitie ekonomicheskikh issledovanii* (Novosibirsk: Nauka, 1980), p. 157.

648. I. I. Adabashev, *Tragediya ili garmoniya? Priroda — mashina — chelovek* (Moscow: Mysl', 1973), pp. 329f.

649. K. Bush, "Environmental Problems in the USSR," *PoC*, No. 2 (1972), [21-31], p. 26.

650. I. Gerasimov, "Nuzhen general'nyi plan preobrazovaniya prirody nashei strany," *Kommunist*, No. 2 (1969) [68-79], p. 69; T. Khachaturov, "Ob ekonomicheskom otsenke prirodnykh resursov," *VE*, No. 1 (1969) [66-74], p. 70.

651. J. Füllenbach, *Umweltschutz in Ost und West* (Bonn: Europa Union Verlag, 1977), p. 235.

652 J. B. R. Whitney, "Ecology and Environmental Control," in M. Oksenberg (ed.), *China's Developmental Experience* (New York: Proceedings of The Academy of Political Science, Vol. 31, No. 1, 1974) [95-109], p. 100. Ph. R. Pryde, *Conservation in the Soviet Union* (Cambridge: Cambridge U.P., 1972), p. 119.

653. I. Fedorov, "Aktual'nye problemy vzaymodeistviya obshchestva i prirodnoi sredy," *Kommunist*, No. 14 (1972), quoted from the German translation, *SW/GesWB* No. 3 (1973) [239-251], p. 249.

654. *Problemy pravovoi okhrany okruzhayushchei sredy v SSSR* (Leningrad, Izdatel'stvo Leningradskogo universiteta, 1979), pp. 80ff.

655. B. Komarov, *Unichtozhenie prirody* (Frankfurt: Possev Verlag, 1978); German translation: *Das grosse Sterben am Baikalsee*. (Reinbek: Rowohlt, 1979), p. 112.

656. D. R. Kelley et al.: *The Economic Superpowers and the Environment. The United States, the Soviet Union and Japan* (San Francisco: Freeman, 1976), p. 275.

657. M. I. Goldman, "Environmental Disruption in the Soviet Union," in Sh. Tsuru, *Proceedings of International Symposium on Environmental Disruption*, Tokyo (March 1970), pp. 171-189.

658. *Materialien*, op. cit. (note 598), p. 392.

659. Castro, op. cit. (note 584), p. 267.

660. H. Förster, "Umweltprobleme in der Tschechoslowakei," *OE*, No. 3 (1974), [205-212], pp. 210f.

661. N. Federenko & G. Gofman, "Problemy optimatsii planirovaniya i upravleniya okruzhayushchei sredoi," *VE*, No. 10, (1972) (German translation in *SW/GesWB*, No. 3 (1973) [229-238], p. 230).

Chapter 9

662. N. Luhmann, *Grundrechte als Institution* (Berlin [West]: Duncker & Humblot, 1965), p. 204.

663. V. M. Chikvadze, "Lichnost' i gosudarstvo: vzaimnaya otvetstvennost'," *SGiP* No. 1 (1971), pp. 19-26.

664. G. Brunner, *Die Grundrechte im Sowjetsystem* (Cologne: Wissenschaft und Politik, 1963), p. 115.

665. I. Lapenna, *Soviet Penal Policy* (London: Bodley Head, 1968), p. 36.

666. J. N. Hazard, *Communists and Their Law* (Chicago: Chicago U.P., 1969), p. 24.

667. Cf.: H. Koschwitz, *Pressepolitik und Parteijournalismus in der UdSSR und in der VR China* (Düsseldorf: Bertelsmann, 1971), pp. 9ff.

668. *Mao Papers* (London: Oxford U.P., 1970), p. 107.

669. R. C. Bush, Jr., *Religion in Communist China* (Nashville: Abingdon Press, 1970), p. 36f.; Ch. Lane, *Christian Religion in the Soviet Union* (London: Allen & Unwin, 1978).

670. *Geschichte der Kommunistischen Partei Albaniens* (Tirana: Naim Frasheri, 1971), pp. 674f.

671. N. Djurisić, "Experience of the Constitutional Court of Yugoslavia," *OE/R* (1970), p. 188.

672. W. Gellhorn (ed.), *Ombudsmen and Others* (Cambridge, Mass.: Harvard U.P., 1966), pp. 336ff.

673. G. G. Morgan, *Soviet Administrative Legality. The Role of the Attorney General's Officer* (Stanford: Stanford U.P., 1962), pp. 22ff.

674. S. G. Berezovskaya, *Prokurorskii nadzor na zakonnost'yu pravovykh aktov organov upravleniya v SSSR* (Moscow: Yurlit, 1959), p. 58.

675. Chile 1975, *Habla Fidel* (Santiago de Chile, Editorial universitaria, 1971), p. 26.

676. T. Ritter, *Eingabenarbeit. Grundsätze und Erfahrungen* (Berlin [East], Staatsverlag der DDR, 1972), pp. 36, 46.

677. P. Reddaway, *Uncensored Russia. The Human Rights Movement in Soviet Russia* (London: Cape, 1972), pp. 250f.

678. K.-H. Kühnau, "Beschwerdeausschüsse und sozialistische Demokratie," *Staat und Recht* (1970) [35-44], pp. 39-41.

679. H. Roggemann, *Die sozialistische Verfassung der DDR* (Hannover: Niedersächsische Landeszentrale für Politische Bildung, 1970), p. 146.

680. J. A. Cohen, "The Criminal Process in China," in Treadgold, op. cit. (note 140) [107-143], p. 143.

Part IV

681. R. R. Fagen, *The Transformation of Political Culture in Cuba* (Stanford, Stanford U.P., 1969), p. 9.

682. E. A. Ivanov, *Profsoyuzy v politicheskoi sisteme sotsializma* (Moscow: Profizdat, 1974), p. 35.

Chapter 10

683. G. Siebert, *Mitbestimmung drüben* (Frankfurt: Nachrichten-Verlag, 1971).

684. P. Vuskovic, "La responsabilidad de los trabajadores," in G. Martner (ed.), *El pensamiento económico del gobierno de Allende* (Santiago de Chile: Editorial Universitaria, 1971) [281-283], p. 282.

685. Schurmann, op. cit. (note 90), p. 87.

686. G. Klaus, *Kybernetik — eine neue Universalphilosophie der Gesellschaft* (Frankfurt: Verlag Marxistische Blätter, 1973), p. 42.

687. Ibid., p. 79.

688. H. Slapnicka, *Die sozialistische Kollektivperson* (Vienna: Böhlau, 1969), pp. 200f., 268; cf. for the people's democracies: D. Granick, *Entreprise Guidance in Eastern Europe. A Comparison of Four Socialist Economies* (Princeton: Princeton U.P., 1975).

689. Schurmann, op. cit. (note 90), pp. 278, 291.

690. V. Prokhorov, "Shirokie prava bol'shie ob"yazannosti," *Sotsialisticheskii trud*, No. 9 (1958), pp. 3ff.

691. H.-E. Gramatzki & G. Lemân, *Arbeiterselbstverwaltung und Mitbestimmung in den Staaten Osteuropas* (Hannover: Fackelträger, 1977), p. 92; H.-H. Höhmann & G. Seidenstecher, "Partizipation im System der administrativen Planwirtschaft von UdSSR und DDR" (Cologne: *BdBfouiSt*, 1980), No. 4, pp. 55f.

692. *Mitwirkung und Mitbestimmung. Die Rechte der Arbeitnehmer in ihren Gewerkschaften in beiden deutschen Staaten* (Bonn: Friedrich-Ebert-Stiftung, 1971), p. 42.

693. Richman, op. cit. (note 196), p. 44.

694. S. Slakovskii, "Podryv maoistami sotsial'no-ekonomicheskoi struktury KNR," *VE*, No. 6 (1969) [76–87], p. 76.

695. P. Harper, "Worker's Participation in Management in Communist China," *StiCC*, No. 3 (1971) [111–140], p. 139.

696. F. M. Leviant, "Obespechenie uchastiya profsoyuzov v upravlenii proiz-vodstvom," *SGiP*, No. 7 (1971) [48–54], p. 49.

697. Richman, op. cit. (note 196), p. 268; P. Harper, "The Party and the Unions in Communist China," *CHQU*, No. 37 (1969) [84–119], p. 111.

698. Voigt, op. cit, (note 43), p. 110. W. Soergel, *Arbeiterselbstverwaltung oder Managersozialismus. Eine empirische Untersuchung in jugoslawischen Industriebetrieben* (Munich: Oldenbourg, 1979), pp. 254ff.

699. J. Ellinger & W. Scholz, *Sozialistische Demokratie im Industriebetrieb* (Berlin [East], Staatsverlag der DDR, 1972), pp. 78f.

700. D. Granick, *Management of the Industrial Firm in the USSR* (New York: Columbia U.P., 1955), pp. 241, 239.

701. *Pravda*, July 13, 1960, quoted in: B. M. Richman, *Soviet Management* (Englewood Cliffs: Prentice Hall, 1965), p. 209.

702. Heuer, op. cit. (note 510), p. 177.

703. A. Tiropolsky, "La participation des travailleurs à la gestion de l'entreprise industrielle soviétique," *Revue de l'est*, No. 2 (1971) [75–130], p. 120.

704. J. R. Townsend, "Democratic Management in the Rural Communes," *CHQU*, No. 16 (1963) [137–150], pp. 141ff.

705. Granick, op. cit. (note 700), pp. 243ff.

706. Dumont, op. cit. (note 425), p. 75; Mesa-Lago, op. cit. (note 218), p. 43.

707. C. Mesa-Lago (ed.), *Revolutionary Change in Cuba* (Pittsburgh: Pittsburgh U.P., 1971), p. 245.

708. I. Kalits et al., "Izuchenie deyatel'nosti deputatov s pomoshchu konkretno-sotsiologicheskogo metoda, *SGiP*, No. 9 (1965), p. 66.

709. J. & V. Fisera, "Cogestion des entreprises et économie socialiste — l'expérience tchéchoslovaque 1967-1970," *Revue de l'est*, No. 1 (1971), pp. 39-67; H. Dahm, *Demokratischer Sozialismus. Das tschechoslowakische Modell* (Opladen: Leske, 1971).

710. H. Kratina, *Polozaj direktora preduzeća u sistemu radnickog samoupravljantija* (Belgrad: 1967), p. 86.

711. H. Roggemann, *Das Modell der Arbeiterselbstverwaltung in Jugoslawien* (Frankfurt: EVA, 1970), p. 69.

712. K. Meneghello-Dincic, *Les expériences yougoslaves d'industrialisation et de planification* (Paris: Editions Cujas, 1971), p. 196.

713. R. Supek & B. Bosnjak (ed.), *Jugoslawien denkt anders* (Vienna: Europa Verlag, 1971), p. 139.

714. Kratina, op. cit. (note 710), p. 69; Soergel, op. cit. (note 698), p. 295.

715. Soergel, op. cit. (note 698), pp. 83ff.

716. *Stat. Godisnjak*, 1969, p. 69.

717. K. Meneghello-Dincic, "Evolution récente des conseils ouvriers Yougoslaves," *Revue de l'est*, No. 2 (1972) [137-168], p. 167.

718. V. Hadzistević et al., *Tendencije i praksa neposrednog upravljanja* (Belgrad: Institut drustvenih nauka, 1963), p. 245.

719. L. Zuniga, "La participación," *Revista sociologica*, No. 1 (August 1972), p. 44.

Chapter 11

720. Mesa-Lago, op. cit. (note 160), p. 113.

721. I. Ceterchi, "La participation des citoyens à la direction des affaires étatiques et sociales en République Socialiste de Roumanie," *Revue de l'est*, No. 2 (1972), pp. 151-162.

Chapter 12

722. Ellinger & Scholz, op. cit. (note 699), p. 78.

723. P. T. Vaslenkov, *Vynbory sovetskikh predstavitel'nykh organov* (Moscow: Politika, 1966), pp. 73ff.

724. "Demokratiya v deistvii," *Sovety Deputatov trudyashchikhsya*, No. 5 (1969), p. 96.

725. Jambrek, op. cit. (note 42), p. 141.

726. Ludz, op. cit. (note 377), pp. 145ff.

727. *Ten Glorious Years* (Peking: Foreign Languages Publishing House, 1960), pp. 248f.

728. Scalapino & Lee, op. cit. (note 121), p. 714.

729. Lethbridge, op. cit. (note 91), p. 176.

730. Kevenhörster, in U. Bermbach (ed.), *Theorie und Praxis der direkten Demokratie* (Opladen: Westdeutscher Verlag, 1973), p. 200.

731. J. I. Dominguez, *Cuba. Order and Revolution* (Cambridge, Mass.: Belknap, 1978), pp. 243ff.

732. R. Debray, *S. Allende: Der chilenische Weg* (Neuwied: Luchterhand, 1972), p. 118.

733. H. J. Lethbridge, *China's Urban Communes* (Hongkong, Dragonfly Books, 1963), pp. 51ff.

734. Klassen, op. cit. (note 538), p. 203.

735. R. J. Lifton, "Thought Reform of Chinese Intellectuals," *The Journal of Asian Studies* (November 1956), pp. 75–86; F. W. Houn: *To Change a Nation. Propaganda and Indoctrination in Communist China* (New York: The Free Press of Glencoe, 1961), p. 56.

736. *Mao Papers* (London: Oxford U.P., 1970), p. 92.

737. Fagen, op. cit. (note 681), pp. 138ff.

738. Mao, op. cit. (note 736), p. 50.

739. E. Gordon, *Freedom is a Word* (London: Hodder & Stoughton, 1971), p. 62.

740. Richman, op. cit. (note 196), p. 37.

741. P. H. Chang, *Radicals and Radical Ideology in China's Cultural Revolution* (New York: Research Institute on Communist Affairs, School of International Affairs, Columbia University, 1973), pp. 35ff.

742. *Der X. Parteitag der KP Chinas* (Peking: Fremdsprachenverlag, 1973), p. 77.

743. F. R. Scheck, *Chinas sozialistischer Weg* (Frankfurt: Fischer, 1971), p. 9.

744. E. Che Guevara, *Ökonomie und neues Bewußtsein* (Berlin [West]: Wagenbach, 1972), p. 139.

745. Hsia, op. cit. (note 138), p. 82.

746. A survey conducted by Volkin; quoted in: W. Teckenberg, "Beteiligung der Arbeiter am Entscheidungsprozeß auf den unteren Verwaltungsebenen und Arbeitskonflikte in der UdSSR," *Kölner Zeitschrift für Soziologie und Sozialpsychologie* (1974) [400-438], pp. 413ff.

747. Gordon, op. cit. (note 739), p. 95.

748. *FAZ* (May 27, 1974).

749. M. K. Dziewanowski, *The Communist Party of Poland* (Cambridge Mass.: Harvard U.P., 1959), p. 260.

750. R. W. Lee, "The Hsia Fang System," *CHQU*, No. 28 (1966), pp. 40-62.

751. *Kritika teorii i praktiki Maoizma* (Moscow: Politizdat, 1973), p. 150.

752. Ch. Bettelheim, *Révolution culturelle et organisation industrielle en Chine* (Paris: Seuil, 1973), pp. 124ff., 140ff.

Conclusion

753. G. M. Shtraks, *Sotsial'noe edinstvo i protivorechiya sotsialisticheskogo obshchestva* (Moscow: Mysl', 1966), p. 103.

754. *Neues Deutschland*, October 15, 1971, p. 3.

755. G. Stiehler, *Hegel und der Marxismus über den Widerspruch* (Berlin [East]: Dietz, 1960), pp. 29ff; G. Kohlmey, *Vergesellschaftung und Integration im Sozialismus* (Berlin [East]: Akademie Verlag, 1973), p. 215.

756. J. Kuczynski, "Gesellschaftliche Widersprüche," *DZfPh*, No. 10 (1972), pp. 1269-1279.

757. X. *Party Congress of the Communist Party of China. Documents.* (Peking: Foreign Languages Publishing House, 1973), p. 7.

758. K. Korsch, *Schriften zur Sozialisierung* (Frankfurt: EVA, 1969), pp. 26ff.

759. J. LaPalombara, "Distribution. A Crisis of Resource Management," in L. Binder et al., *Crisis and Sequences of Political Development* (Princeton: Princeton U.P., 1971) [233-282], p. 244.

760. P. M. Blau, *Exchange and Power in Social Life* (New York: J. Wiley, 1964), pp. 154ff.

761. Cf. R. Hoffmann, *Entmaoisierung in China* (Munich: Weltforum Verlag, 1973), pp. 94ff.

762. Zeitlin, op. cit., (note 42).

763. Y. Dror: *Ventures in Policy Sciences* (New York, Amsterdam: Elsevier, 1971), p. 274.

764. J. Berliner, *Economy, Society, and Welfare. A Study in Social Economics* (New York: Praeger, 1972), p. 45.

765. G. Adler-Karlsson, *Kuba Report* (Vienna: Europa Verlag, 1973), p. 151.

766. S. M. Lipset, *Political Man* (London: Mercury Book, 1963), pp. 45ff.

767. Granahan, op. cit., (note 483), p. 35.

768. St. White: "Communist Systems and the 'Iron Law of Pluralism'," *British Journal of Political Science* (1978), pp. 101-117; A. J. Groth, "USSR: Pluralist Monolith?" *British Journal of Political Science*, Vol. 9 (1979), pp. 445-464.

769. G. Skilling (ed.), *Interest Groups in Soviet Politics* (Princeton: Princeton U.P., 1971); D. Lane & G. Kolankiewicz (eds.), *Social Groups in Polish Society* (New York: Macmillan, 1973).

770. J. Klofáč & V. Tlustý, "Die soziologische Theorie des Konflikts und die

dialektische Theorie der Widersprüche," *Soziale Welt* (1965) [309-318], p. 315.

771. Cf. J. J. Wiatr, *Spoleczeństwo* (Warsaw: PWN, 1964), pp. 95ff.

772. G. Lenski, *Power and Privilege* (New York: McGraw-Hill, 1966), pp. 423, 444.

773. Adler-Karlsson, op. cit. (note 765), p. 35f.

774. J. Wiatr, *Marksistowska teoria rozwoju spolecznego* (Warsaw: PWN, 1973), p. 592f.

775. M. Croan, "Is Mexico the Future of East Europe? Institutional Adaptability and Political Change in Comparative Perspective," in S. P. Huntington & C. H. Moore (eds.), *Authoritarian Politics in Modern Society. The Dynamics of Established One-Party Systems* (New York: Basic Books, 1970), pp. 451-483.

776. Piekalkiewicz, op. cit. (note 43), pp. 159, 327.

777. F. H. Tenbruck, *Zur Kritik der planenden Vernunft* (Freiburg: Alber, 1972), pp. 90ff.

778. B. R. Fry & R. F. Winters, "The Politics of Redistribution," *APSR*, No. 2 (1970) [508-522], p. 509. A falsification of this hypothesis in Germany: M. G. Schmidt, *CDU and SPD an der Regierung. Ein Vergleich ihrer Politik in den Ländern* (Frankfurt: Campus, 1980).

779. V. Bunce, "Elite Succession, Petrification, and Policy Innovation in Communist Systems," *Comparative Political Studies* (1976), pp. 3-39.

780. D. Bahry, "Measuring Communist Priorities. Budgets, Investments, and the Problems of Equivalence," *Comparative Political Studies* (1980) [267-293], p. 285. W. W. Welsh, "On Understanding Budgets and Public Expenditures in Eastern Europe. A Reply to Bahry," ibid., [299-308], p. 307.

781. *Die 15. Tagung des Zentralkomitees der SED* (Berlin [East]: 1971), p. 38.

782. Cf. for a survey study among Jewish emigrés: St. White, Continuity and Change in Soviet Political Culture. An Emigré Study," *Comp. Political Studies* (1978) [381-395], p. 393.

783. A. G. Wishnevskii, "Demograficheskaya revolyutsya," *VF*, No. 2.

784. A. V. Sergiev, *Predvedenie v politike* (Moscow: Ekonomika, 1974), p. 84;

S. Tapeznikov, "Stroitel'stvo kommunizma i gorizonty nauki," *Pravda*, January 5, 1971.

785. M. Weber, *Wirtschaft und Gesselschaft* (Tübingen: Mohr, 1956), 1 vol., p. 60.

786. A. M. Gendin, "'Effekt Edipa' i metodologicheskie problemy sotsial'nogo prognozirovaniya," *VF*, No. 5 (1970) [80–89], p. 86.

787. D. M. Givishiani, *Organizatsiya i upravlenie* (Moscow: Yurlit, 1970), p. 365.

BIBLIOGRAPHY

1. Statistical Sources

"The Agricultural Situation in Eastern Europe: Production and Trade Statistics, 1970-1975." *Foreign Agricultural Economic Report No. 117.* Washington, D.C.: Economic Research Service, 1976.

Anuario estadistico di Cuba, 1974. Havana: Junta Central de Planificacion, 1974 (and earlier issues).

Anuarul statistic al Republicii Socialiste România. Bucarest: 1978 (and earlier issues).

"Ausgewählte Statistiken über die wirtschaftliche Entwicklung in den RGW-Ländern und Jugoslawien." In *Jahrbuch der Wirtschaft Osteuropas/Yearbook of East-European Economics,* Vol. 8. Munich: Olzog, 1979 (and earlier issues).

Bastner, N., & M. Subramian. "Aspects of Social and Economic Growth: A Pilot Statistical Study." In UN Research Institute for Social Development. *Aspects of Social and Economic Growth. Report No. 1.* Geneva: UN, 1965.

Bericht der Bundesregierung und Materialien zur Lage der Nation. Bonn: Bundesminister für innerdeutsche Beziehungen, 1971.

Bureau of Labor Statistics. *Labor Force: Employment and Unemployment Statistics. 1947-1961.* Geneva: 1967.

China: Economic Indicators: A reference Aid. Washington, D.C.: National Foreign Assessment Center, October 1977.

Clarke, R. A. *Soviet Economic Facts 1917-1970.* New York, London: Macmillan, 1972.

Compendio Estadistico de Cuba 1968: Dirección Central de Estadistica. Havana: Junta Central de Planificación, 1969.

The Cost of Social Security: Eighth International Inquiry, 1967-1971. Geneva: ILO, 1976.

Demograficheskie aspekty zanyatosti. Moscow: Statistika, 1975.

Denison, E. F. *Why Growth Rates Differ: Postwar Experience in Nine Western Countries.* Washington, D.C.: The Brookings Institution, 1967.

Drewnowski, J., & W. Scott. *The Level of Living Index: Report No. 4.* Geneva: United Nations Research Institute for Social Development, 1966.

Economic Commission for Europe. *The ECE Region in Figures.* New York: UN, 1972.

First Five-Year Plan for Development of National Economy of the People's Republic of China in 1953-1957. Peking: Foreign Languages Press, 1956.

Gosudarstvennyi pyatiletnyi plan razvitiya narodnogo khozyaist va SSSR za 1971-1975 gody. Moscow: Politizdat, 1972.

Itogi vsesoyuznoi perepisi naselenia 1970 g, Vol. 5-7. Moscow: Statistika, 1973/74.

Jasny, N. *The Soviet Statistical Handbook: A Commentary.* East Lansing: Michigan State University Press, 1957.

Joint Economic Committee, Congress of the United States. *Annual Economic Indicators for the USSR.* Washington, D.C.: GOP, 1964.

Keller, W., et al. *Hauptkennziffern der wirtschaftlichen Entwicklung der europäischen RGW-Länder 1960-1975.* Berlin [East]: 1974.

Keyfitz, N., & W. Flieger. *World Population: An Analysis of Vital Data.* Chicago: Chicago U.P., 1968.

Kiesewetter, B. *Statistiken zur Wirtschaft Ost- und Südosteuropas*, Vol. 1, *Industrie*. Berlin [West]: Duncker & Humblot, 1955. Vol. 2, Landwirtschaft, 1955. Vol. 3, Handel und Verkehr, 1957. Vol. 4, Gebiet und Bevölkerung, 1958. Vol. 5, Währungen, Staatshaushalt, Volkseinkommen, Löhne und Preise, 1959.

Kosinski, L. A. "Statistical Yearbooks in East Central Europe." *Zeitschrift für Ostforschung*, No. 1 (1974), pp. 137-147.

Kuan-Ta-Tung. *The Socialist Transformation of Capitalist Industry and Commerce in China*. Peking: Foreign Languages Press, 1960.

Lewytzkyj, B. *The Soviet Union: Figures, Facts, Data*. Munich, New York: K. G. Saur, 1979.

Maksimov, G. M. (ed.). *Vsesoyuznaya perepis' naseleniya 1970 goda: Sbornik statei*, Moscow: Statistika, 1976.

Maly rocznik statystyczny 1980. Warsaw: Glówny urzad statystyczny, 1980 (and earlier issues).

Marer, P. *Soviet and East European Foreign Trade 1946-1969: Statistical Compendium and Guide*. Bloomington: Indiana U.P., 1973.

Materialien zum Bericht zur Lage der Nation. Bonn: Bundesminister für innerdeutsche Beziehungen, 1974.

Materialni i drustveni Razvoj SFR Jugoslavije 1947-1972. Beograd: Savezni zavod za statistiku, 1973.

Mesa-Lago, C. "Availability and Reliability of Statistics in Socialist Cuba." *Latin American Research Review*, No. 1 (1969), pp. 53-91; No. 2, pp. 47-81.

Mickiewicz, E. *Handbook of Social Science Data*. New York: Free Press, 1973.

Mir sotsializma v tsifrach i faktakh: Spravochnik. Moscow: Politizdat, 1970, 1973, 1974.

Narodnoe Khozyaistvo Mongol'skoi Narodnoi Respubliki za 40 let. Ulan Bator: 1961.

Narodnoe Khozyaistvo SSSR v. 1978 g: Statisticheskii ezhegodnik. Moscow: Statistika, 1979 (and earlier issues).

Narodnoe Khozyaistvo SSSR za 60 Let: Yubileinyi statisticheskii ezhegodnik. Moscow: Statistika, 1977.

Narodnoe obrazovanie, nauka i kultura v SSSR: Statisticheskii sbornik. Moscow: Statistika, 1977.

Pechat' SSSR v. 1978 gody. Moscow: Statistika, 1979.

Rocznik Statystyczny 1978. Warsaw: Glówny urzad statystyczny, 1978 (and earlier issues).

Roberts, C. P., & M. Hamour (eds.), *Cuba 1968: Supplement to the Statistical Abstract of Latin America.* Los Angeles: Latin American Center, University of California, 1970.

Russett, B. M., et al. *World Handbook of Political and Social Indicators.* New Haven, London: Yale U.P., 1964.

Schöpflin, G. (ed.). "Comparative Statistics." *The Soviet Union and Eastern Europe. A Handbook.* London: Heinemann, 1970, pp. 15–33.

The Second Five-Year Plan Fulfilled in Two Years. Peking: Foreign Languages Press, 1960.

SSSR i soyuznye respubliki v 1973 g. Moscow: Statistika, 1974 (and later issues).

SSSR v tsifrakh v 1979: Kratkii statisticheskii sbornik. Moscow: Statistika, 1980 (and earlier issues).

State Statistical Bureau: Report on Fulfilment of the National Economic Plan of the People's Republic of China in 1955. Peking: Foreign Languages Press, 1956.

State Statistical Bureau: Ten Great Years. Peking: Foreign Languages Press, 1960.

Statistical Yearbook 1978. New York: United Nations, 1979 (and earlier issues).

Statisticeski Godisnik Narodna Republika B'lgaria. Sofia: 1970 (and later issues).

Statisticheskii ezhegodnik stran-chlenov SEV, 1980. Moscow: Statistika, 1980 (and earlier issues).

Statistická rocenka CSSR. Prague: 1970 (and later issues).

Statisticki Godisnjak SFRJ. Beograd: 1970 (and later issues).

Statistisches Jahrbuch der DDR. Berlin [East]: Staatsverlag der DDR, 1970 (and later issues).

Statistisches Jahrbuch Ungarns. Budapest: Statistischer Verlag, 1973 (and later issues).

Sukhruchenko, A. N. *Obshchestvennyi produkt i natsionalyi dokhod stranchlenov SEV.* Moscow: Statistika, 1974.

Suslov, I. P. *Teoriia statisticheskikh pokazatelei.* Moscow: Statistika, 1975.

Taylor, Ch. L., & M. C. Hudson. *World Handbook of Political and Social Indicators.* New Haven, London: Yale U.P., 1972.

Trud v SSSR. Statisticheskii sbornik. Moscow: TsSU, 1968 (and later issues).

UNESCO. *Statistical Yearbook.* Paris: UNESCO, 1978 (and earlier issues).

Vjetari Statistikor i RPSh. Tirana: 1972.

Vneshnyaya torgovlia SSSR v 1978 g. Moscow: Statistika, 1979.

Yearbook of Labour Statistics. Geneva: ILO, 1979 (and earlier issues).

Zhenshchiny v SSSR: Statisticheskii sbornik. Moscow: Statistika, 1975.

2. Literature on the comparison of socialist countries

(Only comparative titles have been included. Monographs on single socialist countries are listed in the footnotes).

Adams, A. E., & J. S. *Men Versus Systems: Agriculture in the USSR, Poland and Czechoslovakia.* New York: Free Press, 1971.

Almond, G. A. "Toward a Comparative Politics of Eastern Europe." *StiCC,* No. 2 (1971), pp. 71-78.

Altmann, F. L., et al. *Die Wirtschaft der Tschechoslowakei und Polens: Lage und Aussichten.* Munich: Günter Olzog, 1968.

Anweiler, O. "Gesellschaftliche Mitwirkung und Schulverfassung in Bildungssystemen staatssozialistischer Prägung." *Bildung und Erziehung,* No. 4 (1973), pp. 260-272.

————. Die "entwickelte sozialistische Gesellschaft" als Lern- und Erziehungsgesellschaft. *OE* (1978), pp. 573-585.

———— (ed.). *Bildungsreformen in Osteuropa*. Stuttgart: Kohlhammer, 1969.

Apel, H. "Bulgarien und Griechenland: Ein Systemvergleich wirtschaftlicher und sozialer Nachkriegsentwicklung." *OE* (1976), pp. 271-286.

Beaucourt, Ch. "L'agriculture et la politique d'intégration économique des pays socialistes européens dans les plans 1976-1980." *Est-ouest*, No. 1 (1978), pp. 7-61.

Beck, C., et al. *Comparative Communist Leadership*. New York: McKay, 1973.

Belovic, A. *Planirovanie i finansirovanie kapital'nykh vlozhenij v stranakh-chlenakh SEV*. Moscow: Ekonomika, 1973.

Benes, V., et al. *Eastern European Government and Politics*. New York: Harper & Row, 1966.

Bergson, A. *Productivity and the Social System: The USSR and the West*. Cambridge, Mass.: Harvard, U.P., 1978.

Bernstein, Th. "Leadership and Mass Mobilization in Soviet and Chinese Collectivisation Campaigns of 1929/30 and 1955/1956. A Comparison." *China Quarterly*, No. 31 (1967), pp. 1-47.

Bertsch, G. K., & Th. W. Ganschow. *Comparative Communism: Soviet, Chinese, Yugoslav Models*. San Francisco: Freeman, 1976.

Besemeres, J. F. *Socialist Population Politics: The Political Implications of Demographic Trends in the USSR and Eastern Europe*. White Plains, N.Y.: Sharpe, 1980.

Beyme, K. von. *Sozialismus oder Wohlfahrtsstaat? Sozialpolitik und Sozialstruktur der Sowjetunion im Systemvergleich*. Munich: Piper, 1977.

Blanc, A. *L'Europe socialiste*. Paris: PUF, 1974.

Boeger, K., & H. Kremendahl. *Bundesrepublik Deutschland—Deutsche Demokratische Republik: Vergleich der politischen Systeme*. 2 Vols. Stuttgart: Metzler, 1979.

Bouvier, Ch. *La collectivisation de l'agriculture: URSS, Chine, Démocraties populaires*. Paris: Colin, 1958.

Bovkun, V. V. "O tendentsiyak sblizheniya obraza zizhni molodezhi sotsialisticheskikh stran." *SI*, No. 4 (1978), pp. 73-86.

Brabant, J. van. "Specialization and Import-Dependence of Some East-European Countries." *Jahrbuch der Wirtschaft Osteuropas/Yearbook of East-European Economics*, Vol. 5. Munich: Olzog, 1974 pp. 271–308.

Bromke, A., & R. Rakowska-Harmstone (eds.). *The Communist States in Disarray 1965–1971*. Minneapolis: University of Minnesota Press, 1972.

Brown, A., & J. Gray (eds.). *Political Culture and Political Change in Communist States*. London: Macmillan, 1977.

Brown, A. A., & E. Neuberger (eds.). *International Trade and Central Planning: An Analysis of Economic Interactions*. Berkeley, Los Angeles: University of California Press, 1968.

Brus, W. *Socialist Ownership and Political Systems*. London: Routledge & Kegan Paul, 1975.

Buck, H. *Technik der Wirtschaftslenkung in kommunistischen Staaten*. 2 Vols. Coburg: Verlagsanstalt Neue Presse, 1969.

Bunce, V. "Elite Succession, Petrification, and Policy Innovation in Communist Systems: An Empirical Assessment." *Comparative Political Studies*, No. 1 (1976), pp. 3–42.

Caire, G. "Participation et conflits dans les relations de travail en univers socialiste: Réflexions sur le rôle du syndicalisme dans les pays de l'Est." *Revue de L'Est*, No. 1 (1970), pp. 19–48.

Chen, K. J., & J. S. Uppal (eds.). *Comparative Development of India and China*. New York: Macmillan, 1971.

Chirkin, V. E. *Formy socialisticheskogo gosudarstva*. Moscow: Juridicheskaya literature, 1973.

Ciepielewski, J. (ed.). *Kraje socjalistyczne po drugiej wojnie swiatowej 1944–1974*. Warsaw: Pánstwowe Wydawnictwo Ekonomiczne, 1977.

Cohen, L. J., & J. P. Shapiro (eds.). *Communist Systems in Comparative Perspective*. Garden City: Anchor Books, 1974.

Connor, W. D. *Socialism, Politics, and Equality: Hierarchy and Change in Eastern Europe and the USSR*. New York: Columbia U.P., 1979.

Croan, M. "Is Mexico the Future of East Europe: Institutional Adaptibility and Political Change in Comparative Perspective." In S. P. Huntington & C. H. Moore (eds.). *Authoritarian Politics in Modern Society: The Dynamics of established One-Party Systems.* New York, London: Basic Books, 1970, pp. 451-483.

Crook, F. W., & E. F. "Payment Systems Used in Collective Farms in the Soviet Union and China." *StiCC* (1976), pp. 257-269.

Dellin, L. A. D., & H. Gross (eds.). *Reforms in Soviet and Eastern European Economies.* London: Lexington, 1972.

Die Führende Rolle der Arbeiterklasse in sozialistischen Ländern. Berlin [East]: Dietz, 1970.

Dinerstein, H. S. "Soviet and Cuban Conceptions of Revolution." *StiCC*, No. 2 (1971), pp. 3-22.

Donaldson, R. H., & D. J. Waller. *Stasis and Change in Revolutionary Elites: A Comparative Analysis of the 1956 Party Central Committees in China and the USSR.* Beverly Hills: Sage, 1970.

Douglas, D. W. *Transitional Economic Systems: The Polish-Czech Example.* New York, London: Macmillan, 1953.

Eckstein, A. (ed.). *Comparison of Economic Systems: Theoretical and Methodological Approaches.* Berkeley, Los Angeles: University of California Press, 1971.

Eisenstadt, S. N. "Change in Communist Systems and the Comparative Analysis of Modern Societies." *StiCC*, No. 1/2 (1973), pp. 171-183.

Ernst, M. "Postwar Economic Growth in Eastern Europe: A Comparison with Western Europe." In US Congress Joint Economic Committee. *New Directions in the Soviet Economy,* Washington, D.C.: G.O.P., 1966, pp. 873-916.

Faber, B. L. (ed.). *The Social Structure of Eastern Europe.* New York: Praeger, 1976.

Fallenbuchel, M. (ed.). *Economic Development in the Soviet Union and Eastern Europe,* Vol. 1. New York: Praeger, 1975. Vol. 2, 1976.

Farrel, R. B. (ed.). *Political Leadership in Eastern Europe and the Soviet Union.* Chicago: Aldine, 1970.

Fejtö, F. *Die Geschichte der Volksdemokratien.* 2 Vols. Graz, Styria: 1972.

Feuerle, P. "State Arbitration in Communist Countries. The Differentiation of Functions." *StiCC*, No. 3 (1971), pp. 25-41.

Field, M. G. *Social Consequences of Modernization in Communist Societies.* Baltimore: Johns Hopkins U.P., 1976.

Fleron, F. J., Jr. (ed.). *Technology and Communist Culture: The Socio-Cultural Impact of Technology under Socialism.* New York: Praeger, 1977.

Fleron, J. J. (ed.). *Communist Studies and the Social Sciences.* Chicago: Rand McNally, 1969.

Francisco, R. A., et al. (eds.). *The Political Economy of Collectivized Agriculture: A Comparative Study of Communist and Non-Communist Systems.* New York: Pergamon Press, 1979.

Freedman, R. O. *Economic Warfare in the Communist Bloc: A Study of Soviet Economic Pressure against Yugoslavia, Albania, and Communist China.* New York: Praeger, 1970.

Frolic, B. M. "Comparing China and the Soviet Union." In *Contemporary China,* Vol. 2, No. 2, pp. 24-42.

Furtak, R. *Die politischen Systeme der sozialistischen Staaten.* Munich: DTV, 1979.

Gamarnikow, M. *Economic Reforms in Eastern Europe.* Detroit: Wayne State University Press, 1968.

Garms, W. I., Jr. "The Correlates of Education Effort: A Multivariate Analysis." *Comparative Education Review* (1968), pp. 281-299.

Gati, Ch. (ed.). *The Politics of Modernization in Eastern Europe.* New York: Praeger, 1974.

Gélard, P. "Les constitutions socialistes asiatiques." *Revue est-ouest,* No. 1 (1977), pp. 11-34.

Gella, A. "Le conflit entre l'élite dirigeante et l'élite culturelle: L'exemple de L'Europe de l'Est." *Est-ouest,* No. 1 (1978), pp. 155-168.

Höhmann, H.-H. (ed.). *Die Wirtschaft Osteuropas zu Beginn der 70er Jahre.* Stuttgart: Kohlhammer, 1972.

Höhmann, H.-H., M. C. Kaser, & K. C. Thalheim (eds.). *Die Wirtschaftsordnungen Osteuropas im Wandel.* 2 Vols. Freiburg: Rombach, 1972.

Höhmann, H.-H., G. Seidenstecher, & Th. Vajna. *Umweltschutz und ökonomisches System in Osteuropa.* Stuttgart: Kohlhammer, 1973.

Inkeles, A., & P. H. Rossi. "National Comparisons of Occupational Prestige." In A. Inkeles. *Social Change in Soviet Russia.* Cambridge, Mass.: Harvard U.P., 1968, pp. 175–191.

Interesy v sisteme ekonomicheskickh otnoshenii sotsializma. Kiev: Naukova dumka, USR, 1974.

Ionescu, G. *Comparative Communist Politics.* London: Macmillan, 1972.

Ivanov, E. A. *Profsoyuzy v politicheskoi sisteme sotsializma.* Moscow: Profizdat, 1974.

Jaehne, G. *Landwirtschaft und landwirtschaftliche Zusammenarbeit im Rat für gegenseitige Wirtschaftshilfe (COMECON).* Wiesbaden: Harrassowitz, 1968.

Johnson, Ch. (ed.). *Change in Communist Systems.* Stanford: Stanford U.P., 1970.

Jowitt, K. "The Concepts of Liberalization, Integration, and Rationalization in the Context of East European Development." *StiCC,* No. 2 (1971), pp. 79–91.

Kade, G., H.-J. Zubrod, & R. Hujer. *Organisationsprobleme der Wirtschafts-reformen in der UdSSR und der DDR im Lichte der Kybernetik und Graphen-theorie.* Vienna, New York: Springer, 1971.

Kalinin, L. "O lichnom podsobnom khozyaistve pri sotsializme." *Voprosy ekonomiki,* No. 11 (1968), pp. 52–63.

Kanet, R. E. (ed.). *The Behavioral Revolution and Communist Studies.* New York, London: Free Press/Collier-Macmillan, 1971.

Karcz, J. F. (ed.). *Soviet and East European Agriculture.* Berkeley, Los Angeles: University of California Press, 1967.

Kaser, M. C. (ed.). *Economic Development for Eastern Europe.* London: Macmillan, 1968.

Kelley, D. R., et al. (ed.). *The Economic Superpowers and the Environment: The United States, the Soviet Union, and Japan.* San Francisco: Freeman, 1976.

King, R. R. *Minorities under Communism.* Cambridge, Mass.: Harvard U.P., 1973.

Kirschen, E. S. (ed.). *Economic Policies Compared: West and East.* Vol. 1. Amsterdam: North-Holland Publishing Company; New York: Elsevier, 1974; Vol. 2, 1975.

Kolbasov, G. S. (ed.). *Sotsializm i okhrana okruzhayushchei sredy: Pravo i upravlenie v stranakh-chlenakh SEV.* Moscow: Juridicheskaya literatura, 1979.

Kommunisty mira—a svoikh partiyakh. Prague: Mir i sotsializm, 1976.

Korbinski, A. "Leadership succession and Political Change in Eastern Europe." *StiCC* (1976), pp. 3-22.

Koschwitz, H. *Pressepolitik und Parteijournalismus in der UdSSR und der Volksrepublik China.* Düsseldorf: Bertelsmann, 1971.

Glezerman, G. E., et al. *Razvitie sotsialisticheskoe obshchestvo.* Moscow: Mysl', 1973.

Godwin, P. H. B. "Communist Systems and Modernization: Sources of Political Crisis." *StiCC*, No. 1/2 (1973), pp. 107-134.

Goldzamt, E. *Urbanystika krajów socjalistycznych.* Warsaw: Arkady, 1971.

Gramatzki, H.-E., & G. Lemân. *Arbeiterselbstverwaltung und Mitbestimmung in den Staaten Osteuropas.* Hannover: Fackelträger, 1977.

Granick, D. *Enterprise Guidance in Eastern Europe: A Comparison of Four Socialist Economies.* Princeton: Princeton U.P., 1975.

Gransow, V. *Konzeptionelle Wandlungen der Kommunismusforschung: Vom Totalitarismus zur Immanenz.* Frankfurt: Campus, 1980.

Grant, N. *Society, Schools and Progress in Eastern Europe.* London: Pergamon Press, 1969.

Grechkina, E. *Srednie sloi na puti k sotsializmu.* Tallin: Esti kaamat, 1976.

Gregory, P. *Socialist and Nonsocialist Industrialization Patterns: A Comparative Appraisal.* New York: Praeger, 1970.

Griffith, W. E. (ed.). *Communism in Europe: Continuity, Change, and the Sino-Soviet Dispute.* Cambridge, Mass.: MIT Press, 1964, 1967 (Paperback edition).

Grips, R. *The Political System of Communism.* New York, Toronto: Dodd, Mead & Co., 1973.

Gruenwald, O. "Comparing Socialist Cultures: A Meta-Framework." *StiCC* (1978), pp. 75-95.

Gumpel, W., & D. Keese (eds.). *Probleme des Industrialismus in Ost und West: Festschrift für Hans Raupach.* Munich: Olzog, 1973.

Gumpel, W., & H. Vogel. *Die Wirtschaft Ungarns, Bulgariens und Rumäniens: Lage und Aussichten.* Munich: Olzog, 1968.

Guzek, M. *Ekonomicheskaya integratsia stran sotsializma.* Moscow: Ekonomika, 1973.

Hammon, Th. T. (ed.). *The Anatomy of Communist Takeovers.* New Haven: Yale U.P., 1975.

Hazard, J. N. *Communists and their Law: A Search for the Common Core of the Legal Systems of the Marxian Socialist States.* Chicago: Chicago U.P., 1969.

Hensel, K. P., K. Wessely, & U. Wagner. *Das Profitprinzip, seine ordnungspolitischen Alternativen in sozialistischen Wirtschaftssystemen.* Stuttgart: G. Fischer, 1972.

Kosta, J., et al. *Warenproduktion im Sozialismus.* Frankfurt: S. Fischer, 1973.

Krejci, J. *Social Structure in Divided Germany.* London: Croom Helm, 1976.

Krzyzewski, R. *Konsumpcja spoleczna w gospodarce socjalistycznej.* Warsaw: PWE, 1968.

Kudrova, E. S. *Statistika natsional'nogo dokhoda evropeiskikh sotsialisticheskikh stran.* Moscow: Statistika, 1969.

Kurowski, L. *Les finances dans les états socialistes.* Paris: LGDJ, 1962.

Kursky, A. *La planification en URSS et dans les autres pays socialistes.* Paris: The Hague, Mouton, 1969.

Kýn, O. & L. "Trends in East European Factor Productivity." *Jahrbuch der Wirtschaft Osteuropas/Yearbook of East-European Economics.* Vol. 7. Munich: Olzog, 1977, pp. 141–158.

Lammich, S. *Grundzüge des sozialistischen Parlamentarismus.* Baden-Baden: Nomos, 1977.

Lane, D. *The Socialist Industrial State: Towards a Political Sociology of State Socialism.* London: Allen & Unwin, 1976.

Lavigne, M. *Les relations économiques est-ouest.* Paris: PUF, 1979.

Lesage, M. *Les régimes politiques de l'URSS et de l'Europe de l'est.* Paris: PUF, 1971.

Mansilla, H. C. *Systembedürfnis und Anpassung: Zur Kritik sozialistischer*

Verhaltenssteuerung. Frankfurt: Athenäum, 1973 (on the USSR, GDR, and Cuba).

Matejko, A. *Social Change and Stratification in Eastern Europe: An Interpretative Analysis of Poland and Her Neighbors.* New York: Praeger, 1974.

————. "Les transformations sociales de l'Europe centrale et orientale au cours des années 1950-1971." *Revue de l'est,* No. 1 (1974), pp. 203-228.

Meissner, W., & P. Farkas. "Preisdiskriminierung innerhalb des RGW." *Jahrbuch der Wirtschaft Osteuropas/Yearbook of East-European Economics.* Vol. 4. Munich: Olzog, 1973, pp. 295-318.

Mesa-Lago, C., & C. Beck (eds.). *Comparative Socialist System: Essays on Politics and Economics.* Pittsburgh: University of Pittsburgh, Center for International Studies, 1975.

Meyer, A. G. "Communist Revolutions and Cultural Change." *StiCC,* No. 4 (1972), pp. 345-370.

Meyer, G. *Sozialistische System.* Opladen: Leske, 1979.

Mikul'skii, K. I. *Sotsial'no-ekonomicheskaya politika v sotsialisticheskom obshchestve.* Moscow: Mysl', 1978.

Montias, J. M. "Modernization in Communist Countries: Some Questions of Methodology." *StiCC,* No. 4 (1972), pp. 413-427.

Naville, P. *Le salaire socialiste.* 2 Vols. Paris: Editions Anthropos, 1970.

Oplata truda pri sotsializme. Moscow: Ekonomika, 1977.

Pryor, F. L. *Public Expenditures in Communist and Capitalist Nations.* London: Allen & Unwin, 1968.

————. "Barriers to Market Socialism in Eastern Europe in the Mid 1960s." *StiCC,* No. 2 (1970), pp. 31-64.

————. *Property and Industrial Organization in Communist and Capitalist Nations.* Bloomington: Indiana U.P., 1973.

Rakowska-Harmstone, T. (ed.). *Perspectives for Change in Communist Societies.* Boulder: Westview Press, 1979.

Révész, L. *Die Legende vom Sozialstaat in Osteuropa.* Berne: Verlag Schweizerisches Ost-Institut, 1978.

Riabushkin, T. V., & R. A. Galetskaja. *Dinamika i struktura naseleniya v sotsialisticheskom obshchestvo*. Moscow: Statistika, 1979.

Rochlin, R. P., & E. Hagemann. *Die Kollektivierung der Landwirtschaft in der Sowjetunion und in der Volksrepublik China: Eine Vergleichende Studie.* Berlin [West]: Duncker & Humblot, 1971.

Rolf, H. *Sozialversicherung oder staatlicher Gesundheitsdienst: Ökonomischer Effizienzvergleich der Gesundheitssicherungssysteme der Bundesrepublik Deutschland und der DDR.* Berlin [West]: Duncker & Humblot, 1975.

Ruban, M. E. "Wohnungsbau und Wohnungswirtschaft in den RGW-Ländern." *Deutschland-Archiv,* No. 12 (1973), pp. 1312-1317.

Rush, M. *How Communist States Change their Rulers.* Ithaca: Cornell U.P., 1974.

Rychetnik, L. "A Model of Postwar Economic Growth in Eastern Europe." *Jahrbuch der Wirtschaft Osteuropas/Yearbook of East-European Economics.* Vol. 5. Munich: Olzog, 1974, pp. 195-1.

Sbornik statisticheskikh dannykh o razvitiya narodnogo khozyaistva KNDR (1946-1960). Pyöngyang: 1961.

Schnitzer, M. *East and West Germany: A Comparative Economic Analysis.* New York: Praeger, 1972.

Schweitzer, H. *Sozialistische Agrartheorie und Praxis in China und in der Sowjetunion.* Berne: Lang, 1972.

Senghaas, D. "Sozialismus: Eine entwicklungsgeschichtliche und entwicklungstheoretische Betrachtung." *Leviathan,* 1980, pp. 10-40.

Shishkan, N. M. *Sotsial'no-ekonomicheskie problemy zhenskogo truda.* Moscow: Ekonomika, 1980.

Šik, O. *Der Strukturwandel der Wirtschaftssysteme in den osteuropäischen Ländern.* Zurich: Die Arche, 1971.

————. *Der dritte Weg: Die marxistisch-leninistische Theorie und die moderne Industriegesellschaft.* Hamburg: Hoffmann & Campe, 1972.

Sirk, L. *Economic Devolution in Eastern Europe.* London: Longmans, 1969.

Skilling, H. G. *Communism National and International: Eastern Europe after Stalin.* Toronto: Toronto U.P., 1964.

————. "Opposition in Communist East Europe." In R. A. Dahl (ed.). *Regimes and Oppositions*. New Haven, London: Yale U.P., 1973, pp. 89–119.

Slapnicka, H. *Die sozialistische Kollektivperson: Funktion und Struktur der Juristischen Person in den europäischen Volksdemokratien.* Vienna: Böhlau, 1969.

Sotsial'naya politika kommunisticheskikh i rabochikh partii v sotsialisticheskom obshchestve. Moscow: Izdatel'stvo politicheskoi literatury, 1979.

Spulber, N. *Socialist Management and Planning: Topics in Comparative Socialist Economics.* Bloomington, London: Indiana U.P., 1971.

Sukhoruchenko, A. N. *Obshchestvennii produkt i natsional'nyi dokhod stran-chlenov SEV.* Moscow: Statistika, 1974.

Thalheim, K. C. (ed.). *Wachstumsprobleme in den osteuropäischen Volkswirt-schaften.* Vol. 1. Berlin [West]: Duncker & Humblot, 1968. Vol. 2, 1970.

Tökes, R. L. "Comparative Communism: The Elusive Target." *StiCC*, (1975), pp, 211–229.

Topornin, B. N. *Politischeskaya sistema sotsializma.* Moscow: Mezhdunarodnye otnosheniya, 1972.

Treadgold, D. W. (ed.). *Soviet and Chinese Communism: Similarities and Differences.* Seattle: Washington University Press, 1970.

Triska, J., & C. Gati (eds.). *Labour in Socialist Societies.* London: Allen & Unwin, 1981.

Triska, J. F. (ed.). *Communist Party-States: Comparative and International Studies.* Indianapolis, New York: Bobbs-Merrill, 1969.

Triska, J. F., & P. M. Cocks (eds.). *Political Development in Eastern Europe.* New York: Praeger, 1977.

Veselovskii, V., & M. N. Rutkevick (ed.). *Problemy razvitiya sotsial'noi struktury obshchestva v Sovetskom Soyuze i Pol'she.* Moscow: Nauka, 1976.

Wädekin, K.-E. *Sozialistische Agrarpolitik in Osteuropa.* Vol. 1. *Von Marx biz zur Vollkollektivierung.* Berlin [West]: Duncker & Humblot, 1974. Vol. 2, 1978.

Ward, B. N. *The Socialist Economy: A Study of Organizational Alternatives.* New York: Random House, 1967.

Watrin, Ch. (ed.). *Struktur- und stabilitätspolitische Probleme in alternativen Wirtschaftssystemen*. Berlin [West]: Duncker & Humblot, 1974.

Weralski, M. "Les problèmes de la fiscalité dans les états socialistes." *Revue de science financière*, No. 4 (1969), pp. 735-841.

Wesson, R. G. *Communism and Communist Systems*. Englewood Cliffs: Prentice Hall, 1978.

White, St. "Communist Systems and the 'Iron Law of Pluralism'." *British Journal of Political Science*, No. 1 (1978), pp. 101-117.

Wiatr, J. J. (ed.). *The State of Sociology in Eastern Europe Today*. Carbondale & Edwardsville, Ill.: Southern Illinois University Press, 1971.

————. *Marksistowska teoria rozwoju spolesznego*. Warsaw: Ksiazka i Wiedza, 1973.

Wilczynski, J. *The Economics of Socialism: Principles Governing the Operation of the Centrally Planned Economies in the USSR and Eastern Europe under the New System*. London: Allen & Unwin, 1970.

————. *Socialist Economic Development and Reforms: From Extensive to Intensive Growth under Central Planning in the USSR, Eastern Europe and Yugoslavia*. London: Macmillan, 1972.

————. "Differentiation of Income under Modern Socialism." *Jahrbuch der Wirtschaft Osteuropas/Yearbook of East-European Economics*. Vol. 3. Munich: Olzog, 1973, pp. 467-488.

Wiles, P. J. D. *Communist International Economics*. Oxford: Blackwell, 1968.

————. *Distribution of Income: East and West*. Amsterdam: North-Holland Publishing Company; New York: Elsevier, 1974.

Wiles, P. J. D., & S. Markowski. "Income Distribution under Communism and Capitalism." *Soviet Studies* (1970), pp. 344-369, 497-511.

Woodsworth, D. E. *Social Security and National Policy, Sweden, Yugoslavia, Japan*. Montreal: McGill-Queen's University Press, 1977.

Zaubermann, A. *Industrial Progress in Poland, Czechoslovakia, and East Germany, 1937-1962*. London: Oxford U.P., 1964.

INDEX